The Twe... Dels... Christmas

Sir David Jason was born in 1940 in North London. His acting career has been long and varied: from his theatre work in the West End to providing the voices of Mr Toad from *The Wind in the Willows*, *Dangermouse* and *The BFG*. From *Open All Hours* to *The Darling Buds of May* to his starring roles as Detective Inspector Frost in *A Touch of Frost* and, of course, Derek 'Del Boy' Trotter in *Only Fools and Horses*.

The 1996 *Only Fools* Christmas special 'Time on Our Hands' was seen live by 24.35 million viewers and to this day is the UK's most-watched comedy show of all time.

David Jason is the author of three No. 1 *Sunday Times* bestselling books: *My Life*, *Only Fools & Stories* and *A Del of a Life*.

The
Twelve
Dels of
Christmas

DAVID JASON

PENGUIN BOOKS

PENGUIN BOOKS

UK | USA | Canada | Ireland | Australia
India | New Zealand | South Africa

Penguin Books is part of the Penguin Random House group of companies
whose addresses can be found at global.penguinrandomhouse.com

First published by Century in 2022
Published in Penguin Books 2023
001

'. . . and a partridge up your pear tree' from 'Christmas Crackers',
Only Fools and Horses, John Sullivan

Typeset by 11.88/15.6 pt Goudy Std
by Integra Software Services Pvt. Ltd, Pondicherry

Printed and bound in Great Britain by Clays Ltd, Elcograf S.p.A.

The authorised representative in the EEA is Penguin Random House Ireland,
Morrison Chambers, 32 Nassau Street, Dublin D02 YH68

A CIP catalogue record for this book is available from the British Library

ISBN: 978–1–529–15811–3

www.greenpenguin.co.uk

CONTENTS

INTRODUCTION

'It is at Christmas time that want is most keenly felt, and abundance rejoices.'

Charles Dickens, *A Christmas Carol*, 1843

Not that long ago, over lunch at a rather fancy restaurant in London, an executive from ITV looked me in the eyes and said, 'David, you know what? You would make the most perfect Scrooge.'

Which, I have to say, caused me to pause briefly from chewing on my chicken escalope and take a moment.

Well, how would *you* feel if someone came straight out and said, 'I saw you and thought of Scrooge'?

Because, yes, of course, we all know that Ebenezer Scrooge turns out to be a good guy *in the end*. After the three ghosts of Christmas have pitched up and finished frightening him half to death, the old scrimper's human spirit is unlocked, he realises the true cost of his meanness, and finally grows a heart and puts it to some use. That's the Scrooge story, or what we would now call, on the back of the reality television shows, his 'journey'. (I'm officially old enough to remember when a journey meant actually going somewhere, but let's not get into that now.)

However, our image of Scrooge tends to be, as it were, front-loaded, does it not? By which I mean, if you describe someone as Scrooge-like, you're not generally implying they're the type to knock on your door on Christmas morning with a big grin on their face, a huge turkey under their arm and a bottle of champagne all ready to pop.

On the contrary, you're thinking of the sour-faced tight-wad from the beginning of the tale, the bloke who barks, 'Bah! Humbug!' – the character who is, in Dickens's words, 'a squeezing, wrenching, grasping, scraping, clutching, covetous, old sinner'.

And just to remove any remaining traces of doubt about it, Dickens went on: 'The cold within him froze his old features, nipped his pointed nose, shrivelled his cheek, stiffened his gait; made his eyes red, his thin lips blue; and spoke out shrewdly in his grating voice.'

Hence, dear reader, my moment of personal reflection back there in the restaurant with a mouthful of pricy chicken.

Scrooge? Who, *moi*?

But such, of course, are the daily knocks and setbacks, the low blows and blindside rabbit-punches, for the humble thespian and small-screen entertainer as he goes about his business of attempting to enthral and delight the watching nation. It's called 'casting', obviously, and anyone who goes into acting expecting a life of unbroken flattery in this department is going to be sorely disappointed somewhere along the line.

Saw me and thought of Scrooge? I'd heard worse, frankly. Indeed, I got one of my most important breaks in television when, essentially, Ronnie Barker saw me and thought of a hundred-year-old gardener called Dithers. I was about thirty at the time, with a spring in my eye and a twinkle in my step, but no matter.

And actually, now we're on the subject, 'I saw you and thought of a deluded cockney chancer flogging hooky gear off a market stall' wasn't a completely complimentary thing to hear, either. But that didn't work out too badly.

No, as time and experience have taught me, the only thing to do at these moments is to bite your lip, jut out your chin and think of the work. The fact was, the man from ITV was offering me a part in a new production of A *Christmas Carol* – a starring role in a big and no doubt handsomely budgeted festive number, and, well, you don't go sneezing at those, with a 'nipped' and 'pointed' nose, or otherwise. So, plenty to consider there and much to discuss before they came round with the dessert trolley.

Yet, as I resumed chewing thoughtfully and began to weigh the pros and cons of this potentially nice little earner, another question started rotating somewhat naggingly in my mind.

What *is* it about me and Christmas?

When I survey the wondrous tapestry, if you will, of my acting career, it's extraordinary how frequently Christmas comes into the picture. And not just in the sense of once a year, which you might reasonably expect. No, somehow Christmas bulks much larger than that. So many key moments in my professional life seem to be associated with that time. And it's been that way from the start.

My first ever appearance on television? Christmas Day, 1965. Soon after 4.50 p.m., to be precise, in the BBC pantomime, which was an annual fixture in those days – what we would now call 'appointment television', even. In my family, certainly, we cleared the Christmas lunch away and ritually plonked ourselves in front of the set for it, in various states of turkey-and-pudding-stuffed disrepair, and 1965 was no exception. The only difference that year was that the entertainment for which we all plonked ourselves down (me on the sofa, next to my mum and my aunt, my dad in his armchair) featured . . . me.

Or kind of. More on this monumental occasion and its life-changing consequences for the occupants of the sitting room at 26 Lodge Lane anon. At this point, let the record merely show that the pantomime laid that evening before my proud parents and the rest of the country was *Mother Goose*. And let the record further state that if you strained your eyes at one point, I could be briefly glimpsed playing a swinging policeman.

No, not *that* kind of swinging. *Literally* swinging – by a wire from the ceiling.

So, yes – not one of the greater roles in the theatrical canon, I grant you. And not an especially dignified one, either, because, let me tell you, those theatrical harnesses, when they get yanked up around your softer regions mid-flight, chafe like nothing on earth.

Was it ever like this for the nation's greatest thespians on their various routes to glory? I wonder. For the likes of Gielgud, Olivier, McKellen? Instinctively I feel that it almost certainly was not.

Yet this was where I found myself, as the rocket containing my small-screen career trundled tentatively onto the launch-pad. Never mind Scrooge or a hundred-year-old gardener: someone at the BBC saw me – twenty-five years young, lithe and willowy, his innocent head aflutter with dreams of major parts as a romantic lead – and thought of . . . a flying policeman.

There were other bits and pieces of Christmas panto in those early years, too – even less distinguished, if you can imagine it – and one of them so grim around the edges that I almost gave up acting and went back to being an electrician. But Christmas was already doing its bit to shape my course.

And then there was *Only Fools and Horses*. Now, none of us who were involved in that show had any inkling at the outset about exactly what it would turn into. But I think it's fair to say that it ended up meaning a great deal to an awful lot of people. And it seemed to mean a great deal to people in particular at Christmas.

There were eighteen *Only Fools* Christmas specials in total, beginning with one at the end of the first series in 1981 – the 'Christmas Crackers' episode from which the words of Del quoted at the beginning of this introduction are taken. From then on, our ugly mugs started looming in the corner of the nation's sitting rooms at Christmas pretty much annually. Indeed, from 1991 onwards, after the end of the seventh series, *Only Fools* existed *solely* at Christmas, the team reuniting only to film extended stories for the holiday period – 'our Christmas present to the nation', as the BBC liked to call them.

Would the nation have preferred money or perhaps a gift token? Quite possibly. But instead the nation got given us, doing increasingly daft things in increasingly far-flung places.

Accordingly, it was at Christmas that the world saw Rodney, Del and Uncle Albert set sail in a battered old tub for Holland, pausing to seek directions from an oil rig. It was at Christmas that the entire cast was spotted decamping by coach to sunny Margate, only to watch the coach go up in flames. And it was Christmas that sent Del and Rodney to Miami to encounter both the Mafia and a member of the Bee Gees. (Nice bloke, Barry Gibb. And nice and warm, Miami. No complaints from me and Nick Lyndhurst about that particular location shoot.)

It was also at Christmas that Raquel moved in with Del, that Peckham Spring Mineral Water was first marketed, and that the world's least likely Batman and Robin duo emerged on a foggy street. Those episodes might have been shown at Christmas but they very quickly stopped being *about* Christmas. John Sullivan, the late, great creator of *Only Fools*, seized on those specials as an opportunity to widen the show's scope – to be daring, tell bigger stories over longer time frames, deepen the characters and our attachment to them. John was a pioneer, and it's my opinion that, in those eighteen festive numbers, he pretty much single-handedly rewrote the rules around Christmas shows – about what a Christmas edition of a comedy programme was and what it could be allowed to do.

But more about that later. For now, let me simply try and dizzy you with some numbers that still, genuinely, dizzy me. On the list of the twenty most-watched programmes ever broadcast on Christmas Day, there are seven episodes of *Only Fools*. Well, seven out of twenty sounds like the kind of mark I used to get at school on a good day. But in the context of the entire history of Christmas broadcasting . . . well, I guess seven out of twenty is pretty impressive.

What's more, the 'Time on our Hands' episode, which was the concluding part of the 1996 Christmas trilogy, attracted an audience of 24.35 million. Now, my dear mother taught me not to blow my own trumpet – and also to be careful about blowing other people's trumpets. But at the same time,

unashamedly contradicting herself, my mum also told me
not to hide my light under a bushel, advice I would have
gladly heeded if bushels hadn't been so vanishingly few and
far between in the Finchley area in the forties and fifties –
even fewer and farther between than trumpets, actually.

Facts are facts, though, and, setting all bushels and trumpets aside, 24.35 million is the kind of audience which
tended only to gather in front of television sets for space missions and royal weddings. Yet that number of people eagerly
assembled that Christmas to find out what was going on with
a bunch of fictional wallies in a Peckham tower block.

Just to put this in some kind of perspective, 1996 was the
year England played Germany at Wembley for a place in the
final of football's European Championships – a game of some
interest to the nation, you could say, given what we know
about England and football, and also what we know about
the rivalry between England and Germany. Yet, amazingly,
some six million fewer people tuned in to watch that match
than tuned in to see how much Del and Rodney could get
for the pocket watch that they had just unearthed among the
Showaddywaddy LPs and iffy Eastern European electronics
in their garage lock-up.

Then again, unlike England v. Germany, I suppose at least
our show had a happy ending. Germany, you may not need
reminding, went through on penalties that time, whereas Del
and Rodney . . . well, thanks to that Sotheby's auction, after
years of dreaming about it, they were finally millionaires,

weren't they? And this time next year, no doubt – Del was sure of it – they'd be *billionaires*.

Anyway, the point is, that Christmas, 'Time on our Hands' became the UK's most-watched comedy show of all time, and I think we can be fairly confident now that we're looking at a record there that won't ever be broken. If only the same could be said for those Showaddywaddy LPs.

I can still only shake my head in wonder about it, really. I think back to the beginning of the voyage, the first time the cast gathered together for this completely new sitcom in a shabby room at the BBC's Television Rehearsal Centre in Acton, all carrying the scripts we'd been sent and looking around the place in various states of anticipation, with that first-day-at-school atmosphere in the air, as it always is on such occasions.

Now, imagine if the director had clapped his hands at the start of that session and said, 'Right, listen up, everyone. Come Christmas a few years from now, the world and his dog will be tuning into this show, to the point that, when they all put the kettle on at the same time for a cup of tea afterwards, it'll produce a 1600 megawatt power surge and practically crash the National Grid. So look sharp.'

We'd have assumed he'd banged his head on the way in.

Yet it came to pass. And, incidentally, my formal apologies, belatedly, to everyone working overtime at power stations that Christmas for the inconvenience caused. I speak in solidarity with you as a former electrician who has touched enough live wires in his time to know a thing or two about power surges. However, I can't say I'm not lastingly proud to have been part of something which had that effect. Proud and astonished.

The Christmas connections don't end with *Only Fools*, by the way. In the 1990s, *The Darling Buds of May*, in which I played Pa Larkin, spawned two Christmas specials. Indeed, the second of them went out on ITV on Boxing Day, twenty-four hours after 'Mother Nature's Son', which was that year's *Only Fools* special, had gone out on the BBC. Thus did I straddle two channels for Christmas 1992 – which I suppose was less painful than it sounds, but which should still probably only be attempted under properly qualified supervision and with medical support to hand.

Even *A Touch of Frost*, which, as a detective show revolving around the solution of frequently grisly murder cases, might not automatically have been your first stop for festive frolics, ended up getting a Yuletide spin at one point. In 1999, Detective Inspector Jack Frost took up ninety minutes of the nation's Christmas Day, sandwiched between two bursts of the *Who Wants to Be a Millionaire?* Christmas special.

Or what about the year I was borne aloft in a flying sled alongside a hooded figure – only for the studio to flood and the power to go out, leaving the pair of us hanging in mid-air while everyone else evacuated the building? Again, precise details to follow. But these inconveniences occurred during the filming of Sky TV's adaptation of *Hogfather*, Terry Pratchett's tale of Christmas on Discworld, which

10

eventually, when the power came back on, got completed and went out over the holidays in 2006, with me in the role of Death's manservant, Albert. The producers of that show had the ambition to create something that would be reshown at Christmas every year – and it has.

All things considered, it was no real surprise to me that, when the BBC brought back *Open All Hours* as *Still Open All Hours* in 2013, they chose to make a Christmas thing out of it and launch it on Boxing Day. It was the same when ITV unveiled *Micawber*. That was an idea that John Sullivan had after *Only Fools* – a comedy drama using characters from Dickens's *David Copperfield*. Great hopes attended the Christmas debut of that show – ITV's, John's, and mine, too, because I was playing Mr Micawber. We thought we were really onto something – a potential winner that could run and run. Alas, it didn't work out that way. But the ones that fell on stony ground are part of my Christmas story as well.

All in all, I somehow became someone who seemed to have his own reserved parking space in the Christmas double issue of the *Radio Times*. Indeed, one year the front of that magazine was a picture of me, warmly wrapped in a coat and a red scarf, lightly sprinkled with artificial snow, and smiling suavely. The headline read 'MISTER CHRISTMAS'.

Michael Bublé, eat your heart out! It was as if I had come to define the season: a tree with lights on, a bowl of Brazil nuts that nobody was going to touch, and something with David Jason in it on the telly. Fair play to the *Radio Times* editors, though, for that one. There were spells in my career when I was on television on Christmas Day so regularly that I began to think I knew how the Queen must feel.

And here's the thing: I don't even *like* Christmas that much. Can I confess that here? It's just between the two of us, obviously, and I'm trusting you to take it no further. But I'm someone with a long-held aversion to shopping and a mild anxiety about large gatherings of people, and . . . well, Christmas often seems to be offering both of those things in a sandwich. A turkey sandwich, obviously. Which I'm also not that keen on.

And don't get me started on the cheesy department store ads that nowadays seem to begin in August, the same jingly tunes wherever you go, the heart-sinking corporate Christmas cards ('with best wishes for the season from all of the team at Pepto Financial Planning Services'), the mind-boggling consumption, the enforced jollity, the sense of being held hostage in the house for two days by your relatives, the neighbours dropping in, the obligatory participation in board games and (worse) charades, the faked enthusiasm for unwanted gifts ('A tie-hanger! You really shouldn't have!'), the feelings of intense disorientation and unease which can only occur after forcing a seventh consecutive mince pie into an already bloated stomach . . .

Oh yes, and the tree lights which, despite the fact that you carefully coiled and packed them away last January with an attention to detail which would have impressed the captain of a sailing ship, have just emerged from their box in a knotted clump that is about to cost you seven and a half hours of unpicking before you finally give it up as a lost cause and go out to buy some more.

I could go on. But let me just say (and I suspect my wife, Gill, will meaningfully confirm this), when the season once again looms into view and conversation turns to those apparently urgent 'Christmas plans', the expression 'Bah! Humbug!' has been known to escape my lips quite naturally, and entirely unprompted by executives from ITV.*

So how is it, then, that I, of all people, became a decoration on the nation's Christmas tree at this special time of the year? – the *most wonderful* time of the year, as Andy Williams, among others, will sometimes try to persuade you, although of course Andy Williams never spent it dressed in a policeman's uniform and hanging by a wire from the rafters. Or not to the best of my knowledge he didn't, and he might have had something different to sing about it if he had. And he'd probably be singing it falsetto.

Or to put it another way, by what strange workings of fate did someone like me end up on the cover of the *Radio Times*, dusted with fake snow and labelled 'Mister Christmas'?

That, dear reader, is the subject of this book.

* * *

* Footnote from my wife, Gill: 'I meaningfully confirm this.'

This is my fourth volume of memoirs and musings – the fourth time that I have adjourned to the musky privacy of the library at Jason Towers, pulled up a chair at the antique oak desk, and dipped my freshly sharpened quill in the bronze ink flask. (I really must get round to replacing the cartridge in that printer.) If you've joined me in print before, then welcome back. And if you haven't, then welcome, too, and worry not, because I am assured by my superiors at Penguin Random House that sales staff will be passing among you during the interval with the three preceding volumes on trays, attractively packaged for your further reading pleasure.

Coincidentally, as I began this book – in November 2021 – and commenced the work of gently lifting time's gauzy veil to look back across my illustrious and frequently tinsel-strewn career, another festive season was almost upon us. And yet another one will be drawing near by the time the work is finished and published, this being very much the nature of Christmas, as I have observed it: it tends to come round, whether you like it or not, and very quickly. Increasingly quickly, actually, because in my experience life speeds up the longer you live. Time hurries on its restless way and before you know it, the holiday season is upon us, the lights are going up again (assuming I can unknot them), the geese are getting fat and the amaryllis bulbs are once more planted in the gazunda.

Amaryllis in the gazunda? It sounds like a cryptic crossword clue, or perhaps the kind of thing a spy would say to another spy on a remote park bench in order to identify himself. 'The amaryllis is in the gazunda.' But in fact it's a Christmas tradition for Gill and me. Each year in the late autumn/early winter, we plant three bulbs, with their spaghetti-like roots, in a pot of earth and try to time it so that at least one of them flowers on Christmas Day. This turns out to be harder than it sounds. We've had some near misses on either side, but we've yet to hit it spot on and come down on Christmas morning to be greeted by a freshly blooming amaryllis. Hope springs eternal, though, and, as someone once said, 'This time next year . . .'*

Actually, to be strictly accurate, we've only been using the gazunda since 2021. Various other receptacles for the bulbs have been deployed in the past, but that year, after extensive consultations and a return to the drawing board, we made the decision to up our game. Needless to say, this was not a decision we took lightly. But sometimes in a long-term campaign like this, when you've experienced repeated setbacks, you've simply got no choice but to bring out the biggest weapon in your armoury. So we dusted off the gazunda.

Not that it worked, of course. Far from greeting us brightly that Christmas morn, those bulbs eventually did

---

* Amaryllis: a flowering bulb species native to the Cape Provinces of South Africa, and commonly white-petalled, but occasionally purple or pink. Not to be confused with Amarillo, a city in Texas which Tony Christie was always asking directions to. I guess, in the age of satnav, nobody really needs to ask the way to Amarillo any more. It's pop music's loss.

us the honour of flowering in mid-January. Still, it looked impressive.

'But what's a gazunda?' you may well be asking. It's a bedpan or potty – a 'pisspot', I suppose we might have said in coarser times, but called a 'gazunda' in politer circles because it 'goes under' the bed. My decision to find a home for the amaryllis bulbs in this unusual container met with some initial reservations from Gill, who wondered whether we might regret the overtones implicit in making such an item our Christmas centrepiece, not to mention parking a potty in the vicinity of the place where we regularly eat. But I managed to persuade her that it wasn't just any potty – it was a Victorian potty and, moreover, an artefact of great historic merit which ought to be put to good use.

The artefact in question, by the way, is in china, with a delicate flower motif around the outside, and, seeing as you asked, I bought it back in the eighties while on a trawl of antique shops with Ronnie Barker. It was Ronnie – who was eleven years older than me and in his early fifties at this point – who introduced me to the pleasures of antique hunting, something he loved and was very good at, having a practised eye for it. He was so good at it, in fact, that he eventually opened an antiques business of his own.

When we were in South Yorkshire, filming *Open All Hours*, Sunday would often be our day off, and the pair of us would venture into the surrounding countryside in Ronnie's chauffeur-driven car – something which I found rather grand at the time, though it was a perfectly common perk for the star of the show. It was on one of these trips around the local dealerships that I happened on an old 3D advert for Player's cigarettes, which I snapped up in a hurry and which hung in my house for quite a while. And it was on another of those voyages that I came upon this charming gazunda – a piece of redundant technology, of course, since the invention of the flushing lavatory.

I'm not sure why, really, but this item caught my eye and, with Ronnie's encouragement, I gladly parted with a couple of quid for it. All these years later, it remains in extremely good condition, with the exception of a small crack that has appeared in the handle. But I guess that's not by any means the first crack this particular item has seen. Anyway, it's now been promoted to the role of Christmas planter. And I'm still backing it to repay my confidence in it and come good with the blooms eventually.

While we're all waiting for that to happen, though, here's a view of my life, as seen through a Christmas lens. And, drawing on the example set by Dickens, I'll be compiling it with the help of my own personal Spirit of Christmas Past, whom I've ordered online, at what seemed to me to be a very reasonable hourly rate, or certainly on the basis of the figures I was seeing on the Spirit of Christmas Past price comparison websites. With, I hope, some handy assistance from this hired Spirit, I'll be examining my various interactions with the festive season across the decades, loosening history's ribbons, parting the wrapping paper of obscurity, and peering at what emerges in order to work out what went right, and what went wrong, and, if possible, why it even happened at all. And as I do so, I'll do my best to reach any important conclusions about life, work and the meaning of it all that I can usefully pass on to you – baubles of wisdom if you like. Or certainly a lot of old baubles.

Think of this volume, then, as a Christmas special in book form, from someone who, deliberately or otherwise, has found himself in the middle of a few such – but a Christmas special very much in the John Sullivan style, I hope, being about much more than just Christmas. Or, as Derek Trotter would probably try to flog it, a Christmas special for all seasons.

And who knows? Maybe as a consequence of meeting the ghosts of my Christmases past, not to mention the ghosts of my Christmases present, and, no doubt, the ghosts of my Christmases future, too, I'll end up changing some of my *own* fixed views about the season, as mentioned above. I mean, if it could happen to Scrooge . . .

And mixed in, as usual, will be my latest reports from the frontline of the life I find myself leading as a direct consequence of putting in some of those Christmas shifts – a life which, honestly, remains a source of abiding amazement to me and something I can never quite get my head around, let alone take for granted. For, as I constantly have cause to reflect, none of what has come to pass these past fifty years or so was ever a foregone conclusion on my own 'journey', from north London fishmonger's son and budding electrician with his own van and business card, to multiple-BAFTA-winning television actor, knight of the realm and international man of mystery.

So, will I be recounting herein my recent hours spent in the skies with an astronaut? I will indeed. Will I be attempting to explain my essential and perhaps even history-making duties on the Mall during the celebrations for the Queen's Platinum Jubilee in the summer of 2022? Yes I will. (Those parades don't get watched on their own, you know.) Will I be recalling composing and filming the good luck message I was asked to send the England football team ahead of the final of the 2021 European Championships when they stood so tantalisingly on the verge of trophy-winning glory for the first time since 1966, and just needed that little bit of help from a qualified actor to tip them over the edge? Try and stop me. Ditto my recollections of when *Strictly Come Dancing* came a-calling.

And will I be writing up in detail my recent encounter with fellow dashing screen icon (and fellow helicopter pilot) Tom Cruise? Reader, I may be able to contain myself for, ooh, whole pages before I get round to that one.

So that's where we're heading. And hopefully we'll find something to laugh about along the way, because heaven knows we could do with some laughs in these days when pandemic and warfare seem to be working on a rota basis to mess us all up. Indeed, laughs may be the best means we have of fighting back. For, to quote Charles Dickens in *A Christmas Carol* once more: 'While there is infection in disease and sorrow, there is nothing in the world so irresistibly contagious as laughter and good-humour.'

To which I can only say: good point, Dicko, me old son, and well made.

And that role as ITV's all-new Scrooge, offered to me over lunch that day and for which, as you now know, I was so temperamentally suited?

Well, let me tell you what actually happened there. But before I do that, I just need to get up and let the Spirit of Christmas Past in at the window. He's turned up a bit early, which I suppose is a good sign – showing willing, and all that – but he's been clanking his chains and making a right old racket out there for about twenty minutes now and he'll be annoying the neighbours. So let's get him in here and ask him if he wouldn't mind being an awfully good fellow and spinning us back a few years . . .

ON THE FIRST DEL OF CHRISTMAS . . .

Tinsel and puddings

'The Spirit put out its strong hand as it spoke, and clasped him gently by the arm. "Rise! and walk with me!"'

A Christmas Carol

Right, Spirit: now that you've finished hanging your coat up and plugging in your laptop, your first vision, if you please . . .

Ah, now this I recognise. It's a make-up room at BBC Television Centre. It is 1981, late December, the holiday season fast upon us, and I am sitting in a chair, wrapped in a protective sheet and having a large make-up brush flapped in my face by one of the BBC's crack squad of powder-puff artists. Ahead of me lies an evening of recording in front of a studio audience, an exciting but always nerve-jangling prospect, and no less so on the occasion of the first ever *Only Fools and Horses* Christmas special.

Suddenly there appears, reflected in the illuminated mirror

in front of me, a woman in a bright blue silky outfit and a pair of white high-heeled boots. On her head is a jewelled cap from beneath which falls a long cascade of platinum-blonde hair. She has drifted in from the corridor and it is clear that she is lost.

'Can you help me?' she says.

It is a sight, dear reader, which causes my jaw to drop to the floor – thereby briefly admitting the make-up brush and its dusty contents to my mouth, which is never entirely advisable. Nevertheless, despite the fact that I am essentially trapped under a sheet and have a tongue which is now lightly coated with face powder, I somehow retain the wherewithal to make my feelings clear.

'I think I'm in love,' I say.

The beatific reflection in the mirror acknowledges this open-hearted declaration with an indulgent smile. But before I can rise from the chair, shake off the sheet that binds me, spit out the face powder (but in a decorous and ultimately attractive way, hopefully) and pledge my troth more fully, the make-up artist standing behind me intervenes.

'Where are you meant to be?' she asks.

While I merely sit under my sheet and look on helplessly, like a dental patient mid-treatment, the lost woman mentions a studio number, the make-up artist points her in the right direction, and the lost woman in turn says her thanks. And then I watch as the reflection of this dream in bright blue turns in the doorway and steps back into the corridor.

And with that, Agnetha from ABBA walked out of my life, never to return.

Ah, ships that pass. And what a potentially pivotal moment that could have been for the history of popular culture. In only mildly different circumstances, I could have ended up joining ABBA. Or Agnetha could have ended up joining the cast of *Only Fools and Horses*. Or we could both have decided to throw it all in, there and then, turn our backs on the world and depart forthwith for a life of isolated bliss on a remote Scandinavian island, there to spend the long dark winters happily weaving jumpers for each other. But either way, how very much altered the world as we now know it would be.

As I was discovering, though, now that I was working there regularly, the BBC's various rehearsal and studio spaces were quite the place for worlds briefly colliding. Quite apart from members of ABBA wandering into your make-up session, you might find yourself down in the canteen at lunchtime, tray in hand, queuing for sausage and chips, or whichever other gastronomic speciality the BBC was fuelling its workforce with that day, looking across at someone tucking into a steamed pudding with custard and thinking, 'That bloke looks exactly like Bruce Forsyth,' only to realise that there was a very good reason for that – namely, because the person tucking into steamed pudding with custard actually *was* Bruce Forsyth. And isn't that Angela Rippon over there by the window? And, blimey – isn't that the whole of Pan's People beside the coffee cups?

I can't deny that I got quite a buzz out of it all – this strong sense, which it would be impossible to duplicate today, of being at the British broadcasting industry's beating heart.

Really that canteen in itself, with all its various comings and goings, would have made a good setting for a sitcom. But we already had one of those to think about – and now it was making its first Christmas special. And making it in something of a hurry, I have to say – filming a session in the studio on 20 December for broadcast just over a week later, on the 28th.

Talk about leaving your shopping until the last minute. And it wouldn't be the last time our team ended up going down to the wire in the wrapping of its Christmas gifts to the nation.

To be honest, there was something rather ad hoc and hurried about all of the arrangements around 'Christmas Crackers', as this episode of *Only Fools* was named. It seemed to have been a last-minute gift idea on the BBC's part, too, who commissioned it late and foisted it on John to write at speed. The episode was entirely studio-bound, there being no time for any external location business and perhaps, knowing the BBC, no budget for any, either. Neither Martin Shardlow nor Ray Butt, the director and producer who had worked on the show regularly to this point, were available at short notice, so in came, on a one-off basis, to fill both those roles, Bernard Thompson, who had worked on *Are You Being Served?* and *Last of the Summer Wine*.

Now, I don't think I'll be going out on a limb if I suggest that the slightly slapdash circumstances in which the episode came together ended up showing in the finished product – right the way through to that title, 'Christmas Crackers'. In naming the special editions from here on in, John would never again hit the target so squarely and flatly on the nose. And nor would their content be quite so straightforwardly mainstream, either.

All sitcoms are fundamentally about people who are trapped by their circumstances and yearning in some way to get out. Classically, then, the Christmas special version of a sitcom, when given the standard treatment, will be about those same people being trapped by those same circumstances, but at Christmas – which is kind of a double trap, compounded by the fact that everywhere is closed and the world has shrunk even further.

This is very much the predicament in which we find Del, Rodney and Grandad in 'Christmas Crackers'. Grandad takes charge of the turkey roasting, but leaves the giblets inside, in their plastic bag, and also underdoes the cooking by a number of hours. Nigella Lawson will back me up here: this is not the best way to release the full flavour and succulence of your chosen bird on the big day.

Grandad's Christmas pudding, on the other hand – well, I think we can agree that that could have done with a little less time on the stove. He's basically produced a serving of coal. Again, Nigella will be turning in her apron.

These culinary horrors aside, plus an equally obligatory sequence featuring an exchange of Christmas presents, nothing much develops, apart from a trip to the miraculously open Monte Carlo nightclub where Del and Rodney attempt – unsuccessfully, of course – to pair themselves off. So, not the show's finest hour, let's gently say, and certainly not broadcast at the BBC's finest hour: the show went out at 9.55 p.m. following directly after *Val Sings Bing*, in which the crooner Val Doonican put his silken tones to the songs of Bing Crosby. In that unpromising and very much non-family-oriented slot, our show picked up 7.5 million viewers, which wasn't too bad for that time of night, although many of them, one suspects, were people who, having survived Val singing Bing, decided they could survive anything, and many of the rest were probably just staying awake for the main news, read by Richard Baker.

Not spectacular, though, however you carve it. A bit like Grandad's turkey.

Fast-forward a year to December 1982, though, and things are already starting to move, both for *Only Fools*'s general place in the Christmas scheme of things and for my own. Indeed, by 1982, the show is deemed worthy of not one but two appearances over that Christmas – albeit one of them is only eight minutes long, so perhaps has to qualify more as a head-popped-round-the-door than a fully-fledged visit to the nation's living rooms.

This was for something called *The Funny Side of Christmas* – a set of short skits featuring the casts of already running series, a compendium of miniature Christmas specials, if you will, offered to the country for its delectation on the Bank Holiday Monday, 27 December. Also featured were shows like *The Fall and Rise of Reginald Perrin*, *The Last of the Summer Wine* and *Butterflies* – all well-established sitcoms with their feet well under the BBC table at this point. So this was quite a vote of confidence for our relatively young show, just eighteen months and two series old at this stage, and with its place in the nation's affections still far from secured.

And who is that dapper gentleman in the pink bow tie whose job it is to link together this eighty-minute televisual patchwork on a Christmas theme? Why, that's the raconteur and comedy-writing polymath Frank Muir, of course, the kind of suave, verbally florid presence that, I think it's fair to say, television is simply less inclined to show us these days, at Christmas or any other time. They appear to have gone the way of the pink bow tie.

Often described as a 'lost episode', and not much seen since the night it went out, John Sullivan's contribution to Frank's patchwork was a sketch called 'Christmas Trees', in which Del is charged with going out on the street to flog 150 dismally droopy-looking fake firs – folding tinsel monstrosities, which Del optimistically describes as microchip-driven but which actually seem to need some fairly heavy manual encouragement just to fold away. Needless to say, despite Del's very best sales patter, these items seem to be going down among shoppers, as Del sighingly concedes, 'about as well as Union Jacks in Buenos Aires'.*

I loved doing all those street-selling scenes, and this one in particular gave me some room to get going:

. . . Now, if you went up Harrods you'd pay 27 quid for one of these and you'd think you were getting a right result. Well, I'm not going to ask you for 27 quid. I'm not even going to ask you for a score. Who said 15? . . .

Another vocation missed, clearly. But this was one of those acting occasions when I could genuinely say I'd done my research – specifically on Oxford Street in the late 1970s. While walking to work at the theatres from my place in Newman Street, I would often pause to watch the hawkers who had thrown down a blanket on the pavement and laid out their wares: watches, perfumes, underwear, toys, whatever was fresh off the back of that morning's lorry. The set-up fascinated me. I could stand there in the throng for ages, just watching it all develop, seeing these wannabe entrepreneurs do a roaring trade or die a cold and eerie death, depending – seeing them pack up in a hurry and scarper when the scout, posted up the road to keep an eye out, returned hotfoot to tip them off to the imminent arrival of a member of Her

* Topical joke by John, there: the Falklands War had ended six months prior to this. Probably still works as a joke even now, though.

Majesty's Metropolitan constabulary. You could see a whole story get told in a matter of minutes.

You soon picked up the tricks – the member of the team who pretends to be a customer, handing over a tenner and heading off up the street with his purchase, thereby getting the ball rolling, only to drift back furtively later with the goods tucked under his jacket, ready for resale. But the thing that most hooked me was the patter – the rhythm and pace of it, the reaching out to engage with someone in the audience and, in the process, bring everyone in on it. It was extraordinary to watch those guys cultivate relationships with strangers out of thin air.

How do you persuade somebody that they need something? First of all by persuading them that they can trust you. The manipulating, the tempting, the subtle cajoling – these were, frankly, theatrical tricks. I've said it before and I'll say it again, and in fact I'll keep saying it until the world decides to call it Jason's Theorem . . . but: flogging hooky gear from a suitcase with one eye out for an approaching copper and the noble profession of acting have an awful lot in common when you get down to it.

The slightly odd thing about that Frank Muir compendium is that Nick Lyndhurst and I appear in it twice, both playing roles that were ours before *Only Fools* came along. The inclusion of Carla Lane's *Butterflies* means that Nick pitches up opposite Wendy Craig and Geoffrey Palmer as Adam, the younger of their teenage sons, in a scene set in the wake – yet again – of a clearly thunderously inedible Christmas lunch. Clearly, whether it's a Peckham flat or the middle-class suburban home of a dentist and his frustrated wife, the law of the Christmas special states that crippling indigestion will dominate the conversation.

'What did she stuff the turkey with?' Adam's brother Russell, played by Andrew Hall, asks him from a semi-paralysed position on the sofa.

'A sort of herbal putty,' is Adam's reply.

And then, because *Open All Hours* also got a slot in the show, I additionally graced the screen as Granville the corner-shop assistant, opposite my great friend and mentor Ronnie Barker's Arkwright. It was the fate of *Open All Hours* to be mostly overlooked at the first time of asking (1976, on BBC2), but then to catch fire when the series was casually repeated on BBC1 to fill a hole in the schedules. Suddenly, after a four-year gap in which we'd all reluctantly reached the conclusion that the show was sunk, we were back in business, and the subsequent three series went out in 1981, 1982 and 1985, overlapping with the birth of *Only Fools* and keeping me rather busy, not least, clearly, over this particular Christmas.

In Roy Clarke's eight-minute *Open All Hours* skit, it was Christmas Day – the only day of the year that stingy old Arkwright would consent to close the shop – and nobody had indigestion because it was the morning and Christmas dinner (over the road at Nurse Gladys Emmanuel's) was yet to come.

In the meantime, though, eagle-eyed viewers – and perhaps not so eagle-eyed ones as well – had a moment to ponder the miracle by which, appearing as Granville, I had a dark and lustrous head of hair, which was somehow less in evidence in my portrayal of Derek Trotter in the very same broadcast.

No miracle, in fact – unless you count a little supplementary help with a clip-on hairpiece around the crown area, courtesy of the aforementioned BBC make-up people. Ah, once again, the indignities of the trade. But one is a professional and one weathers them and soldiers on.

The official *Only Fools* Christmas special that year went out three days later, on 30 December, at 7.55 in the evening – so by no means at the centre of the Christmas schedules, but nevertheless glamorously sandwiched between *Top of the Pops* and an episode of *'Allo 'Allo*. This special was called 'Diamonds are for Heather' and, after the conventional Christmas offering which was 'Christmas Crackers' the previous year, it showed pretty quickly that John Sullivan was already loosening the knots a bit and starting to do his own thing when Christmas came around.

OK, so the story was still pegged in time to the Christmas season – John hadn't yet had the nerve to fly in the face of that extremely robust convention, and he wouldn't do so at the next time of asking, either: indeed, 'Thicker Than Water', the 1983 special, will be set, in full compliance with tradition, on Christmas night in the Trotters' flat. There was no pushing the boundaries here in terms of length, either: 'Diamonds are for Heather' was a standard half-hour episode.

But it's quietly revolutionary in its own way, and even pretty daring. For here is a story intended for Christmas consumption, yet not about badly roasted turkeys and cooped-up families getting tetchy with one another while suffering indigestion, but about thwarted love – which can feel a lot like indigestion after consuming the wrong kind of stuffing, it's true, but which is ultimately a very different thing.

Here is a story in which Del falls head over heels for a single mum called Heather – played by Rosalind Lloyd – investing himself wholly in both her and her little son, only to be rejected by her in the end. Out went the full-on festive jollity you'd probably been expecting, then, and in came a heartstring-tugging romance, with an unhappy ending.

And what was on display as a consequence of that move were aspects of Del's character which had only really been hinted at up to now – that sense of Del as a thwarted father and home-builder. For all his striving, boisterous, best-foot-forward nature and for all his ducking and diving and bobbing and weaving, he's a man with this hinterland of tenderness inside him – someone who has had the responsibility for his brother and grandfather dropped on his plate by the death of his mum and has had to make a lot of sacrifices.* All that

* Contrary to some suggestions online, there is no cream you can get for a tender hinterland, or certainly not over the counter, anyway.

was a development for Del's character, and a development for me, playing him.

So, at the end, instead of everyone sitting around a groaning table in a tinsel-festooned room, pulling crackers, you get sadness and melancholy – and a rendition of 'Old Shep'.

Ah, that song – that terrible old song. On 'Spanish Night' in the Nag's Head, just before noticing Heather drinking alone at the bar, a deeply downcast Del orders the pub's specially booked Spanish live music act (more Greenwich in origin than Granada, it turns out) to sing 'Old Shep', a depressing hillbilly tune from the 1930s about a boy and his beloved but now unfortunately dead dog which Elvis Presley famously turned his hips to. So 'Old Shep' effectively brings Del and Heather together – it kicks off the conversation between them – and weeks of successful and happy courtship then ensue, capped off with the application of a 'DEL – HEATHER' sun-strip to the Reliant Regal, than which, clearly, there could be no firmer declaration of a man's best intentions. In the early 1980s, a marriage proposal was virtually a foregone conclusion after a demonstration of loyalty as solid as that.

Lo, over a candlelit curry, Del does indeed propose. But Heather respectfully turns him down, intending to reunite with her previously vanished husband and the father of her child, who has now, it seems, come back on the scene and is happily employed as a department store Father Christmas

DAVID JASON

in Southampton.* Del is back to square one, then, and, in a typically neat Sullivan loop-around, the rejected and thoroughly dejected Del, out on the street, gets some carol singers to sing him . . . 'Old Shep'.

This is a song so dreary, remember, that the 'Spanish' pub singer in the Nag's Head tells Del that there is no way he can sing it and hope to remain employed. Yet John Sullivan manages to get it performed in a sitcom's Christmas special, twice.

Those weren't just any old carol singers, by the way. They were played by the Fred Tomlinson Singers, about whom you possibly know more than you realise because Fred Tomlinson and his people supplied the choral requirements of the Monty Python team. Yes, my old nemeses the Pythons return to haunt these pages yet again. Indeed, Fred wrote the music for 'The Lumberjack Song', which must have earned him a bob or two, and he and his singers performed it with the Pythons for the show, as well as the almost equally notorious 'Spam Song'. Not a lot of people know that, as Michael Caine never actually said.†

* Very good terms and conditions with that job, as Del drily points out. 'Free uniform, luncheon vouchers, forty-eight weeks' holiday a year.'

† According to Michael Caine it was something that Peter Sellers said about him during a television interview as a wind-up – that Caine had the habit of repeating facts from the *Guinness Book of Records* and then saying, 'Not a lot of people know that.' The myth stuck – and so fast that Caine then ended up carrying that catchphrase around with him. He did eventually utter those words in the film *Educating Rita*, which came out in

34

But in between these renditions of that really quite awful song, much that is truly poignant has unfolded, not least in the scenes of Del enthusiastically bonding with Heather's boy, Darren, and embracing the self-appointed role of 'Uncle Del', on a day out round London. And if I managed to make something ring true about Del's predicament in those scenes then maybe that wasn't entirely a surprise, given where I was in my own life at that stage. When we filmed this episode, I was getting into my forties, and surrounded by friends and colleagues who had long since started having families, and naturally wondering if, having wholeheartedly dedicated the last fifteen years to doing all the acting I possibly could and to trying to build a career, I might have missed the boat in that regard.

Of course, with regard to that particular boat, I got exceptionally lucky eventually – as, indeed, would Del in due course. But in the meantime I definitely had the odd bout of anxious reflection in this area about the pros and cons of the choices I had so far made. I tend to resist comparisons between myself and Del, the two of us being – as I am always extremely keen to point out – such different people. But in the case of the kind of melancholy thoughts about his future that Del was having in 'Diamonds are for Heather', and the enthusiasm he brought to those scenes with Heather's child,

1983, but by then the association of Caine with the line was so rife that was an in-joke. Not a lot of people know all *that*, either.

I can make a small exception. Like with the street salesman patter, you could say: this was acting for which I'd done a bit of research.

After the studio shoot was completed, Rosalind and I went out to meet some of the audience, which was something the cast frequently did, just to thank them for turning up, being patient with us when we screwed up and generally being a part of it all. And as we mingled, a woman, still looking a little bit emotional, came up to us and said, 'God, I wasn't expecting that: you two made me cry.'

That was quite a moment for me. I mean, it was a nice compliment for Rosalind's and my acting, and actors will always bite your hand off for one of those. But beyond that – getting people to cry at a shoot for a Christmas sitcom? It made me realise what *Only Fools* was turning into and what it could become.*

All in all, I've got quite a soft spot for 'Diamonds are for Heather'. Coming so early in the show's history and long pre-dating the big set-piece Christmas numbers, it can get over-looked. But it was actually a rather lovely and fully formed episode, in my humble opinion, and in terms of seeding the

---

* Top tip: should you ever find yourself face-to-face with an actor and required to compliment them after a performance that, to be perfectly honest, you weren't entirely sure about, simply look them directly in the eye, beam warmly and say, in a tone of overawed wonder: 'Darling, you've done it again!'

direction for Del's character and the narrative direction of the series as a whole, a formative episode, too.

Even though it went out in what was very much not one of the prime Christmas slots, it still managed to attract 9.3 million viewers, which was nearly two million more people than the previous year's Christmas special had managed to drum up. The slightly disappointing thing was that it was about a million fewer people than had watched the most recent regular series episode of the show, a little less than a month previously – 'A Touch of Glass', which is the one where a chandelier doesn't come off too well from the Trotters' attempts to detach it for cleaning.

One step forward, two steps back, then. But the progress of *Only Fools* often felt a bit that way in those early years. Still, at the time, I wasn't inclined to split hairs. Ten million, nine million . . . these seemed like pretty big numbers to me – a decent chunk of the country.

Little did I know, but we were only just getting started in that respect.

Humble beginnings, then. But that was very much my story, too.

ON THE SECOND DEL OF CHRISTMAS . . .

Ghosts and movies

'The Ghost smiled thoughtfully, and waved its hand: saying as it did so, "Let us see another Christmas!"'

A Christmas Carol

What have you got for me now, my reasonably priced Spirit? Something much older this time?

Ah, yes. It's a cold, clear winter's night, and a small boy and his mother have got their coats on and are heading up Finchley High Road in north London in the direction of the Gaumont cinema.

The small boy in question? Well, draw a little closer, dear reader, because that's me, young David White. I'd be around eleven years old, by the look of it, which would make this 1951 or thereabouts, and I'm a shy and rather cautious little chap at this point in my life, although certainly sharp enough to tell you, if you ask me, how many beans make five. The answer being, 'A bean, a bean, a bean and a half, half a bean and a bean.' (Trust me, this little piece of repartee was considered the height of wit among eleven-year-olds in 1951.)

I'm also slightly on the short side, and a bit self-conscious about it, truth be told. Hard not to be. To my great alarm, a number of my contemporaries at school have begun getting tall before my very eyes – abruptly departing in the direction of the ceiling as if there is something in the light bulbs that they urgently need to get hold of. Some of them seem capable of adding whole feet to their height in the space of a single weekend. I, by contrast, can only watch all this rampant growth from a position closer to the ground and hope that I'm playing a longer game.

Spoiler alert: I am actually in the process of rising by tiny increments towards the giddy height of . . . er, five foot six, actually, where, in three years' time or so, at the age of about fourteen, my body will decide that it's had enough of getting taller, and stop. Here's an encouraging thought, though, gleaned in passing from a documentary I happened to be watching recently: back in the eighteenth century, the height of the average full-grown British male was (small drum roll here, please) . . . five foot five. Something positive to reflect on there, for all of us five-foot-sixers. Only three hundred years – a mere stitch, surely, in the unfathomable trousers of time – has separated us from a place among the giants.

As history shows us, over and again, it's all about perspective.

Anyway, here I am in 1951, fairly tiny, with my mum, who is not so tall herself, now you come to mention it, heading up the street for a night at 'the pictures'. This is not a rare outing for us. On the contrary, this is something we might do twice a week and sometimes even three times – occasionally joined by my father, though he generally, after a long day on his feet at the fishmonger's, prefers to stay at home and read the paper and listen to the radio. Fair enough. But for me and my mum . . . well, why wouldn't we go frequently, when the cinema costs so little – ninepence for a child in the cheap seats, one and six for a grown-up – and when it's basically on our doorstep, or at any rate a simple half-mile walk, up the road and turn right?

And what a cinema, too. The Finchley Gaumont is a majestic, towering, curve-fronted, art deco building whose glass-walled frontage sits behind the splendidly named Tally Ho Corner – not, as it turns out, a part of Aintree racecourse, but a broad road junction, laced overhead by a jumble of wires for the trolley buses.

Don't bother looking for the Gaumont today. It was demolished in the 1980s. And don't bother looking for the trolley buses, either, nor their wires, which, to be honest, were already going out of fashion in 1951, eased aside by the free-roaming diesel vehicles which people seemed to have decided were the future.

And while we're on the topic, don't bother looking for my house half a mile away at 26 Lodge Lane, either, which has long since been knocked down and concreted over, and now takes the form of a municipal car park, round the back of a Starbucks. Alas, then, no blue plaque marks my childhood home. And if it did, it would have to be nailed up somewhere between a Pay & Display machine and a selection of extremely sugary muffins.

Nevertheless, take it from me, on this particular Thursday evening in 1951, both the Gaumont and 26 Lodge Lane are still very much in business, along with these two figures walking out into the night. And if a certain urgency quickens the step of Mrs White and her son along the High Road, it's because they don't want to be late to join the queues which they know will already be forming on the street under the cinema's sweeping glass canopy.

Sure enough, the line when they reach it is already stretching up the pavement, but they take their place in it. And from then on, as the queue shuffles slowly forward, you will notice an eleven-year-old boy repeatedly leaning out from behind the overcoat in front of him and craning his neck to look ahead, in fear of the sight that will spell doom to the whole evening: the uniformed commissionaire emerging from the foyer and plonking down the HOUSE FULL sign.

What a heart-sinker that used to be when it happened – which was quite often, on account of the raging popularity of cinema-going at this moment in history. I should point out that the auditorium at the Gaumont held more than two thousand people and, even then, if you mistimed it, you could find yourself turned away. And there was never a plan B on those cinema nights. Go for a meal or a drink instead, as one might nowadays? Unthinkable behaviour! If the place sold out, my mum and I would simply turn round and walk home the way we had just come.

Tonight, though, after the usual anxious spell on the pavement, we're in luck. We're through the doors. And what a sight it is that greets us, in that immense entrance hall: the red-carpeted steps, the silver pillars soaring upwards into the high ceiling, the hanging globe lights giving off an orangey glow, the walls painted in shades of peach and gold and green. To my young eyes, all of this is unimaginably exotic – and to my mother's older eyes, too, actually, as we reach the window and she pushes the coins under the glass in exchange for our tickets.

And from there it's just a few more paces up another short flight of carpeted steps and we're through the internal doors and into the stalls of that massive auditorium. The enormity of the place never failed to impress my young mind – very different from your modern multiplex. None of that hobbling three miles down a dimly lit corridor to find Screen 14 in what was possibly once a broom cupboard – taking care to leave a trail of popcorn behind you, of course, so that you can find your way back to the entrance later. At the Gaumont, the big screen really did mean the big screen.

And oh, the warmth! I touched on this a bit in my last book, but a large part of the appeal of a night at 'the pictures' in those immediately post-war years had to do with basic creature comforts: things we largely take for granted now, like light and heat. Trust me: if, as was the case for the White family, electricity won't be reaching your terraced street for another couple of years yet, and television not for a couple of years after that; if the main source of warmth in your house is a single coal fire in the back parlour, and most of the other rooms, including the whole of the top floor, simply stay cold; and if the smallest room in your house isn't a room at all but actually takes the form of a tiny and punishingly draughty brick-built lean-to in the backyard, where the cold wind whistles under the door, as well as under several other things . . . well then, somewhere as wonderfully appointed and sumptuously heated as the Gaumont greets you as something which has just landed from the future.

And we haven't even mentioned the gents, with their gleaming porcelain sinks and shining mirrors. What promised land was this?

My point is, they didn't call them 'picture palaces' for nothing, and this, surely, as much as anything, accounted for the powerful magnetism of the cinema in those frequently colourless post-war years, and was what brought us working-class families flocking in such numbers two or three times a week. Never mind the movies – feel the grandeur. Even the commissionaire who minded the queue was loaned the magnificent authority of a peaked cap and a frock coat with gold-braided epaulettes, as if he was the doorman at Buckingham Palace, and for us he might as well have been.

And tonight in these sumptuous surroundings my mum and I will see something called *Scrooge*, a film about which I know very little in advance, but which, it's no exaggeration to say, I will know a lot about for ever more. At this point, though, the limits of my knowledge are that it stars someone named Alastair Sim. I know this because his name is emblazoned right across the top of the poster – 'IN HIS FIRST GREAT DRAMATIC COMEDY ROLE' – a poster which I have already examined carefully under glass outside the cinema, just as I closely scrutinised all the movie posters fixed to that wall, seeking to unlock the promise they contained.

But not too much else is given away in this case, the poster mostly being dominated by a painted image of a smiling elderly man, wrapped up in a red scarf and blue coat and under a top hat, with just a hint of a Victorian London street scene poking itself into view along the bottom edge. The colours on the poster, of course, are something of a liberty because the film we are about to see is in black and white. But it wouldn't occur to any of us to complain about that little detail, nor even really to notice it.

We have barely settled when the room thrillingly darkens and the curtains draw aside and a giant card silently fills the screen: 'RENOWN PICTURES CORPORATION LIMITED'. There is then, suddenly and out of nowhere, a thunderous burst of dark and jagged orchestral music that practically throws me backwards over my seat. The orchestra then gives way to a few voices hesitantly singing 'Hark the Herald Angels Sing', which also sounds threatening and eerie at first but then gradually gets louder, rising in confidence until it sounds strong and ultimately triumphant. Though I don't realise it yet, the whole story of the film is in that overture.

Meanwhile, on the screen, a hand has fetched down a volume from a shelf and solemnly opened it to reveal the film's titles and that name again, 'Alastair Sim', and the narrator has made himself heard for the first time.

'Old Marley was as dead as a doornail. This must be distinctly understood or nothing wonderful can come of the story I am going to relate . . .'

And straight away here comes Ebenezer Scrooge through an ominous-sounding wind, brutally brushing aside the pleading of a debtor outside on a set of icy steps, deriding Christmas in short order as 'a humbug' and crisply dismissing the carol singers outside his house: 'Be gone!'

I'm spellbound already, and I continue to be as I watch this glowering and instinctively mean figure return to his spacious but sparsely furnished and almost entirely comfortless home. With its creepy clock and its long shadows, it's a place set for a haunting if ever there was one and . . . well, what do you know? Before long there is a terrible clanking and creaking out on the stairs while Scrooge sits frozen over the most unappetisingly pale-looking bowl of soup you've ever seen in your life. He continues to stare in open-mouthed terror at the back of the closed door as (brilliant touch, this) his spoon, paused on its way up, tilts and slowly empties its unappealing contents back into the bowl.

By the time that door bursts open and the ghost of Jacob Marley enters, my eleven-year-old self is pinned to his seat, as open-mouthed as Scrooge and, if the lights were up, probably as pale as that awful soup. Because, by the wonders of film trickery, we are now looking at *a see-through man*.

How utterly terrifying is that? I mean, no disrespect to anyone recently hired in this line of work who might currently be sitting on the other side of my study with his feet up, and occasionally looking in a slightly bored way at his watch. But in those days, they knew how to do a Spirit of Christmas Past properly.

Marley's ghost in *Scrooge*, by the way, is played by Michael Hordern. That's the same Michael Hordern whom, some thirty-two years after this, I will stand alongside in a recording studio, creating the voices for the animated film version of *The Wind in the Willows* – him giving the world his Badger while I give the world my Toad. In other words, while Scrooge is encountering his past up there on that screen, I'm staring directly up at my future. But, aged eleven, I'm in no position to know that, and, even if I was, I'm too busy right now gripping the edge of my tip-up seat in horror to really give it much thought.

As it turned out, being in the presence of Michael Hordern was pretty scary, even when he wasn't playing a partly invisible ghost. But perhaps that's a story for further on in these pages. What I'll say now is that, following a preview of the film, the critic from the American trade paper *Variety* felt compelled to warn the world that *Scrooge* was 'a grim thing that will give tender-aged kiddies viewing it the screaming-meemies'.

And what can I tell you? As a tender-aged kiddie, the screaming-meemies – or certainly the nearest British equivalent – were a large part of my reaction, sat there in the stalls with whitened knuckles.

But, of course, that's precisely what I loved about it. Because, let's be honest, there's nothing some tender-aged kiddies like more than being scared witless by a movie now and again, and that was certainly true of *this* tender-aged kiddie. And if it leads directly to some screaming-meemies, then all the better, surely, and money well spent.

'A grim thing'? Well, yes. But that was the point, and what made *Scrooge* so great. This was a story about the consequences of meanness and about meanness overcome – and if you, in the audience, didn't encounter and feel the full force of that meanness in the first place, then there was no redemption in the tale. The director and producer of *Scrooge*, Brian Desmond Hurst, knew that. The film doesn't gloss over the darker aspects of the Dickens story. Even the snow – which falls throughout the film in accordance with the law affecting Christmas-themed movies – has a chilly, hostile bleakness about it.

In the US, the film was released under the more proper title, A Christmas Carol. Well, I say more proper, but if we're going to be pedantic about it, the title that Dickens actually gave his story was: A Christmas Carol, in Prose: Being a Ghost Story of Christmas. So stick that on your backlit marquee.

Anyway, Variety back then didn't care much for the film, whatever it was called. 'Adults will find it long,' the reviewer suggested – which is quite a contention to make about a film that clocks in under an hour and a half. Adult-wise, I can only speak for my mum, who, like me, was agog throughout. Generally there was a quite strong divide in those days between what my mum enjoyed at the cinema (romantic comedies, anything with Rock Hudson and Doris Day) and what I enjoyed (westerns featuring John Wayne and lashings of gunfire). But here, in Scrooge, we found an easy meeting place. This was storytelling which reached across the divides, generational and otherwise.

And as for the Variety critic's allegation that 'Alastair Sim stalks through the footage like a tank-town Hamlet' . . . well, at that point I feel I have no alternative but to reach for the traditional expression at moments of bewilderment while reading film reviews: 'Was this person watching the same movie as me?'

Also, what's a 'tank-town' when it's at home?

OK, I've looked it up: it's American for 'small-town'. But

a small-town Hamlet? Alastair Sim? No, surely not. There was so much that was clever about that performance, and so much that was adeptly done. You laughed at Scrooge, and you recoiled from him, and you understood that there was something monstrous about him. But you also saw his fear and understood it, and eventually came to sympathise with him. It's a rare and deft kind of acting that can command that range of response in an audience.

Anyway, an hour and a half later the credits rolled. Did the young boy in our tale then wander forth from the Gaumont and make his dazed way home, his head a-spin with visions of what acting could do and with the seeds of ambition now sown deep in his heart? Well, if this book was itself a movie, maybe you would play it that way. (And incidentally, film rights to these recollections do remain available at the time of writing: any interested Hollywood producers, please address your approaches to my agent in the usual fashion.)

But in truth, no: there were no dreams of acting for me at this point. There couldn't have been. The place in which there were people called actors, who got together and made entertainments for people like me and my mum, might as well have been another planet entirely. It was so far removed from my own world as to be completely unimaginable – not even, at this point, a fantasy land running parallel to our own that I might dream about finding the portal to. All that was a long way off, in every sense.

So what happened after I watched *Scrooge* was, I went home to bed. I used to love doing that walk back from the cinema – especially in the winter. I loved that burst of cold air as you came out onto the pavement and which caused you to tighten your coat around yourself. And I loved that feeling of tiredness at the end of the day, and knowing that your bed was waiting for you, and not so far away.

But most of all I loved the way that the dark night, as you walked, helped you keep the movie you had just seen running in your head. Summer nights just weren't the same for film-going in that respect. Coming out at around half past nine into the lingering evening light and the warm air somehow made the magic evaporate more quickly. In the depths of winter, when it was properly dark and cold enough to draw you into yourself, you could stay in the world of the film for just that little bit longer.

So I headed home with the story of *Scrooge* rolling around my imagination, and with those ghosts, in particular, accompanying me – and following me up the dark stairs to my bedroom and putting a bit of extra energy in my legs as I scampered under the blankets to get warm. If any seeds were sown, on this and all those other young nights at the cinema, it was in beginning to understand how things can leap off a screen and touch people – how a simple piece of entertainment can reach into people's hearts and minds and lodge there, not just for the whole of the journey home, but for good.

* * *

I saw Alastair Sim in the cinema again several times after that. Most notably, he played the headmistress, Miss Millicent Fritton, in *The Belles of St Trinian's*, that now classic comedy set in the legendarily rebellious girls' school, and which I saw in the Gaumont when it came out in 1954. The character of Miss Fritton was a proper 'grande dame' part originally written for Margaret Rutherford, but when she proved unavailable someone had the bonkers yet brilliant idea of giving it to Sim, who was also cast in the film as Clarence Fritton, the headmistress's brother. What I love about Sim's Miss Fritton is that he doesn't play it as cabaret, which a broader and less capable kind of comedian might have been tempted to do. He doesn't aim for the exaggerations where the belly laughs might have been. He goes for something much closer and more careful – a character study. And it's perfect in every detail.

Sim died in 1976, but he will always be high on my list of the greats. And I'm by no means alone in holding him there, of course. In the early seventies, John Cleese apparently pleaded and badgered and downright begged his way into an episode of the BBC comedy series *Misleading Cases*, purely because he wanted to be able to say he had acted with Alastair Sim. I wish I'd thought of that.

I did at least get to see Sim work onstage, though. I drove out of London to the Chichester Festival Theatre one evening in 1969 to see him play Aeneas Posket in the nineteenth-century Pinero farce, *The Magistrate*. I got lucky, because some now rank that as Sim's finest theatrical performance – stuffed full of unscripted sequences, unique bits of business and tours de force. At one point he spent a long time trying, and failing, to get a pair of braces under control; at another, he spent the best part of five minutes simply washing his face and getting into all sorts of difficulties with the soap and the towel. His control, both of what he was doing and of us in the audience, was masterful. Opposite him as Agatha Posket was Patricia Routledge. It was quite a night, all in all.

I go back to Alastair Sim's *Scrooge* every Christmas, marvelling yet again at the depth of its cast. Patrick Macnee, later of *The Avengers*, is in there, and so are Hattie Jacques and Jack Warner from *Dixon of Dock Green*. And so is George Cole, who would have been twenty-six at the time, playing the younger Scrooge and talking in a slightly higher register voice in order to do so. George's path and mine ended up crossing a lot further down the line, too.

But mostly I marvel at Alastair Sim. He made something there for Christmas which doesn't fade. Which is why, when we wind forward across the ages to that restaurant table in London a few years ago, where the man from ITV was offering me the extremely tempting chance to play Scrooge myself, I didn't have to think too hard or for too long.

'No, thank you very much,' I said. 'I don't think that's for me.'

The thing was, I'd seen other productions of *A Christmas Carol* in the meantime, and . . . well, no names, no pack drill, but I'd found myself sitting there and thinking: 'No! No! Why did you even attempt it?' And now that the carrot was being dangled in front of me, it would have felt hypocritical to snatch at it. It would certainly have felt daunting.

I mean, I was as up for a challenge as any other actor, and always had been, from day one. I was also up for a job, as most actors tend to be, too, acting being a famously precarious business in which you never quite know when the next offer might be coming along – and that's true no matter how successful you are. The problem was, I sincerely believed that Alastair Sim had achieved the summit with that interpretation of Scrooge, and if I were to take it on, I would only end up kicking about in the foothills. His version had left such an impression on me that I didn't see how I could do anything other than a pale imitation of it. So I decided to turn this rather generous opportunity down.

Which either makes me a man of unimpeachable integrity or a bit of a wally, depending how you look at it.

There's a useful saying, though: 'Talent hits a target no one else can hit. Genius hits a target no one else can see.'

Who wrote that? Well, I did, just now, of course. But I believe the first person to set down those words in that order was Arthur Schopenhauer, the nineteenth-century German philosopher whose hugely influential works – I'm sure I don't need to tell you – I am forever taking down from the shelves of the library at Jason Towers and pondering anew. In the original German, obviously.

Actually, I think I might have seen it on a wall somewhere – possibly at the dentist's? Or was it at the recycling centre?

Doesn't matter. The point is, it's true. Talent does indeed hit a target no one else can hit. And genius does indeed hit a target no one else can see.

And just occasionally the wisest course is not even to take aim.

I finished my chicken escalope, thanked the man from ITV for his kind offer – and prayed another part would come along soon.

ON THE THIRD DEL OF CHRISTMAS . . .

Pantomimes and turkeys

And what scene is this now that my reasonably priced Spirit of Christmas Past, who's hanging about over there by the fireplace, bids me contemplate with his bony, pointing finger? Ah yes: I know this vision well enough, and these figures within it extremely well, though it is even older, surely, than the last scene he cooked up for us.

This is 1948, did you say? And if this is 1948, that would make me . . . what? Eight, going on nine – and even smaller than I was in the previous chapter, if such a thing is physically possible. And there I am, in the hall at home with my mother, putting on our coats. But this time the pair of us are heading, not for the Finchley Gaumont, but for the Golders Green Hippodrome, a short bus trip away. And this time, it's not the cinema we're going to. We're bound for the pantomime.

To which you are legally obliged to shout, 'Oh no, you're not.'

And to which I, in turn, am legally obliged to reply, 'Oh yes, we are.'

But wait. Before we finish buttoning ourselves up and set off for the evening, the Spirit invites you and me to put our heads into the Lodge Lane kitchen, just briefly, and observe the scene there.

And what a scene it is. There, piled around the sink and on the table, are Christmas turkeys. Also Christmas ducks and large-size Christmas chickens. Mounds of them. Whole piles of uncooked meat, stacked high. And there, somewhere in among those mounds, sits my father, working away with his bare hands and a sharp knife. You would say it looked like a butcher's in here at the moment, and there's a good reason for that, because it is.

At any rate, being a fishmonger, my father knew the local butcher well and, come Christmas, when the butcher was overwhelmed with orders, my dad could make himself a couple of extra quid by taking in a delivery of fowl at home and preparing it for the butcher's counter: plucking it and disembowelling it, as required. Eventually the butcher's van would come back to load up the now shop-ready meat – and I'm sure the deal was sweet enough to ensure that my father got to set aside a decent-sized bird for the family in part payment.

So this was how my dad would spend his evenings in the run-up to the Christmases of my childhood. He would roll up his sleeves, pull up a dining chair and set to work on a batch of freshly slaughtered turkeys. The smell, like the feathers, would fill the kitchen. I used to pitch in and help with the plucking. I drew the line at the disembowelling, though. Health and safety? Well, we washed our hands, didn't we?

And these, in turn, were the sights and sounds that I came to associate with the festive season, as readily as I associated it with paper chains, glued together at the dining table by me and my sister, June, and then looped across the sitting room through the light fitting in the middle. Christmas at 26 Lodge Lane was about the decorations, yes, and about the stockings hung by the chimney which would end up filled with sweets and nuts, and the pillowcase at the foot of the bed that would miraculously come to contain a clump of presents in the short gap between going to sleep on Christmas Eve and waking up bright and breezy the next day. In that sense, it was probably no different from most other people's. But it was also that time of the year when our kitchen became, briefly, a butcher's outhouse.

Is it any wonder that I later developed mixed feelings about the season and an indifference to turkey sandwiches?

But enough of this. Let us turn away from the kitchen now, and its mounds of partly prepared poultry, and leave by the front door. Me and my mum have got a bus to catch and a pantomime to go to. In fact, by the magic of the written word, we're already there. We're taking our seats in the Hippodrome, which turn out to be in the stalls, but a long way back in this cavernous music hall theatre – so far back that the balcony formed by the circle is not far above our heads, making our position below it quite snug. And this, as we wait for the show to commence, is causing me considerable agitation.

It's nothing to do with claustrophobia because, don't worry, the seating isn't *that* tight. And, of course, my less than exceptional height, which I think I may have mentioned already, has at least one lifetime benefit: I'm normally quite well off for headroom. (You've got to look on the bright side.)

No, my anxiety is entirely about what this position in the auditorium means for my view of the upcoming entertainment. Because the show we have come to see is *Jack and the Beanstalk*. And despite this being my first time at the pantomime – my first time at a professional theatrical production of any kind, actually – I haven't come into this experience entirely unbriefed. On the contrary, I am bringing with me the advance knowledge that the tale of Jack and the Beanstalk features . . . a giant. This I know, as well as I know how many beans make five. (See previous chapter if you're still struggling with the maths.)

And although, as a theatre-going novice, I hardly qualify as an expert in this area, I am immediately certain of one thing about these seats under the circle that fate and the woman in the box office have dealt my mother and me – and that's that they can't possibly lend themselves to the clear and unobstructed viewing of giants.

And this is a worry.

Indeed, as we settle into these seats and wait for the lights to go down, I am leaning forward as far as I can go in my place and straining, unsuccessfully, to peer out from under the circle's low ceiling to get a view of the very top of the curtains. Because that's surely what I'm going to need if I'm going to be able to take in the full enormity of this giant when he eventually pitches up, which will be, by most informed estimates, sometime around the beginning of Act Two.

I mean, you wouldn't want to miss it, would you? Imagine going to *Jack and the Beanstalk* and only being able to see the giant up as far as his knees. That's the kind of disappointment that would live with you for a while afterwards.

So I'm getting up and leaning forward, and sitting down and getting up again, and tilting my head to one side until it's practically upside down to see if that makes any difference . . . doing everything, basically, to work out what's possible, from a sightlines point of view. Meanwhile my mum is trying to reassure me that when the lights go down and the curtains open, all will be well, just you wait and see. (And please, for heaven's sake, would you just stop *fidgeting*.)

And my mum, of course, is right. For it turns out that my childish imagination has rather got ahead of me on this occasion, as childish imaginations are prone to do. In due course, as the entertainment unfolds, it will emerge that the part of the giant is being played, not by an actual giant, flown in from the Land of Giants and appearing by special arrangement with the Land of the Giants Tourist Board, but by a man of slightly above average height in a pair of stacked heels.

I should immediately say that this is by no means a bare-bones production, here in Golders Green. On the contrary, the Hippodrome is a pukka theatre and a landmark home for significant performances from quality performers, and we're not talking Trotter Entertainments by any means. Corners have not been cut. Why, the part of Muggles is being played by Max Wall, no less. This, of course, flies over my eight-year-old head entirely, and perhaps, dear reader, it flies over yours now, too. But in Max Wall I am watching a comedy great at work, a man who will know national fame for his character, Professor Wallofski, and his silly-walk routine – which, as John Cleese readily admits, was the prime inspiration for Monty Python's Ministry of Silly Walks. (I'm sure Wall would thank me for mentioning that he was a great serious actor, too, by the way – strong enough, along with Buster Keaton, to attract the patronage of Samuel Beckett, who was famously picky when it came to actors.)

So Max Wall is playing Muggles – and Muggles, by the way, in case you are drawing a blank or perhaps wondering how elements of J. K. Rowling's Harry Potter books got into a panto in 1948, was the name given in this production to the character of Jack's dimmer brother – the Rodney, I suppose you could say, to Jack's Del. And now I mention it, there is quite a lot of the Derek Trotter about Jack in that panto:

stupidly trading a quite valuable cow for some knock-off magic beans, which then get slung out the window in despair, only for the family to get lucky in a very roundabout kind of way. I mean, if you were to throw a Peckham tower block in there and add a Reliant Regal . . .

But I digress. The point is, you may know the character of Muggles better as Simple Simon. Or maybe as Tommy Tucker. Or perhaps as Simple Sammy, Silly Billy or even Miffins. It all depends on what point in the last two and a bit centuries you saw a production of *Jack and the Beanstalk*. And yes, this particular panto really does go back that far – to a time when Christopher Biggins was but the tiniest of twinkles in a pantomime dame's eye.

In fact, some historians suggest that *Jack and the Beanstalk* may have been the first *ever* pantomime, there having been a production of it at the Theatre Royal, Drury Lane, in London in 1819. Allegedly that Drury Lane production boasted a lavish and, indeed, climbable beanstalk. The problem was, the actor cast as Jack – one Eliza Povey, who was arguably the first ever 'principal boy' – couldn't be persuaded to climb it. Too risky, she felt, and she may have had a point. So a stunt double had to be used. I wonder if you could see the join. My suspicion is that you probably could. Even from a seat at the back of the stalls.

I can't quite recall the state of the beanstalk in this 1948 version, or whether any climbing took place on it, either by leading players or their stuntmen. But I do remember the entry of the giant on his stacked heels, which certainly did elevate him slightly above the rest of the cast, but didn't exactly send him up to the lights or cause him to fill the auditorium King Kong-style, which would have been more in line with what I was imagining as we travelled there on the bus. Less 'fee fi fo', and more 'fee fi . . . oh'.

Now, I suppose another child might reasonably have decided, right there and then, to write off the whole idea of the theatre as a swizz – especially a child who had already started going to films with his mum. Call that a giant? How unlike the cinema the theatre turned out to be. When the cinema promised giants – and also ghosts, for that matter – it generally delivered them. The theatre, less so.

The truth is, though, by the time the giant showed up (Act Two, as expected, after the interval), I couldn't have cared less. By then I was having a high old time, swallowed up by the whole experience, agog at the mayhem that was unfolding in front of my eyes. I was rapidly discovering that pantomime was a form of theatre in which the audience had a speaking part. All the call-and-response stuff, the behind yous, the oh-no-you're-nots, the boos and cheers – this was wonderful, inclusive anarchy to my eight-year-old mind, just the very best kind of fun. Amid such bounty, the giant's lack of authentic giantness was a mere detail.

And that's before I even mention the bike they had up there – a ridiculous contraption that Jack would periodically leap astride and on which, as the wheels went round, the saddle went up and down. This, I would later learn, was a Bucking Bronco bike – made by the legendary company Hawtins. I got to know quite a bit about Hawtins later in my life because what they did tied in with a passion of mine. They were a splendid Blackpool outfit, founded in the 1920s by two brothers, Fred and Percy, who devoted themselves for about forty years to making a vast range of mechanical entertainments – jukeboxes, slot machines, miniature train rides, carousels, mechanical grabbers, dodgems . . . When I started reconditioning classic slot machines for fun in my workshop at home, I came to have great respect for Hawtins and their devices and desires, and not a little envy for their operation, actually – this brilliant, maverick business that started out in a shed and grew to occupy a three-and-a-half-acre site employing hundreds of people, all making mechanical amusements. That's my idea of a business worth minding.

And Hawtins' imagination, clearly, had given birth to the Bucking Bronco bike, bolted together so that the forward motion of the pedals caused the saddle to rise and fall – maybe not a major contribution to road safety but without question a major contribution to theatre-going enjoyment for eight-year-olds. As Hawtins' catalogue description of the bike from the 1940s proudly puts it: 'The contortions of riders mounting the machine for the first time provide spectators with an endless source of amusement.' Endless, indeed.

The catalogue goes on: 'The Ride lends itself to competitions, but in our experience we have never found this stimulation to business necessary.' Well, yes, a Bucking Bronco bike race – that I would very much like to see. Over fences, even better. But in the theatre that time it was enough to watch this fantastic machine make its galumphing way across the stage. I had never seen anything like it. I was in stitches.

Funnily enough, not so many years after this, I inadvertently bought a second-hand motorbike that had quite a lot in common with the Hawtins Bucking Bronco. But maybe that's a story for later on. In the meantime, that mad bike was another detail in a riot of colour and licensed foolishness taking place on that Hippodrome stage which seemed to chime very loudly with a certain eight-year-old.

Put the boy off theatre? *Au contraire. Au* very much *contraire.*

*   *   *

Now, without changing location, let's get the Spirit to pull his finger out and flash us forward seventeen years, if he could be so obliging – to Christmas 1965. Your author is now twenty-five and once more he finds himself in the Golders Green Hippodrome. But this time he's not in the stalls with his mum, he's on the stage, without his mum, having a Kirby harness fitted.

Now, the Kirby harness is without question a wonderful piece of equipment and a great gift to the world of live theatrical entertainment. It is, to your jobbing actor, what a feather was to Dumbo: it enables him to fly. But that doesn't mean it's comfortable to wear, and certainly not feather-like. Basically, Kirby's patented design is a tight girdle with tethers in the back for the wires that, operated offstage, will lift you aloft. And to prevent you simply sliding out of the bottom of that girdle while airborne, there are two leather straps along its lower edge which fasten extremely tightly around the tops of your thighs. So far so practical. But the effect of the wire taking the weight of the harnessed actor is, of course, to tug the girdle upwards. And, in tugging the girdle upwards, it also, by certain unhelpful laws of physics, brings those thigh straps both up and together at the same time, in a devious scissoring motion, whereupon . . .

Look, I probably don't need to go into detail about the nature of the discomfort this scissoring action in the groin area causes, but suffice it to say that my eyes are watering even to remember it, and the Spirit of Christmas Past, over there by the fireplace, actually just crossed his legs.

Anyway, there's muggins, at twenty-five, getting strapped in for his maiden flight, and about to discover for himself just how painful a Kirby harness can be. Alongside me at this rehearsal for the BBC's Christmas pantomime, which is to be filmed in this very theatre a few days hence and then broadcast proudly to the nation on Christmas Day itself, are five or six other cast members, all similarly wired up and ready for take-off. And though all of us are in civvies while we rehearse this flying ballet, come the eventual shoot we will be wearing police uniforms, because . . . well, because this is a pantomime and policemen who can fly and keep bashing into each other are quite funny, or certainly they are if they suddenly show up unexplained in the middle of *Mother Goose*.

So, assuming I don't reach a shocking end in the Kirby harness during these rehearsals, this will be my television debut, filmed at the very same venue where my eight-year-old self once sat in the stalls and stared agog at Jack and his dumb brother and his equally dumb bicycle, and craned his neck in vain to look up at the very ceiling from which he will shortly be swinging uncomfortably by a wire.

I'll be playing multiple roles in *Mother Goose*, actually. Ever-mindful of the bottom line, the BBC has got me doubling up as a villager in some early crowd scenes, and, later on, as the King of Gooseland, no less. Understandably, news of my involvement in this major televisual spectacular has rocked the world's media. Or, at any rate, my agent has managed to get a little item in *The Stage*, the acting industry's in-house journal, complete with a thumbnail headshot. And, publicity-wise, better a thumbnail headshot, I always say, than a head-sized thumbnail shot. Below a small black-and-white snap of me looking all dewy-eyed and promising, it says:

David Jason, who made the first appearance of his professional career at the New [Theatre], Bromley, as the butler in *South Sea Bubble* last April, is to be King of Gooseland in the BBC TV's pantomime this year. After playing the acrobatic waiter in *Diplomatic Baggage* at the New last July he was signed up as a permanent member of the Bromley company.

All true, that . . . well, almost. I did indeed appear, earlier that year, in John Chapman's *Diplomatic Baggage* at the New Theatre in Bromley, south London, and it did indeed lead me to get a full-time gig with the repertory company there. But I wasn't playing a waiter. I was playing a hotel porter – and for we aficionados of the wonderful world of farce, such distinctions are important.

However, as portrayed by me, this hotel porter certainly merited the description 'acrobatic' – and in ways which, I must sheepishly confess, weren't exactly in the script. I worked up a routine around the pushing of a heavy roomservice trolley that lasted whole minutes. Did I overcook it? Well, possibly. But what's a young actor trying to make a name for himself going to do? I saw a chance there, and seized it. My fellow cast members, keen to get on with the play, might have raised a few eyebrows – might even have given me a few frosty looks in the wings afterwards, in fact. But the audience didn't seem to mind. On the contrary, gales of laughter and rounds of applause accompanied me off the stage – eventually – every night. Music to my young and inexperienced ears.

It was a similar story with the butler in Noël Coward's

South Sea Bubble, which had been my very first professional gig since I decided, after months of anxiously mulling it over, to disappoint my parents and abandon my steady and reasonably well-paid job as a self-employed electrician and invite penury by becoming a professional actor. Frankly, as written, the butler was there to serve the drinks and not to dominate the evening. Same goes for butlers everywhere, I guess. But, in collaboration with the play's director, Simon Oates, I managed to get this small part worked up into something a little more, shall we say, substantial.

In particular, there were some ornamental drums as part of the decor in what was a rather fancily furnished garden, and these caught my eye. What if the butler, passing those drums at one point, noticed them and conceived a longing to have a bash on them? Which, of course, would be right out of order for a working butler. If you played it right, the audience could see him having an amusing little struggle with his conscience – his sense of professional duty tussling with his eventually painful desperation to hit those drums. You knew he was going to succumb eventually and let rip, but you didn't know when, and the time in between the audience working out that this thing was going to happen and it actually happening was, I realised, comedy's playing field. That little number, too, turned into a bit of an item and even got me a gratifying mention in the local paper's review of the show. And, again, while I was busy drawing out this moment as far as it could go without cracking, the other members of the cast were probably surreptitiously looking at their watches, but the audience definitely enjoyed it.

So this was where I was, professionally speaking, going into that BBC pantomime. Now, well may you ask, had eking scraps of off-script comedy from bit parts as waiters and porters always been my grand design since I conceived the idea of turning pro? Was it for this that I junked a company van and a steady wage?

Let me put it this way: just before that first job as a reluctant drum soloist in Bromley, I'd auditioned for a place with a repertory company in Margate. My audition piece? The 'Now is the winter of our discontent' speech from Shakespeare's *Richard III*.

Which, by the way, I could deliver very convincingly – or so I genuinely believed. But the audition hadn't gone well. I was so racked by nerves that my legs shook, causing my heels to beat an involuntary tattoo on the rehearsal room's wooden floor all through my delivery. Consequently, my intense portrayal of a mind riven by bitterness and jealousy was slightly undercut by the fact that I appeared to be tap dancing throughout. A tap-dancing Richard III was not what the panel was looking for. Nor me, really.

I left the room with those famous last words ringing in my blushing ears: 'Thank you very much. We'll be in touch . . .'

But my embarrassment on that occasion is not the point here. The point is, just mere days before taking to the professional stage as a slapstick butler, I had presented myself to an audition panel as a serious Shakespearean. Mark, I pray you, the distance that separates the course we envisage for ourselves and the path we end up taking. You go in thinking, *Richard III*, you come out fooling around with bongos and tea trolleys and move on from there, if you're lucky. But 'go with the flow' was always my motto. And clearly I did.

Incidentally, one other important development took place between those two theatrical roles and ahead of my television debut, which your shrewd eyes may already have noticed: I became another person. Or, at any rate, I ceased to be David White and turned into David Jason. The contract I was offered for four weeks' work in *South Sea Bubble* – two weeks of rehearsal, two weeks of performance – was a ticket I could take to Equity, the actors' union, and apply for membership. And that Equity card would itself, of course, be my ticket to further work – a golden ticket.

I rang up as soon as I could. But there was already a David White registered, the woman on the other end of the phone told me. And a David Whitehead, which was my hastily improvised second choice.

'Would you like to go away and have a think about it?' asked the woman from Equity.

But I wasn't going anywhere. I was in too much of a hurry. As I've explained before, my mind now for some reason turned to fond memories of Miss Kent at primary school, reading the class the story of Jason and the Argonauts, a tale which had really connected with me, and a light bulb went on.

'What about David Kent?' I said.

No, I didn't. I said, 'Is David Jason taken?' And it wasn't, so that was me from then on.

What an opportunity for self-reinvention that was. Just one phone call to an office in central London and I was someone else. I guess it felt a bit odd at first – though not as odd as it would have felt if I had also traded in my first name. Everyone had always called me 'David' and everyone carried on calling me 'David', so to that extent my new persona made no difference. But there were a few early confusions on my part. I remember looking at theatre programmes the first few times and seeing the name 'David Jason' in print and thinking, 'Who's he when he's at home?' and then realising it was me when I was at work.

The main effect of it, though, was liberating – emboldening, actually. The idea that David White the electrician had the nerve to think he might give acting a shot had made me feel extremely self-conscious. By no means the boldest of people, I was ready for people to sneer at my presumption. Auditions in which I tried, and failed, to deliver speeches from *Richard III* over the noise of my own shaking legs didn't exactly decrease that feeling.

But it wasn't David White doing that now – it was this other bloke, David Jason, and maybe *he* had a chance, whatever people thought. The change of name made a clean break with the past and allowed me to think that I was now going forward, away from my old self and into whatever this new life as a professional actor was going to bring me.

Which so far was a rapid acceleration from butler, to acrobatic porter, to King of Gooseland, and all in three short steps. Now that's what I call social mobility.

Reporting to Golders Green for BBC panto duty, I really did feel I had been suddenly thrust up the ladder professionally – far further than I had any right to expect. I was mixing with people who were big stars at the time – among them, Terry Scott, Norman Vaughan and Jon Pertwee, who would soon become, in my humble opinion, the greatest of the Doctor Whos (or should that be the Doctors Who?), but who was already familiar to me as a member of the cast of the radio comedy show *The Navy Lark*, which we always tuned into at home. And I was in a production that had the mighty clout and, at the time, considerable glamour of the British Broadcasting Corporation behind it. The BBC was a bit like Britain's Hollywood in those days – 'star central', in as much as the nation had one. It certainly felt a long way from the New Theatre, Bromley. Filming took place over the course of a week, and one day we all knocked off and headed up the road for lunch – me, sauntering out into the street with Jon Pertwee and Norman Vaughan and thinking, 'Oh, if my friends could see me now . . .' I ended up sitting next to Anna Dawson at that lunch. Naturally, I attempted to play it cool and make it look as though I was out for casual meals with familiar faces off the TV all the time, though my gaucheness and the general quaking in my boots must have given me away.

After the filming wrapped, we didn't have to wait long to inspect the fruits of our labours: just a couple of weeks later, it was Christmas Day. In her address to the nation that year, the Queen turned her thoughts to the various ways in which people might be experiencing their 'first' Christmas: 'It may be the first Christmas for many as husband and wife,' she pointed out, 'or the first Christmas with grandchildren.' Indeed. Or, as Her Majesty might have said, your first Christmas with a son on the telly, which is how it was for Mr and Mrs White of 26 Lodge Lane.

The BBC pantomime, by the way, was a regular TV fixture on Christmas Day even before the reigning monarch was. The Christmas message from Buckingham Palace was an audio-only experience at first, and the Queen didn't start showing up in our sitting rooms until 1957, which was a whole year after Eric Sykes, Hattie Jacques and Spike Milligan had given us their *Dick Whittington*. So by 1965 the Whites had had some time to become ritual Christmas Day panto watchers. I'm pretty sure we sat down in front of *Dick Whittington*, and I know we sat down in front of *Babes in the Wood* with Kenneth Connor and Tony Hancock, and in front of *Robinson Crusoe* with Norman Wisdom. It was just what we did.

And now here we were in front of *Mother Goose*, coming

on at 4.50 p.m., right after *Disney Time* and before *Doctor Who* (played by William Hartnell at this point). Meanwhile, in my first and by no means last personal experience of Christmas Day ratings wars, ITV were doing their best to peel the nation's attention away from me with *Moby Dick*, the John Huston film with Gregory Peck, and, after that, the football results.

Football matches? On Christmas Day? Oh yes. A full programme of them in those days, if that interested you, although nobody in my family was all that bothered. Football was someone else's battle in a far-distant country as far as my dad was concerned, and I'm afraid his indifference got passed down.

Moby Dick, on the other hand, might well have diverted my father, although, thinking about it, a film about whale-hunting would have been a bit of a busman's holiday for a fishmonger. Anyway, in our family, by this point in history, there was no contest: the Christmas panto was on. And so was I.

You had to strain to catch me, though. There were no close-ups. Practically the whole thing was filmed in broad shot, from a static position in the stalls, the idea being, I guess, that you, the viewer at home, would feel like you were experiencing this spectacle as if you were in the theatre. 'Can't get to the panto? No matter – the BBC will bring the panto to you!' As a consequence, though, I was but a speck on the screen of the Whites' black-and-white television set as, just after a dance number and Norman Vaughan's opening speech, I stepped forward in my villager's costume and spoke my first televised words:

'*Who comes here?*'

'This is it,' I warned everyone, from my position in the corner of the sofa. 'Wait . . . here it is . . . this is my line . . .'

'That was me!' I said afterwards. 'That was my line!'

Sometime after this, I alerted everyone to my reappearance, on this occasion as the King of Gooseland, and now grandly seated on a throne. A throne, I should say, before which Terry Scott, the star of the show, had to kneel at one point and, as memory dimly recalls, plead with me for somebody's freedom – possibly his own. Imagine that! A bona fide TV heavyweight, bowing at my feet. Did I have any further lines at this point? Likelihood would suggest that I did say at least something. I was the King, after all. That said, I suppose I could simply have been entrusted by the director with staring silently across the scene in a regal manner. Either way, the soap-engrimed shower curtain of time has long since drawn itself across my recollection of this moment, and the BBC appear to have put the tapes of the show out with the bins, as they so often did before archivists started getting cross about it, so more than this I cannot say.

What I can confirm is that I then appeared for my third stint, this time as the policeman in that flying ballet. And then that was me done.

So, how did all of this sudden national televisual exposure

play in Lodge Lane? Well, if my dad saw a glittering career stretching ahead of me on the basis of these short and blurry moments, he didn't exactly say as much. In fact, I'm not sure that he really offered an opinion of any kind from his traditional place in the armchair that afternoon. But then, just to put some perspective on it, my dad, not long before this, had been unimpressed by the Beatles, a group of moptops from Liverpool that I and a few other people had formed a bit of a liking for.

'Turn that off! Never heard such bloody rubbish.'

So what chance did one humble villager from Gooseland have of succeeding where the Fab Four had failed?

My mum and my Aunt Ede, next to me on the sofa, were, as I recall, a little warmer and more encouraging. But then those two inseparable sisters had loyally come to all the amateur dramatic productions I had ever appeared in, lugging themselves up to the Incognito Group's little theatre in an old bottle factory in Friern Barnet, where, much to my surprise, they had uncomplainingly sat through several extremely angry John Osborne productions and a number of nights of Swedish bleakness courtesy of August Strindberg. By contrast, a few minutes of me swinging from the rafters in a policeman's outfit must have felt like a walk in the park on a sunny day.

So they both smiled as encouragingly as they could at my first broadcast efforts, and, I imagine, silently thanked their lucky stars that it wasn't Chekhov. And then it finished and, without any popping of champagne bottles or smoking of cigars, we all went back to our Christmas.

But I'll tell you who was *really* impressed by my appearances that day: me. That, of course, was the thrill of seeing yourself on the small screen and then watching your name – or, at any rate, your stage name – go by in the credits. As little as a month beforehand, the possibility of this would have seemed vanishingly unlikely. It really was quite something, I thought. Something I would like to do a bit more of, if I ever got another chance. What were the odds of that, though?

*   *   *

Worryingly uncomfortable as it may have been, I understood that when you forced yourself into a Kirby harness, as I did in Golders Green that time, you were strapping on a proper piece of theatrical history. What I didn't appreciate was how relatively lightly I would get off, up there in the skies that time.

George Kirby and his company had been working out ways to get actors off the ground since eighteen-hundred-and-frozen-to-death. Indeed, history relates that it was a fully patented Kirby harness that rendered Peter Pan airborne in the earliest productions of J. M. Barrie's play at the start of the twentieth century. The effect was so uncanny at the time that children had to be discouraged from trying to take wing themselves on the way home – or, worse, while actually in the theatre. Legend has it that a young Prince George, who would later grow up to be King George VI but who was at that point a small boy lost in wonderment at the theatre, had to be restrained one night from attempting to jump out of the royal box and join Peter Pan on a quick aerial tour of the auditorium. This probably wouldn't have ended well, either for the line of succession or for the people in the stalls below.

Kirby introduced all sorts of refinements to his system over the years, including the 'quick release' mechanism, which enabled you to land, flick a switch, seamlessly abandon your wires, and then start walking about nonchalantly as usual with (hopefully) nobody any the wiser. But no amount of perfecting the hardware could ever quite remove the possibility that, like the Icarus of the acting world, you might end up flying too high. 'Getting gridded' was the in-house term for this special indignity – meaning getting accidentally flown up into the lighting grid above the stage, where you would find yourself swinging among hot bulbs and bits of scenery. And as Icarus will tell you, it's no fun up there and also very hot.

I wrote in my most recent book about going on tour in the mid-1970s in Anthony Marriott and Bob Grant's farce, *Darling Mr London*, a feast of intellectual entertainment, it goes without saying, at the deeply moving climax of which I had to be flown up into the rafters clinging to an ornamental light fitting.

Look, I did say it was a farce, didn't I? Were my trousers in place at this juncture in the proceedings? I'm not sure, but you would get good odds, in the context, that they were not.

Anyway, those recollections inspired John Schwiller to get in touch with me with some memories of his own. John was the flyman for that production – the person responsible for tugging the wires behind the scenes and launching me into the air at the appropriate time and in the appropriate manner, and then, of course, ensuring that I was lowered to the ground again when no one was looking – with the curtains closed, in this case, and in time for me to get unhooked and then take my bows in the curtain call. Apparently this stunt went off smoothly on all occasions without fail . . . except for the one night when it didn't.

On that particular occasion, I was hoisted with excess vigour off the stage, got emphatically 'gridded' – and then, just for good measure, became stuck. A wire was trapped somewhere and I was lodged, essentially, in the theatre's attic, with only a small chandelier and the lighting rig for company. And there I had to stay while the fault was rectified.

I'm not sure what's more remarkable: the fact that this thing happened in the first place, or the fact that I can remember absolutely nothing about it. You would think that being obliged to hang from a chandelier in a theatre's roof for a period, until the appropriate measures can be taken and you can be lowered to safety and then hastily do the curtain call with the rest of the cast, might have been the kind of thing an actor would have recalled.

But, honestly, I have racked my brains about it here in the study at Jason Towers – the crucible of this memoir-writing operation – and urged the Spirit of Christmas Past to stop looking at his phone for a moment and help me out. Yet, rather embarrassingly, nothing has emerged. I can only conclude that the trauma was so intense that I have simply blocked it out – and the Spirit of Christmas Past likewise.

Anyway, getting gridded happens to the very best of us, clearly – and some of us really do remember it. My correspondent John also told me that once, when Wayne Sleep was performing as Puck in *A Midsummer Night's Dream*, John had the distinguished honour of flying him. Not a lot of people can say they've done that. Certainly not a lot of people can say they have induced in Wayne Sleep a lasting trauma as a result of their backstage work with the ropes and wires.

It happened like this. For one scene, Sleep, as Puck, was meant to arrive on the stage gently – not from a great height but just lightly propelled into view to give the impression that he was landing softly after a flight: more of a twitch on the wire than a full-strength 'haul away' special, then.

Alas, when the green light came on backstage, which was John's cue to go to work, he inadvertently got his calculations wrong and put too much muscle into it, causing an entirely unprepared Sleep, standing in the wings, to blast off in the direction of the ceiling and then to descend again, coming now into the view of the audience, at a steep angle and with some speed, in the manner of a plunging kestrel.

That kind of move is difficult enough for the flying actor if you're ready for it, but if the flight comes upon you by surprise . . . well, even someone as fleet of foot as Wayne Sleep was always going to struggle. The flustered dancer hit the floor hard and then had to force himself into an upright position and wait for his insides to settle down.

Some considerable time later, John was sitting at home watching Wayne Sleep give an interview on the television to Terry Wogan. His ears couldn't help but prick up when he heard the dancer darkly recount the still fresh tale of the night some bloke had 'gridded' him – an experience that had remained etched upon his memory, clearly, as firmly as any number of dances with Princess Diana.

You should have blocked it out, Wayne, like what I did.

All those exertions, though . . . My current self can only reflect with rueful astonishment on all the flinging himself about that my younger self did in those formative years. These days, even when simply bending over to pick something up off the floor, I'm better off booking in advance. Back then, though . . . well, it strikes me that I was almost as much a gymnast as I was an actor in those early years. It wasn't just the typical farce-led comedy pratfalls, either – falling off sofas, tripping over rugs, getting into a tangle with standard lamps and the doors of wardrobes and so forth. I'd go looking far wider for trouble, seeking even more elaborate ways to, literally, stretch myself.

I remember being in a production of Robin Hawdon's *The Mating Game* with Trevor Bannister. Trevor played a super-smooth bachelor whose flat was kitted out with slick remote-controlled gizmos – light dimmers, electronically operated curtains, a television which rose up out of nowhere. Even the double bed dropped out of the wall at the touch of a zapper. Of course, all these kitsch devices were designed to go wrong at some point during the play, for maximum comic effect.

But I recall looking at that automatically self-concealing double bed and thinking: 'What if I happened to be standing on it when it closed? What if it actually ate me?' Cue extensive discussions with the stage manager and the props manager, followed by experiments to see whether the bed could still operate with my weight on it. It turned out that as long as I was up near the pillows at the time, where the bed met the wall, the lever that sprung the bed back into hiding would still function.

So that's what we started doing. I would jump up onto the bed at one point and the bed would slam shut and my character would disappear into the wall. Once the bed had stowed itself away, I was trapped in a tiny air pocket at the back of the set. Fortunately this gimmick took place at the end of an act, so I could be rescued fairly quickly, coming out the way I had gone in. But clearly in those days I was cheerfully ready to risk my neck and even suffocation for an extra laugh if I felt there was one out there to be had.

But how much being crushed by an automated double bed, or similar, can a person's body sensibly withstand? Quite a lot, it turns out. When I was in *No Sex Please – We're British* in the West End, the show would end every night with me sprinting in a panic across the stage in my boxer shorts and diving through a serving hatch in the wall, supposedly to escape into the kitchen beyond. Except that the audience had been primed to realise during the course of the evening that this serving hatch was treacherous and inclined to slam shut at inconvenient moments. Sure enough, in that climactic moment, as I closed in on it at speed in my underpants, the hatch would drop down of its own sweet accord (ably assisted by someone behind the scenes, of course), and I would end up launching myself, not through the hole, but through the panel, along with the satisfying splintering of balsa wood. Lights out and curtain.

Honed by repetition, it was a smooth little number, though I say so myself, and most nights it could be relied upon to have the audience on their feet in advance of the curtain call. Lord knows how I didn't manage to do myself a permanent mischief, though. Never mind two weeks of wrestling with a room-service trolley: I crashed through that serving hatch six nights a week, plus Saturday matinees, for eighteen months. Afterwards, it was a wonder I could still walk and chew gum at the same time, let alone march forward into a life of rich and varied professional experiences including . . . well, falling through another serving hatch, of course, but many other things besides, let's not forget.

And the seed of all of it, as unlikely as it may seem, was that BBC panto appearance. My work that Christmas gave me a television credit, which was invaluable as a calling card. While acting on a stage and acting in front of cameras are closely related, ultimately they are two different kettles of fish, and not every actor can move naturally from one to the other. A great deal of television in those days was live, so it was a real feather in your cap if you were able to demonstrate that you weren't someone who would lose their nerve when the camera was pointed at them.

The appointment also gave me about £75 for a fortnight's work which was a more than decent amount of bunce for a Bromley-based repertory actor who was at that point on £15 a week.

But probably more important than anything else, it also showed me to be someone who could handle a bit of knocka-bout physical comedy. And that, for all my lofty dreams of Shakespearean pre-eminence and Hollywood leading man-hood, was where the wind machine of fate seemed to be blowing me.

ON THE FOURTH DEL OF CHRISTMAS . . .

Grapefruits

'Well, you know me. I never talk about my days at sea.'
Uncle Albert, *Only Fools and Horses*

We interrupt this book to bring you some breaking grapefruit news.

Well, you'd be expecting no less from me after my last volume of memoirs, when I outed myself as one of the UK's leading growers of grapefruit trees – or, at any rate, as someone who, over a period of almost fifty years, had successfully cultivated a tall and weighty plant from a tiny grapefruit pip that turned up one morning in his breakfast.

As I told it back then (and please, by all means refer back to that previous book if you feel you want to flesh out what follows here), the story of the growth of my grapefruit tree from its extremely humble beginnings was a classic, uplifting tale of the triumph of hope over adversity – and also of the triumph of plants over neglectful neighbours whom you've asked to water them for you while you were away but who have forgotten.

Perhaps inevitably, then, the story's publication between hard covers in 2020 led to offers for me to appear in all the big grapefruit-related magazines, such as *What Grapefruit?* and *Grapefruit Tree & Grapefruit Tree Owner*, and to go on all the major grapefruit-related chat shows.

Actually, now I think about it, it didn't. Incredible to relate, two whole years on, the producers of Radio 4's *Gardeners' Question Time* have yet to get in touch to pick my brains on all things grapefruit-orientated, and neither, for some reason, has Alan Titchmarsh. He never writes, he never calls . . .

But the tale also had another crucial human-interest dimension to it because the pip in question – the one I planted, the one that became the tree – had once tried to kill me. As anyone with experience around them will know, your grapefruit is one of your more malicious types of break-fast fruit. Oh, they may look harmless enough, halved and lying there silently in your bowl, with their so-called segments. But when you've spent time around grapefruits, you know better than to be deceived. Unlike the largely passive raspberry and the almost completely uncomplaining stewed prune, grapefruits don't always go quietly. They'll look to take you down with them – or, at the very least, inflict some damage along the way. Not for nothing are they known as the absolute hard-nuts of the citrus world.

It's when you think you've got them completely under control that they're at their most dangerous. When you've got them comfortably in the bowl and are casually moving in on them – that's when they're most likely to go for you, responding to the advance of your spoon by sending a high-pressure jet of juice into one of your eyes, where it works briefly like venom. No other fruit, in my experience, has this kind of power in its armoury. The humble orange, under pressure from the peeler's thumb, can only dream of the grapefruit's devastating accuracy and effectiveness as a squirter of its own liquid. And as for the 'easy-peeler' tangerine, which so often makes its way into the fruit bowl at Christmas . . . well, it's not even in contention as a juice-firing combat fruit. But I learned that you mess with *grapefruits* at your peril.

On the all-important morning in 1973 or so, with spoon in hand in the kitchen of my little bachelor flat just north of Oxford Street in London, I was ready for it. Unbeknown to me, though, the grapefruit that I was about to devour had bigger plans. It wasn't intending to waste its time or energy with any of that low-rent, juice-spraying stuff. Oh no – blinding me was well beneath its ambitions. This one was going all-in.

This one was going to suffocate me.

Fully closing one eye, and half closing the other in nervous anticipation of the stream of juice that never came, I successfully loosened a segment of this devious grapefruit, spooned it into my mouth, chewed and swallowed – and was on the verge of celebrating a great victory for man over fruit . . . only for a devilishly camouflaged pip to lodge itself directly in my windpipe.

Smart move. My face became purple, my eyes inflated to the size of tennis balls and a whining intake of breath ensued which seemed to last a number of minutes. When that whining eventually stopped, there was a brief and pregnant silence during which the whole of London seemed to fall quiet. And then – kerblam! I went into a coughing fit so explosive that it was impossible to believe it didn't involve actual gunpowder.

Frankly, I was grateful on that particular morning to be breakfasting unaccompanied. There are times when a man is better off dining alone, and one of those times is when he is busy hacking up a grapefruit pip that's got stuck in his throat and, in the process, pebble-dashing the surrounding kitchen with bits of fruit and other parts of his recently ingested breakfast. Overnight guests tend not to enjoy that kind of thing, I find.

Let's be as decorous as we can: the pip was in due course, shall we say, 'produced', and thereafter lay before me on the table, giving no sign of the true extent of its menace. As I recovered my breath and my composure and waited for my heart rate to return to something closer to normal, I weighed my options vis-à-vis this unlikely assassin's future. Those options seemed to be numerous. More vengeful people than myself, for instance, would perhaps have flicked the offending item out the window and watched it drop, or angrily beaten it to a pulp with the butter dish.

But I, dear reader, as I have related, chose another path. I don't wish to sound pious, but I have always tried to be someone who believes in forgiveness and in the possibility of redemption, and my feeling is that even the very bad grapefruit pips among us probably have goodness in them somewhere, if we only take the trouble to look for it and give it space to flourish.

Plus I needed a hobby and horticulture was suddenly beckoning.

So space is what I gave that pip – specifically, house space. As previously reported, I went out that very morning and bought a pot and some compost and I duly planted the pip. Then I nurtured and watered it and watched it grow, as the days became weeks and the weeks became months and the months became years, pausing only to repot it every time it outgrew its confinement, and carrying it with me whenever I moved home.

Which is why it is now to be found in a giant tub in my summer house having achieved an impressive immensity, its trunk a pleasingly fat four inches in diameter. Every spring I haul that tree out and place it where it can enjoy the air, and every late autumn I drag it back under cover away from the ravages of the cold for another winter. OK, I can't exactly lie under it during the summer and stare up sleepily into its sun-dappled leaves – or, at least, not without attracting comment. But it's more than big enough to throw shade for at least one of my dogs, and possibly both of them if they budge up a bit.

Here's the thing, though: being written about in 2020 seemed to have a magical effect on my grapefruit tree and force it to new heights of confidence. By which I mean, the following year, to my startlement, a flower appeared among its usual thick clusters of leaves.

And not only did the tree flower. Even more amazingly, it fruited. A little green bud emerged which would, if the stars aligned and the fates conspired, eventually grow up to become a grapefruit.

The tree had done this only once before in its life, shortly after I first moved it out of London, producing, on that occasion, three tiny pods. It was almost as if, freed from the city, it had immediately been driven into overdrive by the richness of the country air. But, sadly, those three pods were incredibly short-lived. Now, after a long break in which no amount of country air could do anything for it, and urged on, it seemed to me, by its new-found fame, it was finally trying again. And this time, more promisingly, it was devoting all its available energy to the one fruit, which duly continued to grow.

I was delighted – and also very impressed. Let me remind you that we're talking about a categorically subtropical fruit. Of all the climates best suited to the production of grapefruits, Buckinghamshire's is not among them, though, likely as not, climate change will alter that in due course. Soon,

Marley's Ghost.

A producer recently told me, 'David, you know what? You would make the most perfect Scrooge.' I'd heard worse, frankly. But Merry Christmas to you, too.

I didn't end up playing Scrooge, but I played Mr Micawber in the ITV series *Micawber*, a comedy drama using characters from Dickens's *David Copperfield*, which debuted on Boxing Day in 2001.

Credit: David Cheskin / Alamy Stock Photo

When I survey the wondrous tapestry of my acting career, it's extraordinary how frequently Christmas comes into the picture.

If only all my Christmases as a theatre actor had been like that West End one of 1974 starring in *No Sex Please, We're British* – spent in comradely warmth, raising a glass with colleagues in a smash hit show after curtain on Christmas Eve.

On set for the 2002 *Only Fools and Horses* Christmas special, 'Strangers on the Shore'. Bon Noël, as they say.

Working has been a very different experience since Covid. Before the pandemic normalised working from home, an appearance on *The One Show* would have been a bit of a day out. Now there's no more professional make-up and no professional camera angles. And certainly no free biscuits. At least the coffee is better.

One of my many lockdown projects. Complete with lockdown beard.

When astronaut Tim Peake offered to take me for a spin in a Gazelle helicopter, I wasn't going to say no, was I?

'Peckham's that way, fellas.'

A bird's eye view of the Isle of Wight.

God bless Derek Trotter. Basically, he launched me into the nation's Christmas tree, and I never came down. It amazes me, the things I now get asked to do simply because I often appeared on the television at Christmas.

Credit: Mirrorpix / Alamy Stock Photo

'Miami Twice', the 1991 Christmas special, would have to feature among my proudest moments from the show. I can vividly recall the Miami hotel we stayed in and drinking cocktails and hanging out in the sun with Nick Lyndhurst thinking, 'Is this actually work?'

Credit: Mirrorpix / Alamy Stock Photo

Bella and Tuffy relaxing after a hard day guarding Jason Towers.

No, it wasn't me. Honest, guv.

The ghostly chair.

From 1991 onwards, after the end of the seventh series, *Only Fools* existed solely at Christmas, the team reuniting only to film extended stories for the holiday period – 'our Christmas present to the nation', as the BBC liked to call them.

Credit: Moviestore Collection / Alamy Stock Photo

Me in my Covid-friendly jumper.

no doubt, you won't be able to walk ten feet in Bucking-hamshire without trespassing on a citrus orchard. On the bits of it that haven't been sacrificed to high-speed railway lines, of course. But not yet. A long history of agriculture amply demonstrates that grapefruits overwhelmingly prefer Barbados to Aylesbury – and in that, I suppose, they are by no means alone. But, look, it's nothing personal. It's just that a grapefruit likes six to eight hours per day of full sun for the whole of its growing life, and you simply don't get that kind of weather in Aylesbury.

Yet here was my tree, somehow inspired by its appearance in print, going into production while being less than an hour from London on the train. I watched in awe as that little bud clung on, and slowly, in a tiny but very definite way, began to swell.

What an exciting development this was. I appeared to have founded a grapefruit dynasty. I was, truly, the UK's Citrus Overlord. Visions began to dance in my head of one day breakfasting on, literally, the fruits of my labour – and, if not choking on one of its pips (too much symmetry there), at least getting squirted in the eye by it. To be temporarily blinded by a shop-bought grapefruit is an ordeal to be wished on no one. But to be temporarily blinded by a grapefruit that you have grown yourself, and on a tree that you personally raised from next to nothing over the course of half a century with your own bare hands – well, that would be something to be proud of, surely.

Alas, though, it was not to be. Only superficially outperforming its three predecessors, my grapefruit grew gradually to the size of a plump pea. And then, perhaps overwhelmed by the effort, or possibly by all the attention it was getting – multiple visits each day from me and Gill, offering encouraging looks and words of inspiration – it dropped off.

I found its little form in the soil one morning – a mournful sight, let there be no question. And thus does this tale necessarily end in sadness and unfulfilment, and not in the blaze of horticultural glory that I had dared to envisage.

Yet, of course, the cycle of life measures out its own consolations and we must be content to understand and accept them. That small fallen bud may seemingly have come to nothing, yet it would now, where it lay, play a small role in replenishing the soil from which it arose. Who knows, it may even have made a hearty breakfast for a family of ants, had they moved swiftly enough.

But they would have had to watch out for the juice, of course. Grapefruits respect nobody.

ON THE FIFTH DEL OF CHRISTMAS . . .

Greasepaint and Pythons

So, obviously, the credits had barely finished sliding across the screen at the end of that BBC pantomime in 1965 when the phone started ringing and the offers of further richly rewarding work began pouring in, directly pointing the way to an unbroken lifetime of high-level cavorting in televisual entertainment's starry firmament.

OK, not really. It was back to the day job, in fact. Which in my case, as a full-time repertory actor, was, of course, mostly a night job. And which, in this instance, meant appearing in Bromley at the New Theatre's 1965 Christmas holiday production of . . . *Aladdin*.

All together now: 'Oh no it didn't.'

Oh yes it did.

From one panto straight to another. What a Christmas that was. As Oscar Wilde so wisely said: to be in one pantomime in a year may be regarded as a misfortune, but to be in two starts to look horribly like carelessness.

DAVID JASON

Or, as the other old saying goes: out of the frying panto, into the fire. For in Bromley I would have a fortnight's paid labour as one half of a pair of comedy coppers rejoicing under the names Flip and Flop.

Masquerading as a policeman? This was apparently becoming a habit. And the lowest rank of policeman, too. If I'd thought being on television on Christmas Day would earn me instant promotion to a cushy desk job, I couldn't have been more wrong. I was straight back out on the beat.

You'll be bursting to know, though: was I called upon to play Flip? Or was I called upon to play Flop? Or did I, employing my full breadth as a character actor, as demonstrated by my smooth handling of those three very different parts in the BBC's *Mother Goose*, Flip and Flop between the two roles as the mood and the evening took me?

Well, I can tell you: I was Flip, staunchly and solidly and without deviation throughout the night – which, of course, made things very much more straightforward for my counterpart as Flop, who was none other than the Scottish actor Robert Fyfe, a Bromley Rep regular, ten years my senior and a frequent colleague on the stage during my stint with the company. Robert was originally from Edinburgh and had dropped out of university to go to drama school in Bradford. The way it seemed to work for the pair of us at Bromley, Robert got the grander of the lower-class roles on offer, and I got the lower of the lower-class roles. Ah, the wonderfully infinite refinements of the British class system.

Flip and Flop, I guess, at least put us on an equal footing, socially speaking.

Robert would later play Howard Sibshaw in *Last of the Summer Wine* – and do so for twenty-five years, spending an awful lot of that time, as I recall, heading off into the Yorkshire Dales for bike rides with Jean Fergusson's Marina and hoping his wife didn't find out. So both of us, then, Flip *and* Flop, were destined for roles in long-running and much cherished British sitcoms. But I wonder if you would have bet on it from the duff slapstick that we were condemned to in *Aladdin* that year. Let us dwell no longer than we need to on the grinding puns, the overcooked pratfalls, the broad slapstick involving truncheons. Let us simply maintain that south-east London had seen more efficient police work in its time. It had probably seen funnier police work, too.

I don't wish by any means to cast nasturtiums on the team in *Aladdin*, least of all my police force colleague, Robert – but things at the New Theatre seemed distinctly to move up a gear, panto-wise, the following year. Never mind future sitcom stars, in 1966 the theatre managed to attract an actual, already established sitcom star. In a positively glittering production of *Robinson Crusoe*, Wilfrid Brambell from *Steptoe & Son* – and advertised on the posters as 'Mr Steptoe himself' – arrived to give Bromley his Mrs Crusoe. And if that wasn't enough glitter for you, Wally Whyton from the ITV children's programme *Five O'Clock Club* also descended from the entertainment stratosphere, bringing the double treat of himself and his owl-shaped glove puppet, Ollie Beak. Did it get any more starry than that? Well, I suppose it did, yes – but not at the New Theatre, Bromley, over Christmas in 1965.

I, however, did not get to reprise my Flip, nor Robert Fyfe his Flop, massive though the public demand for us to do so must have been. By then, I had packed my bags and moved on to other, less police-orientated theatrical pastures. But those months at Bromley had been enormously valuable for me – the best kind of introduction to the acting business, and a period in my life that I'll always be grateful for, even, in their own way, those weeks of Flipping and Flopping. It was all work, and it was all a learning curve.

Remember, I hadn't been to drama school and had pitched up directly from the ranks of amateur theatre – a self-starter at the age of twenty-five and so wet behind the ears you could have grown cress there. And although I was very determined, I was also very mindful of that lack of formal background – worried that I didn't have the qualifications, that I was always going to be inferior in some way to the 'proper' actors who surrounded me and had studied the craft and been taught how things were *supposed to be done*. I, by contrast, was going on instinct, plus whatever meagre experience I'd been able to grab on the way. The knowledge that I hadn't come through the formal route was always nagging at the back of my mind, ready to jump out and ambush me – almost like I was waiting to be found out.

And you could get beyond it while you were feeling confident, but it was a harder wave to ride in those moments when you were less certain of yourself.

However, what you could always be doing was learning – watching and listening and absorbing. In that sense, for a year, Bromley Rep became my drama school. And because of the way that rep theatre worked, with its fortnightly turnover of productions, the education it offered was fantastically broad, and panto just a tiny – if darkly memorable – fraction of it. One minute I was donning a giant wig and a braided smock and becoming Lord Foppington for the Restoration piece *The Relapse*, the next I was crashing about the stage wearing an eyepatch in *Treasure Island*, and the one after that I was putting on a cardigan and ruminatively picking up a teacup in *Murder at the Vicarage*. I took every part the place offered me and tried to learn as much as I could from it.

Somewhere in the middle of all this, I even climbed back into my waiter's outfit for a bit part in Noël Coward's *Suite in Three Keys*. I fell rather heavily for the leading lady in that particular production, an actress who swept in for the fortnight from outside the company: someone with a few TV credits behind her, but no major player, really, in the larger scheme of things, yet who, from where I was standing, seemed fabulously starry and professional – from another planet, really.

At one point in the Coward play, it was my duty, as the waiter in the restaurant where her character was dining, to pick up the napkin from the table-setting in front of her, unfold it, flap it and lay it across her lap, a moment of intimacy which, given my humble status in the hierarchy, not to mention my smittenness, I was more than a little hesitant about.

'You know what waiters do, don't you, at that moment?' she said to me casually while we were rehearsing.

I said that I didn't.

'Well, of course,' she said, 'you're a man, so you wouldn't have to put up with this stuff. Let me tell you, then. When waiters are putting your napkin on your lap for you, they very often take the opportunity to "accidentally" brush their arm against your breasts.'

I think I practically melted into the floor with embarrassment at this point. But if she really was suggesting that we should incorporate this piece of underhand devilry into the performance, then obviously she was the senior actor with the greater authority and it was my duty as the humble apprentice, looking to learn his craft and advance, to dig deep and do my best.

Actually, she wasn't suggesting that – or not exactly. What she was suggesting was that we develop a little exchange wherein, as I moved towards her with the napkin, she would noticeably snap her body back to prevent any contact from happening, while fixing me with a formidable look to indicate she was wise to waiters and their gropy ways. I quietly thought it might be too small and detailed a thing to come across to the auditorium, but I was wrong. It became a little moment in the play each night. The women, in particular, in the audience got it straight away, and it always got an audible reaction. It was all very illuminating for me – and not just because of what it taught me about what 1960s waiters got up to. I already knew I could find extra places between the lines where I could get laughs by drawing things out. But now I saw how a really clever actor could find a tiny and brief piece of behaviour that's nowhere near the script but which instantly adds something and tells the audience about the kind of characters they're watching. Also, if you make sure the audience is focused on the right place at the right time, you can work on a really small scale, even in the theatre. Again, I'm sure none of this would have been news to the drama-school graduates. But to me, picking it all up like a magnet as I went along, these discoveries were real treasure.

Another day at Bromley someone called Martin Jarvis landed briefly among us, fresh out of drama school – RADA, to be exact, where he appeared to have won all the prizes going and a couple more for good behaviour. Martin would become one of Britain's most popular and recognisable actors – and one of its most popular and recognisable voices, too, the voice of Richmal Crompton's *William* books, among many, many others. Even then, you could tell he was going places. He was six foot tall, blond, handsome, debonair . . . the archetypal leading man, it seemed to me. Splendidly attired in a braided frock coat which he wore as comfortably as if it were his own dressing gown, Martin played Captain Jack Absolute in a production of Sheridan's *The Rivals* in which I was the buffoon Bob Acres. I remember following Martin out of the stage door into the alley at the side of the theatre after one of those performances and watching him move suavely through a posse of women from the audience who had gathered to try and catch his eye. 'Oh, to be six foot tall and blond,' was all I could think to myself.

Much later, Martin and I acted together again when he appeared in an episode of *A Touch of Frost*. That time, in a somewhat different vein, and with no braided frock coats in view, he took the part of a male escort in a story titled 'Fun Times for Swingers'. Which may sound titillating, but this was *Frost*, remember, so the fun times were somewhat undercut, as I recall, by a small number of gruesome suicides in the tale, one of which Jack Frost greeted with the typically dry line: 'Oh dear, oh dear, oh dear. Such a mess on the pavement.'

Anyway, did I take the opportunity, during the filming of that episode, to remind Martin of our previous encounter in Bromley? No, actually. I was such a minor part of the scene at the time that I genuinely didn't think he would recall me even having been there. As time goes on and your career advances, you can't possibly remember the face and name of every single actor you've worked with back in the early days. George Cole used to tell a story about first meeting Dennis Waterman on the set of *Minder* – and then, two whole years later, when the series was in full flow, working out that they'd both met ages before, in a 1971 horror film called *Fright*. But neither of them had realised because Dennis's character had died very early in the film and then lain face down on the set for the most part, and George had spent the shoot stepping over Dennis's prone body. Not the simplest way to get to know someone – or even really to notice them, clearly.

I had a similar experience. When I went along to try out as Del Boy in a read-through of scenes from what became the first episode of *Only Fools and Horses*, I enthusiastically shook the hand of the actor who had come along to read as Grandad.

'Nice to meet you,' I said.

'Nice to meet you, too,' Lennard Pearce replied.

It would be many months later, with our working relationship and our friendship both well established, that someone pointed out to us that Lennard and I had been onstage together before – in 1965, in that same Bromley production of *The Rivals*. We didn't remember each other. But I think we both remembered Martin Jarvis.

So, the New Theatre, Bromley, was my unofficial drama school, the place where my learning got under way – a fact which would no doubt be permanently commemorated with a blue plaque on the outside of the building, but for the small fact that, like 26 Lodge Lane, the building no longer exists to nail a plaque to.

I'm starting to notice a slightly troubling theme developing here . . .

With regard to the sad demise of the New Theatre, here are the facts in so far as we have them. In May 1971, several years after I had packed my bags and moved on, the New was all set to host Cliff Richard in a production of Graham Greene's psychological thriller *The Potting Shed*. I'm not making this up. Stepping into the role of James Callifer, once occupied by none other than Sir John Gielgud, Cliff had appeared in the play in the West End and was now bringing that production to eager Graham Greene fans (and perhaps one or two Cliff Richard fans) in the south.

Coincidentally, I believe the last time Cliff had been on the London stage in an acting capacity, rather than a singing capacity, it had been at the Palladium six years previously in a production of . . . *Aladdin*. Small world, eh? It's one of the things Cliff and I have in common, clearly. Though I don't believe he played Flip. Or Flop.

Anyway, what can I tell you? Cliff's much anticipated appearance in *The Potting Shed* was not to be. With the programmes already printed and tickets sold, my personal drama school burned to the ground on the night of 7 May, just a fortnight before opening night. Cliff was later photographed standing rather mournfully in front of the charred wreckage in a flowery shirt.

Highly unfortunate, that. The theatre burning down before opening night, I mean, not Cliff being photographed in a flowery shirt. Six years later, the Churchill Theatre arose, phoenix-like, from the ashes among a new set of buildings on the site and thrives to this day, so ultimately all was well. But next time anyone tries to tell you that repertory theatre isn't a business fraught with hidden danger and complexities, cite the case of Sir Cliff and my old drama school.

* * *

Right, look lively, Spirit of Christmas Past. Enough of this sitting around over there with your feet up, eating my biscuits. Time to earn your corn, son. I need you at this juncture in our tale to sweep us up and carry us forward a couple of years, to the Christmas of 1967.

To Boxing Day, specifically, and to the first edition of an ITV comedy programme for children entitled *Do Not Adjust Your Set*, starring me and my new television teammates, Michael Palin, Terry Jones, Eric Idle and Denise Coffey.

In fact, the episode's full title, in honour of the festive season, is: 'Do Not Adjust Your Set, Or a Happy Boxing Day and a Preposterous New Year', and, on the positive side, that decision to launch the show on Boxing Day, of all the places in the schedules, is a huge vote of confidence in the programme and a major boon in terms of attracting the widest available audience. Our new team can afford to spend Christmas feeling very excited about that outcome.

On the other hand, though, it means our fledgling efforts

find themselves going out opposite the premiere of the Beatles' *Magical Mystery Tour* movie on BBC1, and I don't suppose any new show at this moment in the history of the Swinging Sixties would be entirely happy to find itself fighting the Beatles for attention.

That said, I know which side of that particular battle my dad is going to be on, so we are guaranteed at least one viewer.

Some obvious questions here, though. How have I come to be starring in a children's television show all of a sudden? And how have I come to be teamed up with these young, sharp and rather intimidatingly clever Oxbridge graduates, Mike, Eric and Terry? Well, I can answer all that – which is just as well because when I asked my Spirit of Christmas Past if he had anything revealing to offer in this area, he just looked at me rather blankly and asked me if I wanted him to google it.

I'm a little disappointed with the quality of this Spirit, if I'm being honest. His work seems to fall short of the advertised Dickensian standards. I may have to get on to the agency.

Meanwhile, let me explain to you how this kids' TV opportunity has come about. The man to whom the finger of blame points is a young producer named Humphrey Barclay. Humphrey will have a huge influence on my career, not just here but beyond, eventually pairing me up with Ronnie Barker for some sketch work which will then lead to the pair of us acting together in *Open All Hours*. At this point, though, he is a rising force in TV comedy, who has very successfully produced the satirical radio show *I'm Sorry, I'll Read That Again*, and who, on the strength of that, has now been commissioned to put together a small band of actors who can turn out a comedy programme for children, to be broadcast at teatime on ITV.

Humphrey, Eric Idle, Terry Jones and Mike Palin all know each other from their Oxbridge university days, and have subsequently been involved in various pieces of writing for BBC Radio, so that's all quite convenient and cosy. Humphrey has spotted Denise Coffey, meanwhile, in an Edinburgh Festival production of *A Midsummer Night's Dream*. Like Eric, Terry and Mike, her background is formal and impressive – the Glasgow College of Drama and the Royal Scottish Academy of Music – and while we are making the show, she will get cast in a film production of Thomas Hardy's *Far From the Madding Crowd*, starring Alan Bates and Julie Christie, which I will be deeply impressed by and not a little jealous of, this being the kind of break I was dreaming of.

And me? Well, Humphrey has found me at the end of the pier in Weston-super-Mare. Which I still maintain is better than being found *under* the pier in Weston-super-Mare. I was playing opposite Dick Emery at the time, in a summer-season farce called *Chase Me, Comrade*. Cambridge Footlights, eat your heart out. My CV by this point consists mostly of scraps of TV work, none of it amounting to much: tiny roles in *Z-Cars* and *Softly Softly*. And I have also fallen in and out of the ITV soap opera *Crossroads*. My role there: Bernie Kilroy, a boxing promoter with a shifty edge to him, who also worked as a part-time gardener at the motel. I wonder how often those two professions – boxing promoter and gardener – have been combined. You don't often see Frank Warren doing people's lawns, do you? But then Frank Warren wasn't in *Crossroads*.

Which, actually, now I come to mention it, makes Frank Warren a bit of an exception because an awful lot of people I can name *were* in *Crossroads*, including many that I worked with in other circumstances: Trevor Bannister, for instance, my colleague in the world of rogue stow-away beds, who by the miracles of technology, for which *Crossroads* was by no means famous, played twins in the show; and Bob Monkhouse, with whom I also worked in summer seasons and who was a big enough star that he could simply swan into the motel and play himself.

Then again, would a truly big star have ended up staying somewhere like the Crossroads Motel? Quite the knotty conundrum, that, which I'll leave you to pick away at. It's a bit like Groucho Marx not wanting to be part of any club that would have him as a member.

What I can tell you is that the excellent Lynda Baron did a stint in the motel as a secretary, long before *Open All Hours* encouraged her to go into District Nursing instead. Moreover, my *Only Fools* compadre, John Challis, could also proudly declare himself to be 'school of *Crossroads*', having wandered in for a couple of episodes to appear as a dodgy photographer, many years before he more noticeably became a dodgy car salesman. More on John and Lynda, these sorely missed friends of mine, a bit later.

As for my Bernie Kilroy character, after a six-month stint on the show, starting in the summer of 1966, he ended up having to leave town to avoid conviction on account of some dastardly plot he had concocted to defraud the motel. That should have been the end of him, really, and I certainly assumed so as I caught the train back to London from the ATV Studios in Birmingham. A few weeks later, though, the producers decided that they were prepared to overlook Bernie's problematic past, let him off the hook on this occasion and bring him back into the show as a regular character. There was something about that boxing/gardening hybrid, clearly, that they felt the programme couldn't get enough of.

I, however, saw it differently. And that was nothing to do with boxing or gardening, and nothing to do, either, with the reputation of *Crossroads*, a big red flag though that was for many people, both inside and outside the industry. The show had very quickly become the butt of jokes and used to get kicked about all over the place as a handy byword for the hammy and the clunky. And nobody would deny that it could certainly be both those things from time to time – often gloriously so, but probably no more or less, in fact, than any other televised soap of its era. It was shot quickly and on the tightest of budgets, and that was bound to show from time to time. The walls of the sets were definitely a bit floppy and, wherever you were in the motel, you had to be careful about how you closed doors for fear of giving the impression that the tremors from an earthquake were suddenly being felt in the motel's vicinity. Which would have felt natural in certain parts of the world, of course, but not where we were supposed to be, which was on the outskirts of Birmingham.

But I actually admired the programme – and the more so for seeing how it operated up close. There was no denying the energy around the studio, or how resourceful its production team was – a creative powerhouse, actually, in the sense that at one stage those people were making five half-hour episodes for national broadcast per week, which is an awful lot of drama to be putting together in a hurry. And whatever else you wanted to say about the programme, it certainly knew how to tell a story in a way that made people keep watching.

I should also probably say that I was quite impressed by the wages, too. What ATV were paying their actors – £76 per week in my case – completely outstripped anything I could make in the theatre at that time, which, as I mentioned earlier, was more like £15 a week. And now it was clear that ATV were willing to offer me months and possibly even years of steady employment at these handsome rates. From a financial point of view, I would have been bonkers to leave.

Yet, as new to the business and as unsure of myself as I was, I thought I spotted a trap. What if you made yourself comfy in *Crossroads* for a year or two, and then found you couldn't get out? Because it was clear that roles on long-running and popular television series – especially soaps – could do that to you. You saw it happen to television actors all the time: they would get branded by certain roles, and then discover that nobody, neither casting directors nor audiences, could see past the brand.

I worked out pretty quickly that this was something I would like to avoid if I possibly could. In my youthful and innocent enthusiasm, the whole joy of being an actor seemed to be that you could become as many different people as the world would allow you to be. That was what had been fun about my amateur acting, and that was what my repertory schooling had further instilled in me: that the real pleasure of acting lies in the possibility of ceaseless self-reinvention. Pirate one week, man of the cloth the next, and Restoration-era fop the one after that – that seemed to me the way to go. Finding yourself squashed into one role, or even one type of role, would surely only spoil everything – would defeat the point, even.

Now, it's not always in an actor's own power to save themselves from getting boxed up along the way. Sometimes, as I would discover, it happens through no fault of your own. But for as long as I felt I had the opportunity to keep my options alive, I was determined to do so. Hence my gentle but firm goodbye to Bernie Kilroy, and my fond farewell for ever more to that unique place where boxing had met gardening.

Call me naive, but I had no idea that I would be fighting different versions of that battle for the rest of my life.

For now, though, there I was in Weston-super-Mare. This was where Humphrey found me, driving down from London one night on a tip-off that I might be someone worth having a look at for this new kids' show. And how differently things might have turned out – for this was one of those pivotal career moments, dear reader, at which everything that eventually ensued could have turned out so differently if the scale had tipped the other way, as it so nearly did.

Humphrey had read Classics at Cambridge, was quite a correct, buttoned-up sort of chap with highly intellectual interests, and, as such, he was not really your typical, ticket-holding punter for an end-of-the-pier summer-season farce – even one with Dick Emery in it. Indeed, Humphrey was so unimpressed by what unfolded in front of his eyes that night, that, having somehow made it through the first half without grinding his teeth to dust, he was sorely tempted to cut his losses and leave in the interval.

Which would have been a huge shame for me because my big moment in that production – indeed, my first appearance of the evening – came right at the start of the second half.

Fortunately Humphrey hung on despite the callings of his better nature, and, fortified, I can only imagine, by the stiffest of gin and tonics from the theatre bar, he went back to his seat. And so it was that he saw me do an extended bit of business very much modelled on the Bromley Rep routine I talked about earlier, with the butler and the bongo drums – except that this time I was a man who found himself downstairs in an empty house, weighing up whether or not to inform the residents of his presence by ringing the large ornamental ship's bell that stood in the sitting room.

Different context, different instrument, but same deal, though: as I stood up there, contemplating the bell, in an agony of indecision, the audience knew exactly what was going through my mind, and exactly what was coming – but they didn't know when. With the stage to myself, I could draw that little moment out for several minutes on a good night and have the auditorium in the palm of my hand by the end of it. And luckily, Humphrey came on a good night.

All in all, I've a lot to thank that gin and tonic for.

Flash-forward, then, to the very first episode of *Do Not Adjust Your Set* on that Boxing Day, 1967. We see a mad kind of oompah orchestra, making a horrible but just about coherent racket, with Terry and Mike, Eric and Denise all miming away on various cellos and trumpets and violins, and with me poised at the back, holding a triangle and a beater and clearly waiting for my big moment in this unfolding symphony – my time to shine.

The expression on my face is both expectant and highly anxious. You know that at some point I'm going to hit that triangle, but you don't know when, nor what will ensue when

I eventually do, and in the gap between those things . . . well, we've been here already, haven't we? We are once more in comedy's playing field.

I'm sure I won't be spoiling your fun too much if I tell you that the triangle, when eventually struck, produced the overdubbed sound of a massive, jarring car crash – all crunching metal and breaking glass – to the horrified shock of everyone else in the orchestra. End of performance, end of skit.

And in many ways that was *Do Not Adjust Your Set* in a nutshell, or at any rate in a triangle strike: a cavalcade of absolute and utter nonsense. The show's speciality was extreme silliness, and if it could be swiftly achieved, so much the better. So, for example, in that Christmas launch show, there was a scene in which we all took a moment to display our new Christmas presents. When it was my turn, I looked into the camera with a straight face and said, 'I'm just going to slip on my new shoes.' And then the camera drew back slightly to reveal a pair of shoes on the floor at my feet, which I stepped on and immediately skidded off as if they were a banana skin, landing on my back with a mighty crash.

I had just slipped on my new shoes.

I know: 'sketchy' is very much the right word. But you need to remember that children's television in those days hadn't had much time for the plainly silly, let alone a sense of gleeful anarchy on the part of its presenters. There had always been something rather starchy and upright about it, something responsible – a sense that the grown-ups were always in the room. To that extent, *Do Not Adjust Your Set*, which featured grown-ups but not as we generally know them – the kind of grown-ups, indeed, who were ready to slip on their new shoes – was a giant gust of fresh air.

Each episode, then, was essentially a compendium of nonsense, much of it based on the premise that there's nothing kids like more than adults being made to look foolish. A large percentage of the material was, in fact, parodies of adult television formats – documentaries, news bulletins, discussion shows, all given an absurd twist or made to collapse in some daft or over-literal way. In that, the show very clearly foreshadowed *Monty Python's Flying Circus* – and in other ways, too. Cartoon sequences were dropped in, the work of a big hairy American bloke who used to stomp about the place in a battered Afghan coat – Terry Gilliam. Long before Terry Jones did links between *Monty Python* sketches naked (and seated at an organ), Eric Idle had done the same for *Do Not Adjust* – very modestly shot, of course, given the teatime broadcast slot. The seeds of *Python* are all there, if you want to look for them.

At the time, though, the show seemed – and this was hugely exciting for me – to be drawing tangibly on the influence of *The Goons*, whose radio show, in all its boundary-breaking idiocy, I had absolutely lapped up as a teenager. I had once got a ticket to go and see a *Goons* show being recorded – that's how much of a fan I was. I had sat in awe in the auditorium, watching Spike Milligan, Harry Secombe and Peter Sellers do their thing. To feel that I was now part of something which was working in that same absurdist vein – something that the Goons themselves might even approve of – was truly thrilling.

The absurdity wasn't only what you saw on the screen. It sort of coloured the whole atmosphere in which the show was made. Every episode there would be a musical number by the Bonzo Dog Doo-Dah Band, Neil Innes's highly eccentric pop group, who used to drift around in velvet jackets and silk scarves, smelling of patchouli oil and tormenting the production staff by requesting props for their performances that they didn't actually need or have any intention of using. One time, the band put in a written request for 'a petrol tanker, a plank of wood and a bag of boiled sweets'. Ever obliging, the poor, harried production team solemnly informed them that the plank and the sweets were in hand, but they were having a little trouble securing a petrol tanker; would a large oil drum do?

My favourite slots in the show were the little filmed sequences in which I played Captain Fantastic. A man in a raincoat, with an extraordinary, ferret-like moustache, an oversized bowler hat and a rolled umbrella, Captain Fantastic was intended to be the world's least likely superhero. He, in all his inconsequentiality, was pitted in an endless battle for supremacy with Denise Coffey's Mrs Black, the embodiment of cartoon evil who always had a dark plan up her sleeve to threaten the future of humankind.

Sixties-period surrealism abounded in those skits. Captain Fantastic occupied a world in which alien invaders intent on world domination were best dealt with by engaging them in a custard-pie fight on a deserted train station. I seem to remember getting stuck by my umbrella to a giant magnet in an otherwise empty field at one point, creating an image which Salvador Dalí might have wondered about painting.

At the same time, though, shot properly on film, at a slightly slowed-down rate of frames per second in order to look sped-up when played back at the normal rate, these little pieces were paying obvious homage to the black-and-white comic films that I had grown up with and adored – Laurel & Hardy, Buster Keaton, Harold Lloyd. I got to row a boat across a pond and allude – or so I hoped – to the work of the great Jacques Tati in *Monsieur Hulot's Holiday*, which I had seen in the cinema as a boy and considered for some time thereafter to be the funniest film ever made. It was all great fun, getting sent out into the countryside in the middle of the week and paid to muck about like this. I was living the dream.

Better still, the show seemed to go over well – well enough that a second series was commissioned. It opened in 1968 – with, of course, a Christmas special, 'Do Not Adjust Your Stocking', this time going out on Christmas Day itself. That episode found a moment for me to do my very best impression of Hughie Green, the endlessly sincere television host who was famous for presenting the talent show *Opportunity*

Knocks, and then to introduce Terry Gilliam's extraordinary animation, 'The Christmas Card', a piece for the ages, with traditional festive scenes coming alive in bonkers ways: three wise men on camels going backwards and forwards in pursuit of a strangely unpredictable star, ice cracking under a skater on a pond, a robin on a bough chirruping gaily before getting picked off by a rifle, clumps of snow avalanching from a roof to take out some innocent carol singers down below . . . Christmassy and yet not. In the Captain Fantastic story, I was to be seen rampaging around Gamages, the grand department store in London, and making a risky getaway run along the flat roof of the portico above the main entrance, where the store placed a row of sumptuously decorated Christmas trees. If you were a London kid in the forties and fifties, Gamages, with its vast toy department, held an almost cathedral-like status, especially at Christmas. I had worshipped at that temple of wonders many times in the course of my childhood, and pored over the annual gift catalogue which it issued for convenient at-home browsing, without ever imagining I would one day run amok on the roof of the place. Clearly, saying you were filming a daft television show granted you access to places untravelled by ordinary shoppers.

With the impetus of that big Christmas launch behind it, the second series really began to gather some steam. It was still ostensibly a children's programme, broadcast at teatime in among the rest of the children's output, yet, through no real work of our own, the boundary was blurring. There seemed to be a rising amount of interest from older viewers – slightly bashful about their interest at first, maybe, but then increasingly less so. The story was that people were trying to knock off work early in order to get home and watch it. Adults, too, at this point in history, had not been well provided with surreal madness on television and it seemed that *Do Not Adjust Your Set*, by filling one gap in the market, had exposed another. This was all very exciting. I was involved in something on TV that was getting widely noticed and seemed to have a bit of traction under it.

You'll possibly know what happened next, though. Mike, Terry and Eric decided they didn't want to work on a children's show any more. They had other ambitions for their writing, and they went to Rediffusion and asked if they could make the show exclusively for grown-ups, with a late-evening time slot. And Rediffusion, who understandably thought they were on to a winner with the kids' version, said no. So Mike, Terry and Eric picked up their ball and walked away.

As for Denise and me, we were just onlookers during all this – in fact, not even onlookers. The pair of us did very little writing, so, to that extent, we had no real leverage and, in any case, all these dealings happened over our heads and without our input being sought. When we learned that the plug had been pulled, and the show was over, we were both, naturally, pretty rueful about it.

I was no less rueful a year later when Mike, the two

DAVID JASON

Terrys and Eric, now joined by Graham Chapman and John Cleese, returned, over on the BBC, with *Monty Python's Flying Circus* – the adult version of *Do Not Adjust Your Set* which they had always wanted to make. You'll see, I think, how, from my point of view, it looked as though the band had split up and then got back together without me, and I don't think I would have been human if I hadn't felt quite wounded by that.

Well, I can see that it wasn't the perfect fit – that I was a different kind of performer to those guys and from a different background. Yet, over the next months and years, as *Monty Python's Flying Circus* shot aloft and became a groundbreaking, internationally renowned and ultimately iconic British television show, diversifying into books and albums and films, while my own career was sputtering along and failing to get very far off the ground, I would start to think I knew how Pete Best must have felt about being eased out of my dad's favourite group, the Beatles, just before they made it, and replaced by Ringo.

Of course, my dad, with his strong views on 'that bloody racket', would probably have said that Pete Best was better off out of it. And I don't know how Pete Best felt about it – you'd have to ask him. But in my case, actually, the way it all turned out eventually, I *was* better off out of it – at least to the extent that all the wonderful opportunities that came my way in the 1980s and beyond would most likely not have done so had I found myself tied up in a successful comedy troupe in the late 1960s. Especially one in which I didn't entirely fit.

So, yes, better off out of it, ultimately. But I can't deny that I had a few long years of chipping away forlornly at the show-business coalface after this, and a few quiet bouts of gnashing my teeth in frustration, before I really began to believe it.

ON THE SIXTH DEL OF CHRISTMAS . . .

Hits and misses

Christmas in the West End of London has a special glow about it, no question. And to be in a successful play at Christmas in the West End of London while it glows . . . well, that's very heaven.

Of course, some of that glow which I mentioned is the result of alcohol, liberally applied, as the season seems to insist. But it has other sources too, as I routinely discovered, stepping out of my flat in the late afternoon in the run-up to Christmas, crossing Oxford Street, and descending down through Covent Garden to the Strand Theatre on Aldwych. It would all be there: the lights ablaze in the shops and strung across the streets; the parcel-burdened shoppers hurrying home; the overstuffed pubs; the liberated office workers falling out of bars – all sources of the glow. It would unfold in front of me on that walk to work like my own personal Christmas movie.

Why, even I become sentimental about this.

You could feel it in the audience, too. It used to fascinate me how every audience had a mood and how you could read that mood almost the moment the curtain was raised. There were audiences that were cold and needed to be warmed up, audiences that came in wet from the rain and needed to be dried out, audiences that had been steaming in the sun all day and needed to be cooled off; audiences that needed to be wound up and audiences that needed to be calmed down. Up there on the stage, I learned that you had to monitor the feeling in the room all the time and adapt to it as best you could. And yes, in that week running up to Christmas, before the theatre fell dark on Christmas Day itself, there was such a thing as a Christmas audience: a conviviality, a communal feel, a willingness to engage, a warm energy that simply wouldn't be there at any other time of the year.

And, yes, a glow – especially after the interval.

So here we are: Christmas 1974. I've picked myself up, dusted myself down and got myself a full-time job in *No Sex Please – We're British*, the long-running farce by Alistair Foot and Anthony Marriott, and I'm pleased as punch about it.* The part of Brian Runnicles in that particular play, at that particular moment, was a big pair of boots for my rather small pair of feet. None other than Michael Crawford had been

---

* Nothing to do with alcohol. The punch in that expression is Mr Punch of Punch & Judy puppet fame, a man famous for his permanently pleased expression. Indeed, versions I have seen have tended to have a rather fixed grin.

in the role directly before me, and his was a name you could genuinely put up in lights without being accused of wasting electricity. He'd been in the Hollywood film adaptation of *Hello, Dolly!*, directed by Gene Kelly and starring Walter Matthau and Barbra Streisand, and he'd acted on Broadway. My claims to fame at this point included two series of a collapsed ITV kids' show, some self-terminated *Crossroads* action, and a bit part in *Z-Cars*. Run this past a reputable comparison website if you wish, but it was hardly a fair contest. The reason Michael was leaving *No Sex Please*, by the way, was because he wanted to do a sitcom the BBC were offering him called *Some Mothers Do 'Ave 'Em*. That didn't turn out too badly for him, either.*

So, some large footsteps to follow in – and a big and established play to enter, too. *No Sex Please* was quite the item at this time. The critics hated it. 'Its triviality is beyond contempt,' said the *New York Times*, in a quote which the

---

* It was clear to those who saw both – me included – that Crawford's Brian Runnicles and his Frank Spencer had a considerable amount in common, not least the same seemingly fragile twitchiness and the same hapless propensity to land up in extreme physical peril, which they then somehow survived, in direct and comic defiance of that very fragility. It was as if all the characteristics of Crawford's Runnicles would find their ultimate and most popular expression in his Spencer, not least when being towed along behind a bus on roller skates in what was arguably *Some Mothers Do 'Ave 'Em*'s emblematic stunt sequence. Point of order: as with Tom Cruise and yours truly (when, of course, the insurers allowed it), Crawford insisted on doing his own stunts. All the truest stars of the silver screen do.

producers decided, on balance, not to put on the posters outside the theatre. But audiences adored it. They came in droves – had been doing so for two years before I arrived, and would continue doing so for ages afterwards, until the show broke the record for a long-running comedy piece: sixteen years and more than 6,500 performances.

And it ended up sort of transcending theatre, in a way. Because of its plot (a young assistant bank manager inadvertently begins receiving a slew of Scandinavian pornography after his wife mis-orders some glassware, and then has to be constantly finding ways to dispose of these growing mounds of illicit material in order to avoid social disgrace and professional ruin), it had a slight whiff of scandal about it, even though, in actuality, it was pretty mild fare and definitely not in the business of frightening anybody's horses.

Yet at the time it obviously provided a talking point and its title was both a gift to headline writers and a phrase that ended up entering the language. (Even now you will see the 'no x please, we're y' formula used: I see someone had a show running in 2021 called *No Sex Please – It's Christmas*.) It was that pretty rare thing: a theatre production whose success seemed to resonate in the culture, far beyond the confines of the West End, and it was fantastic fun to stand at the centre of that for a while – really restorative, actually.

Blimey, it was taxing, though; the most physical role of my life – two and a bit hours of crashing through serving hatches (as previously detailed) and bounding over sofas and swinging from door lintels, with all of the attendant bumps and bruises and strains. It felt less like being in a play at some points and more like being in a bar-room brawl – a bar-room brawl that kicked off six nights a week and with matinees on Thursday and Saturday. But I absolutely loved it. And fortunately there were still some functioning bits of me left to walk away after eighteen months when my contract eventually came to its end.

It also put me in the best cast I had ever worked with up to that point, including Simon Williams and Belinda Carroll and Dennis Ramsden, known to us all as Slim. I consider myself privileged to have shared a West End stage with Slim, not just once but twice (we were later together in the Dave Freeman play, *A Bedfull of Foreigners*, at the Duke of York's Theatre), because Slim was quite simply one of the greatest farceurs of his time. By which I mean, among other things, that if there was anyone in the world who was Slim's equal for working a pair of ill-fitting pyjama bottoms for laughs, then I can confidently say I never met them.

OK, nobody was claiming that this was the most delicate of dramatic skills to be famous for, or the most profound in its effects, and it was clear, even in those days, that you wouldn't automatically get into the Royal Shakespeare Company by doing tricks with your pyjama bottoms for your audition.

And of course, comedy has moved on: these farcical skills can appear antiquated and outmoded now, like thatching or making horse brasses – heritage crafts in our digital world.

Yet my respect for Slim and my abiding fondness for the good old analogue form of comedy in which he specialised means that I will maintain staunchly until my dying day that it took a special kind of comic brilliance to be able to yield gales of laughter from a pair of ill-fitting pyjama bottoms.

And to be able to do so six nights a week and with two matinees . . . well, again, let's try and show some credit where it's due.

Also in that *No Sex Please* cast was Richard Caldicot, another vastly experienced British theatre and film actor. Richard played Leslie Bromhead, the bank manager, my character Brian's boss, who at one point catches Brian alone among the recently arrived pornography stacks. I remember the pair of us working up a nice moment out of that encounter.

'Runnicles, what do you think you're doing here?' was Richard's line.

Then there would be a standing face-off between us, with me trying hard to hide a guilty expression, but saying nothing at first. We found we could hold it for ages, staring each other in the eyes. And as long as neither of us cracked up, the audience would frequently come right along with us, their expectation building for whatever it was I was about to say to burst this moment of embarrassment for my character.

On a good night, as we stood there, I was aware that if I just very slightly twisted my hand slowly inside my shirt cuff, it would start a laugh going in the auditorium. That would be the licence to build it, maybe shoot one cuff, and then put my arms back down by my sides, and then, in the fullness of time, shoot the other – all while holding Richard's gaze. As long as the audience were on board and in the right mood for it, we could draw this moment out for a whole minute before I eventually let it go and spoke my line.

'I beg your pardon, sir?'

And that would get a belter – a belter so long that we'd have to go back to staring at each other just to wait for the laughter to clear.

Not for nothing, dear reader, was I known in the cast of *No Sex Please* as 'the milkman'. There was *nothing* – and I mean nothing – that I wasn't prepared to milk if I thought there was a laugh to be found there.

But even the milkman got a day off at Christmas.

Ah, happy times. If only all my Christmases as a theatre actor had been like that West End one of 1974 – spent in comradely warmth, raising a glass with colleagues in a smash hit show after curtain down on Christmas Eve, exchanging a few small gifts and then walking home through the festively inebriated streets of London, with a bed awaiting and Santa on his way.

But no. Alas, 'twas not ever thus. Far from it. By way of acute contrast, permit me to ask the Spirit to show us one last Christmas scene, before I close out this chapter and we leave the theatre behind us for the greener pastures of television.

And perhaps, in fact, this scene can explain *why* we'll be leaving the theatre for the greener pastures of television. Or certainly why I was lucky to do so.

Actually, so deeply etched on my memory is this particular Christmas, and so apt is it to revisit me at random moments of its own accord, that I don't really need the help of a hired ghost for this one. Which is just as well, because he left the room a couple of minutes ago, saying he was going outside for a vape.

I don't want to sound unpleasantly confrontational about it, but I really am going to have to have a word with someone.

Anyway, as I say, I'm fine to fly solo here, because this is a scene that stays vividly with me – too vividly, in fact. Join me, if you will, in Newcastle in the north-east of England, on Christmas Day 1979. And let us arrive, specifically, in the deserted dining room of a determinedly uninteresting three-star business hotel in the city centre – deserted, but for a solitary 39-year-old actor, seated at a table, disconsolately using his fork to nudge a few bits and pieces from the hotel fridge around the plate in front of him. On this great day of convivial cheer and joy to the world, when loud hosannas rend the air and angel voices are heard on high, along with that of Noddy Holder, the occasional scraping of the fork on the plate is literally the only sound in the room.

Merry Christmas to me, then – in town to play Buttons in *Cinderella*, and now well and truly on my Jack Jones on

Christmas Day.* We don't need to spend long gazing upon this mournful picture. I've written about this low point in my career before. But essentially, Christmas has come, the rest of the cast have sped off to their families and loved ones, as recommended in all the Christmas guidebooks, and muggins here has been left to celebrate the birth of the Saviour entirely by himself.

Should I have been driving home for Christmas? History indicates that that's certainly what Chris Rea would have done in my position. Chris, presumably, would have been down to London like a shot, with a full tank of petrol and a bag of wine gums in the glove compartment.

Then again, he didn't have to be back for a matinee of *Cinderella* on Boxing Day. Or if he did, he never mentions it in the song.

Also, unless, again, he thought better of singing about it, Chris Rea didn't have a stonking head cold. That didn't help. Having dragged myself through the Christmas Eve performance like the peerless professional that I was, I had spent most of Christmas Day locked in my room in an unsuccessful

---

* Jack Jones: imperfect cockney rhyming slang replacing the word 'own' or 'all alone' – and nothing, by the way, to do with the smooth, middle-of-the-road American singer, Jack Jones, and everything to do with a music hall song from eighteen-hundred-and-frozen-to-death, entitled ''E Dunno Where 'E Are', concerning a former Covent Garden market porter, Jack Jones, who has come by some money and suddenly developed some snooty and aloof ways, much to the disgust of his former pals. It happens, you know. But no names, no pack drill.

attempt to sleep off the lurgy. Which meant that, having ascertained from the hotel manager the night before that 'Christmas dinner' would indeed be available in the dining room, I then discovered that 'dinner' in these north-easterly parts actually means 'lunch' and I was too late.

Hence the 'cold collation', pulled together by a kindly and sympathetic member of the hotel's skeleton staff but which only had the effect of increasing my self-pity on that day of days, as I suppose a portion of actual, literal hard cheese served in an empty room was always likely to.

Oh, the misery, dear reader – and how efficiently Christmas can magnify it, if you're not careful, just by being there. According to the posters, I was 'TV's David Jason'. Was I really, though? None of the TV I had been in to this point had amounted to much. And anyway, whatever else it meant, being 'TV's David Jason' didn't spare you, clearly, from spending Christmas on your own in a closed hotel dining room.

In short, there I was, a single man, soon to turn forty, finding consistent success a little hard to come by and starting to wonder, in fact, whether he ever would find it; staring out of the window at the dark and deserted centre of an unfamiliar city, and asking himself just what he thinks he's playing at and whether this acting lark is ever really going to be worth the candle.

Still, cheer up, eh? Only six more weeks of playing Buttons to go.

Six weeks!

Christmas bells? Hell's bells, more like.

They weren't all easy, then, those years of itinerant thesping, when I was an actor of no fixed production, constantly moving on, simply in order to keep working. Those were the years in my life when I became deeply familiar with our nation's railway network and all its less than lovable foibles, and especially sensitively attuned to that instruction, so well known to all who were condemned to travel the length and breadth of the country in this manner: 'Change at Crewe.'

Just as the country's travelling rock bands would, in the early hours of Sunday morning, collide with one another at motorway services, so the nation's roaming actors would, of a weekend, find themselves rubbing shoulders at Crewe. That station was almost like our clubhouse. You would know it was Sunday afternoon because there would be all these luvvies calling out to each other as they breezed past on the platforms.

'Where are you headed, darling?'

'Off up to Middlesbrough, love. What about you?'

'Bournemouth for me, darling!'

And because it was Sunday there would frequently be engineering works and the timetable would be up the spout, meaning that a lot of sitting around and waiting was going to be done.

What are the three most heart-sinking words in the English language? That's an easy one: 'replacement bus service'.

And more often than not the station cafe would be closed, so you couldn't even get a cup of tea and a dead sandwich to insert between you and your wandering thoughts.

So you would end up sat on a bench with your suitcase, staring across the tracks, watching the trains come and go – or not, as may be – and you would find yourself, perhaps, with just a little bit too much time in which to think about things and to start wondering what, if anything, was the meaning of it all. Were you living, or was life passing you by? You could feel very detached at those moments, disjointed and uneasy, as though your life was a bunch of unrelated fragments – literally, an assortment of different parts – and you were waiting for something or someone to come along that would link them all together, yet you had no idea what or who that might be.

In 1994, when I was asked to do *Desert Island Discs* – a rite of passage, if ever there was one – I picked among my eight recordings for castaway usage Simon & Garfunkel's 'Homeward Bound', which history relates was written by Paul Simon while he sat on Widnes station in Merseyside, waiting for a train (or possibly a replacement bus service) to take him back to London.

OK, Paul Simon probably wasn't heading for Weston-super-Mare to start a summer season with Dick Emery like some of us were at such times. But for the travelling musician, the feelings of rootlessness and disorientation and all the longings that come with them were, I'm sure, very similar, and the song always and instantly transports me back to those strange and lonely Sundays in transit.*

Incidentally, on that castaway show, I also convinced Sue Lawley, who was then the presenter, to let me have, for my chosen book, a boatbuilding manual, and, for my luxury, a full set of carpenter's tools. It's called planning ahead. I don't think she twigged. But I had no intention of hanging around on my own for any longer than I needed to. What would I do for work?

Oh, and would you care to guess when the BBC chose to broadcast my *Desert Island Discs*? You're probably ahead of me. It was Christmas Day. It could have just been coincidence, of course, but I don't think so. By 1994, this whole 'Mr Christmas' thing had already taken hold.

And I think I know who to blame – for this and many other changes in the shape of my life. It was a bloke called Derek Trotter.

* For the record, my other chosen discs were: Phil Harris, 'The Darktown Poker Club' – a novelty song from my childhood (the chances are you know Harris better as the voice of Baloo, singing 'Bare Necessities' in Disney's *The Jungle Book*); 'Help!' by my dad's favourites, the Beatles; an extract from *The Goon Show* episode entitled 'The International Christmas Pudding'; Rita Moreno and George Chakiris performing 'America' from *West Side Story*; Dean Jones and Susan Browning performing 'Barcelona' from Stephen Sondheim's *Company*; Simply Red's 'Holding Back the Years', for its *Only Fools* connotations, of course; and a quick blast of 'Mars' from Gustav Holst's *The Planets* suite, because you can't beat a bit of Holst.

ON THE SEVENTH DEL OF CHRISTMAS . . .

Hauntings and phone-ins

T he Spirit of Christmas Past has just rung in. Would it be OK if he worked from home today?

He assured me that he would be attending to business just as dutifully as if he were 'in the office' – and possibly even be 'able to get more done', what with saving the time from the commute. And he said that if I needed haunting in a hurry, I could always Zoom him during the afternoon – although if I could leave it until after five, when A *Place in the Sun* finished on Channel 4, that would probably be better.

Is this OK? I appreciate that we're all in a new 'world of work' as we emerge slowly from the two years of disruption visited upon us by the pandemic. And I understand that people are taking this period as an opportunity to reassess their priorities and perhaps reach a new accommodation with the age-old balancing act between work and life.

But to be honest, I'd hoped for a bit more, now the restrictions are off, from someone employed in what we might think of as the 'spiritual hospitality' business – the personal touch, and all that. As an employer – and certainly as someone writing up their memoirs – you want to be in a position to look the ghosts of your past directly in the eye, don't you? To knock a few things back and forth in person? Dickens, I feel sure, would back me up here. I certainly don't remember any of the ghosts in *Scrooge* phoning it in – not even in the Ross Kemp-led 2000 remake.

Ah, well. So be it. It seems I'll be working solo this morning at the memory coalface. And that's OK, as it turns out, because the story I want to tell you now is spooky enough on its own. Indeed, consider it, if you will, my own modest contribution to the venerable tradition of Christmas ghost stories. Except that I'm not making it up. It's about something seriously occult and profoundly unsettling that genuinely happened the other night in the kitchen. And no, it's got nothing to do with my cooking, thank you for wondering.

As I may already have made you aware, parts of my humble home here at Jason Towers – though fortunately not the plumbing – date back hundreds of years. Indeed, a dwelling on this site is apparently recorded in the Domesday Book of 1086, so the house has had a while to accumulate some previous owners. As such, there have been times before now when I've had cause to wonder whether some of those previous owners might still be around – whether the place might actually be haunted. By authentic ghosts, I mean, rather than ones I've ordered in for work purposes from Spirits R Us.

There was, for instance, that episode I recorded in my last volume of reminiscences, involving a moving chair which, in a frenzy of terror (and while, I should probably add, driven quietly nuts by self-isolation during lockdown), I interpreted as poltergeist activity . . . but which actually turned out to be one of the dogs who had crept into the room silently and guiltily (knowing she was not really meant to be there) and who had slid under the chair's legs and was trying to get comfortable there, as subtly as possible.

That incident came on top of a whole period, not all that long ago, which must have gone on for a couple of years at least, when bottles of Diet Coke would keep appearing and then disappearing from the fridge, and mugs and other bits of crockery, similarly, would vanish from the kitchen and not reappear for ages, and when I would sometimes be convinced that I had heard the front door opening and closing and the eerie sound of footsteps on the staircase in the middle of the night.

But then I realised that wasn't ghosts. That was having a teenage daughter.

There was always a gratifyingly reassuring explanation in the end, then. But this new episode seemed to me to be of a quite different order – activity of a kind which only a super-natural presence could explain.

It was the end of the evening, the house was quiet, and I

was out in the kitchen doing a bit of washing-up. You'll be telling me, perhaps, that people have dishwashers for that kind of thing these days, and indeed, many do. And so do we. But I'm old-school: when it comes to washing-up, I prefer to roll up my sleeves and get my hands dirty. Or clean, actually, which is what happens if you're doing it properly.

As I washed and then wiped, I found myself, as so often at such times, free to meditate upon life, the state of the world and the meaning of everything, which I would suggest is one of the great advantages of doing the washing-up manually – that space for reflection. I mean, you could stare ruminatively out of the kitchen window while the dishwasher was going through its cycle, I suppose. But it wouldn't be quite the same, and very few people, so far as I know, take the opportunity.

On this occasion, after scraping some persistent and rather ugly food scraps off a plate, I was thinking, for some reason, about Vladimir Putin, the Russian president, who had recently chosen to celebrate the general easing of restrictions around the pandemic by invading Ukraine and releasing another prolonged bout of suffering and anxiety upon the world.

Thanks a bunch, Vlad. If there was ever a person for whom social distancing was invented . . .

In particular, I was wondering about the origins of the name 'Putin', which you don't seem to hear a lot, outside of conversations about Mad Vlad, of which there have been rather too many lately. And . . . well, this may not do me much credit, but into my casually drifting mind came the thought that maybe, back when Vladimir was just a young lad and restricted, presumably, to invading neighbouring gardens rather than neighbouring whole countries, he had found himself growing up in a remote Soviet-era household without sanitary facilities.

And maybe the rudimentary nature of this accommodation had obliged him and the rest of his family to do their fundamental human business in a large metal can – perhaps a catering-sized baked beans tin, if Soviet-era Russia ran to such a thing – which they stood outside the back door. And maybe this improvised arrangement had gone down badly with the neighbours, causing them eventually to become known widely in the area as the Poo Tin family. And it had stuck. The name, I mean.

Yes, yes – a childish digression, I know. But I swear this was the branch line down which my little train of thought was chuffing as I stood there, staring blankly through the window into the dark garden and slowly rotating a sponge scourer on a dinner plate.

And what do you know? Clearly I wasn't the only person whose mind had gone down that track. At any rate, not long after the evening in question, some simple, home-made signs appeared overnight on the sides of the bins for dog waste on a common in London. They showed the head of Mad Vlad under the legend 'POO TIN'.

Not guilty, your honour. And I have a solid alibi. I was all in favour of the gesture, though. As a child of the forties, I remain a big fan of what I guess we could call the 'Hitler has only got one ball' school of political commentary – the urge to send all puffed-up tyrants into oblivion where they belong by the means of good old schoolyard mockery. And it worked back then, so who's to say it might not work again now?

So there I was, in the kitchen, exploring my feelings about the president of Russia, when I first heard . . . the noise. Actually, it was a sequence of noises. First came a short series of soft taps, four or five in total. And then, more eerie still, came a strange, keening moan.

I paused from my labours and listened. Nothing now. Only the gentle popping of the Fairy Liquid suds in the sink. Had I imagined that other stuff? I must have done. I picked up another plate to dry off the draining board and resumed work.

Hang on, though: there it was again. Exactly the same thing, coming from the hallway just outside the kitchen – a series of gentle knocks, like somebody feebly trying to attract attention, and then that shuddering, baleful moan.

Again I froze. Again it stopped. Again I resumed work, but much more stealthily this time, with my ears fully attuned.

And once more the noise came, unmistakable now – the knocking followed by the eerie moan.

I felt my insides turn cold. I'm not generally given to jumping to conclusions, but as someone who has watched simply hundreds of horror and ghost movies down the years, I would recognise a keening, moaning sound like that anywhere. It was the noise of a lost and tortured soul, condemned to roam the earth in search of ease. Stands to reason, doesn't it? It was the totally distinctive sound of a restless spirit – and not the Spirit of Christmas Past who, needless to say, had knocked off many hours earlier, mid-afternoon, citing a dentist appointment.

And, typical: the part of the earth this particular lost and tortured soul was condemned to roam was apparently the bit of it right next to my kitchen.

It seemed to me that I had two options at this point. I could exit in a hurry in the opposite direction, via the back door, before all the cupboard doors started flying open, the lights started flashing on and off, and it all properly kicked off, *Poltergeist*-style. Or I could head towards the noise and bravely confront the source of it, perhaps with a weapon in hand – possibly a piece of newly rinsed cutlery – thereby doing my manly bit to protect my home and loved ones.

I know which approach I felt more inclined towards: bolting into the garden. Yet something – call it the innate heroism for which television actors and theatricals in general are famous – seemed to be drawing me, almost magnetically, in the opposite direction: drawing me towards whatever this thing was.

I slowly crept to the threshold of the kitchen, braced myself, and peered out into the adjacent hallway, wondering what I would see there – wondering, indeed, if what I saw there would be the last thing I would *ever* see.

Leaning against the wall was my wife Gill's guitar. And below the guitar, stretched out on the floor, was . . . a dog.

A hound of hell?

No. A hound of ours. Tuffy.

Who didn't get up, but who did at least, upon seeing me, offer a small, lazy tail-wag by way of greeting. 'Thump, thump, thump' went the tail, quite softly, on the body of the adjacent guitar. And then, as the tail settled down again, into its reclined position, it passed, on its way, across the guitar strings, like a bow across a cello, thereby producing an eerie moan of the type a person might associate with . . . I don't know – a lost and tortured soul, condemned to roam the earth in search of ease maybe?

The dastardly Tuffy. Spooked yet again by that devious mutt. It took me a while to thread it all together, but I eventually did so. The sound of me moving plates around in the kitchen had, in full accordance with Pavlov's famous old theories on dogs and their associations, triggered in the nearby, half-asleep Tuffy the thought of food. And the thought of food caused the dog's tail to wag involuntarily in anticipation; and thence the thump and the moan, each time another plate moved. I don't think I could have set this effect up if I'd tried. I don't suppose Pavlov could have done so either, and he had more experience of this kind of thing than I did.

So, haunted once more by my own pet. Humiliating, really, and it's turning into a theme. But I have to say, this was another level of haunting. It utterly trumped the poltergeist impression with the dining chair from the lockdown period of 2020. Now deploying musical instruments, the dog had really upped her game, and all credit to her for that. I can't say I'm not worried about what this development portends for even more sophisticated hauntings in the future – and, by extension, the state of my blood pressure. On the other hand, what's that line of Terry Pratchett's? 'Every dog is only two meals away from being a wolf.' So I always think, with dogs, that for as long as I retain ultimate control of the dog food, all should be well.

I should say at this point that Tuffy's record on haunting is almost as impressive as her record on food clearance, a vocation which she shares with our other dog, Bella. When the two of them work together as a team in this area, it's something to witness. In fact, if Crufts wasn't so hung up on trifling things like pedigrees, well-brushed coats and obedient behaviour, and if it had a segment where dogs competed to clear a floorspace of toast crumbs with the maximum efficiency in the quickest time, I think I could be looking at an award-winning pairing and everything that follows in terms of publicity, sponsorship and free bags of Winalot.

Consider this. Quite recently, thanks to the operation of

the principle known to science as Sod's Law,* I managed, while reaching into the fridge for something else entirely, to dislodge a large carton of cream from the shelf, and then watched it drop to the ground, burst open and create a significant lake of double-thick dairy product across much of the kitchen's tiled floor.

I closed my eyes in exasperation, as you do, already entertaining a heart-sinking vision of the practically *Exxon Valdez*-scale clean-up operation that I knew was now upon me. Well, OK, a job that would take up more of the rest of the evening than I wanted it to, and involve, no doubt, the repeated and unpleasant wringing out of cream-soaked cloths, the spreading of the offending liquid even further in the attempt to absorb it, thus making the problem look several times worse before it even began to look better, the likely noticing of deficiencies in my work by my wife a little later on, etc.

---

* The law which states that if something can go wrong it will do. Sod's Law dictates, among many other things, that wherever you stand in relation to the bonfire that you have just lit, the smoke will end up blowing directly in your face. It also ensures that the final tiny screw that you require to complete a complex repair job will, exactly at its moment of need, slip from your hand, drop to the floor and disappear down a crack in the floorboards. The expression is believed to date back to the ancient Egyptian monarch King Sod of the Sodomites (1570–1544 BC), who was the first person in recorded history to get all the way through bagging up a weekly shop at the supermarket checkout and then discover that he'd left his wallet at home. (I may have made that last bit up.)

However, when I finished wincing and miserably opened my eyes, I could hardly believe what I saw. The lake of cream had already practically vanished. Like first responders at a warehouse fire, Tuffy and Bella had instantly arrived at the scene, and they were already close to solving the problem the only way they knew how – by eating it. I could only look on admiringly, and with the deepest gratitude. In due course, not only was there not a drop of spilled cream to be found anywhere in that kitchen, but the tiles were so shiny you could see your face in them. The dogs looked pretty happy about their work, too. Indeed, this will have to go down as a rare instance of a dog looking like the cat that got the cream.

Now, before you get on the phone to the RSPCA, I fully appreciate, by the way, that cream is not a recommended foodstuff for dogs. At the same time, frankly, by comparison with some of the other things those two have found to eat in the course of their lifetimes . . . well, let's not go there, apart from to say that I'm not sure how long something would need to be dead and buried before my dogs would fail to dig it up and find it appetising. In that context, cream practically qualifies as a health food – one of their five-a-day: not so good fibre-wise, but high, at least, in calcium. And if it's only (Sod's Law permitting) once in a lifetime, then, really, I don't think there's cause to worry too much.

The point is, when they're not scaring the living wits out of me, I'm extremely grateful for the work these dogs do. They pay their way, I would say. Tuffy isn't merely in the mess-clearance business; she's actually in the mess-prevention industry. She doesn't just hear food when it hits the floor – she somehow, through some kind of sixth sense available only to certain highly attuned canines, becomes aware of that food in the split second before it leaves the plate. Consequently, she's more than capable of taking any remotely edible morsel out of the air during its descent from the table and she will have chewed up and fully digested it well before it would have hit the ground. Again, Crufts is missing a trick here.

Meanwhile, in terms of her hoovering abilities, she is practically unparalleled in my experience, getting deep into corners and those hard-to-reach areas, completing the job in no time at all and with no operator effort, and requiring no mains or battery power. I should probably license the patent for her to James Dyson and make myself a few quid.

Mind you, she won't do dust – or certainly not dust without a fairly prominent food component. And, in fact, she moults. I guess both of these things would have to be accounted a disadvantage in a household cleaning device. Back to the drawing board, maybe.

* * *

Anyway, where was I? Oh yes: rueing the temporary absence of my hired spiritual help on this current writing project and raising my eyebrow slightly about his decision to work from home. Yet, for better or worse, remote working is now officially with us, and has touched even my humble trade in ways it would have been impossible to imagine as recently as two years ago.

Indeed, there have been quite a few occasions since the pandemic descended on us when I have found myself phoning it in – in the modern sense, obviously, of using Zoom or similar, rather than the old sense of not being all that bothered. And perhaps most prominent among those occasions was the time when Gill came into the study and broke the exciting news to me that *Strictly Come Dancing* had been in touch.

I know what you're thinking: what kept them? I was thinking that, too. But here at last, clearly, was a chance to show the nation the full glory of my paso doble, perhaps in the arms of Oti Mabuse, or maybe Karen Hauer, although, between you and me, both of them would need to up their game a bit, dance-wise, because I wouldn't intend to be messing about.

Looking across at my shelves that day and narrowing my eyes slightly, I took a moment to clear a little space, mentally, between the BAFTAs and the National Television Awards for the fabled *Strictly* glitterball trophy. I have to say it looked pretty good sitting there among the accumulated silverware of a lifetime in show business – maybe almost the crowning glory. It seemed to fit.

'Do you think I should press for something dynamic and

Latin-based in week one?' I mused aloud, sitting back from my desk and sucking ruminatively on the end of my pencil. 'Or do you suppose I should ease myself in gently, and go ballroom – offer them a simple but beautifully executed American Smooth, perhaps? Either way – best book an afternoon at the tanning salon, pronto.'

'Actually,' said Gill, 'they want you to read out the terms and conditions.'

With an almost audible 'pop!', the virtual glitterball on the mantelpiece disappeared and the BAFTAS and National Television Awards shuffled sheepishly back into their places.

The terms and conditions? The yards of obligatory rigmarole relating to the viewers' phone-voting process? 'Calls will be charged at your standard rate' and so on? So much for my shot at dance-floor glory. You can't dance to the terms and conditions. Quite the opposite, in fact. As a long-time viewer of the programme, I knew that for quite a while Claudia Winkleman, *Strictly*'s co-presenter, had had the unenviable weekly task of ploughing through that paragraph of deathless legalese, and even in her terrifically capable hands it had always been a tricky moment for the energy of the show. And also a tricky moment for her, I can only assume. There was certainly one occasion when she completed the job, looked into the camera wanly and uttered the immortal concluding plea: 'Fire me.'

Then at some point the producers realised that it would be an idea to get a guest to perform that function each week and make a little feature out of it. A very smart move: people like Brian Cox and Peter Kay stepped up. John Cleese, as I recall, amusingly read out the rules while unsuccessfully stifling a number of yawns.

Some elite company there, and I suppose I should have been honoured to find myself in the frame for the job. But what about my paso doble? My cha-cha-cha? Overlooked, spurned, cast aside, it seemed, and left to moulder in the darkness of destiny's fitted wardrobe, along with my spangly outfits and my finest slashed-to-the-navel shirts.

In truth, this may not have been an entirely bad thing. And I'm not just referring to the slashed-to-the-navel shirts. All bluffing aside, when it comes to dancing, I make a very good singer. And when it comes to singing . . . well, we'll get on to me and singing in a little while, but suffice it to say for now, it's a somewhat delicate matter.

Anyway, as it happened, some overcrowding in the diary meant I never did get to delight the nation by bringing my very best, theatre-honed tones to the *Strictly* terms and conditions – which was a shame because I had a secret plan to break off, somewhere between 'calls cost 15p from a landline' and 'your vote will not count and you may still be charged', and execute a perfectly timed reverse fleckerl, just to show the producers what they were missing.*

* As any aficionado of the Viennese waltz will tell you, 'fleckerl' is a word meaning 'small spot' and denoting a step in which the dancers cease

However, by way of consolation, I did appear on the show's 2021 Christmas special edition – in keeping, yet again, with the puzzling televisual law that seems to say, 'It's Christmas, so let's see if David Jason wants to be involved.' And again, for some reason my red-hot samba did not seem to be required, but neither was I in the 'terms and conditions' role. This time I was there as . . . well, what I suppose you would call 'an emotional support actor'.

That year, Jay Blades, the presenter of *The Repair Shop*, was taking part in the competition, carefully steered, of course, by a professional partner, Luba Mushtuk, and, I was told, the music they were intending to dance to was the closing theme from *Only Fools and Horses*.

Yes, I know: in all these years of hearing that tune and thinking about its half-price cracked ice, its David Bowie LPs, its pool games, gold chains, wosnames, etc., it never once occurred to me that it was a dance number – any more, frankly, than *Strictly*'s terms and conditions are a dance number. I've heard of people playing the *Only Fools* closing theme at weddings, and I've heard of people requesting that it be played at funerals, and I'm sure an excuse may have been found to play it at all kinds of gatherings in between.

---

travelling across the floor for a few beats and rotate on the spot instead. But, of course, *Strictly Come Dancing* has made us all experts in this area. Never mind fleckerls, I thought a Viennese waltz was a luxury ice-cream dessert made by Wall's until I started watching *Strictly*.

But I'd never heard of people wanting to dance to it in a formal, competitive ballroom setting, and I'm pretty sure John Sullivan never envisaged such a thing when he wrote and recorded it.*

But what do I know? You'd struggle to tango or waltz to it, possibly, but it turns out that, if you know what you're doing, you can get a competition-standard jive going to the sound of John singing 'Hooky Street', in what music critics and aficionados of the genre such as myself now solemnly regard as one of the earliest recorded examples of UK rap. Try it at home in the privacy of your living room.

So, that was going to be Jay Blades's mission on the Christmas special: a jive to 'Hooky Street'. What the *Strictly* people wanted to know was: given his choice of music, would I be prepared to record Jay a little message of encouragement

---

* Just for the avoidance of doubt, John wrote and sang two themes for *Only Fools* – the one for the end credits, which we're talking about here, and the Chas & Dave-style, rolling-piano one for the opening titles. The opening number was requested by the BBC for series two to replace the original instrumental Ronnie Hazlehurst theme, in the hope that it would explain the show's title. Hence that opening theme comes with the emphatic pay-off line: 'Why do only fools and horses work?' It took the BBC a long time, and several million viewers, to stop feeling anxious about the oblique nature of the show's title, but you could argue – and John did argue – that that oddness was exactly what made it stick in people's minds. Anyway, for what it's worth, after much tapping on the table, I've worked out that, if the closing theme lends itself to a jive, the opening theme would more or less furnish a cha-cha-cha, if you fancy a shot at it. I'll just watch while you do it, though, if it's all right with you.

with which they could ambush, and hopefully inspire, him during the show?

Now, I'm as regular a viewer of *The Repair Shop* as I am of *Strictly*. A show set in a workshop where people take things apart and fix them up again could have been designed with me specifically in mind. In fact, that's not really a TV programme, as far as I'm concerned: that's most of my weekends. And it's always seemed obvious to me – even without meeting him in person – that Jay is a good thing. So I said I would certainly be happy to cheer him on.

It was time to dive deep into the wardrobe, then, and pull out what I think of as my ghost's uniform, or alternatively my resurrection outfit – the clothes with which I can bring Derek Trotter back to life on the occasions that I need to. Chief among these is a leather bomber jacket which I actually wore while playing Del on the show but which seemed somehow to make its way home with me when the show finished. I'm not quite sure how that happened, but I assume there is an entirely innocent explanation . . . Anyway, the jacket is in a shade which I think, if it were a car interior, we would be calling 'oxblood', and I feel fairly certain its value has always been more emotional, shall we say, than financial. It was all about the style, really. In the true Trotter tradition, that jacket looked a million dollars but only cost a fiver.

Along with the jacket, I retrieved a bright red pullover and a tweed flat cap – both model's own, let me be clear, and neither of them palmed off from the BBC's ample wardrobe stocks on the quiet. And by the simple application of these three items, and with a few preliminary flexes of the neck and rolls of the shoulders by way of a warm-up, I was more or less ready to stop being David Jason for a couple of minutes and start being Derek Trotter.

You'll imagine, I'm sure, the disruption here at Jason Towers on the day my message for Jay was filmed: the arrival on the drive of various lorries and vans; the offloading of cameras and lights and stands and reflector screens; the wardrobe and make-up teams going about their work; the script people doing last-minute edits; the *Strictly Come Dancing* production staff dashing around with clipboards and earpieces.

And if you imagined any of that, you'd be completely wrong. This was 2021, don't forget. I can list the people and the equipment involved in getting me onto the screen in that *Strictly* Christmas special very swiftly indeed. The people were me and Gill and the equipment was Gill's phone. The whole item was written, produced, directed, lit, filmed and edited by my wife, on location in front of a conveniently blank portion of wall in our house.

Watching the show at home on Christmas Day, my informed opinion was that Jay, bless him, is a better repairer than he is a dancer, and, even allowing for the generous spirit of the season, the judges seemed to agree with me: Jay got turned over by the singer Anne-Marie in the final scoring.

My informed opinion about my own contribution to the show, however, is that it looked . . . well, a touch underlit and a bit . . . *home-made*. Which I guess is hardly surprising in the circumstances.

This is simply where we are nowadays. The same thing happened not long ago when *The One Show* got in touch. As part of BBC 100, the BBC's centenary celebrations, viewers had been voting for their most loved BBC TV programme and . . . far be it from me to shine my own buttons here, but *Only Fools and Horses* had come out top, just ahead of *Doctor Who*.

It's extraordinary, really, and extremely gratifying. It feels like hardly six months goes by without me hearing about the success of *Only Fools* in a public poll of some description. If I had a pound for every time the bar-flap sequence has been voted people's Funniest Television Moment, or similar, I'd probably be able to afford to hire a Spirit of Christmas Past permanently and not just while writing this book. The point is, forty years after our show first went out, and the best part of two decades since its last new episode, people are still talking about it and making clear how fond of it they still are, and that's not something I can ever quite get my head around.

And now here were the viewers of *The One Show* offering the programme another show of confidence and sitting it on top of what, on closer examination, proved to be an extremely distinguished pile, featuring not just sitcoms but BBC-made programmes of all kinds. Just to put this in perspective, *Blackadder* and *Fawlty Towers* were a little way back on this latest list, and Sir David Attenborough's *Planet Earth*, which, whatever else you want to say about it, covered a lot more ground than *Only Fools* and was probably a bit trickier to film, was languishing somewhere down at number 12.

Should have put a few more gags in it, Sir David.

Anyway, the question from *The One Show* was: would I come on the programme and, in this moment of triumph for *Only Fools* and everyone connected with it, say a few words of thanks on behalf of the team?

Now, before the pandemic normalised working from home, an appearance on *The One Show* would have been, for better or worse, a bit of a day out. It would have required a journey to London, for which they probably would have sent a car for you. You would have spent some time behind the scenes in the green room where you would have mingled with the great and good and chatted to your fellow guests, all the while enjoying generous access to the BBC's normally quite challenging coffee and probably some free biscuits.

And then, after having a light dusting of make-up applied to your better side by a professional make-up artist, you would have been ushered by professional production staff into a professionally lit studio to be filmed by professional camera operators – with the result that you might, if you're lucky, end up looking quite professional yourself in the segment that eventually went out into people's sitting rooms.

But of course none of that applied this time. It was me, Gill and Gill's phone all over again, doing our best to put something together and then crossing our fingers that the show would be able to use it. Working from home, in other words. No car, no green room, no day out. More importantly, no professional make-up and no professional lighting and no professional camera angles. And certainly no free biscuits. I suppose at least the coffee was better.

And although I can see there's plenty to recommend this method, it does seem, from the point of view of the finished product, a slightly retrograde development to me. We appear to have gone directly from the pin-sharp, slickly produced, Ultra HD broadcasting era to calmly accepting smudgy and shaky videos off people's iPhones or shot through the slightly dusty lenses of the cameras on their laptops. It's like certain kinds of television programmes are now patchwork quilts, with people working on their own little square of the design at home. And nobody minded during the drudgery of lock-down, because we were all doing our bit and we were just grateful to see faces, no matter the quality of the imagery. But for obvious reasons, relating to convenience and budget, among other things, this approach has continued beyond the pandemic. The self-shot TV appearance seems to be here to stay, smudges, shakes, dust and all.

Of course, that it's possible in the first place to make broadcast-ready images of any kind without leaving your own armchair and employing only a standard-issue phone is pretty remarkable. Why, it doesn't seem all that long ago that I was appearing in adverts for a marvellous technological breakthrough and a dazzling new contribution to freedom and convenience which was about to be unleashed upon the Great British public and which was to be called . . . the British Telecom Phonecard.

Honestly, what would those amazing people in the lab coats think of next? First a man on the moon, and now this. Here was an ingenious, plastic, credit-card-shaped device which, if slotted into the appropriate receptacle near the handset in a public call box, would enable you to – as BT boldly trumpeted – 'buy your phone calls in advance'. The brave new world was truly upon us.

No more fumbling about with coins and frantically feeding the machinery bits of silver to keep the call alive! We were all pinching ourselves in disbelief. Could you even imagine such a time would ever come, let alone in your own lifetime?

This was in the early 1980s, though apparently it was almost a decade before, in 1974, that British Telecom first set up (I'm not making this up) a 'Coinbox Study Steering Group', charged with exploring the future of the coin-less payphone and, by extension, the future of the phone box. Oh to have been a fly on the wall – or even a fly in the phone box – at the proceedings of the Coinbox Study Steering Group. Oh to have been a member of it. I think I missed my vocation.

Of course, history will now demonstrate that the ultimate future of the phone box turned out to be providing storage space for emergency defibrillator equipment or becoming an improvised lending library for the neighbourhood's old paperback books. But I don't suppose anybody on the Coinbox Study Steering Group was predicting that in 1974. And that august committee's big idea, at the conclusion of its doubtless long hours of steering? The phonecard. Because, as the voice-over accompanying my advert for BT patiently explained: 'There will be times when you need to make dozens of calls from a public phone.'

To be perfectly honest, with the benefit of hindsight, I'm struggling to think of a single situation in which you might have needed to make *dozens* of calls from a payphone – unless, I guess, you were doing something like organising a wedding and wanting to save on paper for invitations.

But practically speaking, making dozens of calls from a phone box was never going to work out for you, because, quite apart from anything else, after about call number four, and most likely much sooner, you'd have had a waiting customer tapping agitatedly on the glass with a coin – or with the leading edge of their phonecard – and asking you whether you were planning to be in there all night. There was an unwritten but strictly applied code of conduct around payphone usage, as I recall, and a strong sense that these were shared, public facilities which were to be treated as such. Gumming them up by blathering on for hours on end was very much frowned upon, however much BT might have been trying to encourage it.

On the other hand, quite by contrast, smoking in phone

boxes appeared to be entirely acceptable – indeed, almost obligatory. Some of them even provided an ashtray for your smoking convenience, and in the absence of that, there was always the floor. Or the little metal-lined cubbyhole into which rejected coins dropped. Consequently, there was a long period in the seventies and eighties when the mouthpiece of any public phone had a distinct whiff of smoke and ash about it, as if it had recently been set fire to. Ah, how the memories linger. I can almost re-summon that stale odour of nicotine-impregnated plastic to my nostrils now.

Anyway, in 1982 or thereabouts the all-new British Telecom Phonecard was obviously going to be an absolute boon to you, especially if, for example – like me in the advert – you had broken down in a remote spot and a cloud of smoke while driving a lorry-load of fresh eggs and needed to get a repair service out in a hurry.

I don't mean to ruin the suspense for you, but the gag was that my lorry driver had to place countless calls from a phone box before he could find a garage that was willing to come out to him, with the result that all his eggs had turned to chicks by the end of the ad.

No CGI in those days, by the way: those hundreds of chicks seen spilling out of the back of my lorry were truly hundreds of chicks spilling out of the back of my lorry – imported from a nearby farm for the purposes of our filming. And I probably don't need to say, as extras they were a right old handful. Several hundred right old handfuls, in fact. Never work with children or animals, they famously say, and newly hatched chicks amount, in a sense, to both those things at once – a perfect storm of things you shouldn't act with. I've performed with dogs, who can be bad enough when it comes to responding to cues – and even worse when it comes to learning their lines. But let me tell you, getting hundreds of newly hatched chicks to sit where you want them . . . It was anarchy.

Still, I was proud to play my part, however incidental, at what was clearly such a revolutionary moment in the history of personal communication. It's amusing to reflect, though, that just a few years after making that advert, I would be standing in the Nag's Head as Del Boy, in that episode from the sixth series of *Only Fools* entitled 'Sickness and Wealth', trying to persuade Mike the barman, played by wonderful Ken MacDonald, to part with 'forty nicker' for what Del proudly – indeed, cockily – described as his 'executive mobile phone'.

This was 1989, and you can conclude that a mobile phone was clearly a) still something cutting-edge enough to merit the glossy adjective 'executive', and b) still something that needed to be explained in a sentence or two to the casual observer. Alas, as you may recall, this particular model of which Del was an early adopter, and in which he now tried to interest Mike, came complete with a radio-style aerial that shot upwards during his big sell and nearly took Mike's eye out, causing Mike, understandably, to become sceptical.

As Mike says, after reeling back: ''Ere, that aerial's a bit urgent, isn't it?' Incidentally, I love the word 'urgent' in that line. It's not technically even a punchline, and there's barely any time for the audience to pause and take it in, but there is still something so instantly funny about it. And it's very John Sullivan, of course: the poetry of the pub, for which he had such an acute ear.

And that same urgent aerial would, later in the very same episode, shoot up my nose and become lodged there at an inopportune moment while a bunch of us were trembling behind a curtain, hiding from members of the menacing Driscoll family. And that, I can tell you, was one of those moments where the absurdity of what you have ended up doing for a living comes home to you: during the making of that scene, I found myself devoting a significant portion of my working day to seriously addressing the issue of how best to get a mobile phone to dangle by its aerial from my left nostril. It's very hard to take yourself too seriously when this is what you hesitantly define as 'work'.

A typical Sullivan plot development there, though: the thing that Del is most inclined to be swanky about early in an episode – the thing that gives him new reason to be confident about himself and his place in the world – will be the thing that ultimately undoes him in the most embarrassing way. Developments like that were seeded and knitted into the script so many times along the way, and it was always done so deftly that you wouldn't see it coming.

However, the point is, Del's newfangled yuppy apparatus didn't come across as something that was going to be utterly life-changing any time soon. In fact, as you possibly remember, it merely appeared to be utterly channel-changing – switching the programme on the Nag's Head's telly, to the irritation of Boycie and some other customers, who were trying to watch the horse racing. 'I think I'll stick with the phone in the public bar, Del,' as Mike says – probably speaking for the majority of people in 1989, at that point when mobile phones were first moving among us and looking almost comically unpromising: bigger than house bricks, unreliable in a built-up area, likely to change the channel in the Nag's Head, etc.

Yet before long, of course – literally within a couple of years of that episode – absolutely *loads* of people would be walking around casually with these devices, albeit made a touch smaller and shorn of the urgent aerials. And now look at us all – pretty much in thrall to our handsets and carrying them with us everywhere we go.

Well, I say 'all' of us: to be perfectly honest, my mobile phone tends to live on the windowsill in our kitchen where most of the time it makes me slightly more difficult to reach than our landline. But I know I'm not typical in that regard and for most people now the mobile phone has become a constant companion and, it would even appear, a comfort in times of need.

Which is fine, by the way. Each to their own. However,

I'm not saying near-instant, twenty-four-hour connectivity hasn't been a blessing to our world in so many ways, but I *am* saying that it has brought its own unique inconveniences, too, which sometimes we prefer to overlook. Consider, for example, the amount of communication which is now typically involved when a friend arranges to have lunch with you. There'll be the call, obviously, to make the appointment in the first place. But then there'll be another call, the day before, to check you're 'still on'.

To which my reaction is always: 'Well, why wouldn't I be? If anything had come up, I'd have rung you, wouldn't I? But it hasn't. So I didn't. And I am.'

And then there might be a further call on the morning of the lunch to say your lunch companion is 'running a little late, but just setting out now'. And there will almost definitely be a call, or at the very least a text, to say he's struggling to find a parking space and may not be with you for another five minutes . . .

Which probably, now I come to think of it, explains why my mobile spends as much time as it does on the kitchen windowsill. In many ways, I think I preferred it when people were simply late and you didn't know why. At least there was a bit of mystery and suspense to cling to. And the phone rang less often.

Still, such is the march of technology – and consider how far we have come on that march, and how fast. First came the miracle of transporting our voices from one room to another down a wire – the telephone! Then we found a way to send our voices through far greater distances across the airwaves – the miracle of the wireless! Then we found a way to send pictures, first in black and white, and then in colour – television! And now we think nothing of sending live, moving images of ourselves in real time to and from little handsets that we carry with us everywhere like religious tokens.

What next? we may well ask. Well, as Derek Trotter's representative on earth, I'm here to tell you. Teleportation, that's what's next. Trust me on this. It's coming soon. Scotty on *Star Trek* has been beaming people up and down for years, and only occasionally had a problem with the nuts and bolts, so why not here on earth?

Don't the boffins tell us that we're just a mass of vibrating atoms? They'll find a way to shift those atoms wirelessly from one place to another, sure as my eggs in that British Telecom Phonecard advert were eggs – or eventually chicks. No more shuffling off to the airport and subjecting ourselves to air travel's myriad inconveniences and indignities. Say goodbye to National Express coaches, too, and cars, also, electric or otherwise. Teleporting is the future. Give it a short while, and we'll all be saying: 'I'll be with you in a shimmer.'

Does this sound a touch unlikely? Reflect on this, then. Imagine if you had been around in Victorian times and someone had told you that one day you would be able to make an appearance on a *Strictly Come Dancing* Christmas special via your mobile phone and without leaving your own sitting room. You would have laughed until your top hat fell off. And then you'd have had that person carted away to an asylum.

A couple of boxes at home on the shelf in the hall: an ARRIVA box, and a SENDA box. That's all you're going to need. Straight after breakfast you'll be dissolving yourself in Taunton and reconstituting yourself three seconds later up at your brother-in-law's in Scarborough. And you won't even need to add water.

But you'll still be phoning ahead to say you're just setting out, of course. That goes without saying.

It's the future of personal transport, and I'd be willing to bet good money on it, were I a gambling man. And I'd also bet good money on the equipment being with us about five minutes after they've finished destroying whole swathes of the UK's most beautiful countryside to build the HS2 railway line, instantly rendering that whole project obsolete.

Because technology, as we well know, is temporary. But Sod's Law is forever.

* * *

Our good deed producing and delivering that video message for Jay Blades on *Strictly Come Dancing* did not go unrewarded. Seven months later, Gill and I received a guided tour of the *Repair Shop* barn in West Sussex.

'Wait until the summer,' Jay had said, 'because the barn can get a bit cold in the winter.' So we hung on until July, and ended up going on one of the hottest days of the year.

Good plan. Instead of freezing, we all melted instead.

What a fantastic day it was, though. It was officially Jay's day off and he should have been out basking in the heat somewhere, but he came into work specially to meet us and look after us. As anyone who watches the show knows, Jay is great fun – just a bundle of positive energy and enthusiasm, committed to showcasing dying skills and trades and utterly determined to promote the value of restoration and recycling in our throwaway society. Amen to that. I share his belief in the increasing importance of mending stuff, and it's how I try to operate in my own life, too.

Most of Jay's team was there that day: Suzie Fletcher, the leather expert; Steve Fletcher, who does clocks and watches; Will Kirk, the woodwork man; Dominic Chinea, the metalwork man; Lucia Scalisi, the art restorer; Sonnaz Nooranvary, the upholsterer; Jayesh Vaghela, the milliner; and Richard Biggs, who turns his expert eye to telescopes, and both his expert eyes to binoculars.

I got to chat with every one of them and was so impressed by how much they know and how passionate they are about what they do. I had the chance to watch them at work, too, performing challenging, delicate, sympathetic repairs, all helping each other out and chipping in with their individual expertise when problems arose. A proper team. I'd been slightly worried that getting a peek behind the scenes might spoil my enjoyment of the show, letting light in on the magic in some way. On the contrary: *The Repair Shop* is as you see it. My enjoyment and respect for what that team do and the way they do it only increased.

What a great place to go to work each day, too, in a truly beautiful country location. You could feel how the environment was feeding everybody's enthusiasm and general demeanour. We had a lovely lunch brought in by a local chef and ate under a tree in the fields, and, with the sun shining, it felt like there was, at that moment, no finer place to be.

By lunchtime, I have to confess, I had developed an advanced case of extreme tool envy. The barn inevitably houses an astonishing collection of really quite wonderful tools and I found myself lusting after many of them and wishing I could take them back to my own humble workshop. Dom the metalwork guy, in particular, had this utterly marvellous toolbox on wheels which seemed to contain every single tool one would ever be likely to need, plus a couple of others just in case.

Oh for one of those on the numerous occasions when I have found myself trudging back miserably from a job at the bottom of the garden to fetch the single tool which Sod's Law (see earlier) has belatedly revealed I need. Actually, when Sod is *really* going for it, that can happen three or four times on the same job. A toolbox like Dom's could take whole miles off my working day.

I took along a video to show everyone of Marvo the Mystic – the old, end-of-the-pier, coin-operated fortune-telling machine which I restored with my great film-making friend, Brian Cosgrove. I took it mostly because I thought they would be interested in it, but there was also a little part of me that wanted to make sure they all saw that I know one end of a screwdriver from the other. I'm well aware of the public image we thespians frequently labour under: that we're a bunch of highly impractical, out-of-touch luvvies who couldn't put up a shelf if our parts depended on it – and I suppose, yes, I have met one or two like that, but it's certainly not the whole truth and it's definitely not the case with me. Had the cards fallen differently, maybe I could have been an expert on *The Repair Shop*. Now, that I would have loved. Probably specialising in motorbike restoration, or metalwork like Dom.

Instead, I'll just have to be content to be inspired by those guys, and get on with the work as it arises in my own somewhat scruffier home workshop. Gill has painted me a wooden sign to hang on its door: 'Sir DJ's Repair Shop'. But I know that I can only aspire to operate at the level of skill found in the barn. In my case, it's more like 'The Despair Shop'.

ON THE EIGHTH DEL OF CHRISTMAS . . .

Parties and oil rigs

I'm going to talk in this chapter about when the *Only Fools and Horses* Christmas specials properly took off, but before I do that I want to tell you about a picture I own.

Some while ago I was at a dinner where, after the food had been served and gratefully demolished, they held a charity auction – all sorts of desirable items and opportunities getting flogged off, and all in a good cause, but one of those events where you have to be very careful what you do with your fork or else you go home having accidentally dropped fourteen grand on two tickets for a Spanish cookery weekend and a signed photograph of Alan Titchmarsh.

However, on this occasion I seemed to be managing to keep my fork under control and stay out of trouble. One of the lots, though, somewhere around the middle of the auction, was a giant portrait painting of the late John Sullivan – an excellent likeness of him, my artistic eye told me, with, around the edges, little painted scenes from some of the shows John wrote: *Citizen Smith*, *Just Good Friends* and, of course, *Only Fools and Horses*. Within the spirit of the evening – and indeed, perhaps a little under the influence of the spirits on offer *during* the evening – I felt something of an acquisitive urge come upon me. It would be nice for me to own that picture, wouldn't it? Perhaps I would wave my fork after all.

At the same time, though, somewhere inside my head, a sensible voice which hadn't been entirely doused in the evening's freely flowing refreshments said to me: 'But where would you put it?'

I had to concede, it was a good point that my sober self was making, and he was making it well. This was a properly big picture, the portrait element of it being at least life-size, and there are no rooms in my house that have high enough ceilings to hang a painting like that without it looking . . . well, a bit overpowering, shall we say. A bit urgent, even.

You know that thing which is always said about really good portraits, and in particular about the *Mona Lisa* – that the eyes seem to follow you around the room? Well, in this case, if I'd tried to hang that picture at my place, it wouldn't just have been John's eyes that were following me around the room, it would have been the whole of him, and he would have been practically tapping me on the shoulder and breathing down my neck. And much as I loved John – and as amusing as John would no doubt have found that outcome – I felt it was one I could probably get along without.

So I kept my fork to myself and simply looked on as the picture attracted some hectic bidding and went for a decent sum to somebody on the other side of the room. The auctioneer moved on to the next lot – possibly a Spanish cookery weekend, or maybe a signed photograph of Alan Titchmarsh, I now forget – and I thought no more of it.

When the evening eventually came to an end, I got up and began to leave. As I was on my way out, though, a man whom I didn't know approached me, carrying that large painting.

'Here,' he said, 'I saw you were here tonight, and I really want you to have this.'

This man was the successful bidder for the painting of John, and now he was trying to give it to me.

I was really taken aback and didn't quite know what to say. He'd just paid a fair bit of money for that picture. It was his. I said I couldn't possibly take it off him – that I wouldn't feel right.

Plus – though I didn't say this – the ceilings in my house are too low for it.

But he was really insistent. He said that *Only Fools* had given him a lot of pleasure down the years and had made him laugh a lot, and had also moved him, too, and he felt it was his way of repaying all of that and saying thank you.

'Really, I want you to have it,' he said.

Obviously, I was flattered and touched by his insistence, not to mention his generosity. And he was so sincere about

169

it that I felt I had to accept the painting. I thanked him warmly for his kindness and told him how moved I was that he had done that, and I took the picture from him, got it outside and into the car somehow, and then took it home.

It was all extremely touching. But, of course, none of this meant that my ceilings were any higher.

My quandary now, obviously, was that I was the proud owner of a giant portrait of John Sullivan with no wall space on which to hang it. A number of potential solutions to this problem immediately presented themselves and I mulled them on the journey back that night. The most obvious tactic would have been to quietly pass on the artwork to someone with more suitable ceilings – or perhaps even to put it on eBay and trouser a few quid. But neither of those things would have seemed quite right given the sentimental, and not to mention charitable, circumstances in which I had acquired the painting. Plus I really did like the picture . . .

I continued to mull.

'Move to a bigger house' was, I suppose, an option, but that did seem a bit extreme, not least given that we're very happy where we are, actually, and have spent so many years getting the garden the way we like it.

Another possibility might be to get a special extension built on the side of the house in order to provide some extra exhibition space for the painting, like the National Gallery in London did a few years ago – the Sainsbury Wing, as I believe they call it – albeit, in their case, not just for paintings of John Sullivan, but for other ones too. Maybe I could commission a Sainsbury Wing for Jason Towers. Maybe Sainsbury's would be interested in funding it: they've had enough of my money down the years.

Then again, wasn't the extension to the National Gallery exactly the project that the then Prince Charles famously described, when it was originally proposed, as 'a monstrous carbuncle on the face of a much-loved and elegant friend', causing the original design to be scrapped and the architects to go spinning back to the drawing board? I wouldn't want to court controversy in that way. You have to be so careful, clearly, when you try and make alterations to precious and historic national monuments, such as the National Gallery and my house. The last thing I'd want to do is get the windows all wrong and have Charles turning his nose up every time he dropped round for coffee. (First Thursday of every month, in case you're wondering. And he sometimes brings a bag of washing.)*

Maybe a less controversial – and, indeed, practically invisible – solution would be to dig out the basement underneath the house and create space for the painting in a whole new multi-purpose environment down there. Isn't that what we're always reading about the oligarchs doing to their Kensington town houses? Or at least we used to read about them doing it, when oligarchs were still allowed in the country.

* Just joking. He never brings a bag of washing.

No such problem for me in leafy Buckinghamshire, though, where I still seem to be welcome. So maybe I could call in the diggers, carve out a whole new cavern beneath my house, and create room for the painting, along with a swimming pool, a bowling alley, and parking for fourteen cars.

That would be expensive, though – and extremely disruptive for those of us living upstairs while it was being built. It might just be me, but I find it to be a rule that, the more one can minimise building work in one's house, the more one's quota of happiness rises.

Maybe the simpler and more economical option was to get the scissors out and cut the painting into manageable pieces – bite-size morsels, if you will – and distribute them on various walls around the house, thereby ending up with bits of John in different rooms. But that, too, didn't feel quite right, somehow: it would have seemed like an insult to the fundamental integrity of the artwork, and indeed to the fundamental integrity of John.

Then I had a light-bulb moment. I could put the painting on the back wall of my garage.

Now, I need to be careful about how I explain this because I'm aware that when you say you're sticking something out in the garage, it doesn't necessarily sound like you're offering that thing the warmest of welcomes to your home. I mean, it's not something you find yourself saying to someone when the Christmas presents are getting opened, is it? 'Ooh, how kind of you! And I know exactly where I can put this:

straight out in the garage.' A bit like putting someone's book in the downstairs loo, shoving someone's painting out where the car goes could be interpreted as a mixed compliment.*

But hear me out. The back wall of my garage isn't a place where I stack unwanted Christmas presents and things which have lost their claim to a place in the house – far from it. In fact, it has become something of a . . . well, 'shrine' would be too strong a word for it. But maybe 'wall of remembrance' is closer.

At any rate, it's where I've hung a large picture of Ronnie Barker, my inspiration and mentor and eventually my partner in comedy and close friend. It's a painting based on a photograph taken at the BAFTA ceremony in London in 2003, when Ronnie did me the honour of presenting me with the BAFTA Fellowship award, and, of course, it's a picture of a moment that means an enormous amount to me.

In the compilation of clips from my career that BAFTA screened at that Fellowship presentation, there's a glimpse of a two-man comic play that Ronnie and I did together, right back at the beginning, as part of the LWT series *Six Dates with Barker* – a loopy, quite dark but very funny piece about

---

* Incidentally, dear reader, if the downstairs loo is where you choose to store this particular book, then I assure you that I have no problem with that whatsoever. On the contrary, it's your book to do with as you will, and I am flattered that you should consider giving it house room of any kind. Indeed, if the loo is where my book is currently in front of you, I couldn't be more honoured. As long as it won't shortly be behind you.

a depressed husband hiring an odd-job man to finish him off. Ronnie played the husband and I played the odd-job man. The clip at the ceremony was my line to Ronnie: 'Lucky we met, isn't it?'

Lucky we met: indeed it was. How different the whole path of my career would have been if I hadn't had the great good fortune to meet Ronnie Barker. And the same goes, in equal measure, for John Sullivan, too. Which is why, next to the painting of Ronnie, I now hung the painting of John. So every time I come home in the car from wherever I've been and switch off the engine, I'm looking directly at John and at Ronnie – the two people in my career to whom, by any reckoning, I owe the most. Lucky we met. And they hang together in my private rogues gallery as a constant reminder of those two pieces of amazing, life-altering chance.

However, I have to tell you that, of the two of them, Ronnie is very much the more stable. By which I mean his picture never budges. He just sits there on the garage wall, completely still. John, on the other hand, can't seem to stop fidgeting. At any rate, every week or so, I'll look at that painting and find it's not hanging straight. Which, I confess, is something I'm rather fussy about. It's the legacy of my time as an electrician's apprentice, I suppose – the inheritance from all those days spent running electric cables down walls, stepping back and saying to your mate, 'Does that look right to you?' And he'd give it his best appraising look and say, 'Nah, it's pissed.' And then you'd have to do it again. So even now I can spot a mis-hung picture from a mile away, and if something around the house is on the skew, it offends my eye, and I won't be happy until I've straightened it up.

And so it is with John. I'll come in sometimes and he'll be drunk and I'll have to put him right. A week later, despite my best efforts, he'll have shifted to one side again. It's like he's constantly giving me a gentle reminder as I go about my business: 'Excuse me, don't forget where this success of yours came from.'

And I haven't. And I won't.

* * *

Spirit of Christmas Past! Why do you torment me all of a sudden with this image of a care home and elderly heads in paper hats? What's your point here?

Oh, wait – no, I see where we're going with this. This is 1983, isn't it? That's Russell Harty's care home.

Well, not literally Russell Harty's care home. It's the care home in which, for one night only, Russell's early-evening BBC chat show, *Harty*, has chosen to film its Christmas party – its 'Harty Party' as the producers have by no means resisted the urge to label it, and at which Nick, Lennard and I must now mix and mingle in costume and character as our *Only Fools and Horses* selves.

Ah, the sweet joys of publicity. That said, though, it is at least a positive thing that we have been given some publicity to do. We've been grumbling quite regularly up to now that the BBC aren't pushing us forward for magazine stories and newspaper profiles and appearances on other shows to the extent that they could be doing – things which might put the show under a few more people's noses and expand the audience faster than it seems to be expanding under its own steam.

Sometimes we have even wondered whether the BBC is a touch embarrassed by our little working-class show with its working-class characters and its working-class settings – inclined to sweep us under the carpet a little, in favour of other, less working-class shows. Maybe that was just insecurity on our part. But we did wonder.

Not right now, though. Here in 1983, with the show three series old, the PR machine finally seems to be clicking into gear. Me, Nick and Lennard have already posed for a spread in the Christmas *Radio Times* dressed up as dopey choirboys, in cassocks and white frilly ruffs.

And now here we are, the three of us, with just four days to go until Christmas, in Woking, in Surrey, at the former Railway Orphanage, a giant Victorian building, latterly, as mentioned, a care home. The plan is that, in a large hall filled with tables and chairs and decked for the season, amid plates of sausage rolls and mince pies, Russell and his guests will mingle with residents of the home in party hats. And here, over by the BBC band, which has also been imported into the care home for the evening, Nick, Lennard and I will do our best to drum up some interest in the upcoming, third *Only Fools* Christmas special which, for the first time in its history, has been scheduled to go out to the nation on – trumpet fanfare here – Christmas Day.

Quite late on Christmas Day, it must be said: at 9.35 p.m., to be exact, after *All Creatures Great and Small*. What might be regarded as the season's golden slot – Christmas night, 7.15 p.m. – has gone to *The Two Ronnies*, and we are by no means in a position to argue with the pre-eminence of those two titans at this still young moment in our show's life.

Nevertheless . . . Christmas Day! This is without a doubt the most prominent billing the show has received and we are all, inevitably, highly excited about it, and what it will mean for us and specifically for the chances of our show getting commissioned by the BBC for another series, the possibility of which somehow always seems to be agonisingly in the balance, at every step of the way.

This will also be the first time I have made it onto the nation's screens at the very apex of the holiday period since a certain BBC pantomime almost two decades ago now – and whatever else occurs, it will, at least, be a darned sight easier for my parents to pick me out this time.

So here I sit, in the 'Harty Party' care home, ready to do my promotional bit at this potentially pivotal moment for the future of our show. And, not to put too fine a point on it, I'm a little on edge.

For one thing, Russell Harty and I have, shall we say, some history. Nothing too serious – but definitely some history.

It happened a little while before at an event we were both at, the exact nature of which, I'm afraid to say, has long since boarded memory's barge and floated up the dank canal of yesteryear. What I do recall about that event, though, was that Russell, acting as, I believe, the night's compère, was required to introduce me onstage in front of a quite substantial audience.

What was I going to do when I got out there in front of that audience? A stand-up routine? The 'dogs of war' speech from Shakespeare's *Julius Caesar*? A spot of balloon-folding? Again, memory completely fails me.

But what I do vividly remember is standing in the wings, readying myself to go out, and hearing Russell say the following:

'Ladies and gentlemen, please welcome . . . DAVID JANSSEN!'

At the side of the stage, I looked back over my shoulder, just in case. Nope: no sign of David Janssen, the American television actor, best known for starring in the sixties series *The Fugitive*. No sign of David 'Kid' Jensen, the Radio 1 DJ, either. By David Janssen, Russell must be meaning me.

A slip of the tongue, then, on Russell's part? Well, we all make them, if so. But take it from me, it's quite wince-inducing to walk out in front of an applauding audience to whom you have just been introduced as someone else, and try to carry yourself as normal. You feel pretty . . . foolish.

Could I have handled it better? Probably. Should I have

handled it better? Most certainly. But with ill-concealed irritation, I took the microphone and spoke as follows:

'Thank you very much, Russell Farty.'

Not very grown-up of me, I'll admit. Neither big nor clever. But at the same time, looking back . . . well, kind of funny. And certainly satisfying as a piece of payback at the time. I believe it even earned me a round of applause.

Still, you know what they say: be nice to people on the way up, in case you should meet them on the way down – or, in my case, here in this care home turned TV studio in 1983, still on the way up.

So, that little incident is hovering, a touch unsettlingly, in my mind. Then there's the set-up for this piece we're about to do, which I'm not altogether happy about. The idea is that the cameras will eventually find the three of us seated at our table among the throng, and, on cue, we'll go into a short, scripted sketch, which John Sullivan has written for us. And then, when we're done, Russell himself will appear at our table and conduct an interview with us, during which we are to remain in character.

That last bit is the part I'm dreading, to be honest. Not that riffing for a few minutes in the character of Del doesn't come easily enough by now. And I don't suppose Russell is planning to spring any particularly devious questions on us in this context. Most likely he'll just ask us what we're getting each other for Christmas and lob us a couple of other fairly soft ones, and we'll be out of there.

No, what's bothering me is the potentially awkward transition from the scripted phase to the unscripted phase. That, for me, has the shape of a moment which could go either way. Frankly, I'm worried it's going to look as naff as hell.

And all of this live on one of the biggest and most-watched shows currently on television.

Anyway, stiff upper lip, and all that. Stiff drink, too, wouldn't go amiss, but that's not going to happen, and not just because we're in a care home. 'No drinking on duty' has long since been a mantra of mine. The two don't mix – or not for me, at any rate. I'm very much like a policeman in that respect, or a vicar – and very much unlike someone who used to work in Downing Street. The stiff drink will have to wait until afterwards.*

So, the big moment arrives. Russell, on the other side of the room, introduces us for some reason as 'Grandad, Rod and Del Boy', thereby becoming possibly the only person ever to abbreviate Rodney's name in a public setting. And

---

* I'll tell you someone who wasn't with me on the 'no alcohol while performing' rule: Charles Dickens. When the author did his famous reading tours, knocking 'em dead with extracts from A Christmas Carol on a nightly basis all over the provinces, he apparently adhered to a strict pre-performance routine. Breakfast: two tablespoons of rum with cream. Supper: a pint of champagne. Half an hour before curtain-up: a glass of sherry with a raw egg beaten into it. I feel sick already, but for Dickens that intake would power a high-intensity three-hour performance that would have them either rolling in the aisles with laughter or convulsing with tears, depending. I would love to have seen it. But if it's all right with you, I'll still just have a glass of water.

also, I'm fairly sure, the last. And then the camera swings over, and finds the three of us, getting seated at our table, hunched among the studio guests.

The scripted bit doesn't go too badly: a couple of stumbles, maybe, but nothing to get us hauled up in front of the union. A couple of decent laughs from the assembled care home residents, too. John's script doesn't take a vengeful pop at Russell on my behalf over what we should probably now be calling 'Janssengate', but it does loose off a nice one in the direction of one of Russell's BBC colleagues in the interviewing game.

Del is trying to explain to the other two that he's getting them a Christmas on the cheap by bringing them here, to Russell Harty's party.

'Who's Russell Harvey?' asks Grandad.

'No, you know him,' says Rodney. 'He's like that Michael Parkinson, right, but he's got O levels.'

And if the pace lags, I at least have my cigar to fall back on. When acting, on a Russell Harty show or anywhere else, something to do with your hands is always welcome, and I can report that the cigar delivers exceptional versatility in this area: you can put it in your mouth, chew on it, take it out, examine it, wave it about . . . It's altogether a cracking distraction. And on this occasion I'm more than commonly grateful for it.

With the sketch done and dusted with no noticeable casualties, Russell, as planned, comes into shot rather awkwardly, and, as not planned, blows a squeaky toy at Nick. Well, I guess it is a Christmas party . . . He then asks us a few questions, including what we'll be getting each other for Christmas. Again, we just about get away with it, but it's all a bit nervy, not quite natural. Nick and I both seem to be trying to fight a combination of irritation and embarrassment. The only one of us who appears completely at ease with the situation is Lennard, who, with supreme Grandad-style bluntness, solemnly tells Russell, apropos of nothing at all: 'I don't like you. You're not as good as Parkinson.'

Ah, dear old Lennard, bless his memory. There weren't many situations involving *Only Fools* where he didn't seem to be enjoying himself enormously. The whole experience appeared to come as a fantastic gift to him at a point in his career when he had begun to think he was edging towards that state nearly every actor dreads: retirement. He really relished it.

Actually, now I come to think about it, there was ONE time when Lennard wasn't entirely buoyant about the way things were going, and that was when Nick and I crept into the dressing room, where his costume was laid out ready for him, and nailed his shoes to the floor. That really didn't go down well. Normally Lennard would see the funny side of a prank very quickly – which was a highly necessary attribute to have on the set of *Only Fools*. But with this one I think we must have just got him at the wrong time or something, because he absolutely lost it.

At one point he was even threatening to get the police involved. Which, of course, only made Nick and me laugh harder. But I swear it was the only time, while working with Lennard, that I saw him looking anything other than cheerful with his lot.

It's all the more poignant, then, to think of how much lay ahead of the show at this point in 1983 – and yet the Christmas special we're promoting, 'Thicker Than Water', will be Lennard's last appearance. A year later, in December 1984, just after we've started filming series four, Lennard will suffer two heart attacks, three days apart, and die at home in his flat. The news will hit us like a sack of bricks. We'll all pack up and go home bewildered at the loss of our friend. And we'll also assume the show is finished. Because how can it possibly withstand the loss of Lennard? But obviously we will not be anticipating how John Sullivan will fold Lennard's death into the storyline, allow us to mourn and celebrate him there in the show, introduce the character of Uncle Albert, and take the series forward.

But I'm getting ahead of myself. For now, at least, in this vision from 1983, Lennard is magnificently alive, and baiting Russell Harty like a good 'un. The three of us get through Harty's Party and withdraw for that self-promised stiff drink before heading off to our respective homes for Christmas. It's not, perhaps, been the smoothest promotional appearance that any of us will make. But at least the name of David Janssen never came up.

'Thicker Than Water' goes out on Christmas Day. It's the one where Del's long-since vanished father, Reg Trotter, played by Peter Woodthorpe, walks into the flat on Christmas night, eighteen years after he abandoned the family. It's nicely set up and maybe we think we know which way this is all going, Christmas being, of course, a time for reconciliation, and especially in Christmas specials on television. But John's interest once again is in subverting the form, and he isn't going to let the audience have it quite so easy.

Reg is essentially how Del would be if you stripped out all the nice things about him. There isn't much there for an audience to like – or for Del to like, you would think. The pair of them row quite bitterly and Del feels able to dispense some home truths. Yet before he leaves, Del will end up quietly slipping his dad a bit of cash to ensure he's OK. For all that Del can't stand the man and resents the fact that he walked out on them, that's still his father, when all is said and done, and he's not willing to think of him suffering. It was, I think, another of those poignant passages where you see a deepening of Del's character, and it was certainly a very touching moment to play.*

That Christmas Day slot and our promotional efforts earn the show 10.8 million viewers. That's a million and a half

* As with a tender hinterland, mentioned earlier, there is no reliable over-the-counter cream for dealing with a poignant passage, but your GP may be able to prescribe something stronger that works, so do consult them – especially if you find you are repeatedly having touching moments.

more people than watched 'Diamonds are for Heather' the previous year – so, heading in the right direction. Unfortunately, though, it's a million less than watched the final episode of series three just three days earlier.

So, heading in the wrong direction, actually.

We all feel a bit flat. So much for the power of the Harty Party.

*   *   *

And then, really, the biggest shift of all – the quantum shift: the 1985 Christmas special, 'To Hull and Back'.

Transport me, Spirit – when you've finished taking your cycle clips off, obviously – to the deck of the good ship *Inge*, as it ploughs its way across the choppy North Sea in the general direction of Holland.

Actually, don't. That little tub was like a scene from Dante's *Inferno* most of the time we were on board it. The good ship *Inge*? The good ship *Chunder*, more like. I, fortunately, was pre-fortified with seasickness tablets, but practically everybody else, cast and crew, really struggled during those water-borne scenes, and that alleged old seadog Uncle Albert more than any of us. The shade of green that Buster Merryfield turned that day has yet to be seen on any manufacturer's paint chart, and what ended up going over the side of that boat during the making of this film doesn't bear thinking about.

However, on a happier note, I am using the term 'film' advisedly here. For that's exactly what 'To Hull and Back' was – a ninety-minute film, shot over six weeks with a budget that ran to location shoots on the North Sea and in Amsterdam. Unimaginable luxuries. I remember John's script coming in the post. The story was great, of course – a mad caper about the Trotters agreeing to smuggle some diamonds to Holland for Boycie and deciding to go in the back way, by sea. But what really struck me about that script on arrival was the sheer size of it. It was three times as thick as the ones we normally got. You could have used it, rolled up, to beat back a charging elephant. Moreover, it contained no studio sequences in front of an audience, and the whole thing was going to be shot on film stock, rather than on video.

We all went around saying it to each other: it felt like we had graduated to the movies.

And that meant a whole new way of operating. Without the studio audience to think about, the show could work to a completely different set of beats. You weren't needing to hit a laugh every few lines – things could develop much further, gags could evolve over much longer time frames, with the consequence that the clinching laugh, when it came for the viewer, could be that much stronger.

And, of course, this was the point at which the show could have got utterly lost – more lost than Del, Rodney and Albert on the North Sea, so lost that it might never have come back. We've all seen film-length versions of television sitcoms which simply haven't come off. To pluck one out of the ether at random, I don't think anyone regards the *Dad's Army* movie as among that show's finest hours. (I mean the 1971 film version with the original cast, not the 2016 remake which was a different thing yet again.) Even the makers of *The Simpsons*, a programme which I regard as a work of genius, failed to make a movie version quite click. You can't fit a quart in a pint pot, people like to say, but a pint can also look a bit lost in a quart pot, and that so frequently tends to be the case when sitcoms are offered the bigger scope. The extra length and the different story demands don't always suit what was originally there and what people warmed to in the first place.

The good news for us was that *Only Fools* clearly could survive the transition; 'To Hull and Back' ended up proving it beyond a doubt. There was enough in the writing, and enough in the characters, and enough in the direction (by Ray Butt) to sustain that much bigger act of storytelling. Indeed, the show clearly rejoiced in the freedom and the extra space, as did all of us who worked on it.

Lots of scenes stay with me from that episode, but I particularly enjoyed doing that bit when the motion of the boat on the waves causes Del to be abruptly overcome with a surge of patriotism and to step across the deck with some declamatory oratory in celebration of 'this septic isle', while Rodney is in the background, trying to hold on to the contents of his stomach. That was great fun to do, although Nick barely needed to act at that point.

And then, of course, there was the now famous sequence with Del shouting up to an oil worker to be pointed the right way. We all loved that gag and thought it was an absolutely brilliant piece of imagination by John, as well as a defining Trotter moment. Getting lost in the North Sea and stopping to ask directions from an oil rig? It doesn't really get much more Trotter than that.

That said, Nick tells a story about explaining to one of the oil rig guys how this joke was going to play out, and being a bit disappointed to get no real reaction from him at all, and certainly not the belly laugh Nick had been hoping for.

'Yeah,' the guy eventually said, matter-of-factly. 'You'd be surprised how often that happens.'

So, why this access all of a sudden to time and locations and budgets and film stock – this new 'whatever the show needs' attitude on the part of the BBC? Well, blame Arthur Daley, I guess. The story is that Michael Grade, who had just become the Controller of BBC1, got wind that ITV's big Christmas number for 1985 was going to be a film-length episode of *Minder*, the channel's popular and well-established (it had been around since 1979) comedy drama. Worried that 'Minder on the Orient Express', as this special edition seemed to be called, could come to dominate the season over his first Christmas in charge, and determined to make sure that ITV's Christmas tree got well and truly stuffed up its chimney, Michael scanned the weaponry available to him and decided that *Only Fools and Horses*, now four series old, was the tank in the BBC's armoury to take *Minder* on.

And when I say 'take it on', I mean properly take it on: head-to-head, at 7.30 p.m. on Christmas Day.

Now, Michael Grade was a superb broadcasting executive – one of the finest, with a real feel for what people wanted, expected and needed from television shows. And don't get me wrong: I love a ratings battle as much as the next man. But I have to say, I thought the scheduling aspect of this was madness.

Whoever ended up benefitting from plonking the shows down directly opposite each other, at exactly the same time of night, it wasn't going to be the viewer. Remember that this was 1985, well before the age of streaming and catch-up TV, and even video recorders were still quite a rarity in the British home. Basically, if you missed a programme back then, you missed it for good, or at least until such time as the powers that be saw fit to repeat it, which would normally be a year later if you were lucky. In the case of *Only Fools* and *Minder*, it was self-evident that large amounts of people liked both shows – they had a few things in common, after all – so you were only cutting off your own nose, surely, by forcing them to choose. Cutting off everybody's noses, in fact.

Still, the papers loved it, building up the rivalry between Arthur Daley and Derek Trotter like it was the Beatles v. the Rolling Stones. And we all played along with it, on both sides, because it was obviously gold dust, publicity-wise, and also because, I can't deny, it was quite a buzz, after twenty years of trying, to find a piece of your work at the heart of the national conversation all of a sudden.

Did dirty tricks feature anywhere along the line? Well, far be it from me to accuse anybody of outright lying, but the *Minder* team put out the rumour that this might be the last ever episode of their show. Very crafty – the old Frank Sinatra 'retirement' gambit. Guaranteed to put bums on seats. But if 'Minder on the Orient Express' genuinely was meant to bring down the curtain, then can I just gently point out that the show was around for another nine years after this, until 1994? That's an awful lot of comebacks.

I fought back by giving an interview to the *Mirror*:

'It's got to be us, innit. We will be funnier and better, no doubt about that, my son.'

Did I really put it like that, or did the newspaper automatically hear the tone of Del in my voice and decide that a touch of poetic licence wouldn't go amiss in the circumstances? No matter: all is fair in war. I also seem to have accused *Minder* of only having three viewers.

My honest feelings? I was a huge admirer of George Cole, who, of course, played Arthur Daley – and had been a huge admirer since I'd stared up at him in *Scrooge*, on that formative Christmas trip to the cinema that I wrote about earlier. I thought Dennis Waterman, who played Terry McCann in the show, was a brilliant actor, too – one of those people who makes a lot of difficult things look easy. And I was altogether a huge fan of *Minder*, which made my remark about the three viewers a bit rich. I *was* one of those three viewers. I watched it at home and thought it was a fantastic piece of entertainment. I wished the show nothing but well.

And I hoped to heaven that we would beat it to within an inch of its life in those Christmas ratings.

The final score? When the smoke cleared from the battlefield and all the bodies were finally accounted for, *Minder* had got 12.5 million viewers that Christmas night. *Only Fools* had got 16.9 million. A decent victory for the right team, then, and some payback for all that seasickness, and we were all very pleased with ourselves, especially Michael Grade. Looking back now, though, with the benefit of maturity and sweet wisdom on my side, it all seems a bit bonkers. Again, you don't need to be Rodney to do the maths: there were at least 29.4 million people sitting in front of their television sets looking for something to watch that Christmas. What numbers might both our shows have achieved in 1985 if they had been separated instead of being sent into the field to lock antlers with each other?

Dennis Waterman died while I was writing this book – in May 2022, at seventy-four. Another good one gone. I knew Dennis, and he was a lovely man. He told me how, in bars occasionally, people with a bit of drink inside them would take him on. Well, he was that tough bloke from *The Sweeney*, wasn't he? That plain-clothes cop who fancied he could handle himself in a ruck. So lairy blokes would have a go. When he told me all this, part of me thought: what gets into people? Can they really not separate the actor from the character he plays? Don't they realise this stuff is made up?

But another part of me thought: blimey, though – that's some tribute to Dennis's acting and the degree to which he inhabited the role. Not only could people not see the join, they forgot there was a join there in the first place.

And then yet another part of me (for I am a man, clearly, of many parts) thought: I'm so glad I never played a tough guy. I've had all kinds of public reactions to Derek Trotter, and Pa Larkin, and Inspector Frost, and Skullion, and Granville. But I can honestly say that nobody has ever wanted to sort anything out with any of them in a car park. Not once has anyone fronted up to me in my local and said, 'Let's settle this here and now.' I guess I got lucky.

Also, I don't go to my local. But that's beside the point.

As for where all this high-profile action in 1985 put *Only Fools* in the general scheme of things, perhaps you can get a sense of that from the fact that Nick, Buster and I were asked to represent the BBC in a trailer for the broadcaster's Christmas output that year. It showed us flicking through the Christmas double issue of the *Radio Times*, picking out the highlights.

Del, naturally, seems to be looking forward to watching some of the season's cultural offerings, in particular 'the Royal Ballet doing *The Nutcracker*'.

To which Rodney, drawing the magazine slightly closer to his eyes, replies, 'I ain't surprised in those tights.'

So, not subtle, no: but certainly prominent. (I'm referring to our burgeoning presence on the screen here, not to anything concerning the Royal Ballet's tights.)

And on the cover of the Christmas *Radio Times* which we were consulting in that teaser? Us three, that's who.

Now, that felt like a genuine and unignorable statement about the giddy heights to which we had ascended. People talk about the cover of *Rolling Stone* and the cover of *Vogue* as the twin pinnacles of magazine-based exposure and the surest indications of a person's arrival at the heart of Western culture.

But, dear reader, you and I both know that not to be true. It's appearing on the cover of the Christmas double issue of the *Radio Times* that *really* announces to the world that you've made it.*

In that cover shot, Buster, pouring Nick some champagne into a half-pint glass, is in the obligatory Santa outfit, already having the beard for it; Nick is looking cheerful in a

---

* These days the cover of the Christmas *Radio Times* tends to be a generic illustration of some kind – a Christmassy cartoon, probably featuring Father Christmas, or a snowman, or even The Snowman (as in Raymond Briggs's *The Snowman*), or potentially all three of them. Which no doubt spares the magazine from having to deal with hordes of thwarted, big-star egos, but something – as those of us who are, ahem, multiple recipients of the Christmas front-cover accolade tend to feel – is lost.

knackered camouflage jacket; and I am modelling an exquisite black polo shirt with ultra-suave white detailing, from the Derek Trotter festive-appropriate leisurewear range, and raising a glass of bubbly and a cigar in the general direction of the camera. Cheers!

And frankly, along with the daffy smile, that was a pretty accurate reflection of how I felt about life at that point in the show's history. After all these years of slogging away at it, I was finally part of a truly successful, much-loved show – one that, with Lennard's passing, had weathered a storm that would have finished almost any other programme, yet whose team had pulled together and come through as strong as ever; and, to cap it all, a show that could now attract the best part of 17 million viewers on Christmas Day.

It simply wasn't going to get any better than that. Was it?

ON THE NINTH DEL OF CHRISTMAS . . .

Choppers and gliders

M ission complete and day over. As our two helicopters, blades clattering, rose above the airfield and separated – his heading east, mine pointing west towards the setting sun and home – a voice crackled in my headset.

'Nice to have met you, David,' said Tom Cruise. 'Take it easy and have a nice flight.'

'Good to meet you, too, Tom,' I replied. 'Safe journey and see you somewhere down the road, I hope.'

None of which, dear reader, is invented. None of it. And yes, I'm aware that this tale is something of a digression from the main thrust of our narrative at this point and has nothing whatsoever to do with Christmas, but, frankly, I think I've done pretty well to hold off this long into the book before bashing on about this.

I mean, how often does a person end up chatting, helicopter to helicopter, with Tom Cruise?

Well, I can only speak for myself in response to that

question, and the answer is: once, so far. And I fully intend to tell you about it.

So obviously I'm going to need to explain to you exactly how I came to be in the skies with an open radio channel to the Hollywood A-lister and star of *Top Gun: Maverick*. But in order to do that I'm going to have to tell you first about some work I've been doing recently, exploring the comedy potential of helicopters.

Again, bear with me: I am not inventing this. And I won't be inventing the bit where Tim Peake walks into this story, either. But let me just try and do this one step at a time.

Here's how it panned out. Late in 2021, I found myself invited to attend a meeting with members of the military's Gazelle helicopter display team. They were wondering if it might be possible to create a show involving skilfully flown helicopters which wasn't the usual military display of closely coordinated manoeuvres – as impressive as that is – but was a piece of family entertainment that might be suitable for the Royal International Air Tattoo at Fairford, the world's largest military air display, where helicopters would normally get a bit overshadowed by the Red Arrows doing their business or by fighter jets screaming overhead at Mach 3 and tearing everybody's ears apart.

I was asked to be involved because I am a proud patron of the RIAT, and because I guess, as a pilot, I am known to occupy, somewhat unusually, the ground where entertainment and helicopters meet. So I set aside my labours on this book, picked up a sketch pad and began to come up with some ideas for Olly the Heli – a young helicopter with a friendly face who responds to instructions from the tannoy, does tricks, plays football, helps out around the place, misbehaves a bit, seems reluctant to have a bath before bedtime . . . something perhaps on the Thomas the Tank Engine lines, if you will pardon me that actually rather deft pun.

And then I headed again down to an airfield in Hampshire to explore how this show might work, and what exactly it's possible to do, technically and safely, when you've got helicopters in the air and a crowd on the ground watching. Which is how, among other things, I came to spend a morning in an airfield in Hampshire, carefully scrutinising ways in which the downdraught from a helicopter blows an enormous ball around.

It's dirty work, I admit. But someone's got to do it.

As I quickly discovered, the guys from the Gazelle display team are a great bunch. Experienced servicemen with serious campaigns behind them, they have that military-bred camaraderie which I can only assume comes from being together in situations which bring you close to your own mortality, and so becomes all the more life-affirming for that. At any rate, their constant piss-taking of each other was a joy to behold and their love for flying was off the charts.

It was suggested that it might be useful for me to see what their standard display looks like.

'Excellent idea,' I replied, thinking: what a treat – my own private air show from a front-row seat on the ground.

In fact, they thought I should experience it from a little closer than that – from a seat in the cockpit.

I think I might have swallowed hard at this juncture.

But . . . play it nice and cool, son, nice and cool, as someone once said. So, buckled up tightly, I sat in one of the army Gazelles while the lads ran through their repertoire of tricks – doing formation flying in amazingly close proximity to each other, their skids almost touching, and then going up in unison, practically vertical, before dropping the nose and plunging downwards through the air, prior to rescuing the descent and pulling out horizontal again.

What can I tell you? It was quite a ride. To witness the precision of those manoeuvres from on board was absolutely breathtaking. This stuff requires such faith – faith in your own abilities and the abilities of everybody else in the team, and also faith in the machine you're flying. If you did these kinds of things in my little helicopter, the blades would fall off.

And, of course, it takes a strong stomach, among other strong things. But I emerged in one piece, managed to walk in a fairly dignified manner across the grass with the chaps afterwards, and thanked them all warmly for an experience that I will never forget.

Only the laundry basket knows exactly how frightened I was, and the laundry basket is sworn to secrecy.

Along with us that day was Tim Peake, the astronaut, who

retains strong connections with the Army Air Corps from his time in the military, and was also consulting on this potential display project. Our paths had crossed once before, in a radio station where we were both promoting books, but I will happily confess that I am more than a little in awe of astronauts. Indeed, I have probably never been as discombobulated as I was when I got the chance to shake hands with Buzz Aldrin at a Buckingham Palace charity garden party one year. I'm not much of a person in general for forelock-tugging and standing on ceremony except where it's absolutely necessary, but I am very much of the opinion that one should rise when an astronaut walks into the room. It's just a matter of the respect that's due. Either that, or the lack of gravity.

I have to say, though, that this did not seem to be an attitude obviously shared by Tim Peake's chums in the Army Air Corps Gazelle display team. The liberal amounts of piss-taking I previously mentioned very much extended to include the first British astronaut to walk in space, who was the constant butt of his colleagues' jokes while I was with them all, and continually roasted for being 'a spaceman' – all of which he took in extraordinarily good part and even seemed to enjoy.

When, in a break, Tim offered to take me for a spin in a Gazelle, I wasn't going to say no, was I?

'Let's go and have a look at Downton Abbey,' said Tim. So we did, flying over the Hampshire countryside until we found Highclere Castle, the monumental dwelling where the television series was filmed – all two hundred rooms of it, sat in five thousand acres of carefully tended land, and therefore pretty hard to miss from the sky. It was something special to fly with Tim. This is a man who has jumped on board a rocket, lived in space for six months, and flown home again in a tiny Russian capsule which, he told me, actually had paper maps of the world in its glove compartment. Before he did all that, he was a military and commercial helicopter test pilot. It was literally his job to take helicopters into the sky and see how far you could push them before they broke. His perfectly normal morning at work in those days would involve flying helicopters up to a couple of thousand feet, switching off their engines and seeing what happened.

Suffice it to say, then, that you feel pretty confident when the helicopter you're sitting in is in the hands of Tim Peake. You also get to feel somewhat humble about your own skills as a pilot. Tim handed the controls over to me at one point, which was a bit like being asked to sit down at the piano and bash out a tune straight after Oscar Peterson has just stood up and left it. No pressure or anything. Still, I flew us for a while, without any tricks, fortunately.

'Do you want to land it?' Tim generously asked as we returned to the airfield.

I wasn't going to push my luck.

'I think I'll leave that to you, Tim,' I said.

So, that was how the idea of Olly the Heli got going – a little production journey that's still in development at the time of writing. We'll see where it ends up.

After that initial meeting, though, I flew with my good friend and esteemed business partner, Leon Harris, to Duxford Aerodrome in Cambridgeshire to do some further research there. The staff member who met us when we landed by the control tower pointed down the airfield where, way off in the distance, a large black helicopter was dimly visible.

'That's Tom Cruise's helicopter,' he said.

Which, of course, was exciting to hear. But it was a long way away and we had some business to do, so, to be honest, we didn't think much more of it. Instead, Leon and I had coffee and got on with our work in the officers' mess.

In due course, a guy came up and introduced himself.

'My name's Jack,' he said.

'And I live in the back of the Greta Garbo Home for Wayward Boys and Girls,' I replied, without hesitation, deviation or repetition.

Jack looked at me in stunned silence. Several awkward seconds passed. Beyond his politely puzzled expression, I could sense him thinking: what's he on about?

And fair enough, really. I mean, the guy was about twenty-five. How could he be expected to be familiar with the lyrics to 'My Name Is Jack', the Manfred Mann hit from 1968?*

---

* If you know, you know. For some of us, it's impossible to hear the name Jack without it automatically triggering the next line of the chorus. I guess the guy got lucky, though: at least I didn't try and sing it to him.

Look, just occasionally my flashes of comic repartee are doomed to wither on the stalk, but what can you do?

Fortunately, this sticky moment passed and Jack got back in his stride. He was introducing himself, he said, because he worked over at the Duxford Imperial War Museum, also on the aerodrome site. The museum was closed to the public at that point, but he wondered if I fancied a little look around.

Ah, the advantages of having a known face. It's a pain sometimes, I'm not going to deny, but just occasionally it works out in one's favour – as for instance when someone is offering you a private tour of the country's finest collection of historic aircraft.

Leon and I were delighted to accept, and Jack organised a car to take us all on the short drive across the aerodrome to the museum. It turned out the car's driver, too, was called Jack. Two Jacks now, then. This was turning into a promising hand in poker.

I decided not to repeat the Manfred Mann line.

Touring the museum was a real privilege. I'm always incredibly moved by the sight of World War II aircraft. It's the product of being a war baby. I feel I grew up with the Spitfire and the Hurricane. They're such powerful, beautiful machines and knowing what our freedom owes to the job they did only increases one's sense of awe. We took a good look at the restored Spitfire, discovered in the 1980s where it lay in Normandy, having crash-landed, and brought back to Duxford to be revived and proudly displayed – a truly stirring sight.

In the same hangar as the Spitfire was a bright red biplane. It was being fitted with cameras, after which, apparently, a middle-aged guy called John, who was said to be able to fly anything with wings, was going to take it out and test-fly it. There was a bright blue biplane, too, the wings of which had been reinforced with fibre glass, so they could support somebody's weight. There was also an area of the hangar which had been set aside for desks and computer screens and where people were checking bits of film. It was the *Mission: Impossible* production office. They were working on flying sequences for the next movie in the series.*

As Jack was explaining all this, there was a loud buzz outside and a yellow biplane rolled into view by the hangar's open door.

'Oh, that's Tom coming in,' said Jack casually.

We looked around for a little longer and then Jack offered to show us the place where the museum does its restoration work. We left the hangar and walked out onto the tarmac. There, near the now parked-up yellow biplane, stood a small group of people, including the somehow unmistakable figure of Tom Cruise.

'David!' Tom called out as we passed, a look of disbelief on his face. 'Unbelievable!'

* *Mission: Impossible – Dead Reckoning Part One*, due out in 2023.

He left the group and came barrelling towards me.

'Man, I absolutely LOVE your work. All of it! But who would have thought I would ever get to meet you?'

OK, none of that happened and he didn't say that at all. In fact, I'll be eternally grateful to the woman who, just as we came near, was getting a photograph taken with Tom, but who spotted me and said, 'Ooh, my lucky day! Can I get one with you both together?'

Excellent timing. Tom must have been thinking, 'I might not know who this guy is, but these other people seem to, so . . .'

Anyway, I moved in for the picture, and, when that was done, Tom and I were introduced to each other and fell to chatting. Of course, as I was able to inform him, he and I share many things: a seemingly effortless sex appeal, a long string of leading roles in blockbusting action movies, and a widely remarked longevity at the very top of the global entertainment business. Plus, of course, that famous sun-kissed glow.

What is perhaps less remarked upon in the glossy magazines, however, is that we also happen to share, more or less, a height. Standing with him, eye-to-eye on the tarmac, I had a light-bulb moment.

'I could work as your stunt double.'

Because Tom famously does his own stunts, of course. Absolutely insists upon it, as much as he possibly can. Me too, down the years. Dangling off a ladder, dropping off a bike, falling sideways through a bar flap, bursting through a closed serving hatch . . . As we've amply seen during these pages, whenever the script called for it, I've been happy to put my body on the line. For one thing (and Tom will back me up here), it always looks better if you do it yourself. Nobody gets to see the join. And for another thing, it's good fun.

Or it is if you're the kind of person who, like Tom and me, is drawn to stunt work. Maybe it's genetic. Maybe we just can't help it. Maybe it's just who we are. I certainly enjoyed that line that Tom came up with at the Cannes Film Festival in 2022 when he was doing press for *Top Gun: Maverick*. Somebody asked him why he does so many stunts.

'Nobody asked Gene Kelly, "Why do you dance?"' Cruise replied.

Say it loud, Tom. Say it loud, my friend. I believe I uttered something very similar on the set of 'Tea for Three', in the fifth series of *Only Fools*, when my pleas to do the scenes in which Del gets sent on a madly out-of-control hang-glider journey across the English countryside seemed to fall on stony ears.

I was serious, though. That sort of thing was right up my street – or rather, right up my runway. For a good while in the late 1970s and early 1980s, whenever I got a Sunday off, my idea of getting away from it all was to drive to Dunstable Airfield and take up a glider for a few hours. I absolutely loved it: the silence, the isolation. It took me right out of myself. That was where I first got the flying bug which in due course led to me learning to pilot a helicopter.

So, a spot of hang gliding? I was rubbing my hands with glee. Nothing like combining work and pleasure.

No go, though. The show's insurance wouldn't allow it. Too risky, allegedly. And fair enough, I suppose. If I had fallen out of the sky midway through shooting, it could have had some rather nasty consequences for the rest of the series, not to mention for anyone who had the misfortune to be underneath me at the time. So, reluctantly, I stepped aside and let the professionals take over.

In fact, as it happened, the wind was so blustery on that hill in Hampshire on the day of filming that even the stuntman they'd brought in, a guy called Ken Barker, wasn't allowed to get off the ground. Ken, you should know, was a highly experienced stunt double who had worked on *Superman III* and *Labyrinth*, so had definitely seen some major action in his time. Yet donning the camel overcoat of Derek Trotter proved to be more dangerous and problematic, I think, than any of them.

We had to rig it in the end. For me it became a hang glider in the most literal of senses: I hung from it, roped to a crane which lifted me just a couple of feet off the ground. There, buffeted by the breeze but otherwise stationary, I was a sitting target for the cameraman just below me, who could film me, as if airborne, against a background of pure sky.

Once more, as I dangled there, waiting for the shot to be

set up, I had cause to reflect ruefully how much of my career had been spent, quite literally, hanging about – from that initial BBC pantomime in 1965 to this, some twenty years later. I came in on a harness; it seemed quite likely that I would be carried out on a harness.

Tom Cruise, clearly, would have shared my frustration at being thwarted on that hill. But now, face-to-face with him on the tarmac at Duxford, I sensed an opportunity. Maybe I could ease some of his workload, stunt-wise – take some of the pressure off, make those *Mission: Impossible* movies just that little bit less impossible. I tried to explain to him that he knew it made sense . . .

'If you break an arm or something, the whole production comes to a halt,' I said. 'I could save the producer a fortune here.'

'But I am the producer,' Tom said.

'Then I'm talking to the right person,' I said.

'I'll bear your suggestion in mind,' Tom said.

'Well,' I said, the light going on in my brain again, 'perhaps I could be your double in the love scenes, leaving you free to do the more arduous stuff.'

Tom again said he'd think about it.

We then talked a little about helicopters and flying, before bumping fists and moving on. What an affable and warmly approachable chap he seemed – quite strikingly so for a Hollywood superstar.

Leon and I returned to the helicopter late afternoon, with

the light fast fading. It was as we were talking to the control tower directly after take-off that we heard Tom call in and ask for permission to taxi to the end of the runway for his own take-off. He must have heard us, too, because that was when we had our little exchange of farewells across the airwaves. And with that we went our separate ways.

Probably only a matter of time before I hear from him on that stunt-double proposal, though. All very exciting.

ON THE TENTH DEL OF CHRISTMAS . . .

Cocktails and riot shields

I am often asked which of the *Only Fools* Christmas specials is my favourite, and it's always a question I slightly struggle with. For one thing, there's a lot of riches to pick from here. For another, the shows lodge in my head for different reasons, and often for quite personal or particular reasons.

From my own private perspective, very often I find I am quietly proudest of the moments where playing Del pushed me as an actor. Those aren't necessarily the big showpiece moments that people love and celebrate, like the Batman and Robin chase sequence in 'Heroes and Villains', though I'm inordinately proud of that too, of course. But often what my memory tends to alight on seem to be the much smaller, more nuanced things.

For instance, there's a tiny bit in 'Dates', the 1988 special. That was the one that brought Tessa Peake-Jones into the show as Raquel, changing the whole game for Del, and therefore, by extension, changing the whole game for me, portraying Del. After this there were all these new realms that the character would need to go into – finding love, moving in together, becoming a father . . . There were whole new emotions to explore and whole new layers of detail to find.

But on their first date, Del chooses to go upmarket and takes Raquel to a restaurant at the Hilton Hotel on Park Lane, where the table is very poshly laid. I suggested doing a bit where both of us would get in a muddle about knowing which pieces of cutlery to use – a moment of social anxiety which turns into a bonding moment between them.

Now, I know that's never going to get the big laughs and reruns like falling through a bar flap, but, truly, that's a moment in the show that I'm abidingly proud of. As I tried to explain earlier, finding those little pieces of character-defining behaviour has been what I've loved about acting since the first day I walked into a theatre, and the satisfaction of happening on one that absolutely works is, for me, as good as anything the job offers.*

---

* 'Dates' was the episode that John Sullivan often said was his favourite. It won the BAFTA for Best Comedy the following year. By the way, some eagle-eyed clever clogs claim to have spotted a 'continuity error' in this episode in the fact that Del is seen reading a newspaper in two scenes which are meant to be whole weeks apart – but it's the same newspaper. Well, did you never, at a bored moment, pick up a paper that's been left lying around, find it's days old, but read it anyway? That was no mistake: we were just trying to be true to life as people actually live it. That's my story, anyway.

Similarly, 'Miami Twice', from 1991, would have to feature among my proudest memories of the show, but maybe not exactly for the reasons that other people like it. Yes, obviously I vividly remember that episode for the opportunity it gave me – not one which had come up before in my life, I must say – to shout across the water at Barry Gibb of the Bee Gees, and then, later, take tea and a piece of cake at Barry's gaff overlooking the water.

Where I learned, incidentally, that he was a) admirably down to earth and b) just the most enormous fan of our show. As an ex-pat, Barry apparently used to insist on having two things flown out to him from the UK that he couldn't get in the States: Jaffa Cakes and tapes of *Only Fools and Horses*. Ah, that rock'n'roll lifestyle.

And I vividly recall the Miami hotel we stayed in and drinking cocktails and hanging out in the sun with Nick and mucking about on boats in the Everglades, and thinking, 'Is this actually work?'

I also vividly recall the looks on the faces of some of the cast when the scripts were handed round and they realised that they weren't in those scenes.

But the actor in me likes 'Miami Twice' most for the opportunity it gave me to play two parts – Del, of course, and his mafioso doppelgänger, Don Occhetti – and to try and pull off the scenes they have together, which is a technically tricky thing to do. Another different experience, and another stretch.

I also remember the madness of the press around that trip. Antoni Corone, who played Occhetti's son, Rico, was an American actor (he'd been in *Miami Vice*) who didn't really know how big a deal *Only Fools* was in the UK until he suddenly found himself being taken aside by a reporter from one of the tabloids and offered $500 in used notes for his script.

Antoni, being a man of high principle, declined. Or, at least, I think he did. But that was the level of the temperature around the show at that time. The press were determined to get the scoop on what we were up to, to the point of tailing us all the way across the Atlantic. Whenever I moved around the set in costume as Don, I had to be accompanied by guys holding up blankets to conceal me from view. If a photo of me dressed up like that had leaked out, it would have blown the story and spoiled our Christmas surprise.

Similarly, I feel very fondly disposed towards 'Modern Men', the middle episode in the 1996 trilogy, and in particular the scene where Del and Rodney get stuck in a lift and talk through Cassandra's miscarriage. (It emerges, of course, that Del secretly sabotaged the lift in order to bring about the circumstances in which this difficult but necessary conversation could take place – a highly Sullivan-esque twist.) That was a scene that even John said he was nervous about putting in, and it's one I'm fiercely proud of, and I know Nick is, too. Somehow it makes me love it even more that it comes in the episode directly after the one with the Batman and Robin scene. That we were now part of a drama that could range within an hour of its lifespan from daffy costumed hilarity and caped superhero high jinks to sincerely addressed issues of birth and death spoke volumes about the journey the show had been on and what it had become. 'Christmas Crackers' this was not.

Questions about acting aside, though, if I was picking episodes on the basis of 'moments that made me laugh then and still make me laugh now' . . . well, again, I'd be a long time getting to the bottom of that particular pile, but Buster Merryfield's gasp of horror in 'Rodney Come Home', the special from 1990, will always rank highly with me in this category – and not just because I actually DID laugh at the time.

The set-up is that Rodney and Cassandra are, yet again, having some relationship difficulties, and this time Rodney seems to be planning a crafty date with another woman. Del, who is appalled, instructs Uncle Albert to assist him with the talking-to that he is about to give his brother by injecting an expression of shocked moral horror into the conversation at the appropriate moment. The gormless intake of breath that Buster came up with for that moment is rightly treasured – BAFTA-worthy on its own, if you ask me.

But when Buster produces that gasp for the third, entirely incorrect time, I'm afraid I go. As I swipe at him with the newspaper and deliver the line 'I'll whack you one in a minute, believe me', there's a smile in my eyes that strictly speaking ought not to be there. Simply couldn't help it, though.

Corpsing, dear reader: it happens to the best of us.

In this line, everything about the Peckham Spring Water ruse in 'Mother Nature's Son' continues to amuse me very strongly, too. Or I might go for 'Fatal Extraction' and the scene where Del's late-night, over-refreshed and altogether utterly terrible singing of the Barry Manilow ballad, 'One Voice', starts a full-scale riot on the estate which the police will eventually have to deal with using shields and horses. That seems exactly as funny to me today as it did then, if not a little more so. And finally I had found a part in which my singing voice – never the strongest weapon in my acting armoury – could be used convincingly.

Initially a professional singer was brought in to cover for me. I thought about this development for a while: the implicit assumption was that my voice was so bad that I couldn't even be trusted to sing badly. Was I a little hurt by that suggestion? I may have been. And did I feel a small but satisfying burst of vindication when the singer's recording was dubbed onto the footage and it didn't really sound right, obliging them to come back to me and ask if I could step in after all?

No, actually, because I *really* don't like singing.

Also, talk about up against it. Barry Manilow, I'll have you know, layered his voice forty times for his most famous recording of this song, so he had thirty-nine more chances than I did to make a splash. Hard enough for someone like me to go up against one Barry Manilow, but forty all at once? Not a hope. Anyway, I couldn't help but laugh when, several years later, in 2010, I saw that Manilow had performed this song at a special concert in Oslo to mark the awarding of the Nobel Peace Prize.

Peace? Depends where you sing it, Barry. And who sings it.

On the other hand, if I was picking out episodes on the basis of sight gags, I might go for 'The Frog's Legacy', the 1987 special, which contains, in my humble opinion, one of the absolute classics: Rodney, in the job that Del has found for him as chief mourner at the local funeral directors, leading the hearse the wrong way down a one-way street. John told me he had actually seen this done, in south London. Oh, to have been a fly on that chief mourner's Victorian-style top hat.

But when I think about that episode I also think about how it was the last to involve Ray Butt, who was leaving to take charge of comedy at Central Television. Ray had been on board as producer and director from the start and he was a lovely, easy-going guy who set the tone around the place. His departure caused John Sullivan to wonder about packing up. The show had run for five series at that point, and the Christmas episode had done some tying up of what had been one of the big narrative strands since the beginning – the mild but persistent mystery of Rodney's paternity. It could have felt like a decent enough place to stop. Maybe if 'The Frog's Legacy' hadn't gone down well, John would have gone through with it and the show would have ended at Christmas 1987 – before 'The Jolly Boys' Outing', before 'Miami Twice', before 'Time on our Hands' . . .

Our dear pal Fate may be said to have trembled in the balance here.

But that special did go down well, and John's faith was restored. So, did a mad tale involving a former navy frogman, an explosives expert called 'Jelly' Kelly and a bungled post office raid actually end up saving *Only Fools and Horses*? Well, you could argue the case, and stranger things have happened. Certainly, Tony Dow, who had been production assistant, moved up to replace Ray and the show set off again, bound for its highest heights.

* * *

And then there's the one I remember because it almost didn't get finished . . .

John Sullivan was one of nature's more voluminous writers. He couldn't help himself. When he got going, the ideas flowed and the pages accumulated. I have letters from John that run to a side and a half of A4 and they're just an invitation to lunch. So it didn't really surprise any of us when, asked to come up with a three-minute *Only Fools and Horses* sketch for the Royal Variety Performance in November 1986, John wrote a first draft which was twenty-five minutes long.

Who knows? Maybe the Queen Mother would have enjoyed an almost episode-length edition of *Only Fools* staged in her honour that year. But unfortunately the producers of the Royal Variety Performance had a few other acts to squeeze in as well: Bob Monkhouse, Ken Dodd, Rory Bremner, Victoria Wood, Aled Jones, Nana Mouskouri, Petula Clark, Victor Borge, Lulu, to name only those. Oh, and also Paul McCartney, no less, appearing at a Royal Variety for the first time since being there with the Beatles in 1963, when John Lennon had instructed the people in the cheaper seats to clap along and the others to rattle their jewellery.

Possibly even topping that, in my humble opinion, Angela Rippon had apparently agreed to join us at the Theatre Royal Drury Lane to reprise the high-kicking dance routine she had debuted for the Morecambe & Wise Christmas show in 1976 – regarded as an iconic and vanishingly rare public appearance by a newsreader's legs, which were normally kept entirely below desks in those days and were therefore a closely guarded secret.

And also on the guest list, it seemed, was my old pal Ronnie Barker, who had been given the job of greeting the royal party – the Queen Mother, accompanied by Sarah Ferguson – at the door of the theatre, dressed in a liveried frock coat and in character as Arkwright, the stuttering shopkeeper from *Open All Hours*.

Brave man. And to think I blanched at doing a bit of

in-character improv with Russell Harty. I could only admire the seeming ease and aplomb with which Ronnie would eventually pull this off, handing the Queen Mother a bunch of flowers and then saying, 'That'll be one pound fifty, please. Oh, no, you don't carry money with you, do you? Like Granville.'

So, a crowded bill, all things considered, and, at the end of the day, only space enough in there to treat the Queen Mother to the three minutes of *Only Fools* which John eventually, reluctantly, whittled his script down to.

And just as well, really, because we were busy enough at this point, without landing a whole extra episode on our shoulders. Beyond busy, in fact. We were making what would become the 1986 Christmas special, 'A Royal Flush' – or at least it would become that if we managed to finish it in time, an outcome which was looking terrifyingly unlikely as the shoot wore on and the deadline approached.

That shoot was six weeks long, in various locations around Salisbury and in Derbyshire, and intended to wrap in mid-December. And it had some lovely stuff in it. This was the one where Del ends up chaperoning Rodney at a posh weekend shooting party – and turns out to be rather good at the shooting. That scene contains one of my favourite moments, an instance of what I suppose we can only describe as 'cockney glue ear' – a mishearing by Del which is entirely dependent on London pronunciation. It occurs as Del is preparing to shoot.

'Ready when you are, John.'

'Do you mean "pull"?'

'Oh, sorry, Paul. In your own time, my son.'

It only works if, like Del, you instinctively pronounce 'Paul' as 'pull'. But if you do, it works very well indeed.

That show also gave me the chance to act with the great Jack Hedley, who played the wonderfully scornful Duke of Maylebury. Jack wasn't all that long off the set of *For Your Eyes Only*, the James Bond movie, but I'm sure that experience paled into insignificance for him beside the high glamour of a couple of days' work on an *Only Fools* Christmas special shoot.

But oh, the problems that shoot endured. It was utterly plagued by delays and slippages and outbreaks of our old friend Sod's Law. We fell behind schedule very early on and kept going from there. One step forward, three steps back. When the schedule starts to fall apart on a shoot, a very different kind of energy comes over the place – a sense of growing panic which isn't always the best to work under.

Nick and I didn't help matters by falling ill on a rota basis. I woke up one morning and found I had no voice. You can push through quite a lot of things on a shoot, but when you sound as though you've been gargling nails and paraffin for a fortnight, it doesn't leave you very much wriggle room. My absent voice took me out of commission for three days, following which, with perfect timing, Nick went down with the flu. That was a week lost in total – about a sixth of the available time. I don't think either of us had missed a day's shooting through illness before this. But that was the kind of shoot it was.

As Christmas loomed ever larger on the horizon, we started to wonder whether we would ever get the whole script filmed in time. It reached the stage where the idea was floated that maybe, with at least the location material in the can, we could act the studio scenes in the Trotters' flat live, at the time of broadcast, on Christmas Day itself. Could we not play the recorded material off-tape and then cut live to the studio in between, like on a current affairs show?

This would have been a first in so many directions. I'd spent numerous Christmas Days watching telly. I'd never spent any Christmas Days *making* telly.

Mind you, think of the overtime we'd have been able to ask for. Double time? Triple time, more like. Plus a big fat tip.

Fortunately for our nerves and our Christmases, and almost certainly the show, that particular spare-parachute rip-cord never had to be pulled. Everything we needed did get filmed in the end, including the flat scenes. But it all happened so close to the wire, doing nobody's blood pressure any good. The show was still frantically being edited late into the night on Christmas Eve, with the broadcast slot just hours away. It was skin-of-the-teeth stuff.

So, in many ways, the distraction of a live appearance at the Royal Variety Show bang in the middle of all this chaos was the last thing we needed. But it didn't seem to be an offer the show could really refuse. People fall over themselves to give a performance 'by royal command', as the rather intimidating phrase has it, although, to be honest, I think in our case it was more Michael Grade's command than anyone's specifically at the Palace. But anyway. When you are called . . .

So Buster, Nick and I found what time we could to rehearse John's script, which was very little time, and then, in the middle of the shoot, feeling badly underprepared in one direction and badly behind schedule in the other, off we went to London.

Ah, the unique buzz of the Theatre Royal on a Royal Variety Performance night, with the cream of British show business in attendance and curtain-up nearing. I wish I could tell you something about it, but I can't because we were nowhere near the place at the time. The three of us arrived in the West End to find that we had been – or so it seemed to us – carefully corralled where we couldn't do any damage. The aforementioned cream of British show business was applying its slap in the illustrious, and above all convenient, dressing rooms of the Theatre Royal; we, meanwhile, were among a batch of acts – including, oddly enough, Tyne Daly and Sharon Gless from the US cop show *Cagney & Lacey* – who were stationed over the road in the Fortune Theatre, which had been requisitioned for the afternoon and evening as a kind of overflow car park.

The poor relations again! We stayed in our dressing room for the whole show until our call, at which point a production assistant wearing a headset led us over the road into the theatre, via the stage door, and guided us into the wings. And there we all stood in the dark until she got the signal in her earpiece and we heard her say, 'Go.'

I believe that was the most anxious I had ever felt while waiting in the wings of a theatre. Take it from me, it puts you on your mettle when you know you're about to walk out in front of a packed house containing royalty and a full selection box of la-di-da types to perform an under-rehearsed piece that you've never done publicly before. Everyone else, all those big stars on that bill, seemed to be doing slick routines that they had already honed. Only we seemed to be going where we had never gone before – and doing so in an underprepared and slightly chaotic way which seemed to be entirely typical of our seat-of-the-pants operation.

Still, out we went, fumbling our way onto the stage in the semi-darkness, pretending to believe that we were in Chunky Lewis's nightclub in the West End, dropping off a dodgy consignment of whisky, and only belatedly working out where we actually were. Entirely fitting, of course, that when the *Only Fools* team finally got to join the black-tie-wearing elite of British light entertainment, they would do so in a scenario that had them arriving in the room entirely by accident. The story of our show, you could almost say.

At the peak of that scripted confusion, I found myself squinting up at the royal box and declaiming the immortal line:

'Hello, Chunky – is that you?'

And, as has now gone down in show-business legend, the Queen Mother – working entirely without a script, let's not forget – responded by smiling and giving a regal wave. (I guess any wave given by the Queen Mother was a regal wave. But you know what I mean.)

Now, to be honest, this moment in the skit was a bit of a no-no. Long-standing protocol insisted that none of the performers onstage at a Royal Variety Performance were meant to engage with the royal guests of honour, or bring them into their act in any way. Like speaking to the Queen before she has spoken to you, or stubbing your cigarette out in a Buckingham Palace teacup, this was simply regarded as bad form. At the Royal Variety, any attending royals were to be left entirely alone to enjoy the show, and if you were looking to the audience for a willing assistant for your magic juggling act, or somebody to hypnotise, or whatever, you were under strict instruction to look anywhere other than the royal box. Those were just the rules.

To put it in theatrical terms, it was like a royal version of the fourth wall – a fourth wall with, if you like, metaphorical soldiers in bearskin hats standing guard in front of it – and you were not supposed to break it, even for dramatic effect. In fact, especially not for dramatic effect.

And what had I just done? Well and truly broken it. And for dramatic effect.

Still, if you don't have a little push at the boundaries every now and again, you won't ever change anything, will you? And let's just lend our so-called rebelliousness that night a bit of perspective here. The word was that Max Bygraves had been utterly determined to keep in his routine a pungently fruity joke about Princess Michael of Kent and had only been narrowly persuaded to leave that pungently fruity joke out after some probably equally pungently fruity toings and froings with the producers. In the wider context of what Max seemed to be hoping to get away with, my little exchange with the Queen Mum was surely among the very mildest of indiscretions.

And Ronnie Barker had already asked her for a quid fifty!

Well, whatever the Queen Mother may have felt about it, and whatever discomfort I may have inadvertently caused her, it didn't stop her daughter knighting me, as you may know, in 2005. And closer to the offending moment, Sue Lawley certainly didn't seem to be sucking her teeth too hard about it, either. Sue was doing the commentary for the BBC broadcast, which went out a few nights later. After the show there was that traditional moment where the cast lined up backstage to be presented to the royal party. Nick, Buster and I were graciously allowed to come over from the other side of the street again for this, and at the moment when the Queen Mother was introduced to the three of us, Sue said: 'It used not to be done to incorporate the occupants of the royal box into your act, but I think they got away with it tonight.'

Indeed. In more than one sense.

Afterwards, a car took Nick and me back down to

Salisbury. Slumped in the back seat, relieved at having got through that sketch without drying or otherwise making undue idiots of ourselves, we uncapped a half-bottle of whisky. A little while later, the whisky began to take effect in more ways than one and we asked the driver to pull over.

Standing a touch unsteadily in the bracingly cold, late-November air and looking out across a dark field, I took a little moment to reflect on the great swings and roundabouts of life and how randomly they transport us on this earthly journey. One minute you're performing by royal command, the next you're emptying your bladder in a lay-by beside the M3.

By the time we reached Salisbury, the whisky bottle was empty. Yet somehow the next day we were up at the crack of dawn and back at it on the set. I was running on pure adrenaline in those days. The whole show seemed to be.

* * *

Of the tips I can offer, based on my long and esteemed years at the coalface of nationally broadcast light entertainment, being extremely wary of working with children and animals would be right up there, of course. With a special mention, as we have seen, for recently hatched chicks.

But also prominent would be avoiding filming in a moving coach.

Nothing to do with carsickness, although that could be an issue. No, it's the continuity problems. It stands to reason, really. If your coach is moving, then so is the view out of your coach's windows. And that means that, as you cut backwards and forwards between various shots of people inside the coach, the stuff that can be seen over the shoulders of those people is going to be jumping around all over the place, and a long, sticky and altogether nightmarish session in the editing suite can only ensue.

Another tip: if your plan is later to blow that coach up in front of the cameras, then make sure you get the shot right first time. The same, I can attest, very much applies to shots involving dropped chandeliers. Expensive things, coaches and chandeliers.

This important wisdom about coaches comes to you courtesy of my experiences making 'The Jolly Boys' Outing', the *Only Fools* Christmas special for 1989, where we did indeed manage to blow up the coach correctly first time (admittedly an already wrecked, substitute coach, and not the one we'd been driving around in all day), and where cutting the moving coach sequences was indeed a nightmare. But it was worth it. A Christmas special about an August bank holiday? This was John Sullivan at his most confrontational in terms of the traditional expectations. How far away from stuffed turkey and paper hats could you get? No further, surely, than Margate beach in August.*

* It was August in the story, but we filmed it in May, just in case anybody's wondering. A sunny May, thankfully.

So, yes, as I was saying when we came into this chapter, my favourite *Only Fools and Horses* episode is a question too knotty to be resolved: too much choice, too much baggage, too much history.

But if I could only keep one . . .

And yes, it's partly the exploding coach, because that's such an enormous comic moment – wonderfully framed by the conversation that Rodney is having with Cassandra from the nearby phone box, defending his brother against Cassandra's accusation that something always goes wrong when Del is around.

'I agree that Del gets a bit out of hand. But I think it's unfair to say that everything he touches goes wrong.'

Kaboom!

Nick's reaction shot with the phone receiver still at his ear is one for the ages. But the shot of the rest of the cast, looking on in shock, bathed in an orange glow, will also tickle me for ever more.

But more than that, even, it's the 'Everybody's Talkin'' sequence – the aerial shot of Margate seafront from the camera in the helicopter, which picks up the coach, bringing everyone down for this day at the seaside. And then we go on board with the cast and start switching between interior and exterior, the day's high jinks starting to unfold. And Harry Nilsson's 'Everybody's Talkin'' is playing, setting the mood for what's to come, and it just flows.

Today you wouldn't allow the sequence to do that: you'd

come in and out on the beat, puncture it with lots of shots – cut, cut, cut – and totally destroy the mood. But the director, Tony Dow, had the courage and the sensibility to let the scene run and play itself at length, to take its time, allow us to be in the moment and enjoy it.

And I hate to say it, because you risk sounding like some old fuddy-duddy, but actually, in this case, I don't care because I think it's true: they just don't make them like that any more.

I struggle to write about the way that sequence works on me now. It's a rush of pure nostalgia. Such powerful emotions, so much sentiment, such a massive tug on the heartstrings. Nowadays it reads to me like a cine film of a family holiday. I know we're all acting, all playing characters that aren't ourselves. But it's different from any of the scripted sequences, because it's an assembly of clips of us simply mucking about – charging around on the beach, larking about in the shallows, and so on. And, of course, we're doing it in character, and in costume, and we're making a television programme, not having a holiday. But the way that film gives you the interaction between the cast, it feels to me now like candid shots, as if the camera had just been left to run and caught us being ourselves.

And yes, the show would get bigger than this: the trilogy for Christmas in 1996 would rise to its giddy heights, the 'Time on our Hands' episode would find that 24.35 million audience and break records for good and practically set fire to the National Grid, which, of course, would have been a very Trotter-y thing to happen. And yes, all of that was obviously just the most astonishing and exciting thing to be a part of.

Yet, for me, it's all here already, really, compressed into this single sequence from seven years earlier, down there in Margate – the gang of friends that the cast had become, and the sheer fun of it all. And so many of those faces no longer with us, of course. Nowadays the glimpse of John Challis reaching across to swipe my hat off is so poignant that I practically have to close my eyes, and the whole thing is a world that's gone.

So if someone were to ask me to sum up what, at its very best, it felt like to be in the cast of *Only Fools and Horses*, I would say to them, 'Look, I can't really tell you, to be perfectly honest. Because I've tried many times and I never seem to have the words to do it justice.'

And then I would say, 'But I *can* show you this . . .'

And I would play them that 'Everybody's Talkin'' sequence from 'The Jolly Boys' Outing'. Because that's what it felt like to be in *Only Fools*. That's what it felt like, right there.

ON THE ELEVENTH DEL OF
CHRISTMAS . . .

Tattoos and Kylie albums

Hindi, the official language of India, has no word for 'plonker'. How do I know this? Because I went to a conference centre in a hotel near Bedford in May 2022 and it turns out that it's the kind of thing you learn when you do that – if you go on the right day, anyway – along with a thousand other things including, overwhelmingly, how much people still love *Only Fools and Horses*.

I mean, *really* love it. And not just for Christmas.

The conference centre in question was in the Sharnbrook Hotel, and the occasion was the Only Fools and Horses Appreciation Society's 40th Anniversary Convention, marking forty years since the show's launch, in 1981.

Now, you don't need to be Rodney and have the relevant GCSE up your sleeve to be able to do the maths here and to find the numbers slightly wonky. Don't blame the organisers, though. This anniversary event was originally booked in for

2021, which qualified mathematicians will confirm is properly forty years on from 1981, the year *Only Fools* first appeared on the nation's screens – on Tuesday 8 September at 8.30 in the evening, to be precise, in between *The Rockford Files*, starring James Garner, and *The Nine O'Clock News*, read by John Humphrys. (Television really did boast some mighty stars in those days. And James Garner wasn't exactly a nobody, either.)

But, as with so many carefully planned events at that time, the pandemic got in the way. How often was that the story across the country, as we all did our best to pull together, abide by the rules and put our lives on pause for a while in a unified effort to contain the virus and protect the vulnerable? It seemed the only way you could carry on socialising as usual during those lockdowns was by getting a job in Downing Street.

But the situation eventually began to ease, and in May 2022 we were able to get together and, forty-one years after *Only Fools* was born, celebrate the show's fortieth birthday. I know it wasn't quite what everyone was originally intending, but, on the consolation side, there was at least something rather satisfyingly Trotter-like about that outcome. Indeed, as birthday commemorations go, you might almost say it had a touch of the chunky gold 'Rooney' ID bracelet about it.* It felt somehow right, in other words. Wrong, but right.

---

* Del's birthday gift for Rodney in 'Heroes and Villains' in the 1996 Christmas trilogy – 'Twenty-four-carat gold, no rubbish – it's

Incidentally, were I a less easy-going kind of person, and more swift to take offence, I might have had cause to remark that it was nice of *someone* to make an effort to mark the show's fortieth anniversary. I don't mean to sound touchy, but others – such as, for instance, anybody in any kind of position of eminence at the broadcasting corporation which commissioned the show in the first place – had shown strangely little inclination to mention it. At least, if there was a note or a card or even a one-line email sent out from anywhere in the BBC's upper echelons, saying, 'Blimey, doesn't time fly? Forty glorious years!', or, better still, 'Here's an evening of commemorative programming on BBC2', I certainly never saw it. And when I talked to Tessa Peake-Jones and Gwyneth Strong and Sue Holderness, all of whom also came along to the 2022 convention, they didn't seem to have heard a peep, either.

And now I'm on the subject, neither did we hear anything when *Only Fools* was voted the favourite BBC programme of all time by *The One Show*'s viewers. I sent a

---

even got your name on it, look . . . No, that's a "d" – it's just, like . . . copperplate writing.' And, of course, as with the 'urgent' mobile phone aerial, it's another one of those lovely 'plants', setting up the moment at the end of the story where Albert reads aloud the local newspaper's report on Del and Rodney's inadvertent crime-busting activity, and the part played in the apprehension of the muggers by Mr Trotter's 'younger brother Rooney'. It's just so nicely stitched together, and something which was a great gag in itself ends up paying off all over again.

note about that to John Sullivan's son, Jim, and the rest of the Sullivan family, because it felt like such an honour to the memory of their beloved John. But gone, alas, are the days when BBC bigwigs such as David Hatch and Mark Freeland would send an immediate note of encouragement or congratulations when something happened around the show. David's notes became known as 'Hatchlets' and I have a file full of them. Mark was instrumental in bringing back Granville and Arkwright for *Still Open All Hours*, along with all the energy and enthusiasm to the project that the BBC used to have.

No matter. We took a little time to celebrate the fortieth anniversary for ourselves, near Bedford that weekend.

I had darkened the door of the Sharnbrook Hotel – not to mention its towels – once before this, in February 2020. That was when I went along to 'The David Jason Exhibition', organised by the Only Fools and Horses Appreciation Society, which featured a display of props, scripts, costumes and pictures, and which also featured me, making my first appearance at any kind of fan convention. And, of course, looking back, it could so easily have been my last appearance at one as well – and possibly my last appearance anywhere, in fact.

That February, this thing the scientists were calling Covid-19 was still a gathering threat, somewhere out on the horizon – something which, it was becoming apparent, we would have to confront eventually, but whose exact shape was as yet uncertain and which, for now, seemed to be happening elsewhere.

Now, within a month, of course, the entire country would be under government-issued lockdown orders and we'd all be learning to socially distance from one another and discovering what life was like when you took away, not just *Only Fools and Horses* conventions, but pubs and restaurants and cafes and cinemas and sports events and most kinds of shops and even the chance (No. 10 Downing Street excepted) to have a few people inside your own house.

Back then, though, as I installed myself at that 2020 convention, all that stood between me and a long line of people waiting to come and shake my hand was a single bottle of hand sanitiser, placed on a shelf at the head of the queue. And I remember looking at that bottle and thinking how unusual it seemed – almost exotic. None of us really had any idea how much a part of our lives bottles of hand sanitiser were about to become. Nor how much a part of our lives shaking hands with people was about to unbecome.

As for wearing paper face masks in populated places, we hadn't even begun to think about those at that stage. And therefore it follows logically that we hadn't begun to think, either, about what it would be like to wear a paper face mask during the hay fever season and endure a sneezing fit on a path up to a dentist's surgery – which I only mention because it seems to have become one of

Here I am with my co-pilot Leon Harris and some other guy who photo-bombed us.

My sister June and me, standing where our front room used to be . . .

On set for the 1986 Christmas special for *Only Fools*, 'A Royal Flush'. I never win lucky dips.

Credit: Moviestore Collection / Alamy Stock Photo

Jay and Daryl, my twin bodyguards for the *Only Fools* convention. Dedicated to their duties and, if the situation arose, selflessly prepared to take if not a bullet then at least a thrown Kylie Minogue album for me.

Had the cards fallen differently, maybe I could have been an expert on *The Repair Shop*. Instead I'll just have to be content to be inspired by those guys, and get on with the work as it arises in my own somewhat scruffier home workshop.

How different the whole path of my career would have been if I hadn't had the great good fortune to meet Ronnie Barker and John Sullivan. The back wall of my garage has become something of a shrine to them.

Not guilty, your honour. And I have a solid alibi. I'm all in favour of the gesture, though.

We interrupt this book to bring you some breaking grapefruit news. Buoyed by its new-found fame last year (mentioned in my last book), my humble grapefruit tree attempted to bear fruit. Needless to say, it got as big as a pea and then dropped off.

Me with my wife Gill, who puts up with the *occasional* 'Bah! Humbug!' outburst from me.

Credit: Fiona Hanson / Alamy Stock Photo

Me with Gill, Sophie and her friend Esther on our annual trip down the red carpet.

Credit: David Bennett / Getty Images

All things considered, it was no real surprise to me that, when the BBC brought back *Open All Hours* as *Still Open All Hours* in 2013, they chose to make a Christmas thing out of it and launch it on Boxing Day.

The Platinum Jubilee. One moment the crowds feasted their eyes on the gold state coach, the next they were watching a yellow Reliant Regal Supervan III puttering in the same direction. New York, Paris . . . Buck House?

Credit: Jonathan Brady / Alamy Stock Photo

Merry Christmas.

SCROOGE AND THE TURKEY.

From A Christmas Carol.

I look like Scrooge? Who, *moi*? I hope they mean this warm-hearted geezer and not the sour-faced tight-wad from the beginning of the tale.

Credit: Mary Evans Picture Library / Peter & Dawn Cope Collection

my own most enduring memories of mask-wearing during the pandemic.

Without wishing to go into too much detail, it was one of those pollen-led sneezing attacks that comes out of nowhere, ambushes you from all sides and triggers five or six rapidly consecutive explosions, leaving you a dizzy and watery-eyed shell of your former self. You certainly don't want to be holding a tray of crockery when one of those happens, and neither – I can vouch wholeheartedly for this – do you want to be heading into your dentist's with a face mask on. By the time I gingerly opened the door and entered that surgery, I was wearing a mask so heavily weighted with the expelled contents of my sinuses that it was beginning to sag slightly and gently bounce on its ear elastic.

The receptionist was good enough to respond to my muffled and slightly sticky request for a new mask and I quickly adjourned to the bathroom area to sort myself out – but too late, clearly, to prevent the mortification of this moment from staying with me in perpetuity in the form of a muscle memory. Another of Covid's little gifts.

In February 2020, however, delights like these were all off in the mists of our collective future. And, just to recap: I had cheerfully signed up to do the first large-scale meet-and-greet event of my life, one which brought me into close contact with eight hundred people in four separate sessions across two days, just as a rapidly spreading and cunningly mutating airborne virus was working out the best way to shut us all indoors and make sure we saw nobody we weren't living with for whole months on end.*

Again, if you're not seeing a slight trace of the Derek Trotters in that plot development, I would gently suggest you're not looking closely enough.

But I lived to tell the tale, and I also lived to go back for another helping, a little over two years later, walking up to that perfectly innocuous-looking hotel early on the

---

* I don't know about you, but I remained confused about the nature of the Covid-19 virus all the way through lockdown and beyond. We knew that it was capable of mutating in order to stay alive so it seemed to have some kind of purpose, or at any rate a driven ambition to exist. But what did it actually want? What was it after? What were its hopes and dreams and what was it hoping to achieve by messing us all up like this? Had anybody sat down with it and asked it these questions? If it was just money that it was looking for, could we not have had a whip-round, got a couple of hundred quid together and sent it on its way? It was all very puzzling. At one point during my vexed thinking about these matters, I developed a kind of 'inverse Trojan Horse' approach to battling the virus. On the understanding that the virus was desperate to attach itself to humans, the idea was to wheel giant, laboratory-made and utterly convincing human-a-likes – Trojan Humans, if you like – into deserted town centres around the country to attract all of the virus in the area and then, once the bugs were inside, to tow the human-a-likes out to sea as quickly as possible and dump them. I thought this was a pretty neat solution – classical but with a twist. Oddly, though, nobody at Pfizer or Astra-Zeneca seemed interested in following me down this route. But fair enough, I suppose: the boffins found their own way and had some success, it can't be doubted, with the vaccines. Next time, though, I'm suggesting we go 'inverse Trojan Horse' on the problem. You read about it here first. And yes, don't worry: I've patented it. I wasn't born yesterday, you know.

Saturday morning, where there was nothing to announce to the outside world the full nature of what was unfolding within, unless you count the yellow Reliant Regal Supervan parked by the front door, which, I suppose, now I mention it, was quite a big clue actually.

If I was in a subdued and more than commonly thoughtful mood as I entered the building that day, it was for one reason. No John Challis this time. John, who had been an absolute stalwart attender of these conventions, died in September 2021. He was seventy-nine. We've suffered so much death around *Only Fools* – more than any show's fair share of untimely earthly departures, surely. Lennard Pearce at sixty-nine, Ken MacDonald at fifty, John Sullivan at sixty-four, Roger Lloyd Pack at sixty-nine . . . Buster Merryfield lived to be seventy-eight, which is more like a decent score, but he died while John Sullivan was still alive and the show was still running and there were episodes still ahead of him, so even with Buster there was a sense, among us, of a life cut short.

In the spring of 2022, the world lost Lynda Baron and Denise Coffey, too – two more enormously talented colleagues of mine and greatly cherished companions on the voyage. And not long before that, Terry Jones had passed, also. All these people that I have come through with, now dropping off the perch . . . I find it so hard to reckon with and really difficult to process. I just really wish they wouldn't. I'm starting to feel a little bit exposed up here.

John Challis's death hit especially hard. He had been

ill with cancer since 2019, but was doing OK, it seemed – coping with it. He and I had last been in a room together at this convention, in 2020, and he had been as jovial and as engaging as ever – a truly warm presence in the room. But the illness later seemed to take him over in a hurry and the news, when it came, knocked us all for six – a huge blow. He was just such a lovely man: naturally funny, brilliant company, and a really terrific storyteller.

I mentioned earlier the Beatles' film, *Magical Mystery Tour* – which the launch episode of *Do Not Adjust Your Set* had the daunting job of competing with at Christmas 1967. Well, John was offered a part in that movie. Apparently, at the audition, he'd told John Lennon that he was 'more of a Rolling Stones fan, really' – not necessarily the smartest tactic in the circumstances. Yet, a testament to his charm, he still got the job.

The problem was, John had a prior commitment to a BBC job that he couldn't get out of, so he had to let the chance go. Imagine that: it's the Swinging Sixties and you've got the opportunity to make a film with the Beatles, but the day job goes and gets in the way. Nobody would have found that easy to swallow – with the exception of my dad, of course. I think John was as sore about that twist of fate for a while as I was about being made to surrender a role in *Dad's Army*.*

* The role of Corporal Jones, which was mine for approximately three hours in 1968 – the time it took the BBC to discover that they could have

John was a genuinely talented actor. He'd had roles with the Royal Shakespeare Company and at the National Theatre. In 1995, when he'd become enormously famous for playing a honkingly superior second-hand car dealer from Lewisham, he chose to spend his summer onstage in Regent's Park doing Shakespeare – *Richard III* and *A Midsummer Night's Dream*. And he was equally happy during those years devoting his winters to hamming it up as various villainous figures in pantomimes. Captain Hook was a speciality. He'd seen *Peter Pan* at Christmas as a kid – his first time in a theatre – and been dumbfounded. As he once described it, he'd sat there thinking he was witnessing a chocolate box come to life.

Him too, then. Clearly there is no overestimating those Christmas shows and the impression they made on some of us young ones, staring up from the stalls. They put something in our minds which could never quite be dislodged.

There was something wonderfully unassuming about John. I remember being on a location shoot for *Only Fools* one time in Bournemouth. The show was in its heyday, and, once the

---

Clive Dunn instead. I wrote about this professional disappointment in my first volume of memoirs. It's quite possible that I mentioned it in my second, too. I may also have alluded to it in my third. And now here I am, briefly encountering the subject again in my fourth. Not that it left any kind of lasting impression on me, you understand. Anyway, what became of *Dad's Army*? The programme vanished without trace, didn't it? Some, sadly, wither on the vine.

word had got out that we were filming, people would gather on the street in quite large numbers to have a look at what we were up to. That meant a few security guys would be brought in to mind the perimeter of the set and make sure nothing unhelpful happened.

At one point, during a brief break in filming, John realised that he was running low on cigarettes and decided to pop to the shop. Of course, it wouldn't have occurred to John to send someone out to *get* him some fags, because that would have been too grand and lordly. But he did ask one of the guys on the perimeter if he would mind coming with him to the shop, get him off the set and guide him up the street and back without too much hindrance.

So off they went together and John bought his cigarettes and, mission accomplished, the pair of them returned. On the way back to the set, just by way of conversation, John asked the guy what time his shift ended.

'Oh, no – I'm not security,' said John's guide. 'I just came along to watch.'

John, by the way, was an excellent smoker, and very good at it – by which I mean he could smoke in a full range of styles: the secret smoker, furtively puffing away; the show-off smoker, letting the whole room know; the beginner, still getting the hang of it; the smoker who isn't really a smoker at all and who's only doing it because everyone else is . . . John could hold the room with a whole routine based on people's different ways with a cigarette.

But, of course, wherever he went, it was the laugh that people mostly wanted him to do – that terrible, high, mirthless bray that Boycie specialised in. That was John's personal gift to the show, modelled on the laugh of somebody in his local pub. John offered it up as a suggestion in rehearsal one day and everybody fell about. John Sullivan started writing it into the scripts: '*Boycie does one of his laughs.*'

Given what a solid part of the show he became, it's funny to reflect now how John just drifted in one afternoon to film what seemed to be a casual, come-and-go bit part. We were filming the second episode of the first series – 'Go West, Young Man'. In that story, Boycie has bought his girlfriend a classic E-Type Jaguar and pleads with Del to hide it in the Trotters' lock-up so that his wife doesn't find out. John was there for, literally, that one afternoon and, to be perfectly honest, the car is the thing I remember most vividly about making that episode.

Look, in my defence, it was a very special car, all right? Or it certainly was to me. Back when I was a naive twentysomething, dreaming of life as an international man of mystery from the front seat of an electrician's van, the E-Type Jaguar was, in my overawed opinion, the ultimate set of wheels. I was utterly convinced that the day I took delivery of an E-Type – preferably in red, preferably with white leather seats, and preferably with white-wall tyres – I would know for sure that I had made it, that my personal magnetism had peaked, and that life could show me no more.

I never did get that E-Type, as it turned out – yet now here I was, being handed the keys to one. And at work, of all places. OK, it was white, not red, but beggars can't be choosers. Nick Lyndhurst and I couldn't resist. We asked if we could take the car for a spin round the streets of London during our lunch hour – permission for which was very reluctantly granted.

'You won't be late back, will you?' was the slightly anxious question.

'Of course not!' we replied.

About a quarter of an hour of happy motoring pleasure through the streets of west London later, we realised that we were lost. I blamed Nick. Nick blamed me. Remember, if you can: these were the days before satnav – or 'satnaff' as I prefer to refer to it, having been sent up any number of blind alleys and dumped in any number of traffic jams by those oh-so-helpful electronic assistants. But we had nothing to help us that day apart from our senses of direction, and unfortunately they turned out to be worse than satnaff.

I still don't really know how we made it back that day. I can only think that a higher authority intervened and guided the steering wheel. Possibly a higher authority in the BBC budget department. However, make it back we did, albeit by the skin of our teeth and with filming just about to restart. 'We knew you'd be ready for us about now,' we blithely remarked, in true Del Boy style, as we clambered out. But the truth was we'd come close to holding up the production and embarrassing ourselves mightily. We swore each other to an oath of secrecy about it – which, oops, I seem to have broken. Sorry about that, Nick.

Anyway, that afternoon saw this actor called John Challis pitch up and film his sole appearance in that first series. John Sullivan only wrote Boycie into one episode in the second series, too – 'A Losing Streak', with the famous poker game; 'That wasn't the hand I dealt you,' and so forth. But, unsurprisingly, the character grew from there: Boycie was in two episodes of series three, and four episodes of series four, until it reached the point where those last Christmas specials would have been unthinkable without a part for him. And that was in no small measure because of John Challis showing John Sullivan what Boycie could be. It was the same with Sue Holderness's Marlene, with Patrick Murray's Mickey Pearce, with Roger Lloyd Pack's Trigger . . . The show evolved, far beyond its three-blokes-in-a-flat sitcom premise, and became an ensemble piece because of what those actors brought to their roles.

And that, incidentally, is another reason why programmes need time to develop – time which, I'm afraid, broadcasters are increasingly reluctant to give new shows and which has become a luxury in these more commercially intense times. It's not just about giving the audience time to find the show, although that's obviously important; it's about allowing time for the writer and the cast to find the show, too. Bear in mind that John Sullivan had written the whole of series one of *Only Fools* before the show had even been cast. He had imaginary faces and voices in mind for those characters, which Nick's, Lennard's and my actual faces and voices eventually supplanted. From the second series onwards John could have us in mind when he wrote and could craft the lines and situations to suit our deliveries.

If a show is given space, this feedback loop starts up in which the cast feeds back to the writer and the writer starts writing for the cast, and the programme, with any luck, advances and becomes deeper and richer for it. If the BBC had dumped *Only Fools* after series one – and given the less than spectacular viewing figures for that series on its first showing, they could easily have felt entitled to – none of this would have been able to happen and nobody would have been any the wiser. Fortunately, though, the commercial imperative didn't have to prevail, and the BBC kept faith with the show, and here we are.

When I think about John Challis, I remember in particular how good he was at handling his success in the show – dealing with the changes that inevitably happened in his life when he suddenly became very famous for playing *that character*. I certainly had my own struggles on that score. The success of the show was wonderful – and at the same time quite troubling, even alarming in some respects. Contradictions abounded. Del was the role of a lifetime – I knew that as well as I knew anything. He was an absolute gift, as far as I was concerned. You dream of being given a leading role in a show that really lands with people and embeds itself deeply in their affections, yet how often does that actually happen? I'd had more than a decade of false starts and dashed hopes on that particular quest, and watched a number of well-funded, nicely positioned shows leave the launch pad with a phut rather than a bang. In fact, it had happened to me so often that I'd started to think that my goose was cooked and that the big one would never arrive for me. And then, bingo, along came Derek Trotter.

And yet, at the same time, for all the wonderful things that I could attribute to him, that man was nothing less than a threat to my livelihood. How do you explain that to people? But it was true. Del Boy – lovable, energetic, roguish, playful, eternally optimistic Del Boy – sometimes seemed to be on nothing less than a mission to end my career as an actor.

The thing was, he became such a strong presence in the world, and my face, for obvious reasons, became so firmly associated with his, that he practically threatened to replace me. Wherever I went, Del would come barging through the door ahead of me. Which was all very well in some settings, but if the door in question led into an audition room where I was trying to be considered for another part, it could be less than helpful.

For example, in 1987 I went up for the role of Skullion, the Head Porter, in *Porterhouse Blue*, the Malcolm Bradbury adaptation of the Tom Sharpe novel, made by Channel 4. I had loved the novel and I loved the script and I desperately wanted to be a part of that production. Skullion was an ex-military man, a traditionalist determined to resist the tides of change, a behind-the-scenes wielder of dark power – a truly juicy role, and one that I was really confident I could bring something to.

I read for the part, in the usual way of these things, and it seemed to go OK. But then I had to audition again, this time in Skullion's costume – his dark suit and tightly buttoned waistcoat and his bowler hat. Auditioning in costume wasn't something that anyone had asked me to do before. I think I knew what was going on, though. The producers had to be absolutely convinced that I could come across as something other than an irrepressible, neck-flexing, cockney wheeler-dealer, which, at this point, was the first thing they thought of when they thought of me, and which they were absolutely convinced would be the first thing an audience thought of. And until I'd put on the clothes, and shown them good and proper that I could inhabit another character, one who wasn't going to shout 'Cushty!' at any moment, they couldn't convince themselves. In a strange way, then, I was fighting Del for that part. Successfully, as it turned out – but I had the feeling it was a close-run thing, and I also knew that there would have been other roles at this point in my career for which I wouldn't even have got into the audition room, let alone been invited to try on some clothes. Del would have seen to it.*

---

* I won a BAFTA for my performance as Skullion, which I mention here in the footnotes in order to seem like I'm being modest about it

Of course, Del's popularity brought its challenges beyond the professional realm, too. All of us who were in *Only Fools* saw our public profiles rise and reach a level that was entirely new to us. It worked like a switch. The outside world that you'd been moving around in without really thinking about it suddenly wasn't quite the same place. People were now noticing you, reacting to you, greeting you in the name of your character, quoting the scripts at you . . . None of us, I think, was quite prepared for how that would feel and the differences it would make, and we all responded to it in our different ways.

The morning after the first episode went out with Gwyneth Strong in it as Cassandra – 1989, the 'Yuppy Love' episode – Gwyneth remembers leaving her flat to go shopping, pushing the buggy containing her young son, and suddenly having this feeling that people were looking at her differently, more intently, as if trying to work out whether they knew her, and

---

but, in fact, trust me, in my entire career, it's the award that I'm most stonkingly proud of. And until the Oscar comes along – which must be any year soon, surely – it will remain so. And on the subject of Oscars and auditions, permit me here to recall a favourite story about the great American film star Shelley Winters, who, at an advanced stage in her career, was asked to audition for a role, and also to bring along a résumé and a headshot photograph. Apparently Winters duly attended with a large bag from which she withdrew one of her two Oscar statuettes and plonked it on the table in front of the producers. 'Here's my photo,' she said. Then she reached into the bag again and produced her second Oscar statuette. 'And here's my f∗∗∗ing résumé.' Well, it's an approach. And one, I have to say, that I rather admire. Oh, and she got the part.

if . . . wait a minute . . . it's you, isn't it? Yes! It IS you! Look, everybody! It's her!

We all had moments like that, and it really was an eerie sensation. Again, this can be difficult to explain. It looks, I know, like such an odd thing to complain about. We spend so much time in our culture thinking about fame. Indeed, sometimes it seems to be the thing our culture prizes most: fame, stardom, recognition. For some people the idea of being recognised wherever you go is the dream – an ambition in itself, rather than the unlooked-for consequence of doing something else, which is how it comes to most of us who end up famous, and is certainly how it came to me.

But the truth is, these days when I sit at home and watch the reality shows and the talent contests where the first prize seems to be fame, above all, I can only shake my wise old head and say: be careful what you wish for, my children. Because, whatever it looks like, this may not be for everyone. Indeed, this thing you long for may end up bringing you only unease. Indeed, if there are aspects of your character which are in any way shy, withdrawn, self-conscious . . .

Let me put it this way: I'd never been a wearer of hats – with the solitary exception, I should perhaps declare, of the occasion of my mate Malcolm Taylor's wedding, somewhere in the seventies, where I gleefully discovered that the morning suit I was issued with, in my role as best man, came with a top hat. I was so delighted by this opportunity to look like Fred Astaire that I wore that top hat the whole day, including during the dinner at the reception, only removing it, extremely reluctantly, for the official photographs.*

After Del came into my life, though, hats became a part of my everyday wardrobe – not top hats, in this case, but certainly baseball caps, of which I suddenly amassed a small collection. I tugged their brims down over my face and pulled a scarf up over my chin and hoped to go unnoticed. Nick and Roger Lloyd Pack were very much of the same persuasion, wrapping themselves up tightly whenever they set foot outside the door. It didn't make us particularly comfortable, maybe, but the attention we would get otherwise made us even less comfortable.†

It was another reason I admired John Challis. He didn't let the fuss that came his way as a result of *Only Fools* trouble him or make him anxious, and if he found it tiresome, then he didn't let on. If people wanted him to 'do the laugh' (as almost invariably they did), he cheerfully obliged. I'm sure it must have irritated him sometimes – being asked to do the same thing, over and over, while seeming enthusiastic about it, is bound to – but I never saw him show it. Not once.

* And as a consequence of that heroic hat-wearing, my hair in those official wedding photos is utterly crushed flat and damp. I look as though someone has just dumped a bucket of water over me.
† Be aware that the hat-and-scarf wrap-up is a decent tactic for deflecting unwanted attention, except in warm weather when you end up drawing attention to yourself, which somewhat defeats the point. See also the wearing of sunglasses – especially indoors.

That attitude meant that he signed up wholeheartedly to the *Only Fools* conventions, where others among us, me included, were far more circumspect. John just thought, 'Why not?' When it emerged that *Only Fools* was an especially popular item in Serbia, several of us quietly made a note to cross that country off our list of potential destinations for a holiday. John, by contrast, flew straight out to Belgrade at the nearest opportunity and made a documentary about the show's success there. He greeted all the peculiar repercussions of his fame with wholesome curiosity, an arched eyebrow and a huge helping of good cheer. He was an example to us all, really.

That said, even John needed to be able to escape sometimes, and he and his wife Carol used to like slipping away to the Hotel des Arts in Paris. France, unlike Serbia, has never gone a total bomb on *Only Fools*, and John and Carol knew that, in the charming, quiet seclusion of the Hotel des Arts, John could be anonymous and enjoy his hotel breakfast at leisure, utterly undisturbed.

At least, they knew that until the morning when the journey of John's croissant from his plate to his lips was interrupted by the booming voice of a stranger.

'Bonjour, Boycie! What on earth are YOU doing here?'

Clearly nowhere, in fact, was safe.

But even that was fine by John. It became another story to tell – something else to go into the repertoire of amusing things that people would come out with in his presence and with which John would then merrily regale us all. 'I gather you're some kind of television personality,' a woman once said to him, rather crisply, and upon first introduction. 'Well, I'm here to tell you that I never watch television.' John tipped his head back and laughed loudly at that.

How could you not love a man whose death brought immediate tributes and messages of condolence from institutions as far-flung as Arsenal FC, the British Hedgehog Preservation Society and the American rap artist Ice-T? Well, John loved Arsenal, and he loved hedgehogs, and, as for Ice-T . . . Well, perhaps they were not the most obvious of buddies. Yet John and Ice-T had struck up a friendship on Twitter and every year, when Christmas came around, they would exchange a fond festive greeting – from the man behind Lewisham's most famous fictional car dealer to the man behind the O.G. *Original Gangster* album and back. When Ice-T was asked how the two of them knew each other, he replied, rather magnificently, 'Because I live on earth.'

I'm proud to be able to say that I knew John Challis not only because I live on earth, but also because I had the privilege of working with him and befriending him. I miss him badly. A T-shirt worn by one of the conventioneers in Bedford, and alluding to the florist's card on Del and Rodney's tribute at Grandad's funeral in series four, said it nicely, I thought.

RIP John Spurley Challis. Always in our foughts.

John would have tipped his head back and laughed loudly at that, too.

* * *

Ancient laws, set in stone by the founding fathers, dictate that there can be no fan convention without merchandise for sale. The *Only Fools* fortieth anniversary event certainly had no ambition to flout those laws. A souk to rival anything Marrakech can manage occupied the far end of the hotel's conference hall. But there was something about the fact that it was Trotters Independent Trading that had inspired this cheerful exploitation of a marketing opportunity that made it all the more appropriate, somehow.

I didn't linger too long among the groaning trestle tables for fear of getting purchased and bagged up myself and having to start a new life in, say, St Albans. (Nothing against St Albans. It's just that I'm happy where I am.) But I did observe, among the array of tempting items on offer, a Del Boy 'lounger blanket with sleeves' – a cosy one-piece outfit for at-home television-watching which I thought rather stylish, although my wife might not have agreed. There was also not just a 'Jolly Boys' Outing' beach towel, but a 'Jolly Boys' Outing' deckchair to go with it. There was no time to check the car park, but I wouldn't have been surprised to find a full-sized, limited-edition 'Jolly Boys' Outing' exploding coach out there, too.

There were Reliant Regal door panels and nose cones, with or without working indicators and available in your choice of clean or dirt-smudged finish. One of the oh-so-tasteful orangey-brown carpets used to dress the studio set appeared to have been divided into collectable carpet squares, each for sale, meaning that, just as sometimes football fans get given the chance to own their own small, potted patch of the hallowed Wembley Stadium turf, so *Only Fools* aficionados could take home a little plot of Trotter carpet and tread where the cast once trod.

There were wallets marked 'Loads of Bunce'. And there were bottles of Peckham Spring Water on sale at £3 a pop. Now that's what I call entrepreneurial – a fictional wheeze turned into an actual wheeze. Deeply impressive. I also saw a bloke head off with three rolls of 'Yuppy Flat Bamboo Wallpaper' under his arm. Maybe next time he'll bring photos of his newly decorated yuppy flat.

I lost count of the items from those mounds that I signed over the course of the weekend, and I lost track of the sheer range of those items, too. Plenty of Reliant Regal doors and panels, obviously, but more (as Del might have put it) *retroussé* objects, too: a framed elephant print, of the kind that could very easily have graced the wall of a certain Peckham flat; numerous china cats; at least one ceramic cheese dish (you knew it was a cheese dish because it helpfully came with the word 'CHEESE' printed on it to put the matter beyond doubt); and a sheepskin coat or three. The Monty Python team used to talk about getting cans of Spam thrust upon them to sign, as a result of the show's inadvertent and aforementioned association with that product – and maybe that still happens to them. But I wonder if any of them have ever been asked to put their name to a white leatherette-panelled free-standing cocktail bar, as I was in Bedford. I'd love to know where that ended up. Perhaps in the yuppy flat of the bloke with the bamboo wallpaper.

A small pile of second-hand Kylie Minogue albums now bear my signature, too. Is that OK? Will Kylie object? Too late to worry about it at this stage, I'm afraid. The top was back on my marker pen before I could really reflect on what I was doing. But the next time Kylie's in the house for one of my monthly Jason Towers karaoke nights, I'll try and find a moment to square it with her. If she can hear me above the music, of course. Those nights are always pretty raucous.

I also signed not one but two conventioneers' arms – having been asked to do so, let me make clear, rather than because I got carried away while signing other things, or went for one of the Kylie albums and missed. Both those conventioneers – one of whom apparently owns a barber-shop which is practically a shrine to *Only Fools* – told me that the idea was to create a template. They were intending to head off to the tattoo parlour to have my scribble inked over and rendered permanently.

I didn't know what to say, really – apart from maybe they should have tried it with a chequebook. Except, of course, nowhere accepts cheques any more.

Anyway, I complied to the best of my abilities – I don't know whether you've put your signature on anybody's arm recently, but it's not quite as easy as it looks. The surface moves under your pen in the way that, for instance, the side panel of a Reliant Regal doesn't. Yet, with my scrawl complete and more or less legible, the conventioneers went away content enough, one of them saying she was going straight to the parlour that very afternoon to complete the job.

The following day she returned for the second day of the event. My wife, Gill, spotted her and asked her how she had got on. She rolled up her sleeve and showed Gill her autographed arm – still inscribed in nothing more permanent than marker pen. Unfortunately, the tattoo parlour had been closed when she got there.

Again, correct me if I'm wrong, but the spirit of the Trotters seemed to hover lightly over that outcome, and I can only apologise to her if that was anything to do with me. I hope she found an open parlour before the template rubbed off.

Maybe Jay and Daryl could have pointed her the way of a good one. Jay and Daryl were the security guys appointed to keep guard over me at the conference. I'm sure they've had busier and more physically exacting jobs, because I've rarely felt safer than I did sitting among those *Only Fools* fans. But this was the arrangement, so there they were. They were twin brothers, which somehow made their smartly suited presence seem even more formidable. And, it probably goes without saying, they were both fit, strong blokes, dedicated, I have no doubt, to their duties and, if the situation arose, selflessly prepared to take, if not a bullet, then at least a thrown Kylie Minogue album for me.

They also had tattoos. Quite a collection of them. I know this because at one point, during a break, Jay and Daryl guided Gill and me out of the conference hall and upstairs towards a room on the first floor which had been set aside for me to rest up in and get a cup of tea when the opportunity arose. On the way up, we were talking about the limb that I had recently autographed and Gill asked Jay and Daryl if they had any permanently inked decorations themselves, none being visible, on account of the suits.

Indeed they did. Jay – or possibly Daryl – lifted the leg of his trousers to reveal an extensively illustrated calf. Then Daryl – or possibly Jay – unbuttoned his shirt and slipped it aside to display an equally lavishly decorated shoulder blade. Then Jay – or possibly Daryl – joined in by removing *his* shirt to show what was evidently the extensive diary of a tour of North America. An eagle, a bear and a trout figured, among many other mementoes, all exquisitely rendered. They stopped at their shirts, so who knows what other pictorial delights remained undisclosed to us in other areas, including, perhaps, the full instructions for replacing a filter on a Bosch dishwasher. What we did see, though, was beautifully done and one could only admire and applaud the detail and the craftwork.

Yet now I come to reflect on it, what a little tableau this scene must have presented to anybody who happened to be passing: me and my wife, in a hotel corridor, closely examining the tattoos of two stripped-to-the-waist security guards. I reflected later that it would only have taken one press photographer to have rounded the corner at that exact moment for me to have been left with an awful lot of explaining to do.

Anyway, break over and shirts back on, Jay and Daryl attentively guided me back to my headquarters for the weekend – a battered old armchair in a mock-up of the Trotters' lounge, where conventioneers could come and sit alongside me for a chat and a photograph. And, thus restored to my post, I continued to find myself on the receiving end of an absolute tidal wave of warmth and affection.

People had come from all over – from Leeds, Cornwall, Belfast, Scotland . . . Some just wanted to say thank you for all the laughter, the fun, the good times they associated with the show. Others struggled to speak at all, seemingly overcome by the moment. There were tears, young women going bright red, fanning their hands in front of their faces. 'You're going a bit red,' I would say, not making it any easier.

I would love to put that discombobulation and all those hot flushes down to the sheer awe that people routinely experience in the presence of a man of international jet-set leisure – my pal TC knows all about this – and the pheromones no doubt coursing off me that weekend in Bedfordshire. But I knew the truth: it wasn't me, it was that bloke Del. And that series, *Only Fools*.

A hugely flattering experience, then – but at the same time an enormously humbling one, and a frequently bewildering one, too. What I have quickly learned in two appearances at these kinds of convention is that I will be surrounded by people who know those shows far better than I know them – better than I ever knew them, actually. These are people who can quote whole chunks of dialogue, verbatim, whereas I was cramming those lines into my head as quickly as I could and then moving on to the next script, never really to return. These days, I don't tend to watch the shows, either. Not that I wouldn't enjoy them and be proud of them. I catch clips sometimes when they come up incidentally in other places, and I always think they're funny; they still make me laugh and I'm sure they always will. But it's never going to be my idea of a good night in to sit down with the boxed set and binge my way through a whole series.

Quite apart from anything else, those shows remind me of a time when I had a full head of hair – a time, indeed, when I firmly believed I would have that full head of hair forever. So much for that. I've spoken about this before, but the contrast between the person that appears on the screen and the person that I then have to encounter in the mirror these days is, I find, a little strong for me to take. All in all, if it's OK with everyone else, I'd rather not subject myself to that particular contrast more frequently than I have to.

At the same time, I do entirely relate to the people who watch the show over and over and get it by heart. I completely understand that instinct, because I'm the same way about Laurel & Hardy. I watch Laurel & Hardy the way other people watch *Only Fools*: on repeat, with constantly renewed pleasure, as a fan. That look Oliver Hardy gives the camera when something has gone wrong or he's in the wrong, or he can't work out why Stan has done something – that little punctuation mark that only he does: I will never cease admiring the skill in that. Ditto the sequence in the hospital room, with Ollie's plastered leg in traction and the events that lead to him eventually getting flung out of the window: I will never cease taking pleasure from that, nor exhaust its brilliance. I could watch it on a loop.

Even so, it knocks you into quite a spin to learn so intimately, face-to-face, how much a comedy television series can sink itself into people's lives, and the effect it can have when it's there. I found myself deep in conversation with people for whom the show had clearly been a much-loved companion along the way – and in some cases far more than that. At one point, a guy in pink shorts sat down next to me and immediately started thanking me. The words were pouring from him in a torrent. He was telling me that I didn't realise what I'd done, that I'd saved his life, that he'd been through some really low times, hadn't known what to do or where to go, and had felt he was trapped in a tunnel – but right when he needed it, the show had made him laugh and given him a glimmer of hope, and it had helped him to turn around and start to come out of that darkness.

I felt like I didn't have any kind of adequate response to that. I think I ended up saying something about how if I'd made him laugh then I was very happy, because that was the job, but maybe we both ought to be thanking John Sullivan, because, after all, I was only doing what his scripts told me to do and delivering the lines that he wrote. As Nick Lyndhurst always said, when trying to deflect the praise that came his way: 'John made the bullets, we only fired them.'

Yet my friend in the pink shorts was by no means the only person that weekend who spoke in that way about the show. Sat there in that daft armchair, I heard a host of similar stories, each of them just as heartfelt and each of them just as trenchant – of lives rescued or reshaped or restored by the power of that programme. It made me think: what would it have been like if we had known at the time that the show would have these kinds of effects on people? We were enjoying ourselves – messing about, frankly. We all loved those characters and we loved going to work every day to portray them, and we all had a professional desire to do right by ourselves and do right by the scripts, and that was pretty much the extent of it, really. Beyond that, no pressure. But if we'd known all the ways in which the show would end up reaching out to people, I think we would have frozen solid and been unable to make it at all. It would have been too daunting.

So people came with their stories and some, in addition, came bearing gifts. No envelopes stuffed with cash, alas, which, obviously, I would not have encouraged.* But there were many other touching acts of generosity. Someone, by way of thanks, presented me with a DVD of Jacques Tati's *Monsieur Hulot's Holiday*, knowing (because I have written about it before) that going to see that movie as a child with my mother was a formative experience to rank alongside going to see Alastair Sim in *Scrooge*, and knowing also that I believe that film to be arguably the greatest sustained comedy performance ever recorded. I didn't have a copy, and I'm very grateful to own one. The project now is to try and organise a time when I can sit down and watch it with my wife and daughter – partly because I think they, in common with everybody else who likes funny things, need to see it, and partly because I want to find out if it lives up to my fondly admiring recollections of it, though I think I know the answer to that.

Of course, it's highly likely that I will turn into one of those annoying people who spends the film cajoling everyone else to pay attention and bossily pointing out the good

* I'm firmly of the belief that envelopes stuffed with cash should not be exchanged in the public arena of a fans convention. They should be exchanged afterwards, in the car park, or by prior arrangement at a motorway services.

bits just before they happen – not least that part where M. Hulot is changing a tyre on his car and the wheel rolls away into a pile of leaves in a cemetery, where he picks it up, gathering a bunch of leaves with it, so that he ends up appearing to hold, not a tyre, but a wreath, just as a funeral cortège comes past, all of whom solemnly shake his hand . . . I mean, the whole film is made up of these beautifully threaded-together moments, so I could become a very annoying presence indeed. But I hope not.

The only question is whether we can find a suitable slot between Richard Osman's *House of Games* and the American renovation show *Forever Homes*, both of which seem to be on heavy rotation in my house. When *House of Games* comes on, by the way, I tend to go and make the dogs' dinners. Nothing against Richard Osman, you understand, nor the show. But it's simply not fair to keep two hungry dogs waiting. Or that's my story, anyway.

And then, bearing a gift of another kind, came the person who told me about watching *Only Fools* on television in India, and realising that the all-important term 'plonker' had no natural Hindi equivalent. This I was delighted to discover. In the Hindi dubbed version, apparently, it is rendered simply and consistently as 'plonker'. Don't ask me how the translators got on with 'dipstick', but it seems they found a way. No such luck with plonker, though. As my friend at the convention explained, for her, as a non-Hindi speaker watching the Indian broadcasts, the dialogue would be a long stream of incomprehensible sounds from which, just occasionally, the solitary word 'plonker' would brightly leap out, like the linguistic equivalent of a sore thumb.

Ah, the things that Britain has given the world – in this case, it seems, an untranslatable insult. Or perhaps more likely, looking at it the other way, an insult in no need of translation, whose meaning globally transcends the barriers of language and culture alike, with the consequence that you can say 'plonker' in India and in literally dozens of other countries around the world and be sure that you will be understood. For my own small part in bringing the people of the globe together like this, I couldn't be more proud, I'm sure.*

A hectic weekend, then – one which I spent most of sitting at an odd angle, twisting towards people to hear their

---

* According to the *Oxford English Dictionary*, the actual derivation of 'plonker' is a nineteenth-century word meaning something unusually large that you might have to *plonk down* – a 'whopper', you might also say. The *OED* cites an illustration from 1903: 'That turnip's a plonker.' This notion of something outsized, or bulking embarrassingly large, seems then to have loaned itself to slang usages, particularly in the military, for, ahem, the male member, and also for 'a foolish, inept or contemptible person'. Here the *OED* cites usages dating back to 1955, and also quotes a certain John Sullivan, writing in 1981, specifically for episode three of the first series of *Only Fools*: 'Rodney! I didn't mean drive off! What a plonker!' That, clearly, was Del's first public use of the term, though there were to be many, many more, carrying the word very firmly into popular currency. Again, to be at the heart of linguistic history in this way . . . well, my heart can only swell and tears of pride rise to my misty eyes.

stories, and never stopping talking and engaging. It took me three days at home for my back to recover and my neck to untwist so that I was facing the right way again.

But what a privilege: that was all I kept thinking. What a privilege and a fantastic stroke of luck to end up in a programme that inspired that kind of loyalty, and over such a long period of time. And what a privilege, at this point in my life, to be able to bask in the warmth of it every now and again. What's so striking is that the love for the show holds firm. I wasn't the only member of the cast who watched *Only Fools* become successful and then waited for the backlash. That's the fate of most comedy shows, after all. Comedy, like everything else, with the exception, obviously, of Cliff Richard, ages. If nothing else, I thought, our programme would end up getting found out by changing fashions and new ideas about what's funny and the simple passing of time. In due course, *Only Fools* would be obliged to head off into fusty oblivion and we'd all console ourselves that, well, at least we had a decent run.

But somehow it never happened. The backlash never came.

Why should that be? What was the show's precious secret? People much cleverer than me will be able to come up with some properly smart answers to that question, I'm sure. But when I try to explain it, the thing I keep coming back to is the show's innocence. Which might seem an odd thing to say about a programme whose central character was a dedicated rule-bender and determined tax avoider. (I always used to think that if Derek Trotter had spent half the energy he expended doing things dishonestly on trying to do them honestly, he could have been a millionaire in no time at all. But, bless him, he was too busy trying to get there by the bent route and getting nowhere the long way round.)

What I mean by innocence, though, is that *Only Fools* didn't depend on extremes. There was no bad language in it. It never deliberately sought confrontation in the aim of getting a reaction. In that sense, it was a powerful testament to the power of good, clean entertainment. It remains a beacon for what you can achieve if you try and go down that road, as opposed to going in the direction of comedy that is deliberately divisive, comedy that's straight away spoiling for a fight, comedy in which crudeness replaces wit – comedy that seeks to separate us rather than bring us together on some kind of common ground that we recognise. And I do often find myself wondering whether comedy on television these days has lost its faith in trying to take that route. Maybe the times are just too fragmented to make it possible, but I like to think they're not, and I like to think the abiding popularity of *Only Fools* indicates that I might be right – possibly even reveals a gap that nobody is trying to fill any more.

Then there was the nature of the show's characters and the warmth they generated. Yes, it was a sitcom and its ultimate ambition was to go looking for laughs wherever laughs could be found. Yet it was also obviously built on real people with real dreams, who had the kinds of hopes and aspirations for their lives that ordinary people have. And in the pursuit of those hopes and aspirations, they faced real adversity and real disappointment, things that make up ordinary people's lives and that ordinary people can directly relate to – birth, death and everything in between. It was quietly and gently inclusive, too, without feeling that it had to hammer that point home. It reflected life in London as John knew it, where people from all kinds of backgrounds simply rubbed along together without thinking very much of it.

Most of all, though, the show was, in the most literal sense, family entertainment: it was entertainment about a family – about the relationships between brothers, the relationships between husbands and wives, girlfriends and boyfriends, the relationships with grandfathers, with great-uncles, with absent parents . . . And that would explain, I think, why it worked so well at Christmas, and why Christmas became such a particular niche for it and so strongly bound up with the fate of the show. Because Christmas, too, for better or worse, is about family. And in *Only Fools*, people could see family life, with all its wrinkles and its ruptures, its pleasures and its frustrations, its golden times and its dark spells, played back to them, at a moment in the year when those things were most firmly in their minds. It was inherently a family show for a family time of year.

And on the subject of family, did my 21-year-old daughter gleefully depart the fortieth anniversary convention with, under her arm, the plush mannequin she had purchased of her father looking an absolute idiot? And did my wife quietly descend one evening to take part in the karaoke session, giving the room her renditions of those stone-cold *Only Fools and Horses* classics, 'Everybody's Talkin'' and 'Holding Back the Years'?

Reader, I prefer to make no comment either way on these rumoured developments. I only know that each of us, in our own ways, enjoyed our experience in that hotel conference centre near Bedford that weekend.

Twice in two years, though . . . This might be turning into a habit.

ON THE TWELFTH DEL OF CHRISTMAS . . .

Regals and royals

'To look back is not necessarily to be nostalgic,' said the Queen in her Christmas message to the nation in 1996, before going on to stress the importance of using the lessons of the past in order to look forward 'with courage and optimism'.

Or as Derek Trotter put it, in *his* message to the nation that year, a few hours later on the same channel, at the end of 'Heroes and Villains': 'Not a bad old world, is it, bruv?'

It is – and I think at this stage in the book, we can agree on this – what has ultimately linked Queen Elizabeth II and *Only Fools and Horses* through the years: a quiet determination to use the twin powers of Christmas and television to bestow upon the country a message of comfort and hope to take forward into the new year. Albeit that we tended to get a bigger slot in the schedule for our message and have a slightly greater quotient of punchlines.

That said, for all that obvious sense of a shared mission, I wasn't expecting the Trotters to pitch up during the Queen's Platinum Jubilee celebrations in 2022. Or rather, the 'Platinum Jubbly', as one Chinese manufacturer of chinaware apparently labelled it by accident on about £30,000 worth of commemorative mugs and plates which then had to be scrapped when the error was pointed out. Oops. There were, no doubt, all sorts of ways of sending your very best wishes to Her Majesty on the seventieth anniversary of her ascent to the throne, but 'Have a luvvly Platinum Jubbly, ma'am' probably wasn't a line that even Derek Trotter would have been gauche enough to try.

That said, thinking about it, I wouldn't mind owning one of those plates if you know of any that survived the cull. Collector's item, and all that.

Anyhow, the point at which the Trotters definitively took their place at the centre of the formal ceremonies marking that historic moment in the national life came at Buckingham Palace on 5 June. Maybe you watched the special parade that concluded that holiday weekend: the huge carnival-style procession up the Mall designed to reflect the Queen's seventy-year reign and the years of change over which she had ruled. And if you did see it, maybe you observed in the ceremony a moment of cultural contrast that still makes me laugh to think about now.

One moment the crowds lining the route were being

invited to feast their eyes on the four-ton gold state coach, commissioned by King George III in seventeen-hundred-and-frozen-to-death, and now seen rumbling along the avenue with great dignity behind its eight plumed horses, while a mounted military guard in full regalia rode in attendance; the next (give or take a few moments, and a few bits of marching, and one or two buses with people waving from them) they were watching a yellow Reliant Supervan III puttering in the same direction, with 'Trotters Independent Trading' painted on its side and a camel-coated elbow hanging out of its side window.

New York, Paris . . . Buck House?

I've got to say, I found the sight of that stupid van, in those regal surroundings, both hilarious and moving. Of course, the wonderful incongruity of that vehicle in any kind of grand or formal setting was something that the show itself made merry with on many occasions, perhaps most memorably in 'A Royal Flush', the Christmas special from 1986, mentioned earlier, when Del and Rodney pull into the country estate of the Duke of Maylebury, ready for a weekend of romance (Rodney) and clay pigeon shooting with a borrowed shotgun (Del).

You only had to bring that van into shot in a context like that – show it nosing onto the gravel drive of a sumptuous country house or bumping across a field among the gentlefolk's Range Rovers and BMWs – to be sure of hearing a knowing laugh in the audience when those scenes were screened at the eventual studio recording. There was nothing that Nick Lyndhurst and I needed to do to embellish things, either. In fact, the less we reacted to the van and the more we appeared to think that it was the perfectly natural mode of transport for our characters to be going about in – simply part of the air that we breathed – the funnier it became. And, frankly, because there were very few settings in which that soppy vehicle *wasn't* to some degree incongruous, the van was its own punchline practically every time it appeared.

But for a properly riotous and genuinely deafening clash of tones, this Jubilee pageant set-up, with the Reliant making its way along that famous, broad red-paved avenue in central London and then ceremoniously rounding the Victoria Memorial in front of Buckingham Palace . . . well, that took it, I thought, to another level.

Watching the Trotters' innocent little van perform that magnificent journey, I was reminded of a little royal adventure that once happened to a friend of mine. He worked as a lettings agent and a lot of his job was driving around London to meet clients and show them properties; and one day – this would have been in the late 1970s – heading home after an appointment in Victoria, he found himself taking his car past the garden wall of Buckingham Palace and then up the Mall in the direction of Whitehall. There was a line of quite slow-moving traffic ahead of him, but he simply followed along behind it, having no real alternative.

He hadn't gone very far when a policeman stepped out in front of his car and gestured at him to turn left, which the cars ahead of him were also doing.

My friend, naturally, did as he was told, assuming the road ahead was closed or there was some kind of problem necessitating a detour. Very soon after making his turn, however, he was aware of passing through a broad gateway, after which the line of vehicles ahead of him came to a halt. My friend stopped, too, and noticed in his rear-view mirror that the gate was now closing behind him.

At this point, another policeman appeared, this time in his side window. This one was bending down and he had a searching and possibly rather anxious expression on his face. My friend wound down the window.

'What do you think *you're* doing?' asked the policeman.

'Well, I was told to turn in,' said my friend, understandably a touch confused.

The policeman stood up and did some shouting and some gesturing in the direction behind the car. My friend saw the gate that had closed behind him now reopen.

'Back out,' said the policeman, in a tone which brooked no argument.

So, with no further ceremony, my friend reversed off the drive of Clarence House, which was at that time the residence of Queen Elizabeth the Queen Mother, watched the gates again close after him, and somewhat sheepishly resumed his journey along the Mall. Apparently this is what

272

could happen if you accidentally stuck yourself on the end of a member of the royal family's official motorcade – or rather if a policeman accidentally stuck you there. My friend had ended up going home with the Queen Mum.

It had been but the briefest of visits, of course. If the kettle had been on, no one had mentioned it to my friend, who left without so much as a 'thank you for stopping by'. Still, he was able to dine out on the story forever afterwards.*

The Trotters' van, however, did not owe its place in the procession on the Mall in June 2022 to misdirection, by a policeman or anybody else. It really was meant to be there. And I guess that was what was even more moving, from my point of view, about the sight of it in that exceptionally grand context: the fact that this daft vehicle had been

---

* Just to repeat, this was the 1970s when security was a little less, shall we say, attentive than it tends to be these days. In 1962, during an outbreak of smog in London that reduced visibility to fifteen feet in places, someone was stopped by a police officer driving their car innocently and very gingerly across the parade ground in front of Buckingham Palace. I think it's safe to say that wouldn't happen nowadays, and not just because we don't get smogs like that any more. And on that subject, I was twelve when the properly legendary Great Smog of 1952 descended on London and the winter air was so thick then that a gentleman passing the end of Lodge Lane in a rather superior car asked me and my mate Tony Brighton to guide him to Woodside Avenue – which we did, one of us walking ahead of the car, the other guiding the driver along the kerb. It was about three miles and it seemed to take forever, travelling at a crawl, but we each got five bob for our trouble so it was more than worth it. File under 'wouldn't happen now', although maybe climate change might have its own ideas about that.

selected for the parade in the first place – lobbed in, on this giant public occasion, with all these other wheel-borne icons of British life: the Minis, the Morris Minors, the Land Rovers, the Jags and the double-decker buses.

And once again I could only scratch my head in bewilderment at the niche that this simple sitcom has somehow ended up carving itself in the national consciousness. This, the parade seemed to be saying, is historic Britain: a place defined by hallowed, regal pomp and ceremony dating back centuries, and by iconic feats of engineering that speak for the country nationally and internationally, but also, while we're mentioning it, by a dodgy three-wheeler belonging to a couple of fictional chancers from Peckham.

You can say this much about that battered old Reliant, though: at least it lasted the course under its own steam during that parade, which is more than can be said for the vintage Jaguar bearing the great chef Prue Leith that afternoon. That car conked out and had to be pushed along the Mall by a small team of stewards in hi-vis jackets.

You want to get yourself inside a reliable motor next time, Prue.

Just to be clear about it, I was not at the wheel of the Trotters' Reliant Supervan III that day – and that was not my camel-coated elbow protruding from its window. Nor did I get to be borne along in the class-leading luxury of its passenger seat. And was I disappointed about that outcome? Well, on balance, not exactly.

Don't get me wrong: I associate that vehicle with extremely cheerful memories – some of the most cheerful memories of my working life, actually. Indeed, the first thing that comes to mind when I think of that yellow van is sitting next to Nick Lyndhurst and trying – and frequently failing – to get takes done without one or both of us cracking up. Throughout the filming of *Only Fools* Nick and I were constantly on the verge of setting each other off. 'Giddy' might be the word I need here. Often that was just the irresistible consequence of the scripts, many of which seemed to have the rare attribute of becoming funnier the more often you said and heard them. Containing ourselves in the face of that kind of writing was a constant challenge, not just for Nick and me but for all the cast.

On top of that, though, Nick and I had both worked in the theatre, and we knew from rich experience that, irrespective of how good, bad or indifferent the script was, getting one of your colleagues to crack up and break character – or, as we say, to 'corpse' – was one of our chosen profession's most satisfying pleasures and, indeed, one of its most noble callings. Nick and I duly considered it a point of honour, and practically a duty, to get each other to corpse whenever the opportunity arose.*

---

* To corpse: ancient theatrical expression denoting the unsuccessful suppression of extraneous and inappropriate laughter by an actor, mid-performance. Said to originate from an incident of yore in which an actor, lying on the stage playing dead, got the giggles after somebody fluffed

It was all about not taking things too seriously, I guess – and certainly about not letting your colleagues take *themselves* too seriously. And, yes, in some of the more, shall we say, trying theatrical productions which it had been the lot of both Nick and myself to endure on our thespian journeys, I guess it was also about finding a way simply to get through it all with your spirits intact. When the mission was spirit-preservation, theatre actors could be pretty ingenious. Nick told me he was once in a production where members of the cast organised a nightly game of 'pass the golf ball'. According to the rules of this improvised sport, it was your duty to find a moment during the performance when you could slip one of your participating colleagues a golf ball which they, in turn, had to fob off on someone else – all entirely unbeknown to the audience, and certainly unbeknown to the director of the play, who would almost certainly have taken a dim view. The loser was the actor in possession of the golf ball when

---

their lines, thereby treating the audience to the sight of a body oddly heaving with badly contained laughter. Word spread, and the concept of 'corpsing' was born. This is distinct, of course, from what it could easily seem to describe: an actor forgetting their lines and freezing. The term for that is 'drying'. At moments of drying an actor has essentially two options: to call for assistance from the prompt in the wings or to seek help from a fellow cast member. A stuck Jenny Seagrove once famously took the second, more ambitious option. 'Darling, what do *you* think?' she asked Tom Conti, who was playing her lover. 'I don't know,' said Conti. 'I haven't been listening.'

the curtain came down – or, of course, anyone who gave the game away by corpsing in the meantime.

I think I can honestly say that I never played 'pass the golf ball' during my career as a theatre actor, but I did get involved in any number of pitched corpsing battles – and, indeed, in some of the lesser plays I was in, and during some of the more gruelling tours and summer seasons, I relied upon those battles to keep life interesting and morale high. And I frequently found willing adversaries. That's why I am able to disclose to you here that there was nothing that the great Bob Monkhouse wasn't prepared to reveal to you from a position in the wings if he thought it would cause you to lose your concentration and come out of character for a moment. Absolutely nothing.

Anyway, something about the confines of that Reliant, and being necessarily shut in there for long spells while cameras and lights were being positioned and lines were being run through, only encouraged the emergence from Nick and me of our inner schoolboys, which were always pretty close to the surface in any case. I don't know whether other owners had the same experience but, for us two, extraneous giggling seemed to come that much more automatically when we were in the seats of a Reliant Supervan III.

So, yes, happy memories. At the same time, all these glad associations aside, if you added up all the hours I must have spent in one of those cars down the years, all things considered, it would amount to . . . well, probably whole weeks of my life that I will never have again. And, with all respect to the manufacturer, since the show ended I have rarely found myself bursting to clamber back into one of those tiny cockpits, settle myself into the thinly upholstered seat, fire up its buzzy little engine and take the thing out on a road trip, just for old times' sake. These days, given the choice between driving a Reliant Regal Supervan and watching it go past, I'd generally choose the latter, is basically what I'm trying to say.

And that, as it happened, was the position I found myself in at the Platinum Jubilee parade that Sunday in June: watching it all go past – and from an exclusive front-row seat in the grandstand, I might add. And for this I had to thank my official royal appointment to the status of 'national treasure'.

Seriously. It was there in black and white on the invitation that arrived, summoning me to Her Majesty the Queen's Platinum Jubilee Pageant – and specifically the Marlborough House Reception for 'national treasures'. The accompanying letter informed me that not only would I be enjoying the opportunity to get an extremely privileged view of the parade, from a position 'in the heart of the celebrations', I would also be able to participate in 'the iconic national anthem moment' – taking my place on the stage outside Buckingham Palace at the climax of the proceedings, and, with Her Majesty surveying the scene from the balcony, joining a choir of my fellow 'national treasures' in a rousing rendition of 'God Save the Queen'.

Had these people ever heard me sing? Clearly not. But no matter. Given a fair wind and a decent amount of cover from my fellow national treasures, even I could probably get through the national anthem without the police needing to be called.

And cover it seemed there would be. 'You will be among many other national treasures during this moment,' the accompanying literature informed me. Which I suppose was a comforting thought. At the same time, what *is* a national treasure? I wondered about this for quite some time. Is it something that's recently been dug up? Something that could be cashed in if the economy takes a serious dive? A museum piece? And could one ever be classified as a buried national treasure?

That last question didn't bear too much thinking about.

All I can tell you on this matter is that, around my house, I have never been referred to as a national treasure. Indeed, at home the preferred term for me is 'legend' – pronounced 'leg end', ever since my daughter saw me being referred to as a 'legend' and, honking with laughter, adopted the alternative pronunciation as standard. My wife then gleefully joined her in this act of mockery. I don't see 'national treasure' replacing 'leg end' among the people closest to me any time soon, whatever the organisers of Her Majesty the Queen's Platinum Jubilee Pageant might have to say about it.

Anyway, I was keen to know what a national treasure might be expected to wear at an elite event such as this, and was quite relieved to discover that it was merely 'smart summer attire and comfortable footwear', suitable for an event which would apparently require us to 'be seated in an open-air stand for a number of hours'. I was equally relieved to discover that 'hats, fascinators and morning suits are by no means obligatory'. I always tire of my fascinator – find it less and less fascinating, if you will – and especially on those days when I'm spending a number of hours in an open-air stand.

I also learned that I would be required to produce 'one form of photographic identification' in order to be admitted: none of that 'Don't you know who I am?' stuff was going to wash in the vicinity of Marlborough House that day, clearly. And I also read up on the strictly prohibited items that should not be about my person on the day: 'umbrellas, alcohol, large flags, buggies, poles, knives . . .'

Quite right, too. The last thing you would want, on a royal occasion such as this, would be packs of armed national treasures, drunk on their own alcohol, roaming about the place in buggies, with knives and poles. It's a recipe for disaster.

'It is reasonable to expect large crowds after the show is finished,' the literature further warned me – knowledge which, I must admit, didn't make my heart sing. One huge plus, though: no mention of any kind of red carpet activity prior to the event. I know I made the claim earlier in this book that the three most depressing words in the English language are 'replacement bus service', but I've got to say, from my point of view, 'red carpet activity' runs them close. I'm very aware that this will sound baffling to the kind of people who love that sort of thing, and will only earn me limited amounts of sympathy among everyone else. After all, in the global league table of human suffering, having to walk a red carpet while a few flashbulbs go off is never going to feature very high – not as long as war, famine, plague and pestilence are in the pecking order, not to mention panto-mimes, and none of those show any sign of packing up and leaving us all alone any time soon.

But I can only speak for myself and be honest about it: and the truth is, nothing makes me feel more awkward and self-conscious than having to dawdle in front of the photog-raphers like that. I would almost rather swim to the venue through shark-infested waters than walk the red carpet, and Gill feels exactly the same way.

Anyway, whatever the challenges, physical and mental, of the Marlborough House reception for national treasures and my part in the 'iconic national anthem moment', I could at least assure myself that I had been putting some training in. Indeed, some of us began warming up for the Queen's Platinum Jubilee well before the long weekend in June – even before we had been officially designated as national treasures. In my case the limbering-up for the big anniversary commenced one day in March, with a spot of light cherry tree-planting in Aylesbury.

And by the way, I take back that stuff I said earlier in this book about my position as Britain's leading cultivator of grapefruits having been cruelly overlooked by the wider horticultural community. At any rate, someone, clearly, in a position of authority had noticed that I could be trusted with a bag of fertiliser and a shovel, and that's why I was called in to Aylesbury that day to do my bit for the Queen's Green Canopy initiative.

This was a brilliant, Jubilee-inspired idea that I was all in favour of: a project to get at least three million new trees in the ground all over the UK by the end of 2022. The then Prince Charles had launched this mission in May 2021 by planting an oak sapling in the grounds of Windsor Castle. That was also the occasion, as I recall, when the Prince tried to get a line in about thinking of the Jubilee as a 'Treebilee' – a catchphrase which never quite stuck and which was probably never really going to.

Ah, well: all of us who work in comedy have been there. You've got a line you think is a real zinger and you absolutely can't wait to get to that point in the script where you can land it on the audience – and then it dies on the air in front of your lips and goes for sweet nothing. If it's any consolation to Prince Charles, it even happened with John Sullivan scripts once or twice. Peril of the job.

Anyway, going to Aylesbury for a spot of planting that

morning was a job that I was very happy to do. May that cherry tree flourish, along with all the other 2,999,999 trees that got planted all over the country as a consequence of that initiative.

One morning, very shortly after that, there came another Jubilee-related call. Once again my writerly labours were interrupted by the arrival in the study of Gill, bearing a sheet of paper: I had been summoned to Windsor Castle.

'Given that my horticultural expertise is now a matter of public knowledge, they'll probably be wanting me to have a look at Prince Charles's Treebilee sapling,' I said, 'and offer some tips on upkeep, watering, etc. And maybe I can do something about fixing that "Treebilee" catchphrase at the same time.'

'I don't think so,' said Gill, still examining the piece of paper.

Apparently ITV were organising a television spectacular which would take place in the presence of the Queen and form that broadcaster's main tribute to her in this Platinum year. The idea seemed to be to stage a pageant telling the history of our islands, with more than a thousand performers and hundreds of horses, and with the great Dame Helen Mirren, no less, playing the role of Elizabeth I. This was all set to go off in May, a few weeks before the Jubilee weekend itself. ITV were wanting to know if I was available.

Well, of course, it stood to reason that, at such a moment in history, a national broadcaster would want to gather the nation's beknighted and be-damed thespians and instruct them to lead the country in its celebrating and reflecting. Setting down my quill, I rose slowly and crossed the room to the study's mullioned window. There I stood for a moment and looked out thoughtfully across the rolling lawns of Jason Towers, where members of the estate's gardening staff were busy feeding the peacocks and pruning the azaleas. Or were they feeding the azaleas and pruning the peacocks? From that distance, it was quite hard to tell. And anyway, my mind was on other things. I was wondering which great figure from British history ITV were considering asking me to portray.

So many sprang instantly to mind. Winston Churchill, maybe? The role of our nation's greatest ever wartime leader would be a fairly natural fit for someone with my actorly gravitas and instinctive level-headedness in an emergency, not to mention my way with a cigar and a V-sign.

Or perhaps Sir Walter Raleigh? As I hope I've made clear by now, you don't spend years in repertory theatre in Bromley without becoming a dab hand with a cloak. And maybe it would be good to be back in tights after all these years . . .

Or wait, what about Isambard Kingdom Brunel, the greatest engineering visionary Great Britain has ever known? Wasn't that the role that went to Sir Kenneth Branagh in the opening ceremony of the London 2012 Olympics? Overdue a revival, then. And who better than me to pick up Sir Ken's distinguished mantle, don a stovepipe hat and a frock coat and bring Brunel back to life in a way that the nation might well feel compelled to talk about for years, and even decades afterwards?

But wait again. If this was a history of the British Isles, they were going to have to cover the Gunpowder Plot at some point, weren't they? Maybe I could pitch up in the middle of that as Guy Fawkes, confound people's expectations, play the bad guy, show the more villainous side of my BAFTA-winning range . . . And the more bonfire-lighting side, bonfire-lighting being another of my largely unheralded but indisputable skills.

At that point, however, a thought suddenly entered my mind that caused my excited musings to freeze and a chill to pass like a cold hand around my kidneys.

Great figures from British history . . . Oh no . . . Surely not . . .

I turned to Gill, my tone suddenly full of foreboding.

'They don't want me to turn up as Derek Trotter, do they?'

Suddenly it seemed all too plausible: Dame Helen Mirren as Elizabeth I and Sir David Jason as Del Boy – all in the presence of the Queen. 'Oi! Oi! Have a luvvly Jubbly, Your Majesty!'

In fact, they didn't. Indeed, as Gill explained, they didn't want me to turn up as anybody, actually. Nobody, at least, apart from myself. The idea was that I would say a few words in tribute to the Queen and her long reign. Oh, and this wouldn't be during the show at Windsor, either. It would be filmed beforehand and dropped into the broadcast.

So, my Churchill, my Raleigh, my Brunel, my Fawkes,

even my Trotter – all shelved until the next great pageantry-based occasion in the nation's history.

Still, I refer you at this point to one of the business's most important sayings: there are no small parts, there are only small actors. And for me, at five foot six, this phrase has always held a particularly profound resonance. As has wisely been remarked: for the true actor, every role is an opportunity – even, I'm here to tell you, a role as a police-man in *Aladdin*. And perhaps *especially* a role as a policeman in *Aladdin*. If a brief cameo as myself was where ITV saw me on this occasion, rather than appearing opposite Dame Helen as, for example, a young William Shakespeare, then so be it: I would swallow my disappointment and I would rise to that opportunity and give it my very best.

Plus I suppose you could say, being myself was a role which I was extremely well placed to perform. Better placed than anybody, potentially. Indeed, you could go even further and say that myself was the role I was born to play.

Except that, strangely enough, that's not really the way I see it at all. Tracing it back, one of the fundamental reasons I became an actor, I think, was because being myself was something I didn't seem to be particularly drawn to or excited by, or even especially good at, and because it seemed to me there were all sorts of other roles that I might be better at, or certainly have more fun filling, which acting – uniquely among all the available professions, or definitely the non-criminal ones – magically opened the door to.

And then, as a consequence of performing in some of those roles, people start asking you to come along to things and be yourself again – the person you were doing your best to escape from all along. Ironic that, isn't it? I'm not sure I'll ever quite get my mind around it.

Anyway, once again, the suggestion seemed to be hovering that I might shoot this little personal message for ITV's Jubilee tribute show myself, at home. I guess that would have been the simplest option – Gill and I rigging something up as we had done for Jay Blades on that *Strictly Come Dancing* Christmas special. However, call me old-fashioned – and no disrespect intended to Jay here – but the idea of phoning in a tribute to the Queen seemed borderline treasonous to me. Why, surely, that was the kind of disrespectful behaviour for which you would have got yourself banged up in the Tower back in the day – or, at least, if they'd had television in the seventeenth century. Certainly, being asked to pay tribute to the reigning monarch on the seventieth anniversary of her crowning, and delivering a murky, hand-held iPhone recording shot against a conveniently blank patch of wall in the sitting room would feel to me a bit like turning up at the Palace for dinner in your gardening clothes: not quite the done thing.

So I told ITV that I'd be more than happy to oblige, but we'd need to film it properly, with a camera and some lights, operated by professionals, and maybe also some make-up, also operated by a professional – the way these things were traditionally done before the pandemic rewrote all the rules.

Believe me, I wasn't being a diva here, nor trying to imply that the exquisite nuances of my performance would be tragically lost if brought to the nation via the medium of my wife's phone (although the fact is, frankly, they would); I just thought that, in this special case, if the job was worth doing, it really was worth doing properly. I mean, how often does a queen get to celebrate seventy years on the throne? Fortunately ITV agreed and the message was filmed, using the conventional apparatus, in the distinguished surroundings of Hartwell House, a hotel just outside Aylesbury.

I, of course, can remember watching Queen Elizabeth's Coronation. Not having this new technological marvel called television in our home at that point – very few houses around our way did – come 2 June 1953, with a national holiday declared, we Whites all piled round to where my mate Ronnie Prior lived, a couple of terraces away from Lodge Lane, in William Street. There we were joined by the rest of the population of Finchley and several other neighbouring London boroughs, or so it seemed. The Priors had never been so popular, nor their tiny front room so in demand. We all wedged in as best we could and I – then at the tender age of twelve – remember sitting on the patterned carpet in a huddle of other junior members of the party, and gazing in wonder at the thick, curved glass of the Priors' goggle-box – which was, I'm almost certain, not the Priors' goggle-box at all, if we're going to be precise about it, but more likely a goggle-box belonging to Radio Rentals, from whom they would have had it on loan.

We watched and listened solemnly, as the occasion seemed to demand. Every now and again, not entirely in keeping with that solemnity, the picture would start to roll – literally sliding up the screen and coming round again like the reel in a fruit machine. At which point, it would be time for Ronnie Prior's dad to make an important adjustment to the internal aerial, whose job of decoding the signal on its journey from Westminster Abbey, via the antenna at Alexandra Palace, to the Priors' front room, can't have been made any easier by the presence of half of London taking up all the air in the final couple of yards.*

Yet, the occasional technical hitch aside, I can't even begin to explain to you how magical those pictures coming from the Abbey that day seemed, just by existing at all. Round about this time, I would have been regularly staring in a state of astonishment at Dick Tracy's two-way radio wristwatch,

---

* I may be wrong, but the method of attempting to cure faulty picture reception by slapping or thumping the top of the box came in a few years later, when people started having fixed, external aerials which did not lend themselves to adjustment, short of going outside and nipping up a ladder – broadly considered too much of an interruption to one's viewing. In more recent times, the advent of the flat screen, entirely dispensing with the idea of the television as a solid piece of furniture, has altogether signalled the end for improvised hands-on technical adjustments to the broadcast image – which is probably for the best, all things considered.

the miracle of technology via which, in the comic strips, our intrepid detective could communicate with the rest of his crime-busting force. Utterly incredible it seemed to me then – in a way that is hard to recapture now – the concept of moving images on a television. Yet here it was, the stuff of science fiction come to life. And in Ronnie Prior's front room, of all places.

Those images made a huge impression on me, and on all of us who watched them at the time, and I think the nature of them explains a lot about how people of my generation continue to feel about the Queen – this woman whom we first saw, by the miracle of television, at the centre of this massive ceremonial event. The pomp and the majesty of the Coronation seemed so grand to us, so imposing and other-worldly. Yet at the centre of it all was this young, slight-seeming woman. I tried to speak about some of this in the message that I recorded for that Windsor pageant. I talked about the mettle the Queen had shown, taking over from her father at the age of twenty-five, and how she came to embody dedication – the idea of putting something first. Did I manage to convey what I meant? I don't know. I certainly hope so. But I do think it wouldn't have been the same, some-how, if I had tried to say all this into a hand-held iPhone.

Having done my bit earlier, I didn't go to Windsor Castle for ITV's big show, but I did notice that my colleague in the friendly skies, Tom Cruise, was on hand for that one – covering for me, as ever. We've got each other's backs, you know. I believe the topic of what was then Tom's latest movie, *Top Gun: Maverick*, came up during his appearance that night and consequently a few people raised their eyebrows afterwards about him seeming to use this august, royal occasion as a handy platform for a spot of cross-promotion.

Now, I don't really know what went on, and I certainly don't know what the terms of Tom's appearance on the show were. But what I can say is that, in fairness to Tom, he is, without question, a raging Anglophile. As one of his closest friends – or certainly one of his newest friends – I can vouch for that. He absolutely loves and respects this place and does as much of his work here as he possibly can. So nobody ought to doubt the sincerity of his desire to be part of it all that night.

But you'd expect me to defend him, the pair of us being so close.

Of course, I'm not sure *he* knows that.

* * *

Sunday 5 June, though – that was the big one. Leaving nothing to chance, Gill and I were dropped outside the Ritz, bright and breezy, by my wise and accomplished driver, Les 'there are drivers, and there are drivers' Davis. And then we set off on the walk down St James's Street.

Smart summer attire? Check. Comfortable footwear? Check again. One form of photographic identification?

Naturally. It dawned on me, bantering with members of the security staff as we made our way through the various security checks, that, courtesy of *Only Fools*, I must be one of a very small number of people who can call a policeman a plonker and be entirely sure he'll get away with it. My newly confirmed 'national treasure' status was already yielding dividends.

So now I was inside the grounds of Clarence House, just as my friend had been when he followed that mistaken policeman's signal all those years ago, although I was planning on staying for longer than he did and definitely intended to have something to eat and drink.

It was all very luscious, as you might expect. Waiting staff circulated with trays of drinks and canapés. (I declined the alcohol. Not during the daytime, thank you, and with a national anthem to sing.) Marquees fluttered in the breeze. Flowers nodded in their borders. There was soft seating to sink into, and, of course, there were Portaloos. You shall know the poshness of an outdoor event, I always say, by the grandness of its Portaloos, and in this case I would score Her Majesty the Queen's Platinum Jubilee Pageant (Marlborough House Reception Division) a resounding overall nine out of ten, with strong performances in the key categories of roominess, decor, fragrancing and generally not looking like the kind of thing you see on a building site. Indeed, I would say the Marlborough House Portaloos were outscored only by the Portaloos in the VIP enclosure at the annual

Fairford Air Show in Gloucestershire, which, in this user's humble opinion, continue to set the standard for demountable, mass-use khazi facilities.

I'm glad to be able to share with you the fruits of my hard-won observational expertise in this important area. Remember: I went so that you don't have to. It's a service I'm happy to provide.

It was, of course, both thrilling and strange to be in an isolated enclosure so thickly peopled with faces you recognised – a national treasure island, as it were. As we sat together and took in the scene, Gill and I kept nudging each other, surreptitiously pointing and saying, 'Ooh, look – it's him/her off the telly.' I know that if you yourself are a him or a her off the telly, then people imagine that you don't really do this. But I'm here to tell you that you do – or that I do, at any rate. How could I help myself? It's not every Sunday that I get introduced to Deborah Meaden from *Dragons' Den*, watch the newscaster Michael Buerk make his way across the grass with a glass in his hand, and then, with Sir Chris Hoy the Olympic cyclist hovering in the background, fall into a conversation with Patrick Mower about Leeds, where I filmed *A Touch of Frost* and where he films *Emmerdale*.

Eventually, after this period of gentle mixing and mingling, a nice person with a clipboard came up and told us it was time for those of us who were national treasures and our partners to take our seats for the parade. So Gill and I gathered up our stuff and prepared to join the migration to the grandstand.

Actually, gathering up our stuff took a little doing, now I come to mention it. Because this was the British summer, and because the day was clearly going to be a long one, and because we are British, Gill and I had come equipped for every possible eventuality, bringing two bags between us containing rain ponchos, scarves, sweaters, gilets and other oddments of warm clothing, along with emergency provisions in the form of biscuits and bottled water. None of which, in fact, we ended up needing but, of course, it always pays to be prepared.

Note, however, that at an event at which champagne was served along with food supplied by Fortnum & Mason, I was going about the place with a packet of biscuits that I had brought from home. Old habits die hard, clearly.

Heading, as instructed, across the gardens through the throng in the direction, allegedly, of the grandstand, I concentrated on following a tall and prominent figure in a broad-brimmed hat, a riding overcoat, trousers with leather gaiters and buckles and straps on them, and a pair of magnificent brown boots. It was reassuring to think that, from here on in, if I got lost, I would at least know that Jeremy Irons was also lost.

And that was good news for Jeremy Irons, too, I suppose, because if we got really profoundly lost and hours went by and hunger set in, then I had biscuits, which I would possibly be prepared to share with him.

Although maybe he too had biscuits, stowed in that riding overcoat, or under that hat. I somehow doubted it, though.

Keeping our eyes firmly on Jeremy Irons's hat up ahead, we left Marlborough House and followed the circuitous route to the back of the grandstand – not the one in which the royal party and the political guests of honour were ensconced at various times during the weekend, but the block of seating directly next door to it. Gill and I were escorted to seats in the front row, next to Dame Jessica Ennis-Hill, the Olympic heptathlete, who was there with her mum, Alison – both lovely people. It was sobering to reflect that Jessica has been known to clear 1.91 metres in the high jump, which is nearly 30cm more than I clear when I stand up. Still, I took the opportunity to assure her, athlete to athlete, that if she ever wanted tips on landing a fall through the gap where a bar flap used to be, she should have no hesitation about getting in touch.

Incidentally, on the subject of my height, I was mildly disappointed to realise that, although our seats afforded a splendid and relaxed view of the giant screen mounted opposite the grandstand, the two horizontal metal poles forming the guard rail directly in front of us neatly obstructed my view of the parade itself. However, if I leaned forward and twisted my head slightly to one side I could get a perfect view between the poles. This didn't look especially dignified, and risked giving a bad public impression of my posture. 'Sit back,' Gill kept saying. 'Yes, OK,' was my reply, 'but all I'll be able to see is some tops of heads and some feet with a steel pole in between.'

In due course, the parade began – that famous gold coach trundling along, pulled by white horses and flanked by black ones. You've got to love the way Britain does these things, haven't you? No missiles and tanks, no overt displays of military might or proudly flaunted weapons of mass destruction, but fairy-tale horse-drawn coaches, soldiers in historic uniforms and, shortly after that, a flat-bed truck full of people break-dancing. Well, it made me proud, anyway.

There was also a series of double-decker buses, representing the decades, with various celebrities waving from the top of them. Almost the first person whose wave I recognised was Nigel Havers. Perhaps he was thinking the same as I was: that it's a lot further from Bromley Rep to the Mall than it looks.

At another moment a float went past containing a gaggle of characters from children's television across the years – the Wombles, the Tellytubbies, Peppa Pig and his various relations. And there, in among them, was Danger Mouse. Now, that really did stir something in me. Whisper it, but I think I'm as proud of having given a voice to that little character as I am of anything I've done in my career, and the fact that not only is he still fondly remembered but is deemed significant enough to rub padded shoulders on a bus with such timeless small-screen icons as the Wombles, touches me profoundly.*

And then, eventually, there it was – that only-too-familiar Reliant Regal Supervan III, a mere yellow dot on the Mall at first, but slowly getting bigger and bigger until it was unmistakable in all its tatty glory. I'd had no idea it was going to feature and I couldn't have been more delighted at what its presence said about John Sullivan and the show we all created. And I thought about how hard John would have laughed to see it there that day.

As the van rounded the Victoria Memorial, directly below us, people around me were urging me to stand up and take the salute – just as, earlier in the parade, in the front row of the directly adjacent grandstand, Prince Charles had taken the salute from the passing military. For a moment there, I was sorely tempted. But I thought it might have looked as

---

* Unlike 26 Lodge Lane or the site of the New Theatre at Bromley, Danger Mouse's former home does have a blue plaque. Just as 'Sherlock Holmes, Consulting Detective', is properly commemorated as a former resident at 221b Baker Street, so does the nearest postbox, a bit further up the road, have a blue disc stuck to its base marking it as the erstwhile home of 'Danger Mouse, the greatest secret agent in the world'. So at least one of us got our dues. In truth, though, I think a fan of the show may have stuck that tribute there, rather than the official heritage authorities, and I'm not entirely sure how permanent it may be, so see it while you can. It's an excellent little gag, though. Danger Mouse and his sidekick Penfold really did operate out of a postbox in Baker Street, so the tribute is entirely fitting.

though I was trying to draw attention to myself, and I was also worried that it might have come across as disrespectful. Silly, really. I wish I had done it now. It would have been a good gag.

As the parade drew towards its end, another clipboard-wielding member of staff appeared beside me and asked me to follow him out in readiness for the 'iconic national anthem moment'. Several others stood up and joined me, and we were led out of the back of the grandstand, along a series of paths, through a set of wrought-iron gates at the side of the Palace and into a completely canopy-covered area just to the side of the stage, where we all stood and waited. It was exactly like being backstage in a theatre, with crew, in black and wearing headsets, rushing about, while we, the national treasures, waited for our cue.

I took a moment to look about me. There were people there – no names, no pack drill – about whom my immediate thought was, 'Blimey, they've got older.' Which, of course, is a ridiculous thing to find yourself thinking. Of course they'd got older. That's what happens, if fate smiles on you and you are fortunate enough to stick around for a while. And that's the way to be thinking about it, surely: getting older is what *fortunate* people do. It's the biggest stroke of luck you'll get.

But then my next thought was equally obvious: 'If I'm looking at them and thinking, "Blimey, they've got older," then they're looking at me and thinking the same.'

There were some mixed feelings there, let me tell you.

Because age and fame are locked in a particularly trouble-some tango, aren't they? It's often said that people freeze at the age they were when they became famous – that, to some extent, the age you are when you get well known is the age you will be for the rest of your life. I'm not sure I recognise that phenomenon in myself. But then I became famous rela-tively late on – in my late thirties and early forties – when I'd already had a decent chance to find out the kind of person I was and the kind of work I was interested in doing, so maybe it works slightly differently in that case.

But what I do think is true is that we freeze other people at the age they became famous *to us*. We freeze them in our minds. How we see them from then on is always with ref-erence to how they were at that original point when they most fully entered our lives. So, even as time forges on in the opposite direction, visiting its inevitable ravages, we're always referring back to that first image that we had of some-one. Which is not especially useful and incredibly unfair, of course, but I can hardly complain about it when it happens to me, because I do it myself.

That said, standing just in front of me as we gathered for choral duty that Sunday afternoon was Sir Cliff Richard, to whom none of the normal rules on ageing seem to apply and who appears to be successfully taking all his cues in this matter from Peter Pan. Sir Cliff was wearing an extremely bright jacket made from a Union Jack. He'd been up all night with the sewing machine, by the look of it, and he was moving as spryly as if he had just hopped off a double-decker bus in 1963, rather than, as was the case, off a double-decker bus in 2022. Clearly the day that someone says Sir Cliff isn't what he used to be will be the day we can all give up. That blinding jacket, by the way, even outdid the flowery shirt Sir Cliff was wearing in the pictures I mentioned of the burned-out New Theatre in Bromley, a shared episode in our life stories about which I would have loved to shoot the breeze with him, while also seeking his advice on how not to age in any of the traditional physical senses, but sadly a moment of togetherness for us never arose.

Finally the crew in black with the earpieces began to wave us forward. It took a little while to get us all onto the stage, but once we had sorted ourselves into something like an order, I found myself at one end of the group, quite far back. Again I was struck by the thought of how different this was from the ways in which I might normally pass a Sunday afternoon. In my immediate vicinity at this point were the legendary former newscaster Angela Rippon, the chef Rick Stein, the television presenters Rylan Clark and Holly Willoughby, and the entertainer Timmy Mallett, who had thoughtfully brought a large sponge hammer with him. I racked my brain to recall whether giant foam tools were listed with umbrellas and knives among the items that we were not allowed to carry with us on the day, but self-evidently they weren't, or not in Timmy Mallett's case. He may have applied for and been granted an exemption, of course.

Not that Timmy's mallet formed any kind of obstruction to my view of what was going on. That job was done by a large piece of hanging scenery, dressing the rear of the stage and, just by chance, given the position I had taken up, completely removing the Buckingham Palace balcony from my eyeline.

Nothing I could do about that now, though. Ahead of us, with the parade complete, the barriers had been opened up and thousands upon thousands of people were streaming out onto the Mall and up to the Victoria Monument, massing in front of the stage and the Palace. Whereupon Ed Sheeran, looking almost as young as Cliff Richard, promptly serenaded them, and us, from an open area off to our right. Sheeran completed his performance, set down his guitar and walked off, brushing directly past me on his way through. I toyed with stopping him and running by him an idea that was rapidly forming in my head for an album of duets together, me and him, but, whether he read that intention in my eyes or not, he seemed to be in a blazing hurry to get away and was gone before I could grab his elbow. Maybe he had been booked to do a couple of numbers privately for the Queen. Or perhaps he needed to get to a gig somewhere else for which he was actually getting paid. I wouldn't blame him.

Then, finally, it was our big moment – our 'iconic national anthem moment', indeed. Our cue was supposed to be the arrival of the Queen on the balcony, followed by the usual trumpet fanfare, issued from the forecourt of the Palace. But would she even come out? The Queen had been carefully rationing her public appearances all weekend, had not thus far appeared during the parade, and nobody seemed to know for certain, even at that late point, whether she would now emerge. During those moments, in her continuing absence, a certain amount of confusion rippled through those of us waiting on the stage.

No need to worry, though. After a brief delay, the balcony doors finally opened and a deafening roar peeled off the crowd as the Queen appeared, followed out into the open by Prince Charles and Camilla, Prince William and Kate and Prince George. Or so I was told, anyway. I, of course, was still standing at the back of the choir, with that piece of scenery in the way. I couldn't see a thing. It could have been Alan Titchmarsh up there for all I knew about it. Except that it couldn't, in fact, because he was down here, with us.

Somewhere behind us, though, the trumpets blared and the drums rolled and, waved in by the arms of a producer, the national treasures on the stage launched into the national anthem, joined by the crowd who took over and, with the greater numbers on their side, rather drowned us out which, in my case, may have been just as well. And then the anthem ended, and those in our choir whose view was not obstructed by a piece of low-hanging scenery looked across to the balcony to drink in the celebration's climactic moment: the Queen receiving the acclaim of her subjects on the occasion of her Platinum Jubilee.

There I was, then, uniquely placed to witness history – and

yet, on account of that rogue piece of scenery, not witnessing it, or certainly not witnessing the person at the heart of it. At this point, I had a terrifically good view of Jimmy Tarbuck and, of course, of Sir Cliff Richard's jacket, and I didn't take either of those privileges for granted, but I had not so much as a glimmer of the royal party.

Suddenly I was back in the stalls before the pantomime at Golders Green, in that moment which I wrote about right at the beginning of this book, experiencing an eerily similar sense of imminent deflation. Imagine going to *Jack and the Beanstalk* and not seeing the giant. And now imagine going to the Queen's Jubilee parade and not seeing the Queen.

But what happened next was rather touching. Somehow sensing my predicament, my fellow treasures began to organise a concerted effort to shuffle this particular, shorter treasure across to a position on the stage where he might have a chance of seeing the scene on the balcony. It was very generous of everyone. I felt like a small child, getting passed through a football crowd to a place where he could get a view of the match.

It would be impossible to recount the full list of national treasures with whom I found myself literally rubbing shoulders or thereabouts during these improvised manoeuvres, but suffice it to say that, stepping into a gap created by Anita Harris and Harry Redknapp, climbing around an obliging Sir Steve Redgrave, and taking care not to step on the toes of a sweetly encouraging Bonnie Langford, I eventually, after a long and circuitous journey through seventy years of British celebrity, made it to a spot where, by craning my neck and twisting my upper body, I could lean out and bring the balcony of Buckingham Palace into view.

Just in time to catch a glimpse of a woman's retreating back, the briefest flash of emerald green, returning through the glass doors into the Palace and out of sight.

Damn it. Missed her. And despite the best united efforts of the country's national treasures, too.

Ah, well. With our duties done, and the doors behind the Palace balcony now firmly closed, the choir began slowly to shuffle away to the side of the stage to rejoin our partners, waiting in the adjacent tented village, and head for home. As we departed, some among our number – and, again, discretion being so much the better part of valour, I won't be putting any names to any faces here – were delaying our progress by taking a moment to stop and turn to the crowd and raise their arms, before basking in the cheers and applause that came their way as a result. And I found myself thinking, rather sniffily, 'Oh, come on – you've only been part of a hundred-strong choir that's sung the national anthem. Are you really taking a curtain call here? And also, you're holding some of us up.'

But then I listened to the extraordinary noise washing up from that crowd and looked out at the sea of faces, extending seemingly forever down the Mall. And I thought to myself,

'Well, actually, how many times is *this* opportunity likely to present itself?'

So I, too, stopped and I turned and looked out at all those people, the biggest gathering by a literal country mile that I had ever found myself standing on a stage in front of, and I raised my hand and gave a wave.

'Acknowledging the crowd,' I think they call it in the world of sport. And from those close enough to the stage to see me do it, a huge cheer went up and a host of hands waved back.

And what can I tell you? Those self-indulgent national treasures ahead of me in the queue to get off the stage had had exactly the right idea. It felt absolutely amazing.

EPILOGUE

. . . and a partridge up your pear tree

O*nly Fools and Horses* came back, of course. We'd wrapped up the story with 'Time on our Hands' in 1996. The Trotters were millionaires. The arc was complete. We had reached the perfect end point.

But people wanted more. Five years later, we started making what would become a further set of three Christmas specials, the first of which, 'If They Could See Us Now', went out on Christmas Day in 2001. It was watched by 21.35 million people, suggesting the show had, indeed, been missed.

That was a mixed Christmas for me, though. On Boxing Day, twenty-four hours after the triumphant return of *Only Fools*, ITV launched *Micawber*. Boy, did we think we were onto a winner with that one – my and John Sullivan's second venture together. The press lines wrote themselves really. 'From the team that brought you *Only Fools . . .*'

John was a huge Charles Dickens fan, and had tried to

interest the BBC in an adaptation of *David Copperfield*. They turned it down, though, so he went away and came up with this instead – a kind of prequel to that novel, in the form of a comedy drama series, centred on the roguish but ultimately good-hearted character of Wilkins Micawber.

I have a letter John wrote me, typically long, in the excited build-up to the project, addressing me as 'Wilkins' and using John's own adopted Victorian persona, Adolphus Snuggs-Sullivan. It's on the headed notepaper of 'The Acton Theatrical Touring Ensemble – founded 1803, proprietor: Adolphus Snuggs-Sullivan', a reference to the BBC's Acton rehearsal rooms, the 'Acton Hilton', mentioned before.

'We should meet soon to further discuss our forthcoming theatrical venture,' John/Adolphus wrote, 'with which we shall enthral the denizens of the kingdom with intrigue, veracity, humorous alliterations and fierce battle scenes (apologies, sir, wrong play! By the by, many thanks for that flask of your famous punch).'

He closed with a PS: 'What a joyous day it will be when some clever git invents the telephone.'

ITV apportioned the show a budget of around £1 million per hour, which was serious money, and let us shoot an initial run of four episodes. Each of those episodes got an average of nearly six million viewers, for which terrestrial television would happily bite off your hand at the wrist these days, but which didn't really come anywhere near to cutting the

DAVID JASON

mustard back then – or not when something was costing £1 million per hour. After those initial four episodes, the show was quietly shelved.

And our hopes had been so high. Rogues with golden hearts, people who are nearly always jovial and whose generosity exceeds their means . . . that was Del, and that was Pa Larkin in *The Darling Buds of May*, and that was Micawber, surely. This was a winning formula.

But it wasn't to be. There are no winning formulas, it turns out. There are shows that work and shows that don't work and this was a show that didn't work. I was dashed.

But you get up and move on. A producer called Rod Brown got in touch. He was involved in making a film for Sky of *Hogfather*, Terry Pratchett's Christmas-on-Discworld fantasy story. He wanted to know if I fancied playing Albert, the pork-pie-loving manservant of Death, who is Discworld's rather kindly and philosophical version of the Grim Reaper.

This was 2006, and I'd been playing Detective Inspector Jack Frost in *A Touch of Frost* for fourteen years, so I was rather attracted to the idea of acting the fool again. I was a big reader of Terry Pratchett's novels, but the character of his that I had always dreamed of playing was Rincewind, the hapless wizard from *The Colour of Magic*. So I told Rod I'd sign up for *Hogfather*, but he had to promise me that if they ever made *The Colour of Magic*, they'd give me the role of Rincewind.

We filmed *Hogfather* at Pinewood Studios, out to the west of London. Going through its border-patrol-style gates on the first day, I was transported effortlessly back to a warm Sunday afternoon in the fifties, when I and my pals, Micky Weedon and Brian Barneycoat, taking our motorbikes out joyriding, as we used to on those wonderfully traffic-free weekends, had come upon Pinewood entirely by accident. The sight of it, coming out of nowhere, had a powerful effect on all three of us – the centre of British film entertainment suddenly in front of us. We parked up and just stood and looked at it for a while, as if thinking: 'Beyond this gate lies the world of magic.' And now I was inside it, and part of it. What a journey I had come on.

Not long after that, I got stuck up in its roof. Typical. I was riding the Hogfather's hog-drawn flying sleigh at the time, in the company of Death – as you do. Death's voice in that film was supplied by Ian Richardson, with whom I'd worked on *Porterhouse Blue*. This was to be Ian's last role, sadly.

But Death's body was being provided by a six-foot-seven Dutch actor called Marnix Van Den Broeke, who would later become the requisite cloaked skeleton courtesy of some CGI trickery, post-production. So there we were, the pair of us, a contrast in lengths, you could say, borne aloft in one of Pinewood's cavernous studio spaces by a sophisticated system of hydraulics, and merrily flying our sleigh against a green screen, when – whump. The power went out, along with the lights, and our sleigh froze.

Somewhere below us, an enormous downpour of rain had abruptly flooded the studio. The crew duly evacuated the building, as instructed. But Marnix and I were in no position to do any evacuating. We were left high and dry in the dark for what felt like hours, and would no doubt have got many games of noughts and crosses played, had we only had a pen, and had there only been enough light.

Left hanging about, yet again: it really does seem to have been an unusually strong theme in my career.

Still, the electricity went back on eventually, and the film got made and it seemed to go over well – and still goes over well each year, in fact. In a celebratory mood, I took home, courtesy of the props department, Death's giant hour-glass 'life-timer'. It stands to this day on the stairs in my house and prompts me to reflect every time I pass and notice it, not on Death and our ever-elapsing time on earth, as it happens, but on what a laugh it was making *Hogfather*. Tremendous fun.

Rod Brown was as good as his word, and two years later I got to play Rincewind in *The Colour of Magic*. This time I took home what Pratchett fans know well as the Luggage. Well, nobody else seemed to want it, and I thought it would make a nice ornament for the house – a conversation piece, if you will. After all, how many homes do you know that have large, polished trunks with multiple human feet protruding from the bottom of them?*

Don't get me wrong, by the way: I don't always walk away from shoots with the furniture. There are actors who are a little notorious for backing their cars round on the final day of production. No names, no pack drill. But I am not one of them. My total haul from all those years on *Only Fools* was a pair of bottles of Peckham Spring Mineral Water, with authentic labels (if not authentic mineral water), and, as already declared, a few prize items from Del's exclusive wardrobe, including one sheepskin coat, which my wife is very keen that I shouldn't wear. And though I have fought her on this, I must reluctantly admit, with the passing of time, that she's got a point. Age has slightly withered that coat now, and in some areas slightly expanded it, and it makes me look less like Del these days and more like a moulting camel.

It possibly makes me smell a little like a moulting camel, too. But let's not go there.

However, the Luggage did accompany me home, in all its fibre-glass glory. And when Gill suggested that the kinds of conversation this intended conversation piece would inspire weren't necessarily the kinds of conversation anybody

---

* The Luggage is a highly useful invention: a capacious storage unit which nobody ever needs to lift or carry because it gets itself around on its own many feet. Just to be clear, the feet on my prop version were fibre glass, not human, and didn't actually work.

sensible would be keen to have, I placed it on the little island in the middle of our pond where it could serve magnificently as a feed storer for the pair of swans who descended to live on that island one breeding season. (We seem to be pretty busy with the birds round my way. Swans, geese, owls – you name it. If it's got feathers on, the chances are it will stop by for a free meal.)

And then one evening I got to thinking: props from popular TV shows and films are worth a bit of money. The Luggage probably deserved a more dignified fate than to sit out there in the elements, in the middle of somebody's garden, storing bird feed. Maybe I could auction it off for charity and raise a few hundred quid for some deserving cause. Wouldn't that be a good thing to do?

I resolved to go out there the very next day, bring in the Luggage, clean it up a bit and start to look into ways that I might sell it.

The following morning I set out across the garden. It had been a stormy night – indeed, a dark and stormy night, just like in the very best stories. The grass was scattered with bits of debris torn off the trees by the wind. It looked like the Luggage's last night in the open had been a real tester.

A tester indeed. When I reached the pond, I saw that a tree had blown down and fallen directly on my piece of precious film memorabilia, splitting it neatly in half.

Anybody want to buy half the Luggage? With a bag of related splinters? One previous slightly careless owner?

I didn't think so.

Only one possible conclusion can be formed about this strangely timed intervention. It was a cautionary message from the spirit of Sir Terry Pratchett himself – a warning to yours truly not even to entertain the idea of converting purloined elements of the late novelist's franchise into filthy lucre.

*   *   *

God bless Derek Trotter. I've had some causes to curse him down the years, but I know what I owe him. Basically he launched me into the nation's Christmas tree and I never came down. It amazes me, the things I now get asked to do simply because I once appeared on the television at Christmas, running through the mist in a daft Batman outfit.

For instance, in the summer of 2021, I was asked to record a message of support for Gareth Southgate and the England football team on the eve of their European Championship final against Italy. Now, what I know about football could be written on the back of a stamp and leave room over for illustrations. At Popes Garage, the car repair shop where I got my first job after leaving school, there would often be a bit of a kick-about during lunch hour in the yard, and I would take part in a desultory and frequently satirical manner and in the hope of being regarded as one of the boys. It rarely went well. It was also probably the last time I kicked a ball.

If you had told those guys, during one of those lunchtimes, that one day I'd be giving the England team a pep talk ahead of a major final, they would have laughed themselves so rigid they would have had to go home for the afternoon.

Lo, though, once again that which was unlikely came to pass. Always willing to play our part, Gill and I got the phone out and we filmed a little message. I said hello to Gareth – asked him if he was still over at Southgate, which isn't that far down the road from where I grew up . . . I made a lot of silly jokes, basically, and then told the boys to give it their all, make us proud, win it for England.

After I'd sent it off, I thought about the players, watching this piece of nonsense. Those guys are mostly in their twenties; many of them weren't born when *Only Fools* was regularly on telly. And yet the show would still mean something to many of them. It gets passed down, and I can never quite get my head around that – around having been part of a television programme, not just that families would watch together back then, but that families might watch together now: that generational legacy, each new generation passing the show on to the next and all of them still able to enjoy it. That was the unifying force which John Sullivan dreamed of creating when he was writing *Only Fools and Horses*, and I can only think it would delight and amaze him to see it in action all these years later.

Anyway, I did my bit for Gareth and for England, and then I sat back and watched the game on the night, quietly confident that my intervention would produce the desired result.

And what happened? They lost on penalties.

I felt a bit guilty, really. Could I have done more? Surely not. I gave it 100 per cent – honest, Gareth.

But even this pales beside the invitation that came my way via email in the summer of 2022. A statue was going to be unveiled at RAF Hawkinge in Kent, the former RAF station from which planes flew for the Battle of Britain and many other aerial missions during the Second World War. The statue was of a group of airmen at rest on the grass between missions, and relatives of those airmen would be present. Prince Charles had been going to attend the unveiling, but something had come up. Would I consider stepping into the breach and doing the honours?

Now, I would have responded warmly to this invitation in any circumstances. It's in my roots as a war baby who survived the Blitz to welcome any chance to pay tribute to the sacrifices made by airmen, and so many others, in that awful conflict. And I loved the fact that relatives were going to be there – a really important reminder of something we should never lose sight of about those who served and gave their lives: they were people with families and loved ones.

But I did, I admit, have a little chortle at the thought of the organisers going down their list of possible unveilers.

'OK, so sadly the heir to the throne is out. Let's try David Jason.'

Do I glimpse a hint of a possible future for me here – some kind of job-share arrangement with our new King, helping out when the royal schedule gets a bit tight, and picking up the slack? Well, OK. I do have one or two projects of my own on the go, and, of course, I'm still waiting for Tom Cruise to get back to me on the body-double thing. But we could probably work something out, if that's the direction this is going. Maybe we should put a lunch in the diary and see where we all stand.

But let's get Christmas out of the way first, shall we? By the time you read this, likely as not, the nights will have drawn right in and a tangible sense of anticipation for the 'big day' will be brewing. At Jason Towers, the paper chains will be going up, a warm fire will be crackling in the grate, the cooks will be energetically basting meats in the kitchens, and the peacock pruner will once again be looking forward eagerly to his annual morning off.

I've been given to a little grumbling about the festive season and its various trials and tribulations down the years, I don't deny. But looking back in order to put this book together, I realise that, give or take a couple of pantomime experiences and one or two tight moments in harnesses, Christmas has been quite good to me, really. Overwhelmingly good, in fact.

And yes, there's the forced jollity and the shopping and the possibility of that tricky annual drinks party, and the thousand tiny stresses and irritations the season is prey to.

But maybe, if we're ever tempted to feel vexed about it all, we should cleave to the words of Scrooge's nephew, Fred, in *A Christmas Carol* – words on this matter that nobody, surely, will ever better.

For it is Fred who describes Christmas as 'a good time; a kind, forgiving, charitable, pleasant time; the only time I know of, in the long calendar of the year, when men and women seem by one consent to open their shut-up hearts freely, and to think of people below them as if they really were fellow-passengers to the grave, and not another race of creatures bound on other journeys'.

Well, amen to that, Fred. Amen to that.

Now, if you'll excuse me, I have a pressing appointment with a Victorian gazunda.

Those amaryllis bulbs don't plant themselves, you know.

And this year, surely this year . . .

APPENDIX

Covid and carpet burns

I didn't get to unveil that monument at Hawkinge. Instead of standing in for Prince Charles that day, I was sealed up in my bedroom staring miserably at the ceiling. After two and a half years of dodging it, I had tested positive for Covid-19.

I was bitterly disappointed. I'd been so looking forward to meeting everyone there and doing my bit. (Go, dear reader, if you get the chance, to the Kent Battle of Britain Museum at Hawkinge airfield. Tell them I sent you.)

My symptoms: severe cough, sore throat, loss of appetite, and carpet burns. The last of those was my fault for getting up to go to the loo. Well, when you've got to go . . .

Boom: my legs turned to jelly and I went down like a ton of bricks. Thankfully, the radiator cushioned my fall. I tried to stand, but my limbs had all the strength of overcooked spaghetti. With my pasta arms, I couldn't reach the mobile phone that Gill had left with me, and my throat was so sore that I could only manage a hoarse croak, rather than an audible cry for help.

So I had no choice but to improvise. I set off for the bedroom door, face-down, via the carpet.

In the whole of my acting career, I believe this was the only time I have ever been called upon to portray a caterpillar. With my legs and arms failing me, I resorted to using my head to propel me forward for good measure. It was a long struggle. Doomy thoughts began to overcome me. Was this how it would end? Face-down in the shagpile in my underpants? I began to regret not pinning my knighthood to those underpants – some shred of dignity at the last.

I may have been getting a little delirious.

But then, at the moment of maximum despair, the door flew open and a figure burst in wearing a *Better Call Saul* onesie with its hood up, two face-masks and a pair of disposable gloves. It was Gill in her improvised PPE (*Better Call Saul* is our favourite Netflix series; we've seen it and bought the onesie). At the sight of me face-down on the carpet in my underpants, my wife let out a scream of horror, assuming I had collapsed and banged my head. Her fears were by no means alleviated when she saw two big marks on my bonce.

'Carpet burns,' I explained, wheezily. 'It's a long story . . .'

Gill helped me back to bed and issued me with strict instructions not to venture forth again unaccompanied. She also added a walkie talkie to my communication system and put up a camp bed for herself right outside the bedroom door in case of any more hoarse croaks in the night.

After four days in bed, my limbs resumed the strength of uncooked rigatoni and I was on my way back. I was lucky. I got Covid-19 late, and with four doses of the vaccine inside me. I wonder, though: how many people can add 'carpet burns to the forehead' to their list of Covid symptoms?

INDEX

THE HOUSE OF THE DEAF MAN

T0096823

PARTHIAN

Parthian, Cardigan SA43 1ED
www.parthianbooks.com
The House of the Deaf Man first published as *Dom hluchého* in 2012 by
Marenčin PT
© 2012 Peter Krištúfek
This translation © 2014 by Julia Sherwood and Peter Sherwood
Cover design by Janka and Palo Balik
This book has received a subsidy from SLOLIA Committee,
the Centre for Information on Literature in Bratislava, Slovakia.
PRINT ISBN 978-1-909844-27-8
EPUB ISBN 978-1-909844-28-5
Editor Francesca Rhydderch
Typeset by Elaine Sharples
Printed by Pulsio SARL
Published with the financial support of the Welsh Books Council
British Library Cataloguing in Publication Data
A cataloguing record for this book is available from the British Library.

Peter Krištúfek

THE HOUSE OF THE DEAF MAN

translated by
Julia Sherwood and
Peter Sherwood

JULIA SHERWOOD (née Kalinová) was born and grew up in Bratislava, then Czechoslovakia. After studying at universities in Cologne and Munich she settled in the UK, where she spent more than 20 years working for Amnesty International. Since 2008 she has worked as a freelance translator from English, Czech, Slovak, German, Polish and Russian into Slovak and English. Her book-length translations include *Samko Tále's Cemetery Book* by Daniela Kapitáňová, and *Freshta* by Petra Procházková. She has also translated work by the Slovak writers Uršuľa Kovalyk, Balla, Jana Juráňová and Leopold Lahola, among others.

PETER SHERWOOD is a linguist and translator. He taught Hungarian language, linguistics and literature at the School of Slavonic and East European Studies (now part of University College London) until 2007. From 2008 until 2014 he was the first László Birinyi, Sr., Distinguished Professor of Hungarian Language and Culture in the University of North Carolina at Chapel Hill. He has translated the novels *The Book of Fathers* by Miklós Vámos and *The Finno-Ugrian Vampire* by Noémi Szécsi as well as stories by Dezső Kosztolányi, Zsigmond Móricz and others, along with works of poetry, drama and philosophy.

Peter Krištúfek is an award-winning writer and director. His writing has appeared in Slovak and foreign anthologies, including the *Best European Fiction*, and many Slovak newspapers and magazines. He lives in Bratislava, Slovakia. www.peterkristufek.com

I laughed to hear an elfish spirit, drenched by the shower,
buzz around the lighted house, without
being able to find the door by which I had entered.
(ALOYSIUS BERTRAND: *Gaspard de la nuit[1]*)

The houses of tired feet
have the greatest number of steps.
The houses of crippled arms
have no railings.
The houses of the dying
have bars on the ground floor.
(VLADIMÍR HOLAN)

One is always located at a post through
which various kinds of messages pass.
(JEAN-FRANÇOIS LYOTARD)

But the difference between the present and the past is
that the conscious present is an awareness of the past
in a way and to an extent which the past's awareness
of itself cannot show.
(T.S. ELIOT)

[1] *Gaspard de la Nuit, Old Paris, III, The Lantern, translation © John T. Wright, 1977*

PREFACE

This is not a true story but it could easily be.

To begin with, however, there are two true stories.

Family history is a strange thing. As you get to know people who were here before you, you also learn a few things about yourself. You recognize yourself in the faces in photographs; you detect (whether with delight or shame) your own way of thinking.

One of the stories brushed past me, imperceptibly, as long ago as 1984. My maternal grandfather, Vladimír Kriško, was an elite war pilot. An ace fighter pilot. A veteran of countless dogfights during World War II, he joined the Slovak National Uprising against the Nazis and was the commander of the insurgents' Three Oaks airfield near Zvolen. After the war he continued to serve in the army, working at the Ministry of Defence with the rank of lieutenant colonel until he was suddenly dismissed in 1952 – apparently because my grandmother insisted that her newborn son – my uncle – had to be baptized. Which was, to put it mildly, hardly the thing to do in those days. And so my grandfather spent the rest of his life as a warehouseman (or, to use his better-sounding official title, warehouse executive) and later as a bookkeeper with the State Forestry Enterprise. He died in 1988. In the early 1990s he was posthumously rehabilitated and promoted to the rank of colonel. A classic story with a predictable beginning and end, not worthy of further exploration.

In 1984, to mark the fortieth anniversary of the Uprising, we were given a school assignment to ask any of our relatives who had taken part in the events to tell us about their experience, and write an essay about it. My grandmother, a former teacher, summoned my grandfather into the living room. I got pen and paper ready, we sat down on the sofa and I shot off a starter question:

"So, how many German planes did you actually shoot down...?"

Grandfather responded with an uneasy silence, as if he didn't really know what to say. I put this down to his innate modesty and an unwillingness to rake up ancient history. Grandmother had to come to his rescue, cleverly supplying a couple of standard stories gleaned from books and films of the period. I wrote these up, got an A and a commendation, and everybody was happy.

In 2008, twenty years after my Grandfather's death, a brightly coloured postcard landed in my letterbox. Showing some kind of pleasure boat sailing down the beautiful Rhine, it was addressed to my grandmother, who was no longer with us. On the reverse were a few sentences scribbled in a spidery hand, explaining that the writer (a Slovak who happened to be a steward on the pleasure boat pictured, the *River Symphony*) was researching the history of wartime pilots of the 1940s and would be interested in photographs of the period – or later – that might show my grandfather. I didn't give the postcard much thought and promptly forgot about it until I came across it accidentally while tidying up. I wrote back on a whim. Some two months later, when the sailor's tour of duty was over, we arranged to meet outside the Franciscan Church in Bratislava and then went to a dark and dingy cavern of a pub where, over a glass of disgustingly tepid beer, he introduced me to my grandfather in his full glory, shedding clear light on him for the first time.

He took out a photocopy of my grandfather's funeral card, which he must have got from my grandmother all those years ago, or have acquired in some other way. With a shiver down my spine I recognized my own childish signature ...*our beloved husband, father, father-in-law*... Reluctantly, through the thick smoke and the din of drunken voices, I began to listen.

Having graduated from the military academy in the 1930s, my Grandfather became a fighter pilot, rising swiftly through the ranks in the army of the Slovak puppet state. In 1941, now a lieutenant, he was sent to Karup-Grove in Denmark as part of the 5th Slovak Staffel/Jagdgruppe Drontheim, where he spent some months training as a German Messerschmitt pilot – so that explained why I kept finding wartime Danish coins in our cellar. After his return he was transferred to the eastern front as a fighter squadron commander. To Russia, in other words, since Slovakia had proudly joined the fight for a New Europe alongside the German Reich.

Documents show he flew 156 sorties, shot down nine Soviet planes, earning him the sobriquet *flying ace*, an achievement matched by only two other Slovak officers. Grandfather kept a record of his kills and had to produce witnesses for each of them but he was officially credited with only nine, less than half of the actual number. Although his Messerschmitt Bf109F-4 was heavily damaged in a dogfight on 3 February 1943, by some miracle he managed to fly it safely back to Krasnodar. In recognition of these spectacular achievements he was awarded the Iron Cross, First and Second class for the Campaign Against the USSR, and a number of lesser decorations, including the charmingly named Gold Cross of the Virtutea aeronautică from the Romanian fascist state.

The question is: could he have told his not quite eleven-year-old grandson in 1984, who was writing a school essay on the subject to boot, that the planes he had shot down were not German but Soviet?

After returning from Russia, my grandfather, by then promoted to first lieutenant, was put in charge of the 13th Air Squadron, which was deployed to the airfield in Vajnory and later in Piešt'any to defend western Slovakia from US air raids. By a stroke of good fortune, on the day his squadron was wiped out and on which nearly all the pilots perished he had gone to Bratislava for a medical check-up. Had he flown that day, it is very likely that this book would never have been written.

He had, of course, brought down a number of US fighters in air-to-air combat. The Americans usually ejected, and those who were caught on the ground were interned in a PoW camp in Grinava near Pezinok.

Cut. Enter another man – my father's grandfather, my great-grandfather, an upstanding citizen of the small town of Pezinok. František Tuma owned a quarry and a haulage company with a sizeable fleet of vehicles.

After the Uprising broke out the Germans decided to evacuate the Grinava PoW camp, which in plain English meant that the US pilots had become something of a burden. In other words they were about to receive *Sonderbehandlung*, special treatment, which normally meant extermination. Under cover of night my great-grandfather Tuma loaded 29 American pilots dressed in Slovak army uniforms onto a lorry (or rather, a small bus) – they were armed and a machine gun was ready on the roof – and drove them to insurgent-held territory (in his own words: "It was a clear night, we drove without lights on…"). They reached the Three Oaks airfield (this is actually documented by a photograph taken on 7 October 1944) from where an Allied plane transported them to the Italian base at Bari.

In the early 1990s my father received an official letter from the US embassy. Its final sentence read: *Let me express my heartfelt admiration for your late grandfather's courageous act. He will be remembered with our deepest gratitude. Yours respectfully, Theodore E. Russell, Ambassador of the United States of America.*

In October 1944, the commander of the Three Oaks airfield was my maternal grandfather, Captain Kriško, who had by then – on 30 August 1944 to be precise – joined the Uprising. He was in charge of air reconnaissance, air raids on enemy (now German) positions and, for a while, he was also responsible for the temporary airfield in Donovaly, where an aircraft was waiting to take the rebel generals Viest and Golian to Moscow. However, as we now know, they chose to retreat to the mountains, setting the aircraft on fire before abandoning their position.

But let us return to the US pilots. It is quite likely that they included some actually shot down by my grandfather. But even if he wasn't personally responsible, it would have been a member of the 13th Air Squadron under his command throughout the summer of 1944 who was. And, as we know, it was these fighter pilots who failed to prevent the air raid on Bratislava's Apollo refinery because they had secret orders to save their fighter jets for the Uprising that was being planned.

This is the point at which my audience usually loses the thread. The story seems to fray like some old jumper. The reasons are clear: in spite of all the twists and turns over a short period of time this is the story of two people – my maternal grandfather and paternal great-grandfather. And that's it.

I have no idea if these two men ever met.

And even if they did, I'm sure it would never have occurred to them that they had something in common.

Me.

I'm certain they would never have guessed that one day they

4

would meet in this book, or in any other book for that matter. That someone would bring their stories together in this way.

I am sure they would never have guessed that their encounter would result in *The House of the Deaf Man*.

This book is not a record of my family history and was never intended to be. After all, any attempt at recording it is always doomed to be a piece of fiction, just like any private diary that is published, since everyone feels the need to clear their name and justify the motives for their actions.

The House of the Deaf Man tells how the astounding twentieth century affected the lives of the people of Slovakia.

Astounding in every sense of the word.

Peter Krištúfek
Bratislava, October 2012

PROLOGUE

"Many people have become aware and understand the importance, impact and influence of even only a few principles of Feng Shui, the ancient Chinese art of placement that brings luck, harmony, health, love and prosperity. It is increasingly popular today in the Western world and in our country, too. Many people now apply its essential principles in their environment and in designing their dwellings."

It is almost spring and the trees I see from the car have been gnawed clean by the cold and bleakness. It's been only a few days since snow has retreated from these parts. The white blanket of the landscape is dotted with the black of rooks and crows. I have to keep glancing at my red car from time to time to reassure myself that some catastrophe hasn't bleached the world of colour. As a matter of fact, everything drifts towards greyness. Like clothes that have turned pale and grey through repeated washing. Grey is the queen of all the colours. And also their death.

Oh dear. What a cheerful train of thought! Well, I am seventy so it's quite natural to feel that the end of the world is nigh, and surely this is part and parcel of it?

But then again, it might just be because of the talk I've been listening to on the car radio. Lately I have found that music irritates me. It is charged with too much emotion, something I've been taking care to avoid. Maybe today is the day. Ever since our house started going to seed after my father died, I have been tiptoeing around the place as if it were contaminated. Every time I come back, I am seized by this terrible anxiety. I left Bratislava half an hour ago, heading for Brežany, some 50 kilometres away. I haven't been back for a few months and I'm tempted to ask directions at the petrol station, just to see what it feels like. I would find my way there blindfold – like when you try to walk with your eyes closed for as long as you can. I pay without a word and get back into the car. And lo and behold, the sun makes a brief appearance.

I toss a coin. This is an old habit of mine. I'm painfully indecisive and this technique has often helped me over the years. Heads or tails – heads means *keep going*, tails means *go back*.

It's tails.

But that's not what I want. I toss the coin again.

Tails again. I think about it. No.

Finally, at the third attempt, it's finally heads.

All right then, you've talked me into it. I continue my journey.

I pretend there is an alternative. But the truth is – however theatrical this may sound – this will be my last visit ever to the old house in Brežany. It will be gone the next time.

The radio continues: *"It all starts with the position of your block of land. Evaluating the site and its surroundings, always take into account the placement of your house. The block of land is preferably flat or sloping upwards. As for the surrounding area, it is preferable to keep the mountains at the back of the house (they are then acting as security and stability for the inhabitants). Potential 'water' (or its symbol) should be flowing gently in front of the house in an auspicious direction.*

Taking into account the geomantic survey of your block of land and the location of the ley lines and underground water veins, you should avoid sleeping above those health hazards, and main bedrooms should not be located above them. Your planned design and house orientation should incorporate the best possible Feng Shui principles to maximize your well-being. A grid can be designed showing the influence and impact of this building on various parts of your life (Career, Love, Health, Respect, Prosperity, Personal Growth, Travels, Helpers, Children, Creations, Studies, Openness, Fame and Recognition)."

I turn off the motorway and speed past the mud-spattered sign for Brežany.

What makes life so exciting is that as you throw a message in a bottle into the sea you only know one part of the story. You don't know the ending. That's what my father used to say.

As our old house gradually materializes in front of me, I hear the echo of us children shouting *čik-čik, domček!*, Home, home, our very own! We used to chant this when we finally reached the haven of our house. It was our private spell.

A spell that didn't work.

8

As we set out on our wild, spur-of-the-moment trip to Spain with my father's ashes in a cigar box, my son Bony remarked that no matter what I said, the past didn't really exist. And I still don't know whether those few days we spent together in the car have made him change his mind. His three-year-old son, my grandson Samko, asked me the other day:

"When is yesterday?"

I didn't know what to say.

Part 1

The Fates

1.

Every clock in this house shows a different time.

That's how this place has always felt to me – while I was growing up and also later, when I kept coming back, for whatever reason.

You enter the house from a busy street through a tall gate with an arched portal. Until a few years ago, if you continued straight ahead you would have found yourself in a vast back garden with fruit trees, or you could have taken a turn and entered the house. It consists of a ground floor and a first floor with spacious sunny rooms and high, old windows.

The house has a small front garden. Some of it used to be covered in creeping vines that formed tunnels and passages. This is where my parents would sometimes leave me in the afternoons to nap in my pram.

My mother's face appears to me. She is bending over me. I have just turned one. That's how I imagine the scene, probably from a photo I once saw and have lost long ago. Because you don't normally retain memories like these.

The next thing I remember: I'm four years old and I have suddenly come to life, suspended in the air.

I'm in the garden, in the middle of a fall. I have climbed onto a chair to get a better view but couldn't keep my balance. This is my first and most distant memory.

It was a sunny day in May, one of those when you're supposed to have friends and acquaintances over and have fun. A Saturday or a Sunday. We children played hide-and-seek behind the house while our parents sat around the bonfire, drinking and laughing. They filled the garden. The elderflower was in blossom and the fragrance of the linden trees wafted in from the distance, suffusing the night – isn't it strange how memories are linked to smells? A cat ran across the garden now and then.

I was told to count to a hundred. To block my ears and count out really loud. The other children rushed off to find hiding places. Tightly screwing up my eyes I skipped the odd number but I tried my best. *Forty-five… forty-six… forty-seven… forty-eight… forty-nine… fifty!* Sweating with excitement and concentration I finally shouted – *One hundred!* – and turned on my heels.

13

I turned on my heels and found the huge garden empty.

Just glasses, plates, bottles and a smouldering fire. Not a soul. Silence. Confused, I ran around for a while, gradually gripped by horror. I was the only person left on the planet! So I climbed onto the chair and began to howl.

My father and mother picked me up from the ground. I had grazed my nose. The other grown-ups, who had all conspired to hide quietly, tried to suppress their laughter.

And today, just like then, as I gaze into the overgrown and deserted garden of this house from the street outside, it is empty again. I am all alone on an empty planet. A lonely astronaut, lost in the grass and the thicket, beneath trees untended for years, everything overrun by plants. Plants that had devoured the house, slowly and steadily.

These are the kinds of random thoughts that pass through my head as the engine cools down and the car is buffeted by a gust of wind every time a lorry passes by.

Eventually, I turn off the radio. This time it vies for my attention with news that Abu Sayaf's militant Muslim group has claimed responsibility for the explosion on Super Ferry 14 in the Philippines, in which 116 have died, making it statistically the most lethal attack ever at sea. I catch the beginning of a discussion on our impending accession to NATO and the European Union, open the car door and emerge into a light drizzle that has supplanted the intermittent sunshine from a minute ago.

For the first time in ages I pluck up the courage to clamber to the top of the church tower to get an aerial view of Brežany. The town has swollen and spilled out into the distance.

The church is quite large, and the crypt below contains the usual scraps of cloth, old bones and metal, an assortment of curiosities for the occasional tourist. The spire lost its claim to be the tallest building around many years ago and these days you can no longer see as far as the end of town from the top of the tower.

A sea of roofs stretches away below me, many of them dilapidated and damaged. Modern glass and steel structures protrude from gaps between them like scars. Sometimes only the walls on either side suggest that something is missing – the unfinished brick boundaries of houses no longer there. Housing estates with their regular grid of streets stretch away across the hills to the north and east. The scene is divided by the straight line of the wide and dirty Sálava river – a stream that has never allowed itself to be defied or erased, only straightened out and regulated, something that happened as early as the 1970s, when ironing out its twists and turns, felling trees and changing the direction of rivers was in vogue.

Directly below me in the main square a huge billboard has sprouted up, proclaiming *TESCO 1.2 km*. Štúr Street, nowadays widened to four lanes, snakes around the houses on its way south.

The History of our Town page on the town website, after relating in great detail what Rákóczi, Matthias Corvinus, King Béla IV and anyone who is anyone had to say about Brežany, and enumerating every piece of land they had donated or taken away, goes on to list the new housing estates and all the improvements that came after the Velvet Revolution. However, it maintains a discreet silence with regard to the era that left the most profound mark on Brežany. The era that wiped out most of the town.

The front gardens are now largely empty but when I was young, I remember, there was a walnut tree growing in front of nearly every house. The tree provided shade and its scent repelled insects and mosquitoes. Most of the trees have by now been cut down, leaving only grass or concrete. The present-day inhabitants of Brežany like it that way. That's what they see on TV.

When I wet my finger with saliva and wave it in the air following the direction of the wind and turn off Štúr Street into a gap among the buildings, I come across our house. My house, my father's house, my father's father's house.

Here the wind usually blows from the east.

Our house has always exercised a magnetic pull, which I tried to resist right until the last moment when I could no longer delay entering. Just like now. I've always come up with any number of reasons for putting off the moment. But the house would always catch me in its spider web and wouldn't let go. And it's just got worse as the years went by.

Staying in the same place rots the soul, my father's brother, Uncle Rudo, used to say.

If that happens you must ask someone to come, pack your things, bundle you into the passenger seat and whisk you away. Or it may cost you your life.

15

Or worse. You can never tell.

It happened to me once, and my sister Tina came to my rescue. If it hadn't been for her I would have stayed here forever, under its spell like some deranged Sleeping Beauty.

My mobile has packed up so I go to the nearby post office to phone my son Bony. He sounds grumpy. I tell him I've arrived and ask if he really doesn't want anything from the house. As I stand in the queue my eyes are drawn to a poinsettia in a McFlurry plastic cup.

Well, well. So Mr McDonald has made it all the way here. Well done!

For some mysterious reason the lady behind the counter smiles at me.

People in Brežany used to recognize my face. The first time it happened it gave me a bit of a shock. Then I realized I have my father's face, my grandfather's face, my great-grandfather's face… A family countenance, passed on from one generation to the next. Apart from subtle variations in individual features a face remains basically the same. It is a face that doubles as a business card.

I've never had to introduce myself. The minute I walked out into the street someone would come up and address me (sometimes uncertainly, sometimes without a second thought) as *Alfonz* and patiently I would put them right: *Adam. My name is Adam.* But most of them paid no attention and went on calling me *Alfonz, Alfie* or just *Doctor.*

My father had a small scar on his left cheek. When I was little I used to think that it had happened while he was drinking coffee, that one of those small spoons with a sharp end had made a mark on his skin because he forgot to take it out of his mouth. Nobody was able to persuade me otherwise.

The scar didn't fade with age and my eyes would invariably be drawn to it when I sat with him in the kitchen. By then he was barely able to hear me, which simplified our dealings no end, since he was the one doing the talking while I was expected only to listen. I couldn't tear my eyes away from the narrow slits of his eyes either. They mesmerized me.

2.

When I was small I was convinced that the wardrobe on the first floor concealed a passage into another house. A house identical to ours, only much more mysterious. It might even have been its mirror image. You would open the wardrobe door, push the clothes aside and you'd find another door. You wouldn't need a key, as it wasn't locked. All you had to do was push down the handle and… On the other side there would be similar clothes that would likewise have to be pushed aside, and behind them an identical room…

This is the first thing that crosses my mind as, after a long absence, I enter this house located in what used to be a quiet street in the small town of Brežany. Years ago the town, too, used to be small. It has gradually swollen and grown, turning into a happy, dirty city, indistinguishable from many others in this country.

The house originally belonged to my grandparents, then my parents, and now it stands empty. After a while you might begin to doubt that anyone could ever have lived here. But apparently someone has. Everything points in that direction.

All you need to do is feel your way to the fuse-box, guided by memory, and turn the power on – amazingly, it still works – avoid the dangling cobwebs, exhale to get rid of your anxiety, draw the broken blinds and throw open the windows. Let some fresh air into the place.

I have tonight and all day tomorrow to sort everything out. The following morning a lorry will come and the removal men will load up everything that is still of any value.

The house used to be filled with the scent of vanilla. Actually, it was just me who believed it was vanilla (because my mother used to keep a vanilla pod in the sugar bowl) and it wasn't until I picked up a particular brand of eau de cologne at the chemist's and took a sniff that I realized this was what my father had used as aftershave. Combined with the cigarette smoke in his room this was what gave the house its unique atmosphere. Faux vanilla.

A great many things have vanished. What remains is wallpaper hanging down from the walls, cobwebs, a straight line dividing beige from white, orange from green, dating back to the times

17

Father didn't feel like moving away the furniture every time he redecorated the walls. Now all that's left are these useless lines, like a high tidemark of my childhood. And the wardrobe. The upstairs wardrobe at the top of the spiral wooden staircase leading to the attic. It was Father who came up with the idea of the other door and the other house, a mirror image of ours, and whenever he mentioned it everyone in the family nodded and smiled mysteriously.

I sit down on the stairs and inhale the air thick with the smell of damp plaster and musty clothes. I close my eyes a little to sharpen my senses. My heart is pounding with excitement.

I never dared open the wardrobe door. I suspected it contained nothing apart from a pile of clothes full of mothballs. I wanted to spare myself any disappointment.

My father spent all his life making things up – albeit in a graceful and charming way – and that is why everyone believed him. He would get away with things no one else could. He was a *superman*, as my grandson Samko would say. Few people believed that he had been gravely ill for many years, or even that he died. Indeed, even today people in the street ask me how he is.

"How is the good doctor?"

It seems that some people are immortal.

Here, on this staircase, is where Vojto liked to sit, my friend Vojto. Perhaps my closest friend, my second self – although a mirror-image kind of self. He used to come to this place even when nobody was at home. He liked it here. Once he crept in and caught my father secretly lighting up after lunch – the same man who had strictly forbidden tobacco to his patients and would never tire of telling them off for the habit.

"You're a smoker, doctor?"

From a dark corner my father turned towards the voice:

"One cigarette won't do you any harm, my friend. But you have to be careful not to inhale too deep, just exhale from the corner of your mouth, like this, see…!"

I stand up and climb the rickety wooden stairs. One day, when you've reached a certain age, you'll understand that some things are easier said than done. But once I force my old knees to cooperate they do move. Tina's crazy daughter Jenny, who knew

18

all our childhood stories, once emptied the mysterious wardrobe of ours, unscrewed its back panel and pushed it towards the attic door. You had to go through the wardrobe to enter. So I open the wardrobe and walk in.

If a house possesses a subconscious, it will definitely be located in the attic, together with all the junk people no longer have any use for but dare not throw out.

Dust particles are floating in the air. In the light filtering through the cracks in the old roof they look as if they were made of gold. They remind me of those old Bols bottles with a dancing ballerina inside. Mother used to keep one in the wardrobe, the little flakes of gold suspended, as if frozen in time, in the thick liquid that had gradually evaporated over the years.

I've always had difficulty breathing in the attic.

Asthma bronchiale – Father used to say. My bronchial membranes would get irritated by the clouds of smoke from his cigarettes, which he would light up in secret hoping that no one, including himself, would notice. A doctor at the allergy clinic patiently explained that the composition of dust varies from house to house, making it virtually impossible to devise an effective vaccine that would help the system to adapt to all the microscopic particles of dead skin, animal fur and other bits and pieces to be found in a particular household. The dust here has always made my eyes sting and my throat itch. Perhaps tiny particles of my father also float around hereabouts. He lived in the house longer than anyone else, eventually becoming its sole inhabitant.

I trip over a pile of dusty stuff. I pull out a photograph with a huge head stuck on it, and an old banknote comes to light. Exercise books and shrivelled folders, faded soft toys, Father's medical records.

A notebook. On the back a label with the word *Diseases* scrawled in an ungainly hand. A faded orange endpaper stamped *Alfonz Trnovský, MD,* and Father's signature that he endlessly practised on blotting paper. Next to it a BAYER diary, the year 1937 printed on the spine. I recognise it: it's the one I used for my jottings when I was little.

Under it the *1943 Medical Yearbook*. On page 127 the *List of Physicians in Slovakia registered with the Chamber of Medicine as of 31 May 1939, in compliance with Article 3 of Law 56/1939* features

19

Trnovský Alfonz, of the Rom. Cath. Faith, D.o.b. 30.VII.1912, graduated 29.VI.1935, Bratislava, general practitioner, Brežany.

There is an old chess set in a wooden box (the pieces disappeared one by one, like characters in every good story) and inside it a forgotten round stamp with a circular brown head, ending in metal letters *A.T. MD.*, back to front. And another, oblong stamp, bearing the name *Dr. Trnovský Alfonz, Brežany* with a figure "1" on the right hand side.

A few photos of Father's old consulting room showing various instruments. An X-ray machine, a medicine cabinet, a sunlamp.

So he really was here once, this is proof positive!

When Ötzi the ice man was found in an Alpine glacier there was still some undigested food in his stomach and some kind of mushroom in his pocket, with each newly-discovered detail spawning a new version of his imaginary prehistoric life.

Imagination is a great thing. It's the Achilles heel of the human brain.

But the body of evidence continues to grow.

Septichen inject… Sepsis post partum et post abortum. Pneumonia, ulcus cruris… REMED Prague. I request a shipment of specimens…

Then there's a pile of albums with family photographs, each picture with Father's detailed caption. This is a key family trait – we don't rely on our own memory. Moreover, someone later added comments in felt-tip and ballpoint, in an unsightly spidery scrawl, unwittingly creating two versions of history. I'm not one to point any fingers but I think Mother is to blame, after my parents' relations got sort of complicated. She was an impulsive, restless person, though not always able to channel her energies in the right direction.

Sunday lunches, family celebrations, group photographs of people smiling at the camera. Mother in a photographer's studio, in a white dress and sandals, framed by roses. Mother sitting next to a radio receiver, wearing a hat – obviously listening to some popular song she would later play on the piano… (1951). Mother and Father in the car. The first head leaning out of the back window is that of Polino the dog… (1940). Mother with some girlfriends at a lido… (1936). Our new car … (1940) Me tuning the radio… (1944). My school form – children looking at the camera, a teacher standing behind them by a map of Europe, next to her

20

a stove and further down coats on hangers and a drawing of a human skeleton…

I recognise myself in the third row.

At the bottom of an old box I find a simple funeral card with a black border:

It is with the deepest sorrow that we inform you that our dear husband, beloved father, brother, brother-in-law and uncle, reserve lieutenant colonel Vojtech Roško, passed away on 2 May 1965 after a brief illness in Brežany, where his remains were cremated. His wife Natália… His son Vojto…

Vojto's father.

A postcard has somehow got attached to the back of the funeral card with something sticky – presumably the wonderful, deliciously sweet cough syrup from Father's medicine cabinet that Vojto and I used to sip from in secret. The postcard shows a statue of Lenin sitting on a pedestal in Moscow's Kremlin. He is staring pensively into the distance, as if everything had suddenly dawned on him. Had he been misunderstood? Had his words been misinterpreted? All he wanted to do was proclaim equality for all. Happiness. Peace. Love. Didn't comrade Jesus want to do the same?

The film on the 1960s postcard makes the statue appear as it were floating in space. Comrade Lenin, aloft in the characteristic hue of East German ORWO film that turned all the browns a shade of blue. I know it intimately from the kilometres of film that have passed through my hands as film director in the editing studios of the state TV.

I could go on like this for a long time but my legs are becoming stiff and I'm getting short of breath. Absent-mindedly I stuff an empty box of Luminal into my pocket as a trophy, along with Father's medical diary, and grab a well-thumbed book on Goya with many reproductions in colour.

As I climb down gingerly I recall a summer's day, many years ago. My older brother Peter and I took Father for a swim in lake Senec, one of those rare occasions when the three of us went on an outing together – it may even have been the last. My father slipped on the slime-covered steps, hit his head and lost consciousness. Carefully we laid him down in the grass and tried to resuscitate him. After a while he opened his eyes, slowly sat up, looked around and said, feeling the swelling bump on his head.

"Oh my, I've regained my memory!"

3.

There is a fridge in the kitchen, still in its original packaging. It's brand new, white and pristine. It seems rather out of place in this crumbling house.

Gifts from the Tropics are unloaded from large ships in the harbour. Special carriages at the harbour ramp are ready to transport the gifts to Czechoslovakia, sorted into three categories according to quality – at 25, 20 and 10 Czechoslovak crowns… – reads a scrap of ancient newspaper lying on the floor.

I see Mother standing in the garden at nightfall, bending down, her face illuminated only by a dim light – by now she had become a grandmother, her unruly grey hair boasting a magnificent purple rinse. She is holding a rake in what could almost pass for a classic scene, although she probably wouldn't have seen it that way.

A painter like Millais, or our very own Benka, however, would have found it inspiring.

Dostoyevsky in his classy burgundy binding is still in good shape. *Crime and Punishment,* Father's favourite book. Kafka didn't fare quite so well – five damp volumes, lovingly wrapped in yellowing paper. Now she's picked up Hesse's *The Glass Bead Game* and Rimbaud's *A Season in Hell.* At first she wasn't going to touch them, wanting nothing to do with books he had held in his hands nearly every day.

He had died a week earlier. He had left a bout of pneumonia untreated – as you might, when you're of a certain age and mind. The two of them had spent half a century together. That was quite enough. More than enough! From now on he would stay forever frozen at the age he reached, while she imagined herself turning eighty-seven, eighty-eight, ninety, ninety-two… four… five. The idea appealed to her. She would now start enjoying life at last, she would travel, have the house redone, buy new furniture. Right after the funeral she ordered a new fridge and washing machine.

I can almost see the pain shooting into her lower back, forcing her to sit down for a while and stretch. I'm sure she pictured calcium slowly seeping out of her bones, leaving them stiff and increasingly less flexible, life draining from her drop by drop. Like in her beloved game *Heads-shoulders-knees-and-toes.* Countless illnesses she so loved to talk about.

Now she has picked up the collected works of Tacitus, her fingers trembling with impatience. The November cold and frost makes her skin turn blue. Her coat lets the wind through. Her breath, visible, rises from her mouth.

By the end of his life Father's study, or solitary cell, as he used to call it, was piled high with books, leaving just a tiny space, barely big enough for him to sleep in. It had always got on Mother's nerves. They hadn't been on speaking terms for years and lived at the opposite ends of town. Though they never divorced.

I guess we all have a certain allocation of words to say to another person. And once we've used them up there's nothing more to say. Having spent the greatest part of their lives together, most couples end up resembling each other, whereas my parents ended up being increasingly at odds. By the end their vocabulary shrank to a dozen words they kept exchanging. Father's worsening deafness can't have helped either.

Three days earlier Mother finally had her grand revenge.

I see her again in my mind's eye. I imagine her walking along the gravel path towards a big gate, leaning on a stick, slightly bent over but determined. Black crows perch on the copper church roof, the smell of incense wafts from within.

It must have been a heart-warming feeling for her. She enjoyed every breath she took. She found a seat at the very front, close to the lighted candles. The pompous, tearful sound of the organ made her raise her eyes towards the bright stained-glass windows and look somewhere beyond them, where she sensed him to be. Him, my father, Alfonz Trnovský. As a smile played on her face, his face seemed to materialize here, amid the cold walls, the face of the man who now belonged to her alone, with everything he had ever owned in this world. Not for a long time had she seen a face as ashen yet as furious. Who knows if souls have faces? Who knows.

Father had never believed in God and remained a staunch atheist all his life. He had been baptized and went to Holy Communion (mainly to please his parents – Grandpa Albert would never have forgiven him if he had not) but that was all. During the war it was Mother who almost didn't get baptized because he refused to go to confession. He considered it absurd. He relented in the end. For in those days, as they say in adventure novels, it was a matter of life and death.

Eventually the priest at the recently renovated and rebuilt Dominican church (my mother, who hadn't set foot inside it for over sixty years, must have been surprised by its appearance) gave his consent, just as his colleague did during the war. He promised to celebrate a requiem mass for him. Although it was going to be rather expensive, she could afford it as she knew that lots of people would be interested in the rare 78s of Gershwin that Father had collected all his life. She was as free as a bird at last! She had never felt as liberated as she did now.

The Dominican monk intoned solemnly:

"Alfonz Trnovský was a brave man and a good Christian. A good and honest man. He is a great loss to us all. Alfonz has gone to meet his Maker. May the Lord have mercy on his soul! Amen."

Mother was the sole person in attendance. She managed to keep this spectacle to herself. And she knew very well why. I only found out later when the priest told me about it. As the last notes of the organ died away, Mother slowly rose to her feet and, with difficulty, walked out of the church.

We are back in the garden behind our house. Her violent coughing rings out in the unseasonably cold May night.

There are still a few books left. Lorca, Aloysius Bertrand, Verlaine, and some papers, a whole pile of them covered in Father's handwriting. She throws them into the embers, just like the others before them and waits until they turn into tiny particles of soot and thin slivers of ash. The wind whirls them around like dark powdery snow. She pokes open the hard covers to help the books burn. The flames have got hold of the yellowing paper again. *A black horse, a round moon, there are olives in my pack… death stares me in the face… Cordoba. Away and alone.* The letters are black in the grey ash. Mother inhales the smoke. She can hardly feel her face, her fingers have gone numb with cold. The flames flare up high and then suddenly go out and continue to smoulder. All that's left is a fragment of the burgundy binding… *VICH DOSTOYEV…* the worn golden letters proclaim. A truly superior binding. The icy wind blows her coat open. Chilled to the bone, she draws it tight around her. She is seized by a violent fit of coughing. Her tiny, frail body stands guard over the smouldering embers in the garden of this big house.

The next morning she wakes up with a fever. When the new fridge is delivered later that day, she signs the delivery note as if in a daze.

And now the fridge gleams white and superfluous in the middle of the kitchen. She never got round to unwrapping it.

There is a Slovak proverb that says death always comes to a freshly-tidied house. I don't usually think much of proverbs but this one hits the nail on the head.

4.

The good old days are still to come – Uncle Rudo, my father's brother, used to sneer whenever someone brought up the past. It took me a long time to understand what he meant.

First it was my son Bony who wanted me to draw the family tree and then, much later, years after the Velvet Revolution, his son Matúš, too, asked me to do one. He was told to bring one to school. It was supposed to be very detailed, complete with names, family relations, professions, titles, dates of birth and death.

On that first occasion, in the early 1970s, I suspected this was a sneaky way of using schoolchildren to vet people and dig up some dirt that could be used against their families. Bony drew a big tree with lots of branches on several pieces of drawing paper glued together, and left me to muse over it. Meanwhile, he skedaddled off after lunch into a radiantly sunny day, leaving me to slave over the family tree until Sunday night.

My memory immediately churned up a pot-pourri of family stories.

The man who was to become my grandfather, young Grandpa Albert, had once accompanied his parents on a business trip to Vienna. As they were checking into their hotel, an enormous lift landed in the lobby, thrumming and buzzing. Its doors opened revealing an area flooded with light. Grandpa Albert, who had never seen anything like that in Brežany, thought their hotel room had been sent down for them. He was stunned, his eyes like saucers. Their neighbours' daughter had travelled to Vienna with them. For lack of suitable formal wear her parents kitted her out in national costume. In front of St. Stephen's Cathedral people stared at her as if she had come from another planet. She was his future wife, Grandma Mária. My grandma.

Bony's family tree had Grandpa Albert down as a worker and Grandma Mária as a domestic. Some twenty years later, in Matúš's family tree, he was transformed into a civil engineer, hardworking though not particularly affluent, which at least came closer to the truth. Grandma Mária ran her own small business, giving manicures in people's homes. That's a fact.

Grandpa Albert died young, in a mining accident. An old photograph shows Grandma with little Alfonz, my father, in her lap, flanked by his older siblings and Uncle Karol. Their father is no longer alive: Alfonz was born three months after his death. But he is with them none the less – Grandpa Albert's face had been cut out from another photograph and pasted over Uncle's face – a big head stuck on slender shoulders. The family was complete at last.

This photo is among those I have brought down from the attic, along with a few other odds and ends. My father used to tend it as a family relic. Every now and then, in difficult moments, when he thought no one was looking, he would take it out, and consult his pasted-in father, engaging in long conversations with him.

It is not known whether Grandpa Albert responded.

The situation was trickier as far as my mother's lineage was concerned: her father, Béla Blau, was a Jewish businessman, quite wealthy by Brežany standards. In 1974 I didn't dare include this information in our family tree. So I translated his name, admittedly rather obviously, turning him into a respectable-sounding Slovak, Vojtech Modroch, and making him a clerk at Brežany's post office. I didn't imagine he would have taken offence, as this was also a desk job, after all. To compensate for this little deception I granted him a longer lease of life. At the time we were living in the increasingly anonymous capital, Bratislava, and our block of flats in Malinovský Street was populated by people who had migrated there from all over Slovakia, so discretion was assured. There was no risk of my deception being discovered.

Sixty years after his death, *zeyde* Blau reverted to his original name and profession in Matúš's family tree and I hope it will now stay that way. He managed to die (this time for real) in 1938, just before the war, having been spared everything that was bound to have happened to him. Dying at the right time is a great art. This mattered a lot to him, a man who was exceedingly scared of death. Who knows if he had managed to find the Biblical red heifer without spot, whereon is no blemish, and upon which never came a yoke. In the last carefree day of his life he took his wife Sarah for a ride in the rain and as he was speeding down an avenue of trees that no longer exists, his Laurin & Klement 360, vintage 1926, hit a tree about a kilometre outside Brežany. Some people say this is just the way it ought to be – the advent of motoring has enabled us to leave this world in style and while riding high, so to speak.

Grandmother, also known as *bobe* Sarah, didn't have a job and was a housewife. That was in Matúš's version. In Bony's version of the family tree her name was Štefánia and she toiled in a factory.

As my father used to say: *Nostalgia is the memory of something that never happened.*

This is especially true in Central Europe.

And as for my mother... Her origins remained shrouded in mystery since it was a topic she was never willing to discuss. She was only a little girl when, for reasons best known to themselves, a Jewish family decided to adopt her. That was the official line and I never got her to tell me any another.

In fact, if one believes stories told in books, whenever a girl from a good family happened to bring a child into this world, she would be sent to stay with relatives, preferably very far away. Upon her return the child would be raised as her younger sibling. There are things I shall never know for sure, but that gives me the freedom to use my imagination to fill in the gaps.

During the wartime Slovak State Mother was treated as a Jew, no questions asked. No filling in of the gaps, no imagination. Just cold, hard facts.

Ultimately that makes my son Bony an *echt* Slovak because in his veins there flows Czech, Hungarian, German, Polish, Jewish and, not least, also Slovak blood. A proper Central European *cuvée*. Some of it he's got from me and some from his mother – the mad, maddening and beautiful Zuzana, whom I haven't seen in over ten years, bless her.

5.

To be honest, one of the reasons I've come back to Brežany is the bones. I can't get them out of my mind.

Actually, it all started with the bones. It was sometime in the mid-1980s, when Father was in hospital. We had been drifting apart, even as we sat side by side. He was the one who made me fully realise how difficult it can be to stay alone with someone else, just the two of us, me and Father.

This sounds rather strange, I know, considering I was the one who stuck it out with him to the end. My sister Tina had always had one foot in England (which provided her with plenty of excuses) and my brother Peter, well, he was out of the equation in a rather different way. The first born, the crown prince with his head full of big ideas, he was entitled to a life of his own. He had suffered a lot, oh yes he had, Mother used to say. He could serve as an example to us all, oh yes he could, she said. Habitually adding a story from his early childhood – about the way their hands were shaking when they brought him home from the maternity ward and how his every fart (pardon my language) called for an elaborate scientific procedure. When it was my turn, they would just stick a propelling pencil up my bum without further ado to loosen my bowels. How I loved these stories! There he was, the knight in shining armour, and there was me, younger brother with a pencil up his bum.

One might even say it was because of the bones that I got closer to my Father again – yes, these things do happen, nothing strange about that where death is concerned. Although in this case it wasn't about death, at least not Father's.

Up until that memorable autumn day (an endless flock of honking wild geese was flying above the house and my only witness was the neighbour's cow with a disposition to spend entire days glued to the same spot) I had been deaf and blind, concerned solely with watching my own feet in a desperate attempt not to trip and fall over. I wasn't able to see the whole picture – I don't suppose I can see it now, either, but that's beside the point. But on that day the scales finally fell from my eyes.

To cut a long story short – having just visited my father in hospital, I went to check on the empty house and was about to leave when I remembered something. When I was little I had buried a childhood treasure under an old yew tree. Inspired by Robert Louis Stevenson's *Treasure Island*, I thought it would be fun to bury something and dig it out years later. I could even remember the precise moment – Father was mowing the lawn, a light drizzle was falling and I had collected some big snails and carried them over to the tree. There may have been as many as twenty of them crawling about, leaving trails of slime behind them. That's when I buried my treasure.

The yew tree had been chopped down ages ago, as it had grown out of all proportion and blocked Mother's view from the kitchen window (otherwise it would still be with us today, since yews are hardy trees that, under normal circumstances, outlive humans many times over) and all that was left was a rotten stump. The garden had by now been reduced to its present state, a jungle of untended trees with a half-collapsed wall at one end, covered by an *ad hoc* mesh, which proved little impediment to the local hooligans who could easily jump over it on their regular forays to steal apricots and plums.

Nowadays you have to fight your way through a wilderness, as in Ancient Rome at its nadir.

On that autumn day I picked up a shovel that had not yet been stolen and went over to dig out my childhood treasure. I knew that if I didn't do it then, I never would. I didn't know where to start, couldn't remember the exact spot.

And that's when I found them. First the bones and eventually also a skull, in a shallow grave under a thin layer of soil.

Father was the only one in the family who knew everything about the garden. Hardly anyone else used it.

And although I soon managed to dig out my little treasure chest (its contents didn't mean much to me anymore) I found my other discovery much more intriguing.

I have managed to connect with my father thanks to a small heap of bones that weren't even his – that, too, strikes me as typical of our relationship. It was as if, by pure chance, a minor extra had suddenly turned into a key character in my life.

This was when I became interested in the past. I began to wonder what might have happened here.

6.

It is getting dark, and from the cold street outside comes a gentle hum. I have turned on a few small lights. Two light bulbs are buzzing suspiciously. I've been through all the rooms and picked out the items of furniture that deserve to be salvaged; I've packed a few bits and pieces, and now I'm sitting in a dusty armchair, sunken in time. People always miss their home rituals. At least I do. I have brought a couple of books with me but have given up on both of them after a sentence or two, and laid them aside. Everything in this house conspires to distract me.

I hear an occasional creak, every sound amplified by the empty silence, as if invisible animals were moving about. It's the desiccated furniture groaning. None of it has seen a drop of varnish in years. And then, all of a sudden, I have the audacity to turn up here, open up the doors and let fresh air stream into the stillness, inconsiderately letting humidity in! The dry creaking that reverberates through the room is the furniture protesting against the brutal intrusion.

I lie down on the sofa and watch the shadows flit by.

Slowly, almost imperceptibly, evening anxiety creeps in. It's my favourite kind. Large empty houses at dusk seem to attract it. By the time the night falls I will be wallowing in it like fish in oil. A familiar sensation. Good old anxiety!

To chase it away I imagine all the builders and artisans who laboured away on this place to transform it into a dwelling. They covered the walls with mortar, put in windows and doors, applied several coats of paint, scrubbed off splatters and dried puddles, hung the curtains (to stop people seeing what was going on inside – known as privacy, this usually starts with curtains although in small towns that's also where it often ends), finally they lugged the furniture indoors and set it down, panting... Who were they? Men smelling of plaster and plum brandy, sweaty and muscular, their eyelids caked in paint, covered in cigarette ash and grease, working under the baton of Grandpa Albert who, having earned the money to build this house by helping to construct the Suez Canal, wouldn't let anyone tell him how to go about things or move anything without his permission. His connection to the house was so intimate it almost seemed to me that if I were to grab the big dining table now and push it towards the window – as dear Grandma kept suggesting all her life but never dared to, out of respect – Grandpa Albert would sense it from the far end of the house, across two rooms, the kitchen and pantry and like a spider following its thread, jump out of bed and know that something was amiss. He would fling the door open and make me put everything back the way it was before. Provided, of course, that he was somewhere around here.

Somewhere in this house, where each clock shows a different time. Or all the different times at once.

Anxiety.

I open the BAYER medical diary I have brought down from the attic. When I was young I used its *Daily Notes* section to keep a diary. My funny scratchy script spills out every which way across the green frame of the chart marked *Number / Date / Patient's Name / Medical History / Diagnosis / Treatment / Special Prescriptions / Fee / Paid / Comments.*

Monday, 13 March
When I woke up this morning I heard Mummy and Daddy talking. I opened my eyes just as Daddy asked Mummy how high my temperature was yesterday. I shouted: "Thirty-six". Then Daddy told me I could get dressed and walk up and down the room a little. I was very happy. Airplanes have been flying over all day today, bombing the Sálava because it has frozen over. This year it has frozen over really badly and then snow fell on the ice and now the ice and snow are melting and there is water everywhere and people who live on the banks of the Sálava have had their cellars flooded. Over dinner Daddy told me about skyscrapers in New York. It was very interesting. Especially when Daddy said that if you live on the fiftieth floor it takes five minutes to get there by lift. That's enough to put you to sleep.

And underneath, in tiny letters:

Luminal, SEDATIVE AND ANTICONVULSANT

On that day there was darkness and turmoil in our class. Our

31

teacher, Miss Horecká, even asked someone to draw the heavy curtains, which was normally done only in blistering heat. All you could hear in the darkness was giggling, whispering and her irritated voice. We bumped along in the queue, slowly, one after the other, making our way to the blackboard and approaching the faint, milky-blue glow of a machine. *X-way*, whispered those who couldn't yet pronounce their Rs as well as those who had never heard this outlandish word before. The X-ray machine was mounted on wheels. Each of us had to step onto a round platform, lean back against a small support, place our head upright into a headrest, raise our arms and grasp the two handles overhead. And then the operation could begin.

"Next!" I heard my father's voice.

Father was sitting by the machine wearing a white gown and special goggles. We could see only his silhouette and the slender outline of a child's body.

The faint light went out.

"Next!"

It reminded me of the early evening film screenings at Brežany's Slovan cinema. The audience usually included Father Savický, deputy headmaster at the Catholic school, whose magnum opus, *Romantic Tales of Brežany,* graced the shelves of many a family library (mainly because of its burgundy-and-gold cover with a picture of the local variety of the national costume), which few people, apart from himself, had actually ever read. He ensured that the material being shown was suitably modest. He used to sit right next to the aperture through which images travelled from the projectionist's booth and the minute he thought something in the film was objectionable – be it a kiss or an exposed female forearm – he would cover the projector lens with his hat and announce in his rather funny high-pitched voice:

"Rows one, two and three out!"

That was where the youngest schoolchildren sat. They had to get up obediently and file out of the cinema. Only then would the screening be allowed to continue.

"Next!" My father's voice rang out wearily in the darkness.

It was the turn of a skinny boy. Father took him by the shoulders and pushed him towards the machine. The light flashed.

"Well, well, if if isn't Vojto…." he muttered.

Father couldn't see his face but he had the boy in his hands, so to speak.

"All done!"

He gave him a slap on the shoulder.

"Just don't let me catch you and Adam wandering around town after school again!"

What can I say about Vojto Roško? He was my best friend. The closest friend I've ever had. He is no longer with us, but that's quite a different part of our story.

His mother, Mrs Natália Roško, had a book that said:

A male child born under the sign of Virgo is likely to be inquisitive and self-assured; he will happily contribute to charitable causes but this will not always bring him praise and gratitude. A wealthy widow will fall in love with him but he will seek out a sharp-witted and capable maiden and will sire many children.

I could tell you many tales about the last statement. And I shall.

Just one more thing perhaps: Father's X-ray detected that Vojto had *situs inversus viscerum*. That is, his internal organs were reversed – his heart was on the right and his liver on the left side of his body – as if he hailed from another, parallel world.

And sure enough, in many respects he was my exact opposite. Each of us was lacking something. We complemented each other.

Until the 1920s, roughly speaking, people would be born and die at home. Only later did women have the benefit of clean, sterile hospitals. It was a gradual process and that is why I, too, was born at home. Vojto, on the other hand, was the first child in Brežany to come into this world in the newly built general hospital. As soon as he learned to speak he would boast about this rather inconsequential fact to anyone who would listen, as if he had been accorded some special privilege. I suspect that his mother Mrs Roško was to blame.

In our youth, Vojto became an expert mouse-catcher. He could catch a mouse without hurting it. Then we would get a straw, shove it down its backside and blow. We would pump the poor thing so full of air that it could no longer fit down its hole. It would charge against the wall, desperately trying to get inside and hide. Then suddenly, with a big loud fart, it would deflate and scuttle away.

Vojto's father was a military man, a fighter pilot to be more precise. I often saw him in the garden of their house in his khaki trousers and braces, white vest and perfectly combed hair, chopping wood or cropping trees. The tree crowns reminded me of his hair.

He taught Vojto how to use an air gun. They would practise while Mrs Roško baked a *kuglhupf*. Vojto was so good he could shoot raisins into the cake.

Saturday, 29 April

Tomorrow I have to get up early. I'm going to confession. We had to wait for a long time and then Father Savický sent us over to the Jesuit church. Vojto and I walked down the street and tore up the papers with our sins on them. We tossed one little piece of paper into the street and the other into the sewer so nobody could stick them together. We bought two cones of popcorn and went to the park to play marbles with the other children. I started out with twelve marbles and came home with sixty-three. After lunch I sat down to do my homework. I worked from three o'clock till nine in the evening. I made a drawing, did five maths exercises, wrote an essay about my brother and sister Peter and Tina, and learned a poem by heart. Now I have to go to bed early because I'm very tired.

There's one question I keep thinking about – was Jesus Christ Catholic or Protestant?

Bactifebrin FOR THERAPY OF ACUTE ENCEPHALO-RADICULO-NEURITIS.

Strong family ties always meant a lot to Father. There were rumours that he had married my mother Berta, a Jewish businessman's daughter, just for her money. (This was a rather cheeky claim, you might even call it *chutzpah*. But it never bothered anyone in my family.) They had three children – a daughter and two sons. I am the middle child.

Me.

Some people say if you start your sentences with the word "I" or "me" too often it means you think only of yourself. But this is my story. Or rather – the story of my father whose reincarnation I am. And the story of Bony, who is a later reincarnation of me. And this person – He-Me-Father – will undergo a further reincarnation. In fact, it has already begun to happen. Because there is no long

34

thin white line leading from the past to the future. Everything goes around in circles. That's what it's like, ladies and gentlemen.

Circles.

The pre-war years remain etched in my memory like scenes from colorized movies. Or like photo images showing re-touched people against re-touched backgrounds numbly staring into the camera, desperately trying to look natural. To recognise anything in the picture you need light, lots of light. Dark corners are undesirable and besides, they are impossible to capture anyway.

All that is left is a stylized imprint of life embellished with a bit of poetry: *My love is endless like the sea, in my heart you'll forever be. Like a bird that seeks a nest, you will forever be the best.* The undulating sea in the background is heaving, flooding the whole scene with its romantic waves.

I have this picture of Father and Mother taken heaven knows when.

One of Mother's most cherished possessions was a large oblong scrapbook labelled *Beliebte Filmstars,* in ornamental lettering. Photos of American and German film stars – Cary Grant, Charlie Chaplin, as well as Emil Hörbiger and Marlene Dietrich that came with Lindt & Sprüngli chocolates – had to be stuck into pre-assigned slots to complete the album. Mother tried her best; unsurprisingly, she put on weight at this time, which bothered her.

The album was out of bounds to us children. She got very cross if she caught any of us with it. Only on rare occasions, after Sunday lunch, if she was in a good mood and Father was having a nap on the sofa, would she take it out with great care – *Let me turn the pages, Adam!* – and treat us to a presentation.

Father pretended he was still asleep even as music started pouring from the gramophone, since for Mother music was a natural complement to her beloved photo album. She often played film songs or tunes from the Slovak operetta *Under a Foreign Flag*, starring František Krištof Veselý. I was always transfixed when I heard him declaim, in his gentle Hungarian accent, the patriotic lines: *The most beautiful corner in the whole wide world is my motherland… It is the only country that is so beautiful for me…!*

After cranking up the gramophone, the fragile 78s *Esta, Ultraphon* or *His Master's Voice* (with that little doggie listening to his master's voice coming from the gramophone's horn) began to spin around on the turntable.

Sarah Blau – my Jewish *bobe* – would sometimes join us, only to nod off in an armchair. I only have a two-dimensional image of her because she died too soon, an inanimate image set in motion, her close-cropped hair topped by a wig which she used to cover with a fancy scarf adorned with little pearls, as befitted a practising elderly Jewess.

She adored *matzo*. And everything that went with it. At breakfast she would crush some into her cup and pour white coffee over it. In her golden chicken soup, *goldene yoich*, there floated *matzo kneidlach*, little dumplings made from ground *matzo*, parsley leaves and goose fat, to make sure they stayed light and fluffy.

Although my grandparents had two sets of crockery and kept kosher, they didn't object to their daughter marrying a *goy*. Zeyde Blau spent as much time as he could communing with God – at six in the morning he went to pray at the Ashkenazi synagogue and at eight o'clock to the Sephardic one, just in case. I guess he wanted to make sure he didn't miss any key developments between Heaven and Earth, and that all the debates he had initiated were duly concluded. At Purim, like all the more affluent Jews, he would send the Rabbi a donation for the poor. And in summer, when begging *schnorrers* arrived from Galicia and Mukachevo in the east, he would offer them pastries and make sure they left with a few crowns in their pockets.

Neither my Mother nor my grandparents, nor Uncles Armin and Oskar, had typically Jewish features, as described in detail in the 1925 anti-Semitic pamphlet *The Jew's Mirror*, lavishly the illustrated with bizarrely contorted drawings of the unhinged Czech painter Karel Rélink. The pamphlet detailed how, under cover of darkness, the Jews murdered Christians, seduced their wives, maligned them in every possible way and stole their money and property. In my family there were no long crooked noses, supposedly reminiscent of the figure 6, nor protruding pointy ears, nor even brown eyes.

We would all gather for lunch on Sundays. It was a technicolour dream.

Saturday, 28 April
Today we had firemen's tests. A lot of firemen did clever tricks that made

everyone clap. We don't usually have firemen's tests but we're having them now because there's a heatwave. Lots of people came to watch. I got so drawn in I forgot to eat my lunch. I almost couldn't breathe at lunchtime because it was so terribly hot. Then I took a shower.

Tonophosphan, A POWERFUL NON-TOXIC PHOSPHORUS PREPARATION.
HAS A LONG-LASTING, STIMULATING AND TONING EFFECT ON
WEAKENED CARDIAC MUSCLES.

In the summer the whole town was parched from the sweltering heat.

The air was still and heavy. People said the atmosphere was just as sleepy and languorous immediately before the outbreak of the Great War. Apparently the town councillors, feeling chatty and sociable after work, used to go for a drink to the local hotel, *Zum Goldenen Hirsch,* with its eponymous gold-painted glass stag above the entrance. They had a private room reserved for them at the back of the restaurant, away from the daily hurly-burly.

This is where they must have been sitting on the night of 28 June 1914, as well as the night of 28 October 1918.

They hardly took notice of the excited municipal clerk who barged in, elbowing his way through the tables. Until, out of breath, he shouted:

"The Czechoslovak Republic has just been declared!"

Yes, the Austro-Hungarian Empire, that vast amoeba randomly stretching across Central Europe, was about to pass away.

Turning to the clerk as he downed his glass of red wine, the mayor said with a wave of his hand: "What's all the fuss about, my good man?"

The phrase would have gone really well with Brežany's coat-of-arms, comprised of the customary bunch of vines, the arrow of St. Giles and the letter B. The motto beneath might well have read:

"What's all the fuss about?" How fitting.

Particularly as the nineteenth century still continued in Brežany, its shoots reaching deep into my childhood. And showing not the least inclination to end.

On Sunday afternoons we usually went for a stroll in the main square. My Father, still young, slim and well-groomed, would don his favourite off-white suit, Mother would put on a summer frock (and a summer hat, of course, as her head had to be covered), while my brother and I trailed along in our little sailor suits and my sister in her little dress. This, at least, is what has been captured in the faded photograph now in my hands.

It would have been inconceivable for our family to pass by the patisserie without dropping in, as we children begged for ice cream. The photograph shows us about to enter just as Vojto and his parents are passing by – cordial greetings are exchanged all round, Vojto's father flaunting his dress uniform, as at this point he was a non-commissioned officer, a fighter pilot, though I'm not sure of the rank.

The patisserie belonged to Mr Puškár. This was where Father used to go to play cards with a group of regulars. Their back-room gatherings were his source of the latest news. Sometimes the odd Jew would drop by, too. Mr Schreiber, the vet, was highly influential, as was the lawyer, Mr Reis. The latter wasn't doing too well; people usually prefer lawyers who can whip up passions rather than those who try to talk them out of doing something foolish.

Another regular was Ambi Krebs, who usually walked around bareheaded but always carried his hat pinned to his coat. On a whim, Ambi Krebs had established a small private botanical garden in Brežany. The grown-ups mocked his efforts but the children adored him – for a small fee he used to give them tours of the exotic bushes and trees until he lost them to the harsh winter of 1944.

Puškár loved to recount how his mother suddenly went into labour on her way from the cemetery and gave birth in a stranger's house, the first house on whose door she had knocked. And this was where his patisserie was now located. Nobody believed him.

His vocabulary was very peculiar. For example, if in the heat of a card game someone inadvertently gave a loud fart he would slap the person sitting next to him on the back and shout: *Buenos Aires, amigo!* Mind you, he never dared to treat my father in this way – they had never even been on first name terms. His favourite turn of phrase was: *The God of patissiers has granted me cream slices. The God of diseases has granted me typhoid.*

So, for now, Puškár's patisserie is still in the main square – at least in the photo.

We all pile in. Me, my brother Peter and my sister Tina (her name was actually Marta but she hated it and insisted on being called Tina, which made everyone think that her real name was Martina). Our parents stay outside in the sun.

"I want strawberry…!" I shout.

Puškár says hello to my father through the doorway.

"Good afternoon, doctor!"

Tina gives me a nudge and snaps:

"You have to say *please!*"

"Strawberry… *please!*" I give her a nasty look.

"As you wish…," says Puškár, scooping up some strawberry.

"Vanilla for me," Tina says.

The coins jingle in her hands.

"We say *please!*" I shout.

Peter just laughs. For some reason, he's never liked ice cream.

"That'll be seventy-four plus thirty hundredths," says Puškár with a smile.

"What…?" asks Tina, her eyes popping.

"We say *please!*" I poke her mischievously.

"Seventy-four plus thirty hundredths!"

Tina stares at the change in her hand, not sure what to do.

"Let me give you a hint: one Czechoslovak crown officially equals thirty seven plus fifteen hundredths of a milligram of gold."

"What?"

"Meaning that you can pay me in gold. Or in crowns if you wish. I don't mind either way." Puškár beams at her – he's having a whale of a time.

A confused Tina places two crowns on the counter, licks a small yellow stream of ice cream that's trickling down her arm and heads for the door.

"Bye-bye…!" we hear Puškár shout as we run out.

Outside the shop window Father is talking to Mrs Angyal. My mother used to say she makes little angels, and it took me a while to figure out that this was because, as a midwife, she sometimes performed abortions as I was too young to understand the hint.

We run around trying to get as dirty as possible while the ice cream is melting fast in the blazing summer sun.

"So you say the amniotic fluid was greenish-yellow?" asks Father, rubbing the tip of his nose. I always felt he wasn't too keen

39

on Mrs Angyal. He doesn't trust her, so he chooses his words carefully, to make sure she doesn't read something else into them.

Mrs Angyal nods.

"In case of an apparent death the newborn's skin is bluish-red, the face and the entire body are swollen; the arms and legs slightly taut, the rectum is closed, the heartbeat is intermittent and faint, the pulse in the umbilical cord has ceased or is intermittent... If you stick your little finger down the baby's throat and the throat closes around it, you have to resuscitate it. You have to put the baby on its back and remove the mucus from the oral cavity. From the mouth and the throat, do you understand?"

Mrs Angyal narrows her eyes like a big cat, trying to commit it all to memory.

"Next you have to get hold of the baby's chest and give it a few good thumps. Then you lift its legs with one hand and give it a couple of slaps on the bottom, then get hold of its chest again and shake it up. If this doesn't revive the baby, you have to sprinkle cold water on its face and chest. Then, gradually, it should start breathing and turn pink. But you have to keep going until it starts howling away."

Mrs Angyal thanks him, strokes one us on the head, ruffles the hair of another, and leaves with a smile. Father joins us.

Yes. If someone had released the shutter at that moment and taken a picture, they would have captured a world where everyone was jolly and happy. A world where nothing dramatic ever happened, was happening or would ever happen, a world that was not under any threat, a perfect sunny world on a lazy sleepy Sunday afternoon somewhere in Slovakia, in a town called Brežany.

As a matter of fact, someone did take that very photograph. He has re-touched and colorized it, stamping it with the logo *Nežný et Co. Studio*. The time that had never existed has stood still in the photograph.

As if that wasn't enough, the people in the background include Screwy Igor, bent double and casting around for any bits and bobs he can find in the street – screws, nuts, ball-bearings – to take back home. Whatever it is, he takes it apart and after putting it together again there's always a piece left over. His yard is filling up with all kinds of odds and ends, carcasses of cars and a jumble of spare parts whose original purpose can no longer be divined.

Screwy Igor is a shrewd businessman who keeps selling the same five or six objects, a proud forebear of present-day marketing.

"I've got something just for you! A pair of special flower trimmers and a cigar knife. Here, please take a look!"

"Hmm… But didn't you say last week that these were special French scissors for trimming eyelashes, and that this was a cork knife?!"

"Well, yes, but that was something different. And you wouldn't believe it – they sold like hot cakes! This time, though, I've got two first-class novelties on offer. Great innovations. Don't be misled!"

"Oh, c'mon – I remember the writing on this one!"

"My dear lady, surely you're not suggesting I'm trying to cheat you? Why would I do that? All right, I admit that these scissors could also be used to trim eyelashes, but their primary purpose is trimming flowers. The same goes for this gorgeous little knife – it's meant for cigars but if the master of the house feels like a drop of wine, it'll come in handy as a cork knife!"

"But excuse me – the last time you told me this was a razor for scraping the rough skin from one's heels."

"That must have been a misunderstanding. Nice meeting you, have a lovely day!"

And somewhere in the distance, where apart from me nobody even suspects his presence, is our dentist, Mr Gronsky. An Orthodox Jew, he is enjoying his Sunday stroll with his lady wife, like any respectable citizen. I have no idea what a goldmine might be called in dentist jargon but that's roughly what my father represented to him. He wears a pince-nez and an old-fashioned hat, as if constantly trying to remind people that the good old times did indeed exist, no matter how it might seem these days.

7.

Browsing through the photos I reach for the little bottle of Noax on the bedside table. I let five drops fall onto a spoon and swallow. I've been doing this every now and then ever since that complicated leg fracture. Mostly in the evenings. My doctor prescribed Noax as a painkiller. And so what – it's human nature to try and make things easier for oneself. Cigarettes, alcohol or harmless Ibalgine for elderly ladies: take your pick. Just to make life a little easier. My head clears after a short while. Not too much, just a little. Fine tuning, as Bony would say.

One of the photos that I inspect by the light of the bedside lamp shows the front of our house, still sporting a neat sign made of copper: *Alfonz Trnovský, private medical practitioner.* After a few years it replaced the original, cheap enamel one. What the picture doesn't show is my Father's consulting room – you had to pass through the front door, go up a few steps and make two right turns. Zeyde Blau contributed to the cost; it was Mother's dowry, so to speak. A former kitchen and an adjoining room had been converted into a consulting room and waiting room, though traces of their original purpose remained visible for a while.

Father had studied medicine at Bratislava University, apparently at considerable cost, tempted by the promise of an attractive and prosperous future.

Sometimes he would recall those heady days, including the splendid intravenous hangovers induced by pure alcohol that he and his fellow medical students used to inject. Thinking about it always brought a wistful expression to his face. He passed through the evolutionary stages typical of his day and age: medical student – medical intern – medical demonstrator – assistant researcher – unpaid assistant. Eventually he was able to set up his own practice.

He wasted no time in having business cards printed and sending them out with the following notice:

A. Trnovský MD, former assistant at the Neurology Clinic in Bratislava, external physician at the Urology Clinic of the same hospital and junior registrar at all other clinics in Bratislava as well as Nitra, has the pleasure of informing you that he has established a private practice in Brežany, at 18 Hurban Street, and offers the most up-to-date treatments, electro-physical therapy, sun lamps, solux and diathermy.

Father displayed his medical doctorate diploma inconspicuously in a conspicuous place on a wall for his patients to admire as he wrote out their prescriptions.

There was also a boxroom for the X-ray machine, which he would regularly and proudly show off to all his visitors. Only from the outside, of course, since an X-ray machine is highly sensitive and not meant to be gawped at. The darkroom, containing only a gold-emblazoned sign on a black background, remained empty since Father had run out of money. Inquisitive patients would not have been able to detect the absence of the X-ray machine even if they had peered into the darkness within. The light bulb didn't work.

Right next to the boxroom hung a large orange poster with the photo of a gorgeous lady in a swimming costume and a bathing cap, enthusiastically waving to someone outside the picture. She was smiling from beneath the words PERMANENT SUNSHINE in huge letters, which continued: UNDERNEATH A PHILLIPS "BIOSOL" LAMP and in smaller letters below: *The human body needs sunshine! The few days of leisure and vacation enjoyed by people in full-time employment are rarely sufficient to provide the body with the requisite amount of healthy sunshine. It is therefore often necessary for a physician to compensate for this deficiency by treatment with artificial ultraviolet rays.*

Between the ages of five and six I was madly in love with the lady in the swimsuit costume, throwing myself into an intense love affair marked by passion, jealousy, rows and, eventually, a break-up.

Admittedly, at first Father lived rather beyond his means, as evidenced by the burnished sign on the door, the fancy business cards, non-existent X-ray machine and equally non-existent sunlamp, as well as the actual consulting-room equipment which, on the other hand, did exist, with its gleaming chrome and stainless steel that hurt the eyes. He also liked to pretend he had a full diary – in those early days Mother often caught him holding a receiver to his ear (yes, we had a telephone as well, our number being 46-75), leafing through empty pages and accompanying every attempt to make an appointment with some tut-tutting until, at the fifth or sixth try, the caller finally struck lucky. In short, Father did quite a lot of faking at the beginning and as a result soon became quite successful.

This is a tried and tested method, and not just in this profession.

At first he used to go and see his patients on foot or by bike. At night he slept fitfully, constantly expecting the ominous knock on the door that would yank him out of bed and drag him into the dark night. Then he bought a Praga Piccolo, as – obviously –

driving to see his patients added to the cost of the visits and made the prescribed medication more effective. That is what the smiling company rep in his perfectly fitting sharp suit also said. He offered Father an American cigarette, and bought him a cup of coffee and a piece of cake in Puškár's patisserie in the main square. They had a talk, and after reeling off the virtues of the vehicle, the rep whisked Father off on a ride around the square and the bumpy roads on the outskirts of town.

Some time later my father opened another practice in Nevedovo, a village fifteen kilometres outside Brežany, and started commuting there by car twice a week. The locals were so frightened of cars that they erected a sign saying *Cars 6 kms!* outside the first house in the village. Anyone driving even a fraction faster got fined. Sometimes they also stopped speeding cars in the main square but Father usually got round this by stopping before he reached the police patrol. The obsessive mayor went as far as to check whether drivers blew their horn while driving around a bend, and anyone who failed to do so was also liable to be fined.

This was all because of Ambi Krebs. He was once brought to Father's surgery with a fractured skull, with cerebrospinal fluid pouring out of his nose. He had crashed his car into a tree behind Nevedovo and suffered a severe concussion.

It was Mother who initially took on most of the administrative tasks at the practice; she was also in charge of sterilizing the instruments. As the number of patients grew, Father often didn't manage to eat lunch before six o'clock and dinner before midnight, and he was hardly getting any sleep. The phone in his practice never stopped ringing.

A large loan from the Medical Savings Bank eventually enabled him to buy a Heliodor-Duplex portable X-ray machine ("*offering full protection against high voltage and harmful X-rays*") for his darkroom. And since a certain amount of decorum had to be maintained, he would start each day with a visit to the hairdresser's, who would run around in his white coat brandishing a razor. A doctor couldn't do his own shaving, as that may have given rise to rumours, giving his competitors an excuse to cast aspersions. For the same reason, whenever he went to see patients from upper-crust families he relied on the services of a personal chauffeur (usually

Ambi, if he wasn't too busy) and left him waiting outside polishing the car with a patient smile. People love things that remind them of film scenes, particularly in a small town inhabited by small people who have remained small even after the town has expanded, spilling into its environs and acquiring the designation of a "district" town, but remaining a small town none the less. A town under a spell, proud of its enormous smallness and small manners.

Father used to cross the square with slow and dignified steps and greet acquaintances by raising his hat. While the hairdresser gave him a shave, he read the paper and listened to the latest local news.

Mother's brother, Uncle Armin, a man prone to incessant quipping and the telling of jokes, had just opened a hairdressing salon. Father wanted his peace and quiet and would sit there with a forced smile and an occasional "Hmm" or "Aha" or sometimes a "Really?"

Carrying a black leather briefcase similar to Father's doctor's bag, Armin walked over to the Silbersteins' big house in the main square, as the family insisted on having their hair cut by a Jewish hairdresser. Armin must have been the source of the story about Silberstein, a fabric merchant, summoning to his deathbed his two sons Arthur and Albert, who hated each other's guts, and who would never have agreed to spend any length of time in the same room if it hadn't been necessitated by this unique event, which they might have been secretly anticipating. Silberstein Senior lay in his sweat-soaked bed, with a slice of buttered bread in his hand and a solemn expression. He asked them to come closer and they did.

"Take a good look!"

Not until he took a bite of the slice of bread did the sons notice little oblong pieces of paper on the bread. They were too shocked to stop the disaster from happening. Their father was gulping down his precious stamp collection – his famous 50:50 overprints and other rarities. He just wolfed it all down before his sons were able to move and tear it out of his hands, from under his tongue and between his teeth.

"There – so you can't fight over it! Now I can die in peace."

However, Armin's favourite subject was women, women of every conceivable shape and condition. My Mother used to say he had never got married in order to be always "available".

In his practice Father developed a peculiar habit of addressing his patients in the third person.

"Has he been taking his medication regularly?"

"Where does he hurt?"

"Is she coughing?"

Then he would lay the chrome-plated end of his stethoscope on the patient's bare chest.

"He should breathe! He should take a deep breath! Very deep! He should turn around. That's right."

"She's breathing, she's breathing!"

One of his patients, a man called Monako, was something of a weirdo. He was thirty when Father gave him a thorough examination and told him that the dark spots in the X-ray indicated TB and that he had about a year left to live. And even though he couldn't feel anything, the blood he was coughing up suggested that his lungs were shot. And that he should pack his things and go to the Hágy resort in the High Tatras.

When he left Father's consulting room Monako headed straight for the Golden Stag where, ignoring Father's advice, he ordered a bottle of red wine and a packet of cigarettes. He placed both on the table next to the X-ray of his lungs.

He spent the whole evening looking at the picture, drinking and smoking one cigarette after another and when he finished he ordered more cigarettes and another bottle... And he kept staring at his lungs in the blue-and-black picture with his name at the bottom. In the early hours, as the cockerels began to crow, the bar was closing and he had consumed four bottles of wine and fifty cigarettes, he got up and went home.

He told Father: "That night I came to terms with it, right here, in my head."

And he went on living for many years. Considering the role he was to play in my Father's life this sounded like a badly told joke.

One evening, as my Father was getting ready for his late supper and Zdenka the nurse reported there were no more patients in the waiting room, an agitated young lady entered the surgery. She had fallen in love with a man who wore claret-coloured shoes with metal tips. That was the only bit of information she was able to divulge about the mysterious stranger, – most likely a travelling salesman, probably hailing from a big city, Prague perhaps – she had run off with. They stayed in hotels and everything seemed very exciting and romantic until one fine morning he put on his stylish claret-coloured shoes and walked out of her life. It might have been the shoes she had fallen in love with.

Her name was Klaudia somebody. She wanted Father to perform an abortion. She was Klaudia with capital K, the biggest capital letter you can imagine. A CAPITAL K. Klaudia Horváthová. Father would later have a tale or two to tell about her.

But in the meantime he examined her and told her she was probably not pregnant. However, she didn't believe him and said she understood that as a doctor he had to adhere to certain moral principles and didn't see any reason why she should get rid of the baby. That he just wanted to talk her out of it. She, on the other hand, needed to be absolutely sure – in a few weeks' time it might be too late to do anything. And that was why she would really like the doctor to try giving her an injection (she had heard that an injection might help if the pregnancy wasn't too advanced). She didn't want an operation. She would be very much obliged.

So Father told her to undress, prepared a needle and injected a good dose of distilled water into the silken, supple skin of her upper arm.

Two weeks later she came back, beaming with joy. She thanked him for the intervention: the injection had worked and everything was perfectly fine now.

8.

I had always admired Father's systematic and organized approach to things. For example, he was in the habit of getting up early in the morning and running up the nearby hill in a pair of breeches, a shirt buttoned up right up to the neck and a hat, taking a few deep breaths to warm up and then running back home. But first he would spend a little while on top of the hill watching the morning sun (if it was visible) as he took his deep breaths and told himself what a wonderful day it was and what great times we lived in.

On his way back he usually bumped into Father Peterský, the

47

parish dean. He would greet my father respectfully and always seemed on the verge of asking him something important, apart from the usual gripes about his rheumatism and the early onset of arthritis.

Father thought he was just imagining it until one day he finally spat it out:

"Excuse my prying but… do you go to church, doctor?"

Father nodded.

"That's good, very good! Please forgive me, but I haven't noticed you at Holy Mass. No wonder, our church tends to get very full during the Sunday service, thank God!"

"But I don't go to mass."

Peterský was thunderstruck. "But isn't it our Christian duty to attend Holy Mass every holy day? Still, it is good of you, doctor, to grace the church with your presence from time to time."

"Please don't misunderstand me. I don't go there to pray."

"Don't you? You'll have to explain."

"I go to church to examine corpses, Father. According to the regulations this should be done at the place of death. But then I would have to go all the way up the Volovec Mountain, to the little hamlets in the hills that can only be reached on foot. That way I would waste a lot of time. But all the dead are brought down and laid out at St. Giles anyway."

Dean Peterský turned on his heels and left.

Peterský's chaplain, Jablonický, sometimes accompanied my father on patient visits. They would drive down the paved road in the Praga and then ride up the hill on a hay cart. Father would examine the patient, the chaplain would perform the last rites if he was about to turn up his toes – as the locals would put it –, then they would down a shot of plum brandy proffered by the family and ride back to the car.

Once, they were nearly drafted into a communist march. On that occasion, Father had taken me along so I would have a day out. We had to wait in the car for the Labour Day parade to pass. The foreman from the timber-processing college made his apprentices join the parade and they were happy to get out of school early on such a lovely day. The officials rode slowly on borrowed bicycles with red crepe paper plaited into the wheels' spokes. They were followed by trumpet players adorned with huge red sashes playing an excruciating version of the Internationale, since none of them could play properly. After the rally the chairman of the local Communist Party cell invited everyone to lunch at the Golden Stag to demonstrate how generous and close to the people the communists were.

Father turned his head in the direction of the march and mumbled to Chaplain Jablonický:

"The Lord sees everything and finds us very amusing!"

"You shouldn't say things like that, doctor!"

9.

Vojto's mother had a beautiful name, Natália. Whevever she introduced herself she stressed that her Russophile mother had named her after Alexander Pushkin's great love, Natalia Goncharova, one of the most beautiful women of her day. She would always add that it was because of her that Pushkin was killed in a duel. Who knows if she meant this as a hint to her husband that he should make a similar sacrifice for her. If she really needed a poet to sacrifice his life and writing career for her charms – in other words, if her physical beauty was meant to destroy spiritual beauty just for the sake of destruction – she should have married Ján Smrek, whose poetry she so admired. Unfortunately, her path had never crossed that of the great poet.

She was born into a prominent Brežany Catholic family where there had to be a reason for everything and rules had to be strictly obeyed. As far as other people were concerned, the family knew exactly who were "people like us" and who weren't, and behaved with aristocratic condescension, driven by the belief that members of this distinguished family were the yardstick by which the entire universe was judged. It was they who were used by the gracious Lord to judge what was good and what was evil, rather than the other way round. He had endowed Natália Roško with great beauty – high cheekbones, a wide, round face and huge green eyes, a powerful, imperious chin and long black hair. She looked stunning when she was angry, which happened rather frequently.

I remember one particular day when Vojto and I were playing

with his wooden soldiers in his nursery and heard snatches of shouting from the kitchen, followed by the slamming of a door.

"Silly woman!" Vojto's father said, walking down the corridor.

She ran out after him, shouting:

"And what about those knees of yours, and all the grass stains you've got on them? Well? Tell me where you got them, you whoremonger!"

Noticing that the door to Vojto's nursery room was open, she put on a smile, slowed her step and asked:

"Boys, would you like some lemonade?"

We nodded, she walked back to the kitchen, and the shouting resumed.

It was fairly common (or at least whispered) knowledge in Brežany that Vojto's father had married her basically because he grew up in poverty and because, as the youngest of ten children, there was no room for him at home and the military academy was his only option. Natália liked his pilot's uniform and he, in turn, liked the house into which they were soon to move. Natália's father ran a flourishing haberdashery shop.

The other reason – which Vojto didn't mention until many years later, over a bottle of his favourite Metaxa brandy – was that in order to join the army and have any prospect of promotion in the military, his father had to be a married man. And since he was courting his mother at the time, he thought he might as well propose. Besides, their relationship had apparently resulted in two abortions already so this way it all stayed in the family, as it were, and as a result, Vojto was born, followed by his brother Theo. But Vojto's father liked other women, too – women who were huggable, less complicated and less demanding – as suggested by those green knees. His air squadron was often deployed all over the place but rarely at home.

"Here's your lemonade, boys!" Mrs Roško said, leaving a tray with a carafe and two glasses on the table.

She had to serve it herself because two days earlier she had fired Elenka the maid and had not yet found a replacement. Elenka had to go because of a dalliance with Mr Friedl, the Jewish doctor who was visiting Brežany. And although they were only seen together once having dinner, that was already too much for Brežany. That started the rumour mill and Elenka had to go.

As this was the day of Natalia's regular salon, she had no choice but to borrow domestics from the manor of the local count. A cook and two maids. She usually held her salon in her beloved Slovak Room, replete with shepherds' hatchets, custom-carved folk-style wooden furniture, a plaster shepherd with a sheepdog and an example of the local costume.

Mrs Roško kept meticulous records of every event of this kind in a special leather-bound *Guest Book*. All her illustrious visitors had written or drawn something nice in it. Several inscriptions had come from mayors past and present, Mr Levendovský the notary, Father Peterský, the opera diva Jarmila Kšírová, even the famous operetta tenor František Krištof Veselý. Sitting in front of the fireplace, caressing her precious bear skin and sipping ten-year-old port, Mrs Roško always longed for her home (which she liked to refer to as her "modest abode") to establish itself as a kind of showcase salon in the town of Brežany.

She tried to entice one or two local poets but they fled to Bratislava in search of publishers or the right kind of cafés. The only local artist who frequented her salon was Father Savický, deputy headmaster of the Catholic school, author of a rambling historical opus whose main claim to fame was its feeble plot.

In addition to his other virtues and writing ambitions, Father Savický was also a legendary patient of my father's, suffering as he did from every disease known to mankind, sometimes even from ones yet to be discovered. He loved to discuss his illnesses, exaggerating each of them mightily. He boasted of his arsenal of medications. He had something for everything. He had medicines for pain, the common cold, spots, sleepiness, insomnia, sadness and excessive happiness, depression, excessive depression, over-excitedness, and so on. He used to pop the pills like sweets. He was constantly sucking on something, generously offering it to others, too.

10.

Before the war there used to be a small general store in the main square, where there is now just a gap between buildings hidden behind a Tesco billboard, waiting for a developer to seize his opportunity. It boasted a large sign outside, while inside there was a black, waxed floor and the shopkeeper, Mr Malánek, wearing dazzling white overalls and a smile on his face. The smile was there even when he had no reason to smile, a mask he was no longer able to take off.

Mr Malánek represented the only feature of Brežany that never changed as the years went by. He stood in the same place, with the same expression, come summer or winter, autumn or spring, even when children happily playing by the Sálava made a Russian grenade explode not far from his shop, and when Ambi Krebs came hurtling through the shop window in his new Austrodaimler. He stood there when his general store was nationalized and he was made to wear new, cheaper white overalls made of Bulgarian synthetic fibre and the sign above the door was replaced by angular script proclaiming SELF-SERVICE.

Mr Malánek was still standing at the counter when my father diagnosed him with *morbus parkinsoni*, allegedly a side effect of the Spanish flu he had once contracted – he was trembling, his face had gone stiff and he talked as if he were chanting slogans. He went on standing there because he was too ill to move from the spot, and once he started to move he couldn't stop. So he preferred to stay safely parked behind the counter.

As far as I remember, the most fascinating item his store had to offer a child were sweets kept in glass jars and sold by weight. Today it seems to me that this was the only thing you could get in his general store. I don't recall anything else. Just a clean, airy room with jars full of sweets on the counter.

The thing is, we never bought anything else there. Father used to get every imaginable gift from his grateful patients. They always remembered "our good doctor" – whether they slaughtered a pig or a goose. They would come bearing gifts of roast meat, goose fat, vegetables, fruit, potatoes, chicken, ham and sausages, and home-made wine. We seemed to be living beneath an inexhaustible horn of plenty. That's what happens when your life is in somebody else's hands.

Until the arrival of the radio, divine silence used to reign in our house.

In addition to the occasional orchestra playing on the 78s the only other sound in our house was Grandma Mária singing: *How quiet the night, so dark and fair, / My heart does make me rest foreswear. / The moon sleeps not a wink all night, / What tales it knows, of love so bright. / At dead of night will love change round, / When nightingales in the groves resound.* That is how the folksong went.

But once the contraption arrived, it never stopped playing. At first they broadcast live music, then later someone would play records. Radio plays were presented, complete with every careless mistake and spiteful tiff. Our privacy was later invaded by television – my sweet, beloved, hated television, the device intended to make all brain activity cease. But its advent was still way off.

Now once again silence reigns in the house. As it should at the final curtain. Everything that has ever happened here is long gone.

On the other side of the corridor, almost directly across from the kitchen, is where the dining room, or the drawing room as we called it, used to be. Although it is hard to say what this room might be called these days. The wind is whipping up again outside, making everything within whistle and rattle, as during Father's final years.

Father never tired of trying to keep up family rituals, with everything he thought that entailed. On Sundays there had to be a proper Sunday lunch. A classic Sunday lunch, say in 1938, followed certain fixed rules – chicken consommé complete with chicken necks, feet, stomachs, and cooked vegetables served on the side. The main course was fried chicken with potatoes. Or goose, and sometimes duck from a grateful patient; served with cabbage, dumplings or *lokše*, potato flatbread fried in goose fat. And sweet preserved tomatoes with rum on the side. Or stewed apple. And some delicate crème de menthe.

We sat around the big table, Father taking the place of honour at its head. His brother, Uncle Rudo, with Aunt Julka and their son Filip, my cousin, were regulars, as were several members of Mother's family: Uncle Armin, Uncle Oskar with Aunt Rózka and their children. Naturally, all family celebrations had to be held on Sundays.

I used to help Terka, our maid and cook, serve the dishes.

Uncle Rudo would instruct me, reading out extracts from a dining manual:

"The basic rules of serving at table are as follows… First: Food and drinks must be placed on the table using the right hand and on the diner's right-hand side. Second: Platters are served using the left hand and on the diner's left-hand side. Three: Drinks are topped up using the right hand and on the diner's right-hand side. Four: Plates are cleared away and replaced from the right and left, respectively. Five: While serving you must never turn your elbows towards the diner, except when serving soup in cups. Six: Every service is to be performed in the quietest and most unobtrusive manner possible. All dishes are to be offered twice, the second time also to those guests who had not partaken of the first serving. Food may always be offered, but not imposed, which would be impolite. This inappropriate style of hospitality should also be banished from country feasts, where it has become rampant!"

Uncle Rudo was a few years older than Father. He was a civil engineer who revelled in his atheism. He liked to argue with Father Savický about religious questions (and answers) but they usually tried to keep off the subject because once they got started that was all they would talk about. Both tended to emerge from these debates with their original views reinforced and would end up all sweaty and contented, shaking hands like two bruised boxers.

Uncle Rudo usually concluded with an endearing remark:

"The cross is really a symbol of execution, right, Father Savický? I wouldn't mind a religion that had the gallows as its symbol – or just a noose, wouldn't that be quite spectacular? Imagine everyone wearing it around their neck! Simply delightful!"

Rudo was bald, the tonsure-like little tufts of hair on the sides of his head giving him a monk-like appearance. He used to tuck his napkin under his chin, having always arrived clean-shaven, redolent of soap and eau de cologne, especially for our Sunday lunches. The uninitiated were most likely to take him for a retired colonel, from the days when the military profession still enjoyed an unblemished reputation.

He had spent some time in Africa as an expert in bridge construction (he must have inherited his love of engineering from Grandpa Albert) and he liked to recall what he had seen there.

"They are prepared to stand in long queues for water that is so dirty you can't see to the bottom. It smells as if someone has pissed in it. And these are the people who try to tell us we have destroyed their civilization. Codswallop!"

He had crossed all of Italy, managing to communicate using a single sentence: *Prego, signorina – mezzo litro vino!* He had no

54

inhibitions in this respect and was never in the least embarrassed. He loved wine. It was his favourite thing in life. Like the country itself – this was something he and Father had endless arguments about. Rudo loved Italian food above all. He would enunciate slowly, savouring each syllable: *Pomo d'oro,* adding it translated as *golden apple*, or tomato. The other Italian sentence he had learned went as follows: *I maccheroni sono buoni, ma difficili a mangiare.* The pasta is good but hard to eat. He also learned the right pronunciation of *Chianti* to make sure they understood him at the *osteria*. And he loved the red *Nebbiolo* of the Piedmont, so dark it was almost black.

Food was his be-all and end-all. Uncle Oskar, Mother's brother, nicknamed him *fresser*. And when Uncle Rudo got too chatty, he called him *meshugener*. This just about summed up his role in the family. A glutton and an amateur philosopher or, to be more precise, a clown.

Rudo's wife, Aunt Julka, who rarely said a word and was absolutely unremarkable in every way, didn't mind this at all.

He used to take me to the vineyards.

"I never open a bottle unless I'm sure I will finish it. I know how much work has gone into it. If there's not much left in the bottle it will go off but to throw it out is wasteful."

Sometimes he would wind me up:

"Other people just daydream or go angling or roam the world, while I work on my vines. While others go skiing I bottle wine, locked away in a tiny cellar. And this is real torment for me, believe you me, Adam, because I love working out of doors!"

He loved gnawing on bones. He would pile them up neatly on a small plate after expertly fishing them out of the tureen. He would leave them until the very end. But he also loved animals in their original, living form.

"Nature performs miracles!"

Whenever he talked about nature a dreamy expression would appear on his face. Tenderly he would call out to his wife to come and watch the wild geese fly over their house in the autumn. In October, after the swallows left, another kind of migrating bird, whose name even he didn't know, turned the entire roof black with their tiny heads. They sat there basking in the sun halfway through their journey towards the southern sun. He would stand outside his house and watch them enraptured. I would find him there motionless, holding his breath.

I vividly recall one of our Sunday lunches.

We are all assembled around the table in the drawing room. The children (including myself) are giggling, the grown-ups are talking in hushed voices, and there is the clinking of cutlery. Father is radiantly happy; he is in his element. And Uncle Rudo is speaking with his mouth full: "You may not believe me but… I often think we're living in wonderful times." Uncle Oskar pokes him in the ribs and flashes him an ironic smile. Refusing to back down, Rudo expounds: "Well, yes… If we just compare ourselves to those who came before us: we're not hungry, we have a roof over our heads – and we're quite comfortable…" Oskar: "Hmm, could be better." Rudo continues: "No war. No danger. Nobody is seriously ill. Our country is slightly off the beaten track, tucked away in a corner of Europe. We're actually very lucky. We're living in good times!" Father pulls a face and says: "Halcyon days… eh…?" And he really means it. "One day we shall all live in this house. Like one great big family."

At this moment the window shatters and a bird hurtles blindly into the room from the sun-dappled garden. Everyone starts shouting. I notice in the turmoil that it's a starling or a thrush. It's flapping its wings, crashing into the walls, landing in the food. Arms reach out to catch it. The bird is thrashing about. They've nearly caught it – someone has got hold of it on the table, feathers are flying all over the place, floating in the salad – then the bird breaks free again. "Open the window! Open the window!" Mother shouts. Everyone tries to hustle it towards the window. After a few more collisions with the wall and the window panes the half-crazed bird finally manages to fly out. It has left behind a scene of devastation – broken plates on the floor, overturned bowls, the contents of one plate have ended up on the wall, the meat is scattered on the floor, and the cat has already managed to grab a schnitzel. Relieved and out of breath, the family return to their seats. And all Mother can say is: "Whatever next?!"

For Mother's family Saturday was the holy day. It began on Friday night, before the first star appeared in the sky.

On the eve of the Sabbath the big prayer room in the Letná Street synagogue was packed. Mother and *bobe* Sara had to stay at the back, behind a white muslin curtain – while as a male, albeit very young, I was allowed to sit on the front benches with *zeyde* Blau, Uncle Oscar and Uncle Armin, who wore a black skullcap. Uncle Oskar, unlike Armin, a man of the world, never took off his hat or cap. He carried his own fringed *tallit* to the synagogue and wore short sidelocks. The *shachter*, Mr Stern, stood at the end of the bench with Mr Durchschlag, the *mikve Yid*, who was in charge of the ritual baths.

Everyone prayed in Yiddish while a bearded rabbi, who stood at the front with his back turned to us, read from the Torah. Nobody was allowed to touch the holy scroll with a naked hand: this had to be done with a special little silver hand with a pointed index finger, a *yad*, which I loved. When the rabbi delivered a ceremonial speech, the atmosphere was never as stiff as at St. Giles where I used to go with Grandma Mária. Uncle Armin said the rabbi was the only person obliged to stick to the ritual – the others might exchange a few words, join him in the prayer, then break off again. Someone shows a handful of shiny stones to somebody else, they whisper a few words to each other, nod and go back to the prayer. They sway back and forth and when the rhythm changes to regular chanting, and as the words *Ve'imru omeyn!* are spoken everyone suddenly starts to sing. The rabbi had a wonderfully sonorous voice – I still remember one of the songs. The tune has remained etched in my memory, probably because it's not too complex and includes a chorus: *L'khah dodi, l'khakh dodi liq'rat kalahp'nei Shabbat n'qab'lah, p'nei Shabbat n'qab'lah!* Another verse follows and the chorus is repeated: *Come, my dear, let us welcome the bride; let us receive Saturday!* This is how Uncle Oskar translated it for me when I inquired what we were singing about. The chorus swells and sounds more and more solemn. I keep singing even as we all shake hands, saying *Gut Shabbes!* and walk over to the other room for *kiddush*, the festive meal. A table has been laid and the *shames*, the rabbi's assistant who, I notice, has the keys to everything around here, pours everyone a drop of wine. We sing a song, the rabbi who sits at the head of the table says a short prayer and we clink glasses. I am also allowed a sip, and remember the wine tasting incredibly sweet. Uncle Oskar told me that because of *chames*, the ritual impurity, which only fire or frost can remove, the vine isn't picked until it's nearly winter. Then we go and wash our hands again, rinsing each hand three times, using a metal cup with two handles to make sure both hands remain ritually clean. We go back, take to our seats and the *shames* gives everyone a slice of *barches* bread dipped in salt, symbolising the manna God rained down on the Jews every Friday as they wandered in the desert. Everyone sits down and gets a bowl of *cholent* – as it's already dark, it has been warmed up and ladled into bowls by the *shabbes goy,* Mrs Slavkovská, whose services the community retains for this purpose, and the rabbi tells a story that is both enlightening and amusing. And finally, to greetings of *Shabbes!* all around, we take our leave and go home.

I remember that I kept on singing: *Come, my dear, let us welcome the bride; let us receive Saturday!* – until Mother told me to stop.

Meanwhile, at my grandparents' house, the Sabbath lights had been lit. *Bobe* lit two candles on the table; everyone toasted each other with wine blessed by the rabbi and sang special Sabbath songs.

After the war, in 1946, it was difficult to gather a *minyan*, the ten adult males required for prayers. They had evaporated. Quite literally.

They had to call on the non-believer Mislovič, who always talked more than was necessary, saying things like, "The world is dominated by triangles. Murderers – a green triangle; thieves – a black triangle; communists – a red triangle; homosexuals – a pink triangle. But Jews have two triangles facing each other and forming a star."

He learned this in Auschwitz, which he survived by a miracle, without quite knowing how. Old Grünspan used to remark sarcastically that he must have talked the guards round. When the gas was released, they could still hear him telling jokes and pulled him out so he wouldn't disturb the others in the honest job of dying.

Mislovič loved to tell a joke about Kohn, who wins a fortune in the lottery: when people ask him what he's going to do with it, he replies without a moment's hesitation that he will build a golden monument to Hitler. Why, everyone asks, horrified? And Kohn rolls up his sleeve and shows his forearm: "Because he's the one who gave me the winning numbers!"

Mislovič lived another seven years after the war. Dying at the right time is a great art.

But back then everyone thought they would live forever.

Meanwhile, the entry for *Jew* in the Kálal brothers' Slovak Dictionary of 1922 read as follows: (1) Jew *(kike, jewboy, dirty Jew)*, (2) swindler, usurer, (3) spot, blotch (e.g. after bleaching), (idioms: *to kill a Jew*, to do a somersault, make a mistake; *to have a hard time with a Jew,* to suffer from diarrhoea, *to let a Jew keep his skin*, to graze one's skin).

11.

One chilly morning in 1938, Father Peterský stopped my father as he was running down the hill after his customary morning exercises in his breeches and long woollen socks. After chattering about his angina and swollen feet for a while and perfunctorily asking Father's advice, the chubby servant of God stopped beating about the bush.

"Doctor, we shall be celebrating the great holy day of Corpus Christi tomorrow. I would be delighted to see you in the procession – especially now that a new era has dawned and we will soon have our own republic. Our Catholic republic!"

He said this very emphatically, as if he had carefully planned every word in advance. Then he said goodbye. Father couldn't concentrate on his patients; he didn't really listen to them, and must have been still preoccupied with the encounter as he discussed it with Mother in the evening. I could see only their outlines through the opaque glass of the kitchen door – Mother was sitting and Father was walking to and fro, visibly on edge, his voice rising and falling. Then she, too, rose to her feet, put the kettle on, gesticulated with both her arms, and sat down again. After standing at the window for a while Father opened the door and headed for his isolation cell with his hands sunk deep in his pockets.

The following day he put on a dark suit which he disliked, woke up my brother Peter and myself from our sweet slumbers, and after a grumpy breakfast (we really didn't feel like going – in this respect there was no difference between children and grown-ups) we set out for my first procession, the first of many that lay in wait for me in the future and which have now become a tawdry, multi-coloured blur, full of music, pompous drivel and songs blaring out of tune.

The main street had been festooned with flowers, banners and multi-coloured bunting, and the entrance of every other house boasted a symbolic little altar made of spruce twigs, as well as the odd crucifix and statuette. People lined up in the procession by rank and importance – the dean, the altar boys, the chaplain, the trumpeters, the notary, the postmaster and assorted shopkeepers, followed by the pharmacist, the publicans, foresters, teachers and the doctor, while the common people, the lowliest pawns in this parlour game, brought up the crowded rear. The procession shuffled along from altar to altar at an agonizingly slow pace. Father said almost nothing, but I could see him glancing around in desperation, trying to copy gracefully what everyone else was doing (and trying in vain to pat dry with a handkerchief the beads of sweat dripping from his forehead): when to genuflect, how to beat his breast, what prayers to recite, which words to repeat. And the two of us dutifully repeated everything after him. That was what he took us along for. We were the extras.

At the head of the procession a canopy swayed gently in the breeze and the whole throng echoed its rhythm. Dean Peterský, decked out in lavish vestments, walked below the canopy, sheltered from the sun. Everyone watched the fat nape of his neck and imposing back with fascination, keenly following every gesture of his massive arm.

I noticed that at times Father got carried away by the atmosphere. He allowed himself to be swept away by the current, his movements became automatic, just like those of sheep gently jingling their little bells. He would then come out of his daze and wipe the sweat from his brow, only to lose himself again in the natural flow of the collective rhythm. In his trance he failed to notice that it was now cold and the sky had turned the dark colour of rotting fruit. A gust of wind played havoc with the dean's vestments, exposing the large hairy calves of his legs. There was a clap of thunder and the canopy toppled first to one side, then to the other, until eventually the procession was scattered by a heavy downpour. People ran for shelter and Father, who had kept his wits about him, shepherded us towards Puškár's patisserie in the main square. The owner welcomed him with a broad and understanding grin.

"A drop of brandy, doctor?"

Father nodded, sat down and loosened his tie, which was soaked through.

"You mean to tell me that after some eighty years toiling on this miserable earth what I have to look forward to is another zillion years sitting in a comfortable armchair with a glass of beer doing nothing but listening to the news on the radio? You can't be serious!"

"Would you like to take a look at today's menu?"

"The menu…? Oh yes, please."

Puškár skipped away, smiling and reeling off a stream of similar-sounding words under his breath, as was his habit:

"Menu. Menuet… Menuet, minuet, minuetto, just a minuetto!"

Perhaps it was then that I first noticed that furtive movement. Judging by his expression, Peter noticed it too, although he didn't seem surprised. Father unbuttoned his jacket and his fingers wandered towards the top left-hand pocket of his waistcoat. Fishing out a miniature object and placing it on his tongue, he moved aside the glasses on the table with his other hand to make room for two ice-cream sundaes from the day's menu.

Back at home I had a little snoop around his waistcoat after he had taken it off. I wasn't looking for anything specific; I just wondered what Father could be hiding there. In the bottom right-hand pocket I found a secret cigarette butt he hadn't thrown away for reasons best known to himself, some small change and the stub of a pencil. In the top left-hand pocket I discovered a small blister strip, apparently cut off with manicure scissors. One little cavity was empty, but the other three were intact, containing white pills with a longitudinal groove and a name. The brand name, *LUMINAL O1 BAYER,* was also printed on the silver foil. I replaced it in his pocket, disappointed. I had expected a real secret of some kind.

That reminds me, as night draws on I could do with a few more drops of my elixir, my water of life, although it sometimes gives me restless nights and bad dreams. But then again, I'm not yet asleep. At least I hope I'm not.

12.

The mysterious man with the claret-coloured shoes was back in town. It was with these metal-tipped shoes that Klaudia Horváthová had fallen in love – in fact, it was these shoes that had conceived his imaginary unborn child. And it was my Father who had "discharged" the child from her body, at her own request, which inadvertently brought him into contact with a delicate part of her anatomy, one he was to enter into more regular and more enjoyable contact with some time later, under somewhat different circumstances.

This time the man in the claret-coloured shoes arrived incognito – the shoes he wore now were black, although otherwise identical in shape to the previous ones. His name was Rehor Kohút and he wasn't a tradesman, as Klaudia claimed. He was a healer.

I met him at Vojto's house. He was there at Mrs Roško's invitation. She suffered from appalling migraines and had tried every conceivable remedy – except, naturally, for a regular doctor's visit – all in vain. When she heard that the famous man was honouring Brežany with his presence, she didn't hesitate to call upon his services. He was sitting in an armchair and I heard his deep voice expounding a classification of human illnesses. One kind of illness was brought about by immoral life – masturbation or self-abuse. Another type resulted from lack of neighbourly love. And the third and final category comprised illnesses he ascribed to the influence of the nether world – these included madness, epilepsy and deaf-mutism.

To illustrate his method he cited examples of his patients who had made spectacular recoveries. For instance, he had treated a two-year-old girl who used to masturbate. She had become so weak she couldn't stand up. Her masturbation, Mr Kohút insisted, was the result of her mother – otherwise a person of impeccable morals – indulging in an impure sex life during pregnancy. The girl's mother, declared Mr Kohút in his adorable Czech accent, exuded a *fluidum astrale,* which made anyone who happened to be in her vicinity, including the maid, succumb to masturbation. It was essential to take the child away from the mother.

In Mrs Roško's case the procedure was quite simple. Peering

through the door, Vojto and I choked with laughter when we saw that it consisted primarily in the handing over of several banknotes. Then Mr Kohút, his arms outstretched, slowly approached Vojto's mother who was lying on an ottoman, and laid the palms of his hands on her forehead. He stood silently for a while with his eyes shut, concentrating.

Then he said: "There we are! I must go now. I'm needed me at the hospital. You know these doctors, they can't cope with more complicated cases."

And he vanished as unexpectedly as he appeared.

Some years later the architect Vámoši, one of Father's local patients, tracked Rehor Kohút down somewhere in Austria, where he had opened a sanatorium. Kohút now sang the praises of osteopathy, his personal invention. He claimed that all parts of the human mechanism had to be manipulated by hand to achieve their correct mechanical relationships.

Father said he must have got this from gushing articles praising the process of mechanisation at the Ford factory in Detroit. Vámoši told him that Kohút invited him to his office and told him to strip to the waist. After feeling his spine with his fingertips he showed Vámoši a picture of the human body in all colours of the rainbow.

The healer explained: "The car's transmission shaft sets the whole vehicle in motion, right? If you step on the brake, the wheels stop turning. And nerves, in turn, provide the propulsive force to every organ in the body. If you suppress a nerve, it deprives the viscera of their vital force and they stop working. And this has to be corrected."

He waited for his words to sink in before continuing:

"Every drop of blood, even if it dried up years ago – and every manuscript, even if it is a hundred years old – is comprised of quivering electrons, of vibrations organised in a way that enables us to detect the nationality, religion as well as the disease of the individual in question. These quivering electrons are a new kind of energy, which even the most sensitive physical instruments can't detect. The only way of detecting them is by means of physiological reactions, which is the exclusive province of human beings."

Then he stuck a needle into Vámoši's finger, and after waiting a short while, he inserted a drop of his dried blood into a complex machine so that an electric current could pass through it. From there the blood moved on to an amplifier and into a further instrument labelled *vibration rheostat* and eventually into a *rheostatic meter*. From this, wires led to a small metal plate that was fixed to the forehead of the *physiological indicator*. This was the wretched Vámoši himself, standing in a dark room facing west with his stomach bared. Rehor Kohút stood next to him, tapping his stomach with a tiny hammer – presumably in order to distract himself or the patient – and telling him things about himself he knew anyway.

Although Vámoši's health did not improve, he felt happy. What more can one hope for?

Father was livid.

Father once spotted a glass jar at the pharmacy, which had a metal top and a little rubber hose with a label saying in big letters, some in bold:

The effect of any treatment will be enhanced considerably *if each individual step is performed in a positive frame of mind!*

When inhaling, *the patient should concentrate his thoughts and be mindful of the fact that the inhalation* ***provides him with superior*** *aerial nutrition and thus also with superior and natural mind- and body-fortifying and healing medication.*

By holding his breath *the patient will* ***enhance*** *the effect of any medication taken.*

By exhaling, *the patient is* ***expelling*** *harmful and pathogenic waste matter, which leaves the body with his breath.*

A product of the Rehor Kohút Sanatorium; effective treatments for all diseases.

Asked what the active ingredient was, the pharmacist responded with a smile, as if it were self-evident that the jar contained nothing but healing air.

Father bought a jar and smashed it ceremonially right outside the shop.

When a policeman approached him and demanded an explanation, Father retorted:

"It's my jar, I can do with it whatever I like."

The policeman had to admit this was fair enough and just recommended that Father should make less noise.

"I've finished anyway," Father remarked, throwing the shards of glass into a waste bin.

Since he was wearing his off-white promenade suit and hat and smelled of eau de cologne, the policeman just shook his head incredulously. When he regained his composure he asked Father for "something for his nerves".

13.

Mother rarely left the house of her own accord without a very convincing reason. She often took so long to get ready that in the meantime someone else – often me or Peter, her favourite – dealt with her errands around town, and there was no longer any point in her leaving the house.

On the other hand, she always wanted to hear a detailed account of everything. All her decisions were based on things she had heard. She would use one or two details to piece together a complete picture and know exactly what was what (or so she claimed). And while her idea of the world differed from the real one only in matters of detail, these were quite crucial – like when you stare at a three-dimensional image and all you see is a blur of red and green.

Father used to help her complete the puzzle after coming home, if he still had the strength to talk. He would drop his large black bag in the consulting room, put away the gifts from his patients and sit in the armchair for a while, relaxing. Mother would serve him a glass of wine; he would take a sip, and once the drink had made him feel nice and warm inside, he would begin.

I usually had to listen from behind the door because by then I had been dispatched to bed and was supposed to be fast asleep.

Father's favourite sentence went: "Give me three words from anyone's medical history and I'll tell you what kind of person they are."

Alcohol, phlegm and injections suggest: worker at the Knocht & Marinar factory. Father had several of them on his books. He would administer injections to these consumptives and heavy drinkers who coughed up phlegm mixed with blood. He kept telling them they should go to the Matliary sanatorium in the Tatra

Mountains, offering to make all the arrangements, but most of them refused. Occasionally one of them would die.

Boric acid and clean pyjamas meant measles. Father would prescribe mouth rinses, frequent airing of the room, changing into fresh pyjamas, linden tea, light broth, drinking lots of water and the company of other children whose parents he would personally phone to make sure they also got measles in good time.

Then there were soft boils, sweating and frequent changing of partners, or bruises, depression and a missed period...

When I was little I thought it was Father who had invented everything. Everything I had ever come across or touched. I regarded him as the creator of the Universe. Only later did I discover that, for example, what he claimed as his own cabbage soup recipe wasn't really unique and that everyone in our part of the country made it exactly the same way.

I started using eau de cologne because I had always loved the way Father smelled, and it was also through him that I had gradually acquired a taste for wine.

Father had been trying to get me interested in wine from an early age but since I have always found the vineyard chores intensely boring he was not likely to succeed. That's where our joint bathing ritual came in. Father would fill assorted little cups and moulds with water and let them float around in the tub, scooping up some water and rolling it around in his mouth.

"Mmm, a delicious Grüner Veltliner. Have a taste!"

He passed me the cup and I, too, took a sip: "Yum, excellent!"

"And now try this, it's a Blaufränkisch!"

"I see. But isn't this a St Laurent?" I pulled a face.

Father: "Let me see! Yes, how right you are! I've made a mistake!"

I would laugh gleefully. "You've made a mistake!"

Father would fill another cup. "You really must try this Irsay! It's quite something!"

Long before his hearing began to fail, I noticed that he rarely listened to me. He would pretend to, but would later recall nothing. He had developed a whole panoply of affirmative noises that he employed while I talked, but his thoughts were elsewhere. Peter noticed it as well, and later so did Tina, who mentioned it to Mother.

"You've only just noticed this? Your Father lives in a world of his own."

She laughed, but nobody else thought it was very funny.

Nor was it funny when in the middle of our bathtub wine-tasting he suddenly got up as if he had done his bit, and walked off to his isolation cell. My allotted time was over. At first these sudden changes gave me a fright but later on I took them in my stride.

Every now and then he would take refuge in the garden. He pretended he was working hard and didn't wish to be disturbed. But when nobody was looking he would put the pruning shears aside and sit down in the wicker chair. He needed to be alone.

He hated it if something forced him to leave his own world. Like that time during the wine festival, when Tina fell off the merry-go-round and needed treatment. She had grazed her knees and elbows and bruised her head. Father was furious: she had spoiled his day. At first he tried to persuade her that she wasn't in pain at all and only later, reluctantly, did he take her to his consulting room and dress her wounds.

Late at night, on my way to the toilet, I often saw Father standing in the gloom of the kitchen, having returned from an urgent house call or a childbirth. In the dim light of the fridge that purred like a cat (its sound amplified by the reverberation of the spectacles he liked to place on it, claiming that removing them helped him focus on the taste of his food), he was savouring the salami he had got from a patient, stuffing it into his mouth with a slab of cheese, followed by a piece of stale bread and a bit of dried up green pepper, while promising himself for the fifth time that this really would be the last mouthful, only to succumb to temptation again.

Naturally, the food had to be washed down with some milk. And a generous spoonful of jam. "Add something sweet and something savoury," he would say. To keep the taste buds in a balanced state.

He loved to eat at night, a habit he was not able to kick till the day he died, even though it gave him nightmares and made him put on weight. He usually did it in secret, taking great care not to get caught. The excitement of doing something forbidden increased his enjoyment of the food, and then of course, since nobody knew about it, clearly neither he nor in particular his body, would have an inkling of it either, so it was as if it had never happened.

When he finished, he quietly slipped into the bedroom, undressed quickly and climbed into bed next to Mother. She'd embrace him without waking up, smile and go back to sleep.

We have all picked up this habit of his. White sex, Father would quip, referring to our night-time binges and Mother would give him a slap.

We usually had the radio on low in the kitchen. A weird, tinny voice would introduce a nocturne, and after thirty seconds' silence gentle music would start to play. Whenever I hear Chopin, it brings back the memory of our kitchen at night.

And then came one of the last normal Christmas holidays. I used to confuse it with my name day as I celebrated both on the same day, something I thought was awfully unfair because I would only get one set of presents.

Everyone was jolly and people standing on the garden path covered in snow were swigging *hriatô,* the hot toddy laced with hot melted lard. Also known as *krampampul'a*, it tasted equally disgusting whatever you called it and drinking it was generally considered something of a punishment, although I was considerately not allowed to try it for a few more years.

The taste in the mouth and the overall sensation was usually improved by eggnog, our traditional festive drink.

Fried carp with potato salad followed, all gloriously illuminated by the Christmas tree candles, with presents underneath and a peculiar jingling contraption suspended from the branches, with tin angels on little chains that turned round and round, propelled by the heat of the flame. Everyone is at the table, including a few members of Mother's family, who don't really have anything to do with this circus, apart from the fact that Jesus was also a Jew. The place of the high altar is taken by our brand new radio playing Christmas carols: *The Lord is born this joyous day*, and *The way to Bethlehem*. People drop by to wish us Merry Christmas, presents are being unwrapped. Many have been delivered well in advance, a little something for the good doctor.

"The Lord is born this lousy day…!" Mother's brother Armin mutters under his breath, with a smile.

I hear him and repeat his words in a whisper.
We feel like conspirators.

14.

The war in Brežany began several times.

In 1937, when the Italians invaded Abyssinia, the newsboy carrying a sheaf of newspapers shouted in the square: *It's war!* This was said to have given Mr Levendovský, the notary, such a shock that he broke his pince-nez, dropping it into his coffee in Puškár's patisserie. All right – maybe it just slipped into a half-eaten cream slice and got smothered in cream – but this makes it sound more dramatic. That was the first time.

From that day on Father hated the Italians: he could not comprehend why they had to use airplanes and machine guns to attack half-naked savages who just ran around wielding spears. He fumed about the degenerate Romans, the last stage of a great ancient civilisation in decline, a nation that had once proudly conquered Europe but these days all it could manage was to loiter in the streets wolf-whistling at girls. Although that too was an art form of a kind but still…

He didn't change his mind even when Fellini appeared on the scene and we all fell for his films, which also featured loitering and wolf-whistling.

The second time the war broke out was in 1938.

Mother later recalled that calm and serene summer as the most beautiful in years. As if something in the air was trying to persuade us that the world was safe and fragrant. The cellar was packed with freshly preserved plums and apricots and whenever we managed to sneak in and open a jar prematurely, its pressurized lid made a hiccupping noise. That was when Vojto's father gave him a fabulous brown boomerang and we spent every day playing with it. Sometimes it would disappear into the raspberry bushes but eventually we learned how to throw it so that it flew back into our hands.

Meanwhile some curious fellow (Father said his name was

Hodža and he was Czechoslovakia's prime minister) bleated Jeremiads on the radio and when he wasn't lamenting, mournful music was played. In those turbulent times Father couldn't tear himself away from the set in case he missed the latest news. Our Sunday lunches started to resemble a funeral feast without the deceased. Everyone looked grave, and every time Uncle Armin was about to make a joke (he was particularly fond of jokes about funerals and corpses) the withering looks that greeted him wiped the smile off his face. The radio took over our house.

Then in September 1938 my parents went to our local cinema, Slovan (this was just before the letter "n" was replaced by a "k", changing Slav to Slovak) to see the operetta *The Land of Smiles* with the tenor Richard Tauber, whose monocled grin adorned many of the cards then found in the packets of cigarettes Father received from his patients. As they emerged from the auditorium into the main square, humming *Dein ist mein ganzes Herz*, they learned that general mobilization had been declared and that we might soon be at war with Germany. It was 23 September – I remember the date because at that very moment I was spilling hot chocolate all over myself at Vojto's birthday party. Father bought a paper from the newsboy on the corner and there it was, in block capitals. He stopped in the street to read the article by the light of the street lamp, until a tense Mother gave him a nudge and asked what exactly it said.

Vojto and I were in his garden playing with the boomerang and heard Vojto's father turn up the radio. A swing tune was interrupted by an agitated voice: *Attention! Attention!* Vojto's dog Letov – named after the type of aircraft Lieutenant Roško used to fly – raised its head as if it understood what was going on, and began to tremble and howl. It huddled up to Vojto's father for protection and would not leave him. It kept getting under his feet and Mr Roško had to stroke it until it calmed down a bit, which was only achieved with the help of a chunky slice of ham. When I told Father about this strange occurrence he said the dog must have sensed the alarm in the announcer's voice and perhaps also a change in the body odour of those listening in the room.

The tension in Brežany culminated with the departure of the young men drafted into the army. The local radio kept reminding people to observe the blackout. Vojto and I spent hours staring at the sky in anticipation of the first air raid. We could not imagine it at all and were almost looking forward to it.

Vojto told me that one night, when he went for a pee, he noticed a light on in the kitchen. He found his father sitting there, lost in thought and cleaning his service weapon. He was making a very thorough job of it, while the announcer went on and on about a German city somewhere miles away. Munich. For me its Slovak name, Mníchov, conjured up monks and monasteries – stone cold walls, shaven heads and anguished statues of Jesus in dark corners.

The next day someone stopped Father on his daily stroll across the square to Armin's hairdressing salon, sounding very agitated about the fact that we had given the Sudetenland to the Germans. I couldn't imagine what that could possibly mean. I assumed they were talking of some kind of building blocks, or perhaps sweets. To my great disappointment aircraft failed to materialise, even though they appeared in my dreams more than once.

A few days later, in early October, an independent Slovak government was formed, headed by a priest who was later to end up on the gallows. Jozef Tiso was on the tubby side and I gather the hanging didn't go at all smoothly. But for the time being things were working out for him. There was joy over Slovakia gaining independence and much talk of "intolerable Czech oppression". Books began to disappear from libraries – those that had kind things to say about the common state of the Czechs and the Slovaks. And those that said the Soviet Union was a great country whose example should be followed by all.

All sorts of weird things started happening. One Saturday Father took all of us – Mother, Peter, Tina and myself – for lunch at the restaurant of the Golden Stag. We found a table with a view of the sunny autumnal street.

Our starters had just arrived when a short, stout man, who was neatly dressed, rose noisily from a nearby table. He had a badge with the Slovak double cross pinned to his chest, and as he passed us on his way out, he remarked in a low voice that he wasn't prepared to share a restaurant with a Jewish woman. Everything froze for a moment and Mother stopped eating. A waiter cleared the man's table, brushed away the breadcrumbs, pushed the chair back and mechanically picked up his empty plate, all the while casting sidelong glances at Mother. When she caught his eye, he turned away pretending he was looking somewhere else. Father wanted to say something but was speechless. We quickly paid our bill and left.

The short man hadn't introduced himself but since all roads, however winding they may be, lead to the doctor's, a month later Father found him cowering in his waiting room. He looked so miserable as he entered the consulting room that Father only recognized him by his badge. Father was about to give him an injection but the man protested, squealing that his aunt had been given one of those and died the following day. After refusing an X-ray on similar grounds, he left, deeply aggrieved. His name was Gajdoš and he was the secretary of the local branch of the ruling Slovak People's Party.

A few days later, while giving Father a shave, Uncle Armin mentioned a rumour he had heard that someone wanted Father removed from Brežany. The Hlinka Guard, the Slovak People's Party's militia, was behind it and Father's colleague, Dr Ducký, was also rumoured to be involved. Ducký, whose surgery was right in the main square, claimed that Father was poaching his patients, undercutting the going rate and couldn't be relied on to make a proper diagnosis. Father knew that this kind of baseless gossip was more effective than if Ducký had lodged an official complaint with the Medical Council.

And then, one evening, as he returned from his round, he found a letter waiting for him. The letter said:

"*We have received a report indicating that your ancestry may not be purely Aryan. The Town Notary's Office therefore requests that you present, at your earliest convenience, the birth certificates of your ancestors, going back five generations.*"

With some difficulty, Father managed to gather the documents and peace was restored. For a while.

A week later he received another letter, this time with an application to join the Hlinka Guard. He spent a couple of days deep in thought, giving only monosyllabic answers to every question. In the end, without consulting anyone, he completed the form and sent it off. He confessed this to me only many years later, at the point when our conversations had two participants but only one listener. Father claimed he did it to protect Mother but maybe he just wanted to preserve his peace of mind.

He took out a subscription to *The Guardsman*. The paper's front pages featured articles and speeches by prominent German Nazis interspersed with peculiarly bellicose rhymes, enthusiastically churned out by poets such as Vojto's mother's favourite Ján Smrek or the young and promising Ján Kostra. One of the poems was entitled *Before the Battle* and we were supposed to learn it by heart at school: *May Slovak rock / Harden in our catapults / Hey, someone will be beaten up / Hey, someone will fall face down / Hey, someone will end up licking their wounds / On our Slovak soil...!* The job of editor-in-chief was entrusted to the writer Milo Urban. After the war he was one of the first to realise there's nothing people love more than a reformed sinner and wrote a history of the Slovak Republic from the point of view of a committed communist. After all, even the Bible is full of stories of radical conversions – they are among its greatest hits.

And since you could never be sure you weren't under someone's watchful eye, in early 1939 Father also ordered a magnificent monograph on the Hlinka Guard complete with an impassioned introduction by the journalist Emo Bohúň, who later penned the idyllic memoir *Stories of Dust*. However, the book remained in its wrapping, with the delivery note casually stuck to its side. It was still untouched when it eventually found its rightful place in the recycling bin.

The same fate awaited the sumptuous coffee-table book on the Hlinka Transport Guard, which Father received with this recommendation: *The task of editing and overseeing the present publication,* The Hlinka Transport Guard – Its Origins and Activities, *has been entrusted to brother Eduard Gajdoš for the purposes of sales and distribution. It comes with the warmest endorsement of the HTG Command in Brežany, since it includes the history of Brežany's own HTG unit.*

This being very recent history, all the contributors beat their chests and swore they had heroically attended the huge pro-autonomy rally in Bratislava on 5 June 1938, at which ardent speeches lambasted the Czechs for breaking the terms of the Pittsburgh Agreement. Attended it if not in flesh, then at least in spirit.

I realised long ago – not just now as I sit here at night in this empty, almost non-existent house, having taken some of my usual painkillers – that the history of Slovakia boils down to proving that you were in the right place at the right time.

Let's see what a questionnaire on some crucial dates might look like. It might include the following questions: What were you doing on 14 March 1939? Pick the right answer and cross out the one that does not apply: I was in Hlinka Square shouting my head off and my windows were festooned with garlands. / I most certainly did not attend any noteworthy event that day, I was busy planting gladioli in my garden.

Were you in Banská Bystrica on the day the Slovak National Uprising broke out on 29 August 1944? Of course I was there, first thing in the morning! / Where exactly is Banská Bystrica?

Were you present in Stalin Square, roaring "Hurrah!" on 25 February 1948, when the communists took power? (Alternative option: Have you gone round the bend? Why would I do that in the middle of the flu season?)

I trust that on 21 August 1968 you made sure you stood in front of a tank, its terrifying turret pointed straight at your bare chest? (Alternative answer: I welcomed the fraternal troops of the Warsaw Pact with a bunch of red carnations, which from a distance may have looked as if I were standing in front of a tank, its terrifying turret pointed straight at my bare chest.)

Were you among the crowd marching with candles during the first mass rally in Bratislava on 25 March 1988 and did you end up drenched by the water cannon? Or did you phone the police from your flat in nearby Jesenský Street to complain you've just come off your bloody night shift and can't sleep because the street is ablaze with light?

And last but not least, on 17 November 1989, were you among those who were beaten up yet never stopped chanting: "Unity is strength"? I am sure you were. Because, right now, you have only one option, although who knows what the future might bring. As the protests raged, the capacity of the square that first bore the name of Hlinka, then of Stalin and later of the Slovak National Uprising, was exceeded many times over.

Dalí hit the nail on the head with his melting clocks – that really is what time looks like.

People also changed, like chocolate Santas mashed up by a child's hand.

There was something medieval about the Hlinka Guard's torch-lit processions at dusk. The same old faces flickered in the torchlight, at their head a commander on a white horse, followed by two former communists, out-shouting and out-singing everyone else. After 1948 one of them resurfaced as a regional secret police officer: without breaking sweat, he just shaved off the little tuft of a moustache under his nose and stopped greasing his hair. It was all like a parlour game, though one underscored by a military choir whose singing chilled you to the bone.

By October 1938 things cooled off. Vojto's boomerang was still in good shape. We tried to hit the pigeons sitting on the ledges of houses in the main square, mostly without success. Our hands were numb with cold.

During a Hlinka Guard oath-taking ceremony in Trnava just before Christmas both synagogues in the city went up in flames, allegedly by accident. The Hlinka Guard commander-in-chief Šaňo Mach (the diminutive Šaňo, for Alexander, may have been meant to underline his friendly, or perhaps even artistic, outlook – either way it now strikes me as rather fatuous) gave a speech venting his outrage:

"*Following yesterday's events in Trnava, where a synagogue was set on fire and Jewish shops were vandalized, our message to the city is as follows: these people have betrayed the interests of the Slovaks. These shops will belong to you, sons of Slovakia, my fellow Guardsmen! All the broken windows and everything you have burnt or destroyed could have passed into the ownership of Slovak people.*"

I had no idea that this type of warfare originated in Bratislava in 1936. Christian university students from the Svorad hall of residence were so outraged by the screening of Duvivier's film *The Golem* that they marched to the heart of the old Jewish quarter and smashed a poor rag-and-bone merchant's shop windows to Christian smithereens shouting "These fucking Jews own all the property in Slovakia", and accusing them of having crucified Jesus.

This particular claim was said to have so upset Uncle Rudo that a stewed cherry he was eating went down the wrong way, and when it was eventually extracted, he yelled until he was blue in the face that it was the Roman soldiers who had crucified Jesus and, besides, Jesus himself had undoubtedly been a Jew. So it would have been historical justice if the Jews had invaded bloody Rome and smashed up the Colosseum, since those bastards had crucified one of their own, an *unsereiner*.

Everyone did their best to calm him down and get him to bed.

The war broke out for the third time in early November 1938.

The border between Slovakia and Hungary was decided by arbitration although, ironically enough, neither of the two countries actually attended the negotiations. The meeting resembled a medical triage about which of your legs should be amputated and which should remain. As a result Slovakia was forced to hand over the southern part of its territory to its southern neighbour. Joachim von Ribbentrop, Germany's Minister of Foreign Affairs, working with the Italian Foreign Minister, Count Ciano, Mussolini's son-in-law ("Those degenerate Romans again!" – fumed Father) had apparently covered the map with their doodles until their pencils went blunt, making the border several kilometres wide in places. The Germans consoled the Slovaks like some gravely ill patient: they should take comfort in the fact that it could have been much worse and they could have lost the cities of Nitra and Bratislava, not just Levice and Košice. To cap it all, Poland picked up some crumbs in the north while Germany occupied the Bratislava district of Petržalka on the other side of the Danube and the nearby village of Rusovce. Everyone had their bite of the cherry.

Regardless of the repeated outbreaks of war, life in Brežany went on as usual.

Except that Father received a letter from Dr Levius, a colleague in Levice, by then occupied by the Hungarian army. He wanted to consult him on some minor medical matter. In addition to the usual postage the envelope boasted a memorial stamp declaring *Léva visszatért! – Levice has returned to the fold!* Greetings from the hot south. I asked Father if I could keep the envelope because I liked the stamp.

I kept it along with an advertisement that shows a smiling yellow crescent moon admiring a nightshirt drying on a line. *OVERNIGHT AND (please turn over) EFFORTLESS – half your work is done if you let your laundry soak overnight in Schicht's "Frauenlob" laundry concentrate. This astonishing dirt-dissolving preparation removes most of the dirt all by itself. All you need to do the next morning is give your washing a light rinse using SCHICHT'S SWAN SOAP, the finest soap in the world.*

This has popped into my head because moonlight suddenly flooded the room. But the floor and walls were illuminated for barely a minute before clouds covered the silver orb again.

On the eve of parliamentary elections, seven days before Christmas Day 1938, Chaplain Jablonický burst into the Green Tree pub, later known as The Tower. His frock was all crumpled and some claimed he reeked of drink. He was accompanied by a band of men shouting: "Jews out!"

The regulars were speechless. The publican, Mr Bernauer, and the football club chairman, Novacký, tried to mollify the chaplain and show him out. But he just ranted on and on.

Eventually one of the Jews, a well-built chap called Hugo Jungreis, got up and gave him a resounding slap that sent him to the floor.

When the other customers began to rise to his feet, ready for a fight, the chaplain's drunken companions helped him up and took him away.

The next day the town was awash with gossip. People debated who had started the fight, how many slaps were received by whom, and rumour had it that Dean Peterský had given his chaplain a dressing-down although Mother thought the opposite was more likely to be the case.

Uncle Rudo commented, "Free will is wasted on some people."

The war broke out for the fourth time in February 1939.

The chairman of the Slovak-German Society declaimed in Hitler's presence that he was *"entrusting his nation's fate to the Führer's hands"*. Father remarked that he could say the same and entrust the fate of his nation to Ambi Krebs's hands.

This was not to the liking of the new Czechoslovak President Hácha either, a man who usually looked as if he had just been resurrected from an autopsy. He ordered the Czech army to occupy Slovakia, had a few politicians imprisoned, abolished Slovakia's autonomy, and declared a state of emergency. The Czech soldiers, all muddled and decent in a confused sort of way, didn't stay very long. Vojto and I watched them as they wandered the streets of Brežany, looking at a loss. One of them wanted to show us how to use a boomerang and threw it so vigorously it got stuck in the telegraph wires. It was only brought down by wind some time later.

Over Sunday lunch Uncle Oskar told us about his visit to Bratislava, where he sat with a colleague in the Berlinka Café watching the local Germans gather on the bank of the Danube and shout across the river to Petržalka: *Führer, please take us as well, we are yours, too!* Apparently young Nazis handed out leaflets saying *Pressburg will Anschluss!* Bratislava wants to join! A time bomb exploded in a small car parked between the Old City Hall and the Jesuit church, killing a street vendor who had the misfortune to be passing by.

Shortly afterwards, on 14 March 1939, the Slovak parliament held a formal vote, declaring independence and establishing the Slovak Republic.

Before going to bed that night, Uncle Armin allegedly insisted that none of this was true. It was just a ploy to make people buy newspapers – we would wake up the next morning to banner headlines announcing that nothing had really happened.

But then he turned on the radio and heard that the Hungarians had invaded Subcarpathian Ruthenia, justifying their action by nostalgia for the good old Austro-Hungarian Empire. This war lasted four days before the two parties declared a truce. Thirty-six people lost their lives and another chunk of our territory was hacked off.

Brežany, meanwhile, remained an island of peace.

Except that one day in April our Slovak teacher, Mr Štermenský, walked into the classroom struggling to hold back his tears, and without further ado told us to open our textbooks on page one. We were asked to take hold of the frontispiece and then, at his command, in a single collective movement, rip out the portrait of Czechoslovakia's founder, President Masaryk, and drop every copy in a pile in front of the blackboard, next to the poster celebrating the Führer's fiftieth birthday.

Czech teachers were sent home and gradually left our school, while Czech books disappeared from the school library. Suddenly they were not to be found in the catalogue and the librarian went around with a peculiar look. Peter had taken out a Czech book, *Insights into the Animal Kingdom*, by Bohumil Bauš. He was notified that the book was to be returned urgently and a week later, when he wanted to borrow it again, it no longer existed. It had vanished off the face of the earth.

A circular was delivered to Father's consulting room:

Dear Sir,
Please find enclosed the decree concerning changes in the generally applicable forms of address whereby all forms of address previously reserved for party members are to be adopted by all traders, entrepreneurs, as well as all civil servants and everyone else whom it may concern.

Na stráž! – *"On your Guard!", the greeting originally used by members of the Hlinka Guard, has rapidly acquired the status of a nationwide greeting, underlining national solidarity and the patriotic feelings of the Slovaks. It is advisable to use this greeting not only in the street but also whenever entering offices and public premises. It is also to be used in the closing formula of all public notices and speeches.*

Originally two varieties of this greeting were in use: the so-called small one and big one. From now on only the big variety is to be used. That means that in addition to uttering the greeting aloud, everyone must raise their right arm to eye level.

The response to the greeting consists of its word-for-word repetition or its abbreviated form: Stráž! – *"Guard!"*

In some parts of the country schoolchildren may supplement the Guardsman greeting with a Catholic greeting, which is equally acceptable.

I hereby charge you with ensuring that all your subordinates within the remit of your activities are notified of this ordinance and with ensuring that it is observed by the said employees.

signed by his own hand,

Minister of the Interior of the Slovak Republic
Alexander Mach.

As Father read the letter, frowning, a lovely song played on the radio.

Being an optimist, I know for sure, / it's those who haven't been born who are happiest of all. František Krištof Vesely's tenor had a certain charm. Mother was particularly susceptible to it.

"Do you know, Berta, that your idol only ever speaks to his butler in Hungarian?" Mother's Jewish grandmother, *bobe* Sara piped up from her knitting and joined in the catchy tune. This was shortly before she and her Jewish grandfather, *zeyde* Béla, died in a car accident.

79

She didn't live to see the new definition of "Jew" officially promulgated not long afterwards. A Jew was defined as: *A person originating from Jewish parents who was not baptized before 30 October 1918.*

Father was sitting in his armchair leafing through a copy of *The Slovak Physician*. Reviewing a book on medical ethics, one Dr Chovanec wrote:

"An overview of the ethical principles of the past with reference to Kant, Eckhardt, Rosenberg and Dietrich is followed by the presentation of a new medical ethics, free of the past's negative attitudes and infused with the national socialist worldview. The first and foremost duty of the new medical ethics is to foster the belief that, however interesting it may be to study the healing of a colli femoris *fracture in an eighty-year-old, from the point of view of the nation as a whole this fracture is of little significance. The same applies to pioneering pulmonary thoracoplasty. In Gauerbruch's view surgery is indicated for this type of patient if and when all else has failed; however, the patient should also undergo castration because, in the interests of national health, a person who is thus disfigured is merely a procreator of inferior individuals. While it is commendable that medical science has succeeded in prolonging human life expectancy by an average of two or three years, this has, on the other hand, resulted in a growing pyramid of old people incapable of work."*

That night Father was woken up by the insistent ringing of the phone. It was the Guardsman Gajdoš. He claimed that Dr Ducký had told him he would swell up overnight but nothing had happened so far and he found this extremely alarming. He said he had lost faith in the other doctor and wondered if an injection might help.

"Drop by in the morning," Father said drowsily.

On that ordinary and rather dull Friday at the end of the summer of 1939 Peter and I wished something would happen, but time seemed to have ground to a halt.

In the afternoon the smell of marble cake wafted through the house. Mother dusted her collection of china ballerinas and closed the glass cabinet. She turned on the radio and listened to a Brahms concerto under the baton of the great Alexander Albrecht. The sun and warm air streamed in through the open windows from the garden. Everything was quiet and peaceful.

Peter and I shattered the tranquillity by barging into the drawing room. Peter, brandishing a broomstick, chased me into a corner while I shouted:

"You must believe me. Honest Injun!" I always used this argument as my trump card, and surprisingly it usually worked.

"Shush!", hissed mother.

At that moment Father walked in and announced that Hitler had invaded Poland. After making this a matter-of-fact announcement he went back to dealing with a case of appendicitis.

I heard Mother pottering about in the bathroom before going to bed. She brushed her hair, then exhaled slowly and whispered:

"Poland…"

As if it was a foreign word she had just picked up on a language course.

It was the end of the first day of September, the day of St. Giles, the patron of our parish church, protector of nursing mothers, shepherds, huntsmen, the shipwrecked, archers, beggars and lepers, the one who lends a helping hand during fire and drought, thunderstorms and accidents, in poverty and loneliness, during confession, in epilepsy, mental illness and infertility. Father Savický insisted we always rattle off the full list and I still remember it today. The Saint is also one of the fourteen holy helpers in need.

That was when the war broke out in Brežany for the fifth time and for good. It was 1 September 1939.

Ab fünf Uhr Morgens wird an der polnischen Grenze geschossen…

The 15 October 1939 issue of *The Slovak Physician* had the presence of mind to feature a fine article entitled *The Honourable Fight*. Mother and Father discussed it over breakfast but wouldn't let us read it although, of course, that was the best way to make sure we would want to.

"*From early on misunderstandings have bedevilled the relationship between the German Reich and what used to be Poland. With a bleeding heart the German nation, suffering under the yoke of the diktat of Versailles, watched the war of extermination waged by the ruling aristocracy against their kinsmen. For a long time, with fists clenched, they were able to exercise restraint. However, what the leaders of the Polish people have demonstrated to the world in the past few weeks may be called anything but an honourable fight. How self-regarding they must have been*

81

to see as a sign of weakness their adversary's invitation to resolve the
situation by peaceful means. Their prejudice and overweening pride drove
them to actions that forced the Leader of the great German nation to heed
a call to arms and hasten to the assistance of his persecuted defenceless
compatriots. The savage acts and atrocities perpetrated against German
nationals have been fully exposed only since the German army has entered
individual German settlements and cities. Thousands and thousands of
Germans – old people, women and children – have been abducted, maimed
and murdered. Men have disappeared without trace. Extremities were
chopped off, eyes gouged out, noses cut off and tongues cut out, corpses
deprived of their manhood, girls and women defiled – these acts stand as
an eternal indictment of those who had whipped up the animal instincts
of an inflamed mob. Bereft of all humanity they stooped so low they did
not recoil from crucifying children, dousing people in petrol and setting them
alight, burying them alive. Age-old customary international military law
demands that prisoners of war be treated humanely. We have recently
marked 75 years since the adoption of the Geneva Convention by the Red
Cross. Poland too was bound by this Convention!"

The author illustrated his text with a dramatic, and artistically
quite powerful, photograph of defiled female corpses, one of them
draped across the picture in a perfect golden section.

Thus, once and for all, did Slovakia's nineteenth century come
to an end, having overstayed its welcome by several decades.

From then on nothing would ever be the same.

15.

I had no idea where to begin my search for clues in the bones
puzzle.

I fetched Father's magnifying glass and inspected the bones
closely. There seemed to be a hole in the skull, just above the
forehead – but I decided not to disturb the bones any more.
I examined the scattered ribs – assuming they were ribs – and
something that may have been a brachial bone. I don't know what
I was expecting – perhaps that the Lord, in His infinite mercy and
providence, had furnished the bodies of all His children with tiny
identity tags attached to every body part?

The most dramatic events in this part of the world occurred during the war. Everyone took it more or less for granted that people just vanished. This was probably the key. I decided to draw up a list of names and to start ticking them off, one by one.

I also examined the ground in the surrounding area but did not detect anything noteworthy. So I piled some soil on top of the bones and covered them with branches and leaves, just in case.

I went to the TV archives and dug out some crime stories, which I watched in a dark and lonely projection room. All in vain.

I realised that this would not get me very far and although I had no intention of initiating anyone else into this matter, I thought it was time to pay Igor a visit.

16.

A shot rang out in the vineyard.

The arrival of starlings spells disaster for a vineyard – a huge flock descends on the vines in a black cloud and can devour an entire vintage in a matter of minutes. Father and I spent all day walking up and down the rows making a hell of a racket. We banged lids and pots and used sticks to pound everything that was likely to make a frightening noise, and every now and then Father fired his old pistol into the air, which I just loved.

"I might hire a falconer next year," Father said.

The section of the vineyard nestling at the foot of the hill was a buzzard's stamping ground and the starlings never dared go near it. A neighbour used to catch crows and nail them to two crossed sticks by the chest, basically crucifying them, head down. They looked menacing, even I could see that, but the ruse only worked for a while.

Deer from nearby woods would come at night and gnaw on the vines. Father had had enough:

"C'mon, it's time to visit the hairdresser's…!"

Normally I wasn't keen on going to the hairdresser's – I thought it was a waste of time that I could more usefully spend doing lots of other things. But I loved having my hair cut since we started going to Uncle Armin's salon. Father, Tina and two other children and I seated ourselves on a bench, each of us holding a serial number.

Uncle Armin was tall and well-groomed. He paid regular visits to the *shachter*, Mr Stern, the Jewish butcher, who slaughtered poultry and cattle in the kosher way. People would bring him their chicken, geese and ducks; he would pluck the back of the creature's neck, make an incision with a very sharp knife and let the animal bleed. At the end he carefully removed all the veins from the meat. To get to his house you had to walk down Hangman's Alley (the name caught on even though Brežany never had its own executioner and used to send the local criminals to Nitra for hanging and beheading). When Jewish children walked down the alley carrying pitchers of milk you could hear the clatter of their feet in all the nearby streets. Jews didn't grease their cows' udders for milking because they wanted to make sure not a drop of fat got into the milk.

Armin offered shaves and haircuts. If he happened to nick someone's face, he would stop the bleeding with a white stone he called lapis. It worked like a miracle, all you had to do was hold the stone to the wound.

"Your chin is strong and your skin is delicate," he would say to customers prone to bleeding. Mostly my Father. This may have been a reason why he disliked Armin.

Uncle Armin was in the middle of styling the hair of a plump lady I knew by sight. He kept talking and smiling while his nimble fingers did their job.

"Oh, but you're the only reason I haven't given up this business, Mrs Škridla! If it weren't for you I would by now be lounging about somewhere... on the Riviera!"

Mrs Škridla gave a flirtatious laugh: "Don't exaggerate, Armin. But do go on, you're flattering me!"

"Happy to oblige, madam!"

He kept working on her hair.

"By the way... have you heard this one, madam ? Two men are travelling in the same train compartment, without saying a word. Two hours go by and then one of them turns to the other: "Excuse me, you're not Jewish by any chance?" The other one looks up from his newspaper: "Yes I am. But how did you know?" The first one smiles: "It's your accent!"

All the grown-ups in the salon laughed.

After a few final adjustments with his scissors Armin ceremonially whisked the sheet off her shoulders in his own inimitable way.

He bowed: "I have been aware of your beauty for years. But now, suddenly, I feel it may be too late for me…"

"Oh Armin, Armin!" said Mrs Škridla, admiring her reflection in the mirror.

It was my turn. Armin had my wild mane trimmed in almost no time. A young lady entered the salon just as he finished sweeping up my hair with a little broom and stuffing it into a paper bag he had ready for this purpose.

"I'll be with you in a moment, madam. I see you slept well last night. You weren't alone, were you? A man's embrace works wonders!"

The lady blushed but didn't take offence. Armin must have known that she could take his teasing.

"If you're such an expert, why are you not married?"

"Well… I've been saving myself for you. And besides – I'm not the one who misses a man's embrace. So, how may I help you today?"

"Just a little trim."

"Please take a number and a seat."

Armin sighed and draped a sheet around my sister Tina's neck.

"A man is like the sun. A round, hot sun, always beaming. Provided, of course, it's not hidden behind a cloud, if you know what I mean."

He stared at my sister's head for a while as if wondering which side to tackle it from.

"A woman, on the other hand, is like the moon. Always different – a crescent, full moon, new moon, half-moon – inscrutable, forever changing, never the same. Aren't I right, Alfie?" he said, addressing my Father who was the only one not smiling, and giving him a wink in the mirror.

"Aristotle compared man to a joiner carving a child from a block of wood. And the block of wood is woman!"

The young lady started to giggle.

Father frowned and felt his jacket. He pulled a cigarette out of his inside pocket, put it between his lips and stood up. He took out matches from his trouser pocket and gave the box a shake in the direction of the shop window. Armin nodded and gave another wink.

"What a clown…!" Father muttered through clenched teeth and went out into the street.

He almost collided with Gajdoš in the doorway. He hadn't spotted him because of his small stature. Gajdoš worked at the post office and was always scowling. People said he was five centimetres short of being normal.

Our hair ended up in paper bags, each of us having contributed their share. We were back in the vineyard, walking up and down. Father stopped at regular intervals to hang the bags onto posts.

"Deer are repelled by the smell of humans, especially males. If a stag catches the scent it won't come anywhere near it. That's how powerful hair is," Father explained.

Last November Bony and I went for a stroll in our former vineyard. It was untended, overgrown with weeds and rosehips, and crippled concrete posts protruding from the growth. My feet kept getting caught in some rusty mesh. Wisps of faded hair were still wound around it, protecting non-existent vines. The sun had bleached the hair white and the bags had disintegrated.

The vineyard hut had been taken over by bats. They were hanging from the beams heads down, their babies clinging to their chests. They squealed, hiding from the light. Rusty bits of tools and a few yellowed photographs – these are the remains of an extinct civilization.

And the hair, which Father kept collecting, just in case, even when he no longer needed it.

Frozen time, laid to rest. All the memories, all the meals eaten, all the alcohol consumed, all the medicines taken…

Thinking about it I taste the grapes in my mouth.

You put a grape on your tongue and gently press it towards your palate. The grape splits open, its magenta-coloured skin cracks and it slides down your tongue. It is smooth and tastes of nothing. You squeeze and it bursts. The sweet and tart jelly-like pulp makes you clench your teeth. You bite into it. The last to burst between your teeth are the pips, somewhat spoiling the pleasure but enhancing the overall effect. Like a bird dropping that lands on a clean tablecloth. The shredded grape, the fibres, torn tissue, sweet juice spilling onto the tongue.

You might even taste blood. Like that time when an agitated man barged into Armin's salon and sat down in a chair, gasping for air. He didn't seem quite with it.

"Sir, how can I help you?"

"I've just… out there … I've run over… I've run over a man. But I need a haircut."

Did I taste blood then? Or was it just my imagination?

17.

It's the middle of the night. The temperature outside is a few degrees below zero, if Father's ancient thermometer can be trusted. There is a blustery wind. I watch the flowers the frost has painted on the windows. There are just a few, branching out and blossoming on the left-hand side of the glass.

It's been a long time since I last saw this. It's become a rarity. Just like so many other things. Frost flowers don't grow on perfectly vacuum-sealed plastic windows like the ones in my Bratislava flat.

Vojto's father kept pigeons.

I had often seen him delight in them, before he was dismissed from the army in 1952. They used to fly above our part of town wheeling in large circles in the air and I never tired of watching them from our garden.

He used to enter them in competitions in cities hundreds of kilometres away and they always came back. Vojto once told us that only males are sent on long-distance flights, while the females stay locked inside. The males long to be reunited with them and that is why they never fly away. The females are held hostage. As a reward, Vojto's father would let the males inside the pens so that they could spend some time together.

Lieutenant Roško's voice had an unusual timbre. However, he didn't use it as an instrument of seduction, unlike those men who impress women with their deep bass cadences, flirtatious modulation and sophisticated vocabulary. He didn't use it as an instrument of persuasion either, or to attract attention or win over an enthusiastic audience. For him, his voice was merely a tool of essential communication and that's exactly what it sounded like: as if it had been dried out by a harsh sun and – if a voice can have a colour – utterly grey. He was barely audible because he never strained his vocal cords, which may have completely atrophied as a result of being used so sparingly, as if their owner was saving his energies for another, more strategic part of the body.

A couple of words, the odd noise, a clearing of the throat, a yawn, a discreet cough… That was enough. It invariably made everyone draw closer, move nearer and prick up their ears to hear him better. As a result Vojto's father gave the impression of being rather popular with those who listened to him. He even acquired the reputation of being a skilful storyteller, perhaps precisely because nobody had ever heard him speak more than a couple of sentences at a time.

Vojto was very sensitive to his father's voice. In the early hours of the day, he could hear its hushed tones when his parents held a quiet conversation over breakfast, before his father's vocal cords had a chance to warm up. The minute he spoke Vojto would prick up his ears even though the words weren't addressed to him. He could pick up their frequency from far away, as I often noticed.

Lieutenant Roško's voice must have sounded very resolute over the radio transmitter when he communicated with base during sorties.

Vojto and I had our favourite places in Brežany.

At the far end of town, just beyond the last houses, there was a brickyard with a small pond. The place was called Behy. It was just a patch of stagnant water with some frogs, fish and Mr Mislovič – hirsute, with a big belly – always immersed in it, whether it was summer or winter. He was a stoker and his wife was a seamstress. He was bald (we children used to say that if you wanted to make him angry, you should ask him for a comb) and his skin was black with soot and coal dust. In addition, his arms and his back were covered in all sorts of scrawls and images – this was very peculiar since Jews were not allowed to have tattoos, Uncle Oskar used to say. Except for the number on the forearm, Mislovič used to counter jokingly.

He taught Vojto and me how to catch crayfish – we would follow him to the Sálava and he would point to a hole in the riverbank: "Stick your finger in!"

Hesitantly I would put my finger inside, and it was immediately grabbed by claws.

"Pull it out, pull it out!" We caught two in this way.

Nowadays you won't find any crayfish near the brickyard. When the Knocht & Marinar factory changed its name to Slovlina and started producing synthetic fibres and plastic in addition to paint and varnish, the crayfish moved away, as the euphemistic saying went. It could have meant that they moved away on little crayfish lorries or tiny crayfish trains carrying their miniature suitcases, the way people sometimes took their leave. Yes. A nice image, that. If it hadn't been for the odd sighting of their little bodies carried downstream, away from Brežany, along with dead fish, white bellies up. Yes, well, one might say they were just happily basking in the sun, imitating people. As a matter of fact, no one ever proved otherwise.

Mislovič's grandfather was called Mislowitz. His father had changed his name to Miszlovič since he worked for the railways and in those days it was better to have surnames that sounded Hungarian or were at least spelled in the Hungarian way. His son, in turn, became Slovakized, maybe with a little help from an absent-minded clerk at the register office. His name was Nándor, or Ferdinand. Not a practising Jew, he didn't pray and used to say he wouldn't recognize Him if he met Him in disguise. After the war the surviving Jews from Brežany used to seek him out when they wanted to pray in the Letná Street synagogue, since at least ten grown men were required so that Jehovah would accept their prayer as a plea on behalf of the whole of Israel.

If they were a bit late Mislovič would stamp his feet outside the entrance thinking of better ways to spend his time and shouting:

"C'mon, you stinking Jewish bastards! You make me shlep all the way here so you can talk to that God of yours and you can't even be bothered to get here on time!"

Mislovič's house stood in a secluded spot close to the river. He had built it on the site of an old farmstead that had survived every flood. The island where Mislovič's house stood was usually the only thing that stayed dry in the middle of inundated fields and meadows. When the flood of the century came – and they seemed to be coming with increasing frequency; I myself have experienced three of them – people in dinghies would call out to him offering to take him away and save him from drowning. He refused every time and sent them packing. And every time his house on his island survived. People still call that spot Mislovič Island, even though it has been almost devoured by the spreading cancer of the satellite districts on the outskirts of town.

Mislovič would sometimes turn up at our house with an empty sack and leave with a full one, with something kicking and pulsating inside it, and his visits always happened to coincide with our Ikebana's litter. Father would give him some small change, the two men would shake hands and he would be on his way. We all guessed what was going on but no one spoke of it in our family. Tina was the one who found this the most difficult to take but Peter was quite upset, too. But since no words were ever uttered, the assumption was that the kittens had simply vanished into thin air, or turned into ginger cat angels, carried by the big omnipresent Tomcat straight to Heaven, and all seemed to be well with the world. Ika later got into the habit of hiding her litter soon after giving birth. We never discovered where.

In addition to the Behy pond – which we were strictly forbidden to dip even a toe in – in the summer a lido was set up on the bank of the Sálava. And since Father was not supposed to know that I was making progress in swimming with the help of Mislovič's wolfhound – his owner instructed me to hang on to the dog's tail and it worked brilliantly – I let him pay for a coach.

The following image keeps coming to mind: I'm immersed in water with a harness around my chest, a lifeguard slowly walking along the pool's tiled edge carrying a pole I'm clinging to, to make sure I don't suddenly vanish into the depths. Father is standing next to him, dressed to the nines in spite of the sweltering heat – his off-white suit complete with jacket and waistcoat, his sun hat pulled down to shield his brow.

He frowns and says from time to time, "Adam, why don't you make your strokes longer, like Mr Kopasný says?"

Once I got a bit better at it, Tina, Peter and I used to go

swimming with Mother. She used to pack milk mixed with strawberry syrup and for us this became this became the taste of our swimming outings, with the odd raspberry seed crunching between the teeth offsetting the absolute perfection of the drink. The seed would get stuck in a molar, right at the back of the mouth, impossible to extract, even if you rinsed your mouth with water or tried to scrape it out with your fingernail. It was only after you came home and brushed your teeth before going to bed would it come out, empty and devoid of taste, like the faded memory of a summer's day spent by the water.

My parents, by contrast, would blend a litre of pure medicinal alcohol with a litre of raspberry juice. That was their grown-up version of raspberry lemonade.

Vojto and I loved to go to a dead arm of the Sálava to catch fish – just like that, by hand. The best we could manage was burbot, for in order to catch a decent sized catfish you would have needed a hook and line. We would bake our catch on a bonfire right there, by the river.

Bellies full, we would lie down in the grass as dusk fell and the air cooled off, talking for hours on end. That is, Vojto did – he was the one who loved telling stories. I loved to listen.

The last time I came to Brežany, last autumn, I went back there.

I stood by the river and watched it stubbornly trying to find its original bed. After an astonishing amount of rain had fallen the previous week, particularly somewhere up north, the Sálava easily found its former bed and started meandering again, breaking free of the straight irrigation lines that had turned it into a gutter.

Both banks of the river flooded, inundating the nearby copse. The people of Brežany rushed over to take a look at the spectacle but they didn't last long in the cold. They stopped for a while, thrilled by the sight of the rushing water wearing down the banks, turned around and stared at me wondering who I might be. A stranger with a familiar face. Then they went back home in the gloomy light of winter.

A dog barked at a crow sitting on the fence but could not reach it. There were still quite a few nests left in the copse; many birds had arrived from the north to spend the winter.

A few years after the war Vojto and I lugged some branches and planks of wood onto the top of an old willow by the Sálava and built a hideaway there. It must have been May because the May beetles were swarming.

We watched a group of people partying on the riverbank. Men from Brežany, including Mislovič and some of his friends, ordinary folk by my Father's and Vojto's mother's standards at least – we would be told off if we talked to them. It was early evening, almost dusk.

The men had dug two pits on the riverbank. They lit a fire in both pits and laid sheets of metal over them. For a while nothing happened, they just sat around drinking and talking. A bottle of transparent liquid went around, and there was much laughter.

Then some huntsmen came out of the woods carrying crows – plump and young, the kind that still only hop about on the branches, just before they take off on their first flight. They made an incision under the crows' necks and skinned them. Thighs, stomachs, hearts – everything was taken out and placed on the metal sheets. Mislovič, who turned out to be the head chef, added some lard, pepper, salt and paprika and started cooking.

"Dinner! Kosher dinner!" he shouted, laughing. "Everything I touch is kosher!"

Before long he begun throwing the first pieces of meat onto plates. It smelled wonderful! They ate it with bread and washed it down with wine.

By then the sun had set. The air smelled of the cooling earth.

While the first lot was cooking, the hunters went back to the woods to shoot more crows. We heard voices, distant gunfire, more laughter.

At this point a strange figure emerged from the woods. But, in fact, he was no stranger to us. The man was wearing soiled camouflage gear and carrying a rucksack on his back. He walked past our tree. Vojto watched him particularly intently. For the man walking under our feet was none other than Mr Roško. He gave the company a nod and walked on without a word or a smile.

"Hello, General! General!" an inebriated Mislovič called after him.

Vojto's father shook his head, trying to protest against being given a rank that was too high – but anyway, whatever Mislovič may have said, it was no longer true. A week earlier the postman had delivered a letter from the ministry and he had been wandering around ever since and was hardly seen at home.

"Come and join us, General!"

Vojto's father hesitated and turned around reluctantly.

"C'mon! Have a bite to eat!" The others joined in.

Slowly he approached the pits and the group of men, and sat down in the grass.

"Good evening...," he said in that peculiar voice of his. Mislovič introduced him to his friends and found him a plate.

"Here, have some kosher pigeon!" he roared with laughter. He loved to repeat successful jokes many times.

"Ferdinand is my name..." he said, offering his elbow as his hand was greasy, and Vojto's father took it and shook it.

"Vojtech," he exhaled.

"I know. Welcome."

Mislovič gave him a pat on the back and returned to tend to the meat.

By then Vojto and I had climbed down from the tree and started to approach the men slowly.

"Oh, look who's here!"

"Good evening," we said shyly.

Vojto went up to his father cautiously. Both of them were here illegally, so to speak, and both were out of their depth – but his father was getting bolder, and the more wine he drank the more he laughed at the jokes. He spoke very little, as if scared that someone might whack him on the head. He leaned close to Vojto.

"But not a word at home. This will be our secret, OK?"

Monako shouted at his wife: "Hey, Zuza! Leave something for the others!"

His wife found the crows repellent and refused to eat them at first, shouting hysterically that she would never touch the meat and telling Monako to leave her alone. He just laughed and made her try a little piece. After that nobody could drag her away from the metal sheets.

"Leave some for the others too, do you hear me?"

"Another piece of kosher pigeon! Help yourselves!"

Paper plates were pressed into Vojto's and my hands, each laden with a thigh, a piece of bread and a hot pepper.

Gingerly we took a first bite. It was delicious.

We heard gunshots from the woods. Somebody sang a song and played the accordion. Other voices joined in, happy and out of tune.

A ferry with more revellers arrived; they were quite tipsy, too.

The ferry service on the Sálava continued until 1976 when the river washed away the three large oak trees to which the ferryman's cable had been tied – one on Christmas Eve and two the next day. The Sálava formed the boundary between our district and Nevedovo and many years ago, to show off to the kids "on the other side", Monako's son had made a bet that he would shimmy across the river on the cable. He was about halfway there when he got cramp in his hands, fell into the river and drowned.

The river's appetite was insatiable.

18.

Familiar period film footage mingles with my memories. The setting is always the same sunny street. Sometimes it's raining, sometimes the street is covered in snow. Nothing at all is happening. The general atmosphere is *gemütlich*, as the Germans say. Noble boredom.

The film might also include fast-motion scenes of people darting through the main square of a provincial town. The camera gets everywhere – now it is inside the crowd, now it hovers above it, wandering around ignoring every law of physics, peering into every nook and cranny. People… hurrying, smiling, exchanging greetings, enjoying their daily routine.

The camera pans from one street scene to another, all in fast motion – a chestnut-seller, a glass-blower, a few cars zooming past, a horse-drawn carriage… Gentlemen in hats in the middle of a convivial chat… A beggar on a street corner… A market… Women laughing… Life runs its quiet course, nothing seems to be happening…

And on the edge of the pavement a gentleman in a hat is reading a newspaper, smoking and biding his time. The camera zooms in on him like a pesky fly and films the headline.

The gentleman is my Uncle Armin Blau, apparently on a date.

Even though our house was in a side alley, we could hear all too well the endless stream of tanks, cars and combat vehicles rumbling day and night down Adolf Hitler (formerly Masaryk) Street, the wide boulevard that ran the length of town and was now out of bounds to Jews. The moment the street was re-named, the impudent Jews were swiftly evicted from their homes and hustled into half-ruined houses on the outskirts of town – who did they think they were, anyway? Father said that an army convoy was marching on the Soviet Union.

"The Soviet Union... Hmm...," Mother whispered in the bathroom as she brushed her hair before going to bed – she uttered the words in one breath, like in a phonetics exercise. A brilliantly constructed tongue-twister you have to repeat over and over again until a new, dirty meaning is revealed. A great party trick.

A bit like the parlour game *Whose eyes are these?* or *Whose feet are these?*, in which you had to cover your face with a piece of paper or hide the rest of your body behind a curtain. The grown-ups loved to play this when the company reached the right state of inebriation. They would laugh their heads off.

Whose eyes are these? – Hitler asked. *Whose feet are these?* – Stalin countered.

Both men had their way with lots of feet and eyes.

At school we were given Michael Herbert Mann's *Great German Reading Book*, which taught us a great deal about our allies, the German people.

The teacher made me stand in front of the class and read out aloud:

"What is Greater Germany? What is this great European, 'Middle Kingdom'? The land of poets and thinkers, uniforms and ringing ceremonial marches, castles, cathedrals, palaces and enchanting historic towns, smelting furnaces, shipyards and laboratories, where learned dreamers seek to re-invent paradise or hell. What is it like, this empire in which a symphony of labour, prudence and combat holds sway? What is it like, this country in which extensive legislation for the protection of animals co-exists with the death penalty? What is Greater Germany? And who is this dreamy, hard-working and belligerent 'German Michael', whose heavy-footedness did not stop him from learning to fly? A concise and

factual answer to these questions follows. The Great German territory has provided the stage for a significant part of the momentous history of the West, indeed of global history. Furthermore, the Germans have been also active beyond Europe and overseas, as the origins of the United States of America demonstrate. The Diktat of Versailles turned Germany into a mutilated, unviable rump. But the seeds of a new beginning had already been sown. The existential struggle imposed on the German nation in the world war, regardless of tribal affiliation and national allegiance, has awakened the thirst for a harmonious, united empire of all Germans. Hitler has now quenched this thirst. The national socialist movement came to power on 30 January 1933 with Adolf Hitler's appointment as Chancellor of the German Reich. Having transformed the country from a parliamentary republic into a new German People's Republic, with a strong centralized power, he was able to embark on the step-by-step creation of the Great German Reich. Parts of the German nation that had been separated from Germany under the Diktat of Versailles were re-incorporated: the Sudetenland (1938), Bohemia and Moravia (1939), the Memelland (1939), Danzig (1939) and Eupen-Malmedy (1940): the dream of German Austria to be re-united with the Reich finally came true in the spring of 1938. In the autumn of 1939, following the victorious military campaign against Poland, the provinces of Posen and Western Prussia were re-established, with the General Governorate set up at the same time. We might say that the variety and mix of character traits and skills typical of the 20th-century German make him one of the most perfect human types in the world."

The text was illustrated by a map showing *Greater Germany as the Heart of Europe*. The following pages featured black-and-white photographs of a *Miner from the Silesian coal region* and a *Heligoland Fisherman*, a photo of the *Munich to Salzburg Reichsautobahn, Modern workers' housing: light, air and sunshine* and finally a picture of *Hitler watching German soldiers marching in a military parade*.

At Christmas we were taught to sing *O, Tannenbaum!*

My son Bony, in turn, had to sing a song about *yolka*, the Russian Christmas tree.

But at home we always played *I'm dreaming of a white Christmas, just like the ones I used to know*, on one of Father's old 78s, until Uncle Rudo sat on it and broke it.

We learned from German propaganda that on 22 June 1940 the French agreed to an armistice with Germany and that Hitler – who had a particular penchant for symbolism – had tracked down and sent to Compiègne the very restaurant carriage in which Germany had signed the armistice at the same site in 1918. Then he had the carriage sent to Berlin and put on public display, where it was thankfully destroyed in an air raid in the final months of the war, otherwise the game might have gone on forever. And who knows what that might have led to. Providence, or whatever Hitler called it, sometimes works the way it should.

Others called it God. Father Savický used to declaim soulfully:

"The Lord is everywhere. He is pure spirit, He is the air all around us, He is the air we breathe. He is omnipresent."

I was daydreaming, gazing out of the window, when I suddenly heard an angry voice:

"Trnovský! What is God?"

"God is… pure air!"

Before I knew what was happening, Father Savický was standing next to me, barking:

"Fingertips together!"

I stretched out my arm and whoosh! Down came the cane.

Before it was made compulsory I hadn't been going to church very much. Only now and then would I accompany Grandma Mária to Holy Mass. Under her dress she wore a scapular – a glass medallion with miniature prayer beads her late mother had given her – with a picture of a doleful Mother of Christ on one side, and St. Anastasius on the other.

Inside the church I stared at the ceiling where naked contorted figures jutted out from the walls, inhaling the exotic and exciting scent of incense. I gave a start whenever Grandma touched my forehead with a cold hand dipped in holy water.

I remember being six years old and Grandma telling me off because of the way I described a place I'd been to with Uncle Oskar: "You know this place at the end of town, there's this man, Imri and he's showing the way." What I had in mind was the crossroads with a statue of a man whose one hand pointed west and another east to help pilgrims find their way to Brežany. The man's name, written above his head, was IMRI.

Father couldn't stop laughing when he heard this.

That is why I was taken aback on that Saturday morning when he took me along to Our Lady of Sorrows, a little church in a side street. It was a hot summer's day, I remember it well. I also recall tugging at my Father's sleeve and asking him, as we followed a priest who wore a black cloak over his white habit, down the aisle to the vestry:

"Is he here?"

At first Father didn't hear me, or he didn't understand my question. Either way he seemed a bit agitated and didn't respond.

"Is he here?" Now I was no longer whispering but almost shouting.

"Who…?"

"God, who else!"

Father raised his hand and slapped me on the head, sending flying the hat which I had forgotten to take off. He gripped my hand firmly.

The small church of Our Lady of Sorrows was run by four Dominicans, also known as *Domini Canes,* which translates as Hounds of the Lord, Grandma explained. She said that in the Middle Ages they administered the Holy Inquisition, but that didn't seem plausible. They looked so peaceful, diffident even.

The oldest one – with a sweaty tonsure – joined us on the bench.

"So what is your idea? How will you proceed?" Father asked.

"This is not a theatre production, doctor," the careworn Dominican sighed.

"I understand, but still…"

"Well, you go to confession and take holy communion; and then I shall perform the wedding ceremony and finally I shall baptize your wife. We shall have to backdate her baptismal certificate, of course, otherwise it won't be valid, as I'm sure you understand."

"And there's no way it could be done without my confession?"

"But my dear doctor, you are a man of impeccable character, a law-abiding citizen. You lead an exemplary life; I don't understand what your problem is."

"It's more the principle I'm concerned about."

"Ah, principle…!" The Dominican smiled. Then he turned serious and said, rather sternly: "I'm sorry but that's the only way. It can't be done without going to confession."

Father heaved a deep sigh.

I've always had a strong, visceral response to the sound of the organ. Its music makes my body reverberate and my heart vibrate to its rhythm. We were sitting in the front row – Father and the three of us children. The godparents – Ambi Krebs and his wife – were also present. The Dominican sprinkled some water on my Mother from an aspersorium.

Then he spoke solemnly:

"Berta Rozália, I baptize you in the name of the Father, the Son and the Holy Spirit. Amen!"

The church was completely empty and every sound echoed back from the walls. Mother received the body of Christ while Peter picked his nose. It was all over very quickly.

Outside on the gravel path an elated Uncle Rudo was waiting with a bouquet of flowers. Winsome in his rotund majesty he sang out as Father and Mother emerged from the church:

"So you've now joined the bone collectors? My heartiest congratulations!"

Father tried to stop him with a serious look on his face since it wasn't a good idea to attract too much attention. Uncle Rudo went quiet but couldn't stop a smile playing about his lips.

Over lunch he began to expound his pet theory.

"Isn't it wonderful how attached the Catholics are to all those holy giblets?" What he meant, of course, was holy relics such as the tiny metacarpal bones, cervical vertebrae and bits of fabric. "Yet in the same breath they insist that they don't care about this transient world of ours. Matter is irrelevant, while the spirit is all-important. How ironic. It seems to me that there's something crucial here that the Christian philosophers have missed."

Mother was lucky in a way – and the rest of us along with her – since according to the laws of *Halakha,* Jewishness is passed on through the mother, whereas the dutiful Slovak authorities have traditionally held the father responsible. Isn't life a great parlour game?

The following Sunday afternoon Father and Mother sat in the wicker armchairs on the veranda drinking coffee. I was playing nearby. Screwing up his eyes as he looked at the sun, Father kept nodding off. For several days Mother had been tense and unable to conceal her agitation. She seemed to be on the verge of saying something, but couldn't pluck up the courage. People tend to think that children live their own lives without noticing what goes on around them but that's not true. They miss nothing and the grown-ups wouldn't believe how much they remember.

Mother cleared her throat, swatted a fly away and mumbled as if to herself:

"I wonder what will happen to Uncle Armin. And … all the others…"

Father said nothing for a while, then he pushed up the straw hat he especially liked wearing while sitting on the veranda, whether or not the sun was shining.

"Why should anything happen to them? They're in no danger."

"In no danger?!" exclaimed Mother and I could see she was seething inside.

"It's all just idle talk. Because of Hitler."

"The Reinfeldts have already been evicted."

Father, by now fully awake, sat up and topped up his coffee.

"But they went of their own accord."

"Well… that's not what I heard… And old Katz, too. He's gone and someone else is running his café. It's been Aryanized."

Father shrugged, digesting the news that yet another Jewish business was being taken over by a non-Jew.

"Oh well… these things do happen. Especially nowadays…"

"But it's been taken away from him, Alfie!"

"Hmm…"

Father stayed calm on this sleepy Sunday afternoon, with goldfinches singing in the garden and the sun shining. He sank back into his wicker armchair and covered his face with his hat again. He was thinking of the Suez Canal and Grandpa Albert.

Mother blurted out: "They've been to see me. Lazar and Samuel, Oskar, aunt Tilda, Eduard…Armin…"

Father sat up abruptly. His face had gone red.

"About what?"

"In case something happens…"

Now he was really angry.

"Nothing's going to happen!"

Mother took a deep breath and let it all out in one go:

"They want you… they want you to Aryanize the hairdressing salon and the shop."

"Me?"

"Well, who else?"

Father was speechless and just stared ahead into the garden. This idea had never entered his head.

Mother pressed her point, which was quite rare for her: "Otherwise everything may be lost! My family will lose everything!"

"But... I... I can't do that."

Mother was so upset that tears welled up in her eyes.

"Oh, I see!" she burst out. "Family means nothing to you."

When she was upset she looked even more beautiful than usual, that's what Father used to say. As she walked angrily back into the house she dropped the cup with what was left of her coffee. It shattered on the floor, giving me a start. Mother left it there.

"Wait! Let me think about it," Father shouted after her.

He watched the dark stain slowly spreading on the floor.

"I'll have to see what can be done."

Mother reappeared in the doorway.

"Everyone gets ill from time to time, people always need you. There are so many people who owe you. You have so many contacts. Do something, Alfie, please!"

She snuggled up to Father and planted a kiss on his cheek.

"Surely it can't be that difficult for you. All roads lead to the doctor. Sooner or later. Am I quoting you correctly?"

"All right. I'll give it some thought."

The shrivelled summer was slowly drawing to a close. Chrysanthemums, asters and autumn crocuses started to bloom in our garden.

In September the government adopted the Jewish Code, as we learned from the Slovak Radio, which – in addition to Gejza Dusík's operetta *Under the Foreign Flag,* and mindless drivel about family happiness and pure joy – sometimes broadcast actual news of this kind. It didn't come as a surprise. Over the past year things had been building up and now they had just been brought together neatly under a new name. And legally codified.

Mother and I and Uncle Oskar, who had just come back from a business trip, were eating chicken soup, which – except for the missing *matzo* dumplings – was identical to Grandma's *goldene yoych.*

101

A voice on the radio enunciated slowly and solemnly:

"*Article 8, paragraph 1. Jews must display a special symbol on their clothing. Details of the form of the symbol and the manner in which it is to be worn, as well as general exemptions agreed by the relevant ministry, will be decided by the Minister of the Interior and the decree will be published in the Official Gazette.*"

"Berta my dear, could you please pass the salt."

"Here you are."

"*Article 10. A Jew or a Jewess knowingly having sexual intercourse with a non-Jew or non-Jewess commits an offence punishable by up to five years' imprisonment.*"

"Hm… It needs more salt. Or something…"

"*Article 16, paragraph 1. A Jew may not hold the position of a) public notary or public notary's clerk, b) practising lawyer or clerk in a legal practice or c) civil engineer.*"

"How about some black pepper?"

"Yes, please."

"*Article 18, paragraph 1. Jews may not practice medicine or veterinary medicine.*"

"The soup tastes a bit strange today."

"So sorry about that, Oskar."

"*Article 20, paragraph 1. Jews may not dispense medicines.*"

"I'm really very sorry."

"It's not your fault…"

"*Article 28, paragraph 1. The Central Economic Agency, in consultation with the Ministry of Interior, may oblige Jews to move out of a certain locality or town, while at the same time it may oblige them to move into a certain locality or town.*"

"Perhaps it could do with some more salt after all…"

"*Article 43, paragraph 2. Jews are forbidden to own photographic equipment, binoculars, as well as gramophone recordings of folk songs and tunes.*"

"Oh, now I've put too much salt in…!"

"*Article 191, paragraph 1. All immovable assets belonging to Jews and Jewish associations will become the property of the Slovak Republic, represented by the Central Economic Agency, on a day to be decreed by statute.*"

"I'm so sorry… Please forgive me, I don't think I can finish it."

"I'll throw the soup out."

"I'm sorry, Berta."

"Oh, don't worry about it."

"I think I've got an upset stomach."

"Why aren't you eating, Adam? Eat up, at once!"

That evening President Tiso spoke on the radio. We sat around the kitchen table listening to him. Mother waited for her favourite music programme, her face gradually clouding over.

Tiso's voice seemed to emanate from the depths of his voluminous hollow belly. I imagined his fleshy jowls wobbling as he spoke.

Later, many years after the war, after I had moved away from this house, my next-door neighbour Steffi, who spoke an adorable mix of German, Hungarian and mangled Slovak, used to clean my tiny flat in Bratislava for a few crowns. When she liked something, she said *finom* in Hungarian. This was also how she remembered the war years, the period when she made a living as a high-class prostitute. She was much sought after by men who could afford her – a pretty dusky Jewish girl. I have seen some photographs.

She shared a flat with three of her colleagues in Zelená Street, across the road from the Perugia Hotel. Each had her own room. Quite often, however, a car was sent for her – that's what was so *finom* – to take her to the Koliba hill above Bratislava where the Leader and President had set up a love nest in a cosy villa that had originally belonged to a non-Aryan and resembled a miniature castle. He paid generously and apparently wasn't too bothered about that vow of celibacy. She claimed he was great in bed but I'm not sure how reliable that information was. But perhaps this was why he was sometimes referred to as Father of the Nation – the nickname may have been based on the number of children he sired. Steffi cried when they hanged him after the war. (I've heard that hanged men get a real erection.) That might be true. But for the time being he was wearing a dog collar around his massive neck rather than a noose.

President Tiso said:

"It is high time we drove the Jews out of this country. And took over their property. By doing so we shall be following the Holy Scriptures, which tell us that property should change ownership every fifty years."

Plain-clothes policemen, or "stargazers" as people called them, patrolled the streets of Brežany checking that every Jew wore the star of David. Anyone who didn't was fined or arrested. People took to carrying their briefcases in such a way that their star would be covered up. They had no inkling what fate the strange constellations might foretell. If they had been able to read the stars they would have seen incredible things. But even if they had seen them they wouldn't have believed their own eyes.

Vojto's father had been sent to Denmark to train on the new Messerschmitts, and when he came back he told us the King had caused a scandal when he decided to wear a yellow Magen David to show his solidarity with the Jews.

Uncle Armin, on the other hand, had no choice. He had to wear one. So did Uncle Oskar. And so did everyone else.

In the middle of one night in March the whole house was woken by the ferocious ringing of the doorbell and banging on the door. Father, assuming this was an urgent case, threw a robe over his pyjamas and went to open the door, all drowsy and with ruffled hair.

"What is it? What's going on?" he muttered as he unlocked the door.

Outside in the cold night he saw a gendarme, the diminutive Guardsman Gajdoš and several of Mother's relatives, including Uncle Armin. Mother, terrified, peered out from behind the curtain, covering her mouth with her hand. She didn't even try to send us back to bed.

Puzzled, Father stared at this motley group.

"What's this all about?"

"Good evening," Gajdoš said in his high-pitched voice, then continued blandly: "I've got a deportation order for you."

A little while later Father was pacing up and down the room in his nightgown, smoking one cigarette after another, scattering ashes all over the floor. Since nobody in the house was officially a smoker we didn't have any ashtrays. Mother sat on her bed, biting her fingernails and pretending to ignore his cigarette.

"Gajdoš promised he would have the transport delayed."

"So they want to take them to Poland…"

"Yes, apparently they have whole towns there ready for the Jews."

"Pull the other one!"

"Nonsense!"

"People say…"

"People say, people say! It's all just stupid British anti-Hitler propaganda. Or Goebbels's propaganda to discredit British news. It's wildly exaggerated. Oskar thinks so too. And so do the Silbersteins."

Father went over to the wardrobe and started going through his clothes feverishly.

"I need the new black suit ironed."

"Do you have a meeting tomorrow?"

"I'll go and see some people tomorrow morning. Old Schmetterling gave me an idea. I'll stop by the bank as well."

"Why at the bank?"

Father gave her a wan smile: "You should go to bed now."

Mr Schmetterling, co-owner of the local button factory, was rather foolhardy, to put it mildly. He didn't heed the warning of his Aryan partner Konečný (who suggested, among other things, that he should immediately buy an airplane ticket for France – that wouldn't have been too difficult, surely), opting instead for a heroic life of staying at home. Before long he was under arrest. With only the vaguest information regarding his possible whereabouts, his family did their utmost to have him released and eventually succeeded, though at considerable cost.

At that point Schmetterling "appointed" Konečný as his own Aryanizer (telling him *Er ligt nain el in der erd*: in short, he was in trouble). The two of them drew up a co-ownership contract and had it approved by the authorities. Schmetterling sold his partner fifty-one per cent of the company, which made it non-Jewish. It was as simple as that. The arrangement worked quite well for a while.

He wasn't the only one – for example Poničný, the landowner and proprietor of the Vindobona winery in Brežany, asked the Chamber of Commerce and Industry to help him recruit Mr Klein, who owned Nevedovo's Vinum Bonum winery, as his manager. So the officials at the Chamber came up with a scheme whereby Poničný would Aryanize the Nevedovo winery and Mr Klein, an eminent wine expert, would administer both companies under joint management.

However, the authorities' favourable attitude didn't last long, so Mr Klein chose to pack his bags and emigrate to the US. Impoverished and starving, but overjoyed at having managed to get away, he indulged in all manner of delicacies and fancy meals in such quantities that it killed him.

Uncle Armin pondered whether it was better to starve to death or die of gluttony. This led to quite an interesting philosophical debate over Sunday lunch, although I wasn't quite up to following it in detail.

However, I did understand Uncle Oscar's succinct summary: on the whole it's preferable not to die.

When the court jester, a dwarf at the court of King Henry II, faced execution because he had been selling dangerous snake oil, and the King gave him a free hand to decide the manner of his death, he said: *In that case, I choose to die of old age.*

19.

The silver eagle with a double cross – the Hlinka Guard coat of arms on the lapel of Father's black suit – looked as if it had always been there. The eagle was sitting on what looked like a pile of twigs, but Peter later explained to me that it represented the sticks in the legend of King Svatopluk, symbolizing the country's unity.

Brother Kružliak welcomed Father to the Brežany District Hlinka Guard Command with open arms – after all, years ago Father had cured him of the complications of gastric flu. He offered him real coffee and German cigarettes and after quoting the Führer's remark in the journal *Gesundes Leben* to the effect that cigarettes were just "the idiotic revenge of the Redskins on the white race for introducing them to firewater", he lit up as well. He ushered Father into a cosy leather armchair and as he listened to his problem the smile slowly faded from his face. He did show a certain amount of understanding since Father put the emphasis on his business interests, which might suffer if the authorities proceeded with their plan of action.

Kružliak kept repeating, "It won't be easy, brother Trnovský, it won't be easy." He gave him a few names, promised to put in a word somewhere and suggested he try his luck at the Central Economic Agency.

The Brežany branch of the Central Economic Agency, the office in charge of Aryanization, was located at 69 Adolf Hitler Avenue. It resembled a traditional institution, with offices and clerks dealing with a variety of cases, shuffling papers around and strictly observing lunch breaks and official opening hours. Father knocked on door number 12 and a surly voice asked him to come in. It sounded as if it was suggesting that this was well outside working hours. Father entered with a smile.

A lugubrious-looking man got up from his desk and hurried to shake his hand, his eyes aglow. He was Július Vašíček, Monako to his friends. He coughed uneasily, a reminder of his lung problems.

After pointing out that he was just a rank-and-file official, a tiny cog in the system who really had nothing to do with this sort of thing, he gave Father a piece of advice ("but don't quote me, doctor!"). To secure an exemption the doctor would have to sign a statement and list the names of the Jews who were indispensable to his business and why. Monako could handle the paperwork but it was up to the doctor to secure the actual approval. From someone "in authority".

Father had no idea if Monako even knew what that phrase meant and whether he had the Almighty himself or something of that nature in mind. But eventually he did let slip a name. It meant a trip to Nitra.

So Father got on the phone.

With the help of several other patients (second-degree burns, an appendicitis, and haemorrhoids) an audience was arranged: another patient (exudative pleurisy) helped to nudge Father a little higher up the waiting list; while the third patient (a timely diagnosis of a wife's postnatal complications combined with sepsis) really set things in motion.

Father travelled to Nitra together with uncle Armin and three of Mother's other relatives.

The negotiations were brisk and tough. After two hours he was getting fed up. He went into the courtyard to light a cigarette. He was followed by an indignant Rabbi Weissmandel:

"Mr. Trnovský, what kind of Jew are you? Smoking on the Sabbath!"

Father responded with a tired smile.

"But I'm not Jewish."

The rabbi was dumbfounded.

"Really...? But what about that nose of yours? And where did you learn to speak such good Yiddish?"

"I picked it up from childhood friends... In the park." He made a face. "At Hanukkah we used to play with the *dreidl* and I would always clean them out. I kept getting *gimel*. Their parents kept chasing me away."

The rabbi shook his head.

"*Gebojrn in a saydn hemdl!* All right then... Come on in, we'll work something out."

Before going back he turned to Father and said in Yiddish:

"But it will cost you, Mr Trnovský. If a Jewish merchant's scales are not accurate they have to be adjusted to make sure they show the same for every customer. If we give someone a present we do so only to make sure that the officials apply a yardstick that is as realistic as possible. You get my drift?"

"He should have bought a special wallet made of cock skin!" Mislovič laughed when Uncle Oskar told him the story. "You stroke it and it grows into a trunk!"

This was how Father earned the label "white Jew" – the endearing term given to people who helped Jews in those days.

The following Sunday they all came for lunch at our house, ruefully hiding their stars of David. Uncle Oskar wore a Magen David made of bakelite which – as Uncle Armin explained to me – designated an "economically beneficial" Jew. The others were issued with yellow identity cards.

Both Oskar and Armin had shaved off their beards and sidelocks and had their hair cut short. Father sat at the head of the table as usual.

We helped ourselves to soup and bits of beef and boiled carrots.

Armin spoke in a low voice:

"But we can't take any risks. We ought to get baptized, like Berta."

Father took a spoonful of soup.

"That won't be easy now. The Catholics won't do it anymore."

108

He shrugged his shoulders. "The amount of money they charged was hardly Christian anyway." He gave Mother a dig in the ribs. "Don't you worry. You were worth every penny!"

Mother poked him back. Uncle Oscar chipped in from the far side of the table.

"Well, I don't know… We could try the Lutherans. Baptizing Jews has been banned but they like to be contrary."

Father shrugged again.

"But will it help, given the way things are…?"

Mother cleared her throat.

"We'll see what happens… Let's not talk about it in front of the children."

Armin's star of David was attached with a safety pin instead of being sewn on so that he could take it off whenever he wanted. This wasn't allowed but he didn't care. After lunch, while we were playing and the grown-ups were taking coffee and brandy in the dining room, he joined us.

He took off his star and pinned it to my chest. It looked great. He wetted his fingers and slicked down my hair. I had always hated that but didn't mind when he was the one who did it.

"Let's have a look at you! What a good-looking young fellow you are!"

Armin broke into a laugh and patted me on the shoulder. I started laughing as well and ran to the dining room where the others were sitting.

"Daddy, daddy, look what I've got! I got it from Armin, isn't it lovely? May I keep it? Please, please…! I will wear it just like everyone else!"

I will never forget Father's red face. He ripped the star off my chest. Then he marched out of the dining room and he and Armin locked themselves in the isolation cell.

I heard Father shouting at him.

20.

A group of men were playing cards in the private room at the back of Puškár's patisserie. There was Father; next to him was

Levendovský the notary, as well as two Jews with yellow star exemptions, Mr Schreiber and Mr Reis.

Father,who was losing and on edge, lit up one cigarette after another.

"Have you heard this one, doctor?" Puškár asked, laughing. "Two men meet in the street. One of them is smoking and other says to him, "Do you know that cigarettes shorten your life?" "How old are you?" "I'm forty." "You see! If you didn't smoke you would now be forty-six!"

Everyone laughed.

"Stop looking at me like that – I'm not a smoker!" Father said, offended, picking at his cream slice and managing to smear it all over his plate.

"Well, from a distance it looks just as if you were!" said Puškár roaring with laughter.

Father exhaled some smoke and looked at Puškár.

"So how is Lila, eh?"

Puškár's face assumed a tender expression, if such a thing was possible.

"She's just written. I got a letter yesterday."

Puškár lived on his own. His parents had left him a large, nicely furnished flat above the patisserie. He was over forty but nobody had seen him with a woman for years. Perhaps it was because of his pot belly or the fact that, whenever he found himself alone with a lady, he started to resemble a polar bear that had drifted to the Equator on a detached floe of ice.

"It's really difficult to meet an interesting woman these days, doctor."

"To be honest, I don't understand you," Father had said to him once.

"Why?"

"Have you never tried placing a classified ad?"

Puškár admitted this wasn't a bad idea and immediately went off to put an ad in the *Slovák*. Father told him what to write.

"*A sophisticated man of independent means….*"

"Sophisticated? What's that supposed to mean?"

"Just look in the mirror. *Good-looking* doesn't exactly fit, you have to admit. *Well-preserved* will make it sound like you're eighty, *youthful* like you're fifty."

110

"All right. But why not put my actual age?"

"Tactics, Mr Puškár, tactics. Now, where were we… *A sophisticated man of independent means with a pleasant demeanour seeks a young and intelligent lady…*"

"Intelligent…?"

"Do you want a stupid one?"

"No, but… She ought to be… pretty."

"*Young and intelligent* sounds like pretty, doesn't it?"

"Well, yes… but…"

"All right… *with a young, good-looking woman with a view to a long-term relationship.*"

"Right?"

"Right! *Photo required.* Add to the box number '*Meet me in my patisserie*'."

"Is it a good idea to mention the patisserie?"

"You've got to do something to make it stand out. Now off you go and put it in the paper!"

The first response arrived a week later and was soon followed by a few more.

Father stopped by Mr Nežný's photo studio, to hand over a prescription for his persistent cough, and asked if he could look at some of the photos that had never been collected. Over the years the photographer had accumulated quite a few. Father selected a couple of old studio photographs and paid without going into too much detail about what he wanted them for.

Eventually he picked a pretty, slim, darkhaired woman, a *beauté phtisique*, a consumptive beauty – slender face, pale complexion, sad eyes – which permitted a cautious guess that she might no longer be alive. He put the photo in an envelope with a letter expressing interest in a meeting. He signed it Lila.

Now her second letter, a response to his reply, was in Puškár's hands. He read out:

"*Dear Sir, by way of introduction let me admit that I am very flattered by your compliments regarding my hair and… and….*"

Puškár blushed and began to stutter.

"Well…. I can't read out this bit. But listen to this: *I would very much like to meet you in person.*"

Father and everyone else watched him with amusement.

"Let me tell you… Let me tell you… The God of love has granted me a woman!" Puškár exclaimed poetically, pirouetting out of the private room.

Voices rang out in the square, audible even in the back. As customers were coming in, the door stayed open for a while.

A uniformed guardsman was reeling off names through a loudhailer. The back room fell silent. As the determined but monotonous recital continued, sometimes the names drifted away on the wind. Finally the patisserie door slammed shut and a silent film continued to roll behind the shop window. Flashes of men in black uniforms, families with suitcases and other items of luggage, bewildered faces… Two guardsmen had great fun forcibly cutting off an old man's sidelocks. The regulars, sipping coffee and gorging themselves on chestnut puree, cosy and comfortable in the patisserie, found it hard to imagine what was going on in the heads of the people outside.

After the last name was read out the gaggle of folk with stars set off for the railway station. Everyone stopped talking or lowered their voices, trying to look elsewhere. The patisserie was transformed into a fish tank.

Somewhere at the front a voice shouted: "They should give back everything they've stolen from us! In Poland they'll teach them what it means to work hard. Fucking Jews!"

The Lutheran church was some distance away from the hubbub of the town, sort of tucked away inconspicuously. Brežany has always been a proud Catholic town.

Two people, the sexton and his wife, stood at the altar. The godfather and godmother.

The pastor waved the aspersorium. With a single gesture he baptized two hundred people in a church full of yellow stars. It was almost beautiful.

Armin turned to Uncle Oskar and whispered:

"I read somewhere that under the Ottoman occupation entire villages converted to Judaism. Suleiman regarded Christians as infidels but he treated the Jews well; he respected them. Some Jews may have been created this way, through necessity, the survival instinct… Who knows… Isn't that amusing?"

Uncle Oskar shrugged and scratched his head.

112

"So how can you be sure you're really Jewish?"

Oskar tapped his yellow star.

"I'm dead certain, Armin."

They walked out into the dusk just as evening mass was about to begin. Each went his own way.

Two old men were chatting nearby:

"We've been Lutherans since the tenth century!"

"Tenth century? That's not possible!"

"Oh yes it is. Only we were called something else back then."

On Sunday Grandma Mária, Peter, Tina and I went to church. The Catholic one, of course, St. Giles'.

As we entered, Father Peterský was reading from the Holy Bible:

"Now Peter and John were going up to the temple at the time for prayer, at three o'clock in the afternoon. And a man lame from birth was being carried up, who was placed at the temple gate called "the Beautiful Gate" every day so he could beg for money from those going into the temple courts. When he saw Peter and John about to go into the temple courts, he asked them for money. Peter looked directly at him, as did John, and said, "Look at us!" So the lame man paid attention to them, expecting to receive something from them. But Peter said, "I have no silver or gold, but what I do have I give you. In the name of Jesus Christ the Nazarene, stand up and walk!" Then Peter took hold of him by the right hand and raised him up, and at once the man's feet and ankles were made strong. He jumped up, stood and began walking around, and he entered the temple courts with them, walking and leaping and praising God. All the people saw him walking and praising God, and they recognized him as the man who used to sit and ask for donations at the Beautiful Gate of the temple, and they were filled with astonishment and amazement at what had happened to him. While the man was hanging on to Peter and John, all the people, completely astounded, ran together to them in the covered walkway called Solomon's Portico.

In addition to the Christians, people in the pews included some newly-baptized Jews who had managed to convert in the nick of time. But the others tried to keep their distance from them. The Brežany synagogue had been appropriated by the state a few months ago and was scheduled for demolition.

Father Peterský was just getting into his stride when someone in the back row – it was Mr Lazar Stern, the *shakhter* – calmly

113

unpacked his *tefillin*, prayer straps, bound them to his forehead and arms and began to recite a Jewish prayer, standing in the aisle between pews.

Father Peterský continued undisturbed:

"When Peter saw this, he declared to the people, "Men of Israel, why are you amazed at this? Why do you stare at us as if we had made this man walk by our own power or piety? The God of Abraham, Isaac, and Jacob, the God of our forefathers, has glorified his servant Jesus, whom you handed over and rejected in the presence of Pilate after he had decided to release him. But you rejected the Holy and Righteous One and asked that a man who was a murderer be released to you. You killed the Originator of life, whom God raised from the dead. To this fact we are witnesses! And on the basis of faith in Jesus' name, his very name has made this man — whom you see and know — strong. The faith that through Jesus has given him this complete health in the presence of you all."

The others, too, pretended they didn't notice anything unusual.

Now Mr Stern was no longer just muttering to himself but declaiming in a loud voice, almost shouting, in Hebrew:

"Yitgadal v' yitkaddash sh'mei rabba. B'alma di vra khirutei v'yamlikh malkhutei, b'chayeikhon u-v'yomeikhon u-v'chayei d'khol beit yisrael, ba-agala u-vizman kariv."

Peterský suddenly stopped. Everyone stared in astonishment.

"V'imru amen!" Mr Stern said loudly.

"It's the Kaddish Yatom, the Mourner's Prayer," I whispered to Grandma Mária, who was dumbstruck.

Peterský decided to hold himself in check. He began to sing: *"Oh Lord, we call upon thee in Heaven, during the day as well as in the night, oh help us…"*

The organ started playing.

The other clergy joined in: *"…Come, oh come, Redeemer!"*

Stern's voice mingled with the Christian song: *"V'imru amen!"* came again, at the end of the verse.

"Y'hei sh'mei rabba m'varakh l'alam u-l'almei almaya!"

"Show us the way to the eternal city, give us joy, give us mercy, redemption, come, oh come, Redeemer!"

"Yitbarakh v'yishtabbach v'yitpa'ar v'yitromam v'yitnasei v'yit'hadar v'yitaleh v'yit'hallal sh'mei d'kudsha b'rikh hul'ella min kol birkhata v'shirata tushb'chata v'nechemata da'amiran b'alma v'imru amen!"

The hymn began to break up until it disintegrated entirely and

114

everyone fell quiet. People held their breath, horror-struck. Nobody dared move.

"Y'hei sh'lama rabba min sh'maya v'chayim aleinu v'al kol yisrael. V'imru amen!"

The organist resisted longer than anyone else. The organ's majestic cadences merged with the Jewish prayer, echoing around the vast church.

At last the organ's pipes came to a dissonant halt.

"Ose shalom bimromav hu ya'ase shalom aleinu v'al kol yisrael v'al kol yoshvei tevel. V'imru amen!"

Eventually three strong men in suits pulled themselves together. The sudden silence woke them from their trance. They grabbed Mr Stern under the arms and carried him out.

He didn't try to resist.

If at that moment, on top of everything, someone had shouted: "Jews out!" Jesus would have been the first to break loose from the cross (I can hear the clatter of falling nails, the cracking of bones and sinews straightening for the first time in centuries, the pad-pad of bare feet…), followed by all the apostles. One by one they would pass through the door into the sunshine, screwing up their eyes, hitherto accustomed to twilight, and gradually vanishing among the respectable lanes of Brežany.

Uncle Rudo told me about a German *Hitlerjugend* march in the streets of Bratislava. The youths wore woollen knee socks and *Lederhosen*, shouted *Heil Hitler* and banged their drums as their flutes wailed. They shouted: *Jesus war ein Judenbub und Maria eine Hure!* – Jesus was a Jewish lout and Mary was a whore! Apparently nobody intervened. Perhaps they all forgot their German at that moment, or the word "whore" wasn't in their dictionary.

Or they were all suddenly gripped by an epidemic of deafness, which is actually our typical national trait. A re-touched photograph published in *The Slovak Physician* offers a perfect illustration of the gang of the deaf. Deputy Prime Minister Vojtech Tuka has the look of a mad prophet, a cross between Franz Liszt and a longhaired collie. As for writer and parliamentarian Tido Gašpar, he seems completely mesmerised by uniforms, just like Göring, who also had a predilection for them. In the photo they both look like actors after a demanding operetta performance, or like deranged revellers at a cross-dressers' party. Minister of the Interior Šaňo Mach looks as if he has taken laxatives instead of indigestion tablets. And the most dignified thing about President Tiso is his belly, or more precisely, its size. And of course the incredible bulge of blubber at the back of his neck, which makes pork lovers salivate and head for the nearest butcher's.

However, above this chorus of the deaf the odd timid voice did occasionally make itself heard.

In March 1942 Catholic bishops appealed to the Slovak government against the anti-Jewish initiatives, saying they contradicted the Lord's natural law. The Lutherans joined in the protest a month later:

"We have been forced to witness unnecessary and unjustifiable blunders and excesses that run contrary to basic human compassion, as well as the Lord's law and Christ's teaching of love."

21.

I was at an age when I enjoyed imitating everything my father did.

He had discarded an old stethoscope and I begged him to let me have it. Vojto and I then used it in the attic it to examine Vojto's five-year-old cousin Táňa. We managed to talk her into taking off her blouse and not to be so shy about showing off what would later become known as breasts and of which there was still only the subtlest hint. The metal stethoscope felt cold on her skin, she said, as Vojto and I took turns listening to her heartbeat, from the front as well as the back.

"She takes a deep breath… Deep…! Now she holds her breath. That's it… Now she's breathing!"

Next came the turn of the thin sticks for checking that Táňa's tonsils weren't enlarged.

"She opens her mouth! Wider, wider!"

Táňa protested that this was making her sick so we stopped and decided to operate on her instead. While we debated our next steps, explaining the details of our proposed intervention, I tested her knee-jerk reflex using a little rubber hammer I had appropriated from Father's surgery. Táňa got angry and started to chase me around the attic.

After Vojto calmed her down she lay down obediently – and almost naked – on an old sofa. Holding a kitchen knife, I indicated the line of the incision on her stomach but I pressed too hard and drew blood.

Screaming, she ran off to Vojto's parents.

When she grew up she would sometimes show me the scar above her belly button. I always protested I didn't remember anything.

I was there when someone broke the window of Armin's hairdressing salon. A stone landed on the floor, wrapped in a piece of paper that read *The Jew is our enemy!* A week later someone daubed the words *The evil Jew has caused the war!* on the wall of his house. The clumsy handwriting was accompanied by the drawing of a grotesque face with a crooked nose. I couldn't understand how my Uncle could have caused the war. Armin almost stopped laughing and even developed a tic in his left eye.

Many of his regular clients deserted him. Presumably they too thought he was to blame for the war.

I never figured out what it was about Armin that my Father found so irritating. Perhaps it was his eccentricity, perhaps the fact that many women still considered the ageing bachelor so attractive. Male rivalry is a force to be reckoned with. And Father had a great capacity for envy. He was just as keen on women as his brother-in-law – as I only discovered years later – but Armin had the advantage of being able to indulge in an independent life, unhampered by marriage and aspirations to a cosy, glowing family hearth.

One day he was in a particularly good mood as he said goodbye to Mrs Škridla. He had just finished devising a complicated hairdo.

"Thank you so much, Armin! You're simply the best!" Mrs Škridla said.

Father and I had just walked into the salon. Father frowned, overhearing the last comment, which Armin uttered as he drew open the drapes covering the shop window and opened the door for us.

"Well, you see – it's just a fact that we Jews are more interesting than the ordinary folk you see in the street. I mean men, of course, only men! Actually, we're also long-distance runners, if you get my drift… Thanks to a certain thing down there, you know what I mean."

Armin smiled and gave a wink.

"So take care of yourself and I'll see you next week. Please remember me to your husband. This way, if you wouldn't mind."

"Goodbye, doctor."

Mrs Škridla gave him a flirtatious wave and headed for the back entrance. Armin let her out through the storeroom, which led into a side street. The salon was empty.

Father took off his hat. "Armin... listen to me. You really ought to be more careful. Can't you see you're rubbing these people up the wrong way?"

Armin furrowed his brow.

"How do you mean? I'm not sure I understand you, dear boy. There's something wrong with my hearing today."

He showed Father to a chair in front of the mirror and started to strop his razor. He applied shaving foam to his face with a brush.

"People are saying all sorts of things and that's not good. Not good for any of us."

Armin responded light-heartedly: "Why should it be good or bad for anyone? We all live our own lives."

"You should leave women alone, at the very least!" Father gestured towards the back door. "Do you know who her husband is? He's the district treasurer of the Hlinka Guard."

Putting on a show of surprise, Armin exclaimed: "Oh! Really?"

"Now listen...!"

Father realised he'd better keep his emotions under control. After all, Armin was giving him a shave, moving the razor up and down his neck.

"Why would she come here in secret otherwise? I'm the only one who can assemble that bird's nest she wears on her head. I'm the best. I'm like a secret lover!" He made a face.

"Stop clowning about, I beg you! We must have a serious conversation!"

Armin pretended to be surprised.

"But I'm as grave as a judge. Look – not a scratch anywhere!"

Father turned red with fury.

"You know what, Armin?" he shouted. "You of all people ought to show me some gratitude!"

Armin grinned.

"Of course I am profoundly grateful for everything…! May I wash my hands, sir? Thank you, sir!"

Father yanked the sheet off his shoulders and furiously wiped off the lather as he got out of the chair.

Armin was shaking with anger, razor in hand:

"I haven't finished yet!"

Father stared at him, eyes blazing.

"Neither have I!"

He left, slamming the door. The shop front rattled. I stayed behind, not moving. Armin took me by the shoulders and thrust me into the seat. His hands were trembling. I heard the door creak behind me.

"How nice to see you, my dear lady!"

A wide smile spread across his face.

I don't know what else happened between them and what was going through my Father's head in those days. He would regularly send Mother to bed with the words: "Now, let me be!"

He would pace up and down in his isolation cell.

Late one night I was on my way to the toilet, half-asleep, and saw him take out the photo of Grandpa Albert with his head glued onto somebody else's body. He stared at his father's face for a long time. He would spend hours smoking on the balcony. The smoke wafted through the open windows into my room at regular intervals through much of the night.

What happened next I know only from hearsay but the following Monday at dawn there was an insistent ringing of the bell at Uncle Armin Blau's door, followed by impatient knocking. A sleepy Armin ran to the door in his pyjamas and silk dressing gown, hastily smoothing down his greying hair.

A voice behind the door shouted: "Open up!"

"Yes, yes, coming… coming! What's going on?"

There was a man in a leather jacket outside accompanied by two soldiers. They barged in.

Armin blinked in surprise.

"Mr Gajdoš… Can you tell me what's happened?"

"You are Armin Blau, hairdresser?"

"What's up, Mr Gajdoš? You used to be a customer of mine."

The man's expression was far from friendly. He handed him a piece of paper.

Armin took it.

"The administrator of your hairdressing salon has signed a declaration stating the firm no longer needs you. Your transport leaves in a few hours."

Armin went pale. He seemed about to faint.

The man asked: "Are you all right? Did you understand what I said, Blau?"

Armin nodded and clutched his chest, unable to utter a word. He staggered towards an armchair but before he could reach it he collapsed onto the parquet floor, face down. As he fell he brought down a bowl of apples, sending them rolling everywhere.

They were still there days later. My brother and I would rake them out from under the wardrobe, shrivelled and rotten.

Another strange thing happened that day. Armin's dog Gaštan was found dead in the courtyard, under Armin's window. It must have fallen from a great height.

Some time later I walked into the hairdressing salon and found someone else working there – it was a young hairdresser in overalls and glasses. Old Mrs Drotár had just settled into the chair in front of the mirror. Like so many others, she once had a Hungarian-sounding surname but she and her husband changed it – as the current fashion dictated – to something genuinely Slovak. The name Drotár – meaning tinker, the traditional Slovak trade – was almost too genuine to be true.

I stood in the doorway, not sure what to do.

"So how would you like your hair done?"

An offended Mrs Drotár muttered to another woman, whom I didn't know.

"Armin would never ask a question like that. May God have mercy on him!"

The other woman frowned sarcastically: "Which God do you mean?"

"Well… his one. The Jewish one." And she snapped at the hairdresser: "Just a little trim. Here, and here," she said, showing him in the mirror.

The other woman leaned over to her:

120

"By the way, I heard the autopsy found that Armin's lungs were full of hair!"

"You don't say!" Mrs Drotár exclaimed, shocked.

"I heard it from old Kucbelová's son – he is a trainee at the pathology department in Trnava."

"But how on earth can that be?"

"It seems this does happen to hairdressers. It's the hair they inhale as they work. Their customers' hair. Mine. And yours!"

"You mean in Armin's... in his lungs? Oh no! I can't believe that!"

She frowned, casting a distrustful glance at the young hairdresser who was trying to construct something on her head.

I couldn't make head or tail of what I had heard. Where had Uncle Armin gone? And what was that about the hair? And how could anyone know that thing about the lungs...?

Tears streamed down my face.

Even nowadays I get goosebumps at night whenever I remember that my Uncle Armin Blau carried a little bit of all of his customers with him wherever he went.

Later I found a poster trampled on by guardsmen's feet on the floor of Armin's flat. It showed a smiling gentleman in tails, with glasses and a straw hat in his hand, peering out from behind a curtain.

*I BRING YOU THE JOY OF LIFE! I take it you have not yet come across our Friends of Classical Books Society, which boasts as many as 20,000 members these days, or else you would have joined too. Please read the attached brochure (if you are too busy now, read it later at your leisure). From the detailed information it contains you will see that we distribute luxury editions of **the greatest works of world literature, novels that will enrich your life and bring you joy, volumes that will adorn your home**, all at an exceptionally reasonable price, payable in easy monthly instalments.*

*An application form with a stamped addressed envelope is attached: **complete the form and send it off to us today!***

22.

It is the middle of the night. The night is as deep as a well into which you can keep falling forever. For as long as you like. I feel a little night-time cocktail is called for. Nudge, nudge. I don't mean a drink. My friend Noax will keep me company. Interestingly enough, instead of putting me to sleep he just endlessly prolongs the time before sleep comes.

Or perhaps it's this house that is to blame. I'm lying on my bed and feel the house spreading, seeping through my head.

In the months following Armin's death Father had trouble sleeping. In fact, I never saw him sleep in those days. He smoked a lot, trying as usual to keep it secret from everyone else and especially from himself. I even saw him drunk a couple of times. That wasn't like him at all. But he would be fine in the morning – apart from his pallor and the bags under his eyes – as he set out in a cheerful and businesslike manner on his rounds, carrying his black doctor's bag. Attending to cases of flu, fractures and asthma. Or to a child that apparently chose a particularly difficult way to come into this world. Either too early or too late.

One day he came home exhausted after assisting at a childbirth – the mother had died but they were able to save the child.

"Someone has to die in order for someone else to live. That's life," he said to Mother, and she burst into tears.

She used to cry a lot in those days.

Father pretended not to hear anything as he shaved in the bathroom, whistling a tune he had heard on a radio. He eased the razor up and down his face, tossing the lather into the basin and never cutting himself.

A prominent chin and delicate skin, I thought.

Once, he woke up with a start in the middle of the night. He sat up listening for a moment, and even put the light on.

Mother drowsily asked what on earth was going on. Father was fuming – what's the neighbour up to? He's been banging on the wall with a hammer for a full hour, he must have gone mad. I'm going over!

But Mother couldn't hear anything. The night was quiet; total silence reigned.

Father didn't believe her and it took him a while to calm down. He kept touching his ear and blocking it.

On another occasion, thinking he heard persistent tapping on the window sill – an urgent case, a breech birth or something like that – he ran over to the window but there was nobody in the street. Not a soul.

This would happen more and more often. He didn't regain his composure until he managed to find the reason. The explanation was obvious – the sound he was hearing was his own extrasystoles. The right vertebral artery was knocking against the bones of the thoracic wall, resulting in tinnitus. I am not quite sure about this – his colleague Dr Ilavský actually thought these were the first symptoms of hearing loss – but Father found this explanation satisfactory.

It was worst before he went to sleep and at night. The regular pulsating noise was driving him mad. He found that music helped. In the middle of the night I would often find him standing by the radio or the record player. He was trying to drown out the tinnitus.

Puškár received another letter from Lila.

She was responding to his request that they should meet soon. He received twelve replies from her altogether. He dismissed all the other responses to his classified ad as too reserved and demure. Or their looks were not to his liking. That's what he told Father.

Lila asked for more detailed information about him, while telling him a little about herself.

Father made use of some details of a case he had heard about from a colleague in Nitra.

She was an Aryan, who had married a Jew many years previously. It was a happy marriage which produced a son. She adored the boy and would do anything to ensure his future happiness.

Now she was doing her best to prove in court that her husband was not the boy's father. The husband, who also wanted only the best for his son, which in this case meant a pure Aryan origin, went along with this.

Mrs X testified in court that she had had a number of affairs and had been unfaithful to her husband when the child was conceived. Her father even helped her find a geneticist, someone he knew from medical school. The geneticist presented his expert opinion confirming her version of events (for a not inconsiderable fee that did not, however, pose a problem for the family). Eventually they resorted to cutting up photographs of the Jewish father and of the son, combining them and re-assembling them in various ways, examining the facial features, endlessly speculating whether a child might or might not be descended from this man, whether it was completely out of the question or at least, well, conceivable.

The trial was deliberately dragged out, and by 1944, as the Red Army approached Slovakia's borders, it turned increasingly relaxed and entertaining. Nobody – especially the lawyers, of course – objected to the endless adjournments and fresh hearings, which finally came to nothing.

Lila, on the other hand, told Puškár that her divorce had eventually come through and that she now had no contact with her former husband; she wondered if the fact that she had a child was a problem. Gazing at her picture, an enraptured Puškár wrote back to say it didn't bother him at all and that he couldn't wait to meet Leo (that was the boy's name). Although he hoped she would come to their first meeting alone.

Unfortunately, Lila cancelled the meeting in her next letter as she suddenly fell ill. Nothing serious – she wrote – but it was enough to prevent her from travelling to Brežany.

"The God of love has granted me sorrow. But I'm not giving up."

23.

Father Savický approached the blackboard in our classroom with a dignified gait.

"To achieve redemption we have to have faith in what the Lord has revealed and abide by what he has ordained. The teaching of our Holy Church is based on the revelation of everything the Lord has granted and done for our redemption."

He opened the Bible and began to read:

In the beginning, God created the sky and the earth. But the earth was *formless and darkness covered the deep waters. And God said, 'Let there be light.' And there was light. It was the first day. On the second day, God created the celestial heaven, which is the air that surrounds the earth. On the third day He separated the water from dry earth, and the earth, following God's command, began to bear many different kinds of plants and fruit trees. On the fourth day God made the two great lights, the sun and the moon and the stars. On the fifth day God created fish and other living animals in the sea, and birds in the sky. On the sixth day God created many different kinds of animals living on earth. Then he made people who were images of himself. God rested on the seventh day. He rested on the seventh day from all His work which He had done. Then God blessed the seventh day and sanctified it. Besides the visible world God also created the invisible world, that is celestial spirits or angels. At the beginning all the angels were good and beatific but later many of them sinned against God by being proud and disobedient. God punished them by driving them out of the celestial bliss and casting them into eternal damnation.* What are you chattering about there, Roško?"*

Father Savický pointed a bony finger in our direction.

"Sir... we're talking about evolution. Trnovský and I think something's not quite right here."

"Evolution is a load of nonsense, mark my words! And now be quiet! *When God completed the creation of the world and filled the earth with plants and animals, a being that would rule over everything was still missing. And God said: 'Let us make people who will be images of ourselves and let them rule the earth.' – Then God formed man of dust from the ground, and breathed into his nostrils the breath of life; and man became a living being. God gave the first man the name Adam, that is, the man of earth.* What is it now, Roško?"

"Sir... He made man out of dust? That's strange..."

'This is the word of God and there's nothing weird about it. One more interruption and I'll throw both you and Trnovský out of the class! *Our ancestors' bliss in paradise did not last long. A bad spirit envied their happiness and tempted them to transgress God's command. Disguised as a serpent he said to Eve: 'Why did God forbid you to eat of any tree of the Garden of Eden?' And she replied, 'From the fruit of the trees of the garden we may eat; but from the fruit of the tree which is in the middle of the garden God has said, 'You shall not eat from it or touch it, or you will die.' And the serpent said to the woman: 'You surely will not die! For God knows that in the day you eat from it your eyes will be opened, and you will be like God, knowing good and evil.' When the woman saw that the tree was good for food, and that it was a delight to the eyes, she took of its fruit and ate; and she gave also to her husband, and he ate. By doing so our ancestors abused their free will, disobeyed God's command and thus committed the first sin. The consequences of this sin were terrible."*

"For example, we were born."

"Right! I heard you, Trnovský! You and Roško are both in detention! And I shall be asking to see your parents, too!"

His menacing figure came closer.

"Fingertips together!" he said grimly.

The cane came swishing down through the air.

Father Savický could preach to his heart's content about original sin and similar things. But when, in the catechism class, Vojto produced a faithful and realistic drawing of Adam and Eve – after all, legend says they ran around the Garden of Even stark naked – his mother, Mrs Roško, was summoned to school. Although Father Savický and several priests on the school staff gave her a stiff talking-to, they were reluctant to show her the dreadful incriminating picture. And that really made her angry.

She never discovered quite how her son managed to capture details of the female anatomy so accurately without ever having laid eyes on one.

But it was on me that this episode had a far more powerful effect. On the night of the "day of the drawing" I put on a small torch under the bedcovers. I had removed a certain book from Father's bookcase in his isolation cell, making sure nobody saw me. This must have been the first time I tossed a coin to help me decide whether to do something or not. Five times it came down tails, which meant I was not allowed to open the thirteenth door until, finally, on the sixth try, I struck lucky. And in I went.

The magic word "sex" featured in the actual book title. I leafed through it eagerly, paying particularly close attention to the drawing headed *Cross-section of the female body* with a caption underneath that read: *External feminine sex parts.* I was immediately aroused. The next caption said: *Areas of sexual stimulation in the female body.* My hand reached down as so often before. My breathing got faster, I closed my eyes in bliss and suddenly I felt something wet on the sheet under my belly. My head sank down onto the book, blazing with a cold flame.

The caption *Self-abuse (masturbation)* leapt out from the crumpled pages in the depths of the book. Turning the pages quickly I read:

The other, though not infectious, yet no less and perhaps more serious threat to young people's health – apart from venereal diseases – is self-abuse.

I read on: *The earliest indication of how grave a transgression this was can be found in the Old Testament, which says that this was the reason God killed Onan. In the present day, too, it is a serious disease that not only devastates one's physical health but, more importantly, paralyses the vital functions. In no time previously vigorous young men turn into total human wrecks. While frequent stimulation upsets their nerves, the rest of their body is weakened by the enormous loss of semen, which in healthy youths may occur during sleep from time to time, without any ill effect. Vigorous youths, whose eyes used to radiate health and strength, are transformed into depressed and irritable individuals of a cowardly disposition. Such a shocking transformation and sudden aging in a young man will be immediately obvious to every caring mother and father.*

Horrified, I closed the book and tossed it under the bed. I stared wide-eyed into the darkness, agonizing about my future. I imagined the slow and cruel death that lay in store for me.

Initially, on a purely theoretical level at first and lacking the relevant practice, I spent a lot of time meditating over how that stuff is supposed to work. How can this thing called a condom stay on the willy without slipping off? Surely it will tear if you're clumsy. How does the man find the opening in the woman and how does he even fit in there? I once examined my sister Tina while she was asleep but I just couldn't figure out how you are supposed to fit in there. (Plus she woke up in the middle of the examination and ticked me off). What if I make a mistake and end up in the place meant for peeing?

I was no more enlightened after a more detailed exploration in the school toilets where Apolena – a girl two years older and much bolder than me – and I showed "ours" to each other. Sitting on the toilet bowl she spread her legs, as well as what was between them, and I had a chance to examine it to my heart's content. In exchange I pulled down my trousers and allowed her to touch my part of our secret. I managed to stand my ground as she expertly moved my foreskin up and down several times in a businesslike manner, in spite of a tingling sensation at the bottom of my spine and some slight giddiness. We put our clothes back on and left the school toilets deep in thought and mingled with the crowd of children frolicking during break.

The following years, however, taught me that when it comes to that act which, as the Bible would have it, was first performed by Adam and Eve, with some unpleasant and fateful consequences, one could safely rely on instincts thousands of years old.

24.

On 22 June 1941, when Slovakia joined Germany's war against the USSR, I was deployed on the eastern front as a pilot with the Second Squadron, equipped with Letov Š-328 surveillance biplanes, although I did not see any significant combat action. I was mostly sent on reconnaissance missions. I returned to Slovakia on 20 August 1941 to complete my fighter pilot training. On 25 February 1942, after several months' service, I was one of the pilots selected for re-training on the German Messerschmitt Bf 109 with the 5th Staffel / Jagdgruppe Drontheim on the Danish airfield of Karup-Grove. Following my return to Slovakia on 6 July 1942 I was assigned as deputy commander of the first front crew of the 13th Fighter Squadron, specifically commanding its terrestrial echelon. On 28 November 1942 I was one of the first to participate in a battle between Slovak and Soviet aircraft in the Caucasus. During air-to-air combat, which took place in the vicinity of Tuapse, the two-man planes under my command shot down three enemy aircraft, without sustaining any losses on our side. These kills have not, however, been formally recorded. In the course of nine months' fighting in the Kuban, Caucasus and Black Sea area I carried out a total of 156 missions, with a total of 36 confirmed kills, and was awarded several decorations of Slovak and German provenance, of which I would specially mention the Slovak Silver Medal of the military Victorious Cross, the Silver Cross of Military Merit, gold, silver and bronze medals for Heroism, the German Iron Cross (First and Second Class), an Ehrenpokal, a German Gold Cross and the Croatian silver cross of the Crown of King Zvonimir. With effect from 1 January 1943 I was promoted to the rank of senior air force lieutenant.

Snr. Lt. Vojtech Roško

One day Vojto came running to our house blabbering something so excitedly I couldn't understand him. He dragged me off to the cinema. He had even bought me a ticket.

They were showing the documentary *From the Tatras to the Sea of Azov*, featuring Slovak soldiers who took part in the Russian campaign. Vojto's father appeared in it for a full ten seconds! All of Brežany crowded into the Slovák cinema to watch him. Everyone held their breath during those ten seconds. The appearance of Vojto's father in uniform, his chest bedecked with medals and a plane manoeuvring in the background was followed by thunderous applause. We went to see this brilliant, heroic, patriotic film at least twenty times. People later regretted that a follow-up documentary, *From the Sea of Azov to the Tatras,* somehow never got to be made.

On several occasions the film was screened together with a newsreel in which the commander of the German air force in Slovakia, Lieutenant General Keiper, could be seen awarding Vojto's father the German Gold Cross.

The commentator intoned soulfully: *"A small group of Slovak fighter pilots battling the Soviet hordes at the eastern front alongside the pilots of the Luftwaffe has truly proved itself, particularly in action in the Kuban region."*

To mark the Führer's birthday, the writer Jozef Cíger Hronský, director of Matica Slovenská, Slovakia's foremost cultural heritage organisation, gave a speech from the institution's balcony in the city in Martin:

"The map of Europe will change after we Slovaks hammer it with our fists!"

This was duly reported in all the newspapers.

The calm, endless current of the Sálava flowed by in the autumn, bringing plenty of fish and a pleasant coolness.

Vojto and I were sitting in an oak tree, just as its leaves were beginning to turn brown, each of us on his own branch. We watched the milky daytime moon hanging over the Volovec Mountain but we didn't really see it, as our romantic imaginations were taking us to a rather different place.

During a recent week-long leave back in Brežany, Vojto's father told his mother that the Slovak pilots were astounded by the devastating impact of twenty years of communism on the Russian countryside. And he was even more astonished by the fact that instead of treating them as occupiers, the Ukrainians welcomed them as brothers and liberators.

Vojto's eyes glistened as he described his father's sorties.

"You've got to be faster and target the enemy first, otherwise he will shoot you down and you won't survive. At such high speeds in the sky you can't start explaining to someone that you don't want to fight him."

His father and another pilot in the 13th Fighter Squadron once accompanied a large German Focke-Wulf 189 on a reconnaissance mission. Their nickname for the Russians was Redskins – and his father spotted three of them on the horizon, flying Ilyushin 153s. Vojto's father liked to pick one plane and focus on it. He chose an Ilyushin that was moving into position to take aim at the Focke-Wulf. He shot it down and the other Russians tried to escape. He gave chase but then six more planes arrived, accompanied by some bombers. When they saw him, they dived, protected by the Russians' anti-aircraft flak. He wanted to attack but they came closer, so close he could feel the turbulence from their engines. They fired their machine guns. In the confusion he lost his comrade-in-arms in the other plane and learned later that he had been hit from the ground – whether by Russians or Germans he never discovered. Vojto's father managed to escape without injury even though his Messerschmitt, nicknamed Gustav, sustained fifty-nine hits from gunfire and two cannon grenades. He totted them all up once he managed to land back at the base.

On another occasion four Redskins pursued him over the Black Sea. One of them seemed to be quite inexperienced, as he started firing from a long way off. Vojto's father fired as well but his machine gun jammed and he was so preoccupied with releasing it that he nearly crashed into the Russian plane. The Russian flew off in a panic.

He breathed a sigh of relief, turned around and noticed two more Redskins pursuing him. Fortunately for him they were unable to position themselves well and kept getting into each other's line of fire. As his father swung around again, Gustav went into a corkscrew dive, thanks to three large holes blasted in its wings. He didn't regain control over the plane until he was nearly down, too late to bail out. For a while he flew above a Russian village. He saw smoke belching from chimneys and people running for shelter. He was certain this was the end and that he would crash. But by some miracle, he managed to limp back to base.

A week later a Redskin he was chasing flew into a cloud. Vojto's father followed and after pursuing him through the clouds for a while he saw a huge explosion. He rammed down his joystick as hard as he could and managed to steady his Gustav just above ground level. The Redskin was obviously not so lucky, crashing into a building at full tilt. He put that down as a kill.

Dusk was falling over Brežany as we started walking back home down the narrow path across the field, excited and daydreaming. Neither of us said a word.

Years later, after the war, Vojto's father recalled his last Russian flight. After a fierce dogfight he returned to base on a badly damaged plane. He lost control on the landing strip and crashed. He could smell kerosene and moments later the jet went up in flames like a piece of paper.

A military ambulance drove him to the main dressing station, almost jolting the life out of him on the bumpy terrain. He found himself in a dilapidated shed, newly and hastily painted and fitted out with an operating table and medical instruments. A dose of *morphium hydrochloridum,* a four per cent solution, was injected into his thigh. Four minutes after the shot he felt the pain slowly easing. Seven minutes later it was completely gone and he drifted off into a light sleep and dreamed weird, confused dreams.

He underwent an operation, lost a great deal of blood and needed several blood transfusions. His body turned into slab of meat. He was given more injections. They sent him to a field hospital set up in a former aristocratic mansion – a sign announced that until recently this had been home to the local branch of the Communist Party of the Soviet Union – where he was treated by military medical officers. He thought it strange that there were no women on the front line. Only once he was transferred further into the hinterland did he see some female nurses.

Due to the inhospitable conditions in Eastern Europe and the unreliability of rail connections it was several weeks before a medical train could be dispatched. Not until he got back home did he see a decent bed with clean white sheets, and the sight brought tears to his eyes. On the other hand, this may just as well have been caused by withdrawal symptoms after coming off the morphine.

During those days he spent a lot of time reading. At the field hospital a caring nurse gave him a copy of a book that graced every self-respecting home library at the time and had recently become a bestseller in India. *Mein Kampf.* This rather worn copy, a special wedding edition, in a slipcase with the golden seal of Bavaria embossed on its parchment-like cover, was handed out free to newly-weds as a gift from the government. Since Vojto's father had always been rather bad at foreign languages, he understood only a few words in each sentence and guessed the meaning of the rest.

He was enchanted by the book right from the first sentence: "*It has turned out fortunate for me today that destiny appointed Braunau-on-the-Inn to be my birthplace.*" He empathized with the Führer's childhood and the hardships he had endured in his years in Vienna. He shed a few tears over the hero's hostile and cruel fate – the morphine certainly played a role here – and since he never finished the book (the nurse asked for it back when he left) he remained convinced it was a powerful social novel on a par with any Charles Dickens masterpiece.

He would often begin a sentence by quoting *Hitler, the writer…*

In the middle of the hot summer of 1944 Vojto's father suddenly disappeared.

As a member of the 13th Fighter Squadron, which had meanwhile returned from Russia, he was responsible for defending Bratislava from British and American bombers. The pilots were under secret instructions from General Čatloš not to strike first and to save the planes for another, more important mission. On 26 June, ten days after the bombing of the Apollo factory in Bratislava, Vojto's father went on leave to celebrate the seventh birthday of his second-born son Teo. This turned out to be a very fortunate decision.

That muggy but clear day with excellent visibility ended in a sudden summer storm. By then it was all over. At 9.30 a.m., just as Vojto's father finished repairing the propeller on a model airplane and the smell of freshly picked strawberries wafted in from the kitchen, Slovak fighter pilots, who were on high alert, were ordered to attack the 15th US Army. The Germans had accused them of cowardice and injured pride is no laughing matter.

The 13th Fighter Squadron thus ceased to exist.

From August onwards there was no news of Vojto's father. Vojto guessed that his mother knew something but her lips were sealed. Everyone sort of pretended that his father had just popped out to the corner shop for a packet of cigarettes and would be back any minute. Whenever Vojto started asking questions, Mrs Roško immediately changed the subject – usually she quickly found an excuse to tell him off for something, so he learned to keep his mouth shut.

Newspapers and the radio increasingly talked about bandits and terrorists who called themselves partisans. Fences and walls were plastered with a variety of decrees and the Minister of the Interior proclaimed martial law.

And Peter's tiny battery-powered radio, a Christmas present from last year, started to proclaim *London calling!* and *Govorit Moskva!* He and Father held their breath as they lapped up the news of the Americans capturing Rome, of uprisings breaking out in Warsaw and in France and about the Red Army's invincible march from the east.

I imagined them as tiny little red soldiers in red uniforms and red beards. With red guns firing red bullets. Spreading scarlet fire.

25.

The summer of 1944 was initially cold and rainy, turning hot and humid only towards the end. It wasn't rare for the thermometer outside our living-room window to show 38 Celsius in the shade. Peter, Tina and I would go and check it regularly and couldn't believe our eyes. Mother, her friends and our home-help Terka talked about the fighting on the Russian front and the insurgents in the mountains as they made apricot jam.

A long and glorious Indian summer followed. Father and Uncle Rudo sipped cider in the cellar, discussing the air raids on various cities. Later someone told me that people whose houses were bombed but who survived the air raid actually felt relieved afterwards because it made everything much simpler. No address, no worries.

People also said that the Germans deployed several army divisions to crush the Slovak Uprising and that they were intending to occupy the whole of Slovakia.

I had only one direct encounter with the Germans.

One afternoon in October Mother sent me to Puškár's for a few slices of her favourite *Dobostorte*. I heard Puškár bustling about at the back as I waited for him to wrap up the cake. The bell above the entrance tinkled and three tall Fritzes in black uniforms walked in. Their loud talk and laughter filled the empty patisserie.

It was just them and me. Puškár was nowhere to be seen. They approached the counter where I stood waiting. One of them addressed me in broken Slovak:

"Ah, nice boy... What... your name?"

I don't like talking to strangers but on this occasion decided to respond, though quietly.

"Adam."

"Adam! Nice name!" he said, his heavy hand with a gold ring ruffling my hair. He raised his index finger: "A German name...!"

"Are you mad? It's Slovak!" I snapped.

The German laughed, I guess he didn't quite understand what I said. If only he'd known he was talking to a cross-breed, a mongrel, he wouldn't have taken it so well.

"Also! Na ja... Mein Name ist Horst!"

One of the others drummed his fingers on the counter and said something. They all laughed again. The curtain behind the counter rustled but Puškár didn't appear. I went around the counter to get him.

I nearly collided with him. He was watching the scene from behind the curtain. He shook his head and put his finger to his mouth, begging me to keep quiet.

"*Hallo...!*" the German called out.

Puškár bit his lips. He was sweating. Suddenly one of the Fritzes leaned against the counter and picked up a bottle of rum. Puškár couldn't take it any longer.

He emerged from behind the curtain, smiling and wiping his forehead.

"Hello. How can I help you, gentlemen...?"

134

"Please. You have…?" The German got stuck, waved his hand and continued in German.

Puškár kept smiling, as if his mouth were full of wire and rubber bands making it impossible for him to speak.

"I don't understand."

The German went on and Puškár kept smiling at him.

"I don't understand what you're saying!"

I stepped back waiting to see what would happen.

Eventually, with much gesturing and pointing, the Germans managed to order a selection of gateaux and strudels as well as coffee. Puškár didn't dare to offer them ersatz coffee. It was all too much for him and I wondered where his sense of humour had gone.

He slowly removed the slices of *Dobostorte* for my mother from the glass counter while we both watched the Fritzes stuffing themselves. They wore black uniforms decorated with golden badges and the stark, menacing letters SS, reminiscent of two lightning flashes. As they placed their hats on the table I noticed the skull and crossbones on them. They must be pirates – that was my first thought – and I moved closer to take a better look at the badges. Puškár put a hand on my arm to stop me.

By now his shirt was completely soaked through and he whispered:

"I didn't want to serve them, you're my witness! But I was scared they might smash up my shop. I'm no hero! Stay with me, Adam, just in case. Everything is on the house. You do speak German, don't you?"

I nodded.

The Germans savoured the pastries, traded jokes and looked out into the street through the window, commenting on the girls passing by. I couldn't get the words on their belts out of my head: *Gott mit uns!* Which one did they have in mind? The one who protected my mother?

While they were enjoying themselves, nobody entered the patisserie even though this was the usual time for couples in love and old ladies to start trickling in. Afternoon visitors, families with noisy children. People would pause uncertainly outside the entrance and move on.

"I hope they get the hell out of here soon!" Puškár was imploring silently. "Otherwise I can forget today's takings!"

135

They ordered brandy – Puškár kept some in stock for his friends, just a few drops at the bottom of the bottle, but now served the soldiers with trembling hands.

"Ich hatt' ei-nen Ka-me-raden, / ei-nen bes-sern find'st du nit. / Die Trom-mel schlug zum Strei-te, / er ging an mei-ner Sei-te / in glei-chem Schritt und Tritt, / in glei-chem Schritt und Tritt."

"What are they singing about…?" Puškár asked, shaking like a leaf.

I started to translate. Combat song lyrics are always very simple. As simple as death.

"I had a friend, you couldn't find a better one. The battle drum sounded and we marched side by side, side by side."

"Ei-ne Ku-gel kam ge-flo-gen; / gilt es mir o-der gilt es dir? / Ihn hat es weg-geris-sen; / er liegt mir vor den Fü-ssen, / als wär's ein Stück von mir, / als wär's ein Stück von mir."

"A bullet came flying, is it meant for me or is it meant for you? It has mowed him down and now he's lying by my feet, like a piece of myself, like a piece of myself."

"Will mir die Hand noch rei-chen er, / weil ich e-ben lad': / 'Kann dir die Hand nicht ge-ben, / bleib du im ew'gen Le-ben, / mein guter Ka-me-rad, / mein guter Ka-me-rad'!"

"He wanted to shake my hand while I loaded my gun: 'I can't shake your hand, but in eternal life you'll be forever my good friend, forever my good friend!'"

Their eyes glazed over as they sang the last verse.

To this day I don't know what got into me but I started singing right there and then:

"Treu-e ist ein lee-rer Wahn, / schon Courts-Mah-ler sagt! / Man ist treu, doch täg-lich ei-ner an-dern. / Ei-ne klei-ne Lie-be-lei für das hei-sse Blut, / Gott, ich fin-de nichts da-bei, / a-ber merk's Dir gut."

They joined in: *"Küss' nie die Frau von Dei-nem Freund / und wenn's Dir noch so süss er-scheint! / Er könn-te Dich beim Küs-se fas-sen / und sie vie leicht Dir gleich für ewig überlassen! / Küss' nie die Frau von Dei-nem Freund / und wenn's Dir noch so süss erscheint / Schmeckt auch der Kuss Dir je-den-falls, / doch Du hast sie dann ewig auf dem Hals!"*

This was Mother's music, and all I remembered was the first verse and the chorus. I still recall that we used to sing it accompanied on piano: *Küss nie die Frau von Deinem Freund! (Fox-Trot u. Charleston). Text und Musik von Willy Rosen.*

The Fritzes applauded and laughed. One was moved to tears by the silly song.

It didn't seem appropriate to continue: "*Frau Levy mensendiekt / schon morgens früh, / weil nur die Schlankheit siegt, / beugt sie das Knie. / So zwischen 9 und 10 / treibt sie's energisch im-mer…*"

The song was about a certain Mrs Levy, whose background can't have been entirely Aryan.

But they would certainly have known the song, just like the previous one. Willy Rosen, real name Willy Julius Rosenbaum, one of Berlin's most famous cabaret singers, had penned many songs that were popular all over Europe from the 1920s on. After a failed attempt to flee to America via Holland he set out on a train journey in the opposite direction – eastward – to a certain distinctive sleepy Polish town known by its German name Auschwitz – where within a few weeks he breathed his last in a Siemens gas chamber, generously supplied with Zyclon B gas produced by I. G. Farben. Best quality guaranteed, advertising brochure provided free of charge on request, please use the stamped self-addressed envelope. Unmistakeable quality.

26.

Himmler visited Bratislava in September 1944 and rumour had it that he was beside himself, raving about Germany being in ruins and food being rationed, while people here were just strolling in the streets and spending money in the shops like there was no tomorrow.

The idyll was short-lived. More and more goods were rationed.

The production of cream was banned and Mother had to go on secret milk-hunting expeditions so that she could make Peter's favourite French cream cake for his birthday. Puškár came to the rescue at the last moment; he had his sources, as always.

Another rare dish she served at the party was smoked beef tongue, a present from a patient of Father's. The meat was quite tough because Mother didn't boil it long enough but everyone pretended it was a treat they would not miss for the world. Uncle Rudo broke a tooth on it. After lunch the grown-ups withdrew to finish off the supplies of fine pre-war coffee. It was Monako who slipped it into Father's pocket. It must have come from the Wehrmacht officers' store, Mother claimed.

The golden age of Puškár's patisserie was slowly coming to an end. He kept serving cream puffs and his legendary chestnut puree to his favourite regulars until someone snitched on him. An inspector discovered bags of coffee as well as huge supplies of sugar and cream in his storeroom. His licence was taken away.

And to cap it all Lila had left him for good.

The God of postmen had delivered a letter.

At the beginning of October Father had her emigrate because he'd had enough of the charade. She did not reveal where she was headed, explaining that her German background would make a free life in this country impossible in the future. There was a mention of Rio or Paraguay, I forget which. In any case, in her final letter Lila said she would remember him as long as she lived and that she was sure they would meet again although it might be in many years' time.

This was the last straw for the poor man. He disappeared, nobody knew where. He left the city.

Puškár never stopped waiting for Lila. The love of his life.

How true: nostalgia is remembering something that has never existed.

The Germans gradually occupied all of Slovakia and the Jewish exemptions were suddenly no longer valid. Preparations went ahead for a fresh round of accelerated transports.

Before escaping to Switzerland, Mr Gronský the dentist managed to fit Father with a special platinum crown. I heard him whisper into Father's ear:

"I could get the death penalty for this!"

It was quite obvious that Mr Gronský took morbid pleasure in saying this.

In the 1930s he was a fanatical adherent of the theory of focal infection, a dental sickness that affects the area deep within the gums that lurk under the teeth. As a result he deprived many a patient of their coveted and carefully tended ivories. But at least they had nothing to worry about for the rest of their lives. Luckily, Father had resisted this siren call.

Father used to say, "Teeth are a strange thing, Adam. Would you believe that what we have inside our mouths are actually thirty-two joints? But they can hurt like hell!"

When my friend Tonko Grün, who was my age and blessed with amazingly delicate fingers – he was an expert in bending copper wire and fashioning it into various animals and flowers – packed his child's suitcase covered in coloured paper, he threw in a pair of pliers because they were supposed to be going away to work somewhere. Mislovič was also included in the transport, even though he didn't know a single Hebrew prayer. Mrs Kluger had given her cats away.

Throughout this period Uncle Oskar tried to keep a low profile. If he had to go out he stayed off the main streets, taking special care to avoid his concierge who might have reported him. He spent hours in other people's homes but they, too, were frightened whenever the doorbell or the phone rang, as if some invisible person might have slipped in via the sound-transmitting devices. He and Aunt Rózka took to visiting acquaintances they would never have dreamed of seeing before, as well as strangers they happened to strike up a conversation with in the street and who looked like decent people. Anything to avoid staying at home. But the postal service had no mercy on Oskar or his wife. Or their children.

People wondered what to pack. All sorts of rumours circulated about Poland but few believed them.

On the eve of the transport Mother and I were sitting in Uncle Oskar's living room, talking and drinking herbal tea. He sat on the sofa looking out of the window and barely said a word. Everyone else spoke in hushed tones or chatted about things that were quite irrelevant, pretending that nothing was happening. Gardening, the weather in Krakow, a football match…

The doorbell rang. Nobody moved. Aunt Rózka looked at Mother, who nodded and went to answer the door. People from the neighbouring flats were standing outside. One after the other they filed in, slipping past Mother. They were silent. At first they were embarrassed. Then they started taking pictures off the walls. They helped themselves to vases, opened the chest of drawers and took out the silver cutlery. All in total silence.

Aunt Rózka began to talk again. About gardening, the weather in Krakow, a football match… I saw tears welling up in her eyes – if she had stopped talking she would have broken down. Her voice trembled slightly but she managed to get a grip on herself.

Meanwhile the neighbours – the same neighbours who used to beg her for her cake recipe or chat about yesterday's weather – removed objects from glass cases, helped themselves to china cups, small statuettes, pulled a crocheted tablecloth off the table… Uncle Oskar and Aunt Rózka just sat there watching them and suddenly realized that none of this mattered anymore because *malach hamoves,* the Angel of Death, had taken hold of them. The neighbours were just his innocent altar boys.

Oskar's favourite song played on the gramophone:

The world doesn't like tears, / they're just mockery. / It only loves those who laugh all the time. / You must never cry, / even if your heart is bleeding…

Ever since then hearing this song makes me nauseous.

A few years ago I was on the night train from Kraków. I finally managed to get to sleep on a couchette, despite the usual discomfort and the noise. I sank into a dull, bottomless sleep. It must have lasted only a moment because something – the switching of points, or the sudden braking of the engine – woke me up with a start. As I opened my eyes, an enormous illuminated sign *OŚWIĘCIM,* filled my field of vision. The word shone into the darkness. My heart skipped a beat.

The supreme irony was that some people in the compartment next door were conducting a noisy conversation in German. Suddenly they fell silent, as if the earth had taken a deep breath and time had come to a halt. I know that may sound theatrical, and they must have thought so, too, for they soon resumed their conversation while I spent the rest of the journey (between short naps and the changing of engines) wondering about the locals who still live there today. They had no reason to move away after the war, of course, it was all over. But perhaps at least they could have changed that spine-chilling name. To live in a city bearing that name, even as late as 1999, was something I could not fathom. Every time I opened the window I would smell burned bodies.

I was shocked when Bony told me that on his travels around

Europe he once spent the night there, staying with a friend. They went to a karaoke club in the evening and had a whale of a time. Hearing the name *Oświęcim* made his eyes light up. He may even have mentioned an interesting woman he met there, if I remember right.

Can anyone still have fun in a city bearing that name?

Some of the transports were headed for Lublin and Treblinka. Day in, day out, special trains would stop at, or leave from, Brežany or rattle through the town, a key junction on the way north.

Just before Christmas I overheard a grey-haired gentleman in an overcoat and hat, a thoroughly hard-working and virtuous denizen of our city, complain that he had spent all night tossing and turning because the endless clatter of trains disturbed his sleep.

"Can't even get a good night's sleep because of those bloody Jews!"

On my way home with a packet of Father's Bystrice cigarettes in my pocket (I was allowed to keep some of the change, provided I didn't tell Mother) I noticed piles of old Jewish religious books that had been thrown out of the windows of the house on the main square that used to belong to the fabric merchant, Mr Silberstein, and his sons.

They stayed scattered on the ground for a while, getting wet, but since the winter of 1944 was harsh, the good citizens of Brežany used them as kindling in their stoves. And if they happened to be short of toilet paper, the books found another use. Guardsman Gajdoš, who suffered from haemorrhoids, was particularly pleased with the exquisite, century-old pages.

27.

Six years later in May, sitting on the bank of the Sálava with a fresh crow thigh on a paper plate in his lap, his tongue loosened by Mislovič's cheap Blaufränkisch wine, which at least temporarily assuaged his severe headache, "the General", Vojto's father, stripped of every military rank, told us what it was like in the mountain village of Donovaly during that cold, rainy autumn towards the end of the war.

The Sport Hotel, normally the playground of happy holiday skiers, was packed to bursting. The Germans, under SS Obergruppenführer Höfle's command, launched a massive assault against the Uprising. During the hasty retreat from the Three Oaks airfield, Vojto's father and his colleagues salvaged three courier planes to maintain contact with other insurgent groups and the advancing Russians. They also brought a storage tank containing four thousand litres of diesel. Vojto's father had spotted the airfield next to the hotel during a reconnaissance mission and drove over to inspect the terrain, carrying a passenger – Rudolf Slánský. He sported a red beard in those days. He had just flown to Donovaly from Moscow for a meeting with one of the leaders of the Uprising, Gustáv Husák.

The names caught everyone's attention.

"And now they've both been arrested," said Mislovič, smacking his lips.

No one would ever forget the night of 27 October 1944. At seven a.m. Free Slovak Radio made its final broadcast and the leaders of the Uprising, who had been evacuated to Donovaly, spent all evening holed up in their last joint meeting.

Captain Vojtech Roško and his colleagues were put up in a hotel staff room – some in beds, others on the floor. All night long they heard shouting and agitated voices from the corridor. The hotel was in turmoil, as a few days earlier the Germans had started bombing Donovaly and firing mortars. The insurgents pored over maps, wary of the SS divisions that were drawing close. But since the hotel guests included Generals Viest and Golian, along with part of the Slovak insurgent army quartered in the village, they all tried their best to convince themselves that, since the front was advancing, it would be the Russians coming in rather than the Germans.

From time to time the mood of despair would be relieved by someone singing Grandma Mária's favourite song with updated lyrics:

How quiet the night, so dark and fair / The partisan fights in his forest lair. / The moon sleeps not a wink all night / The partisan it must guard with light. / When he leaves the forest's shade / With fighting spirit his heart does blaze. / Slovaks, onward! Into battle's might: / Our homeland summons us to fight!

Vojto's father bumped into General Viest at the hotel bar and

142

informed him that the plans for relocating the HQ to Soviet-held territory were ready. They could set out at any time. Viest acknowledged the news but didn't give an unequivocal response.

The general whispered that General Höfle had just phoned him from the occupied city of Zvolen, insisting on capitulation. He downed a small glass of French brandy and was about to say something but the drink went down the wrong way, making him cough.

"Do you like France, Captain?"

"I do."

"Well, I don't."

And with that he left.

After a tumultuous night, at about four in the morning, the insurgent leadership retreated into the mountains. Rumours started going round that the army was being disbanded, but they remained just rumours, since nobody actually knew anything.

The dawn of 28 October 1944 brought a bitterly cold wind, as well as rain turning to snow. Flying was out of the question. With frozen hands Captain Vojtech Roško and his colleagues doused two of the planes with kerosene and set them alight. The third one wouldn't catch fire in the rain so they riddled it with gunfire to make sure it could not fall into the hands of the Germans, who were poised to burst into Donovaly any moment.

An eerie, apocalyptic mood reigned. Fires were lit everywhere to get rid of documents, and the heavy, damp air was filled with smoke. It came from the hotel garages as well as from the cemetery.

Vojto's father and the other two pilots commandeered a car. Vojto's father, the fat from the crow thigh trickling down his chin, recalled that it was a fabulous 1940 Opel Kapitän. They had their pick of dozens of superb cars parked outside the hotel. They drove up the mountain on a forest path as far as they could. When the Opel got stuck in the mud, they wrecked the engine and pushed on without any idea where they were going, since nobody had managed to get hold of a decent map.

Mislovič topped up his glass and Vojto's father, munching away, went on with his story, recalling the astounding number of horses that had escaped from the villages and were now roaming the woods. They caught one but it wouldn't do what they wanted and couldn't carry their gear.

143

"Do you know what horse meat tastes like?"

Everyone nodded.

"It's sort of… sweetish."

"It's quite tough, though, it needs roasting for a long time."

"Oh, c'mon! Have you ever tried a two-year-old foal, you fool?"

Vojto's father waved his hand and continued.

They spent several weeks wandering in the forest. First there were three of them, then they were down to two because one of the fighter pilots had a breakdown, probably from the cold and exhaustion, and ran off. They spent nights in sheds and haylofts. As for food, some they got from generous folk, some they stole. Eventually, at the end of his tether, Captain Roško sneaked back to Brežany.

The Germans crushed the Uprising within two months.

After the war it transpired that Generals Viest and Golian, hiding in plain clothes, were arrested by Einsatzkommando 14 in Pohronský Bukovec as early as 3 November. Someone betrayed them after they had made the arduous trek across the Pol'ana and Prašivá mountains, a journey that was particularly challenging for General Viest, who was in poor health. They probably perished in a German concentration camp or in another, similar establishment in the Soviet Union, having been dispatched there by the NKVD. You can fill in the blanks yourself. History is whatever you choose to believe.

"I think that Viest was scared of flying…" Monako speculated.

"Another piece of kosher pigeon? Have some, they're almost gone!"

Some say that the Germans, on a high after successfully burning down several villages and hamlets, and probably also on metamphetamines which, it was said, the Wehrmacht as well as the SS divisions were especially partial to, wanted to raze to the ground the insurgent cities of Banská Bystrica, Zvolen and Brezno.

It wasn't a bad idea in principle, but eventually they settled for helping themselves to war booty in the form of cars, cattle, telephone and telegraph parts, typewriters and a few trifles (collections of stamps, coins and paintings) from private homes that had been abandoned.

President Tiso referred to the brutal suppression of the Uprising in a letter to Pope Pius XII in 1944 as a "special kind of pastoral care" (true enough, shepherds also have to slaughter the odd sheep from time to time), stressing that it was just an embarrassing little rebellion by a bunch of Czechs and Jews.

A few months before he died, Vojto showed me some entries in his father's pocket diary for 1945. He found it while rummaging around his parents' old house, when he had nothing better to do after the 1989 Velvet Revolution and his subsequent rise and fall from grace.

Monday, 22 January – travelled: Brežany-Leopoldov-Prievidza-Štubňa-Zvolen – train by night
Tuesday, 23 January – travelled: by train – Zvolen-Banská Bystrica. Bought a car – B. Bystrica-Brezno-Tisovec. Night.
Wednesday, 24 January – waiting, Tisovec
Thursday, 25 January – waiting, Tisovec
Sunday, 28. January – Tisovec: 8:30 am, Germans vac. the city, 9:20 a.m. Russian soldiers arrive, 12:15 left for Hrachov. 16:00 reached sister's house in Hrachov.
Thursday, 8 February. Poprad: reporting for duty and call-up.

Vojto's father joined the First Czecho-Slovak Army Corps, a Red Army division. The same army he had successfully fought against in Kuban two years before.

28.

The POW camp Brežany-Behy consisted of a couple of barracks hastily knocked together and surrounded by some barbed-wire fencing. It had been hurriedly set up in the storage depot of a disused wine cooperative. Most of the inmates were English-speaking. Uncle Rudo could see the camp from his balcony from where he admired flocks of redstarts that for some reason tended to congregate on the shiny metal roofs of the barracks to soak up the remaining rays of the waning autumn sun before their migration south, chattering and arguing loudly.

The redstarts had arrived in the wake of swallows, which, in turn, had alighted on the roof after the swifts had left.

On his way from the woods, Rudo often passed the barbed-wire fence and watched the men lounging about the camp perimeter, drinking or playing volleyball. Neighbours told him they were American pilots who had been shot down in the summer over southern Slovakia.

From time to time one of the men would chat to him over the fence, offer him a cigarette and ask about the latest news. Uncle Rudo spoke passable English, having picked it up on his business trips. He turned down the offer of cigarettes and told the men about the Russian, French and Italian fronts, while they shared stories of their life in Cleveland and Boston. When one of them mentioned that he came from Fresno in California, Uncle Rudo questioned him eagerly about Monarchs, the migrating butterflies that fly in huge swarms from Canada across the US to winter in Mexico. He had read about them in *The Global Source of Entertainment And Knowledge*, the Czech journal he received from a friend in the Protectorate.

The Americans weren't too badly off in Behy. Sometimes the guards let them to go for a swim in the pond, and once they were even taken to a wine cellar, where they apparently got quite drunk. In this idyllic state they waited for the war to end, killing time as best they could.

But then the Uprising broke out and two regiments of the SS Galizien division occupied Brežany. One of the guards overheard that the Germans regarded the "keeping" of Americans as an unnecessary luxury and a potential risk, and that they were waiting for the first opportunity to get rid of them on the quiet.

One day, when the first flocks of redstarts took off from the roof of the barracks before heading south, Captain Woldow, the man from Fresno, whistled to Uncle Rudo, who was on his way from lunch at our house, still replete with memories of the pheasant *au vin* that Father had somehow managed to secure.

This was Rudo's chance to demonstrate the romantic and adventurous side of his nature. When the guards showed up at night with Slovak uniforms for the American soldiers and opened the entrance, he was waiting with a lorry he had borrowed from Ambi Krebs without telling him why. Ambi used it to transport limestone from the quarry and wanted it back by dawn. No questions asked.

Just in case, Captain Woldow pointed out to Rudo that it was quite likely he wouldn't come back and that he might not receive any reward for this service but Rudo just waved him off and opened the door resolutely to let the captain and a fellow pilot take the front passenger seat. The others piled into the back under the tarpaulin along with a few revolvers and a machine gun.

When people later asked about this unusual and indeed shocking act, Uncle Rudo explained that for a long time his life had seemed boring and he had been too set in his ways. He felt the need to rush headlong into the night with his eyes half-closed, to get a little taste of the excitement of a hunter. To feel the pounding of his heart in his throat, the smell of blood. To make love to naked war – these were the exact words he said to my father, who almost choked on a liver dumpling. Rudo lived off this experience for the rest of his life.

They set off. It was a clear night and they didn't put their headlights on. There wasn't a soul on the road.

Rudo drove mainly along minor, potholed dirt roads, avoiding the towns and villages strung along the night's necklace of smouldering blacked-out pearls.

At the railway crossing in Zbehy a military patrol accompanied by two guardsmen waved at them to stop but Uncle Rudo, although sweating with anxiety, just accelerated and passed them without slowing down. He expected to be fired at but nothing moved behind their vehicle. And when Captain Woldow suggested they open the bottle of plum brandy he had in his rucksack, Uncle Rudo readily agreed.

Woldow started telling his story, recalling that memorable 26 June, which happened to be the birthday of Vojto's brother Teo, when the boy received a splendid toy Messerschmitt Bf110E complete with a Schräge Musik cannon from his father. (According to a horoscope Mrs Roško had seen, "Boys born in this month are brave and always keep to the straight and narrow. While they exact vengeance on those who have done them wrong, they are also prepared to make their peace easily. They are not lucky in married life and are disappointed in their loved ones, which makes their lives unusually bitter.")

This was the day Vojto's father's 13th Fighter Squadron was

147

annihilated. However, before that happened, one of the Slovak fighter pilots shot down Woldow's Liberator in the hot but clear air above Bratislava.

The US bombers released clusters of tinfoil strips that glistened in the sun, which were intended to confuse the enemy flak's sights, but the anti-aircraft guns started pounding, and when Woldow's plane appeared above the forest it took several hits from an approaching Messerschmitt. Woldow's colleague bailed out and his parachute was hit by machine gunfire. The plane was going down; only two of its engines were still working and shells were bursting all around. He lost radio contact and both right-hand propellers were shot to pieces. As he saw the curtain of fire and smoke Woldow realised he had to bail out as quickly as possible. He reached for the cabin lock, loosened the belts, found the parachute straps and jumped. As he fell, a powerful jerk slowed his descent and he floated down slowly from quite low, watching his Liberator explode. He hit the ground and before he managed to disentangle himself from the parachute a military vehicle stopped by and men in grey uniforms jumped out. The Gestapo.

If all this had happened fifty years later he would have landed on the crossroads of two streets in Petržalka, named after two meritorious female communists, Klara Zetkin and Jožka Jabůrková. Uncle Rudo, by then an elderly gentleman, used to visit this spot in the late 1970s with a map. He would stand on a corner for a while lost in thought, before walking slowly to a nearby café, enjoying the sight of the redstarts flying about.

Back in 1944, in the middle of the night somewhere around Kozárovce, Rudo began to feel tired from the endless, protracted journey. He asked Captain Woldow if they could make a brief stop so he could have a little nap with his head on the steering wheel, just to give his eyes a rest.

When he woke up he was alone in the car. A worn cigarette case with the picture of a monarch butterfly lay on the passenger seat. Rudo waited for a few minutes and then returned to Brežany.

Only much later did he learn that the Americans had made it to the shrinking insurgent territory at the Three Oaks airfield, which had just, for a short period, come under the command of one Captain Vojtech Roško. In early October they were flown out to the Italian base of Bari.

29.

A newsreel at the Slovák cinema screened before the feature film on Count Münchhausen showed Hitler in person pinning medals on Wehrmacht officers. It didn't take Father long to make a diagnosis. What struck him in particular was the tremor in the Führer's hand, which he tried but failed to hide behind his back. Father's guess was *morbus parkinsoni* – the same illness Mr. Malánek suffers from, Adam, – it can be caused by excessive use of Pervitin, a kind of metamphetamine, as he learned from a fascinating study in *The Slovak Physician*. Its use was said to be quite widespread among the SS and Father had indeed received several requests for prescriptions. The medication reduces tiredness, hinders sleep, "inhibits the baser instincts, promotes the urge to move, talk and keep busy", but eventually results in addiction, irritation and a state of anxiety.

When the film ended we walked out into the darkened city. Slovakia had been under a state of emergency and since the front was slowly but inexorably approaching, a blackout had been imposed.

There weren't many people in the street as nobody had much reason to go out. Father, Mother, Peter, Tina and I walked home. Father strode ahead of us, crunching the freshly fallen snow and showing the way with a battery-powered torch firmly held in his hand. It made a droning noise that irritated all the dogs behind the fences and walls that we passed.

We came to a German patrol – a few soldiers standing on both sides of the road. I sensed danger. I knew that the Germans had, like us, blood coursing through their veins, brains inside their skulls, that some had just been to the toilet while others suffered from stomach troubles, but nevertheless... They scared me.

A shot rang out, making me jump. A man was running down the street with soldiers in hot pursuit. One fell onto the pavement and lay there writhing. The uniform on his stomach was stained with blood. He screamed and his bulging eyes stared ahead. Father rushed forward and knelt down by his side.

Mother dragged us away but Peter and I were spellbound. We heard the sound of gunfire in the distance.

"Go home!" Father shouted at us.

A German armoured car passed by and braked sharply. A man in uniform climbed out.

He held out his hand to Father and introduced himself as Doctor Johannes Atlas of the SS-Sanitätsabteilung.

By then Mother had dragged us around the corner and we hurried home.

Over breakfast Father told us that the Waffen-SS soldier had suffered a bout of peritonitis. He said this was what had killed Alexander Pushkin, after he was shot in the stomach in a duel. But this fellow was likely to survive.

Apart from this incident war was still something far off and I couldn't really imagine what it was like. All I knew was that you could lose a head or a leg. Sometimes even your senses.

I loved our Sunday afternoon strolls around town, combined with window-shopping. For Father this was the only way of enticing Mother out of the house as she was now prone to increasingly frequent and serious spells of depression and lethargy, so much so that she was sometimes unable to move or even get out of bed.

We peered into the window of a dressmaker's. A range of silks and ladies' dresses of various styles were draped on mannequins; newspapers and magazines for their male companions could be seen in a dark corner. In the old days before the war Father often sat there while Mother tried on a new outfit.

Mr Malánek developed an interesting strategy for his general store. At first he kept his shop window full, even though none of the goods on display was available inside. One by one, however, the items disappeared from the window, until eventually he covered it with white paint and replaced the goods with a slogan appealing to the citizens to save water, power, coal and gas.

Mr Stern's kosher butcher's was Aryanized by old Rozgoň, a Hlinka Guard member and great Germanophile. The first thing he flaunted in his shop window was a giant map of the Soviet Union, on which he marked the progress of German divisions into Russia's heartland with pins and tiny flags adorned with swastikas. Once the situation on the Russian front began to change (which the powers-that-be presented as a "planned withdrawal" and a "tactical manoeuvre" aimed at reducing the length of the front), he became less ardent with his pins and flags and gave up on them completely once it seemed that he would have to start pinning his flags outside the map – into the photograph of a smiling Bavarian girl holding a basket of smoked meats.

By then the Russians were positioned on the outskirts of Warsaw.

30.

Just before midnight, early in February 1945, someone knocked on our gate.

Father went down, prepared for the worst. There was a cold wind howling outside and since everyone observed the blackout religiously, a bulletproof darkness reigned.

It might conceivably have been the three Wise Men bearing gifts and singing a carol, but to be on the safe side, Father hung a stethoscope around his neck as a badge of his profession, hoping it might deter any potential assailant. Then he opened the door.

A German officer, accompanied by two soldiers and a man in plain clothes stood outside. Caspar bearing gold, Melchior frankincense and Balthazar myrrh for the baby Jesus. And the Angel was hopping around them wiggling a paper star.

But then everything morphed into reality.

After giving a salute the officer apologized for disturbing him at this late hour. Father recognized him as Dr Johannes Atlas of the SS-Sanitätsabteilung, the man who had helped him treat that gunshot wound to the stomach. He came to ask for a small favour, at the suggestion of Mr Levendovský, the notary. He was about to perform an urgent operation but had run out of morphine.

Father showed him into the consulting room. He took out a few vials from the cabinet and offered him some glass syringes as well, but these the German doctor declined. He complained that the heating in the hospital's operating theatres was inadequate and that he had to operate with fingers frozen to the bone. Before leaving he asked Father if he could occasionally consult him on difficult cases. Father didn't hear him at first so he had to repeat his request.

"One good turn…" Father nodded.

Gradually they warmed to each other and although their friendship lasted only a month – for this was the exact amount of time Dr Atlas had left to live – it developed in a rather interesting and bizarre way. Dr Atlas was an excellent surgeon, a skill he had perfected during the years spent at a field hospital where accurate and fast interventions were required. He had a few unusual hobbies – for instance, he kept count of the number of penises and limbs he had amputated in the course of his practice (the number and dates were meticulously recorded in a little red notebook). And he collected cockroaches.

The airspace above Brežany was increasingly becoming the scene of fierce combat between Russian and German fighter planes, which sometimes woke me up with a start and made me climb into my brother's bed in fear. The roaring of engines was answered by the rumbling of the German anti-aircraft guns.

During one of these firefights Father had to get out of bed to attend to an urgent case. A deeply unconscious patient, hunched up under a blanket, was stuffed into the boot of Ambi Krebs's old Austrodaimler, quickly driven through the garden gate. The man wore a Russian pilot's uniform and was bleeding profusely from a head wound.

Father recognized him in spite of his bloodied head.

Later, much later he told Father that he had asked to be redeployed at the Second Ukrainian Front, with the Fifth Air Division, so that he could participate in the battle for Brežany – this was the only thing he had to offer and felt he was any good at – but for the time being he didn't seem to have long to live.

The man was Vojto's father.

His Lavochkin had been shot down by a German Messerschmitt Bf110E.

The three men who brought him in laid him out carefully on the table in Father's consulting room. After a brief examination Father diagnosed a perforation of the cranial bone and *impessio calvae*. It required surgery and the draining of a haematoma.

Having given the matter some thought Father asked for Peter to be woken up and sent to fetch Dr Atlas.

A drowsy Peter first went to look for him at the SS-Sanitätsabteilung, then at the hospital and eventually found him in his room at the Golden Stag hotel, interrupting the mounting of a particularly oversized specimen of *Blattella germanica* (commonly known in Slovak as *Russian cockroach*). As he was getting dressed, Dr Atlas mentioned in passing that in this respect Slovakia was a paradise. Peter alerted him to the urgency of the case and, as instructed by Father, asked him to pack a set of scalpels.

Meanwhile at home – after stopping most of the extensive bleeding from the head – Father managed with Mother's assistance to strip Captain Roško of his Russian uniform and dressed him in his own civilian clothes as far as possible.

Dr Atlas arrived a few minutes after Father had carefully laid the patient back his consulting room desk, making sure he was accessible from every side. They shook hands and set to work without too much ceremony.

Anaesthesia was induced by inhalation of diethyl ether from my father's supplies and Dr Atlas personally injected the patient with morphine. He didn't ask any questions, though he must have figured everything out from the Russian tattoo on Roško's left shoulder and the fact that rather than using hospital facilities, this night-time operation was taking place in Father's consulting room, woefully ill-equipped for this kind of intervention. Nevertheless, he remained professional and discreet.

And just as two Greco-Roman wrestlers reach a kind of intimacy through the commingling of their sweat, Father and SS-Hauptsturmführer Dr Atlas formed something of a fraternal bond as their hands were sprayed with Vojto's father's blood.

Their tentative conclusion was that the operation was successful. The anaesthetized patient lay on the impromptu operating table with a bandaged head while they, exhausted, enjoyed a cigarette on the veranda, talking about their wives.

"Is your wife Jewish?"

"What?"

"Your wife…"

"What gave you that idea?" Father asked, chilled to the marrow. As the wife of an Aryan she was exempt from wearing the star of David. So were we, the children.

"I've seen the next transport list," Dr Atlas stated dryly, scratching his back and shoulder.

Father was completely lost for words. He stared into the murky

Brežany morning. The cigarette burned down his fingers and he tossed it into the grass, where it landed with a hiss.

Dr Atlas watched him for a while. "I had her name deleted. Also those of your three children. By the way – do you have any morphine left? For my patients."

Father recovered from the shock, while Dr Atlas chatted casually about Berlin where he hadn't been for four years, suggesting that next time it would be my father's turn to visit him in his flat in Potsdamer Platz, even though his consulting room was much less charming.

They sipped some fine German schnapps and Father noticed that the contracted pupils of Dr Atlas's eyes did not dilate in the dark, and also that his forearm was covered with needle marks, which he took scrupulous care to cover with his shirt, after he had taken off the upper part of his uniform with the SS insignia of three silver stars to the right of the collar and two stripes to the left.

That was how Father's accountant, Mr Kvapka, whom my Father forgot about in all the chaos, found them at eight the next morning.

The following night Vojto's father, who had regained consciousness but was still very weak, was handed over to Mrs Roško. He was nauseous and kept heaving from time to time but he was alive and surely that was all that mattered. Father attended to him for the next few weeks, regularly changing the bandage on his wound, which was healing quite well. When Brežany was liberated he had him transferred to a hospital.

Captain Roško didn't remember anything from this time. These few months were completely erased from his memory. Which didn't return until the summer of 1945.

31.

As the front drew closer, the police organized sporadic raids, sometimes confiscating the odd radio – this was how Uncle Rudo lost his set. He was extremely upset about it. The reason was that the Slovak government had detected a "diminished level of

154

resistance among the population to propaganda broadcasts from Moscow and London".

The Germans ordered Saliny, the village on the outskirts of Brežany, to be evacuated in anticipation of the Russians' arrival. Father's medications and medical supplies were confiscated. Dr Atlas personally came to collect everything and they agreed on what he would actually take and what he would accidentally fail to find and seize. As before, he was particularly interested in morphine and Father gave him an inquisitive look as he packed his supplies into his briefcase with a smile on his face.

By then the rumbling of cannon fire could be heard in Brežany. Every now and then night would turn into day. Stalin's lamps illuminated the city – you could easily have read by their light if only you had nerves of steel. The advance guard of bombers dropped flares on parachutes. Descending slowly, their spectacular magnesium light in various shades of green, white and blue lit up the countryside below. You suddenly felt transported into another world full of colour. And then the Ilyushins started raining bombs.

The Russians didn't drop many bombs on Brežany. They were mostly interested in the German ammunition depot and the Wehrmacht positions on the Volovec Mountain.

People hiding in cellars and bomb shelters would dash out into the cool of the night from time to time, whispering to each other, "I heard the Russians have reached Nevedovo…!" Because the power lines were down, there was no electricity and radios didn't work either, except for those on batteries. Rumours were rife.

The mayor, Father Savický, the notary Levendovský, butcher Rozgoň (having cleared the Nazi flags and frontlines from the map of the USSR in his shop window, painting it red, to be on the safe side, and drawing a crude and crooked hammer and sickle in the middle), as well as the chief of the fire brigade – all in their Sunday best – prepared to welcome the Red Army. They hung about the main square, smoking nervously and once an hour Mrs Levendovská and her daughter brought them ersatz coffee and cake.

In the early hours of the morning the first Russians started trickling in. They were silent and tired. They were followed by lines of soldiers on horseback, carrying submachine guns and wearing hats and helmets with red stars. Some were blond but there were also Mongols, Georgians, Turkmens and Kazakhs. I had seen a few

155

of them before, in the SS. They all seemed the same, like paid extras.

At dawn the town representatives asked to be received by the army commander to report that the German soldiers had withdrawn and the population was not putting up any resistance. The colonel gave them a tired nod and promised that nobody would come to any harm if they handed in their weapons.

In the course of the following days Brežany's leading families invited Russian officers to lunch or dinner. Candles, specially put aside for this kind of festive occasion, were lit so that they wouldn't have to sit in the dark as power had not yet been restored.

Most of them took the sensible precaution of dispatching girls of any age to relatives or, at the very least, made them wear dirty and tattered clothes and hid them somewhere. Because, as a military leader once remarked, "Rape is the trophy of a good combatant!"

There was singing and plum brandy. Schnitzels, fried chicken and roast pork with cabbage appeared out of nowhere. So did some Brežany Blaufränkischer, vintage 1944, with a visceral nose and a bouquet of blood, sweat and tears.

Only a few months earlier Waffen-SS and Hlinka Guard officers had received the same treatment when they went hunting for partisans. A tiny picture of the Führer in a gilt frame landed in the stove at the last minute. Phew, what a relief.

The Soviet soldiers went in and out of Brežany's homes at will, shamelessly rummaging through wardrobes and drawers. But they didn't dare to behave like this in our house – they knew Father was a doctor and came to him for advice and medication. A field hospital was set up in the garden next door, right under the blossoming apple trees, and Father attended to the wounded there. Most of the time he was called to deal with serious cases.

During one of their unannounced visits the Russians swiped Peter's radio off the table, cutting off our only connection to the outside world.

Father didn't notice until they were gone. He shook his head:

"This is the first time these people have seen civilized Europe. It must have come as a shock to them. We have to try and understand them."

That night drunken soldiers, roaring with laughter, shot to smithereens the gilded glass stag outside the Golden Stag hotel. Then they snatched their watches off all the regulars and set them all to Moscow time, two hours ahead.

Military proclamations and notices in Russian were posted on every corner.

At first our parents wouldn't let Vojto and me out of the house but later we were allowed to go down to the Sálava.

We spotted something big and white in the reeds. Gingerly we crept up through the blossoming cat's tails and marigolds. When I pushed the flat sedges aside my heart gave a leap. It was a dead woman, caught in the growth on the riverbank. Her hands were tied behind her back and she had several shot wounds to the chest.

The first naked woman I'd ever seen! Vojto hadn't seen one before either. Her left breast was mangled by the gunshot but the right one was full and beautiful, with a bluish-tinged nipple. Our water nymph also possessed a hairy pudendum, which came as a shock to me, since little Tina was still completely hairless down there. Vojto didn't have a sister so for him it was even more of a revelation.

"What should we do about her?"

"What do you mean – do about her? She's dead, we can't help her any more. Let this be our secret."

I tossed a coin, just in case.

My proposal was confirmed.

For a whole week we kept coming back to look at her. We subjected her lips, the skin on her thighs and stomach and her stiffened breasts – so rounded and exciting – to detailed examination. Once Vojto went so far as to move aside the hair between her legs and relish the crevice leading into the depths of her fascinating body. Then he pushed the slit asunder with two fingers. For a few seconds he stared at something pink and mysterious, seemingly delicate and surprising but let go with a scream as a huge black beetle crawled out. It must have chosen this, of all places, as a temporary shelter. It scared us to death.

That's when we knew that our heady moments with the naked dead woman were drawing to an end. The blood on her chest was beginning to decompose and the body started to get bloated.

I told Father about her.

Vojto and I wanted to see our beloved being pulled out of water but we were sent packing as soon as we got closer.

I could see from afar that her lower half had been gnawed off by fish.

Anglers were particularly happy with their catch that year. The pike and catfish grew fat and chubby, having feasted on human flesh.

There is a place in the woods under the Volovec Mountain where until recently you could see a German army Kübelwagen 82 mouldering away. Children used to go and play soldiers there and parts of the vehicle that gradually fell off were piled up next to a small wooden cross.

All that is left now are a few bits of metal and small chunks of rubber in the grass – and a plaque commemorating, in the context of some anniversary or other, the events that took place here.

It states the bare fact that just before the Russians liberated Brežany a German military doctor drove to this place and committed suicide. His name was Dr Johannes Atlas. He shot himself.

He certainly chose a beautiful spot to die. Centuries-old oak trees, fresh spring air. The sound of birdsong all around. The smell of fresh, moist soil. The shot through the mouth at a sharp upward angle must have been heard far and wide.

The autopsy was carried out by my father. When he asked for the body to be turned over, dozens of empty morphine vials fell out of the jacket pockets.

The plaque mentions that he took his life "when he realized the desperate situation of the German army as it withdrew before the Soviet forces", suggesting a sense of guilt. Personally, I don't believe that any death can be heroic and honourable. There is no such thing. The only people who need drama are those who are alive and lack imagination.

What's honourable about bits of brain splattered all over a car's rear window?

"Adam…! Adam…!" An urgent voice hissed from a small cellar window in Hitler Street, soon to revert to its earlier name, Masaryk Street.

I came closer and saw a dusty face. It took me a while to recognize the tall SS-man with whom I had sung Willi Rosen's songs in Puškár's patisserie a year ago. Horst was his name, if I'm not mistaken.

He was still wearing his black uniform, from which he had torn off the insignia, but the attempt at camouflage wasn't much use. The hand stretched out towards me was clutching a golden chain with a deformed Jesus. He wanted to trade it for my Father's clothes. Nice of him to have remembered my name.

I pretended not to hear and went on.

"Adam! Adam! Good boy…!" He was almost shouting now.

"But I'm a Jew," I said over my shoulder.

"Adam!"

I pulled down my trousers and offered him my behind.

Peter was taken to the vineyards under the Volovec Mountain to help search for dead bodies.

The Russians were put in coffins and taken away in lorries. The Germans had to be buried on the spot, their valuables and identity cards removed and placed into a wax paper bag, signed, witnessed and sealed. Some of them had been roasted like *bratwurst* and there was not much left of them. That's what happens when you overindulge on Molotov cocktails.

It was around this time that Grandma Mária, my Father's mother, vanished from my life. I'm not even sure when exactly she died. She kept shrinking and shrinking, until one day she was simply gone. What remains is a sort of translucent image, riddled with holes. I could almost poke my hand through the image she has left in my memory.

This is how I remember certain people. They don't take long to disappear from memory.

32.

Many years later Father confessed to me that during the war he had often wondered which one of their neighbours, acquaintances or other townsfolk would have dispatched him to the next world without hesitation if push had come to shove.

Which one of the people with whom he exchanged greetings in the street or passed on his way from the shops, would have made a beeline for him with a gun and bumped him off. Just for the heck of it.

The May after the liberation arrived. The Red Army organized a big Labour Day parade in the main square – there was always something to celebrate. Like the fact that you had survived, at the very least.

Uniformed Russian officers sat on the rostrum side by side with the interim local officials. The band was about to start playing a festive military song and hardly anyone paid attention to a tall, dignified figure in a gown that had dashed out – not exactly in a dignified way – of the gates of our school, gesturing frantically.

The man on the run was none other than our venerable Father Savický, author of the rambling *Romantic Tales of Brežany*, based on semi-fictional events from days gone by, which he had apparently studied rather superficially. He had a great propensity for this kind of behaviour, as was clear from what happened next, when he headed for the rostrum steps. He pushed his way up and then forward, elbowed two Soviet colonels aside and squeezed onto the bench between them. He took a seat in the front row, his usual place in this town. The music started to play.

"Savický is my name…!" he said, holding out his hand to a general. "Savický…!" he said, turning to the other.

The poor fellow. Hardly a month had passed since the town honoured him with a medal, yet now it seemed that in the confusion the so-called "liberators" had somehow forgotten to invite him. So he came on his own initiative, to save the organizers from ignominy. Surely a festive event of this kind couldn't take place without his presence!

He could not understand why the soldiers immediately took him by the arm and dragged him off the rostrum, leaving him to watch the parade down in the dust in blessed ignorance, amid all the flowers and laughter.

For some reason, his invitation to Mrs Roško's salon also failed to arrive. Had it perhaps gone astray in the post?

The Russians marched through Brežany again on their way back after conquering Berlin. Their march took several days, on horseback and lorries, accompanied by vodka and songs. Occasionally they would ransack a house or a garden.

"Their last taste of Europe!" Father commented drily, as he changed the bandage on a soldier's burned hand and treated the wound with boracic acid.

33.

The war was as sticky as American chewing gum.

I managed to piece together the following half-forgotten story from scraps of conversations and the odd footnote.

On the last night in May there was general merriment and drunkenness in Brežany's Green Tree pub as people were still celebrating the victory. After a few drinks a man nicknamed Papír proposed that they all go and take a look at the Germans in Behy. The local German community, mostly vintners from Brežany and surrounding villages, had been assembled there, with stripes fastened to their sleeves. They were temporarily interned in the same POW camp barracks that had housed Woldow's Americans only six months earlier. All because President Beneš had recently issued a decree declaring Germans "persons with an unreliable attitude to the state". And it was the state that would now administer their property.

The carousing regulars joined him.

Papír, who had once played the drum in the Brežany brass band, was popular at local weddings. The peasants used to invite him to entertain their guests with his jokes and funny faces when the atmosphere started to flag. Though he was one-quarter German himself, in the heady weeks after the war he got somewhat carried away. He donned a rakish red shirt emblazoned with a five-pointed star and took command of the Brežany Revolutionary Guard, which reported to the communist National Council and the NKVD, and helped to arrest local Germans. Naturally, the first to be targeted were the owners of the largest vineyards. The red guardsmen identified them in advance and shared them out

161

amongst themselves. They would generally smash in the windows of a German house and help themselves to as much as they could carry away.

Papír and his fellow revellers were quite merry by the time they reached Behy, where the Germans were held while awaiting transport to an internment camp. Mrs Kroneisl, who had brought some soup for her husband and son in a mess tin, was sent back home and assured it would be delivered.

The men burst into the barracks where the Germans were having dinner. They dragged five of them out at gunpoint, got hold of some pickaxes and shovels, loaded everything onto a tractor trailer and drove to a brook in a meadow about a kilometre from Saliny, so that the noise wouldn't be heard in the city centre. They handed the tools to the Germans and told each of them to dig a pit about a metre deep and two metres long.

Mr Šimon, one of those who took part, later told me what happened next. Whenever he got tipsy in the smoke-filled Tower pub, it would come pouring out of him like sewage from a drain that had been blocked for a long time.

The Germans dug the pits. Under Papír's direction the Slovaks picked up spades and shovels and started beating them. Šimon and another man came to their senses and wanted to run away but Papír ordered them to stay put and watch. The Germans were battered to death. A teacher, two peasants and a local landowner from Nevedovo. The fifth one was Ambi Krebs. A random selection, as these selections go. From then on they were listed in the police records as missing persons.

The following day, Šimon told me, he had gone back to the meadow outside Brežany – known to this day as Papír's Meadow – and saw that the men didn't even manage to bury the bodies properly: there was a hand sticking out here and a knee there. Someone boasted in the pub of having split the landowner's head with a single blow of his spade. This man lost his new farm in Nevedovo in the 1950s, when he was declared a *kulak*. Beneš's next decree retrospectively granted an amnesty for crimes committed against the Germans after the war.

Nobody remembered anything more, except that old drunk Beňo, a tractor driver at Brežany's cooperative, who once claimed that in the early seventies, during deep ploughing in Saliny, some bones were dug up. After that, nothing was ever planted in Papír's Meadow.

All sorts of things went missing after the war.

I once saw a man without an arm standing in the corner of Brežany cemetery. He was silent.

His arm was buried under a cross bearing his name, in the slimy clay, decomposed and gnawed to the bone. The ligaments and muscles had atrophied.

Perhaps he was wondering if he might end up in several graves without ever being properly buried – one grave for his other arm, one for his right and left leg and a separate one for each of his fingers… Perhaps only the one with his head would be the real one, who knows? Can you live without a head? Or without a heart? Oh yes, the heart should definitely be buried elsewhere.

A voice whispers in my ear: War is a toy for big children. It has the shape of a meat grinder.

But this is just sleeptalking. I've nodded off for a moment, I have to confess.

It's all because of my usual little bedtime cocktail. Faces and fingers flickering in restless opiate dreams. I wake up, realise what's going on and sink back into listless sleep.

Part 2
The Witches' Sabbath

1.

Father's monograph on Goya's "black series", which turned up in the attic last night, includes the reproduction of a mural I've always found fascinating. Art historians have dubbed it *The Witches' Sabbath*. Goya himself didn't give the painting a name, nor did he provide it with a signature or any commentary. He just left it on the wall of a room on the ground floor opposite the main entrance to his house.

The painting is dominated by the figure of a big black goat, the customary representation of Satan, presiding over a coven of brightly dressed women. I first saw it in real life at the Prado in Madrid, on that crazy trip Bony and I made with Father's ashes in the car boot. I remember being astonished by the picture's enormous size – 140 centimetres by 438. The mural was retrieved and transferred onto canvas towards the end of the nineteenth century.

As I examined the figures in the folds of Satan's clothing, in the interplay of light and shade, I suddenly seemed to discern a blurred, indistinct face. And somewhere in the background there was a room with barred windows where someone seemed to be moaning with pain. On closer inspection the scene dissolved.

A guide hurried over and sternly reprimanded me for standing too close to the painting. Then, switching into another register, he rattled off his practised script about Goya having painted the fourteen murals on the walls of the *Quinta del Sordo*, The House of the Deaf Man, near Madrid, at the age of seventy-two, having survived two grave illnesses and the turmoil and savagery of the Napoleonic wars. Plagued by anxiety, depression and nightmares, he shared his house with the young and beautiful Leocadia Weiss, whom he tried, in vain, to teach how to paint.

It is with this thought in my mind that I wake up to a brilliant morning and luxuriate in the sheets, still a bit woozy from the Noax. When I raise my head to look out of the window I can see the feeble orange glow of the spring sun. The noises of the night have died down and all I can hear is a gentle hum in the street and the ticking of my watch on the bedside table.

"Every clock in this house shows a different time...!", Mother would say every so often. She tried to adjust and synchronize the clocks but as soon as we looked away they would stop altogether. Or they would unexpectedly restart of their own accord, as if obeying an invisible command. "It must be the house that does it…," Father used to say. But the culprit may have been time itself, for it never kept a steady pace around here. It would jump about at will, sometimes leaping ahead, then falling behind again. There were always plenty of clocks and watches around the house.

Except, that is, for a few days during the passage of the front, when Russian soldiers went from house to house. They snooped around drawers and linen cupboards, looking for Germans. Two of them came to our house, too, just as we were having lunch. One had slanting eyes while the other was tall and fair-haired, with a pockmarked face. They wore green uniforms and caps adorned with stars. Generally speaking, stars were fashionable all through the twentieth century and this was when red, five-pointed ones, became all the rage.

"*A nu ka…. Davaj chasy!*

They claimed to be collecting watches as a birthday present for Marshal Malinovsky. The fellow must have been plastered with watches. I imagined Marshal Malinovsky as the world's greatest clockmaker. And the Soviet Union as a country where time was so plentiful not even all those watches could measure it.

I didn't mind giving them my watch, it was broken anyway. Father put on a stern face but he was helpless when the smiling soldiers fished out the Rolex on a chain from his pocket. They took a clock off the wall and were finally satisfied. They left with a salute.

At that moment time came to a standstill in this house, just for a while. It would soon re-start again.

And now: get ready for take-off!

Our camera rises into the sky…

The streets of Brežany are almost deserted and we can fly from one side of the street to the other, between lamp-posts and pointed roof gables. Somewhere a radio is playing, broadcasting from Bratislava and promising Hitler's final victory, which is imminent, almost tangible.

Piles of documents are being burned in the Municipal Office courtyard.

A little further away we catch a glimpse of the Count in his manor house, hastily stuffing jewellery and valuables into a small suitcase. He raises his head for a moment – outside the large window, close to the park gates, he sees the smoke and light of explosions of the front, now approaching fast. The tremors bring pieces of plaster crashing down from the ceiling and make glasses topple over. A fragment of plaster falls into his glass of wine; in his distress he doesn't notice and shudders when he takes a sip.

At that very moment in the other wing of the house people start to clamber in through a window, grabbing everything that can be carried away before the Russian soldiers come and shove the mahogany furniture and bookcases into the grand majolica-tiled stoves and large fireplaces in order to heat the place – spring is slow coming to Brežany, and who's got time to collect firewood now?

Not far from the manor house, at the small military airfield in Lehota, German pilots are on standby. The Count climbs aboard, the plane takes off.

A few hours later and the manor house has been ransacked – mirrors, cabinets, everything the Count couldn't pack has taken off in the direction of the town.

A few more hours and the tanks have churned up the park, two ancient oaks and plane trees have become shattered cripples. The manor house has been turned into the Red Army headquarters. The cold creeps in under the fingernails. Vapour rises from mouths. The soldiers have found axes behind the glasshouses. They are happy. Vodka is best drunk cold but it tastes much better in a heated room.

Vojto and I sat on a wall watching the events unfold like a film in a cinema, for in these unreal times nothing seemed real, not even reality itself.

"Look over there!" Vojto pointed to a huge object under what used to be a stained-glass window.

It was a splendid telescope, complete with a tripod, all sorts of gears and levers, taller than either of us. It must have been too heavy to haul off. We hid it in the bushes and returned to lug it to our house in a wheelbarrow under the cover of darkness.

For good measure, we also took the Count's Remington typewriter and two small dark stones. They must have been a part of the Countess's onyx earrings once; now they rolled under a wardrobe when Vojto tripped over them. He managed to fish them out eventually. Looking at our distorted faces reflected in their shiny black surface, we decided to keep one stone each. And we resolved that, should either of us ever want to abandon the other, all he would have to do was press the stone into his hand. Without having to say a word.

But that would never happen. Both of us declared we would be friends forever.

The Count used to be quite a globetrotter, collecting all sorts of things on his travels. A large statue of Buddha stood in the big park, next to a genuine Thai pagoda. This was where in 1961 Comrade Kominár, Chairman of the local National Committee, would host a confused President Novotný, who had come to Brežany on an official visit. The President was relieved to learn no one would be shaving his head and making him put on an orange robe – instead the pagoda had been converted into a bar flowing with wine.

The Count's grandfather had once owned extensive vineyards in the shadow of the Volovec Mountain but by now they had been swallowed up by Brežany's sprawling and shabby housing estates. The old Count used to ship his legendary Château Sálava to Pressburg, Vienna and Budapest. A clever businessman, he located the company headquarters right on the edge of town, just five metres beyond the tax district boundary, so he could pay only the bare minimum of tax. An eternity of bliss beckoned. However, he suffered serious setbacks after World War I. The Count had been a generous lender of money but after the currency reform his outstanding debts were no longer honoured. From then on savings books filled with six-digit figures would crop up around the manor house, reduced by history to worthless scraps of paper. Soon afterwards, because of the steady expansion of the town, the liberator-president Thomas Garrigue Masaryk shifted the tax district boundaries out into the fields and suburbs.

On an unusually cold autumn day of that the same year, 1918, the Count's beautiful sixteen-year-old daughter Agnes caught a chill after running barefoot down the grand stone spiral staircase and out to the gate. She contracted the Spanish flu and ended up paralysed. In addition to being unable to walk, poor Agnes also lost the power of speech. All she was able to do was scream and suffer.

And so she suffered and screamed until the day she died at the age of about forty, during World War II.

To support his family of nine, the Count began to sell off the family heirlooms – precious jewellery and antiques, even offering the family letters patent to a museum for next to nothing.

Eventually he took off from the Lehota military airfield in a plane with a German crew and disappeared. As an ethnic Hungarian, and thus a member of another "unreliable" minority, he had an additional reason to flee.

Father was once treated to a bottle of Château Sálava 1918 from the Count's former vineyards, by a patient who had built a house on the very spot the vines used to grow, as a grateful gift for successfully treating his spotted fever.

These days it is the site of the huge box-like Volovec logistical centre, a creature from outer space with long container lorries attached to openings all around its perimeter like suckling pigs.

We continue our flight…

A gaggle of lads are using a flat anti-tank mine to warm up an UNRRA tin of beans. It seems perfect for this purpose. The boys scatter about to look for brushwood: only the smallest, a chubby little fellow, is too lazy – he stays behind to keep an eye on the fire to make sure it doesn't go out. No sooner do they disappear into the thicket than the mine goes off, taking his legs with it.

A handful of Jewish survivors are wandering around town in their tattered camp rags. People cross over to the other side of the street, trying to avoid their emaciated faces.

Father Savický, surrounded by children carrying bouquets of flowers, bursts into the hospital eager to find a wounded hero, any hero. He is humming a brand new partisan song.

An inexperienced, high-pitched voice drones from the loudspeaker:

"Citizens… The Local National Committee and the People's Militia request that all items of furniture and valuables looted from the manor house and its adjoining properties prior to the arrival of the Red Army be returned under threat of the death penalty!"

So all the stuff is being carried back, as in a film that's being rewound. And it's the film negative, because while the looting took place in the middle of the day, people are creeping back to the manor house under the cover of night. Few are willing to return the loot in broad daylight. Fearing house searches, politically conscious citizens hurl furniture over the walls and fences. Vases that used to decorate drawing rooms end up in the stream that flows through the park, only to be invaded by fish and the nymphs of caddisflies.

It may have been in the middle of the summer of 1945. Or in very late spring. Either way the nightingales had already arrived, filling the nights with their song.

Walking through the manor house park Father nearly tripped on the broken crystal chandelier that had once hung from the tall ceiling of the entrance hall but had now been dragged out into the plundered rose garden. Black bag in hand he was on his way home from a patient who had drunk some exquisite white wine "liberated" from the German officers' warehouse to celebrate the liberation. Suddenly the man turned deathly pale, and started to cough and choke, unable to breathe. He asked to be taken home, certain that his end had come. His wife called Father from a neighbour's phone but by the time he arrived the patient had made a miraculous recovery.

Father examined him and as he could find nothing wrong with him, he asked to see the bottle they had been drinking from, just in case. It was Hungarian Tokay.

"You see, Mr. Ďuratný, the grape used to produce this wine is naturally infested with noble rot. And that's what caused your allergic reaction. As a native son of a winemaking region you should have known that! And for the same reason, you must stay away from sherries and Sauternes!"

And now Father was taking a short-cut home through the devastated park of the manor house. The remaining three bottles of sweet, 4-puttonyos Tokay, which he had received in addition to his fee, clinked in his bag. The pond he passed was full with fish, though they were all floating belly-up and beginning to smell.

A man in rags was sitting on a bench beneath a statue of St Giles with a deer and an arrow in his chest. He caught Father's eye at once as someone new. The man was staring vacantly ahead. Below one of his eyes there was a wound covered in dried, blackened blood. Under his arm he clutched a crumpled bag from a food store.

He was oblivious to everything around him. The charred trees towering above his head were beginning to blossom.

Father sat down on the bench next to him and touched the wound with the tips of his fingers. Only then did the man take notice of him, flinching with pain. Father shook his head. He opened his bag, took out a small bottle of carbolic acid and dribbled a few drops on a piece of cotton wool. He wiped the wound to disinfect it and prevent it becoming inflamed and filled with pus, then dressed it with a bandage.

"What have you got there?"

Father prodded the paper bag the man was clutching under his arm.

Slowly and hesitantly the man took out a blue album with worn covers, and with infinite care, as if time had ceased to exist, opened the album and started turning its pages.

"This is all I have left," he said feebly, almost inaudibly.

He said he was a local German and that his house had been destroyed during the passage of the front and its aftermath. He had no one left. His sole possession was this album, containing his collection of old banknotes. He had been wandering around town and with nowhere to go.

Father thought for a while.

"I will swap you the album for two shirts, this wine and a loaf of bread."

The threadbare man tried to haggle but being on the verge of starvation in the end he agreed. One loaf of bread turned into three, and as well as the shirt he got two pairs of trousers Father couldn't stand because they scratched his skin. And a jumper into the bargain.

Father delivered the goods to the park and slipped the man some money. Its value was impossible to determine at that time. That was part of its allure.

The blue album contained the distinctive banknotes that were used in POW camps in Germany and Austria during the two world wars. The plain though beautifully coloured pieces of paper had been inserted like photographs into corners on the sheets, some attached loosely with ordinary brown tape.

One of the banknotes said: *Quittung über fünfzig Kronen. Theresienstadt am 1. Jänner 1943. Der Älteste der Juden in Theresienstadt:*

173

Jakob Edelstein. It depicted a blue star of David and on the reverse an old bearded man holding the commandment tablets in Hebrew lettering.

Father said the banknotes were sure to be very valuable and their worth would only increase with time. He put the album away "for a rainy day" without really knowing what that might mean.

That year everyone was after one piece of paper or another.

For the moment Father was issued an *Interim Confirmation of Political Reliability*, which read as follows:

The Brežany National Committee, based on references provided by Ambróz Krebs and Dr Levius and in line with the NC Vetting Commission's decision dated 12.5.1945, hereby provides Dr Alfonz Trnovský with this interim confirmation of political reliability which will be valid until a final determination by the commission set up by the Brežany National Committee.

Chief of Staff
signed, Dr Haluzický

Next Father had to procure an official certificate: *The Brežany District National Committee (DNC) hereby certifies that the owner of this document, Dr Alfonz Trnovský, a physician, has been continuously resident in Brežany and practising as General Practitioner. Throughout this period no incidents or facts have come to light that might disqualify the aforementioned person from being regarded as a loyal citizen of Czechoslovakia in accordance with the prevailing criteria. The aforementioned person – who is, incidentally, married to a Jew – is well-known for his impartial views and as someone who did not demonstrate his support for the former Slovak State regime and was not involved in any activities outside his medical profession.*

DNC Secretariat

And last but not least, in December 1945, he obtained a *Certificate of Loyalty to the nation, the state and to the people's democracy*, signed by the secretary and chairman of the National Committee.

2.

Still groggy with sleep, I get up in the morning and dash to the shops to get something for breakfast.

Spring is coming and "impoverished" tradesmen are descending on the town in their Hyundai Jeeps, eternal tinkers filling the fragrant air with the din of endless drilling and hammering.

Where Mr Malánek's general store once stood there is now a small CBA supermarket. I pile my usual combo of cod salad, rolls and Coke into the shopping basket. All my life I've eaten like a labourer – and let's face it, that's what I've actually been all my life (notwithstanding the fact that in every official document I've ticked the box labelled *artist*). That's another thing I learned from my second mother, Television. You've got to wrap it up fast, as neither the crew nor the weather will wait. "Lunch" usually means deep-fried cheese with sauce tartare, my favourite. I love it so much I might as well get it through an intravenous drip. But then again, I'd miss the delicious taste. In my book sauce tartare ranks among the greatest inventions of man.

The problem is that not even cod salad is what it used to be ten or twenty years ago… These days you just can't find decent cod salad anywhere.

"Your taste buds are messed up, that's what it is!" Vojto would say, laughing.

Fair enough. You can't argue with the dead.

But perhaps my taste buds really are messed up.

Butter, too, has fallen victim to my dissatisfaction. It tastes too sweet nowadays. It's the sweet butter of our sweet post-communist present.

Under communism it used to have a slightly sour aftertaste because the comrades were frugal with cream.

But the most delicious butter I've ever had was the kind we got from UNRRA after the war. It replaced the revolting yellow margarine, supposedly invented by the Americans as a by-product in the manufacture of turkey fodder or feed for some kind of vermin. The UNRRA butter tasted… salty.

I remember the packages wrapped in wax paper. They were

originally intended for soldiers on the front line, and that's why they usually came with a condom and three *Lucky Strike* cigarettes. Plus some dry biscuits, tinned frankfurters – my brother Peter's favourites – and tins of ersatz goulash, which (for reasons unclear to me) my sister Tina loved. Fig jelly. Jam. And fantastic butter. That terrific salty butter.

Ah, that amazing post-war butter!

Unfortunately, it was accompanied by another delicacy. We all had to bring a small spoon to school and take a spoonful of fish oil every day before class. So that we would grow stronger, as many of us suffered from anaemia. I didn't, but like it or not, I had to take the fish oil anyway.

When Father called on his patients during the school holidays he would take me along.

We drove to the house of Mr Rozgoň the butcher, who managed to negotiate the rocks and ravines of the early post-war months with the skill of a tightrope walker. Janko Belan, who joined a partisan unit during the Uprising, started to frequent Mr Stern's former kosher butchers', which Rozgoň had Aryanized. He'd turn up for a friendly visit, for a glass of wine or brandy, usually staying for dinner and leaving loaded up with bags of meat. Until, that is, by the end of June, he finally signed the butcher's Certificate of Loyalty. Rozgoň sighed with relief. He was quite frightened because soon after the front passed through Brežany, two fellows like him ended up hanging from lamp-posts with less than flattering cardboard signs around their necks. He immediately applied to join the Communist Party, to be on the safe side.

And now his son had fallen ill.

Rozgoň's wife opened the door and ushered us in. We followed her across the living room.

"Don't take any notice of this, doctor!" she muttered over her shoulder as an extraordinary scene unfolded before us. The shop at the front had been closed for over three months due to a lack of meat and to rationing. But the living room presented quite a different picture.

Veiled in Rembrandtesque twilight, for the blinds had been drawn to make sure nobody could peer in, the master of the house, clad in a bloody apron, was butchering a cow. Pieces of meat

176

dripping with blood were scattered all over the place. There were kidneys and liver on a silver platter under the window, and a thigh nestled in the marble washbasin in the bathroom. A fillet, a knuckle, bones… And swarms and swarms of flies.

The master of the house emerged from this apocalyptic scene with a smile and welcomed Father joyously, adding: "Mind if I don't shake your hand? It's covered in blood," and offering him an elbow instead.

While Father was examining his son Jurko, who had scarlet fever, Rozgoň's wife brought me some sour sweets and a piece of freshly baked cake. Just as I took a big bite, my eyes fell on the cow's eyes, which had inadvertently been left on a plate lying on a little table in the corner. I began to tug at the blood vessels. Father walked in with his sleeves rolled up to get the stethoscope from his bag, slapped me on the hands and told me off.

Our fee was a bagful of meat. Wrapped as thoroughly and as inconspicuously as possible it resembled a package of books.

I'm munching on a roll and rummaging in the old wardrobe.

I open a small drawer and a withered bunch of lavender falls out. I pick it up and smell it. The scent has almost completely faded. But what's left of the intense bouquet hasn't lost its capacity to conjure up memories.

For me the wardrobe has always been a symbol of order, peace and safety. I loved to rummage through Mother's things. Before Mother, her *bobe* Sara used it to store her lace, batiste and muslins. All these things exerted some mysterious pull. Much more than Mother's clothes, which were becoming increasingly drab.

Now the wardrobe is empty, like the belly of a gutted fish. I close the door and images assault me with renewed vigour. They're much more powerful than real objects. Invisible objects, that's what they are.

I swallow a mouthful of cod salad and sniff the lavender again.

The smell of lavender is part and parcel of the atmosphere of this house.

It was me who picked up the telephone – one of the few telephones in Brežany – and heard crackling and strange sounds in the receiver, as if someone were calling from a phone booth in the street.

Someone shouting in an unknown language, the clatter of carriages… I even thought I heard a donkey braying in the distance and dogs barking.

It was Mr Gronský, Father's Jewish dentist, calling from South America. He and his entire family managed to get there via Switzerland and he now had a thriving practice in Buenos Aires. I guessed there was a delay on the line as Mr Gronský's answers to my questions were preceded by a short pause…

He asked to speak to Father, who had gone to his isolation cell to read the paper.

"So what do you think, my friend, should I come back to Europe? How are things back home?"

"Absolutely, my friend, sure it's safe to return, *gerecht?* Everything is quite wonderful here, *gerecht?* Everything is running like clockwork, *gerecht?*"

That's exactly what he kept saying: *gerecht…*, right, followed by a question mark.

Mr Gronský took Father's advice to heart. In 1948 he sent him a thank you letter, as well as a box of Argentinian chocolates. It arrived almost empty. All that was left were a few fondant truffles, which nobody in our family liked. He could have sent something more sensible. Actually, he may have included something else, but it certainly never reached us in Brežany. In the brave new world we now lived in everything belonged to everyone.

Mr Gronský attached a lovely photo of his family taken against the backdrop of mountainous countryside with vineyards stretching into the distance. It was the first colour photo I'd ever seen. Until then I thought photos came only in black and white. Or colourized, at best.

Dr Gronský set up his Argentine practice with the help of Dr Weiszmann, an oto-rhino-laryngologist from Nitra, whose life was saved by an advert in the *Medical Gazette*, which he had reportedly framed and kept on the wall of his consulting room. It read as follows:

Medical Congress in TEL AVIV!

Our luxury boat for Tel Aviv sails on 21 April 1936. 15% discount on return tickets for departures booked by 10 April. Further information: Palestine Shipping Co., Ltd.

He never used his return ticket.

Dr Weiszmann had a good nose. The names of many of his colleagues later appeared on the pages of the monthly *The Slovak Physician,* in the Physician's Chamber minutes, in column *III. No longer listed on the grounds of: a) having relocated beyond the chamber's territory,* with the comment *Destination unknown.*

In this case, if you pronounced "destination unknown", with a German accent, it read "Tre-blin-ka", "Maj-da-nek" or "Auschwitz".

Names that sound a little like a nursery rhyme.

3.

The equipment from Dr Ducký's consulting room in the main square, next to Mr Štiepka's tiny bookshop (which I used to visit more and more often to hunt for books to buy with my meagre pocket money), went on sale. He was offered a job at the Ministry of Health and was moving to Bratislava.

Father took the opportunity to buy a second-hand electrocardiograph, and then spent entire days playing with it. His patients were also involved, of course. He daubed their skin with gel and attached suction pads to their chests. It pleased him no end to pore over the electrocardiograms.

He was in the middle of studying one when, all of a sudden, Puškár turned up in his consulting room.

He had returned from the front with a small gift. *The God of war has granted me a surprise.* Innate discretion – and Father's aloofness, which had never disappeared even though they were friends – prevented him from asking which side he had fought on. Both sides had their fatalities, as well as their sick and wounded. What was astonishing was the fact was that Puškár had taken part in fighting at all.

Father got up, turned off the machine and called the nurse: "Zdenka, spirit please!"

Zdenka came back directly with an apothecary bottle marked *Spiritus vini conc.* Father picked up a drinking glass, half-filled it with spirit and topped it up with water. He thrust the glass into Puškár's hand and mixed himself a drink.

"Well then… To our health! To your return!"

Father clinked glasses with his guest and knocked his drink back in one gulp. His face turned red and tears welled up in his eyes.

Puškár told him that he had spent some time in a field hospital, where he noticed that he had swollen nodules and that a hard, though painless, boil had appeared on his private parts.

The military doctor insisted on being addressed as Doctor Kotúček, which lent him gravitas and an air of trustworthiness. In fact, he had been a hairdresser in Malacky before the war. He must have been recruited because he wore scrubs and there was a shortage of doctors. Kotúček administered medication based on whatever packet he happened to have just opened, for pills were quite scarce, too. The only afflictions he recognized were diphtheria and hepatitis, which for some reason were his favourites, plus shot wounds. His field hospital boasted an isolation ward with two patients – one who was feigning an illness and the other whose wisdom tooth was playing up. This was where Puškár ended up.

Kotúček dispensed pills and tablets by the fistful through a hole in the door, and in order to reduce his dealings with the infectious patients to a minimum he made them swallow all the medication immediately in his presence. Within twenty-four hours Puškár was teetering on the brink of life and death, sweating profusely, suffering from the most startling hallucinations and shortness of breath. At the last minute he was rescued by a doctor from the adjoining battalion – a Russian or a German, who knows – this time a proper doctor, who needed to clear a few beds for his wounded. He concluded Puškár had most likely contracted syphilis and recommended a more thorough examination. Discharged by Kotúček, who didn't have the first idea of how to treat him, Puškár's condition improved miraculously and he stopped taking his boil and nodes seriously, particularly as they soon disappeared.

Sometime later he broke out in a rash. Copper-coloured marks appeared in his massive armpits and eventually the rash covered his entire forehead and he developed canker sores in his mouth as well, and later also persistent headaches.

"This is an illness nations keep blaming each other for, did you know that? Each one claims to have been infected by the enemy."

"I'm not sure I get it."

"Well… To begin with, the Germans call it the French disease. And here, in our parts, it's sometimes referred to *morbus hungaricus*, the Hungarian disease. Do you get it now?"

"Hmm…"

"To Poles it's the Russian disease, in French it's known as Spanish smallpox. The Japanese refer to it as Chinese smallpox and the Indians call it the Portuguese disease. And if we also bear in mind that one of the Russian words for prostitute is *vengerka*, Hungarian woman…"

"All right doctor, that's enough!"

"So I see you're no longer waiting for your Lila?" asked Father, drawing blood from his friend's forearm into a big syringe.

"Oh no, I'm still waiting."

"So how come…?"

"That was just a moment of weakness, you see. I told myself – I've never even met her after all."

"But she did send you a photo, didn't she?"

"What use is a photo?"

"Here we go – now you see where this kind of thing gets you. All that doubting."

"I hope Lila doesn't find out. She would never come back if she did! Is there something you can do about this?"

"We'll send a sample to the Institute of Hygiene in Bratislava and we'll see. Then we'll get on with the treatment. Injections."

"Oh dear…!"

"Was it worth it, at least?" Father gave him a wink.

Puškár waved his hand dismissively.

The last letter Lila posted from Slovakia arrived in 1944. Puškár was quite prepared to get on a train and scour the whole town, leaving no stone unturned (I can tell you in confidence that the city in question was Nitra – Father used to go there to pick up medicines from a central warehouse). He would have done anything to find her and convince her to stay, to change her identity, name, even her face if necessary, but by then it was too late. The stamp on the letter was two weeks old and Lila must have travelled across the continent to Berlin or Munich, to stay with one of her aunts.

He went on waiting for a few lines from her, for at least some information on her new abode, followed up any clues, and remained faithful to her.

The test results from the Institute of Hygiene arrived. The document stated that the blood serum was examined using Bordet-Wassermann's deviation, followed by the Sachs-Witebsky test as well as the Meinicke test. The column headed *Test results* read: *Positive*.

Father diagnosed Puškár with secondary-stage syphilis with advanced symptoms and started treating him with Neosalvarsan – he managed to unearth some old, pre-war supplies from somewhere. He was concerned it might be out of date but as it turns out, arsenic preparations last only too well. Under normal circumstances he would have put him on a course of the new magic antibiotics he had read so much about, if only they had been available in Brežany.

Father once told me, laughing, that a few years after the war venereologists complained that this fellow Fleming had deprived them of the most spectacular cases of progressive paralysis and *tabes dorsalis*.

It was around this time that Uncle Oskar returned.

After being put on a transport in the autumn of 1944 along with Aunt Rózka, their daughter and two sons, they spent several days jolting along in a cattle car. The smell was unbearable, as people had to defecate inside the car. There was no other option. Eighty people had to share two buckets of water. A quarter of the passengers didn't survive the journey. Those who did were whipped out of the train into the vicious frost and told to line up on the ramp. The corpses of those trampled to death by the others or who didn't manage to stay upright were unloaded. Uncle Oskar felt more hungry than cold. A few apples and some potato peel tossed inside were all they had been given to eat on the whole trip.

Flocks of jackdaws took off from the frozen ground and landed in a nearby field. A man approached them. Uncle Oskar claimed it was Mengele himself, but Father had his doubts – he might as well have claimed it was Hitler himself who marched up to them to pinch a little boy's cheek. At that moment every doctor's name was Mengele. But Oskar protested – he saw the infamous doctor's photos later and besides, he was making no secret of his name, and why should he? So this Mengele came up to him and asked: "Is this your daughter?" Oskar was taken aback and glanced at Aunt

Rózka, who looked ten years younger than her age, her hollow cheeks radiating a certain fragile, doll-like beauty despite the dirt. He managed to string together a reply that wasn't completely devoid of pride: "She is my wife."

Mengele nodded, touched her with his gloved hand and pointed to the other line, which Rózka, now almost drained of any willpower, dutifully joined. He ruffled the grubby boy's dark hair with a smile and moved on.

It looked like a mere formality but later it emerged that everyone in the other line was headed straight for a door marked *BRAUSEBAD*. A shower that happened to have no running water.

"I should have said she was my daughter…!" Uncle Oskar said in a broken voice.

There was something that might be called a bit of luck, for he ended up in the old part of the Auschwitz camp. His hair was shaved off and a number was tattooed on his forearm with a steel pen.

He had two options. Those who were emaciated faded away slowly like candles or were plagued by painful swellings brought about by starvation. In his own words, Uncle Oskar survived only by a miracle. After returning to Brežany he suffered anxiety attacks and fits of rage. At moments like these he would start shouting, and screamed until he was hoarse or lost his voice altogether.

He recounted his story while Father felt him all over and listened to his chest through his stethoscope. He exhibited symptoms of epidemic typhus. There had been a few other cases in Brežany at the time so Father was rather scared. He tried to recall the title of the Turgenev novel whose hero, a medical student, cuts himself with a scalpel during surgery and then dies of spotted fever.

The typhus developed into meningitis. Oskar often felt as if he were lying in bed next to his double. As he recovered, Oskar's two bodies were slowly moving closer to one another. Closer and closer. Until they eventually merged into one.

Father had a brilliant instinct for diagnosing illnesses. Once he explained to me that the skin and breath of people with typhoid fever smell of freshly baked bread. Smallpox, on the other hand, gives people the odour of sweating sheep. Pneumonia sometimes makes their breath smell of honey. I found this quite amusing.

He noted all these observations in his notebook, the one I'm browsing through now, an empty Coke bottle in my hand.

4.

When Vojto and I saw each other again in school after the summer holidays, he raved about the celebrations of the first anniversary of the Slovak National Uprising in Banská Bystrica, which he attended with his father and the whole extended family in late August of 1945. Captain Roško's head injury was healing nicely, largely thanks to Father's treatment. Apart from the occasional persistent headache and sudden bout of dizziness, his health was not affected in any major way.

A year earlier most of those who attended the celebrations wouldn't have dreamed of saying: "This time next year in Banská Bystrica!" Vojto's father was awarded the Order of the Slovak National Uprising, First Class, and proudly wore it pinned to his air-force uniform.

The Roškos sent us a special edition postcard sporting a tricolour, a big stamp and the printed text: *Regards from the celebrations of the National Uprising in Banská Bystrica 1944-1945.*

Following the festive opening of the school year, when all the tiresome speeches and music-making were over and while everyone burbled on about freedom and a happy new life, Vojto and I set out to filch some pears from the church garden lovingly tended by Father Peterský, the juiciest pears to be had far and wide. We stayed out until dusk, just hanging around the streets of Brežany.

As we approached the Roškos' family home in St Adalbert Street, we could see a bonfire blazing in the garden. It was getting dark. We crept past the shed and crouched down beneath an old elderflower bush – thrushes had built a nest in its boughs and a bit of white goo landed on my sleeve but I didn't make a sound. Vojto's father was standing by the bonfire, coughing and raking the embers. Every now and then he would cast a nervous glance in the direction of the gate to see if there was anyone coming but nobody did. He puffed on his cigarette, clearly on edge. We noticed there was something in his hand and heard something rattling and the fire crackling. From time to time the captain would toss some into the fire and poke it with the rake.

We watched him for a while. Then I whispered to Vojto:

"What is he doing?"

"He's destroying his war decorations…"

"His decorations? But why?"

"Oh, never mind!" Vojto snapped, staring at his father and holding his breath. His face looked grave in the light of the flames.

"But why?"

"Because!"

There was something in Vojto's father's hand again and I could see more now as the fire flared up. He tore off a piece of cloth, used his pliers on some bits of metal and started cutting it into tiny pieces with secateurs. Then he tossed the lot into the flames.

All of a sudden I felt sorry for the medals, I had really liked them. Why did he have to do this when he could have given them to us, I wondered.

Once, when his parents went out, Vojto had unlocked one of their wardrobes and took out a cigar box wrapped in a piece of cloth lying at the bottom. That was where his father had kept them. I had felt their weight in my hands and read the inscriptions: *Memorial Medal for the March On the USSR First Class… Iron Cross, Second Class… Iron Cross, First Class… Chalice of Honour… The German Gold Cross… Silver Medal of the Crown of King Zvonimir…* I liked the last one, from Serbia, the best.

Now Captain Roško put away the pliers and scissors, sat down in the damp grass and stared into the fire, raking it over from time to time. The live coals smouldering in the embers looked like a living creature. And Vojto's father was engaged a silent conversation with them.

Then he brought a garden hose and poured water over the embers. He shovelled the burnt scraps into a bucket. The smell of damp smoke enveloped the trees in a mist. An anaemic moon rose above the garden. We ran around the shed, appearing from under the trees nearby, pretending we hadn't seen anything. Vojto's father hesitated for a moment, but he, too, pretended that nothing unusual had happened.

"Hello…" Vojto said as we passed him. "What are you up to?"

"Nothing."

His father's face resembled a slab of stone.

"Mother was getting worried. Where have you been…?"

A few years ago Vojto and I found another version of his father's

CV in the wardrobe. This one was typed and was much more legible than the earlier one.

Around 1 November 1942, I was despatched as a fighter pilot, together with my squadron, to the eastern front, to fight against the Soviet Union, and remained there until returning to Slovakia in early March 1943 to attend my father's funeral. At the end of April I was deployed again, and did not return to Slovakia until I was relieved of duty in early July 1943. The fighter squadron deployed in the Caucasus comprised the Maikop, Krasnodar, Slavyanskaya, Karch and Anop units. As a fighter pilot I carried out some 150 sorties altogether. In the winter months, i.e. until my departure for Slovakia on account of my father's death, the squadron was not very active. Its activities intensified during my stay in Slovakia. Before being deployed again in the Soviet Union in April, I went to see Air Force Commander Colonel Velen, who stated (in the presence of Captain Zápražný), that we ought not to get too involved in combat activities, that it was pointless and that our priority should be to ensure we returned home safe and sound. The account of my activities corresponds to the information I provided during the investigation into my activities in the spring of 1945. I did take off on several occasions, only to make sure I wasn't accused of shirking my duty or cowardly conduct, but at no time did I actively seek combat, and my encounters with Soviet pilots throughout my period of deployment did not exceed around 12; even though a larger number of kills was recorded, in actual fact I did not secure a single kill. Furthermore, even though all the pilots in my squadron recorded far more kills than I did, I declare now just as I declared at the time, that I did not witness any kills by anyone in my squadron, although I concede that some may have had some kills. Let me provide an example. When the flight squadron crews were being redeployed in late June 1943, while on a joint flight with First Lieutenant Kučkár, I briefed him on the real nature of our activities by firing several shots in the absence of any planes and by reporting a kill after landing. However, he did not keep this information to himself and following my departure confided in the squadron commander, Captain Zápražný. Afterwards, beginning around November 1943, I was in charge of a fighter squadron deployed initially in Vajnory and from about 1 March 1944 until 28 August 1944,(i.e. until I joined the Slovak National Uprising), in Piešt'any. This was an emergency squadron, charged with defending our territory against Anglo-American pilots. After a few take-offs, the squadron was destroyed in battle with Anglo-American pilots in the air space above

Bratislava in mid-June 1944, while I was on leave. By August 1944 I had joined the preparations for the Slovak National Uprising in Piešťany. On 29 August, jointly with the Piešťany crew, I left for the territory controlled by the Slovak National Uprising partisans, serving as fighter squadron commander at the Three Oaks airfield. My flying activities during the Uprising involved some 20 combat sorties, a number of bombing raids and reconnaissance flights. In the last days of October 1944, as ordered by the commander of the air force division, I flew three planes to the village of Donovaly. Just before the arrival of the enemy in the village highly unfavourable weather conditions prevented our departure for the USSR; I ordered the planes to be destroyed and left for the mountains.

When I came home Father asked me where I'd been so long and I told him everything – I felt very sad about the loss of the medals. Father just nodded his head thoughtfully but said nothing.

He was in the middle of dressing a rather nasty wound on Janko Belan's hand, which wouldn't heal. It kept festering and weeping, and would bleed from time to time for no reason.

"It's those bloody fucking Catholics!" he kept swearing which made me very confused. Did he get shot in church?

Father later explained that it was mostly the Catholics who had joined the Hlinka Guard while many of the Protestants had joined the partisans. The war was a convenient pretext for settling old scores.

Uncle Rudo commented: the best kind of killing is in the name of love. People have enjoyed doing that for two millennia now.

5.

Out of the blue, Father received a typewritten letter with the following letterhead: *The Society for Cultural and Economic Relations with the USSR, Bratislava Headquarters, Captain Nálepka St. 19/I. tel.2598.* It read:

Bratislava, 3 April 1947. Attached: 1 membership form.

Dear Dr Trnovský,

The Society for Cultural and Economic Relations with the USSR wishes to invite you to join us, trusting that you will not turn down our offer and complete the enclosed membership form. We call upon you to join us in our efforts to contribute to one of the strongest, healthiest and most beneficial traditions for our nation, the proud tradition of Slavonic reciprocity.

We believe that our Society should consist not only of all representatives of the intelligentsia, who are better qualified for a scientific exploration of the Soviet Union than anyone else, but that it should attract good workers from all professions.

On 18 April 1947 former President Tiso was executed by hanging.

Bells tolled all over Slovakia and people dressed in black.

Father came home from his round and commented drily:

"Artificially induced brain anaemia."

Tuka, Tiso's prime minister, had already met the same fate a few months earlier. He had to be lifted out of his wheelchair and helped into the noose.

Dr Dérer, a professor at the School of Medicine, requested the eyeballs of Waffen-SS Obergruppenführer Hermann Höfle and recycled them in the glaucoma treatment of a young patient by the name of Tomáš Hovorka. Höfle was infamous for his many bloody and brilliant successes in crushing the Uprising in and around the city of Banská Bystrica, an accomplishment he crowned by providing a very passable organ accompaniment to the *Te Deum laudamus* following Tiso's celebration of the mass at the local cathedral.

These were the kinds of things my parents talked about over Sunday lunch.

A film magazine Mother had borrowed from a friend reported an exotic new discovery. While we were having soup, she enlightened the assembled company:

The origins of so-called "television" (a blend of the Greek tele and the Latin visio – i.e. seeing into the distance) date back to 1873, which means that this invention pre-dates radio, film and the gramophone. In 1873 a telegraph operator discovered that his machine performed differently on sunny days and on days that were cloudy and rainy. That was how electrical engineers realized that it was possible to transmit the interplay of shadow and light via electromagnetic waves. The first attempted television broadcast took place in London in 1912, by means of a cable. In 1926 television was used in the US as a spectacular operetta interlude. In 1928 the General Electric Company transmitted the inaugural address of America's new president, the broadcast being picked up by two receivers.

However, the new technology is still far from perfect. The transmitted picture often resembles a blizzard. The actors sometimes appear split into two or even three. When an actor gets up from an armchair to take a few steps on the stage, his shoulders often stay in the original position while his feet move further down the screen, with the rest of his body floating somewhere in between. In addition, viewers complain that during hockey matches they see twenty-four players instead of twelve on their screens. On the other hand, they appreciate the fact that, unlike the experience of watching a match in the cinema, they don't yet know the outcome and feel almost as if they were watching the game at the sports stadium.

Actors who are used to the radio find it hard to get accustomed to not being able to read their lines on television and having to learn them by heart instead. In addition, the cameras require a lot of light, which generates tropical heat in the studios. In a Chicago studio, while shooting a scene depicting the meeting of two lovers by candlelight, the candles on the table began to melt. The apple that the lover was supposed to hand to his beloved got stuck in the wax and couldn't be lifted off the table. Many problems have yet to be resolved before television becomes a fixture in our households.

One Sunday some weeks before the fateful day of Father's arrest, his sister, Aunt Antónia, exceptionally accepted our invitation to Sunday lunch.

She scowled into her soup, her face framed by her long, dry hair, behind which she liked to hide. She was known by her childhood nickname, Tonička, as if she had forever remained a small child. Although she resented this, her behaviour was indeed rather reminiscent of a spoiled and capricious little girl. Tonička rarely came to see us – she lived in a distant part of town that, to all intents and purposes, was almost another town altogether, and hardly ever left her house. She wasn't interested in the world around her, men included, and was therefore considered an old maid since she was by now on the wrong side of thirty. She usually announced herself around the time of her birthday, for she drew the line at spending this day entirely on her own. Although we all pretended that his wasn't the case, we all knew that we were celebrating her birthday. With Terka's considerable assistance Mother baked a cake and pretended this was an everyday occurrence. Father handed Tonička a present, which of course he had to do very unobtrusively to avoid a scandal. The gifts she received from my family at the end of May usually re-surfaced under our Christmas tree as Tonička lacked the imagination or the willingness to look for anything else.

This time her gift was a paperweight, the kind I had always dreamed of. It was made of glass, with an exquisite colourful flower inside. I'd love that for Christmas, I thought. It disappeared into her bag immediately.

Aunt Tonička feared men but she liked to say it was men who were scared of her. She did manage to overcome her inhibitions on at least one occasion, however.

The said gentleman walked everywhere in the company of a black greyhound.

After lunch and coffee Terka cleared the dining-room table for a game of bridge. Mother, Father, Uncle Rudo and Tonička were playing.

"Did he really say he needed the money for a motorcycle?"

"Double!"

"Deal again."

"But he was such a darling.."

"All right, but…."

"His dog was very sweet, too."

"A sweet greyhound?"

"A black greyhound!"

"Pass!"

"Pass!"

"How much did you lend him?"

"Everything."

"Double!"

"Re-double!"

"But afterwards Helena told me she lent him some money, too."

"Did he propose to her as well?"

"Let's drop the subject, shall we? Pass."

"Love is…" Rudo said with a smacking sound.

"Quiet!"

6.

The first act in Father's drama took place back in 1945.

The Levendovskýs were one of the most distinguished families in Brežany. Old Levendovský had served as public notary for many years. Just before the end of the war, after the passing of the front, he felt so moved that he thought the best thing to do was to put on his Sunday best and walk across town to the Count's manor house, his heart pounding, to ask to see the Russian commander. He just wanted to show his gratitude by inviting him and his men to a celebratory dinner at his house in two days' time. The Russians accepted. Levendovský beamed with pride and joy, relishing the prospect of hosting the heroic liberators at his villa.

Everything went well – there was much eating, drinking, cracking of jokes, broken Russian mixing with broken Slovak. And then, suddenly, in the middle of dinner, the lights went out and the soldiers gang-raped young Mária Levendovská, the notary's daughter. People said that when she was born, her parents couldn't decide on a name – at that moment a neighbour dropped by and said: "Come now, have you forgotten about the Holy Virgin Mary?" This is how she became Mary's namesake, although there was no doubt that the manner in which she conceived was far from immaculate. The Holy Spirit isn't known to wear a Soviet army uniform.

The family was shocked and horrified, all the more so as some time later Mária discovered that she was "late" and that a new life must have started growing in her womb. They tried to dispel her fears, assuring her it was just shock after what she had been through and saying she should just wait a little longer, things would turn out all right. Levendovský didn't confide in anyone – Brežany couldn't be allowed to know that his daughter had been defiled. And by the liberators to boot!

Eventually they had to accept the truth.

Mária resisted for a long time; she wouldn't hear about an abortion, but her father and mother insisted.

"What will people say…?"

Initially they considered the option of finding her a husband at short notice to keep matters above board. But there were no suitable candidates around. And meanwhile the clock was ticking. Eventually Mária gave in.

Aborting a foetus was prohibited by Article 144 of the Criminal Code. Nevertheless, Father had performed illegal abortions before. Partly out of necessity, to prevent Mrs Angyal from taking matters into her own hands, since she had a very poor reputation. Over the past few years three young women in their prime had died in Brežany and it wasn't difficult to guess what caused their death.

And so the inevitable happened…

It is summer and the sweltering heat continues well into the night. Moths hover around the lamp above the kitchen table, crashing into it, falling on the tablecloth with a rustle. Shadows dance on the walls… At least that's how I picture the fateful scene. There might be a storm raging outside but perhaps my imagination is running wild.

He had already tried other methods – first pituitrin and then pituglandol – but Father's supplies were running low and he had almost nothing left. The medication didn't help. The baby was thriving and showed no inclination to leave the haven of its mother's womb.

Nobody knew how it happened. Father had carried out dozens of similar interventions before. He knew every nook and cranny of the female body. The wall of Mária's uterus, consisting of thick vessels bubbling with blood, was as soft as butter.

As his scalpel did not encounter any resistance, Father pierced the uterus and continued all the way into the abdominal cavity. If he had realised in time and abandoned the intervention immediately, there would have been no serious consequences. But he had been plagued by insomnia for several nights, his head was about to explode that night and he didn't notice there was anything amiss. Instead of Maria's uterus, it was her abdominal cavity that he began to empty onto the Levendovskýs' kitchen table. He damaged her peritoneum and intestines and it wasn't until he started pulling out the tangled knots of her bowels instead of the stubborn child that was apparently not keen on its development being halted prematurely, that he realized his mistake.

They agreed to keep the tragic accident a secret, but somebody snitched on him some time later. Only three people knew what happened: the fourth didn't survive. It must have been Mr or Mrs

Levendovský, feeling desperate or vengeful, although revenge seemed pointless. The perpetrators had returned home to the vast Russian steppes where they would wax lyrical about the best days of their lives over shots of vodka. Father was the only one available.

Bad news was usually delivered by telegram.

Like when grandmother and grandfather Blau died in the car accident, when Grandpa Albert disappeared off the face of the earth, when Armin landed face down on the dirty parquet floor, when Father was summoned to court and when he was told that after all the mitigating circumstances had been taken into consideration he would serve two years in prison.

7.

Father used to say that however strange it may sound the one thing that kept him alive and sane in prison was an apple. Yes, an apple. The apple that usually came with breakfast.

He would stare at it until he was able to give an accurate description of every detail of its red, yellow or green peel. He would polish it and gaze at it. The whole cell was reflected in the apple. It was his private television set with its very simple and soothing schedule. As he lay on his bunk the apple was the only thing – apart from the dirty barred window – emanating some light. It seemed to concentrate all the brightness until night fell and the dreadful grey electric ceiling light came on. The apple went on glowing until lights out at ten. As if it had absorbed light, it went on shining until all the other lights were turned off for good. And only then would he eat it.

He stuck to his habit of staring at an apple even when he had to share his cell with two other inmates.

A Black Maria drove him to Pilsen, to the Bory prison. At first he assumed there was a shortage of doctors, given the turmoil and circumstances of the times. He got out of the car and found himself in a sizeable prison yard. His name was read out and he was allocated a cell.

He was received by Officer Barkl. The prison felt like a temple run by a sect of prisoners with sickly white faces, some flabby, others emaciated, and the wardens with their feline movements. If prisoners ran into them while cleaning the corridors, they had to stand to attention and yank the caps off their heads. The ubiquitous silence was sometimes interrupted by a faint distant noise. Father held his breath as he entered the circular central room on the ground floor. A space strongly resembling a church nave rose upwards, with endless corridors radiating in all directions and forming an eight-pointed star.

Barkl led Father to the basement and made him take off all his clothes. He wasn't even allowed to keep a handkerchief. Following a body search, during which he had to endure all sorts of indignities, he put on prison garb consisting of some thick shaggy grey-brown material, a faded shirt and underpants. Next came a cap, foot clouts and heavy boots, and off he went – down long corridors, stairways and galleries with protective netting, among bars and walls painted peculiarly depressing shades of grey, pea green, khaki and brown – and into a small cell with a judas hole, through which guards in dark-blue uniforms kept peering and shouting whenever they saw something they didn't like. Father was scared he might end up having to share a cell with hardened criminals, or wolfhounds as they were called. They could be extremely dangerous – if they didn't like someone, they would simply kill them. Eventually he was moved to the prison hospital, to people of his own kind.

On the first night he was surprised to hear knocking, the prison Morse code, messages tapped on walls, water pipes and radiators to communicate all manner of news. Father was not yet familiar with it and spent his first nights sitting about in his cell feeling deaf and blind. Hopelessness and depression descended on him; he was frightened of the prisoners he met in the corridors and the dining room or with whom he polished artificial pearls and various stones in the basement. Many enjoyed boasting of their misdeeds – he'd heard a hundred and one variations on the story of the forester's corpse tossed by poachers onto an anthill to make it vanish without a trace, or of the wife battered to death by her husband and then neatly rolled into a rug on the balcony where her children might play and ask when mummy was coming home from her business trip.

The little money he earned he spent mostly on cigarettes. After apples they became his second joy.

The best times were those he spent smoking and staring at the apple.

When he discovered that the prison rules allowed him to participate in services at the prison chapel, he decided, quite unexpectedly, to avail himself of this opportunity to escape the numbing routine. Walking past the guards positioned along the walls, he was as amazed to see the barrel of a machine gun, hidden casually behind the altar, as by the fact that Father Zikán used "confession" to pass on the latest news of the political turmoil of that autumn.

Father's situation improved somewhat after Dr Čeňka, the prison doctor, had him transferred to the prison hospital because he could no longer cope on his own. Father's first case was a prisoner who started to pass blood in his urine during an interrogation and was prone to frequent and intense epileptic fits. An examination revealed extensive internal injuries.

While Father was in prison, Mother struggled to make ends meet. From time to time she would sell off something of value, and sometimes our uncles came to the rescue. But she had to let go of Terka, our home help.

In search of a job, Mother stopped by the Golden Stag to ask if they could use a waitress. She even went to the trouble of procuring a textbook and in the evenings she crammed the French restaurant terminology at the insistence of Mr Tóth, the hotel owner.

"*Abricot*… apricot brandy, *Aigrefin*… cod, *à la* – in the manner of…"

"*Canapé*… a thin slice of toast garnished with paté or caviar, *Casse croûte*… hearty breakfast with wine, *Chablis*… white Burgundy…"

In the end the hotel job didn't work out. Times are bad, said the manager, we have enough staff already. But I still remember many of these expressions, for Mother asked me to test her in the evenings just like she tested my knowledge of Slovak geography.

"*Forestier au four*… dishes baked in the oven, particularly potatoes, *Fricassé*… stewed chunks of meat in a spicy sauce, *Jurassienne*… a starter of shallots, mushrooms and bacon, *Pièce de résistance*… the main course."

195

Eventually she landed a job with UNRRA, which at least ensured a steady supply of chewing gum.

Meanwhile a new doctor, a permanently huffy fellow, fresh out of medical school, stood in for Father. His name was Škorica, which means cinnamon, though he smelled more like a billy goat. The patients wished it were the other way around.

One evening I caught Mother taking a tiny key out of Father's desk in his isolation cell and unlocking a small drawer where he kept his valuables. By the light of a weak light bulb she took out the album with the precious banknotes and began leafing through it.

When I passed her half an hour later, she was still sitting there, staring at the blue covers and lost in thought. Then, in an instant, she made a decision, replaced the album and returned the key to its home. This isn't the right time yet, she thought and for a moment she must have felt like the character from the hoary old fairy tale who finds a magic ring that will make three wishes come true – and keeps postponing that last wish.

Harder times may yet lie ahead.

The first film Vojto and I were allowed to see on our own was a Hollywood production, *The Pirates of the Caribbean*, in colour. It was showing at the Slovan cinema.

Actually, I was going to ask out Zuzana Kabátová, the zany, beautiful Zuzana. I got as far as buying two tickets for the 6:30 show but each time I was about to take the final step – and believe you me, I tried several times, in the street, over the phone and at school – my legs turned to jelly and I lost the power of speech. As if someone had put a spell on me.

Asking Vojto wasn't difficult at all. Besides, he was going through something similar with Jana Podobová.

Since our discovery of the beautiful woman's corpse in the papyrus bushes on our side of the Sálava during the passing of the front, Vojto and I were haunted by the female form. Male and female private parts exert a magical pull on children. Particularly thirteen-year-old boys... We engaged in lengthy discussions of various unexplained issues.

Once, in order to gain more clarity, I remember climbing to the roof of Vojto's house when his parents left to watch an air show, and watching Magda Levendovská, the late Mária's older sister. She was sunbathing stark naked on their terrace between two tall houses, certain that no one could see her.

We were fascinated and repelled at the same time. It was that damned pubic hair, which, in the case of the woman from the river, we put down to an anomaly caused by drowning. To us it seemed impure, disgusting and mysterious – something akin to a spider's nest. But at the same time we couldn't tear our eyes away.

One evening, hidden in the reeds of a blind channel of the Sálava, we spied on a man and a woman skinny-dipping. (For me the river will always evoke the feminine, which was confirmed by a later experience at this very spot or a little further away.)

I don't remember much of the film because I kept imagining what it would have been like if Zuzana Kabátová had been sitting next to me. To make my fantasy more realistic, I almost took Vojto's hand at one point. Luckily he didn't notice.

Every Christmas for years to come Father would tell us about the Christmas Eve of 1947, the only one he spent in prison. He told the story so many times that Peter often felt compelled to leave the room in disgust and go to the bathroom, where he would whistle loudly.

On Christmas Eve the everyday hustle and bustle of prison life stopped by three p.m. Father and his colleagues, doctors Mayer and Hájský, listened to German prisoners behind a wall quietly intoning *Stille Nacht, heilige Nacht*, while the sounds of the Czech Christmas carol, *The glorious day has arrived, let everyone be merry,* drifted over from the other side, and from some other place the cinnamon-like fragrance of Christmas frankincense, smuggled in and lit by some crazy fellow, wafted in. Father was about to open the Christmas parcel that we had handed over during our visit the previous day. Before he could untie the string a guard came over and marched him to the prison office. There he was given another parcel, covered in illegible writing (the only thing Father could make out was that it was German) and four block capitals: *LILA*. The guard informed him that it had been personally delivered to the Bory Prison by a lady in the company of a gentleman from the Argentine consulate and it was his intervention that my Father had to thank for receiving it. The parcel was roughly the size of our old Tungsram radio.

Inside it Father and his colleagues found a selection of delicacies – cheeses, sausages and pastries. They were taken aback to discover that the package also contained sixty eggs, wrapped separately, a rather unusual thing to send to prison.

Besides, some of the eggs had leaked, Dr. Hájský pointed out, and licked the yolk that seemed to be coming out of one of the eggs. He stiffened, swallowed and shouted that this was no ordinary yolk but real eggnog. "Let's have some then!", a delighted Father said and they all got out their tin mugs and started breaking one egg after another. They found that each had a tiny opening sealed with wax: the contents of the eggs had been replaced using a syringe.

Father never found out who had sent the parcel.

It was from Father Zikán and the other doctors that he learned about the events of February 1948 – the fall of the government and the communists' eager grab for power. This didn't come as a surprise, for the politicians on the right did nothing but squabble, representing a hundred different opinions, while the communists stood for just a single cause and were ready to pounce at the first opportunity to get rid of their opponents. The writing was on the wall; you could feel it in the air, in the language, even in the food, which was getting steadily worse. The Bory prison was suddenly inundated with new customers nicknamed *kopečkári* ("over the hillers"). These were would-be defectors who had tried to flee the country discreetly, hoping for a better life over the hills, in Germany or Austria. They were led from the border like lambs to the slaughter. After debriefing they landed in the prison hospital.

Before very long Father was summoned by the lilting voice of Barkl or another guard:

"Doctor dear, we need you!"

There was a blond man who had been assaulted with rifle butts and beaten about the face until he happened to fall on a filing cabinet and break the door with his head. Reinforcements were brought in, pummelling him with whatever came to hand, until he stopped moving. He was lying in a pool of blood, his teeth scattered around like dice.

"Doctor dear…!" came the sweet siren call from the corridor.

Underground cell number 3, its bare walls lit by a dim light bulb dangling from the protective rail on the ceiling, was furnished with an iron ring embedded in the wall opposite the door, covered in rust-coloured stains. The guard ordered a tall man, frightened and battered, to climb onto a chair, and fastened him to the ring by his tied hands. The guard kicked the chair away, leaving the prisoner hanging and screaming, with the handcuffs cutting into his wrists. The guards gave him a good going-over and after a few blows to the head and stomach the man fainted. The wall acquired some fresh stains in addition to the rusty old ones.

"Doctor dear…!" The lock rattled and another almost lifeless man landed in the hospital cell. Father had met him before. Strong and full of energy only the other day, he was just a piece of rag now. Three years ago the Germans failed to see him off at Pankrác prison. Their successors might finish the job now.

Father told us that Officer Barkl once took him to see a patient in Sector 6 where he saw a scene straight out of a Baroque panting. Fifty Catholic priests were sitting plucking feathers in a huge workshop. They worked in silence, filling the air with floating wads of down that descended slowly, covering everything like a soft layer of snow.

Then came the news that on 19 June 1948 President Eduard Beneš resigned and the National Assembly elected a new President of the Republic, Klement Gottwald. The following evening was the last time Father feasted his eyes on an apple.

On 21 June 1948 – it was a Monday, as Father remembered for years afterwards – he was summoned to the prison office, where a dumpy elderly lady with a stern look on her face was waiting for him (he also remembered that it was a hot day and he could tell from the odour of her sweat that she was a diabetic). She informed him that he was to be released immediately as a result of an amnesty issued by President-elect Klement Gottwald. Father almost fainted. He had to sign a few papers, and went to pack his things and say goodbye to his two cellmates, who asked him to pass on some messages. He was escorted to the prison yard swarming with convicts about to be released just like him – they clustered around tables where the prison guards were dealing with the paperwork. There was laughter and animated chatter.

A little while later a camera crew turned up and Barkl asked Father if he knew German or English. Father said he had a smattering of both languages. He was introduced to a short man in a blue suit, a BBC reporter who asked him – on camera – how he felt about the amnesty. Since Barkl was standing right next to him, and a prisoner with chiselled features whispered the translation into the guard's ear, when Father was asked about the conditions in prison he knew his only option was to reply with a few clichés about "adequate food" and "friendly guards". The whirr of the camera stopped and after shaking Father's hand and wishing him good luck, the reporter, cameraman and a few guards went up onto the prison roof, which offered a fascinating view of the crowded courtyard.

Barkl told Father to return to his place in the queue. Some of the more impatient inmates didn't like that but the whole process seemed to take hours anyway, as the guards were unprepared for this kind of event and apparently lacked the intellectual capacity required to handle it. Father looked around – he knew most of the prisoners from medical interventions and examinations. Violent criminals stood alongside would-be defectors, wartime collaborators, thieves and hooligans, smugglers and political prisoners: in short, a motley crew of teeming humankind.

It was nearly seven o'clock by the time Father reached the last prison gate, the one leading out to freedom. He emerged into an early summer's evening and joined a throng of people who had come to meet the prisoners. There was nobody waiting for Father, for we had no way of knowing about his release, and he didn't object when an exuberant stranger, a woman he'd never met, fell into his arms and gave him a big kiss. Then another woman embraced him. Some wore Sokol sports club uniforms, presumably in honour of the National Sokol gathering that was taking place in Prague at the time. Father stumbled out of the human throng and after taking a few steps felt tears rolling down his cheeks. He couldn't stop them. He hadn't wept for years; it wasn't quite his style.

Somebody gave him a nudge from behind. It was a fellow inmate convicted of rape, who had been in another queue in the prison courtyard.

"Doctor, doctor…," he whispered imploringly into Father's ear, so close that Father could smell his bad breath, and grabbed him by the arm. "Hurry up, and don't look back!"

Wiping away his tears, Father rummaged in his pockets for his crumpled handkerchief as his nose, too, was running.

"Do you hear me, dammit! Get a move on! This is all just for show!"

The man let go of Father and started to run towards Bory Park on the far side of the road.

Father quickened his steps. He was tempted to turn around and see what the supposed danger was but he checked himself. He bumped into a few more happy smiling people, pushed his way through a group of elderly women and spotted a group waiting at a bus stop on the other side of Klatovská Avenue.

He started to sweat in a sudden grip of panic. Mustn't look back! He thought he heard some stamping of feet behind him and began to walk even faster. He stepped off the pavement into the road and had to swerve to avoid a car. A dusty bus trundled lazily up to the stop. Father could feel that his back was drenched in sweat; it poured down his forehead like a flood from a sea within.

He started when he saw two plain-clothes men jump on a prisoner whom he vaguely recognized from the prison canteen, and arrest him in the melee.

The noisy bus ground to a halt at the stop. The door opened, Father pushed aside an old man with a walking stick and dashed for the platform. All he could think of was: "One to the railway station…" The old driver, whose rheumy eyes resembled those of a tired fish, nodded and carefully tore off a ticket. The old man behind Father was grumbling loudly and to make things worse somebody farted, filling the whole front of the bus with a terrible stench. Father felt that in the time it took the driver to place the ticket in his hand and for him to pay with some loose change, he could have lived several lives in another dimension. So the station it would be. He took a seat at the back and pulled down the blinds.

After a few seconds that seemed to last an eternity the bus finally pushed off. Father's heart was pounding; he had no idea what he would do next. The other passengers knew nothing of what was going on and met his eyes with the blank stare of tired workers whose only thought was of home and a hot dinner. Father pulled the blinds aside and was observing the swarm of humanity outside the prison when someone thudded into the seat next to him.

It was a face he knew. He had once treated this man's wounds after an interrogation; his broken nose had healed well although it was now slightly skewed to the left. Father asked him what on earth was going on. The man explained that the entire amnesty was a sham for the benefit of foreign journalists, a spectacle that was meant to demonstrate that the communists had a human and tolerant side. State security was re-arresting those who were released outside the prison gates. Except that they hadn't counted on the crowds of waiting relatives and friends and were wary of causing chaos and problems, and in the commotion quite a few people managed to get away. The ones who had no inkling of what was happening were the most likely to do so.

Over the next few days, filled with tension and suspense, Father managed to make his way to Brežany, to our immense surprise. He later learned that he was one of the few to actually benefit from the amnesty.

After he came back from prison his hearing deteriorated. He put it down to the ill-treatment. He didn't have any particular symptoms – it was just that sometimes he wanted us to repeat what we said. He always came up with a plausible reason – a background noise, traffic or whatever – and laughed it off.

The only benefit of his stay at Bory Prison was that he learned the lyrics to the *Cantata for Stalin* in Russian. To his dying day, try as he might, Father couldn't get it out of his head: *Po krajam, po gornym vershinam…*

> All over the land, high above the hilltops
> Where the mountain eagle soars
> In praise of Stalin, the wise, the beloved, the dear
> From the people rises a beautiful song
> A song that wings past every bird
> Enraging the exploiters' world
> No border post can curb its flight
> No boundary can block its path.

For the last few months of his imprisonment it was played on the prison radio every day. Father returned home just in time.

8.

Now what about those bones, I hear you ask.

My neighbour Igor's office was in the unprepossessing building of the Institute of Forensic Medicine of Comenius University's Department of Medicine, in Sasinkova Street. He lived in one of the anonymous courtyard balcony flats one floor above mine and at one time I was, let us say, quite intimately acquainted with his wife Dorota. For many years Igor and I had passed each other in the street or shopping at the market before we got talking one day and ended up sharing a few bottles of plonk. His wife had moved out by then, taking their children with her and leaving him to his own devices, while he stayed embalmed in his present state like a boulder overgrown with moss and lichen. All he cared about was his work, pathology and forensic science.

After reporting to reception I walked down a maze of corridors, unable to shake off the image of walking among dead bodies lying in their refrigerated boxes like cakes displayed in a pastry shop.

This is how Igor had once described it to me, adding that everyone who worked here was affected in one way or another. It was something you could never get used to. The coffee machine was just behind the door to the room where the boxes were kept and only a thin wall divided the stiffs from the showers. Before performing an autopsy Igor would put on several layers of clothing, overalls, gloves and a surgical mask, which helped to put at least some distance between him and grim reality.

He received me in his "cabinet". In addition to various curiosities I would rather not go into here, he piqued my interest with a study he'd been working on for years. It was a detailed analysis of the way our world had been shaped by drugs.

His basic thesis went as follows: People have a natural tendency to improve their lot. It is part of their nature and character to try and relieve the heavy burden of life at least for short while.

"For example, ladies in the nineteenth century favoured ether because it wasn't deemed proper for them to indulge in alcohol and to have its smell on their breath. They ingested it mostly in the form of Hoffman's drops, by affecting a cough. Under this name it is still quite popular with Lithuanians on the lower reaches of the Neman river and on the coast of Curonia. It is dribbled onto a sugar cube, its popularity a boon for smugglers who bring it in from Kaliningrad.

"In the nineteenth century the opium tincture known as laudanum was a household staple, popular with artists and ordinary folk alike, even children. Used as a remedy for headaches and freely available without prescription, it usually led to severe addiction and degeneration of the faculties.

"In the 1930s chemists discovered a methamphetamine which was sold under the brand name Pervitin. During World War II it was widely used by the Wehrmacht and the SS. Amphetamines in general became wildly popular in the sixties, particularly with housewives in western Europe – they came in handy if they had to deal with the ironing, the laundry and the shopping, fix dinner and help the children with their homework. The little yellow pill, known as Mother's Little Helper, was immortalized by the Rolling Stones. The stuttering lyrics of *My Generation* by The Who exemplify the way ideas can take the place of articulated words. Our very own beloved dextromethamphetamine, known locally as *dexík*, is also a type of amphetamine.

The social role methamphetamines used to play has now, to some extent, been taken over by various forms of Ibuprofen and anti-anxiety pills or anti-depressants."

"What about Luminal?" I asked.

"That's a phenobarbital, a barbiturate used in the treatment of epileptic fits and also as a sleeping pill, tranquillizer or sedative, or for treating anxiety. It is highly addictive. Maybe that's why it has been prescribed far less since the late seventies. Years of use can lead to anaemia, confusion or depression. So – what is it you've got for me?"

I was happy for him to go on talking and said I found it fascinating but I knew I was just putting off the moment I would have to tell him about my gruesome discovery. A strange paranoia suddenly gripped me and my courage drained away.

So he began to hold forth on how, if several members of a family are killed in the same car accident, it is particularly important to determine the precise sequence in which the passengers died, which is crucial in legal cases involving inheritance.

I left after two hours. Without even mentioning the bones.

Back at home I examined my list. Gajdoš – cut. He died ten years ago, having lived to a ripe old age. Albert, Artur and Sára Silberstein – cut, cut, cut. They never came back from Auschwitz.

9.

The colour of the Victorious February of 1948 was red. What I mean is that the town of Brežany was painted various shades of burgundy, crimson and scarlet by all the banners, flags and drapes. Momentous events were soon to follow.

It all began with Jan Masaryk – son of the esteemed President T.G. – who committed suicide in such an ingenious manner that he contrived to close the window in his bathroom after leaping out of it. Since this happened in Prague, far from Brežany, to our ears it sounded like a fairy tale. Hlinka's Guard was replaced by the People's Militia, the main difference being that they dressed in a more formal and foppish way.

While Mother sorted out and dusted her 78s an exuberant Uncle Rudo sat on our "White Christmas" and as a result we wouldn't hear the song again for many years.

The lobby of the Golden Stag – once so quiet and pristine that upon entering you felt you had come upon a strange kind of religious ceremony from which even the quietest sound had been banished, except for the odd discreet whisper and squeaky shoe – suddenly came to life and was filled with a loud commotion and roars of laughter. It was invaded by a troop of tipsy workers in dirty overalls from a nearby construction site. They lounged about on the velvet upholstery, burping and shouting. They would nick the odd piece of silver or drop a china bowl, and wipe their hands on the tablecloths.

The attempt to rename the establishment Stalingrad Hotel had failed. The name of the aristocratic building, set back from the main square, was simplified to plain old Stag Hotel. A plastic stag with twelve antlers was hung above the entrance, replacing the glass original smashed up by the Russians.

Today, as I walk through the lobby of the hotel, once again graced with the epithet Golden, I find it hard to believe all that has happened. Discreet silence and unostentatious luxury are again the norm, further enhanced by soft anodyne piped music. This is how hotels survive – basically by not giving a toss and offering everyone the scent of hotel soap and an eleven o'clock checkout.

I order a Coke at the hotel bar and look around, sensing that this is my last visit.

If I remember correctly, the first time I saw Coca-Cola was after the war in newspaper cartoons by Bednár and Weisskopf. A fat (fairly un-Aryan looking) imperialist would invariably be perched on a sack of money, smoking a cigar and drinking Coke from the signature bottle or a can. How I envied him! A few years later, when actors in our TV and theatre productions supposedly drank this mysterious capitalist libation they acted as if they were drunk because they were convinced it contained alcohol.

I love the tickling of the bubbles on the roof of my mouth.

After Father came back from prison, he was no longer quite himself. I would sometimes see him at home, sitting in an armchair with a vacant stare, unaware he was biting his fingernails and his feet were twitching nervously. When I asked what was wrong he would quickly get up and say casually, trying to sound carefree:

"What do you mean, what's wrong? I'm absolutely fine but what about you…? There must be something wrong with you to ask a question like that!"

When he thought I couldn't see him he would reach into his pocket, behind his books or into the cupboard and pop a Luminal.

Sometimes it gave him constipation, made him lose his appetite or made him dizzy. The patient information leaflet listed a variety of side effects from higher doses, including impaired co-ordination, confusion, sleepiness and depression. Father didn't mind any of that. But he was tired a lot of the time, and it showed in his eyes and drooping eyelids.

He took to drinking lots of coffee and strong tea. When my son Bony lived in England and the Netherlands, he also started his day with considerable quantities of caffeine and said it was quite common there. I still remember Father's mug, stained brown with caffeine. He never washed it.

And at night he suffered from insomnia. It was a vicious circle.

He would stand by the fridge, his eyes half-shut, studying the label on a beer bottle. His ophthalmologist used to say:

"I know, I know, your eyesight is fine – it's just your arms that are too short!"

I have no idea what his ear doctor said to him.

He was brilliant at pretending he could hear everything.

In those days Tina, Peter and I led a secret life at night. During the day we all did our own thing but at night, when everything went quiet and the kitchen was bathed in yellow light, as if it had been torn away from the world like a ship on a dark river, illuminated by a single lantern, it turned into a universe of its own.

Following Father's example, we indulged in midnight binges. We would be lying in our beds quietly, and then, all of a sudden, we would leap out of bed and go and get a snack. The minute one of us opened the fridge the others would be there as well.

Peter used to come home quite late. What he told us and the way he said it offered reliable clues as to who he had spent the evening with. Whoever he'd been with, something of that person would cling to him, leaving a mark just as if the Lord had crafted him out of plasticine. As if nothing of his real self remained.

And so we would feast on cheese, salami and sausages provided by Father's patients, on slices of bread and butter, washing everything down with gulps of cold milk. And we would talk, all at the same time, each from a different end of the kitchen table. It was as if we were in different time zones.

Tina wanted to change gender and envied us. For a while she used to pray every night: "If only I could be a boy!" Every morning she rushed to the mirror and examined her lower parts. Nothing. She regarded it as a disgrace and injustice.

What made things worse was that people kept holding up Peter as an example for her to follow. He was always interested in the right kind of things, held the right kind of views and interests, and he didn't mess around or chase girls.

When Tina was little, she had the makings of an obedient little girl. Later she began to give vent to her feelings by tormenting other people's cats and dogs. She would also torment our dog Polino, who would come home scruffy and covered in blood.

Tina grew up to be something of a rebel. She mostly took it out on Mother. She longed to get the hell out of the house and did try to get away a few times but always came back. She hated Mother for constantly comparing her with us; she hated school and she hated Peter, although they didn't have it out until many years later, when they were much older. It was an extremely long conversation lasting well into the night.

But all that was yet to come. Meanwhile we were still deep in the past, sitting in the kitchen that echoed to the munching of peppers, tomatoes and cheese.

That night Tina was very quiet. Father had made her, his favourite daughter, believe that she could pass through the wall, if only she was sufficiently focused. She had been trying all day.

With arms stretched out in front of her and eyes closed. Nothing.

"Poly! Polino!"

When our old dog – who still remembered our grandfather and who like most Slovak dogs was called Dunčo – died of old age, Tina brought a new puppy from a neighbour's house – and because our first dog had an ordinary name, she named the new one Polyester, after the new type of fibre that had gone into industrial production earlier that year and was now all the rage. She liked the name, not least because its local abbreviation was PES, which is the Slovak for dog.

"Poly! Polino!" she would call out to the dog. It followed her everywhere.

It was the first one in a long line of Polyesters that passed through our Brežany household.

Our succession of cats on the other hand, mostly looked after by Mother, wandered around the table during our midnight feasts. They were habitually named Ikebana. Probably because of the flowers they gnawed on and destroyed. Ikebana I was followed by Ikebana II and so on. Ika for short.

Ikebana IX kept Mother company until she died.

10.

One day in March our long-standing Slovak language teacher, Mr Štermenský, who had been promoted to the secondary school because of the teacher shortage and was by now all grey and faded, as if he had spent years lying in the sun being slowly coated in dust, walked into class. Fighting back his tears he asked us to hand in all our readers.

He brought them back to the next class. The books had a number of pages glued carefully together, those that featured authors and extracts from their work now deemed unsuitable.

The Brežany National Committee sent out a new circular. The text was also broadcast on the local radio, whose loudspeakers had now invaded every corner of the city, churning out non-stop news of births, deaths, meetings, details of volunteers, plenary meetings and saboteurs, sounding like the alluring pop singer Melánia Olláryová's rendition of the song *Do you still remember, my darling?*

In the spirit of the preamble to the Declaration of our new Constitution, the Czechoslovak people declare their determination to develop their state into a people's democracy, thus ensuring peaceful progress towards socialism.

By liberating labour, socialist society has ushered in a new attitude to work. This no longer humiliates man the way it did when capitalist society morals prevailed, having been transformed into a joyful creative necessity, a creator of new values that will embellish and enhance the lives of all working people.

I have therefore issued the following decree, which comes into force with immediate effect, regarding the use of the greeting Čest' práci! – *"Hail Labour!" and the form of address "Comrade".*

I charge you with ensuring that all subordinate workers within your sphere of activity are familiarized with this new regulation and observe it.

Jozef Kominár, Chairman of the Town National Committee.

The announcement was followed by Stalin's favourite song, *Suliko*.

"I have searched for my sweetheart's grave, but it's so hard to find..."

The Georgian choral performed by the Alexandrov Ensemble came booming through the streets.

Father Savický, the former deputy headmaster of the Catholic secondary school, skulked around under one of the loudspeakers. Yet again no one had thought of inviting him but he was no longer angry. He would turn up at every festive occasion, welcoming esteemed guests and profusely thanking the performers on behalf of the town, shaking their hands and patting their backs as if nothing had changed.

There was something strangely symmetrical about the year 1949. It made a sound like slapping your hand on the table. All my life I have enjoyed matching numbers with sounds, and cities with colours. It started when I was a little boy. And I do it to this day. For me Berlin is blue, Paris green, Vienna orange and Brežany is tinged with brown.

The year 1949 felt like a car, a sports car, perhaps a convertible, well-tuned and run in. A cool breeze is blowing through your hair and you feel that all's well with the world and life is full of promise. The first half of the century was behind us, the second half lay ahead. Naturally, the worse part was over. Prosperity was just around the corner. That's what the radio proclaimed.

The family gathered around the table for Sunday lunch was in a good mood and not only because of the particularly pleasant spring we were having, without a single cloud in the sky. Everyone was having fun and cracking jokes. Only Father was shrouded in gloom. He was about to carve the duck, something he was very particular about (the manual says: "The head of the family carves the bird..."), when Uncle Oskar took the knife out of his hand as he chattered merrily on.

Four of Mother's relatives survived the war. Oskar was one of the few to come back from Auschwitz (he managed to escape during an US air raid on the branch of the I.G. Farben factory to which he had been assigned) and made an effort to forget this refined form of hell as quickly as he could. He never dwelled on the subject unless absolutely necessary, except to mention once that in order to survive, he was forced to be a Kapo for a while, i.e. volunteer to be a traitor. People had to resort to all kinds of strategies, for example, a young nurse was ordered to inject children's hearts with phenol, otherwise she would have been injected herself. Although Aunt Rózka hadn't survived the first day, their children Rebeka and Izák crossed the Hungarian border at Miloslavov and stayed with relatives in Budapest for a time before being deported to Mauthausen, where they died of typhoid. Cousin Samuel survived because family friends hid him on their farm in a pen where they kept goats and pigs. He lost his toes to frostbite but one can live without toes.

Uncle Oskar changed his name to Novan, chosen from a list of surnames on offer at the register office. It was meant to remind him that he started a new life. A few hundred years ago a list of names was compiled by a decree of Emperor Joseph II's; now a new one had been drawn up. It begs the question: what is the point of a name if you can choose it freely?

After exposure to Hitler's tender mercies Oskar Novan lost his faith for good, though he continued to consider himself a Jew, but without any of those bothersome rules. God was no longer entitled to tell him what to do and what not to do. He remarried. And he developed a strange habit: the kitchen cupboard had to be full of bread at all times even though there was a bakery down the road from his flat. Just in case, he used to say.

He had come back as a zealous supporter of the Soviet Union, communism and Stalin, believing them to be the only ones who could save the world. He stopped going to the synagogue and observing the Sabbath, and mocked all Jewish customs as well as the people who observed them. Trembling with thrill and joy, he ordered his first pork schnitzel at the Stag Hotel for the first time, on a Saturday afternoon to boot – he was tempted to go to the kitchen and ask the chef if he could personally tenderize the meat, coat it in breadcrumbs and fry it but he restrained himself, blushing at such blasphemous thoughts. He did it so often it turned into a ritual – a Saturday schnitzel at the Stag Hotel.

Of course, he would come to regret bitterly that he had taken me along and waxed lyrical about the schnitzels because many years later, when he would come on his visits from Israel, crinkled like an apple in March, and nostalgia drove him to look for the synagogue, the very one of which he had once said that it should be torn down, I never missed an opportunity to remind him of this. "There used to be a wall here, right, Adam?" he asked, tugging at my sleeve. "And this is where the *rebbe* used to stand, isn't it?" His grandsons, who no longer spoke Slovak and wore *kippahs*, gloomily surveyed this no-man's-land overgrown with weeds that for some reason had been left empty. "No, this is where the rostrum was, from where Comrade Široký gave a speech when he visited Brežany in 1950," I chipped in. It wasn't very kind of me, I know. But who could have resisted?

Ancient and half-blind, Uncle Oskar shuffled down the streets of Brežany like a wandering Jew, beaming with joy whenever he came across an *unsereiner* – someone, so to speak, of the same breed. It didn't happen very often, though.

But on that Sunday of that annus mirabilis of 1949 Oskar went on carving the meat and chattering.

To mark the occasion he had put on a red tie, which went well with his white shirt and dark jacket, and also with the slim booklet he kept fingering every now and then. Along with many others, he had just joined the Communist Party. A brave new world was nigh, a world where everyone would be equal. Not just after death, as the Christian and Jewish God would have it but here: in this life, on this earth.

"Now the Jews will finally be left alone!" Oskar shouted, almost choking on his duck, which he stuffed straight into his mouth in the heat of carving. The new Aunt Rózka nodded in vigorous agreement.

"The Central Committee is full of them. Secretary General Slánský, for instance."

"Oh yes, Slánský is an *unsereiner*, he used to be called Salzmann!"

My cousin Samuel piped up: "I bet Dr Rais at the Ministry of Justice is one too!"

"Definitely!"

"And so is Artur London at the Foreign Trade Ministry, Fischl at the Ministry of Finance, Löbl and Margolius at Foreign Trade."

Father stared at his plate, lost in thought. Oskar slapped him on the back and gave him some cabbage and another piece of *lokša*.

"I know, Alfonz. But you wouldn't understand!"

"I'm sorry…?"

"I said you wouldn't understand!"

Mother nodded and topped up their glasses.

"Pre-war vintage!" Oskar praised the wine, letting it dribble down his chin. "Come on, have some, Adam!" I offered him my glass and glanced at Father. After all, I was going to be fifteen soon. Father gave a wordless nod.

"To Gottwald!"

"Isn't he Jewish as well?"

"Who knows? Probably not."

"The wine is from the abandoned vineyard under the Volovec Mountain."

"Must be."

"What do you mean? The wine…?"

"No, I mean Gottwald. He must be Jewish."

212

"I can't believe that."

"Can I have some more wine?"

"The world will be different. Completely different, Alfonz. You may not believe it but you'll see."

"I think the main thing is peace and quiet. I don't care about anything else."

"Or maybe he isn't?"

"Who?"

"Gottwald."

At that point Uncle Rudo looked up from his de-boned duck thigh:

"When people start talking of equality and love of mankind – it's a sure sign that prisons and scaffolds will soon get crowded. All in the name of love, of course. Medieval Christianity is a case in point, and so is Nazism, and Russian communism."

"Shut up, you *meshugener,* you!"

Meshugener Rudo's tongue had already got him into trouble two months earlier.

The secret police went after him after he blabbed at the Stag Hotel, emboldened by two bottles of St Lawrence. They tried to charge him with spying for the US. They got as far as concocting a file with a false confession, which he learned about from an almost illegible copy a patient of Father's had secretly made and asked Father to pass on. It was a risky operation because all typewriters were strictly registered in those days. The confession read as follows:

Engineer Rudolf Trnovský, landowner and traitor.
On 29 September 1944 CIA agent Captain James Woldow came to see me to propose collaboration after the war and to recruit me as an agent. Based on the pledge I made to him, in 1948 I began to organize subversive activities aimed at bringing about an armed uprising in Slovakia at the time of the conflict brewing between the East and West, and installing a capitalist regime.

He was briefly detained but Uncle Oskar came to the rescue, interceding on his behalf with the Minister of Justice Štefan Rais, an *unsereiner* and a friend of Gottwald's.

He had to sign a declaration of loyalty and join the Communist Party of Czechoslovakia.

The two uncles had a long discussion about it. Rudo resisted at first but when he remembered what Father had said about prison food he agreed to sign.

Oskar's son Samuel got hold of a poster and displayed it proudly on his wall.

One half depicted an emaciated worker in rags standing in front of a factory, with a capitalist sitting on the factory roof astride a sack full of money and waving him away with his hand.

The caption underneath read: *THE PAST…*

The other half of the poster showed a throng of workers marching towards the factory gates, one of them giving a tiny chubby scared capitalist a kick in the bum with an enormous shoe.

… AND THE PRESENT.

"What do you think?" Samuel asked me.

"Nicely drawn," I said hesitantly.

"Is that all you can say?"

"Well, hm… but our *zeyde* Blau was… also a bit of a… capitalist, you know that, don't you?"

My cousin waved his hand dismissively and planted himself in a chair.

"Stop talking and pass me some tape; it's a bit torn here."

"I don't want to be a spoilsport, but our *bobe* Sára…"

"Hang on, tacks will be better. I'll be right back… Keep talking, I'm listening to you."

By now he was at the far end of the flat.

"Adam, did you know that Comrade Gottwald was once so poor he had to take his books outside and read them by the light of a street lamp?"

11.

The third version of Vojto's father's CV read as follows:

I joined the Communist Party of Czechoslovakia in 1946 in Brežany (at the Lehota Military Airfield), after my application was approved at the Communist Party of Slovakia headquarters in Bratislava. I joined the party because of my political convictions. Membership card number: E-110350.

I was born the eighth of ten siblings. I was raised in very modest circumstances. I completed 8 years of elementary education in Brežany. I was very keen to go to an engineering college but this was beyond my family's means. I held a number of part-time manual jobs until 1 October 1928, before volunteering for military service at the age of 18, at the military air-training school of Prostějov, the air pilot section.

On 15 November 1933 I was admitted to the military academy, graduating in August 1936. In early 1940, after working at the Lehota Airfield for several years, I was deployed as a member of a reconnaissance air squadron to the Vranov nad Topl'ou airfield, with no military activity. I was subsequently sent for re-training on the Bf-109 aircraft as one of a group of 125 pilots. After returning to the 13th Fighter Squadron in Piešť any I had a number of conflicts. To give an example – the squadron commander, Major Stréženský, placed me under house arrest for regularly avoiding evening meetings with our German instructors. Major Stréženský told me: "Your officer's credentials are obviously made of manure!" (He was probably alluding to the fact that I had achieved the rank of officer without the benefit of secondary education.) As I learned upon my return, my reference stated that I was not suited to be a section commander. Sometime around 1 November 1942 my fighter squadron was deployed to the Eastern Front, where I served as a pilot until early March 1943, when I returned to Slovakia upon my father's death. At the end of July I was deployed again, returning to Slovakia in early July 1943, when we were replaced after the German armed forces complained about our unsatisfactory performance and lack of reliability.

Afterwards, from about November 1943, I was in charge of the 13th Fighter Squadron, first in Vajnory and later in Piešť any. Sometime in June 1944, while I was on leave, my squadron was deployed in an emergency capacity to defend our territory against Anglo-American pilots and was wiped out in air-to-air combat above Bratislava.

In August 1944 I was invited to join the preparations for the Slovak National Uprising. I was sent to the Three Oaks airfield. My air force activities during the Uprising consisted of some 20 sorties in the Bf-109 aircraft with German markings, which had the effect of thoroughly confusing the enemy; the sorties mostly involved air strikes, bombing and reconnaissance missions. In addition, from 29 August 1944 until 17 September 1944, I held the position of commander of the technical squadron at Hájniky barracks. From 18 September 1944 until the partial crushing of the Uprising I served as a commander of a combined Three Oaks Fighter Squadron and airfield commander. In the last days of October 1944, on the order of my section commander, I flew to the village of Donovaly, taking three aircraft. Since highly unfavourable weather conditions made it impossible to depart for the USSR before the enemy reached the village, I ordered the planes to be destroyed and left for the mountains.

In January 1945 I waited in Tisovec for the front to pass and after crossing through Hungarian territory joined the 1st Czechoslovak Army Corps in the USSR. In March 1945, at my own request, I was redeployed to the 5th Air Division on the Ukrainian front, where I participated in military action until I was severely wounded.

After the war I was promoted to the rank of air force staff captain (1 January 1946), and on 1 March 1948 to the rank of major. I served as air force regiment commander at the Brežany-Lehota airfield, 1948-1949.

Decorations awarded: Czechoslovak Military Cross 1939, Slovak National Uprising Award, First Class, Czechoslovak Medal of Merit, Second Class, and Czechoslovak Commemorative Medal for participating in the building of a new Czechoslovak army.

A tanned and soot-covered Mislovič wiped his forehead. "That's it, chaps!" He moved the pan from the smouldering pit. The last crow had been roasted.

He sat down in the grass next to Vojto's father, who was gnawing on a thigh. He took a swig from the bottle and passed it on.

"Well, well, General, it seems that at the end of the day neither side wanted you, eh?"

"Oh no, no. They did want me… In May 1944 I graduated from a German air force commander course. In Vienna. And in the spring of 1950 from a military command course at the officer school in Prague."

"Well? What's the problem, then?"

"I wish I knew."

"Oh, never mind…!" Mislovič laughed and slapped him on the back, almost making him drop the bottle.

"Your dad is quite a fellow, Vojto! He's one of us! Boys – have another bite of the kosher pigeon – catch!"

On the first day of spring 1949, soon after breakfast, Mrs Natália Roško read in a dream book: Seeing and talking to an angel means promotion.

She went on to read the cards, drawing first a leaf nine, meaning you will go on a journey, followed by a bell eight and a leaf ace, both portending a life of bliss and prosperity.

As a result of these omens (plus a few other factors) I was soon to be deprived of Vojto's company for nearly a year. His father was appointed squadron commander at Kbely airfield in Prague and the family relocated to a stunning huge flat in the capital's Dejvice district.

The Stations of the Cross on the hill behind the Brežany parish church underwent a transformation. Initially the authorities wanted to get rid of the Stations altogether. But taking a leaf out of the Christian book, the communists realised it was not enough to destroy a place. To make it disappear you had to overlay it with a new meaning.

So the hill was turned into a pantheon of prominent comrades. The brilliant idea was the brainchild of the new chairman of the Brežany National Committee, Comrade Kominár, whose wife used to proclaim with pride: "My husband has always been a chairman. Only once in his life was he deputy chairman!"

Right after the war, on that memorable May night, he was one of those wielding spades near Saliny. But that was a taboo subject.

His idea was vaguely reminiscent of the original Stations of the Cross, except that the figures' eyes weren't turned towards heaven, as we're used to in the fourteen depictions of Jesus, but instead gazed ahead like sleepwalkers, as befits proper revolutionaries.

The project was based on an original idea by Comrade Kominár, a qualified joiner. He was also the author of the project guidelines and design.

The new sequence went as follows:

1. Jesus is condemned to death – Lenin in exile
2. Jesus takes up the cross – Lenin takes the train via Germany to St Petersburg
3. Jesus stumbles under the weight of the cross for the first time – Lenin engages in a lively debate with his comrades
4. Jesus meets his mother – Lenin meets his elderly mother and assures her that communism will prevail
5. Jesus is helped by Simon to carry the cross – Lenin meets Stalin

6. Veronica gives Jesus her veil – Nadezhda Krupskaya wipes Lenin's perspiring brow while he is struggling

7. Jesus stumbles under the weight of the cross for the second time – Lenin on board the Battleship Aurora gives the order to attack

8. Jesus admonishes the weeping women – Lenin addresses the working masses

9. Jesus buckles under the weight of the cross for the third time – Lenin survives the assassination attempt by Socialist Revolutionary Fanya Kaplan

10. Jesus is deprived of his garb – Visiting steelworkers, Lenin dons workmen's overalls

11. Jesus is nailed to the cross – Lenin stands in front of a big red cross with his arms stretched out in victory

12. Jesus dies on the cross – Lenin dies a heroic death in battle (!)

13. Jesus' descent from the cross – Lenin is embalmed

14. Jesus is laid in the tomb – Lenin's body is placed in the Mausoleum

Comrade Kominár's chest swelled with justifiable pride. In an extravagant gesture he proposed a fifteenth Station, the biggest of them all, which was to be the gateway to the whole procession: three Wise Men (Marx, Engels and Lenin) follow a blazing red star, accompanied by a young pioneer carrying gifts (hammer, sickle and a pair of compasses) for baby Jesus Stalin.

However, the project was soon shelved. First Stalin fell out of favour; next came Gottwald, who was added for a while as the first steelworker, only to be removed again. Then they ran out of material – white sandstone from the island of Brač – because the fraternal nation of Yugoslavia chose to go its own way and the "running dog" Tito fell out with the Russians.

Eventually they left the hill alone. The monks from the nearby monastery who used to look after the place had been sent packing to all corners of the republic for re-education and the bare hill was taken over by the forest that grew uncontrollably from everything blown in that direction. The roots of the trees penetrated the foundations of the Baroque angels, which can now be seen gracing the gardens of the expensive villas on the hill, alongside smiling gnomes and plastic Micky Mouses.

On the last Friday of April 1949, Father, feeling exhilarated after his morning run up the hill and back again in the fragrant air, and after savouring a cigarette and taking his shower, went to open his consulting room only to find a National Committee delegation in the waiting room. Three comrades, two women and one man, obediently waited their turn and the man, who complained of palpitations, let Father examine him with a stethoscope. Father took a cardiogram and reassured him that the best thing for the heart was not to pay it too much attention. One of the female comrades asked for a prescription for headache pills.

Then they began:

"Now that we have our new people's democracy, comrade doctor, we hope you will take part in the May Day parade. We must all demonstrate our solidarity and show that new times have arrived!"

Father nodded absent-mindedly but they insisted on a firm commitment.

"What is it you were saying?"

"We were saying that your absence, comrade doctor, might have a negative impact on…"

"Oh, I see. Very well then."

When they left, he told Zdenka to see to the prescriptions and went to see Mother.

I don't know if they had a row or if Uncle Oskar had given him a talking-to, but come next Sunday, instead of a lie-in the whole family had a quick breakfast, and in our Sunday best we took to the streets, filled with relentlessly strident, upbeat music.

The parade wound its way along formerly Hitler, formerly Masaryk, now Stalin Street, crossing the main square, which boasted a podium shrouded in red cloth. The entire route was festooned with bunting, flowers, balloons and peace doves. The Stag Hotel sported red banners with yellow lettering: *We pay tribute to the 4ʰ anniversary of Czechoslovakia's liberation by the Soviet Army with new achievements in the struggle for socialist construction* and *With the Soviet Union, for ever and ever!*

The organisers carried portraits of Marx, Engels, Lenin, Stalin, Gottwald and Široký – as well as a few other odd, pasty faces which, someone explained, belonged to members of the *Politburo*. I thought the word "Politburo" sounded lovely and wrote it down in my diary as a new acquisition, next to "chiffonier" – Grandma Mária's word for the wardrobe – and *"kocinkrát"*, the folksy word for the medicinal plant allheal.

At exactly nine o'clock the head of the parade marched past the rostrum on the main square to the sounds of the Czech and Slovak national anthems. Comrade Kominár delivered a solemn speech standing above his own, larger-than-life portrait:

Four years ago in the glorious days of May the heroic Soviet army completed the liberation of Czechoslovakia from German Nazi occupation. On 9 May 1945 Soviet troops crushed the Nazi hordes besieging Prague, crowning the liberation of our country with victory. This year we shall join progressive peoples across the world for the traditional celebration of Labour Day, marked this year for the fifty-ninth time. The May Day festivities are the expression of the radiant and rich life of our working people and of the mighty and invincible power of the global progressive forces as they strive for peace and socialism!

Then the Internationale was played. Neither my parents nor we children had any idea what to do, as we didn't know the lyrics, but when a gentleman with a blue band on his sleeve prodded me and started shouting: "Hurrah!" and "Long Live May Day – the holiday of all the working people of the world!" I joined in. Looking confused, Father followed my lead and nearly lost his balance as the thousand-headed Labour Day serpent lurched forward. People sang and waved their pennants and little red flags. I have always been afraid of crowds and this was now beginning to get to me. Peter was the only one who really enjoyed the whole thing.

Behind us trundled an allegorical float representing a Soviet tank with a red star. On top of it rode an actor from the Brežany amateur theatre in the guise of Field Marshal Stalin. He greeted the masses with grand gestures, smiling under his moustache. Someone standing behind him tossed handfuls of toffees to the crowd. Old women, who had come scuttling out of their houses to revel in the sight of the parade, began to cross themselves and ran as fast as they could to kiss his hand.

Uncle Oskar and the new Aunt Rózka elbowed their way towards us with joyful shouts. Oskar shook Father's hand happily and gave Mother a kiss. Tina had stuck a pennant with Stalin's portrait into her cleavage and walked around with his face covering hers. Oskar gave her a slap on the face, replaced Stalin with a stick with multicoloured ribbons and wagged his finger at her. So she took my Marx, whose thick beard I admired.

Father was fidgety, acknowledging greetings from time to time, tugging at his hat nervously and casting searching glances around, sweat trickling from his brow.

He took the first opportunity to slip away from the crowd. Mother had to stay behind as Uncle Oskar was walking arm in arm with her but I, along with Tina who had a Picasso dove stuck in her panties and colourful crepe ribbon in her hair, followed him into the narrow Sálavská Alley, emerging at the other end of the square. We headed straight for Puškár's patisserie.

Father ordered a glass of Georgian brandy and we were treated to lemonade and pastries. He reached into his pocket and managed to swallow a pill just before Puškár came up to us and started telling us about his beloved Lila:

"I keep waiting, doctor, I keep waiting. The God of patience granted me endurance."

From the square we heard festive music, interrupted by more speeches and chanting: "Long Live May Day – the holiday of all the working people of the world!" and saw a red helium balloon, released by a child, rise into the sky. Tina ran out of the patisserie to take a look but it quickly disappeared.

Just at that moment our view was blocked by a large canvas, which was being carried past by four workers. The picture, painted in autumn colours, depicted a partisan and a Red Army soldier fighting side by side on a high cliff, against the backdrop of a thick forest.

Puškár later told Father that after the crowds and allegorical floats had rumbled past and the rally was over, some of the local women descended on the deserted platform, wielding knives and scissors. Snip-snip, they went. The material would soon be turned into sports shorts and trousers.

12.

Cousin Samuel was becoming a real pain in the neck. In early 1950 he decided to join the construction of the Youth Dam. He was so keen to volunteer he pretended he was over sixteen, and since I was soon to be of age, he brought me an application form from a recruiting officer at the National Committee. I smiled and shook my head, planning to throw it out when no one was looking.

But Father took it from my hand.

"Look, Adam, we live in difficult times. We don't want people pointing fingers at us, you know we're being watched all the time. I'm sorry but you'll have to go. Otherwise people might say we're sabotaging the project."

"Out of the question!"

We argued for several days but in the end I gave in. Father assured me it would be just a month or two and I would earn some brownie points – everyone who wanted to go to university had to take part. Peter had also spent last summer as a volunteer building the Youth Railway. I gritted my teeth. I wanted to tell him it wasn't me who had messed up that bloody abortion, it wasn't me who'd been imprisoned, so all this nonsense had nothing to do with me. No one was going to suspect me of sabotage. But I thought better of it and said nothing.

So there I was at Brežany station in late February or early March 1950 with a small suitcase, waiting for a train. The steam rising from everything – the engine and the mouths of passengers – merged with the dark, leaden clouds above the station roof. My parents came to see me off. As Mother kissed me goodbye, I thought I saw a tear roll down her cheek.

I was supposed to get off in Púchov and then take a bus to Nosice. Cousin Samuel had gone ahead. No sooner had he arrived at the camp than he started walking around with a little red notebook pestering everyone about not meeting their targets.

I first spotted Zuzana Kabátová when I arrived at the station, dusted in fresh snow. She was standing there in her little sheepskin coat, blowing on her hands. Her cheeks were red with the cold. I walked down the carriage looking for a seat but couldn't find a decent one.

I found her sitting alone by the window in an empty compartment and when I asked if there were any free seats (this is a question I've always found quite funny – if you have a compartment all to yourself how on earth are you going to take up every seat), she nodded and I went in. I took the seat across from her, by the door.

Neither of us said anything for a long time. She watched the countryside roll by and seemed lost in thought. That gave me a chance to steal a sideways glance at her face. It was oval, framed by ginger hair, which she kept sweeping out of her face with a characteristic gesture. It was tied together at the back with a simple clip. Her nose was small and slightly retroussé, typical of some English people or northerners. A strong chin under a delicate mouth harmoniously complemented the picture. Her eyes seemed slightly sleepy but cheerful.

Her lips opened up into a radiant smile, she looked at me and I was so captivated by her warm voice that it took me a while to concentrate on what she was saying. I've suffered from this minor aberration all my life: if I hear an interesting voice I can't get enough of it. I'm a voice fetishist.

"Pardon me...?" I said.

"I've been saying..." But I stopped listening again. I was on edge, giving monosyllabic answers.

"What do you think?" she asked finally, but for the life of me I had no idea how to respond.

"Because, you see...." I was back in the fish tank. Hypnosis. A voice without words. A magnificent voice.

The beautiful, graceful Zuzana. When she got off the train I watched her walk down the platform and wave to me before disappearing in the crowd. I vaguely remembered she said something about visiting her grandma in Nové Mesto.

"See you. It was nice to chat."

I was given a pair of work trousers, a quilted jacket and a pair of boots. I had never worn clothes like that before. They made me look like an idiot. Together with other idiots who, unlike me, knew why they had come here and demonstrated a greater or lesser degree of enthusiasm, I was supposed to build barracks for future volunteers. I thought their idealism would make them more resistant to the cold but they seemed to shiver as much as I did. But it's possible that in their case this may have been from the thrill of socialist construction.

What surprised me was that the camp was guarded and nobody

223

was allowed to leave without permission. Unauthorized departure was tantamount to escape and was harshly punished, usually by expulsion and a bad cadre reference. At first I didn't understand the full meaning of this phrase but later realized that this was a form of labelling people that would remain with them for the rest of their life, just like the number tattooed on Uncle Oskar's lower arm. The magic phrase was "working-class origin". It was the holy grail. Just like membership in the SYU, the Socialist Youth Union and CPC, the Communist Party of Czechoslovakia. These six letters comprised the code that opened the door to a career.

Without them the doors remained firmly locked.

Our leaders were a duo of zealous young communists, Hrdlička and Lavrátková, fresh out of secondary school. Some other leaders were even younger than me. The person everyone feared most was Samuel, my brilliant cousin, who specialized in uncovering "dual collectives", a term covering any relations with the opposite sex, including "dating". This was strictly forbidden and anyone caught in the act would be immediately expelled from the camp and the incident noted in their cadre reference. Communism, just like Christianity, seems to have a thing about sex.

This was why boys and girls slept on hard bunks in separate barracks, each holding thirty people. We were allowed to put some straw on the bunk but that was the last thing I wanted as it immediately made my eyes water and I would start sneezing so loudly the others threatened to smother me with a pillow if I didn't stop at once.

When Uncle Rudo later asked me about the food the only thing I could remember was *bryndza,* the Slovak ewe's cheese, and jam so tough it had to be cut with a knife. It tasted like rubber. Perhaps they made a mistake and dished up chewing gum instead. The soup we got for lunch was the same every day; the only thing that varied was its colour, texture and the proportion of tiny bits of something coloured floating in it. The chef left the taste completely to our imagination. Anyone could taste whatever they felt like tasting – presumably in the spirit of communism.

Except for Sundays, every day was the same. Reveille at seven o'clock, exercise, breakfast, roll call, allocation of tasks... We worked eight hours a day.

Our job was to dig foundations in the frozen soil. One of us would wield the pickaxe and the other shovel the earth after him. Before long I had blisters on both hands and the exertions made my whole body ache. When there was no frost the whole countryside dissolved into slimy mud. My shoes were filled with mud, my face was caked in mud, there was mud all over my body.

While outside it was mostly bitterly cold, our barracks were heated by a small white-hot stove. The omnipresent whiff of sweaty unwashed bodies smothered everything like a mysterious veil.

The walls were adorned with huge posters.

Protect the potato harvest from the Colorado beetle! Immediately report any sighting to the National Committee!

Men into key industries!

Another poster I quite liked showed a worker driving a steamroller as it pushed a mountain of bottles, one of which had a poisonous adder coiled around it, menacingly showing its forked tongue.

We won't let drunkenness derail the Five Year Plan!

The first time I had my face smeared with shoe polish I knew I had made it as one of the boys. The person who laughed most was Pal'o Suchý, who hailed from somewhere near Topol'čany and was as enthusiastic about our involuntary stay there as I was. The next evening he promptly asked me to accompany him on an expedition to the girls' barracks and to help him attach a condom filled with milk to their door. In the morning a furious Hrdlička burst in with my cousin Samuel and launched an investigation into who was responsible for this outrage. But they never got to the bottom of it.

The first thing I learned here was to retreat into myself while working. I perfected this art to the degree that I was able to conduct a conversation while in this state. I turned into a zombie who had allowed himself to be carried away and now couldn't understand what was the point of all this building and exceeding quotas at all costs, and destroying the beautiful countryside around the river Váh in the process – the old willows, the wetlands and birds' nests. I was surrounded by people who radiated happiness, longing to "change life on earth" and blabbering about electricity and "harnessing the element water". Some claimed that in the Soviet Union they had managed to reverse the flow of a river, inadvertently causing a large lake to dry out.

Our only entertainment was provided by cultural evenings.

Before the main programme started, Hrdlička and Lavrátková would assess our work performance, announcing which crew was the best at meeting the targets and handing out Stakhanovite badges and the camp flag to the winners, whom we were expected to applaud.

When everyone took a seat at the clubhouse a budding actor recited poems by Vítězslav Nezval in a fine resonant voice (back then he had just finished school; these days I often see him on TV and imagine he would rather not be reminded of this episode). Nezval's most recent poem was simply entitled *Stalin*, subtitled *A Poem for the 70th birthday of Field Marshal Joseph Vissarionovich Stalin*.

> *That land where every season reigns at once,*
> *That land where snow falls as the roses bloom,*
> *There boil-covered Jobs did once confront*
> *A life they lived in despair and gloom.*
> *In Minsk, in Kiev they lived in shame and loss,*
> *In Moscow too and, stained, in Gori,*
> *Where like Jesus upon the cross*
> *The Caucasus spreads its limbs in glory.*
> *And there towers above every throne*
> *A shining light of adoration:*
> *The God of the Dollar, Pound, and Crown*
> *Playing pool with all creation.*

I had never read poetry before, let alone heard it read aloud, and found this so stirring – in part perhaps because the rendition made the barracks walls shake – that I learned a few stanzas by heart.

The young thespian took a deep breath and reeled off the next poem, this time in my native Slovak:

> *Over yonder, by Spasskaya Tower,*
> *Where time counts out the astral hour,*
> *It's history's time, breaking bars of iron.*
> *Over yonder, by Spasskaya Tower,*
> *Our thoughts reach out to you, our*
> *Leader, called by the bell's pure clarion.*
> *Where man's muscles try to seize*

Unruly Nature by its sleeves,
Where the leading pioneer lands,
Where roll and toss the taurine seas:
There our culture's beacon gleams,
That's where Father Stalin stands.

When he got to the "pure clarion" I noticed a dark-haired girl sitting in the first row: "culture's beacon" revealed her breasts which, under the brushed cotton shirt, resembled freshly picked apples (I only caught a sideways glimpse but that was enough to impress me) and by "the Party badge on the coat" in the next stanza I could no longer concentrate on the poem as I couldn't get the girl out of my mind. It was as if we were the only two people in the room.

As the Komsomol activist Hedviga Lavrátková showed her appreciation of the performance by clapping vigorously, and launched into an analysis of the poem with revolutionary zeal, I tried to inch closer to the girl.

"Ján Kostra's poem *To Stalin* was inspired by the solemn occasion of Joseph Stalin's seventieth birthday. The work begins at the time when Europe is in the throes of fighting Hitler's Germany. But the Soviet army comes to the rescue, forever sealing the fate of the pirate flag through the glorious victory at Stalingrad. In this historical period Stalin plays the role of leader and theoretician, simultaneously putting theory into practice. That is what enabled his army, inspired by the teachings of Marxism-Leninism, to advance victoriously to its glorious goal. However, at the same time, he continues to steer our ship and watch over our freedom!"

I asked Pal'o Suchý to swap seats with me so that I could sit right behind her, taking deep breaths of her mysterious fragrance. I found myself getting turned on and spinning wild fantasies, rehearsing in my mind every kind of scenario that my adolescent imagination could come up with. Meanwhile Hedviga went on with her speech intended to boost our revolutionary zeal. Pal'o just shook his head as he noticed that something was stirring in my nether regions. He later admitted he ascribed my obvious erection to Hedviga's lecture.

"Under Stalin's leadership the living standards of the working people have improved and the entire country has been overcome with unbridled enthusiasm for socialist construction. In place of infertile deserts there are now vast processing plants and thriving cooperative farms. For all this the Soviet people are profoundly grateful to their leader, comrade Stalin, the genius who has transformed the vast Soviet lands into a socialist country! Stalin has been hardened by a life in battle. That's what has predestined him to be a leader, organizer and teacher of the working classes. He is a far-sighted and bold commander who leads us into battle against the onslaught of the enemy!

The poet concludes by describing how our beloved Stalin unleashes the creative forces of this great historic era, inextricably linked with his name. Kostra's poem is not just a tribute to Stalin; it also demonstrates a profound understanding of Stalin's personality and his achievements. It is a work of great poetic power and a declaration of faith in the future!"

Hedviga's presentation was followed by thunderous applause. Everyone rose to their feet. I managed to stand only with great difficulty, blushing and with uncontrollably wobbling legs, as my revolutionary zeal was by now all too evident. I tried to cover it with my cap and forced myself to think of something else. Something totally, totally different.

I strained to remember a poem I had discovered in an old copy of the Slovák newspaper from 1938, written by the same, yet very different Ján Kostra. The poem was entitled "14 March" – the day the Nazi puppet Slovak state was founded. It went like this:

A gaze proudly raised from ignominy flutters among the flags, / hearts like fists, hearts make church bells ring in the steeples, / Too unworthy to cheer I lose myself in the throng / Swept along by the deluge I pass shattered gates / Long shadows of scaffolds flee before us / Come along, come along, To arms, to arms…

And I said to myself (with my member sagging as normality started to return) – this guy is a real pro! He's a dab hand at strong words.

We had to attend regular meetings where we analysed various "relevant events of the day".

Hedviga Lavrátková informed us that a Slovak translation of a work by Maxim Gorky, dedicated to Vladimir Ilyich, was in preparation. Its first line read: *Lenin is dead.*

"Can a book containing such text be published in socialist Czechoslovakia at all? Lenin is dead. Doesn't it sound sacrilegious?", she demanded to know.

Lavrátková and Hrdlička penned a joint open letter to the Soviet Book Publishing House and made us all sign it.

By April morale was beginning to flag alarmingly. People in the nearby villages were not keen on the construction and kept making trouble. They would gather outside the gates, shouting abuse and threats.

"You'll pay for this one day!" a voice yelled from the crowd.

Someone broke Hrdlička's nose. They must have known red was his favourite colour.

In response one of the camp leaders ordered everyone to march to the nearby village of Nosice. To give speeches and to campaign.

Somehow I managed to get out of it and stay in the camp. I needed a rest. After a little nap I stared out of the window at the grey, messed-up landscape.

I noticed that the lights in the girls' barracks were on.

I got up and fished out a coin, my heart pounding. On the tails side a woman bending over a sheaf of wheat was wiping her brow gazing into the distance. I tossed her up in the air. She appeared again on the back of my hand.

I'm going!

I knocked and on hearing someone answer, opened the door.

The dark-haired girl with breathtaking breasts, whom I had admired during the evening of Stalinist poetry, was sitting on a bunk with her back against the wall, a book on propped up on her drawn-up knees.

I was sure I would faint.

"What are you reading?" I managed to stammer out in a choked voice. It sounded as if I'd been caught in the middle of town wearing women's clothes.

"Holan."

"I see…"

"Poetry. Poems," she added by way of explanation. She glanced at me and returned to her book.

"I know a poem, too:

As the ploughman with his oxen wends his way,
as the woodsman stores his pile of wood away

229

so our Stalin's solemn oath does mark
as he stands by Lenin's catafalque:
To you, our Lenin, do we truly swear
To you whose spirit for us all does care,
That we shall for ever more fulfil
This your commandment and your will.

"That's bullshit!" she interrupted me.

"But it's Nezval."

"Rubbish!"

I gave her a sheepish look and didn't move.

"Let me show you some real poetry! Come over here…!" She patted the place next to her. I approached her timidly and sat down.

"Take a look at this!"

She pointed to the middle of the page and started moving her finger along the lines. My eyes followed obediently.

The poem was about lamps swaying above a garden restaurant and the people below. I surrendered to the rhythm: *We're swaying, we're rocking to and fro, like graceful flowers we glow…*

Before we knew it we were kissing. I didn't even have time to ask her name – not that it mattered at that moment.

Clumsily I reached between her legs. She was moist and velvety, with a bush of pubic hair! We tore our clothes off. Her breasts, her naked breasts swayed to and fro like the arched lamps in the poem. I couldn't stop looking at them. Not quite sure what I was supposed to do, I planted myself on top of her and tried to penetrate her. She just shook her head and pushed me away.

Rummaging in the beside table she produced a condom. I lay on the bed, half-naked, watching her. She unwrapped it, blew it open and gently rolled it on me.

"My father is a gynaecologist, a specialist in venereal diseases," she said, as if by way of explanation.

I still remember that my mouth was dry, my eyes were popping and my heart was pounding so loud I was sure it was echoing around the building. She calmed me by caressing my face and pressing my eyelids down as you do to the dead, then gently placed my head on the bed and sat on top. It all seemed surprisingly natural. The sensation was quite overwhelming.

And so, unexpectedly, what I had spent long nights dreaming

about and mulling over in my father's medical books, I ended up experiencing under the light of a newly-installed flickering light bulb rhythmically swaying to and fro. Our bodies would plunge into darkness and then emerge again into the light, their flickering at one with our rhythm. *We're swaying, we're rocking to and fro, like graceful flowers we glow…*

And right at the end I heard a booming chorus sing out:

"*Where the axe rings out today, tomorrow will the turbine roar …!*

Pure joy flooded my body. Then I realised that the chorus wasn't in my head but coming from outside. The Stakhanovites were coming back from the village. I could distinctly hear Samuel's voice, which seemed to resonate above everyone else's.

"What's your name?"

"Adam."

"Nice to meet you. Eva."

And suddenly I recalled:

Disguised as a serpent he said to Eve: – Why did God forbid you to eat from any tree of the Garden of Eden? – And she replied – From the fruit of the trees of the garden we may eat; but from the fruit of the tree which is in the middle of the garden, God has said, 'You shall not eat from it or touch it, or you will die.' – And the serpent said to the woman: – You surely will not die! For God knows that in the day you eat from it your eyes will be opened, and you will be like God, knowing good and evil. When the woman saw that the tree was good for food, and that it was a delight to the eyes, she took from its fruit and ate; and she gave also to her husband, and he ate. So this is was how I came to regard sex as a wonderful socialist achievement.

I'm a socialist and don't need Matthew 5: 28 to stick its oar in: *But I say to you that everyone who looks at a woman with lust for her has already committed adultery with her in his heart.*

I didn't feel at all guilty for having too fertile an imagination. Socialist man is free to enjoy his own body and those of others whenever and however he fancies, without any guilt.

During the regular criticism and self-criticism sessions everyone was expected to confess their sins and misdemeanours, just like they used to confess their sins to the priest in the confessional, except now we had to do it in public. Eva and I just glanced at each other and smiled, and it seemed to me as if everyone else could tell by looking at us but they didn't – so when it was my turn, I admitted to…. And

231

then, some time later, she also got up with a contrite smile and admitted to... Then we both kept quiet and listened and kept smiling and giving each other a wink from time to time. What a wonderful criticism and self-criticism session that was. I often recalled it – the two of us against the world. The two of us and the world.

When it was finally time to leave it rained incessantly. I stood on a hillock sadly surveying the enormous sea of mud and sludge stretching all the way to the river Váh. I saw a brook flanked by willows and poplars. The excavators were fast approaching and the blows of the axe sounded like a drummer trying unsuccessfully to tune into the right rhythm of some hackneyed song.

A blue flag fluttered over the camp. Our session was coming to an end.

– *Hail labour, peace to the world!* – sighed Eva on the sweat-soaked blanket and fell asleep almost immediately, her naked breasts spilling out like two mounds of jelly that had been left on the table for too long. I watched her until darkness fell. Then I got dressed and slowly made off.

I was holding the book I received from comrade Hrdlička in recognition of my hard work at the farewell ceremony (on my last day I noticed that his longed-for moustache had finally started to sprout), Julius Fučík's *Notes from the Gallows*. An untrained eye might have found it hard to tell the difference between this and a beautiful Christian hymnal bound in black leather – its back was even embossed with something resembling, from a distance, the biblical tablets with the Ten Commandments that Moses received from the Almighty. On the inside the book was the spitting image of a Catholic missal, with its division into chapters, dark red uncials and headings, only the text seemed different. But again, only at first sight because the content was almost identical. Julius Fučík had long been beatified, indeed declared a communist saint par excellence – the man ticked all the boxes, having also endured brutal torture and held on to his faith, which is why he had to die a martyr's death in a Nazi prison. And his book had become holy writ. Just another variation on the worship of a symbolic corpse. The more brutal the sadistic excesses endured, the purer his soul, and the more convincing his sacrifice. Few communist saints could boast this – even though many may have longed to die a brutal, martyr's death.

People are animals who need flesh and blood, that's what makes them capable of believing anything.

Such were my thoughts on the train journey from Púchov back to Brežany. The woman sitting opposite gave me a conspiratorial smile – she was quietly telling her beads and because of Fučík's book took me for a brother in suffering, admiring my courage in those harsh times. Just to be on the safe side, she held her small silver cross well concealed in her folded palm as she let the tiny wooden balls pass inconspicuously through her fingers.

The poor woman, she never knew how wrong she was about me.

Meanwhile clouds drifted casually past and the sun shone on the fields that didn't care who would eat the bread made of the wheat they would bear.

13.

It strikes me that back in Balzac's day you could still write: The events described in this book took place in Paris in the year 18.. In his day and age the pace of life was slower, a particular day, month or year was very much like another, and the writer could leave it to the reader to fill in the exact date. People walked or travelled on horseback. There were no telegrams or telephone calls. When you wrote a letter it took a week to receive a reply.

A contemporary author can't write something like: The events described in this book took place in Brežany in the year 19..

When exactly, dammit!, the reader would scream. Was it in 1914? Or in 1922? Or did it happen in 1947 or 1949? Or 1988? Well...?

While I was away, Puškár's patisserie was nationalized. He had no idea why or even that such a thing was possible. It was his baby, he had built it with his own hands. These things were happening all over the place but surely not to HIS patisserie...?

Puškár refused to believe it. One day he owned everything and the next day he had nothing. All because of a piece of paper. He was furious and ranted that this was a revolution brought about by a bunch of layabouts who had never done a day's work in their lives, which was why they were jealous of everything other people had achieved through their hard work, and were determined to rob them at all costs. And things like that. He shouted a lot, whether he was sober or drunk, and for the second time in a short period he came to lose his sense of humour.

He wanted to protect his property and call to account those who had invented this nonsense. Yes, Jesus Christ had also called for everything to belong to everyone but he had never taken anything away from people. That's what he shouted too. Puškár wanted to find the self-proclaimed Jesus, the God who wanted to appropriate something that belonged to him alone but all he achieved was to get himself locked up as a speculator and profiteer. He spent a year contributing to the common good of mankind somewhere in central Slovakia. He was sent to toil in a quarry and we never learned what exactly he'd been through – he wouldn't discuss it when he came back – but it left him with a limp for the rest of his life.

He said the only thing that had kept him alive was the thought of Lila, the beautiful and sublime, whom he had never met and who had once, in the good old days (I quote) written him wonderfully affectionate letters before escaping to South America after the war. Not a day passed without him expecting that a letter would come from her. Or, better still, expecting to find her on his doorstep with her suitcase.

He spent all his free time gazing at the photograph showing her blurred and faded image in all its consumptive glory. Slender, beautiful, and inaccessible.

Oh well. *Cherchez la femme.*

Cherchez la femme… indeed.

Mrs Natália Roško browsed through her dream book until she found what she was looking for: Seeing a Jew – good fortune. She kept dreaming of Jews although there weren't many left in Brežany. In Prague, on the other hand, they seemed to be everywhere.

Major Vojtech Roško was assigned to the Ministry of Defence. His red star was very much in the ascendant. Everyone in his family enjoyed the generously proportioned flat in Dejvice, especially Vojto and his younger brother Teo.

Air Force Major Vojtech Roško demonstrates a positive attitude to the democratic people's regime of our country. He supports the progress of our people's revolution and zealously promotes its achievements, such as the land reform, nationalisation and the new constitution. Signed: Commander of the 4th Air Force Division, Air Force Colonel Julius Trnka. Such was the reputation he enjoyed.

Mrs Roško was in charge of the household and "representation", as she herself used to put it. Since in those days everyone had to have a job, for the sake of appearances she signed up to train as a nurse. She didn't need to do the cooking, having hired a cook who had access to the military's generous supplies of meat and milk, while ordinary mortals were obliged to enjoy the austere regimen of rationing.

Her visitors' book was filling up with prominent trophies. Her most treasured autograph belonged to the Prime Minister, former railwayman comrade Viliam Široký, who was in her good books even though he once spilled some French brandy at a party, because he kissed her hand every time they met, an indication that he might be interested in a meeting *à deux*. And he was quite good looking, although he didn't speak any French at all. He wasn't terribly fluent in Slovak and Czech either. At least in Mrs Roško's view.

She kept all the invitations to official parties, air shows and grand balls lovingly in a special box that once contained Lindt & Sprüngli pralines.

The first letter from Vojto came as early as April 1950, covered in his tiny, nervous handwriting and a stain left by Malcao, the new cocoa drink he loved to distraction. It gave a higgledy-piggledy account of everything and anything that happened to cross his mind.

The nearest place to Dejvice where we live is Letná, a sort of huge park or, rather, a garden. I often take a walk there and watch the world go by. What struck me was that dogs channel their owners' feelings before they are even aware of them themselves. Mum has bought a poodle named Míla. The other day she was taking ages getting dressed for the opera, it took her two hours, and we were running late. Father was waiting in the kitchen, he was livid and his headache came back, but she wasn't in the least bothered. But Míla kept barking and Mum said, "Why is the dog so restless? You ought to take it for a walk!" By the way, we were going to the National Theatre to see Eugene Onegin. Tchaikovsky. Fabulous. Seriously, it doesn't really compare to football or ice hockey. When people leave the opera they sip champagne and don't feel the need to smash in other people's heads or shop windows with beer bottles.

During the interval dad met a Czech colleague of his who said that the Slovaks are a truly heroic nation. Dad said he agreed but wanted to know what made him say that. The man said that 26,000 people fought in the Slovak National Uprising, yet 52,000 people were now on the 255 (oh, you won't know what 255 is – it's an official certificate of participation in the Uprising). The Czech thought this was very funny. Father didn't know what to say but later he told Mum that people would sign the certificates for each other and testify that they had fought in the same partisan unit. He said if all of them had really taken part in the fighting we would have had the Germans on their knees in no time.

Never mind. Back to school, homework. My classmates in seventh grade are all children of my father's colleagues, officers and diplomats, all bigwigs. They pretend they've never been to the loo.

Regards to your family, Adam!

Vojto

Mrs Natália Roško considered herself a staunch and faithful Catholic (in spite of having a soft spot for a variety of quacks). At least in Brežany. Her home turf.

With a pious expression she would make the sign of the cross on her children's (and later also grandchildren's) foreheads. In church she had a regular pew. At home she had her very own private kneeling bench by her bedside. Mind you, whenever I came to see Vojto, it was covered with corsets and knickers. While getting ready for Sunday lunch she used a large crucifix – or rather the arms of Jesus Christ, which were particularly suited to this purpose – to hang her bras and slips on. Once dressed, she would make a dignified entry into the dining room. Everyone had to say a prayer and cross themselves before lunch; she saw to this herself, in person or via her huge portrait, commissioned from a local artist. Her eyes in the picture followed you round the room wherever you went, a fact she was particularly proud of, and never tired of pointing it out.

But now she had to keep her religious beliefs secret. When visitors were due, she would hide the crucifix under a pile of jumpers in the wardrobe. Or somewhere among her Persian lamb and black fox furs.

Before the war, when her uncle died of a heart attack, she took several hours to decide which fur coat to wear to his funeral. The uncle's body had been displayed in all his finery. His nose became thinner and thinner, gradually acquiring a strange purple hue as he lay in state surrounded by sundry relatives. Meanwhile Mrs Roško was trying on her fur coats.

"Which one suits me better?" she shouted into the living room.

Mila's late predecessor Letov just barked restlessly.

Hello, Adam!

Blanka said I have a lovely voice. Sort of deep and sonorous. I guess I forgot to mention this girl, Blanka, in my last letter. If only she'd heard me before my voice broke! Do you remember how old Mislovič said that Ambi Krebs had a "peristaltic" voice? And you asked what the word peristaltic was supposed to mean? And Mislovič said: "Young man, it means that women wet themselves when they hear it!"

I've got a bit of a cold so I went to see a doctor yesterday. He prescribed something but didn't let me off school. This strange woman was sitting next to me in the waiting room. She gave off something very weird. It was like something from the underworld, a kind of strange perfume or something. A bit like chrysanthemums or damp earth, I'm not sure. Anyway, she asked whose turn it was and we got talking. Her husband had been hanged as a traitor six months ago. He was a soldier, a general, who had served in England and Moscow during the war. But she said she couldn't talk about that.

Since you're into collecting unusual words, I've got a new one for you: "vidmo", or glory. A classmate of mine who comes from Mýto under Mount Ďumbier told me about it. He says it's a phenomenon that can only be observed in the mountains – when the sun is low behind you and you see your own huge shadow reflected in the fog or in the clouds.

Apparently some scientists have calculated that a day lasts exactly 23 hours plus 93 hundredths of an hour. That means that a whole four minutes are lost somewhere every day. And nobody knows where exactly they disappear. It's precisely these minutes I'm always short of.

I'm going on a date with Šárka, there's too much going on…We're off to Letná, to take a look at the new pedestal for Stalin's statue they're building there. I've heard that Masaryk was supposed to have a statue there, designed by the same architect. It's a lovely spot, right above the Vltava. It overlooks the Svatopluk Čech bridge and there's a fantastic view of the

237

whole city. Stalin will be 15 ½ metres tall and the whole statue will be 22
metres. The papers say it will be the largest sculptural group in Europe. Bye
for now!

Vojto

On 9 May 1950 Lieutenant colonel Roško gave the opening speech
at the military pilots' ball at Waldstein Palace:

Dear guests, dear comrades!

On behalf of the entire 6th Air Regiment please allow me to express our
gratitude to the staff of the trade union of the ČKD engineering plant in
Prague for taking on the patronage of our unit. We pledge that we will never
cease to defend the interests of the working people – the interests of peace.
This pledge is all the more solemn because I am making it, on behalf of
our regiment, at this very moment, when our glorious celebrations are linked
to the 5th anniversary of our victory over Germany.

May the ties between the army and the working people flourish and
continue to grow stronger, following the example of our great ally the Soviet
Union and in the spirit of our great teachers Marx, Lenin and Stalin!

Specially for this occasion, Mrs Natália Roško had a ball gown
made to measure at the Klasik Elegant fashion salon. The
resplendent green dress with a deep décolleté was complemented
by a pair of elbow-length black gloves.

Everything went well until the first round of dances, when she
noticed something that gave her a grievous nervous shock (in her
own words), forcing her to leave the ball immediately. The staff
commander's wife was wearing the same dress! After this
outrageous incident Natália Roško stopped receiving guests for a
full week, Vojto told me in a letter.

Soon afterwards, a devastated Mrs Roško left for her annual
holiday in Karlovy Vary. As usual, she spent a few weeks there
accompanied by several friends, officers' wives. They had sent their
luggage ahead by train. Her bags would arrive back home first and
she would turn up later, refreshed and with many stories to tell (or
to keep discreetly to herself).

On one of the first occasions when she met her daughter-in-law
– Vojto's first wife – she warned her that she would never let her go
to a health resort. She must have had her reasons.

The swifts had just started to build their nests in Dejvice and juicy black cherries were beginning to ripen in Ambi Krebs's derelict botanical garden in sleepy, sun-drenched Brežany, when a live radio broadcast broke the silence in the hot summer air:

Thousands of responses from all walks of life have reached this court to voice the great outrage of our working people at the disgraceful conduct of the defendants! The defendant Horáková recruited criminal gangs whose goal was to destroy our Republic, while our Stakhanovites in the Jihlava steelworks toiled to meet 159 per cent of their gruelling targets!

14.

My sister Tina recently reminded me of the smell that used to permeate our house in Brežany.

Mother used metal curling tongs. She would stick the gadget into the flames or directly onto the red-hot stove to heat it up. Then she curled her hair. The temperature of the tongs could not be regulated, and as a result her hair gave off a slightly burnt smell. We could tell from afar whenever Mother was doing her hair in the kitchen.

Now a similar fragrance is carried on the wind from the distance. Somebody must be burning spring grass. Or is it rubber? I go out into the neglected garden for a breath of fresh air. I can't get those wretched bones out of my head. Although it ceased to matter a long time ago.

After much hesitation and procrastination I finally spilled the beans to Igor.

I said to myself – the bones are old, the issue must be beyond the statute of limitations, Father is dead. (Mind you, who said it was Father who did it? But on the other hand – who else could have done it? It's hard to imagine anything happening in the house or in the garden without his knowledge.) I told him I suspected that it had something to do with the war, the passing of the front, or something of the sort.

Igor brought his whole crew along. He kept stuffing himself with biscuits and sweets while they worked. He unwrapped another chocolate bar and came up to me, noticing my curious look.

"Do you know what American Indians call the brain?"

"The brain? No, I don't."

"The one that devours sugar."

I laughed.

"When I work I have to eat something sweet. It helps me think. Other people smoke cigarettes for the same reason."

He and his colleagues took pictures of the whole scene, made drawings of the exact position of the skeleton, even though I had moved it a bit, which they didn't appreciate. Working gingerly, they dug out individual bones, cleaned them with soft brushes, left them to dry, wrapped them individually in paper and carefully placed them in a padded box. They coated the bones they considered too fragile in a thin layer of paraffin. They paid special attention to the skull. Now only the face, filled with soil, protruded from the earth. Parts of it had cracked along the seams. The skull was also carefully placed in a box next to the other bones.

Finally they dug up the grave and sifted the dry soil. Chewing on a coconut bar, Igor explained that this way you could find some vertebrae and bones from the hands and feet. And teeth.

They discovered tiny scraps of clothing and the odd button. Finally they took a few soil samples, to help estimate the time of decomposition. Because the body decomposes at different rates in different types of soil.

"But I'm not holding my breath about the wartime scenario," he said. "I don't think it's that old. Anyway, we'll soon find out."

They packed up and left.

I must have been barking up the wrong tree with my list, like a young hunting dog. Perhaps it all happened later, much later. After Ďuratný appeared in Father's life.

Yes, I did look for him, checked the nameplates on doors after finding his address in the phone directory, but found that only his widow lived there. He was dead. She refused to say any more. Could he be the one buried in the shallow grave?

Ďuratný …? Names, names, names…

Father often mentioned a recurrent dream he had.

His nursery, which is on the first floor of our house, is immersed in darkness. He is still a little boy, sitting on the bed and looking out of the window at the street below. Shadows flicker on the wall behind him but when he turns around there's nothing there.

And then, suddenly, a huge face appears in the window – an enormous figure is peering in, a sneer on its face. Its feet are down in the garden. Its nose is pressed against the glass and it is looking for the child in the dark. Father tries to hide but the eyes keep following him. The fat, grinning face fills the entire window. The wardrobe is full of stuff, the bed is too low – Father knows he can't hide under it. He starts to scream.

He would always wake up with his heart pounding. There was nothing outside.

Whenever I try to visualise my Father's isolation cell, what I see in my mind's eye is a battered white table fan – on muggy days its four blades would make ripples in the air as if it was water, generating a draught, making a high-pitched buzz as it swivelled to and fro. And I see Father's grey radio, actually just one big oddly-shaped loudspeaker, which filled the air with crackling noises.

*Stella. When the stars shine above the Adriatic… Only once, Stella, did I taste the sweetness of your kisses… Without you I shall never be happy…
!* – came the plaintive tango fittingly accompanied by a syrupy orchestra.

In the afternoons Father would stretch out on the bed to rest, trying, unsuccessfully, not to fall asleep. Whenever someone happened to come in, he would start up firmly and say:

"I'm not asleep." Or he would mumble in his sleep: "I've got everything under control…!"

I often walked in on him just to hear that. It always made me laugh.

"I've got everything under control…!"

And then, all of a sudden, the big black telephone rang. Father usually tried to guess from the sound of the ringing who was at the other end and sometimes I also seemed to make out different kinds of ringing. A louder and more persistent ringing announced a restless patient, say a case of appendicitis, while a somewhat lower and softer tone might have indicated a young mother who just needed to be reassured that baby's temperature wasn't anything to worry about, and the even softer, calmer, more drawn-out tone was old Mrs Krebs, who wanted to consult Mother about her recipe for pound cake.

Father walked over to the desk but this time he didn't have a clue. He picked up the receiver.

"Dr Trnovský speaking!" he said as usual.

It was only many years later that I learned, from old files and various documents fallen victim to the sun, dust, humidity or simply the ravages of time and memory, what actually happened after he picked up the receiver on that warm autumn day. I have gradually gathered the pieces of the puzzle until at some point they started to fall into place because before that I often found Father's behaviour absurd, puzzling and unpredictable. He was moody, absent-minded, inscrutable and suspicious of everyone in that perfectly symmetrical year of 1950, another of those perfectly symmetrical years that lay in store.

A voice at the other end of the receiver curtly conveyed a few simple facts. At first it seemed like a casual conversation and it wasn't until it was over that Father realized what it was really about.

Then he received an official summons to report to the local office of the ŠtB, the State Security police, located in an anonymous grey building tucked away in a cul-de-sac next to the police headquarters. He was to report within five days, inform his superiors of the reasons for his absence and ask to be relieved of work on the said date.

As he was still his own boss, Father just told Nurse Zdenka that he wouldn't be in his surgery next morning. He put on his best suit, the one he wore to funerals, and set off, without any idea of what it was all about. These kinds of documents never give away more than absolutely necessary.

I picture him walking down the corridor looking for room 24 and almost colliding with the runt-like Gajdoš. The former guardsman greets him formally – he's wearing a uniform, not of a high rank, and Father is probably unable to conceal his amazement. He follows him for a while and since they have stopped outside room

24 (which is only one room down from where his temporary consulting room used to be), he knocks on the door. A brusque *Enter!* comes from within. Behind the desk sits a State Security officer, Captain Ďuratný, whose mucous membranes Father had become intimately acquainted with five years earlier due to the anaphylactic shock brought on by the Hungarian Tokay wine.

There is another man in the room, standing with his back to Father, who has just fetched some papers from the archive. He turns around to say hello and Father recognizes Papír. The drummer of the Brežany brass band and famous entertainer, the man who can't stand *heroisches deutsches Blut*, heroic German blood.

Captain Ďuratný has a strange habit. At the beginning of every meeting or interrogation session he takes from his drawer a blank sheet of paper and places it on the desk. As if he were about to take notes. But instead he just tears off tiny bits of the paper and puts them in his mouth. In the course of the encounter the sheet of paper disappears – as a matter of fact, the meeting is over when he places the last bit on his tongue and chews it up.

Father told me about this years later, adding that Ďuratný evidently suffered from vitamin deficiency. A weird reason.

So Captain Ďuratný takes a blank sheet of paper from the drawer.

"Good morning doctor! Come in and take a seat. This is just a formality."

He stands up, putting his hand on Father's shoulder in what might pass for a friendly gesture, and shows him to a seat opposite his heavy wooden desk. Father sits down and Ďuratný returns to his place behind the desk piled high with files and reports.

Father asks: "So how's your good lady wife?"

"Thank you, she's much better. The labour was quite tough, but she's going to be all right."

The officer leafs through what is presumably Father's file, taps a pencil on his knee and rip! – tears off a little piece of paper. He has a tic in his left eye – I have noticed it as well, when I saw him and Father chatting across the garden fence like two old friends.

"Member of the Agrarian Party before the war. Member of Hlinka's Slovak People's Party during the war. Rather convenient, wouldn't you say? Joined the Communist Party of Czechoslovakia after February 1948 – not too active – an undistinguished rank-and-file member. Quite a chequered past. Any comments, comrade doctor?"

He's looking at Father.

"Sorry, what did you say?"

"Well, what do you have to say to this, comrade doctor?" says Ďuratný, raising his voice.

Father shrugs.

"Now I understand where my allegiance should lie."

"I see. But that's not all," Ďuratný says with a mysterious air.

Father is visibly startled. Until this point the threat had not felt serious, just a bit of intimidation, although he had no idea what had prompted it.

The officer pushes a piece of paper in his direction. Father examines it and the characters on the page begin to blur. It still hasn't dawned on him. Ďuratný picks up the paper.

"Let me just read you this bit: *Fully aware of the above facts I truthfully declare that the Jew Armin Blau is not needed in the hairdressing salon at no. 49, Svätopluk Street, Brežany, which I have Aryanized. The operations of the salon will not suffer as a result of the above Jew's detention and transportation, nor will this be to the detriment to the economy of the Slovak Republic. I have found a replacement, the Aryan...* And so on, and so forth... Well?"

Father stares at him in surprise. He recognizes the piece of paper, that's for sure. But Ďuratný's voice sounds as if it were coming from next door. He doesn't understand what's happening to him. He's starting to feel hot. And the acoustics are really bad. What is the man saying?

"Did you hear what I said...?"

"Excuse me?"

"I said, did you hear what I said!"

Father remains silent.

Ďuratný continues: "Surely you don't want anyone to find out about this, do you, comrade doctor? Your wife, your children, your brother-in-law Oskar Novan..."

I had often seen Father turn his head slightly and screw up one of his eyes, which made him look as if he literally pricked up his ears, trying to sharpen them because he had trouble understanding something. A thin furrow would appear on his cheek. This is exactly what happens now.

"Do you want your wife to find out about this? We could phone her right now. Or we could call her in and show her this piece of paper right here in this office."

244

I suspect that this was something my Father did hear, although I wouldn't stake my life on it. At all events, now everything began to make sense.

I see him making a quick grab for the piece of paper. Desperate, he stuffs it into his mouth and begins to chew. He chews it up and is about to swallow it.

But Ďuratný is faster, makes a grab for him and starts hitting him. Another man, who was apparently waiting behind the door, bursts in and joins in the beating. It is Gajdoš. ("Every era needs capable men", he later told Father with a smile). Father falls to the floor. They force his mouth open and pull the paper ball (or whatever remains of it) from between his teeth and tongue. He tries to resist but doesn't stand a chance.

There's blood on Father's face. At home he tells us some nonsense about having slipped on the stairs after seeing a patient. At least, he doesn't claim banana peel was involved.

Ďuratný smoothes down his hair and tries to compose himself. He goes back behind his desk.

"We're not here to play games, comrade doctor!"

Father scrambles up from the floor and leans his head against the filing cabinet. Gajdoš takes him back to his chair.

Ďuratný continues casually: "A waste of effort. That was just a copy. I've got the original here."

He takes out another piece of paper from his desk and waves it in Father's face.

"So. What are we going to do about this?"

Father says nothing, he has no idea what should be done about it, but the existence of the document is obviously undeniable. They can show it to anyone they like whenever they feel like it without asking his permission.

"I have a proposition for you, comrade doctor."

I imagine my poor, frightened Father clutching a packet of anti-anxiety pills in his pocket. He is as pale as a sheet. He asks for a glass of water and is given one. Someone opens the window. He takes out a pill and swallows it with water. Everything seems to be taking an eternity.

This time it is Gajdoš who speaks:

"We've been to your consulting room today, comrade doctor."

He grins sarcastically.

Now I imagine secret police turning my Father's desk and card index upside down. They go through his medical notes and files. Horrified, nurse Zdenka Pavlovič stands in the doorway. There's nothing she can do; she can't even tell Father about this. The gentlemen in plain clothes have sworn her to secrecy.

"Now look what we've got here, how interesting! An impressive consumption of Luminal! Is it really without side effects, doctor?"

Father shakes his head.

"We all need something to calm us down," remarks Ďuratný, stuffing another strip of paper into his mouth. "But it's not good if it makes you fall asleep while seeing patients, as a reliable source informs us."

When Father finally returns to his consulting room, the traumatised nurse hasn't quite managed to clean up the mess the men left behind. He gives her a hand, for the waiting room is full of patients. It's the start of the flu season.

Many years later I found the following document in Father's ŠtB file. It survived the ravages of time as well as the wave of shredding.

On 15 October 1950 the recruitment of CSI (Candidate for Secret Informant) "LUMINAL", a.k.a. Alfonz Trnovský, took place in the local ŠtB superintendent's office. The informant's binding pledge was secured by ŠtB superintendent lieutenant colonel Valent, Dr Jur, and Captain Ďuratný, MSc., in line with standard procedures. In the course of the initial discussion on domestic and international political issues the CSI demonstrated a correct political outlook. He was asked to comment on whether he would be willing to provide the National Police Corps (NPC) agencies with information of the above-mentioned nature or whether he had any objections to maintaining contact with NPC officers. He responded that he understood the type of work carried out by NPC officers and was willing to take on certain tasks to the best of his abilities.

Since he had consented to cooperate, he was asked to write a declaration, in his own hand, to the effect that he was accepting the offer of cooperation. He drew up a handwritten declaration stating that he has agreed to cooperate of his own accord and that he would write reports, signing them with the code name "LUMINAL". After this he requested that his work and contacts with the NPC officers be kept strictly confidential, as exposure would deprive him of the trust of his patients and the general population of B. and would make him a social outcast. In response it was stressed that it was in the mutual interest of the parties to maintain confidentiality, and that NPC officers undertook to do this in a consistent manner. CSI LUMINAL will be handled by the deputy head of the ŠtB department, Captain Ján Ďuratný, MSc."

Father's first task was to write down everything he knew about people in his immediate circle and in Brežany in general to give the ŠtB an idea of his contacts and how they might be exploited. I have seen that report. It was laconic and straightforward.

Father typed up his first report on the Count's old Remington, which I had brought home from the manor house at the end of the war. I recognized it by its letter O, which veered slightly to the left and had a characteristic way of snuggling up to every character preceding it like a loyal little dog, except when it occurred on its own or at the beginning of a sentence.

The name of Vojto's father was one of those that cropped up several times. And so did mine, in this context. As did Vojto's father's wartime activities and the destruction of his medals. Father said he had heard about this from Captain Roško's son, who was a friend of his own son's, but didn't really believe it to be true. He said he knew very little about his patients, citing the Hippocratic oath, and that he wasn't interested in his patients' private lives in any case. He didn't know how he might be of assistance to the agency although, of course, he would do his best to try and help unmask enemies of our socialist motherland. And so on.

A jubilant captain Ďuratný added a few comments to the report. Alfonz Trnovský was held in high regard in Brežany, and as the scion of a prominent family enjoyed the trust of a wide circle of acquaintances. This confidence was further buttressed by the medical profession, his regular contact with patients making him an ideal candidate for the task in hand.

After returning home Father calmed down a bit – at least I imagine he did – like a man who, after wandering for miles through a snowstorm, spots a house with brightly lit windows and walks in. Once he has warmed his hands above the stove and has had a few spoonfuls of hot soup, the winter no longer seems so harsh (even though at first the rush of warm blood suddenly flooding back into his cold hands hurts a little). Now he'd be quite happy to go out again and continue his journey, if necessary. He looks out of the window at the beautiful snow and at the frost painting strange patterns on the windowpanes. Nothing bad has really happened. What matters is that he's alive.

In everyday life even the most treacherous acts can become routine.

16.

Doctors tend to fix everything with a plaster, just like guitar players do with guitar strings.

When Father bought his second car, thereby increasing traffic in the streets of Brežany by about ten per cent, it was soon all covered in plasters.

The splendid four-door Tatra 87 sedan resembled a beetle with shiny, hard wing-cases. I was pleased to discover that my favourite poet Vítězslav Nezval also drove one.

Peter was happier than anyone else, especially as he was sometimes allowed to drive the car, which he christened the Chevy. He was a reckless, impulsive and aggressive driver. Sometimes, when he took me for a drive around town in the evening, he would move off so fast I'd get nailed into my seat as if I was in a Formula One cockpit, and he would step on the brakes at the very last moment before reaching an obstacle (such as a traffic light). In those days safety belts were still unheard of and you had to hold on tight if you didn't want your head to hit the windshield. And since Peter would exceed hundred kilometres an hour even when the roads iced over, even the police didn't dare give chase.

On his patient rounds Father drove much more sedately and with dignity, a certain grace you might say. The car seemed to cry out for such treatment.

His private practice was closed down and he had to move his consulting room to the local health centre, where he set up as general practitioner.

Over the years he had developed a variety of effective tricks. For example, when parents brought an injured child who needed stitches – Father was loath to make things complicated by calling in a surgeon for simple cuts to the forehead, nose, lip or head – he told them to accompany their offspring and help hold them down, to teach them a lesson and ensure they took better care of them in future. He took a certain pleasure in pretending he couldn't restrain the children on his own, even with Nurse Zdenka's assistance.

Comrade Kominár, the Chairman of the local National Committee, often came to see Father. He became particularly fond of hunting – preferably deer – in the dense woods on the Volovec Mountain. It gave him such a thrill he had to take a tranquilliser at least three hours before the hunt. Father regularly gave him Hysteps, a weak barbiturate that was safe enough even to help children who couldn't sleep.

However, comrade Kominár once mixed up the packets and instead of Hysteps took Isacene, a powerful laxative. He didn't get much hunting done that day.

I passed my school-leaving exam with flying colours and managed to avoid the draft by faking a combination of high blood pressure, weak eyesight, flat feet and, last but not least, thanks to Father pulling a few strings. And although this made me something less of a man in the eyes of a few Brežany regulars, I appreciated the fact that Father's divine intervention spared me two years of military service, which was bound to have involved much crawling through mud and the hazing from the old hands. I didn't really mind that it deprived me of the chance to look back nostalgically in later years and claim that the mud was, in fact, wonderfully velvety and warm, the officers friendly and that the old hands had actually greatly contributed to my fitness and flexibility.

I still had no idea what I wanted to do with my life. Meanwhile, Vojto said in one of his last letters from Prague that he was applying to study psychology at Charles University.

And that's when it happened.

Vojto's father was discharged from the army. Nobody knew why. Most people suspected it had something to do with the baptism of his newborn daughter Ela, Vojto's little sister who, instead of bringing joy to her parents – who were no longer in their prime and hadn't really planned her (Vojto said she may have been the result of a combination of a torn condom and high spirits after an officers' ball) – gave them nothing but trouble from the minute she was born. The labour was difficult, with both Natália and Ela hovering on the brink of life and death, as the girl tried to leave her mother's womb in the breech position, forcing the obstetricians at the Central Military Hospital in Prague to resort to a Caesarean to relieve the suffering of both mother and daughter. Because of this, Natalia's Catholic family insisted that all these trials and tribulations made a christening indispensable. It would also send a signal to heaven that the baby had indeed survived.

The christening was shrouded in complete secrecy, but news of it leaked out nevertheless. It was a big mistake. Vojtech Roško should have known better and realized that having his baby christened wasn't the appropriate thing for an officer of the democratic people's armed forces, a lieutenant colonel at the National Ministry of Defence.

But maybe the key to this mystery was buried elsewhere and had something to do with the medals Vojto's father had destroyed and the Soviet pilots he had shot down. I often saw them in my dreams. Who knows if they had managed to bail out? "Things happen in wartime, I was just following orders!"

Be that as it may, the leaf eight and an ace of acorn that Mrs Roško drew from her deck of cards, certainly portended something. Something not at all good.

An express letter arrived in the post. It read:

The Ministry of National Defence, ref. no. 035157
Order
As of 30 June 1951 you are relieved of active military duty. Your current salary is suspended, and as of 1 July 1951 you are redeployed to reserve duty in line with Article 7d of regulation 86/1950 of the Military Code. Following article 13/1 of the above regulation you will no longer be entitled to military pay for inactive duty. As for your redeployment in a civilian post, please report to the regional military command at your place of permanent residence.

Prague, 19 June 1951

Minister of National Defence
signed: Army General Alexej Čepička Dr Jur.

I know from his file that Father deliberately missed his first few meetings at a safe house in Kirov Street (formerly known as St

Adalbert Street – the atmosphere of the street changed as soon as it was renamed). He claimed to have forgotten or to have been too busy. They must have done something to clip his wings, to tighten the screws or the rope or something of that kind. So eventually he went. Reluctantly, but he did.

The safe house was rented in the name of a Mr Kišš, a notorious local drunk, and its location hadn't been chosen by accident. It was right above the Tower bar. You could pretend to go for a drink and then, when nobody was looking, you'd quickly scramble up the stairs and down a narrow corridor. The door opens, you are expected. A small flat, just a few pieces of furniture, a quiet and cosy atmosphere, ideal for confidential conversations. As you leave, nobody notices anything. You've had a drink at the bar, that's all.

"Hmm, so from what you're saying, comrade doctor, your son is friends with the son of Lieutenant Colonel Vojtech Roško, currently retired."

"Well… Yes…."

"They get up to all sorts of mischief together, go swimming, have barbecues… Is that right?"

"More or less."

"Excellent."

"They're friends, that's all. They're good lads."

"I don't doubt that, comrade doctor. Lieutenant Colonel Roško is of interest to us."

"Why? He's been sacked…"

"He's been relieved of active duty! Not sacked, comrade doctor. There's a difference."

"He's now working for the State Forestry Enterprise. In Brežany."

"We are aware of that, comrade doctor."

"I don't understand…"

"It could have been much worse!"

"What do you mean?"

"He holds rather dubious views. And his past is, how shall I put it, problematic, from the point of view of our people's democratic regime. You have said as much yourself in your report."

"I've never written anything of the kind!"

"Calm down! We know what's in the file."

"He took part in the Uprising for several months."

"You keep going on about the Uprising! Anyone could say that! And what about before that? Well?"

"I don't understand."

"Oh yes, you do. Do you know him?"

"We just say hello to each other in the street."

"So you're not friends?"

"I wouldn't say so."

"Does he have a medical record with you? Have you ever treated him?"

"Not recently. I suppose he had his own doctor in Prague."

"And before that?"

"Before that... no, I never did."

"You will establish closer contact."

"Closer contact?"

"Via your son. Two fathers of two boys who are friends. Do you understand?"

"Yes, but..."

"We need you to report on his views, attitudes and contacts with other soldiers who ended up like he did. Including his contacts abroad."

"Have you gone mad? I'm the last person he would confide about with that sort of thing!"

"That's enough of your fucking excuses, comrade doctor! We have you by the balls, don't you ever forget that!"

17.

Before the war Father had passed on to Uncle Rudo his share of the vineyards on the southern slopes of the Volovec Mountain. Now Rudo had it taken away from him. Or, to be precise, party activists (including Uncle Oskar) had spent so much time persuading him to join the cooperative, and the quotas he had to hand over under the threat of fines and prosecution were so huge that he eventually gave in and joined.

But he never stopped grumbling about it. He was quite right, for in a few short years the quality of Brežany wines deteriorated so drastically that people would say with a bitter grimace: "You've got to finish the Irsay by Christmas and the Müller-Thurgau by Easter. After that it's undrinkable."

The united agricultural cooperative had been established two years earlier on Mr Katz's former lands behind the pond at Behy. Mr Poničný's erstwhile winemaking company, Vindobona, became the Brežany Winemaking Cooperative.

One day we were having a barbecue in the steep meadow at the edge of town, at the foot of the Volovec Mountain, right by the fence of Rudo's former vineyard in Dudrová:

"So why did you join then?"

Rudo dodged my question. "Not now, I'll tell you later, when I go for a pee."

I went with him. The wind was blowing from the Volovec Mountain.

"Come over here," Rudo said.

"So why did you join?" I asked him.

"Take a look at yourself. Can you piss against the wind?"

He laughed. I peed on my trousers.

"Sod it!"

"There you are!"

A whiff of smoke drifted over from the bonfire and I heard Father laughing at a joke. Uncle Rudo shook his head sadly as dusk fell enveloping the countryside in a ghostly gloom.

"Just look at the moon…!"

We stood there for a while, lost in thought, watching the orange disc that looked like a pockmarked face.

"Never mind, you will always come out on top, come what may. And so will I, and your father and mother. Everyone, all of us. All the people who live in this world."

"Why?"

"Well, when you look at it – somewhere at the beginning of your life there had to be a single sperm that managed to win out over several million others to fertilise the egg. Don't even ask how minuscule its chances were. But it did happen, however incredible it may seem. And then… We are the descendants of people who survived the Black Death, all the wars that swept across this land and all manner of other disasters and misfortunes – and yet we've managed to beget offspring. How does that make you feel?"

"I don't know."

"It makes you a winner!"

Uncle Rudo watched me for a moment, his eyes gleaming with joy.

Then he pointed towards the fire flickering in the growing darkness, and smacked his lips in happy anticipation: "Come along, there's some lovely crispy bacon waiting for us. I can smell it in the air."

That smell of grilled bacon filling the evening air was extremely precious, coming as it did from Rudo's last pig, Julinka. His neighbour, Jožko Čierny, managed to raise it for him in secret by going around and asking people for pigswill.

To make sure they didn't lose everything, people revived some of their wartime strategies. When they were about to slaughter a pig, they claimed it had died of an ailment. Then they would strangle it with a chain so that they wouldn't have to shoot it, which somebody might hear. It took several grown men and enormous effort, and the poor porker ended up squealing and groaning so desperately that anything seemed better than this solution. Sometimes the pig managed to escape. A wild pig-run through the streets of Brežany would ensue.

Julinka breathed her last in a relatively peaceful way. Nevertheless, Jožko's neighbour Čavojec noticed some commotion in the shed and reported him. By the time the comrades from the National Committee came to check if a pig had been slaughtered, all they found were a few items of indirect evidence – a tripod and a slaughtering knife with a few splatters of blood. The blood sausages had been stashed away in the larder. The comrades left without pursuing the matter further but Uncle Rudo was livid. He took a crumpled piece of paper and wrote on it: *Čavojec, go eat shit and don't tell anyone about it!* And he threw it in his neighbour's letter box.

As was to be expected, a few obstinate kulaks remained in and around Brežany, deaf to the enticements of the cooperative and spurning the joys of collective ownership. Not for them the posters declaring: *After completing the harvest and threshing the wheat in good time we are giving the state its due.* The poster showed an old man with a pipe and a hat, a heavily lined face and a moustache, with two people behind him hauling hay on a tractor with a trailer. One of them was waving cheerfully to someone in the distance.

Although nobody talked about it, it was common knowledge that Captain Ďuratný had recruited a bunch of Gypsies who lived at the edge of town in a place known as the Hole. He supplied them with cars, money and drink and asked for only one thing in return – every night after dark they were to knock on the door of an unsuspecting farmer resting after his well-deserved evening meal, and rough him up, breaking the odd window here, ransacking a barn there, trashing a tractor perhaps, or digging up the man's potatoes, stealing his chickens or laming a horse… This technique gradually brought the kulaks to their senses. Ďuratný was determined to make them see the light, even if it meant killing them. Which did happen now and then.

The harvest was certainly completed in short order.

Years later Uncle Rudo showed me something he had found in the estate of Jožko Čierny, who had joined the cooperative as a combine-harvester driver.

Only the cover was left of what had once been a fine red membership booklet embossed in yellow with "Association of Cooperative Farmers" (*Dear comrade! United agricultural cooperatives are social organisations and production units that play a key role in securing our nation's nutrition. Hand in hand with the growing tasks of our national economy, the tasks and the significance of the cooperatives' membership are also increasing. In line with the resolution adopted at the cooperative meeting, its members have joined the Association of Cooperative Farmers – a national social organisation affiliated to the National Front. If this certificate is lost, damaged or destroyed, or your personal details change, this must be reported to your cooperative officials.*) The cover now contained a brochure of the same size and even the same length – *Celestial Flowers*, compiled by J. P. Kysucký, 15th Edition, with an introduction that read: *Divine grace will accompany you on your journey through life if you pray regularly. May you take heart from the Slovak proverb "He who keeps to the path of the Lord shall not be abandoned by Him until the end of his days."* The brochure featured *Prayers every good Catholic must know by heart. Praise be to Jesus Christ. Amen.*

For the Roško family the return to Brežany was like being driven from paradise. Their earlier life now seemed like a fanciful dream. Mrs Roško no longer had to hide her crucifix under her fur coats – not least because she had been forced to sell them. The house remained eerily quiet; sometimes it seemed uninhabited, as if everyone living there had turned into a ghost. They barely spoke to one another.

The books they brought back from Prague included Kostra's poem *To Stalin*. It was a gift Vojto's father received to mark his promotion to lieutenant colonel.

Where man's muscles try to seize / Unruly Nature by its sleeves, / Where the leading pioneer lands, / Where roll and toss the taurine seas: / There our culture's beacon gleams, / That's where Father Stalin stands.

Vojto typed up these lines and sent them to prominent comrades in Brežany – party secretaries, chairmen and deputy chairmen, heads of departments and all kinds of bigwigs whose addresses he managed to collect – *Think about it, dear comrade – shouldn't this magnificent poem appear on the cover of every newspaper and journal in all the people's democracies? Please respond to this survey by post to: BREŽANY POST OFFICE, marked "The greatest man who has ever lived."*

Within a few weeks Vojto's former nursery room was inundated with replies. All those he had approached responded eagerly, outdoing each other in heaping praise on the person of Joseph Vissarionovich. Their replies were full of concern or fear that this may be just a provocation.

Vojto and I read the letters out aloud, laughing so hard Mrs Roško had to tell us off as we were distracting her from her evening prayers. We crammed all the letters into a suitcase and lugged it to the top of the hill, then over the hill to a house above Nevedovo that could be reached only by a narrow dirt road. The house had no water, sewage or electricity and in the corners still possessed remnants of Auer's filament lights, installed by the original owners. The current owner filled them with paraffin oil, when he could get hold of any, and they bathed the musty walls in a weird greenish glow.

We passed through the garden, which was hopelessly wild as the new owner didn't have a clue about how to look after it. Here and there gigantic wild kohlrabi sprouted from the ground and onions were left to blossom freely in the tall, tough grass.

The current inhabitant of the house had been exiled to this isolated spot from Bratislava as part of what was known as Action A. He was forced to leave behind a large flat in Peace Defenders' Street, which he stubbornly called by its original name, Štefánik

256

Street. His flat was immediately reassigned to someone else who had been salivating after it and who was able to pull the requisite strings.

The man, the poet Klaudius Kolár, had been labelled a class enemy and Trotskyite. Although he did have a vague idea of what that might mean, the label never stopped amazing him. His wife and children couldn't stand living in this godforsaken place and had left him after a week. Two days after their departure, in an act of desperation, Klaudius pierced the tops of all the preserve jars his predecessors had left behind in the larder, like someone who vents his fury by felling all the trees in a garden.

When he finally pulled himself together he went to the larder to check – the fact that he remembered to do so helped him realise that he was slowly recovering – and discovered that all the preserved cherries, plums, raspberries and strawberries had miraculously fermented. He decanted everything into one large container and carried it to a distillery.

He would later offer the resulting brandy to all his friends and visitors. He claimed it tasted divine and contained life in its purest form. He finally understood why the northerners called this drink the water of life. Aquavit.

As there was no fridge in the house, Klaudius Kolár preserved meat by rubbing it with salt or black pepper and, in winter, by letting it freeze outside. He would boil a pot of soup to last him a week and leave it to cool suspended in a grubby well behind the house, just above the surface of the water, where the temperature was steady. He picked up these tricks from some fellow from a nearby hamlet, on the other side of the Volovec Mountain. The man also told him that in the local dialect the metal cream jug he was about to throw out went by the endearing name of *lovíšek*, so he kept it.

Vojto knocked. A voice called from within:

"Who's there?"

"It's me. Open up!"

"Open up what?"

Vojto and I entered, laughing. We were met by an unshaven, emaciated man with tousled greying hair and translucent blue eyes. He didn't rise from the table where he was slicing mushrooms. He just put on his glasses to take a better look at us in the greenish gleam of the filament.

257

"This is my friend Adam."

"Nice to meet you."

"Hello… The person you're meeting is not me. It's my body language cheating. I mean – my body is cheating." He touched his head. "The real me is here, inside!"

He kept touching his head, in a kind of unconscious, involuntary gesture.

"I see."

"Don't take any notice of my mortal coil. It's twisted and repulsive, though not entirely. Only to the extent that it is grey and uninteresting. Glasses, greasy grey hair, all average, here today gone tomorrow. But the real me is here, living a thriving spiritual existence. Deep inside there are other worlds, colourful and rich. Right here."

He touched his head again.

"Aquavit?" he asked.

We nodded. The strong smell of alcohol emanating from him reminded me of Father's medicine cabinet.

"It's the same when you drink. It gets you either in your head or in your legs. Either you get a headache or you can't walk."

He poured some clear liquid from a sticky green bottle.

"In the village down below, in the valley that you can see from here, a little girl who lives in one of the cottages was told to keep an eye on the family dog while the rest of them went to the woods. But she didn't keep an eye on it, and the dog broke its chains and ran off. They tracked it down and brought it back home. And to teach her a lesson, they hanged the dog in front of her. I heard this from a chap who just passed through today."

"Awful!"

"Volovec is a wild place."

"So is Brežany. Just read this."

Vojto fished out a small pile of letters from the suitcase and tossed them on the table. Klaudius glanced at a few lines and roared with laughter.

"Have they all been hit on the head by a shit torpedo?"

Every now and then Mr Tóth, former owner of the Golden Stag Hotel, stopped by on his walk in the woods. The hotel had been nationalised and all he was allowed to keep was his flat on the top floor, where he could dispute with the clouds and watch May Day parades to his heart's delight. If he were able to get as far as his window, that is, for he crammed the tiny flat with all the valuable furniture from the hotel to make sure he didn't lose it. He could only get to the kitchen and bathroom by walking along narrow aisles between chairs and chests of drawers. Mr Tóth decided he would live in a maze. Whatever he wasn't able to fit into the flat he stored in the attic among the pigeons.

His space problems were partly resolved by comrades from the health and safety inspectorate. One morning they banged on his door, muttering something about birds and fire hazard that sounded almost biblical. In any case they issued an unconditional and immediate order for the attic to be cleared out completely.

Mr Tóth had no choice but to give some of his furniture away. He tried to sell some but ended up chopping up and burning most of it. Out of sheer spite. There's a price to pay when you revel in destruction. Vojto said he would never forget the smell of inlaid mahogany and cedar veneers as the hotelier chopped and sawed them up in the hotel backyard, assisted by his son Mário, who was a friend of Vojto's. During that winter he certainly had no shortage of firewood. It was a very harsh winter too. The Sálava froze over completely.

The next spring it flooded as thoroughly as only our river can.

The restaurant at the Stag Hotel never failed to respond promptly to local and world events. During the flood, the day after the Sálava's level peaked, a soup they called Deluge was added to the menu. It contained barbel, catfish, pike, gudgeon and carp and it stayed on the menu until the authorities banned it. That took approximately a day and a half but our family managed to get a taste of it. We also got to taste their Hiroshima steak – well done and tender, served on a bed of a rich mushroom sauce. That one lasted on the menu only for a day.

The restaurant later introduced Soviet-style service, championed by a certain comrade Gusev. It had supposedly proved highly successful, especially in top Moscow restaurants, as the new chef, Mr Svinický, had read in the weekly *The World of Socialism*. After giving it some thought, he put on a spanking clean suit and a white tie and donned a freshly starched chef's hat. He downed two shots of pear brandy for courage, walked into the dining room and homed in on a guest, who had just arrived. With a courteous bow, he asked how he was and if there was anything special he could prepare for him.

"Just give me the menu and a shot of gin, and leave me in peace!"

Mr Svinický turned around and went back to the kitchen and drank two more shots of pear brandy. He never repeated the experiment again. As luck would have it, the man he picked on was Mr Tóth who, curious and anxious in equal measure, had just dared to set foot in his own restaurant for the first time in ages.

18.

To experience the full benefits of stereophonic music playback you must make sure your loudspeaker system is in good working order. Your speakers should form an isosceles triangle with the spot from where you are listening, with the left-hand loudspeaker attached to the left-hand amplifier output and the right-hand one to the right-hand amplifier output. Try the following test to check that your speakers are correctly positioned and properly connected. The whirling sound of the drum should emanate from the left-hand speaker first, moving slowly to the right-hand one, where the solo will end.

I am fascinated. I have just brought from the cellar Father's old Tesla Moderato radio gramophone, complete with speakers. The only record Mother didn't manage to sell along with the old 78s is the *Introduction to stereophonic listening*. It must have rolled under or behind something, and anyway, nobody would have been interested in it.

I attach the speakers, switch from radio to record player and after the inevitable crackling I hear a languorous, incantatory voice.

When the A-side finishes playing, the voice introduces a sample of stereophonic playback on the B-side and stops. I turn the record over and hear music that is intimately and heartachingly familiar, evoking fragmented images that gradually merge together. The piece is innocent enough – the worn and hackneyed *Entry of the Gladiators* by the composer Julius Fučík, namesake of the hero of gallows fame.

The summer of 1951 was drawing to a close, with everything that entailed. Autumn had dug its first claws into the warm air, and after the occasional hailstorm skies were swept clean and radiantly blue again. Pears were ripening in the local gardens and the air reeked of burning grass, leaves and wood, as you might expect on a day like this.

Peculiar characters started wandering around Stalin Street (ex-Hitler, ex-Masaryk and future Štúr Street – in our twentieth century, the streets, too, became turncoats). At first we saw faces covered in make-up, clowns and dwarves followed by a gentleman in a top hat leading an elephant on a rope. An acrobat in a shiny leotard rode on its back. And there was music. The band played the *Entry of the Gladiators* slightly faster or slower than necessary – certainly, something wasn't quite right (perhaps it would have sounded like this, had it been composed in the final years of the Roman Empire) but it still made all the children rush out into the street and gawp. They ran excitedly alongside the horse-driven carriages and caravans.

Overnight a huge multicoloured big top sprang up in the meadow on the edge of town, where back in 1891 a vineyard had been destroyed by an outbreak of phylloxera. Muscular circus builders erected the tent, driving wooden poles into the ground with heavy mallets. The ringmaster stood at the tent entrance, shouting into a tannoy:

"Ladies and gentlemen! The largest circus in Europe has arrived in your town! Roll up! Roll up! New attractions and exotic animals! Bingo the elephant! Trained dogs and ponies! A real African cobra, well, American actually! Roll up!"

His calls were accompanied by circus music, whooping and laughter.

All this mixed with an optimistic song blaring from every loudspeaker:

> *Come nation, oh loyal nation*
> *Let's follow President Gottwald*
> *Who leads us higher and higher*
> *Into a reality that is no longer a dream.*
> *You who fought the victorious battle by his side*
> *Stand by him now.*
> *Up we go, comrades, don't give an inch!*

We went to the circus because Tina wanted to see an elephant – as a little girl she couldn't get enough of the story of *l'elefante* from the Italian circus that had been stranded in our town during World War I and whom the good citizens of Brežany saved from starving to death, by helping to feed it through a whole winter. And so the next night we went to see Circus HARRY, now on its last legs, during one of its last tours of the country. In those days circus didn't yet have to face competition from TV – our roofs had not yet been covered in fish skeleton-like aerials and its only rival was the brand new Moscow Cinema that had opened in the main square. However, something akin to the climate change of the late Tertiary, which resulted in the extinction of the dinosaurs, was already looming on the horizon.

We all got dressed up. Father wore his trademark off-white suit, which showed every spot, forcing him to steer clear of wine or ice cream when he wore it. He suggested that I invite Vojto, in case the Roškos hadn't seen the show yet. Vojto came with his father and brother, while his mother stayed at home with baby Ela. We took our seats in the auditorium. Among the audience I spotted Mr Malánek from the shop in the main square (his face the picture of respectability and greyness) with his wife holding an infant grandchild in her lap. His legs were too unsteady to be entrusted with this task.

The beginning of the show was delayed and the irritated audience started to make muttering noises. Eventually, some fifteen minutes later, the ringmaster in a shiny suit entered the ring, looking mournful. He announced that for some reason the band had failed to turn up. At that moment the drummer staggered in. Still trying to knot his tie and smooth down his hair, he began to play. Soon two saxophone players emerged and joined in. Tina started to clap. The other instruments gradually joined in as well and we all recognized the tune. *On the Brežany tower*. Huge applause ensued.

Lights in the circus tent were gradually lit, starting from the top and moving down to the main entrance, the circus band played a fanfare and the circus director, wearing a black coat and tails, cream gloves and a top hat, stood in the middle of the ring, waving a baton and welcoming the audience.

The ringmaster bowed and announced the first number: *The one and only Harry Houdini!*

A distinguished-looking old gent in a jacket that had seen better days walked into the ring to the accompaniment of music and started demonstrating card tricks, pinpointed by a spotlight and accompanied by the ringmaster's running commentary. The alleged Houdini made an expansive gesture and a card fell out of his sleeve, giving the trick away. To cap it all, he dropped the entire pack of cards. The audience started to whistle and boo. The old fellow collected the cards hurriedly, wiped the sweat off his brow and continued, blushing. But things went from bad to worse. A spectator shouted: "Fraud! Get lost!" and the audience became increasingly vocal, telling him to get out. People stamped their feet and whistled. The ringmaster leapt towards him and tried to lead him away, two clowns darted out of nowhere to defend Houdini, a fight broke out. The ringmaster vanished, then his voice rang out over the empty ring. The spotlight located him at the card table.

"Attention please! I am the real Harry Houdini!"

The cards began to flash between his fingers with breathtaking speed. He was rewarded by great applause.

The next number featured Lipizzaner horses and an acrobat rider. The clowns were a yawn. Wearing shoes that were five sizes too big, the mouths of their whitened faces wide open, they teased each other and the ringmaster, who never stopped smiling. The poodle drill was passable and the trapeze artists made my neck hurt. Father changed seats to get a better view, somehow ending up sitting next to Vojto's father. I sat next to Vojto as Tina stamped her feet on the other side.

During the interval Father surreptitiously shook a box of cigarettes in the direction of Vojto's father, who shrugged and smiled. Fobbing us off with small change for candyfloss, not exactly my favourite treat, they went behind the tent for a cigarette, as smoking wasn't allowed inside. Tina demanded a Coca-Cola, which was hard to get in those days. Even if it had been available, it would have cost a fortune. The sound of the elephant trumpeting behind the scenes provided enough excitement and she made do with damp potato crisps and lemonade.

"So you're a smoker?" Vojto's father asked.

"Only occasionally. The latest research shows that cigarettes are harmful only in forty per cent of cases." He smiled. "How has your head been?"

263

"I had it X-rayed a few times in Prague; it seems the bones have healed well. I don't remember anything from the moment of the plane crash. Until the summer."

"Oh, so no serious consequences then…"

"Well… I wouldn't go that far. I get severe headaches. They come all of a sudden and disappear just as suddenly. Sometimes I find myself just staring into thin air and losing the thread. I never had that before."

"Drop by the health centre sometime. I'll give you a once-over. No late nights and not too much alcohol."

They were silent for a while. Father was about to ask something but thought better of it.

"It's going to be a lovely autumn this year," he said finally. "It must be a wonderful sight. From above… From a plane…"

"That's all in the past now. I applied for the job of flying instructor in the air club but I've lost my licence. I don't really want to talk about it."

Vojto's father stepped on his cigarette butt and let the smoke out from the corner of his mouth. "We ought to go back inside."

"Pardon…?"

"I said we ought go back."

"Oh yes, right."

That was all they said to each other that evening.

The show continued with a knife thrower. I remember a beautiful brunette in a blue leotard standing in front of a wall, her outline marked by twenty blades thrust into it. The knife thrower shouted: "Ali!"

She replied: "Up!" and quickly bent down to let the knife pierce the heart drawn on the wall roughly where her own heart was. At least that was the idea. But the man threw his knife before she finished bending down. The sharp blade cut into her neck and nailed her skin to the wall. She screamed as blood streamed from her neck onto her breasts. The knife thrower stiffened but the ringmaster lunged towards her, pulled the heavy knife out of the wall, took her in his arms and carried her backstage, frenziedly signalling to the band, which, rather incongruously, started playing *Entry of the Gladiators* again.

Father got up, leapt over the low edge of the ring, colliding with a clown rushing to the stage to limit the damage, and followed the bloody trail. The clowns did what they could but in the ensuing commotion the horrified spectators started leaving in a chaotic scramble.

By the time we caught up with Father at the hospital later that evening the brunette had been bandaged up and the surgeon was explaining that, luckily, the knife had missed the artery and the larynx, although she would be left with a nasty scar. She had lost a lot of blood and had to be given a blood transfusion.

Tina and I sat in the waiting room next to the ringmaster in his shiny suit. There was a look of terror on his face and he couldn't stop jabbering – probably to drown out what was going on inside his head.

His first story concerned a hammer-and-nails trick, a *pièce de résistance* that was part of their wartime show and concluded with the performer, Gigi, on his knees with his tongue nailed to a table. To reduce his suffering, they decided that instead of hammering the nail in gradually, they would do it in one big blow. The ringmaster hit the hammer, driving the nail through Gigi's tongue, the plank and the table underneath. At that moment the sirens began to wail, announcing an American air raid. Spectators started running in all directions, tripping and falling over each other. And in the middle of all this there was Gigi on his knees, with his tongue nailed to the table. One by one, each member of the troupe tried to pull the nail out. To no avail.

Gigi survived only because the bombs actually fell on the other end of town.

"Can you imagine what would have happened if the bomb had hit the circus?"

The ringmaster laughed hysterically and his right eye started to twitch.

"C'mon, Adam, we're going!" Father shouted at me from the far end of the corridor. He was cross.

A full moon, huge and red, rose above the gardens. A few stragglers were still coming out of the big top. The circus lights were going out. The rattling of dishes could be heard from the caravans, the acrobat rider sat on the steps with a cigarette and the clowns were unrecognizable without their make-up, which had disguised their stiff, tired faces. They looked like dried fruit. Well kept and candied though.

The next day the circus declared itself bankrupt. I heard they tried to sell off the animals but ended up having to put most of them down, including two elephants and a giraffe.

"Fancy some giraffe steak?" Rozgoň the butcher asked someone.

19.

Limpid January stars shone above the house like perfectly cut diamonds. That night Tina was at home alone. My parents and Peter had gone to see some friends a few houses down the road while she stayed at home nursing a cold, if I remember rightly. Before we left, Father stressed that the keys had to be left in the lock, and on no account was she to let anyone in. So she sat on her bed dangling her legs and listening to the radio which, judging by the crackling and occasional rasping noises, was playing music from an old record.

The doorbell rang. Tina decided to ignore it. After a while it rang again. The bell was new and its clear sound echoed across the drawing room and the hallway.

Barefoot, Tina tiptoed down to the front door and peered through the letter flap. Her feet were cold. She heard someone cough and mumble at the door. The person shifted a little and Tina saw a stranger in a leather coat.

"Who's that?"

"Is your father home? I've got something for him," the man said.

"Wait a minute, I'll open up!"

Tina felt for the keys in the lock but couldn't find them in the dark. So she got on all fours and felt around the floor for them.

"What's going on? Open up!"

A frosty wind blew from the garden. The scarecrow rattled in the wind as if skeletons were dancing all around the house. The smell of burning coal stung the nostrils. Somewhere in the distance a dog barked.

"Open up!"

"I can't find the keys!"

"What?"

"They're not here," said Tina, crawling on all fours, having just stuck her hand into something moist and slimy, which she couldn't properly make out.

"Damn it …!" The man in the leather coat banged his fist on the door and Tina heard his steps squelching in the snow. Irritated, he mumbled something, his voice slowly moving away.

She went back to her cosy room and her radio and sat on the bed for a while, her teeth chattering. Something else was playing now and Tina frowned, trying to figure out where the keys could possible be. They had to be somewhere!

She ran out into the hallway again without bothering to put her shoes on, her bare feet padding on the tiles. She reached the front door. The keys were in the lock.

She began to tremble with fear. She hurried indoors, locking every door on her way and crawled under her bed.

That's where Father found her asleep, after a long search.

In those days I often saw him sitting at the desk in his isolation cell looking at the old photograph with his father's head glued on. Whenever someone passed by, he would close the door. This happened particularly during long, sleepless nights.

But in our presence he was all smiles and jokes.

In the Middle Ages, if you wanted to undo an evil act, you had to eat dirt from the four corners of a room. That was what kept going through my mind on the day the astounding twentieth century ended, as I walked from my flat to do something I had told no one about. I'm not sure why: maybe I was ashamed to put my suspicions into words, I was scared that I would make them come true. But above all, I was scared of having my suspicions confirmed. I was prepared to get on my knees and eat any dirt I might come across.

I often find it hard to explain my own actions. Admittedly, those lists of ŠtB collaborators did exist and although they hadn't yet been officially released, I decided to look through them – I guess there was a reason, even if I hadn't articulated it yet. It had to do with the *magnum opus* I was planning to shoot in the late 1990s, at the time of the great intake of breath, when skeletons started coming out of cupboards.

I told myself, as usual: "Toss a coin to decide what you really want want to do. Heads or tails?"

My toss was too high. The coin fell to the ground and I couldn't find it. I was in a lousy mood.

And so I found myself in the library of the Institute of National Remembrance, reading one of Father's reports:

This is to report that I have paid a visit to the subject in question under the pretext of organising a joint birthday party for our sons. I raised the issue of comrade Čepička but this didn't elicit any specific reaction. A detailed analysis of the subject's attitude to our comrade President can be found in my previous report. The conversation was not very interesting until Vojtech suddenly drew my attention to some books his brother had brought from abroad which – as far as he knew – had been banned in the ČSSR, which is why he keeps them hidden in his attic. I took this as a sign that I have finally gained his full confidence. I continued to follow my handler's instructions but didn't learn any new material facts. Luminal.

I couldn't tear myself away from the file. I opened the window and stared out into the cold air, at people who had no idea of any of this.

This was the moment that changed my life.

A teacher once told the young Leo Tolstoy that if he didn't stop thinking about a polar bear, he would be punished by being made to kneel in a corner. Tolstoy ended up spending a whole day in the corner. He was trapped. It's impossible to get out of your mind the polar bear that has caused your suffering.

By then Father was out of this world, so to speak. Like when you switch off the lights as you leave a house. I watched his aged face while I cut his toenails – this job was a privilege I had reserved for myself, maybe because it allowed me to touch him, I'm not sure – and wondered how doing all that must have made him feel.

"Would you like a glass of water?"

"What?"

"OK, let me fetch you some."

I wanted to tell him I knew what he had done and bombard him with questions but I realised I wasn't up to it.

"So, would you like a glass of water?"

"What…? What did you say, Adam?"

There he was, sitting before me, helpless. I had come from Bratislava specially. I had sent his Leocadia home early. I needed some time alone with him.

"Can I get you a glass of water?"

I sat on the sofa hesitating, listening to the wind rattling the double-glazed windows and the compressed air wailing inside them. Like the horn of a train rushing through the night, illuminated by a single lightbulb.

I had to toss for it again. Heads or tails? Tails or heads? Heads means saying something, tails means keeping quiet.

Tails. Tails and tails again.

"Would you like a glass of water?"

"By the way, any news from Bratislava?"

"A slice of bread perhaps…?"

"You'll have to speak up, Adam."

20.

The end of 1952 was ushered in by a long series of birthdays and name days, which brought our family together quite frequently.

On one such afternoon, instead of chatting about health and family affairs we all gathered round to listen to the radio.

Uncle Oskar, usually cheerful and calm, stood by the receiver, visibly on edge. He was listening intently to the live broadcast from a courtroom. The state prosecutor had just given the floor to the presiding judge.

After clearing his throat, the judge said: "Defendant Rudolf Slánský, step forward! Do you understand the indictment?" "Yes, I do," Slánský replied. The judge asked: "Do you plead guilty to the offences listed in the indictment?" Slánský: "I do." The judge: "The first criminal offence is espionage; is that correct?" Slánský: "Yes." The judge: "Treason?" Slánský: "Yes." The judge: "Sabotage?" Slánský: "Yes." The judge: "Military treason?" Slánský: "Yes."

It seemed that he could go on asking these questions forever and receive the same answer.

A few other people spoke and then it was the turn of the presiding judge again:

The verdict, in the name of the Republic!

The court has decided as follows: Rudolf Slánský, born on 31 July 1901, former Secretary General of the Communist Party of Czechoslovakia, of

Jewish origin, son of a merchant…, Bedřich Reicin, born on 29 September 1911, former Deputy Secretary for National Defence, of Jewish origin, from a bourgeois family…, Artur London, born on 1 February 1915, former Deputy Secretary for Foreign Affairs, of Jewish origin, son of a self-employed tradesman…, Vavro Hajdů, born on 8 August 1913, former Deputy Secretary for Foreign Affairs, of Jewish origin, son of the owner of the Smrdáky spa…, Rudolf Margolius, born on 31 August 1913, former Deputy Secretary for Foreign Trade, of Jewish origin, a wholesaler's son… , Otto Fischl, born on 17 August 1902, former Deputy Secretary of Finance, of Jewish origin, a merchant's son…., Otto Šling, born on 24 August 1912, former Chief Secretary of the Brno Regional Committee of the Communist Party of Czechoslovakia, of Jewish origin, a factory owner's son…

… are guilty of having, over an extended period of time up to their arrest, in Prague, as well as in other locations, conspired together as well as with others, in an attempt to destroy the Czechoslovak Republic's independence and the country's constitutionally guaranteed system of people's democracy, having jeopardized this system to a considerable degree by entering into relations with a foreign power and foreign officials; Slánský, Reicin and Šling have misused the armed forces to this end…

… are hereby sentenced to death…

Uncle Oskar held his breath. When he finally did breathe again, he sucked out all the air from the room.

"Let me open the window…" said Mother, breaking the silence.

"Please do," said Father and picked up the knife to carve the cake, as nobody else showed any intention of doing so.

"Yes… yes… That's a good idea," Oskar muttered absent-mindedly.

In the evening Father sat down to type up his medical reports, quietly whistling a tune. Somewhere at the back of the house a radio was playing. A voice spoke, sounding as if it had to force its way through rainy streets and walls in the bleak November weather.

Thanks to the vigilance, foresight and decisiveness of the leader of the Czechoslovak people, Comrade Klement Gottwald, thanks to the invincible unity and support that the Central Committee of the Communist Party of Czechoslovakia has shown Comrade Klement Gottwald, thanks to the indomitable loyalty of our people to the Soviet Union, the conspiracy was crushed and the criminal plot thwarted.

Father stopped whistling and closed the door to his isolation cell.

Uncle Rudo, who was still finishing his dinner, remarked drily from a fish skeleton he had thoroughly cleaned:

"An evolutionary duel of predators fighting for juicy bits of meat! We are just small animals that happen to have mastered the art of standing on our hind legs. Along with the ability to speak. Otherwise we're no different from a pack of wolves."

And he smacked his lips with satisfaction.

But except for Polyester 2 and Ikebana III, who hoped to get some titbits from the table, no one paid him any attention. So Rudo turned to address the animals: "This is what an interrogation looks like: Defendant, do you know the words of the song *Row, row, row your boat? – Row, row, row your boat… –* Go on! *– Row, row, row your boat… –* Keep going! – Damn, I know it! *Gently down the stream… –* Go on! – It's on the tip of my tongue…– Go on! – I'm sorry, comrades, I can't remember. – What comes next? – I really don't know, I'm so sorry! – So he gets a whack on the nose. – What comes next? Sing, you idiot! – I don't know. – Sing! A whack on one side, a whack on the other. – So you won't sing, eh? I'll beat it out of you! C'mon, start again, right from the beginning *– Row, row, row your boat, gently down the stream, merrily, merrily…* Whack! Here, Ikebana, have a piece of fish. There's nothing left for you, Polino. Good night, I'll see myself out!"

I read somewhere that execution by hanging followed roughly this scenario:

A court representative read out the verdict in the prison courtyard and then, for appearances' sake, he read out the president's refusal to grant a pardon. Then the court representative handed the prisoner over to a state procuracy official.

The executioner, wearing a suit and white suede gloves, tied the prisoner's hands with rope, which he passed under his arms and, climbing on a ladder, threaded through a pulley. His assistants pulled the rope up, the executioner climbed down, tied the prisoner's feet and threaded the long rope from his feet through the gallows pulley. He handed the end of the rope to the assistants. Then the executioner climbed up again and placed the noose around the prisoner's neck.

At his command the assistants let go of the prisoner, tugging at the end of the rope in one abrupt, well-rehearsed movement. The weight of his body and the pull from below made the prisoner fall into the noose around his neck while the executioner tried to break his neck vertebrae. If he didn't succeed the prisoner would choke, gasp and jerk about, opening and closing his fists.

Finally rigor mortis would set in. After a while the procuracy official asked a doctor to climb up the ladder and listen to the prisoner's heartbeat with a stethoscope. This was repeated at intervals until the doctor confirmed that death had occurred.

We were chatting to pass the time on the trip to Bratislava airport as I drove Uncle Oskar through a frozen landscape. Electricity cables along the road dipped from masts rising again to the next masts in elegant arcs. Up and down they went. Inhaling and exhaling. All the passengers' eyes were on these power lines as we drove past white plains with a scattering of bare, sleeping trees. Up and down, up and down. This was the rhythm of the road breathing.

"You know, Adam, as a matter of fact, we Jews have always been on the run," Oskar said.

Mother, sitting at the back, stared pensively out the window. She shook her head wearily and caught Oskar's eye in the rear-view mirror. Oskar just waved his hand.

"Tragedy is what has kept us going all these years. Maybe that's why we're so fond of dark humour. It all started in Egypt, in slavery. After God appeared to Moses to tell him He had picked us as His chosen people. Everything was fine for a while, until the next spell in captivity, this time in Babylon, in the sixth century B.C. That was when we began to cultivate all those myths about our history, the only God, Sabbath and kosher food – all those rules, you know. And then bang! In the year 70 A.D. the Romans destroyed the Holy Temple in Jerusalem and ever since then we've been scattered all over the world. Diaspora, centuries of pogroms and the Holocaust followed. This is what has held us together. These are our favourite topics of conversation. That, plus the memory of Old Jerusalem. And that's why we long to return to the Promised Land."

I didn't say anything, or ask any questions; I just kept driving Father's car calmly along the icy road. But Oskar answered his own questions.

"Diaspora is actually a Greek word – it means dispersal or exile. It began with the destruction of the Temple. About sixty years later we staged a botched uprising and then the Romans rapped our knuckles for good. We were banished from the Temple and the city of Jerusalem. We were driven out and enslaved, and so we dispersed around the world. Only a few thousand stayed at home, while a million and a half left. The great exodus, that's our lot. Mesopotamia, North Africa, Italy, Greece... Some crossed the Alps, heading for the North. Ping! Like the turning point in a game of billiards."

We were passing a farmstead on the right and I had to overtake a horse-drawn carriage that was turning off the main road. A man in a sheepskin coat and hat sat in the coach box and raised his arm in greeting. A car was a rare sight for him, even on the main road to Bratislava.

"For many centuries we had worked in various professions, drawn mainly to trade and finance. Christians were not allowed to lend out money for interest; nor were we – but only within our community. We were able to offer them loans and we prospered. It was a risky business but quite profitable. Some guilds shut their doors to us, some kings wanted us to administer their treasuries, others forced us to live outside the city gates. That was the beginning of the ghettoes."

"Could you turn up the heating a bit, Adam?" Mother said from the back seat.

"OK, Mum."

"Some Jews made it to Spain together with the Arabs, and became known as Sephardim. They worked as advisers, doctors, teachers, translators, cartographers, mathematicians and astronomers to the caliphs. In the fifteenth century, following the *Reconquista*, the Christians drove them out of Spain. As a result, their economy collapsed like a sandcastle. On the run again... Africa, France, northern Germany. The Sephardim from Amsterdam were among the first to reach America. Others – the Ashkenazi Jews – travelled through Germany to Poland, Ukraine and Russia. We were driven out during the bubonic plague, accused of poisoning the wells. We were accused of using the blood of young virgins as an ingredient in *matzo* bread. What a fascinating notion!"

I felt the taste of blood in my mouth; I must have bitten my tongue. I had some tea from the vacuum flask.

273

"In the fourth century, when Emperor Constantine converted to Christianity, the church started to claim that God had transferred his grace to the Christians and the Jews were no longer his Chosen People. They had killed Christ, and after being disowned by the Lord they began to sow evil. New laws were introduced to limit our free movement, and following the Fourth Lateran Council in the thirteenth century we had to pay high taxes and wear clothes that distinguished us from others. That gave rise to prejudice and all sorts of myths, but ordinary people believed the drivel they heard in churches. We had no choice but to withdraw into family life, our community, into ourselves... Do you know what's interesting, Adam? Jewish merchants could always rely on their Jewish business partners even if they'd never met them. And through all these years we have dreamed of Jerusalem, the Holy City, the destroyed Temple... Who knows if the Jews would still exist today if it hadn't been destroyed? We would have dissolved in Europe like sugar in tea, my dear Adam."

Uncle Oskar also took a sip from the flask and fell silent for a while. The road was full of potholes and I had to drive carefully. The jolting woke up Mother who had dozed off. "It was all Theodor Herzl's idea. Kibbutzim were established; people flocked there from all Europe, from Germany and Russia. The luckier ones. If they missed the boat to America. By then Germany started making plans for the Final Solution. Six million of our people died."

The jagged skyline of Bratislava was deep in winter sleep. Thin wisps of smoke rose from its chimneys.

"Five years ago the British Mandate of Palestine was terminated and the squabbling between us and the Arabs began, resulting in a pile of corpses. On 14 May 1948, in Tel Aviv, David Ben-Gurion proclaimed the establishment of the state of Israel. That same night it came under attack from the neighbouring countries. We have won the war but the problems have continued. We'll just have to see what happens."

Our Chevy swept into a car park outside the lounge of Ivánka airport on the outskirts of Bratislava. I helped Uncle Oskar unload the luggage. It was the end of January. The air was frosty and our noses immediately turned red.

The previous autumn Oskar had applied for permission to emigrate to Israel with new Aunt Rózka and Samuel. They flew from Bratislava to Prague and then, via Berlin, to Tel Aviv. Exactly 5714 years after the creation of the world.

New Aunt Rózka and Samuel had gone ahead while Oskar stayed behind to make the final arrangements, but now everything was sorted out and suddenly the day of his departure arrived. Mother was tearful, sniffling into her handkerchief. Every parting was hard for her and this promised to be a very long one. To make matters harder for her, this was the first time she had left the house in a long while. She had been going out less and less often and preferred to be told about everything while she sat by the window, watching and listening.

Uncle Oskar managed to get hold of a book on the Slánský trial, recently published by the Ministry of Justice. He waved it in my face and treated me to an extract from time to time. First he sounded sad and confused, then he started to laugh.

"I'll take this with me. In case I ever feel homesick. Have a look at the errata at the back – that's the best bit!"

I didn't feel like touching the book but in the end I agreed to take a look.

On page 138, line 4 from the top, after the words "in their hypocrisy they…" insert the word "also"… On page 21, in line 5 from the bottom, before the last word in the phrase "taking over the organisation" insert "company"…

I didn't understand.

Uncle Oskar smiled:

"The defendants didn't learn their lines properly."

He gave Mother a peck on the cheek, and with a wave of his hand, disappeared.

We watched him walk to the Czechoslovak Airlines aircraft amidst the first signs of a blizzard.

Just before Oskar left, I remember reminding him of something he had once told me. According to Marx the dominant class had to impose its own ideology on the whole of society in order to convince the exploited classes that the exploitation they had been subjected to was essential and fair. He pretended not to hear me. Perhaps I had misunderstood the whole thing. Or maybe he was the one who had misunderstood. Anyway, I thought Marx was a moron. Uncle Oskar had convinced me of that.

While we were still waiting in the airport lounge, Mother took off in search of the well-concealed toilets and I just went on about whatever popped into my mind, just to kill time until their departure.

No longer listening, Uncle Oskar looked distracted and gave me a look that suggested he had something important to say. He leaned close.

"Sometimes one has to do the strangest things to survive, Adam."

He sounded so serious that I stopped in my tracks.

"Back in the camps, one of the doctors, SS-Untersturmführer Kreutze, had a crush on me. First he had me transferred to the crew that sorted the luggage of the newly-arrived transports. At least there was always something to eat there. All the stuff ended up in the warehouse, which we called Canada. Then he had me transferred to the infirmary. I was basically his butler."

Uncle Oskar watched people walking up and down before us.

"His way of showing affection was to come to me every night and give me a blow job. He didn't ask for anything more. It was revolting and tender at the same time, do you understand? The only reason I survived was because I let him do it."

He fixed me with his stare.

"Don't tell anyone. You are the only one who knows."

By then Mother had returned and flung herself into his arms, weeping.

21.

I couldn't get the bones out of my mind.

I tried to find out what had happened to Colonel Ďuratný and if it could have been him who ended up buried in our garden under the fallen yew tree.

There was every indication that he had started working for Czechoslovak intelligence before the war. During the Slovak State he was active in the illegal Communist Party, but some suspected him of links with the secret police. He took part in the Uprising as one of the rank-and-file soldiers and after the war joined a special intelligence unit at the Ministry of the Interior. He was in charge of investigating Nazis and the Brežany officials in Slovakia's Democratic Party, which won the 1946 election. In 1949 he turned up at our local State Security department and gradually rose through the ranks from captain to colonel.

In 1968, when special hearings were held to rehabilitate victims of the Stalinist trials, the details of many 1950s cases came to light. And Ján Ďuratný, MSc., was suddenly out of the game.

He hanged himself at the foot of the Volovec Mountain on 20 April 1968, a few days before he was due to testify before the state procurator. His grave at the southern Brežany cemetery, overgrown with decorative zinnias, didn't explicitly cite *laesio medullae spinalis transversalis* – as Father would have said – but I got this information from a former neighbour of his. She served it up as a forgotten piece of gossip with tea and home-made pastries hard as stone.

22.

More and more people from villages near and far started moving into Brežany. They came for jobs at the Slovlina factory, formerly Knocht & Marinar. Another factory, the Karl Liebknecht Lumber and Paper Mill popped up virtually from one day to the next, filling the air with its sweetish smell, especially at night. The Brežany synagogue, which had been plundered during the war and had stood empty until now, was turned into a warehouse.

To accommodate all the new arrivals, hastily constructed blocks of flats sprang up at Behy. Uncle Rudo was in mourning because the nearby forest, where he used to go every day to "meditate on life", as he liked to say, fell victim to the new development.

The entire Roško family gathered to celebrate the fiftieth birthday of Vojto's uncle.

One of the guests talked about foreign lands, mentioning the new state of Israel, which he said was located at the northern tip of Africa.

"No, you're wrong. It's Western Asia," Vojto said.

His father, who was rather worse for wear, got up and leaned on the chair armrest to steady himself. A mischievous smile played on his face, spurred on by a headache, as Vojto could tell because his father kept touching his temples.

"Well, well, well, listen to our clever clogs…! Our know-it-all!" he shouted, approaching Vojto on unsteady feet. Everyone fell silent.

"Now tell me, what use is that school-leaving exam of yours? Nobody in my family has ever taken one. You want to show off, or what? And as if that wasn't enough, he wants to go to university as well…!"

He came right up to Vojto and grabbed him by the collar.

"You always had to be different! You won't even talk to us! You're just wasting your time keeping your nose stuck in books all the time. You don't belong to us! You don't belong in our family! You're not Jewish by any chance?"

He raised a glass of plum brandy above his head.

"Our little Vojto is a Jew! Do you hear me? He's our family Jew!"

"That's enough," Mrs Roško said, grabbing him by the hand. "That will do!"

Vojto got up and left angrily.

That night Vojto's father threw open the door to his room, felt his way along the wall looking for the light switch, and then, still unsteady, turned on the light, swaying by Vojto's bed for a moment. Vojto wasn't asleep.

"I'm sorry, I didn't mean to… I didn't mean it that way…"

"Right…"

He placed his heavy hand on Vojto's forehead.

"These are bad times. Very bad. We may even have to move out of this house."

He wiped away a tear that coursed down his cheek, hoping that Vojto wouldn't see. But Vojto did. He wanted to take his father by the hand or stroke him to show he cared, but he couldn't bring himself to do it. No one in their family was given to displays of affection, not even at moments like this.

"I know, Dad," Vojto said into the darkness.

Looking back years later, he said this was when he realized he really was his family's Jew. That's how he had lived his entire life. Always on the run, in exile, on the wrong side of the barricades.

I admired his courage.

The next morning was Mrs Natália Roško's first day at work, her first chance to make use of the nursing training she had had in Prague in 1950. Gritting her teeth she reported to Dr Alfonz Trnovský's practice, replacing his loyal Zdenka, who had now retired.

Looking at her you might have thought she found the patients repulsive. A second look would confirm this impression: she would much rather have meditated or gone out for a cup of coffee. Or perhaps played solitaire.

She was immersed in the latter activity when she was interrupted by a mother with her three year old who was running a fever. The mother provided a graphic account of the rasping cough at night that had turned her daughter's face almost blue. She also mentioned a sharp noise during intakes of breath that could have indicated whooping cough.

Nurse Natália looked up briefly from her cards and pointed out that the doctor was busy with more urgent cases and she wasn't going to disturb him just because someone had come down with a cold. Give her some lime blossom tea, apply compresses, keep her in bed.

This would have been quite sensible advice if the child hadn't died within a week.

Overall, March 1953 proved to be a time particularly conducive to the grim reaper, who must have found this was a perfect point for going on the rampage.

It all started with Field Marshal Stalin dying of a brain haemorrhage. He might have lived longer had his doctors not been too scared to enter his room (as instructed by his chief of secret police) but that was not yet common knowledge. We heard it on the seven o'clock news on Radio Vienna and later it came bleating from our radio. The streets were teeming with people convinced that the end of the world was nigh.

It took everyone a while to realise what a monster he had been. And when the skeletons finally came out of the cupboard at the Twentieth Congress of the Communist Party of the USSR, the poet Kostra was said to have changed the title of his celebratory "Ode To Stalin" to "I've Been Done In".

Our beloved comrade president Klement Gottwald met his Maker nine days after Stalin. The flight to the Field Marshal's funeral had dealt a final blow to his blood vessels, already weakened by syphilis, and poor old Klement died of an aortic aneurysm. That wasn't common knowledge either. I mean – it was common knowledge but it wasn't to be mentioned in public. Soviet medical experts refused to hand over the President's brain and released only his heart. Maybe they meant to emphasise that emotions are what matter rather than cold rational consideration. Especially after someone's demise.

In ancient Egypt the haruspex used to place the heart of a deceased person on the scales to divine their afterlife from its weight. We'll never know how much (or rather, how little) Gottwald's heart weighed, since the Czech doctor who was asked to issue the death certificate was rumoured to have exclaimed indignantly: "What am I supposed to do with these giblets?"

Father didn't let Tina invite her girlfriends to her eighteenth birthday party because state mourning had been declared. She was livid.

23.

The job in the Brežany Forestry Enterprise didn't just fall into Vojto's father's lap. After much pleading Comrade Kominár, Chairman of the National Committee, pulled some strings at the Ministry of Forests, Groves, Swamps and Meadows (or whatever).

Nevertheless, Comrade Kominár, whose name means chimney sweep – a calling that is said to bring good luck to those he meets – was a staunch communist, firm and invincible in his faith. For the benefit of the kind reader, in whom this creature may have aroused ambivalent feelings and who may favour an unambiguous and edifying outcome in the eternal struggle between good and evil, let me fast forward and reveal that Comrade Kominár eventually drank himself into the grave. I regret to inform you that by then his own family had given up on him, and that his wife and daughter had kicked him out of the house.

But it's so hard to turn down a drink when people constantly want something from you, turning up with a bottle or inviting you out – alcohol is a social lubricant and the machinery needs to be constantly greased… He usually came home late at night, often in an unspeakable state.

But at this point of our story he still enjoyed robust health. And apart from the occasional mix-up between tranquillizers and laxatives, he might well have considered himself immortal.

Vojto's father had to show his gratitude by helping to build Kominár's cottage on the Volovec Mountain, a palatial log cabin in the middle of the woods. Mr Roško and other grateful comrades devoted entire weekends to hauling the building materials on their backs up a narrow waterlogged road.

Thanks to this "voluntary" job Vojto's father was eventually promoted to warehouse manager, where he met a former priest, Father Čerešník, and a former Communist official, comrade Németh. The three men became inseparable.

They would have great rows about God and Marx over copious quantities of St Lawrence wine. Once, in their cups, they decided that both had been Jewish – Marx certainly and God most likely, at least according to the Bible.

Such unanimity usually brought them closer together, as it provided them with a great excuse to curse the Jews.

Since he wasn't allowed anywhere near airplanes, Vojto's father could only watch from the ground as they drew broad swathes across the sky before disappearing below the horizon. Or late at night, standing in the doorway smoking his final cigarette of the day, he could follow the steady blinking of their red lights as they glided slowly among the stars.

To demonstrate that he was done with flying once and for all, he got rid of his pigeons too. Their plucked little bodies started to appear on Vojto's plate and he had to force himself to eat them. He would put a bit of boiled potato into his mouth, toss a bit of meat to the dog, then have a little drink and *whoosh*! half a thigh would land under the table… The deserted wooden dovecote was taken over by mice. For many years it continued to loom pointlessly over the Roškos' garden.

Vojto and I used to visit his father in the forest – we had to climb up the Volovec Mountain and then down the valley on the other side.

On our way we would drop in on Klaudius Kolár, who continued to slide downhill, pickled in alcohol like a lizard. In fact, his dwelling, illuminated by the good old filament, was somewhat reminiscent of menthol liqueur. In every respect, including the smell. Its dim light inspired him to produce great decadent poetry. Sometimes, when he was in a good mood, he would read to us. One of his poems was called *The Chimney*.

> *Life is a chimney and I'm a chimney sweep – as you well know.*
> *A deep vagina or a rectum? But before*
> *You ask me how I know – leave me alone, go!*
> *I have no idea. Whatever. Yesterday or tomorrow*
> *I'll howl at the moon like a stray dog.*

"That's fantastic! Really fantastic!" raved Vojto. He even wrote it down in his notebook.

He told me that our versifier was quite upset when a neighbour, who also lived in a solitary house in the woods, brought him a newspaper that carried the following notice:

I, the undersigned Ivan Kolár, hereby declare that my father Klaudius Kolár is a class enemy, a saboteur and an enemy of the people. After careful consideration I have decided to renounce him. I haven't been in touch with him for several years now.

We went off into the woods and had some fun catching ground beetles. Their metallic backs glistened in the moist forest grass and we could still smell them on our hands afterwards as we lay sprawled on our backs, staring at the crowns of the tall beeches and elms.

Vojto's dog was scampering around happily, panting into my ear one minute, barking somewhere far off the next. The dog was in its element, revelling in nature's smells. As far as it was concerned, everything made sense: the sun, hay, the smell of manure carried on the wind. The freshness of the air after rain, other dogs and distant creatures, the stars, the night, the warm earth, the damp forest... I was caught by the dog's unalloyed joy and I sighed with delight, saying this was how freedom felt.

Vojto turned onto his stomach:

"Freedom is in your head. It rarely has anything to do with external circumstances."

"What do you mean?"

"Well, take things like your character, or where you were born. Or who you were born to? And also what mood you happen to be in, how often it changes and how you respond to things. All this keeps you locked in a cage. You can never be really free of all that."

I didn't contradict him, enjoying the sun on my face.

"Anyway, the greatest challenge is being able to stand your own company."

A tick climbed up my elbow. I didn't notice it but Vojto brushed it away in a swift gesture. I got to my feet and began dusting myself off.

"You should have someone look you over in case you've picked up a tick. They're all over the grass and the bushes," he said.

We walked back. I wondered who I could ask to look me over. Then I got an idea, and was suddenly so excited I had to toss a coin. Heads is yes, tails is no. Tails. So I tossed the coin again – tails again. I shrugged. That's settled, then. But I couldn't get the idea out of my head. I tossed the coin really high and let it fall on the back of my hand. Heads!

"Look at the mountains – doesn't it look like they're smoking?! I bet it's going to rain."

Zuzana Kabátová lived halfway across town, in a new detached house her parents had built right after the war. I was pleased that she answered the door, but that was about as far as I had got with my planning. Although I had taken her out to the cinema a few times (I wouldn't claim I got much out of the films, as I spent the whole time glancing at her and wondering whether and how I could touch her pristine arm), I'd always been rather shy in this department and didn't think of myself as particularly good-looking. Nor was I sure that in a delicate situation I could rely on my great eloquence.

We sat down in the kitchen and she offered me some lemonade. We didn't speak. There was no one else at home. We looked out of the window at some sparrows hopping on the laundry line, dropping their excrement on the concrete pavement lined with an assortment of bottles.

I started speaking out of the blue, so suddenly that it took me by surprise.

"Can you check me out for ticks?"

Zuzana laughed and blushed demurely.

"All right… Take your clothes off."

Without giving it a second thought I undressed. Zuzana stifled a little burst of laughter with the palm of her hand, then assumed a serious and professional air.

I was standing naked in the middle of the kitchen and she knelt in front of me.

"Raise your arms!"

She carefully inspected the skin under my arms, on the chest and neck, touching me gently with her fingertips, presumably to make sure that any protuberance was a birthmark rather than a tick. I felt as if I was at the doctor's.

She focused on the area between my legs and I felt something stir. I tried to cover my slowly advancing erection.

"Raise your arms!" she said threateningly. "You're blocking the light, I can't see anything."

I swallowed hard as a pleasant tingling sensation spread through my body.

Very slowly she moved to my back and legs. And my bottom. I felt awkward when she separated the two cheeks and inspected me, stifling a chuckle.

"All clear."

Her finger wandered along my thighs and down to my calves and toes.

"Nothing there."

I lowered my arms, and only now realized I'd been holding my breath all that time. I reached for my trousers absent-mindedly.

Her beautiful blue eyes glanced at me from below and her sultry voice asked:

"Don't you want to check me out as well? I might have caught a tick too…?"

When it was all over Zuzana fell asleep on the bed. With her body next to mine and the air filled with her fragrance I felt high, as if cold air were running through my veins. We were naked. I admired the suppleness of her breasts and her clear white skin with tiny freckles that shone in the semi-darkness, smooth and delicate.

I reached down and pulled off the condom. Zuzana rolled over to one side. Her eyes were closed and her breathing was regular. As

I gently covered her with a blanket, she purred something incomprehensible in her sleep and cuddled up to me.

Holding the delicate elastic object I examined the condom against the sunlight streaming from the window. Tiny veins like white paths coursed in it in various directions. The creased plastic with a little cap at the end looked like a miniature breast engorged with milk.

This is me inside and her outside, I thought. How magical.

I watched Zuzana as she slept. The sun was slowly setting behind the Volovec Mountain, casting long shadows, and for a brief moment her lovely youthful oval face suddenly appeared aged, with droopy eyelids and shapeless cheeks, with wrinkles around her joyful sleepy eyes and delicate mouth. A body that would turn soft and pulpy as gravity exerted its pull, making it slacken and sag. I chased the image away and leaned close to her face. She smelled wonderful. Only the present was real.

Zuzana woke up and stretched out sensuously. Suddenly she didn't seem all that pretty, more average, indeed plain. But then the light fell on her from another angle, or perhaps I looked at her from a different direction, or maybe it was just the muscles under her skin settling into another configuration. She smiled, flaunting her curves, and her beauty had me under its spell once more.

We made love again. As I climaxed I felt something cold shooting up my spine and suffusing my whole body. My mind clouded over. When my hand traced Zuzana's face I felt tears. This was how it would always be after we made love. Unless she fell asleep, she always wept. I have never asked why and I guess she wouldn't have been able to explain anyway.

Zuzana, my mad, maddening Zuzana!

By the time her parents came home we were both dressed. Zuzana was cooking dinner and I was keeping her company in the kitchen.

I only knew her parents by sight. Mr Kabát shook my hand and looked me up and down. He was an austere man of few words. He owned a shop after the war and rumour had it that he was still dealing in one thing or another.

Zuzana's mother was a portly red-haired woman. She went over to the cupboard to get some plates.

"I hope you will stay for dinner."

"Yes, he's staying," Zuzana said, giving me a gentle kick.

Her father didn't say a word throughout the meal. Her mother was in charge of the conversation.

She gave a detailed account of how her brother-in-law had lost his eyesight in a car accident six months earlier. He was hit by another car although he had right of way. Since the damage was negligible they agreed not to report it to the police; the other driver gave him some money to cover the cost of repairs and they parted amicably. Her brother-in-law wasn't in a lot of pain, he had just hit his head on the side of the door. But when he woke up the next morning he realized he couldn't see anything. Absolutely nothing. At the hospital they told him that he must have had a brain haemorrhage and the spilled blood had damaged his retina.

Zuzana's mother apologized for raising such an unsuitable subject over a meal but there was something about the story she found irresistible and she couldn't help adding more and more juicy details.

I happened to glance down at the soup, the usual mix of carrots and greasy globules that I normally don't take much notice of. There was a big fat flour worm floating in it. The fact that it was no longer moving didn't improve matters. I felt a nasty taste in my mouth straight away.

I looked around. Mr Kabát was spooning his soup and Zuzana listened, spellbound, to her mother describing her brother-in-law's surgery.

"The optical nerve…" she said, pointing her finger at me. Both of them stared at me. I nodded.

"Is the soup too cold?"

"Oh no, it's… delicious!" I said with a forced smile.

She went on talking.

I sighed. The last thing I wanted was to make a fuss. We had only just met, I had just slept with their beloved daughter for the first time and now this! I knew I couldn't embarrass them or make them feel bad. If I threw the worm under the table everyone would see. Beads of cold sweat appeared on my brow.

"Let me open the window," Zuzana said.

I took a deep breath. Just grit your teeth, I told myself. For some reason it seemed like a good idea to cut the worm in two. It was quite easy. Dipping my spoon in the soup I fished out a piece of the corpse. I closed my eyes and took a spoonful. I thought it touched my teeth but I might have been wrong. I felt nauseous.

"Would you like some more?" chirped Zuzana's mother.

Something touched me gently under the table. It was Zuzana's hand on my knee. She was stroking me. Hurriedly I dispatched the second half of the worm. By the time I finished eating my T-shirt was drenched in sweat.

It was getting late and I said I had to go. Zuzana gave me a shy kiss when nobody was looking.

"Wait…" her father stopped me at the door.

A cold wind was blowing outside. A swarm in May is worth a load of hay. I expected the customary lecture about his daughter, about what should or should not happen – the smiles and the warning finger, that sort of thing…

But there was none of that. Instead, he remarked casually:

"People say there will be a currency reform, have you heard?"

I shook my head although I had heard some rumours.

"It's going to happen, make no mistake."

He stared at me for a moment.

"I have it from a reliable source."

I shrugged. He lowered his voice.

"Should your father, the good doctor, by any chance wish to change crowns into dollars or forints at an excellent rate…"

He made a eloquent gesture with his hand.

I nodded.

Again, he stared at me for a while. His loosened tie was slightly askew. He smiled.

"Well, take care of yourself."

"Goodbye."

"Tell him to get in touch."

24.

The most refined kind of revenge is the kind you haven't planned. And it's most satisfying when its instigator is completely unaware of it himself. This is what happened after Screwy Igor died. His body wasn't found for two days. He had had a stroke. This was what Father assumed, and the autopsy confirmed it.

Sighing with relief, his relatives sorted out the rubbish in the house and the courtyard – all the broken gadgets, useless ball bearings, nails, screws, copper wires, hubcaps, chassis parts – and lugged everything over to the scrapyard. It took them a full three months and fetched an astonishing 150,000 crowns.

They had pleaded with him for years to stop hoarding but he wouldn't listen; they even considered having him locked up in a loony bin, at least for a while, so that the house could be cleared out. Eventually they gave up and stopped contacting him, wondering all the while how to get rid of this dead weight.

The big clearout was finished on 29 May 1953 and the money was shared out among the relatives.

Yes, the most refined form of revenge is the kind you haven't planned. Screwy Igor hadn't planned it but he chose just the right moment to die.

For several days communist bigwigs kept assuring all and sundry, on the radio and in the papers, that nothing was brewing and that the currency reform was only a rumour trumped up by Western imperialist propaganda. Those swine, who had sold their souls to the devil, wanted to sabotage our thriving socialist economy. Comrade Kominár gave a passionate speech on local radio.

Although the rumours circulating for over a week were quite contradictory, the denizens of Brežany did not hesitate. They besieged the clothes shops, the grocers' and the chemists', buying up anything they could lay their hands on. The more expensive goods discreetly vanished from the counters and eventually even sales of tinned food and smoked meats had to be banned. The goods were sent back to the warehouse. Over-the-counter sales were terminated and those unfortunate enough to have no ration cards went hungry. In the end even the sale of petrol was prohibited by special decree and rationed only to state enterprises and government cars. The streets were patrolled by police.

On Saturday morning Czechoslovak Radio broadcast a speech by President Antonín Zápotocký, also known as Torpedo Ears. He referred to rumours spreading among the people of an impending financial collapse and a currency reform and swore blind:

"There's not a grain of truth in it, our currency has never been more stable. Anyone who claims the contrary is a liar!"

The evening news carried the information that was to appear in the Sunday edition of the party dailies *Pravda* and *Rudé Právo* the next day: between Monday 1 June and Thursday 4 June 1953 a currency reform would take place.

All you needed to do was report to the exchange centre of the Czechoslovak National Bank and exchange 300 old crowns for 60 new ones, i.e. at the rate of 1:5. Any additional currency would be exchanged at the rate of 1:50.

People's savings melted like ice cubes in the sun. The two hundred thousand crowns Father had deposited in a state investment fund disappeared without any recompense. And since he employed a nurse, he was classified as an exploiter to whom only the 1:50 exchange rate applied. I can still see his expression as he read our bank statement. Our family savings had dwindled to 420 crowns.

People tried to spend as much as they could on Sunday, as if that would solve anything. But nothing remotely useful was available. Cinemas, restaurants, patisseries and pubs stayed open. As the citizens of Brežany were determined to get in, some waiters ended up getting slapped in the face in the melee.

Zuzana and I went to the cinema and watched three screenings one after the other. We didn't mind seeing the same film. I've become an expert on Pal'o Bielik's *The Wolves' Lair*. For anyone who hadn't had the pleasure of experiencing the Slovak uprising in real life the film offered a chance to make up for it. Afterwards we got hammered at the Stag Hotel bar and we were by no means alone. A man in a suit asked: "What's your most expensive drink?"

By the time we left he was lying under the table, spewing up some partially digested five-star French brandy.

The hotel sold off all its kitchen supplies to the staff. All that was left for Chef Svinický was a small crate of Portuguese sardines. It gave him nightmares of drowning and lying at the bottom of the sea, with swarms of little fish swimming in and out of a hole in his belly.

Puškár couldn't think of anything better to do but to live it up in a house of ill repute outside Brežany's fortifications. Any trace of the old fortifications had disappeared a long time ago, of course, and carnal relations were taking place in secret in an establishment outside the city limits, which exercised an irresistible pull and continued to function through inertia after prostitution was banned. Officially it was home to Mrs Škarniclová and her daughters.

Puškár left none of its attractions untried.

The minute his well-worn body crossed the threshold of the establishment, he was gripped by guilt of such tremendous proportions that he holed up at home and didn't go out for several days.

Meanwhile people threw hundreds of worthless banknotes into the Sálava or set fire to all the Štefániks, Kollárs and Karel Havlíček Borovskýs and other historical figures whose portraits had graced them. At night they used the notes to plaster the walls of the three currency exchanges in Brežany with a fetching new wall-covering.

On Tuesday night my parents had a tense discussion in the kitchen. I was later told that Father had been wondering what to about the German's banknotes that were gathering dust in the blue album.

But who would want them now?

So for the moment the treasure trove remained untouched. At night Father leafed through the album, feeling the firmness of the old paper.

Mr Kabát, Zuzana's father, had no such concerns. They came for him first thing on Monday morning. Their doorbell rang, followed by loud hammering on the door. Zuzana gave me a lively account of how they had taken him away without saying where he was going. It wasn't until a month later that the family was told that he had been accused of smuggling and illegal speculation with the national currency.

A week or two later Vojto came to see me unannounced. Before he even took his coat off he told me he had been expelled from university. Because of his father. He was in the first year of a psychology course. The family was told they could count themselves lucky they were allowed to keep their house.

We sat in the kitchen for a long time saying nothing. He said the other reason he came was to say goodbye. We grabbed a bottle of wine intending to go to the manor-house park.

As we were putting on our shoes in the hallway Father hustled past with his medical bag. He was greatly agitated and hardly noticed us. He knocked over a bottle of raspberry syrup, which slicked out over the kitchen floor, overwhelming the ants. They flailed their little legs until their heads disappeared in the sweet liquid they had always so desired, and they drowned in their sticky paradise.

Father swore. He wiped the floor with a rag without so much as looking at us.

"I'm leaving for Podbrezová tomorrow. I have to report to the rolling mill there. So that I can mingle with the working classes on the production line," said Vojto when we got to the park.

He had a glass of wine, smiling sadly. "Not bad. One of ours?"

I nodded.

"At the university youth union meeting the majority voted against me. They said there was no place for me there, as the son of a Nazi. Some people found a pretext not to attend."

We sat on the bench drinking. I couldn't think of anything to say. I guess I should have comforted Vojto but I didn't know how. Dusk was falling.

"Do you still have the stone we found at the manor house?"

I nodded and took the black onyx out of my pocket.

Vojto placed his on the palm of his hand.

"And the telescope... One day we'll watch the stars through it."

I looked up towards Venus shining above our heads.

"We don't need the telescope to see them."

On the production line Vojto was immediately assigned to work at a dangerous hydraulic press that regularly jammed and refused to function. If the factory had done everything by the book it wouldn't have made any money, so whenever the machine got stuck, to get it going again the workers would just reach inside it with their hands without turning it off.

As a result Vojto's boss was the proud owner of a jar full of chopped-off fingers preserved in formaldehyde, which he showed to newcomers by way of warning. One still had dirt under the fingernail, with a vein and transparent scraps of skin hanging from it.

When Vojto shook the jar a little finger would point, as if beckoning to him. Or it would rise in warning. All that was missing from his boss's collection was a fist of the working class, as the popular saying of the day went. It was just a question of waiting for the right kind of accident.

291

25.

One day, many years before, Father's father, Grandpa Albert, had gone abroad to make some money and landed a job as an electrical engineer and pump supervisor at the construction of the Suez Canal. The work was very dangerous and many people died. But within a year he made enough to build a house. This house. The only surviving photograph shows Grandpa standing proudly in bright sunshine, the water of the canal rippling in the background, below a high dam.

The house was built with the money from Egypt. Sometimes I saw Father walking along the walls as if trying to catch the scent of something. Perhaps I was just imagining it, but at times I thought I detected the merest hint of the Mediterranean in the smell of the walls and plaster.

"If only I could get away from here, escape, run away," Father must have thought.

I am lying on my bed exhausted, with my eyes closed (they are itchy and I'm sneezing; my allergy is taking its toll but it's not bad enough to make me run away, it's just making my nose run) and I imagine exotic fragrances. And for the hundredth time I take out the vintage photograph with grandfather's face stuck on top of great-uncle Karol's head. Yes, the family is back together again.

The main thing is to stay calm, Father used to say, admiring the same view (he too used to lie on the bed in his isolation cell, the way I am now doing), then you can take anything, you can stand anything. Just stay calm, don't worry, everything will be all right. Everything will be all right! The louder you say it the more likely it will be. Or will it?

The northern cemetery has always been the quietest place in Brežany.

For the umpteenth time I admire the memorial to the fallen of the First and Second World Wars. Typical Brežany names – Levendovský, Puškár, Krebs… I catch myself again at not being quite sure if anything is really worth fighting for. Isn't it more sensible just to make sure you survive? What is the point of laying down your life in battle?

The cemetery lives a life of its own. A black cat trying to bask in the cool spring sunshine between the tombstones looks at me as if I were an intruder. This is its sovereign territory and it is ready to defend it. But for the time being it just crouches behind a weeping stone angel, watching me with distaste.

I follow the highways of ants, two-way traffic that goes all the way up to the fence where the advance guard has detected a dead frog. Ant throngs swarm towards it and away from it, taking it apart. Perhaps they will reassemble it like some puzzle back at the anthill if they're bored.

I remember these warm early evenings when the air is as heavy as before a storm, with ants swarming. Clumsy copulating couples somersaulting through the air, bewinged and confused, having just hatched, and fulfilling their one and only obligation in this world: that of multiplying.

The swifts didn't have to work hard to swallow them in mid-flight, pouncing on them from the sky.

My innate indecisiveness has resurfaced. I take out a coin and toss it in the air. I am determined to keep tossing until I get the desired outcome. But then I put it back into my pocket and finally approach Father's grave. There is nothing in it but not many people know that.

On one of his rare visits to Brežany Vojto told me that his mother, Mrs Roško, had overheard a bit of a conversation behind the consulting-room door. A patient had just walked in, complaining of difficulty sleeping. Ďurovič was his name. Or was it Ďurica? She couldn't remember exactly.

"You always have an excuse. This is not good enough. Don't you forget our agreement and your pledge!"

"But it really couldn't be done! Why won't you believe me?"

"Someone has walked away with the Silbersteins' possessions; perhaps you were involved in that as well, comrade doctor. People say you treated the old man's broken leg…"

"But that's not true!"

"Come now, comrade Trnovský! There are moments when there is no such thing as truth. Whatever you believe *becomes* true. It's been like that for thousands of years, as long as the world has existed. Don't you forget that!"

The door opened and Ďurovský or Ďurina, or whatever his name was, flashed a grateful smile.

"Thank you, comrade doctor. I hope the new medication will work."

She said Father had walked with him all the way to the main hospital entrance.

When Father came back, Natália reminded him that the issue of their house had not yet been resolved. That had nothing to do with him, Father snapped. She told him that she'd overheard their conversation and Father went pale. She said that if he, as a respected citizen, would put in a good word for the Roškos, God would most certainly look upon this as helping a neighbour in need. Father asked what exactly she'd heard and she asked if she could assume that they wouldn't be evicted. He just nodded and left.

"A strange story, isn't it?" Vojto commented.

"Yes, very strange."

Sometimes when I crossed the main square on an errand I saw Father in an armchair in the lobby of the Stag Hotel staring at the stained glass in the ceiling. He once told me he liked the design, because it reminded him of a kaleidoscope filled with multicoloured fragments of glass and mirrors that rearrange themselves into dazzling new patterns every time you move it. (I read somewhere that the proper Slovak word for it should be *krasohľad*, "beauty viewer", but that doesn't sound right to me – although the word *kaleidoscope* doesn't fully convey the sensation of looking into it either). Father said it calmed him to just sit there and watch the world go by.

Whenever Father thought no one was looking, his features would harden and go strangely pale. His left leg, crossed over his right, would twitch convulsively when he was thinking.

I knocked on the window and he gave a start. He quickly put on a smile and sprawled in the armchair as if nothing was happening. I said something to him but he pointed to his ears to indicate that he couldn't hear.

I imagine that every time he wanted to suppress his anxiety, he reached for a Luminal and each time the word would remind him of the cause of his anxiety.

Klaudius Kolár seemed to be on his last legs. I begged Father to go up to the hills to see him urgently because Kolár was adamant he wouldn't see a doctor. He used to say, perhaps as a romantic pose, that "it will be best to leave it in the hands of fate". Vojto successfully argued that fate might be "Adam asking his father the doctor to come and see you." Before Klaudius had time to change his mind I turned up with Father.

Ileus, Father concluded after a brief examination: obstruction of the bowel. It may have been caused by a nervous shock or physical strain, and although Klaudius couldn't recall having experienced either, the cause was immaterial. He urgently needed surgery tremove the obstruction in the gastrointestinal tract, Father said. So Kolár came down from his mountain.

As a preventative measure against high fever Father put him on Chloramphenicol. Later that night Kolár had horrific hallucinations of fluttering pieces of burned fabric with blackened edges, which he was unable to dispel. By the time morning came he was so desperate he felt suicidal. This didn't prevent him from later recalling this episode as the most powerful spiritual experience of his life.

Father pulled some strings at the National Committee so that Kolár did not have to return to the mountain, and he was allowed to stay in Brežany. He was allocated a tiny basement flat, dark and damp. His favourite pastime was watching the feet of unsuspecting people walking by.

After giving his blessing to the move, Comrade Kominár was slightly cross when he came across the poem featuring chimneys and chimney sweeps:

> *Life is a chimney and I'm a chimney sweep – as you well know.*
> *A deep vagina or a rectum? But before*
> *You ask me how I know – leave me alone, go!*
> *I have no idea. Whatever. Yesterday or tomorrow*
> *I'll howl at the moon like a stray dog.*

He summoned Kolár and demanded an explanation.

"So this is what you call socialist art, is it?"

Klaudius shook his head.

"And what about the allusion to my person, eh? Am I supposed to be the dog? Am I?" Comrade Kominár liked to say everything twice.

Kolár pooh-poohed this: "That's just a metaphor."

This must have been the first time comrade Kominár had heard this word, so he wasn't sure whether he should take offence or not.

"I see, I see. Well, that's a different kettle of fish. A different kettle of fish."

He patted the poet on the back and let him go, confiscating the poem, just in case.

Klaudius was in a hurry, as he was every Saturday.

Saturdays were when weddings and funerals were held in Brežany. The local drunks were among the first to turn up, eager to shake everyone's hand and congratulate everyone, particularly anyone who had a glass and was likely to offer them a drink. After the third ceremony they were usually done for. The register office and the funeral parlour faced each other across the street.

Klaudius was a regular at these events. Afterwards he often invited his buddies to his basement flat.

"Congratulations to the bridegroom and the bride... To your happy day!"

"My deepest commiserations. He was a wonderful man. It's a real tragedy."

"A toast to the beautiful bride! A splendid wedding. To your big day!"

On Easter Monday he went from house to house, carrying the traditional willow whip as well as a huge demijohn.

When the lady of the house offered him a drink, as was customary, he said: "Thanks, not now, just pour it in here." Whatever it was – wine, vodka, eggnog, plum brandy, gin – he would take it. He would later offer the resulting exquisite mélange to his visitors.

His street buddies came and went. One, in particular, was unforgettable, a man with a massive head. I heard he had sold his brain in advance five or six times over for scientific purposes. When he died, the pathologists ended up fighting over him.

26.

Working at the hydraulic press Vojto had plenty of time to think. Since he always met his quotas, they left him alone, immersed in the smell of metal and oil and his own thoughts. On Saturdays he did extra shifts "for the benefit of Korea" even though he had no idea what that was supposed to mean.

One day Vojto and I were waiting for a bus outside Progress, the brand new Brežany department store, and I asked him how he was coping.

"It's all relative… We can't even predict when the next bus is due. There are too many possibilities – the time that your watch shows doesn't necessarily match the time on the driver's watch, he might be running early or late, something might crop up along the way. And, last but not least, the time shown in this timetable doesn't necessarily have to match yours or his… Basically, nothing is certain. For example, the bus should be coming around that corner any second now – fifteen, fourteen, thirteen, twelve, and so on… six, five, four, three, two, one. Can you see it? No, you can't. Well, and that's what everything is like. It's all incredibly relative."

"I see…" I said. "Shall we go?"

The bus had arrived and was waiting for us to get on.

Well yes, everything is relative.

Like the family party many years later, to celebrate Father's birthday. It may have been 1967 or so, long after I had moved to Bratislava. The party was held in the drawing room; somebody even played the piano which, out of tune as usual, produced the most pitiful wail, but everyone put on a brave face and lavished praise on the performer.

Meanwhile my six-year-old son Bony was chasing Monika, the daughter of family friends, across the drawing room and into the living room, all the way to my parents' bedroom, through all the doors, whether they were open or closed. Driven out by the sound of the piano I pretended to join them, and sat down in an armchair to browse through a book.

Little Monika poked me in the ribs.

"Count to a hundred and then come and look for us!"

"We're going to hide. Close your eyes and start counting!"

It reminded me of the game of hide-and-seek we played in the garden of this house many years ago. Ever since then I'd been scared that if I closed my eyes and began to count something might happen. A secret would be revealed, as if in some magic ritual, a strange forgotten spell. You count to a hundred – and nothing is the same as it was before.

But I did as I was told; I closed my eyes and started to count, leaving the odd number out. I heard rustling, the moving of furniture and giggling.

"... ninety-nine... a hundred! Here I come!"

I got up from the armchair and started looking round.

A curtain fluttered. I flung it aside, expecting to find Monika. Bony's usual hiding place was under the furniture so I knew it wasn't him, but the little girl proved to be smarter than that. A picture, caught by a sudden movement of the curtain, fell off the wall. I had never seen it in our house before although it seemed familiar. It depicted a scene in a night bar, painted in brown, yellow and blue, showing tired female faces from an unconventional perspective.

Luckily the frame was not damaged. I was about to replace the picture on the wall when something on the reverse caught my eye. It was the stamp of the German military headquarters in Brežany with a handwritten note on Aryanization. I froze.

Bony kept mum in his hiding place but Monika wasn't as patient. She crept out of the wardrobe and came up to me quietly. When she realised I wasn't paying her any attention, she tugged at my sleeve.

"What's up? What are you doing, Adam?"

The guests next door were obviously in high spirits. The aspiring piano player had just finished his seemingly endless clumsy piece.

"It's nothing, nothing."

I examined the stamp. It seemed unreal and I shivered.

"What are you doing?"

"I haven't finished counting... Go and hide!"

Monika left, disappointed.

A little while later Bony crawled out from under the bed and ran after her. I looked around the room and discovered a few more objects I hadn't noticed here before – a silver sugar bowl, a candlestick, a tray.

Everything was labelled and meticulously catalogued. I heard

Father howling with laughter as if there were no tomorrow. He was partying. Gradually I began to recall where I had seen these objects before. It was in Armin's flat, which I had visited many times as a boy.

I sensed someone moving behind my back and I turned around. Father stood in the doorway looking at me. He must have been on his way to the toilet when he spotted me. I had no idea how long he'd been standing there. I hadn't heard him – there's something about this house that makes everyone lose their hearing. He was staring at me. I tried to look nonchalant and even flashed him a shy smile but it can't have been very convincing.

He turned around and walked away without a word. I heard his steps in the corridor. The company in the drawing room took up another song.

Yes, everything is relative.

Reluctantly I had to admit that I didn't really know my Father at all.

Especially when the registered letter arrived – *To be opened only by the addressee – A REMETTRE EN MAIN PROPRE.* I signed the delivery note with trembling hands and tore open the envelope:

RE: Your request for access to documents, as provided by the Law on National Remembrance.

I went through the documents in the reading room, quite certain all this had to be just some embarrassing mistake. Including the following, handwritten statement:

I declare, upon my honour, that I will keep all matters discussed with the Security Officer completely confidential. I will not mention these facts to anyone, including my colleagues, acquaintances or family members. I am willing to help uncover any criminal activities that may come to my attention. I have no objection to meeting with a Security Officer. I am aware that any breach of this declaration will make me criminally liable. Alfonz Trnovský.

I laughed – but this isn't Father's handwriting! And it's not his signature either. And besides – Security, that's basically the police, right? So Father helped the police uncover criminals, surely there's nothing wrong with that.

I went on reading. Of course I did recognize Father's handwriting as well as his signature. And the pledge of silence sounded ominous.

The archive contained sombre, impersonal reports and their evaluations by higher-ranking ŠtB officers. A grey imprint of life.

The Secret Informant Alfonz Trnovský enjoys a high reputation in Brežany, his place of residence. He also enjoys the trust of his patients. He appears to possess all the qualities required of a SI, provided he is given proper training and guidance. So far he has provided only information of a factual nature that can be documented from other sources. There is no indication that he has divulged his contacts with ŠtB officers. He has taken great care to observe confidentiality in his dealings with ŠtB officers. The SI displays a positive attitude to our people's democracy. We anticipate that it will be possible to deploy him extensively. The Informant was vetted by Secret Informants ĎUSO, GARDENER, GERMAN and Agent ISAAC. The SI will be tasked to target individuals listed in his recruitment plan, as well as other persons with whom he is in contact and who are of interest to the ŠtB. The SI will be handled in a responsible manner. He will be given a full explanation of the tasks assigned to him, appropriate cover stories will be devised and he will be guided towards strict observance of confidentiality. Following his recruitment, the SI will meet his handler at regular biweekly intervals in accordance with a predetermined timetable. Should a scheduled meeting be missed, a replacement meeting will be held one week later. In the event that contact with the Informant is disrupted telephone contact will be established. Drawn up in the original on five pages.

Operative officer:
Captain Ďuratný, DSc.

The documents in the archive are like walls of an old house that has been abandoned by people. All the furniture is gone and it now stands completely hollow.

I had photocopies made of all the reports and statements. I walked down the corridor thinking I would definitely have to pay Ďuratný a visit. I remembered that somebody by that name did live in Brežany. I wanted to talk to him and find out what really happened. I harboured no hatred towards him; I just felt the need to learn more. I would have been prepared to pay him for the information if necessary.

For the umpteenth time I rang the doorbell in Hviezdoslav Street. For a long time there was no answer. And just as I was about to leave, an old woman opened the door and told me that her husband had died in circumstances she'd rather not discuss.

I half-expected her to ask me if I wanted her to pass on a message.

Part 3

Fantastic Vision

1.

I am looking at *Fantastic Vision*, another in the series of Goya's wall paintings in the House of the Deaf Man, featured in Father's monograph. It shows two figures floating in the air, one of them pointing towards a distant hill with a castle bathed in mist.

I'm sitting on Father's bed. Through the window I can see the countryside, with the Volovec Mountain enveloped in haze. A glider is sailing through the sky. It soars high in the air, gracefully weaving its way in and out of the clouds.

Earlier in the morning there was a feeble spring sun, glowing orange. As it slowly disappeared a light drizzle, mixed with the occasional wispy clump of snow that would immediately melt on the pavement and in the gardens, drove me out of the cemetery.

Now I feel like doing something I loved to do as a child. Undeterred by the creakiness of my joints, long past their flexible prime, I slowly lower myself on the ground and lie down. My decrepit body has turned uncomfortably stiff over the years. It's petrifying to look back at everything that one has been – and been through. It feels humiliating to have to go down on my knees first and only then slump down gradually.

But the resulting sensation has certainly made the effort worthwhile. Stretched out on the moist mouldy carpet in the middle of the living room, I stare at the ceiling, with its damp stains and cracks. The plaster has peeled off in places, revealing older layers underneath. Traces of green and yellow left by a paint roller, faded shades of lilac, tiny shreds of wallpaper torn down a long time ago...

A map of constellations and mysterious continents.

"Every clock in this house shows a different time...!" Father grunted irritably as he hastily put on his scarf, coat and hat in the hallway. Not that it was cold outside – this was how he always went out. He thought it dignified and appropriate to his standing in society. He was in a hurry to get to the health centre.

Back then he still believed I would go on to study medicine, that I would eventually come to this decision of my own accord. And he wanted me to believe it too. Whether I liked it or not. That is why he insisted I took every opportunity to visit him in his consulting room and observe him at work.

The consulting room was austerely furnished – just a few pictures from old copies of the *Medical Journal* pinned perfunctorily to the wall along with a couple of Matthias Walter engravings marked *Engraved by hand*. One showed the outline of a paediatrician with a stethoscope examining an unkempt child sitting on a bed, while in another the smiling doctor was speaking to a babe in arms, a hammer for testing the knee reflex hidden behind his back, apparently waiting for an unguarded moment when he could put it to use.

On Father's desk there was usually a medical report, fresh from the lab, with the patient's name and details: *red blood cell count: 3,340 cells/mCL, white blood cell count: 16,200/mCL, Hb: 61%, Colour Index: 0.9. Institute of National Health, Department of Microbiology… Test number… Patient's name… Sample… Result…*

The one thing that really impressed me was the X-rays. After they were delivered by Nurse Natália Roško, Father would inspect them, holding them up against the window or clipping them to a glass surface lit from below.

There was an extraordinary beauty about them – the patterns of bones and fine tissue seemed to have been meticulously arranged and accurately drawn by a painter. If I were a painter, I would copy X-ray images.

Father showed me an X-ray of splayed fingers. I picked it up and examined it against the light. Standing behind me and sipping hideously bitter coffee from his stained mug, Father said:

"Fingers are really an extension of the soul. They are magic. They're the first thing I notice in a woman."

He placed the mug on the desk and took the X-ray from me.

"I can't help looking at my own hands, either. The way they work is truly miraculous! Observing your fingers helps you stay in touch with yourself. Whenever I feel tense or insecure, I inspect my hands."

We said nothing for a while, observing the various interconnected bones in the palm of the X-rayed hand. In four of the fingers the digits seemed slightly skewed compared to the rest of the hand, with tiny spots around forming irregular constellations. I was fascinated.

"What's this?"

"What do you think… These are broken fingers, Adam."

I sensed that he was itching to light a cigarette. Although he never smoked in my presence, I recognized the fidgeting as he furtively felt for matches in his pocket.

"What's happened to him?" I asked.

I noticed a name in the corner, in tiny, almost illegible letters: *Puškár*. I have always imagined that the teachers at medical school devote a significant part of their time to destroying the students' handwriting until it degenerates into an illegible scrawl, while the other part focuses on teaching them to decipher it. Of course, would-be pharmacists also have to be let in on the secret so that they can deal with prescriptions. They all use a code or a secret alphabet to avoid upsetting patients. The salient facts are included in the typed medical reports but those, too, are phrased in such a way that nobody can understand them. But I had cracked Father's code.

"What was it you were asking?"

"I was wondering how this happened."

"He said… it happened during an interrogation. They asked him to take something out of the drawer, then slammed it shut on his hand. These things happen. I guess he wouldn't talk, or something like that…"

Father broke off and started rummaging through other X-ray images, picking some of them up and absent-mindedly clipping them onto a string stretched above his desk. I don't know why he did that, I guess he liked looking at them. I sat down and watched.

Backlit, against the backdrop of shades of blue, gray and black and the gleaming window, among all the ribs, skulls, elbows, pelvises and spines, he looked like the Almighty in His archive of human forms.

It's too dark in here! Please turn on the light!

Yes, he did look a little bit like God. As if he could hear what I was thinking, he turned around, and said, framed by the morbid pictures behind him:

"Someone said to me the other day: 'God sees everything. He doesn't have a choice, he can't look elsewhere or turn away. He is the all-seeing God after all!' I replied: 'But what an enormous effort that must be! It must really make His eyes hurt!'"

305

Father grinned.

"What is Mother making for lunch?"

I've already mentioned that people used to confuse me with my father, especially once I was older. It wasn't so much our appearance (although there was quite a resemblance) and besides, they must have known I wasn't *the* Doctor Trnovský. Rather, it was as if something of his profession had rubbed off on me. Some of the iodine smell and the glint of the stethoscope must have left a permanent trace on me.

And so it came about that sometimes the good people of Brežany would consult me on their health problems. At first I thought this was just a coincidence or small talk, like discussing the weather. But more and more often I had to accept that they were genuinely seeking my advice. I demurred, of course, and explained that I was not qualified, that it was Father's advice that they really needed, but they wouldn't listen and kept sharing their stories. Eventually I found myself dispensing advice, recommending medications (I did pick up a thing or two by observing Father), offering a preliminary diagnosis or suggesting a more thorough examination.

Once I went as far as to inspect the contents of a carrier bag containing Mr Malánek's potpourri of medications and insisting that he replace one particular medicine with another.

In 1956 the socialist camp (the communist cliché had always conjured up for me the image of a bunch of jolly Bedouins crossing the desert) was buffeted by a fierce sandstorm. From the sparse, carefully filtered reports that reached us we gathered that mendacious Western propaganda had provoked protests in Poland and that Hungary had suffered a counter-revolution and assault on the fledgling people's democracy. We also heard that loyal communists were hanged from lamp posts. And other similar stories.

It wasn't until much later that I learned how Soviet tanks had destroyed entire districts of Budapest and that some three thousand Hungarians had been killed. How strange – barely a decade ago the soldiers of the same army had been welcomed as liberators. Now they were occupiers. History has some tasty morsels to offer.

Soon afterwards Albert E. Kahn's *The Game of Death* was

published. My brother Peter was quite excited to show us the book on one of his rare visits home. He had left it for us to read, and Tina and I lapped it up by the light of our new fridge during our midnight kitchen binges. We were hooked as soon as we read its opening lines:

In the autumn of 1950, barely five years after the end of the Second World War, certain strange and ominously warlike lessons were introduced into the classrooms of American schools. They were lessons which had never previously been taught to any children anywhere in the world. For the first time in history, children began learning to crouch under desks with their eyes tightly closed and their heads buried in their arms, to stand motionless with backs to windows and faces pressed against walls, and to lie on the floor with pieces of cloth covering their bodies.

The children were advised by their teachers that these measures would help protect them from flying glass, falling debris and flash burns in the event of an atomic bomb attack. If they followed instructions carefully, they were told, they would be spared fatal injuries, unless of course a bomb happened to fall too close to their school…

"In order to save your children from burns in the case of direct exposure to an A-Bomb," the principal of a New York school wrote in a form letter addressed to parents, "we are asking him or her to bring to school a piece of sheet large enough for him to curl under. Will you send it with him? Write his name on it in ink. He is to keep it in his desk for use in emergencies."

On October 11, 1951, with considerable fanfare, the New York City Board of Education announced a special "emergency safety measure" in the city's schools. The measure consisted of the distribution of 200,000 identification tags among all second- and third-grade pupils in public, private and parochial schools. Press reports noted the hardly consoling fact that the metal out of which the tags were made had a melting point of 1400 degrees centigrade and could therefore withstand heat which would incinerate bodies.

Our reading was accompanied by the unremitting sound of Gershwin emanating from Father's isolation cell.

Someone To Watch Over Me – sang the young Frank Sinatra on His Master's Voice in Father's collection. In the evenings he liked to sit in his armchair, put on a record and sip a glass of sherry, which was becoming increasingly rare in our parts, just like the old 78s, soon to be forever replaced by vinyl.

His other favourites were *Do It Again* and *Soon*. And with Sporting Life in *Porgy and Bess*, intoning *It Ain't Necessarily So,* the Gershwin brothers created the perfect illusion that the world was a happy and peaceful place and nothing bad could possibly happen.

It was while listening to music – in fact, while listening to this very piece – that I realised Father's hearing was rapidly failing. He would play the song more loudly each time. One of us would have to ask him to turn it down. We all pretended everything was fine otherwise, as Sporting Life's voice reverberated through the house.

Eventually Father's hearing went completely, cutting him off from the world of sound. But he never stopped playing Gershwin. Old habits die hard.

2.

Father wanted me to become a doctor but Fate, "lurking behind the curtains of reality" (as the great Klaudius Kolár aptly put it in one of his poems) had other plans in store. It all began quite innocuously.

I went to Bratislava to pick up the papers exempting me from military service, which had been finally issued by the army command. Vojto's father asked me to deliver a handful of blurry photographs from the Uprising. On the train I took them out of the unsealed envelope and had a look. There were men in fatigues standing by a crashed Gustav plane; a bunch of armed men in friendly conversation with a shepherd; Vojto's father playing with the shepherd's dog; a couple of people outside the Donovaly Sport Hotel; an airstrip with some aircraft. He had asked me to drop by Slovak Radio's headquarters in Zochova Street, find his former comrade-in-arms, air force officer Július Mazanec, and hand them over to him.

Bratislava always seemed a vast and complex city to me, the embodiment of a metropolis with all its snares and temptations. Both seemed equally attractive as I walked up Židovská Street and past the tram tunnel below Zámocká Street, bundled up against the cold. It was early November and the neo classicist façade of the Radio headquarters sported a huge banner asserting our country's indissoluble friendship with the Soviet Union. Mazanec came down to meet me in the lobby. Visibly on edge, he hastily shoved the envelope into his pocket without giving it a glance. He grabbed me by the shoulder.

"Can you drive, young man?"

I nodded.

"Come along then!"

He ushered me into his second-floor office and introduced me to Ludvo, his production assistant, a red-faced man who was popping tranquillizers as if they were M&Ms.

I stayed the night in a hostel in Karlova Ves down the Danube where I had my first encounter with a live cockroach, having previously admired them in Dr Atlas's splendid collection of dead and neatly mounted specimens (who knows where that ended up). The next morning I read a jubilant article in the paper:

This evening carries special significance for the people of Slovakia. As of tonight, our working people will be able to watch on their own receivers cultural and sports events in our country and all over the world. Preparations for this great moment have been underway for some time now. Television aerials have been mounted on rooftops and their settings are being double-checked. In Bratislava, in particular, aerials have mushroomed. Do-it-yourself enthusiasts have fashioned their own makeshift aerials, to make sure they don't miss the first broadcast. TV screens have been showing Czechoslovak Television's test card for several days now.

The first TV programme produced in Bratislava was to be broadcast from one of the Danube Fair exhibition halls, which required complex waterproofing. While the work was being finished, the hall presented a scene of total chaos. Ludvo handed me the keys to a rickety old Skoda 1200 and asked me to be on standby, ready to make a dash for the TV studios, located inside the transmitting station on the Kamzík Hill above Bratislava. As a humble messenger I was relegated to the sidelines but, as it happens, I found myself standing next to the announcer, Hilda Michalíková, and in the commotion overheard her referring to Július Mazanec – the man who had the honour of presiding over the whole pandemonium and was on the verge of a heart attack – as a part of the male anatomy. These were her exact words, fortunately uttered before the show went live. All this just goes to show how inarticulate and inadequate people can be if they try to maintain decorum at all costs, since in my view the simple word "prick" would surely have been much more apposite in this context. But it was none of my business.

The first broadcast from the Bratislava TV studios, eagerly awaited by a grand total of some five hundred viewers nationwide, was a live performance by the Slovak Folk Art Ensemble, SL'UK, staged in honour of the fortieth anniversary of the Great October Revolution (give or take a year, give or take four days) as well as the thirtieth anniversary of radio broadcasting in Slovakia. I was hanging around the TV van equipped with three cameras when Ludvo grabbed me and off I went to the makeshift studio on the Kamzík Hill.

On my way up I spotted a crowd in front of a hardware shop. It had gone dark by now and the shop assistant had tuned the sole black-and-white TV set to the test card. Excited citizens of Bratislava jostled to get closer to the shop window, stamping their feet in the creeping November cold, their eyes glued to the wondrous image on the screen. When the hand on the clock reached the top of the hour the announcer appeared. Children whooped with joy and adults were suddenly lost for words. I pulled over and joined them. The announcer dissolved into darkness for a few seconds, and eventually a stage emerged. After a brief pause the dancers in national costumes, who had been waiting in the glare of powerful spotlights, started to dance to music – or at least so I assumed, as no sound penetrated through the thick glass of the shop window. Unbeknownst to the sniffling crowd pushing and shoving around me I felt elated to be part of this momentous event.

And that feeling hasn't left me to this day.

Sometimes when I'm at home in Bratislava I watch the footage of Father I took with a black-and-white 8 mm camera. He is sitting in his isolation cell, talking. He smiles at the camera. In those days he sported a moustache. He walks over to his safe and removes the blue album. He opens it to take out some banknotes. *Quittung über fünfzig Kronen, Theresienstadt, am 1 Jänner 1943. Verrechnungsschein für die deutsche Wehrmacht. Zehn Reichsmark.* Mother sticks her head in the frame and disappears again; she hated to be filmed. Father drags

310

her in front of the camera; she resists. Finally she manages to get away.

I have kept the sound recording, too. If I play it at the same time as the film the silent room comes alive with the sound of birdsong from the open window, and I hear Father's distorted voice.

"… it's like the fairy tale about the magic ring. You can have only one wish. You are just about to make it but then you get another idea and put the magic ring aside. And nobody realises that someone swapped the magic ring for an ordinary one a long time ago. Stop filming me now…. Do you hear me, Adam…? Do you hear me?"

I bought an 8 mm AK8 camera as well as a tape recorder. I took to making home movies of anything and everything. It was all fascinating for me. I would film Father, Mother, Uncle Rudo, Vojto and others, birds, cats mating, everything.

Perhaps I wanted to capture them on film so that I could take them with me, because by then I had moved to Bratislava. I lived in one sublet after another, in all sorts of dumps, but I felt a new and unexpected surge of happiness. Ludvo, the assistant producer, had hired me and since they were short of staff I got a chance to try my hand at every kind of job, from lighting engineer to assistant director.

On Sundays, if I was too busy to go back home, I would put in a reverse-charge call from the post office in Kollár Square. I'd wait for a post office clerk to call out: "Brežany, booth 2!" and storm into the booth. After a quick call to my parents I would spend longer on the line with Zuzana.

My "Licence to install and use a television receiver" was finally issued by Bratislava Post Office No. III. It stated: *Adam Trnovský is licensed to install and use a TV receiver as specified in the Radio Fee Directive and the regulations enacted therein.*

Every day after work I would sit in a small café in Radlinský Street, doing a spot of people-watching. There were no streets like this in Brežany. A tram trundled by and a gentleman in a hat missed it. A car hooted at him, frightening a dog peeing on the corner. As it ran away, the dog almost collided with another car and then with a bus that was huffing and puffing at a stop. The number of cars just kept growing.

311

The first time I parked my brand new burgundy Skoda Spartak by the fence in front of our Brežany house the whole family gathered round to admire it. Father gave the bonnet a professional pat and seemed about to produce his stethoscope and listen to the throbbing of the engine. But he thought better of it.

Once inside the house I noticed that after the great silence of my childhood and the subdued radio of later years the television had assumed complete and permanent control over the internal soundscape.

As the proud owner of the second TV set in Brežany, Father had to contend with twenty-one boisterous people – not counting three children asleep on the sofa and in my former bed – who would converge on our smoke-filled drawing room to watch the sports broadcasts.

Father must have been quite pleased to finally see coming true his dream of sharing a large and welcoming house as one big happy family, at least to some degree. He would walk to and fro regally, a smile playing on his lips.

Czech sports broadcaster Karel Mikyska was in the middle of a stirring figure-skating commentary: "She is competing in a periwinkle-green skating costume, her partner in a plum-blue outfit…." Picturing the colours on the gleaming black-and-white screen required a bit of imagination. Mikyska didn't make it easy either. By the time you found the word "periwinkle" in the dictionary to work out what damn colour she was wearing you would have missed the skater's turn on the ice.

Christmas was around the corner (so was my name day, although no one had ever seemed to care about that) and the house was filled with the delicious smells of baking. Father, Mother, Tina and Peter were all there. Aunt Tonička, a little the worse for wear after overindulging in cherry brandy, was slightly unsteady on her feet. Also in attendance was Uncle Rudo with his wife, Aunt Julka, whom we saw very rarely and suspected he kept hidden among mothballed fur coats. Which is exactly what she looked like. Cousin Filip was also there.

From the moment I woke up I knew exactly what was going to happen that day and in what sequence. The same story played out every year. First the Christmas tree would collapse because it hadn't

312

been set up properly, which would prompt Peter to tell the same joke he told every year, too corny to be reproduced here. Mother would exclaim: "My God!" and Father would say "Thank God!" or vice versa. "We must get a new stand next year!" A row about Christmas tree decorations would follow – should we use round baubles or the shiny fish-shaped ones? – and, predictably, Father would end up fetching a third set of decorations from the cellar. Ikebana IV would swallow some tinsel and be sick in the kitchen. After deliberating for a long time Peter would kill the carp that's traditionally kept in the bathtub in the days leading up to Christmas Eve, and declare this was the last time he'd let himself be talked into doing this job – he had always been a soft touch but as the oldest child he ended up with a fair share of unpleasant chores. The potato salad would be even more scrumptious than last year, at least that was the verdict on it from Tina, who had prepared it.

Mother doesn't feel like frying the carp: we urge her to get on with it; she complains about aching joints and a headache before she finally gets going. Everyone is on edge: we can see from the window that all our neighbours started their Christmas dinner a long time ago. Aunt Tonička faints. Father puts it down to hunger and carries her over to the sofa in his isolation cell to endure the last moments of the fast. Another hour and dinner is ready and Father, as is the custom, tosses walnuts into every corner of the room to ensure that the coming year will be one of plenty. He racks his brains to remember the accompanying jingle, only to get it wrong, to Uncle Rudo's great glee. Aunt Julka bursts into tears; Father puts it down to an excess of emotion.

After we've shared the traditional honey and wafers, the proceedings come to a temporary halt while half the family insists on unwrapping the presents before supper and the other half wants to wait until after the meal. The second faction prevails. Tina starts to cry, Father puts it down to disappointment. Each table setting includes a small goblet filled with plum or cherry brandy. We clink glasses and drink, then move on to the soup. Wine glasses are half-filled. We argue whether the cabbage soup tastes better than it did last year. Next the slain carp sails in, accompanied by potato salad. Someone chokes on a fish bone, a role performed by a different family member every year. Finally *opekance,* the special Christmas honeycakes, are served as dessert.

After that all you can hear is the rustling of wrapping paper. Aunt Tonička hands out presents she has received from us for her birthday. Uncle Rudo remarks this is the natural life cycle of gifts.

Then it's time to go out into the snow-covered yard for a drink of *krampampul'a*, to gaze at the stars and wish each other joy and happiness. Father complains that his tinnitus is becoming unbearable. There's a whistling sound in his ears and at times he can't hear anything at all. As we file back into the house he keeps opening and closing his mouth like a fish and shaking his head to try to get rid of it. And as if that wasn't bad enough, he thinks he heard the doorbell ring.

Someone really is at the door. It is Puškár who has come to wish us Merry Christmas. Peter answers the door and invites him in.

Worn out by the wait for Lila, Puškár is about to lose all hope. He has resolved to try and to forget her. It's not easy.

He tries so hard that he has subconsciously started dropping his "L"s, the letter her name begins with. He replaces all his "L"s with "W"s, which makes him sound as if he has a speech impediment.

"Merry Christmas to the assembwed famiwy!" he hollers as he enters the drawing room.

When Mother asks what happened to him, he says, without batting an eyelid, that he's bitten his tongue.

Try as he might to forget Lila, he thinks of her all the time. No wonder – she is the only long-term requited love of his life.

"Some people don't know what they want – and then they want what they don't know," Uncle Rudo remarks.

3.

My memory of the first years in Bratislava is rather bitty.

I remember my first TV staff meeting. A colleague raised the following burning question:

"Is it acceptable for animals to smile in animated TV stories even though it contradicts the findings of natural science?"

A stormy debate ensued, splitting the participants into two opposing camps. I took the opportunity of a break to sneak away unnoticed.

314

A few doors down, a documentary on Soviet architecture was being pre-screened in a projection room.

The film included footage of a flat with movable walls. *This extremely convenient innovation enables the new residents to choose the size of their rooms or change their layout whenever they wish. The flats don't have kitchens*, the commentary went on, *only space for a small samovar, as present-day comrades take their meals on the ground floor, in a common kitchen and dining room. The new socialist woman will be completely free of the chore of cooking.*

"Oh yeah? Pull the other one!" Zuzana said, when I told her about it on the phone.

In hindsight this was a time of great dreams and plans, yet somehow I always ended up doing the same old thing. I even came to be regarded as something of an authority in my area. I specialised in filming government and party dignitaries from fraternal Eastern bloc countries visiting our country. They parade in front of my eyes.

Ethiopia's communist Prime Minister, Colonel Mengistu Hailé Mariam and his retinue step off a splendid white aeroplane and are greeted by a double row of state and party officials waiting on the red carpet. Girls in young pioneer uniforms appear on cue, presenting him with a bouquet of red carnations.

Touring Kablo, Bratislava's cable factory, President Antonín Novotný expresses genuine interest in and engages in comradely discussions with carefully selected workers, and participates in a meeting of the Central Committee of the Communist Party of Slovakia.

The first female Soviet cosmonaut, Valentina Tereshkova, addresses a crowd assembled in the square under the balcony of the Slovak National Theatre. People wave flags and flowers and the façade behind her is decked out with Czechoslovak and Soviet flags. Top officials deliver their speeches and everyone piles into a gleaming Tatra 603 and a humungous Soviet-made Chaika limo to visit the International Women's Day yarn factory where comrade Tereshkova engages in a lively discussion with the female workers and is handed a bouquet of red gerbera.

The former Tatrabanka headquarters in Slovak National Uprising Square was converted into the TV editorial offices; editing suites were set up in what was now a derelict former market hall a block down from the square. Editing often went on late into the night, before the editor and I would call it a day and go for a drink to Krištál's Bar or the Lesser Franciscans wine cellar, staying until the small hours.

Soon after I joined the Slovak TV I met Arnošt, a make-up artist from the Barrandov film studios in Prague. Ludvo had asked me to show him round and after spending the whole day going around Bratislava we became firm friends.

I used to drop in on him whenever I was in Prague on business. While the illustrious year 1969 has left the strongest impression, there were other years, illustrious in their own way. The first time I visited Arnošt, he was in the middle of creating something resembling a clay cylinder topped with fingers.

"Take a look – what do you think this is?"

"The Golem?" I speculated.

"Hardly. This is Gottwald's hand, my friend!"

"What film do you need it for?"

"It's not for a film, it's for real."

Arnošt explained that the former president had been embalmed in 1953, just like Lenin and Stalin, and put on display at the National Monument on the Vítkov Hill. However, it soon turned out that the embalmers had messed up. Gottwald's arms, legs and body started to decompose and specialists from the Barrandov Film studios had to keep replacing them.

"But this is strictly confidential, Adam. Not a word to anyone, you understand?!"

Gottwald's corpse was on display until, finally, in 1962 the authorities got fed up with the whole charade and had him cremated.

4.

Shortly before Father died and a few months before the infamous garden episode that claimed Father's entire library as its victim, and a few moments before the final chapter starring rampant pneumonia and streptococcus, Mother suddenly turned old and shrivelled up.

I recall a day, or maybe two at most, when she was really young and beautiful. I remember it well. The random footage I managed to shoot while she was off her guard, before she threw a towel over her head or hid behind a curtain, also testifies to the beauty of her mature years.

Another roll of film shows her raising her head and exposing her face to the sun. The wind has blown her hair into her eyes. That was the day when freckles appeared on Mother's skin. They stayed there until the day she died but you had to look closely to see them.

Father used to say that she had green fingers. Everything she touched would bloom. The fragrant valerian on our windowsills, for example, which she had to watch constantly because whenever she carried the flowerpots into the garden, an Ikebana or another cat would break their stalks and gnaw on them. Mother used it to make calming herbal infusions.

With her you always had to expect the unexpected, and Father used to say she contained two or three personalities that were not acquainted with one another. I think he hit the nail on the head. The very fact that she doesn't loom large in these jottings of mine is because she had always behaved like an angel. Except that the jury is still out on the question of whether she was an angel of light or of darkness. She was always somewhere in the background although where exactly it was hard to tell. That's all I can say.

The same applied to our Sunday lunches, which just about managed to hold our family together through a network of name day and birthday celebrations and other minor holidays spread throughout the year. Our weeks and months were framed by these communal rituals, over which Father presided. After all, walking around in circles and regularly repeated patterns are the natural form of locomotion for inhabitants of our mild climatic zone. Even though I had lived in Bratislava for over a year now, I was still connected to this house by an umbilical cord, a vital link that kept my bodily functions going.

There's Mother, smiling as she passes through the drawing room and sits down without a word. The whole family has assembled for dessert and Father regales us with a story he alone finds amusing.

"So Armin had this shaggy dog, Gaštan. One day I went to see him and found young Sára Silberstein in his living room. I sat down next to her. She played with Gaštan, throwing him a ball. It was a scorching hot day and I remember the windows were wide open. She would throw the ball and the dog would duly catch it and deliver it back to her feet. Then it would wait. So she threw it again. The ball bounced off the wall and whoosh! – it flew out of the window. Gaštan jumped out to fetch it. I quickly closed the window and handed over whatever it was I had brought for Armin, I forget what it was. Then I rushed off.

I also remember they were in a hurry to go somewhere and as they walked downstairs Armin asked Sára: *Have you seen Gaštan? – Not really* – she replied."

"Hmm, I seem to remember it didn't happen quite that way. But never mind," Uncle Rudo said, his mouth full.

"Well, you've got to make up the odd story every now and then to spice up your life, don't you think?"

The phone rang. Father went over to the desk and picked it up.

"Your friend Jano sends his regards," a voice said at the other end of the line. "He needs a prescription for Luminal. But he can't collect it himself, he's had to go away for a while."

"Thanks, I'll be there in twenty minutes."

Father replaced the receiver.

"An urgent case," he said and went to his isolation cell to pick up his doctor's bag. He packed his stethoscope and an enema, put on his coat and stuck his head round the living room door.

"Have a nice time, I won't be long."

The episode had gone out of my head but now I know he drove his Chevy to the outskirts of town, took a sharp turn onto the muddy potholed road leading to the former Behy Brickworks, by then derelict and overgrown with weeds, and pulled up next to the shallow pond where I had once learned to swim.

That's where an official Volga was waiting for him.

5.

Igor took a couple of weeks to examine the bones in his lab. He seemed to enjoy it. Eventually he came over to report his findings, which we discussed over a bottle of wine. He said that in a normal grave soft body tissue takes about ten years to decompose. The house in Brežany was built on humus soil mixed with fine sand, meaning the process wouldn't have taken very long but wouldn't have been too rapid either.

Bone is affected by the loss of water, fats and organic matter, he explained. The bones get lighter in weight and often darker in colour through contact with iron oxide or sulphates. They start to disintegrate after ten years and this skeleton was definitely older than that. Judging by the degree of dryness, the low fat content and absence of cartilage, Igor estimated that the bones had been buried for between twenty-five and fifty years. However, he couldn't be any more specific. He showed me a picture of the skull, enthusiastically pointing out traces of plants that had taken root in it.

Nor was it possible to draw any conclusions from what little remained of the clothing – cotton and linen usually take about five years to disintegrate, while wool takes ten and silk twenty years. Buttons, on the other hand, might offer some clues for dating. Any rings or monogrammed articles would also be helpful.

"By the way – it's a woman," he said with a meaningful look, and I was stunned to realise that this possibility had never crossed my mind. It had never occurred to me to ask him if the skeleton belonged to a male or a female, as I had automatically assumed it to be the former. I was flabbergasted.

While all this was going through my head, freely mixing with the wine – I seemed to be topping up my glass more frequently, which wasn't exactly conducive to clear thinking – Igor explained certain characteristics of skulls that can be used to identify gender, such as the arching of the forehead, traces of ligaments, the bump at the back of the skull and its overall size. Thigh bones provide further clues, usually being thinner and shorter in women; the pelvic inlet is a particularly good indicator, being heart-shaped in males and circular in females.

In terms of age – and here, too, the skull provides the greatest number of clues – any changes become less marked after the age of thirty. The bone composition as well as the position of the lower jaw change in old age and some cranial sutures may grow together after age fifty, but none of this is very reliable. This woman would definitely have been more than thirty and almost certainly less than sixty years old. That's as much as he could say.

One thing we can be quite certain about is that the smashed skull shows marks of a blow from a blunt instrument, which may well have been the cause of death. He demonstrated this in a close-up photo, pointing out that the edges were sharp where the bones had been damaged at the time of death and the surface of the fractures was the same colour as the rest of the bones.

"Murder?" I asked.

"Everything that happens during wartime is murder," Igor replied with a strained smile and had some more wine. And he added that the bones weren't all that old.

As he took his leave he said that the Institute of Criminology would hold on to the bones, just in case. It was unlikely that the murderer would be caught but you never knew. The same went for the identity of the skeleton's original owner. He mumbled something about checking old missing persons lists if he ever had a bit of spare time but right now he was inundated with work. And with that he left.

Leaving me with the mystery.

People like to quote statistics claiming that most victims are murdered by the people closest to them, particularly their relatives. Nevertheless I ruled out this hypothesis. Which left all the other women in this world. Great!

6.

Our family album shows everyone aging gradually. Actually, every family photo collection shows this, provided it's been put together methodically and chronologically.

The photo with Uncle Karol's head cut out and replaced with Grandpa Albert's borrowed head is at the top of the pile. It is crumpled and worn as might be expected of a frequently used object.

I take a closer look at the next photograph – because if you've looked at photos of familiar people too often, all you see is their imprint stored in your memory – and something surprising leaps out at me. At first I dismiss it as coincidence. There's a woman in the background of the family photo taken outside Puškár's patisserie, the one with Father in his off-white suit and me wearing my little sailor suit – I've seen her before but apparently haven't paid her enough attention. The same woman is also visible in the picture that shows Father in front of his consulting room, with a busy street in the background. And I can identify her in three other pictures. I put her under a magnifying glass.

Now I recognize her even though she's aged and her face has been marked by the passage of time.

Klaudia Horváthová lived in Brežany so there ought not to be anything unusual about her being in the pictures. Nevertheless... She appears in ten photos in our album, in all kinds of situations, behind Father's back. In one portrait in particular she seems to be growing out of his head.

Klaudia. Her name reminds me of the English word 'cloud'. It always has.

A clearer picture of her emerges from surveillance reports on "target" Luminal, which I found in Father's file. Between 1954 and 1964 they used to meet roughly twice a week, usually in her flat in 25 Voroshilov Street "for sexual purposes", according to Agent Samaritan who lived across the street. Although the frequency of their meetings later decreased they never stopped seeing each other.

I wanted to know what happened to her. I had to find Samaritan.

7.

It is hard to believe that what is now an impenetrable jungle behind the house was once a vegetable garden. But I have photographic evidence to prove that, too. In some photos the garden appears bare and ploughed up, asleep in anticipation of winter. In others everything is in bloom, with beds full of vegetables flanking a cold frame and two Ikebanas – numbers IV and V, I guess – strolling down the paths. As well as one of the dogs, Polino, who knows which incarnation? The scent of dill, marjoram and linden blossom immediately tickles my nose.

When the cherry, apple and plum trees were in bloom we used to go out at night and stand in the garden watching their branches heavy with blossoms and inhale their powerful scent. Those were moments of sheer magic.

In the springtime Father used to burn the grass by the fence. I often gave him a hand since Peter was constantly away and Tina always had plenty of credible excuses. So it became something of *our* moment, a time for chatting in a cloud of smoke rising from the burning grass. We both pretended not to notice my constant allergic sniffling and runny eyes.

"Anything interesting happened in Bratislava?" Father asked, just to wind me up. He knew I hated questions like that. Really, how can you answer that?

But I gave it a try anyway. We were in the middle of filming a newsreel on a major exhibition, *Soviet Satellites and Hydroelectric Construction in the USSR*. The Soviet Union had by then notched up three successful satellite launches, capping this with the first artificial sun satellite, all in the course of a single year. Each time they managed to beat the Americans, but only just, by a couple of months in the first case. That's what the commentary focused on.

"Isn't that something?" I said, resorting to a phrase that, for a change, Father couldn't stand. It's another question you can't answer. Father nodded, raking a pile of smouldering embers.

I told him that we kept the TV lights, props and sets in the Neolog Synagogue in Rybné Square, which had been converted to a storehouse. When a production assistant first took me there I noticed many features similar to those of the recently demolished Brežany synagogue.

Father stopped listening. His eyes glazed over after a few sentences. His mind was obviously wandering. He kept repeating:

"I see, I see."

He had always dreamed of owning a huge garden somewhere far from all the hustle and bustle. He wanted to grow mighty trees and give them lots of room. A solitary tree looks quite different in the countryside, when it has no need to compete for space and isn't fenced in. If a tree planted very close to a house grows too tall, it would normally be chopped down, since its heavy branches and trunk might pose a risk. A single storm or gale may be enough to cause damage. The smallest crack that appears in the wall is enough for the houseowners to put a metal band around the tree.

Solitary plane trees, on the other hand, grow far and wide, spreading their branches at almost right angles to their trunk in expansive gestures. Walnut trees grow fast, so Father would plant one at the centre, giving it an area some fifty metres in diameter because they need a lot of space. Finally, he would plant chestnut trees and maybe also a horse chestnut. For its beautiful blossom and leaves.

Father used to say that people, too, resembled trees (comparing people to flora and fauna was a peculiar family trait – Uncle Rudo was likely to compare people to insects or birds). For example, Father saw himself as something like a cherry tree. One with many branches, garlands of fruit and blossoms, an explosion of red, black and white and perhaps a little green, a cherry tree bursting with life. A beech tree, by comparison, was taciturn and austere, unblemished and harsh.

"That's what your brother is like, Adam."

Ivy, on the other hand, needed support – something it could creep around, slowly choking its host to death.

"You don't mean to say that's me?"

Father laughed and shook his head.

"You might be an elder tree. Elders are interesting. That is, if they eventually grow into proper trees."

He went on to tell me what Rudo used to say about elders. They are trees with an abundance of discreet and secretive life. Aphids love elders, secreting droplets of honey to entrap ants, which is why people protect the aphids from ladybirds. Sometimes people specially colonise a new place with aphids, constructing leaf shelters for them to make sure the precious liquid is not washed away by rain and rearing them almost like cattle. What looks like honey is actually their excrement, a sugar solution produced by their digestive tract. According to Rudo the aphids have special tubes that secrete a sticky resin to put off predatory aphid "lions", by gluing their mandibles together.

"The garden is a bloody battlefield!" Rudo would exclaim, gesticulating wildly. If we didn't look after it, the plants would wage a brutal war for access to light and water. The gentle fragrant wildflowers growing in a meadow – the buttercups, bluebells, lungwort and dandelions – all play their part in this ferocious warfare.

"Hello, comrade Doctor! How are we?'

A smiling Major Ďuratný was leaning against the fence.

Father walked over and offered an elbow as his hands were dirty.

"How's that cough doing?"

"It's improving but I'll need something. I'll drop by the health centre."

Father gave him a wave and Ďuratný went off. Some turf under the trees had just caught fire and the thick smoke made me cough and wheeze.

"Leave it, Adam; just sit down and take a rest."

I leaned against the old apricot tree. It may well have been the last one to grow this far north. Apricots don't thrive in winter and Brežany is situated on the northern periphery of their geographical distribution.

Father put out the last smouldering coals and sat down next to me on the cold ground.

The smoke dissolved in the air, with the last wispy plume still rising, driven by the wind over the tall park wall behind which the Brežany manor house was slowly falling into ruin. We used to go to the park whenever there were problems in our family. No problem was too knotty not to be disentangled on its endless, brick-lined winding paths strewn with white gravel. That was always where we looked for a way out of the maze.

The time to start looking was coming closer, slowly but inexorably.

The Sálava River broke its banks that night. We had been on alert for several days because the snow on the mountains was melting unusually fast.

Once the water subsided, the locals picked up the fish that had washed up in the growth and hollows along the banks and threw them back into the river while peasants, who flocked into town on their carts from the neighbouring villages of Nevedovo and Lehota, came to pick up bleaks and roaches for duck feed.

Monako, who had landed a job as a lowly official at the Town National Committee (he would smile and shrug his shoulders: – *I've always been a bureaucrat!*), found a huge catfish, over two metres long, stranded in a puddle and unable to get back once the water receded.

Vojto's father used to join Monako on poaching expeditions along the Sálava River, along with Németh and Čerešník, the two chaps he had met at the forestry enterprise. While they engaged in futile annoying discussions about Jews and God, Vojtech Roško sat in the boat tossing dynamite into the water, never more than ten to fifteen grams, Vojto said, although sometimes he had to have nine or ten goes before it worked. Stunned by the explosion, the fish would float to the surface with their white bellies up. Some fifty metres downstream, men would stand ready with a fishnet spread out against the current, waiting for the Sálava to deliver the fish into it. Vojto claimed the stunned fish would come to after a while but I didn't really believe him.

The fish had to be eaten fresh and you could tell it was fresh by the firm flesh, shiny translucent eyes and agreeable smell. Someone usually thought of the good doctor, too, as with most things in Brežany that moved, flew or grew.

8.

I've done another round of cleaning and walking around the dilapidated house and need to take another break. I take my shoes off, and being too lazy to bend down I slide my socks off by rubbing my feet against the bed frame. It's a bad habit of mine.

It reminds me of Father. When he was exhausted that's what he used to do before going to bed. He would fall asleep straight away. I had often watched him as he did this and found it disgusting. I took this to be a quintessence of male messiness.

But as usual, here I am doing the doing the same thing.

It's easier for me than for Father because his socks clung to his legs, held up by suspenders.

I haven't had many opportunities to use this turn of phrase in my lifetime but in those years, the early sixties, I really had the time of my life. You know what I mean – the days when everything and everyone you can think of seems to be surrounded by a sort of golden halo. It's something that usually happens only when you look back. That's what life is like, the good old days are always in the past, never in the present.

In 1961 I married Zuzana Kabátová and five months later Bony, our only son, was born. A few days earlier Zuzana dreamt that her mouth was full of broken glass. It wasn't a proper nightmare because she knew that broken glass meant good luck. But it gave her a fright. She had to be careful to hold the shards between her teeth and tongue in such a way that they didn't fall out or she didn't swallow them or cut herself on their sharp edges. In other words, she had to make sure her happiness didn't hurt her. Happiness is a fragile thing, as we know only too well.

We were allocated a one-room flat accessed through a courtyard balcony in No. 43 Malinovský Street in Bratislava. Every time I see the name Malinovský I'm reminded of clocks ticking. And I remember – the fellow must have been plastered with watches.

Sometimes we were so happy we stayed in all day.

When we didn't, we would climb the hill that rose right behind the slowly disappearing Blumental cemetery and the railway line, leading to the woods below the Kamzík Hill, covered by vineyards on one side. The Straw Shack restaurant at the trolleybus terminus, a former shepherds' hut after which this neck of the woods was named, was a perennial favourite with hikers. L'udovít Štúr and his fellow Slovak national revivalists came here to carouse in the nineteenth century; nearby was the last battlefield of the Prussian-Austrian war; on New Year's Eve 1919 it was the first place in the city – still known by its Hungarian name, Pozsony – to be taken by Czechoslovak legionnaires, and it was from here that the Red Army launched its covert advance on the city one night in April 1945.

Zuzana was nurturing a baby inside her warm, velvety, heavenly womb. We went for a walk in the sun-drenched oak grove that seemed so much more gentle and friendly than the Volovec Mountain above Brežany. We felt as if we were walking in a strange primeval forest, with large insects – stag beetles and longhorns – like shiny olde-worlde limousines, their wing cases reminiscent of car bonnets from some distant world, from a different era and a different universe, far away and filled with light. In the rays of the sun rippling through the dark green foliage it was all too easy to succumb to daydreams. We were surrounded by myths spun long ago but not yet articulated, quiet, dead and forgotten.

I introduced her to Father's tree theory.

She took it a step further, suggesting that beech trees were Calvinists, since they are so orderly and their trunks seem so reserved. The animals and insects that live on them are also like that. Oaks, on the other hand, were Catholic, with their baroque, robust and broad crowns, and their furrowed bark brimming with scents and sounds.

Novelists tend to admit that they don't have much to say about happiness. My own experience confirms this observation.

9.

Father fell ill. An old superstition says that medical cases in doctors' families are invariably idiosyncratic, atypical and unusual, as if nature wanted to take revenge on those who pit themselves against it.

When Father finally allowed a colleague to examine him, the two doctors performed what seemed like a curious and cautious peacock dance. Dr Levius was keen to come up with the best possible diagnosis to minimise his pain and save him time, while Father, wary of offending his friend, would not admit that he was in fact getting steadily worse and the treatment wasn't working. Instead, he claimed he was making progress and feeling better.

By the time it all came out in the end, Father needed surgery. He was in great pain and lost a lot of blood. The doctors suspected cancer and were concerned that the excessive loss of blood might make him anaemic. "It's the fish, it must be all the fish I've eaten!" Father kept repeating in a faint voice, sounding like an illiterate bricklayer who has no idea how his body functioned and was clutching at straws. He was terrified of surgery.

This was his first encounter with anaesthesia under gas and his interest was piqued. When we came to see him at the Brežany hospital, he was thrilled to tell us that as he went under his eyesight had gone first and then he stopped feeling pain. He claimed he heard a colleague say, "You can start, he doesn't feel a thing now." But he did feel the pressure of the knife on this stomach before he lost the ability to feel anything. Enthralled, he told us that when your hearing is "poisoned" everything you hear sounds like somebody striking metal rods at regular intervals.

Some time later he went to see Vojto's parents and this

experience helped Father detect a gas leak from the stove and save everyone's life. They were chatting over a cup of tea. After about an hour Mrs Roško's face turned bright red and she fell uncharacteristically silent but she didn't complain of feeling unwell. Everyone felt strange and dozy and eventually Vojto's mother started vomiting. That's when Father heard that special sound – like metal rods being struck – inaudible to anyone else. He realised what was going on and yelled:

"There's a gas leak!"

Vojto's father later told us that some bricks had fallen into chimney, blocking it. Windows were thrown open and before long everyone was back to normal.

Following his surgery Father was in pain, kept vomiting and had stomach cramps but whenever we came to see him he played the hero and insisted that he was fine. The doctors prescribed morphine. He became lightheaded and when we talked to him, each word seemed to be coated in velvet. Except that he didn't sound like himself. But I suspect that he had really enjoyed it. Nurses helped him sip his tea and applied cold compresses to his head. After ten days he was taken off the morphine, to prevent the risk of addiction, and was immediately convulsed with pain, sweating and screaming at us furiously. But with the doctors he pretended everything was fine.

The ward came alive the minute Ada walked in. Ada with her sparkling blue eyes and long dark hair. Tall and statuesque. My sister's new friend. Tina wanted to smuggle in some cigarettes for Father and as they were passing by, she brought Ada along.

As soon as Father laid his eyes on Ada he managed to get his pain under control, colour returned to his cheeks, he sat up in bed, smiled and put on his special, seductive voice.

"Rubens or Rembrandt? Too early to tell…"

"Ada," she said, shaking his hand.

Mistaking this for the delayed effect of the morphine, Tina just rolled her eyes and tossed Father a packet of cheap Mars cigarettes.

He opened it, held it to his nose and said with eyes half-closed, savouring the aroma:

"Spices and the thrill of temptation."

"Are you feeling better, Dad? Mum has sent you some apples."

"Do you have delicate hands? Are you a smoker?"

"No," Ada replied with a smile.

"Good girl."

At this point Zuzana, Peter and I walked into the ward. At the sight of Ada, Peter's eyes lit up and I felt a pleasant tingling in my loins. Zuzana realized what was happening and kept a watchful eye on me from then on.

Father gave us an angry look. And I realized that sexual preferences, too, are hopelessly hereditary. We were transformed into three hummingbirds flitting around a single flower.

"Mum said Ada could stay the night at our house."

"Did she, now?" Father said.

I blurted out: "We're staying the night too."

"We can have a game of canasta in the evening. I'm not in a hurry," Peter chimed in.

Zuzana gave me a furious poke in the ribs.

"Time we went home!"

She started to drag me off immediately. "I've got work to do."

"What work?"

"Shut up!"

10.

There was something dormant in our genes that kept triggering all sorts of weird coincidences. I discovered this while rummaging through our family history. In each generation of our family there was someone who had veered slightly from the straight and narrow.

Let me present a hit parade of our family follies.

Aunt Tonička hated the outdoors. Uncle Rudo once managed to talk her into joining him on a hike through the woods on the Volovec Mountain and visit his favourite spots. She prepared herself thoroughly, mainly mentally but also investing in a complete hiking outfit, which took Rudo by surprise.

They set out around lunchtime. Soon after leaving town they came to some low bushes. The place was swarming with flies and before long one flew into Tonička's ear. Rudo told her that everything would be fine but the fly struggled frenziedly to get out and they had to return home. For two days and nights the fly

329

buzzed incessantly in Tonička's ear, driving her to distraction. Finally, at dawn on the third day, it fell silent.

Father gently removed it with a pair of tweezers and concluded that it must have battered itself to death as it thrashed about in desperation against the walls of the inner ear.

When Tonička complained about the incident to her confessor, he planted in her the obsessive idea that the fly must have been God's punishment for her sins. He told her that while consecrating the monastery at Foigny, St. Bernard kept shouting *Excommunico eas!* thus driving away swarms of importunate flies.

Then there was Grandpa Albert's brother Jacob. When he was a little boy, going through the joyful phase of discovering his body's orifices, he managed to insert a bean up his nose while he was playing. The bean went in easily enough but showed no inclination to come out. Little Jacob was ashamed to mention it to anyone. Knowing his strict parents would tell him off and give him a walloping, and fearing that even worse might lie in store, he pushed the bean further still, down to the root of his nose, so that he was able to breathe normally.

As he grew up he began to talk gibberish, was slow at school and generally behaved like an imbecile. When his state deteriorated further, medical help was sought but the doctors couldn't figure out what was wrong, until one of them had the idea of X-raying Jake's head. He found the bean next to the root of the nose and discovered it had come to life, sprouting in the damp and warm environment. It had pushed its way through various cavities into the brain, causing serious damage.

Jacob had surgery to remove the bean, which was preserved in alcohol and exhibited in a museum of curiosities. Come to think of it, it was the real magic beanstalk, as it had grown all the way to the sky as in the fairy tale, transporting Jake to another, magic country. He remained backward for the rest of his life although people who knew him said he always seemed very happy.

My brother Peter was a man of many different guises and faces, which all ultimately merged into a single form.

His visits to Brežany were usually unannounced and unexpected. He would turn up out of the blue bellowing: "Anybody home?"

from the garden gate. He used to divide his time between Bratislava and Prague and I was never quite sure what he did for a living, as he never talked about it. I never asked, although occasionally my work happened to bring us together. Admittedly, as his brother, I ought to have shown more interest, but I was swamped with work and too preoccupied with my own problems to find time for anything else.

When Peter finally went off the rails, Tina recalled an incident from many years before. After one of our midnight binges she found him sitting in the kitchen with bulging eyes. He had lit dozens of candles and was lost in a Chopin nocturne playing on the radio. He slowly turned his head to face her and said he'd seen the future and knew what that was going to happen.

And I recalled the day when he packed his bags at dawn and said he was setting out for the Equator. He asked if I wanted to come along. He was back an hour later as it was raining heavily.

But I suppose none of this proves anything. It's just that looking back we tend to invent warning signs retrospectively. The human brain is great at that.

The game of canasta went on till late that night. Peter played with Mother, Tina and Ada. His face was flushed and he couldn't take his eyes off her.

Ada was put up in the guest room. As she lay in bed, the door opened gently. Someone slipped inside and sat down on her bed without a word. It turned out to be Peter.

He took her hand and whispered: "My heart is filthy! I am evil! Everything I do is just a sham!"

Ada turned on the light and he started telling her about his German shepherd dog that he had named Joshua. For a long time he was convinced that he had to be kind or Joshua would suffer for his sins.

Later he realized that if the dog died for him, he would be cleansed of his sins. So he killed Joshua to spare him further suffering.

I had managed to sneak a look into Peter's medical record:

Mr P.T., 30 years old, was admitted in an agitated mental state and was incoherent. On 15 September he started to exhibit symptoms of anxiety and paranoia. He suspected he had been narcotized by chloroform, refused to accept food believing it to be poisoned and claimed that his soul had escaped from his body. He complained that time has slowed down. In a sudden fit of anxiety, while talking to a doctor he lashed out, biting everything around him. On 17 September, while being transported to the sanatorium, he had to be restrained and kept snapping his teeth at the accompanying medical staff.

The medical records from the sanatorium show that he refused food, claiming it was poisoned and that he had been hypnotized. He suffered a breakdown on 20 and 21 September, despite being administered camphor and caffeine injections. He claimed that his mother had died and when she came to visit he said it wasn't her.

His behaviour has been extremely self-centred right from the start; he believes that he was the cause of everything that was happening and that he was being tricked. The illness had been brought upon him.

Medical report dated 25 October 1961, 12:00 p.m.

The patient seemed calm when he came for his check-up and appeared to recognise me. He thinks it odd that doctors know his address, adding that he suspects a younger colleague is involved with his sister (?) Ada. His gives calm and appropriate answers. His response to general questions is adequate. He has an approximate idea of time, is aware that it is the middle of October. He knows he is in a sanatorium. He claims he doesn't know how he got there and says he heard he had been hospitalised on doctors' orders. He has only a hazy recollection of being admitted . "Why were you admitted?" – "That's what I'd like to know too." – "Were you ill?" – "Yes, I was very ill; I was feeling awful!" – "How are you feeling now – are you ill or well?" – "I don't think I'm quite OK… I don't fully understand it, I don't know if this is reality or dream, I don't recognize myself. I may be on drugs. When I see myself in the mirror I don't recognize myself. Everything is different – my moustache, my hair, my expression – it's as if I'm looking at a picture that's gone wrong." – "Have you noticed any changes in your mind?" – "I don't know, I haven't really been myself. I do whatever I'm told. I follow orders." – "How come someone else is directing your actions?" – "I don't understand it, I could do with some guidance, a manual of some kind. I must be under some kind of hypnosis. I find the variety of phials in this office quite stunning. Maybe it's just my imagination. I can't understand how they can make me see all this detail. I feel quite befuddled… sometimes I feel I am … in the nether world and am only reliving the earthly life." – "What is the cause of your illness?" – "I wish

I knew. They made me believe terrible things – that I'm evil, terribly evil. That's what they've told me!" – "Could you hear them?" – "Yes I could, and I answered them too. They were male voices." – "How do they speak to you?" – "They don't make any sound when they speak, obviously, they're not audible to the ear, it's all inside my head. The ear is not aware of it. If the internal voice comes from a distance I don't look around for it. With the voice from within I know it is a distant being that's connected to me. It's telling me things that are alien, not mine."

After the consultation of 12 December 1961 he states that he now accepts me for who I am for the first time.

The psychiatrist's report concludes: *The prerequisites for declaring the patient mentally incapable are present and he may be sectioned for six months. The patient is not to be notified of this decision since this might be detrimental to his state of health.*

Father was appointed Peter's legal guardian.

I dropped by the flat Peter was renting in Bratislava to pick up some things for him, and apart from an unspeakable mess I found a diary. What I read gave me quite a shock. It turned out that Peter had been an ardent and committed communist. During filming I had often seen him at party receptions and meetings but thought he just happened to be there. His diary proved otherwise. I stayed up reading until I heard the thrushes' dawn chorus.

12 December 1958
Our President, Comrade Novotný, is a wonderful man! He's a great human being. Truth be told, he is no big fan of the Slovaks but that's just a detail, a minor detail. Yesterday, at the grand reception, he told us how after Slánský was executed and he was chosen to succeed him, I mean when President Gottwald picked him as his successor, his wife was out working in the fields, at a cooperative or something. Some women who were working further down the field called out: "Boženka, some men have come looking for you!" The women sent these men her way but before the comrades in suits managed to explain what it was all about, the women told her: "Would you believe it, they wanted to know if your husband Antonín is Jewish?!" Comrade Novotný is a truly devout Communist! He knows exactly what that means. For example: when he travels abroad and his delegation receives gifts,

he puts everything in one big pile, including the gifts he himself was given, and of course he gets more gifts than anyone else, and he adds it all up. Then he shares the pile out evenly among the comrades. A true communist!"

11 January 1959

I try to make an entry in my diary whenever an interesting date comes up. I enjoy that. Numbers are very meaningful. They are strong and firm. Like the number ones in today's date. Lately the cadre of time-tested comrades, those who have been in charge of the party since the twenties, has dwindled quite markedly. A number of younger comrades have emerged, people not forged in the fire of the class struggle. They're too young to remember that holding party office used to mean constant risk of being thrown into jail, being sacked, or not getting a job and receiving only meagre social benefits. After the Victorious February of 1948 this threat was lifted: party office meant financial security and a much higher social standing. And as a result a new and unexpected trend made itself felt, shocking to the honest old comrades – the younger comrades started competing for office. They no longer tried to earn promotion through honest work but by plotting and scheming, and eventually the entire apparatus, right up to the highest echelons of the party, was caught in this morass. It's true, because I remember that in the past every trade had been represented on the Politburo: comrade Gottwald was a trained carpenter, comrade Zápotocký a qualified stonemason, comrade Novotný a skilled metal worker. Before they got to the top they had worked in factories or were unemployed, and suffered harassment from the police. They had to work their way up and for this reason they had felt a stronger bond with the man in the street. But now their generation is on its way out. It has just started snowing outside.

2 February 1959

At a recent party meeting someone whispered to me the story of the head of the ŠtB, Osvald Závodský. He'd been convicted in one of the big trials in the early fifties. The president, comrade Zápotocký, insisted that all those convicted men be executed, but members of the Central Committee thought that enough was enough. So they agreed among themselves not to carry out the sentence: instead, they would keep Závodský in prison and let him out after a while once things had calmed down. However, comrade Zápotocký didn't attend the meeting where this decision was taken and wasn't informed of it. A few months later he suddenly remembered Závodský and ordered his execution, saying it had been delayed for too long, chop, chop. The others learned about it only by accident, when they received a letter from Závodský's wife who said she had had no news of her husband for a long time and wanted to know what was happening. The Minister of Interior tried to wriggle out of it but eventually had to admit that Závodský had been hanged on the President's orders. That must have been quite painful. I came, I hanged, I conquered.

9 September 1959
(Dinner with Honza. Notes on a napkin copied into the diary.) A convincing symbol of communism was necessary and lo and behold! Július Fučík was made into one. Everything the poor man did is just a myth and a fabrication. In real life Fučík didn't even look like his portrait. After Victorious February, Minister of Culture comrade Václav Kopecký went to see the painter and National Artist Max Švabinský and asked him to paint Fučík's portrait. And Švabinský is supposed to have said:
   "Tell the boy to come and see me ..." and Kopecký says to him: "That won't be possible, he's dead..." "My God, so he's already dead? What a shame – what happened to the poor chap? Tell me Minister, was he run over by a car?" "No, he was executed by the Nazis." "Poor fellow... Well, send me a photo then." And even though Fučík was unrecognizable in the portrait, Švabinský was given a Peace Prize for his work. Nobody looks the way they do in reality. They're all our Doppelgängers.

11 November 1959
More brown envelopes today! That's the problem with the brown envelopes. I knew it! People used to hand them out as early as in 1918. Masaryk and Beneš used to hand them out, as did Comrade Gottwald and Comrade Zápotocký, and so does Comrade Novotný now. It's always people who have made a contribution to the country who get them. And fair enough, we have added the requirement that they should have made a contribution to the party

335

as well, nothing wrong with that. Comrade Novotný told me he'd never gone over ten thousand; he used the presidential fund but the comrades weren't happy and said that wasn't enough. They got accustomed to bigger gifts under Comrade Gottwald – Comrade Machačová of the National Reconstruction Fund, for example, used to wear a huge diamond ring until Comrade Gottwald put a stop to it. I've never seen a living breathing diamond.

10 October 1960

I've done a lot of thinking today. A huge amount of thinking. Wine is red, blood is red, our flag is red. That's what the voices say. Actually, they sing it. Our generation will live to see the triumph of communism. Regardless of the doomsayers who claim that our trade and industry hasn't reached the requisite standard, that we are short of cadres and programmes, that we lack educated people and even for them we can't find proper jobs. These people want everything to be 100 per cent but that's not possible! Comrade Khrushchev said that we would defeat capitalists not only in terms of industry and technology but especially in terms of economy. His optimism is no delusion – it is based on real facts, real statistics! Yes, some people say we have set the bar too high, but Nikita Sergeyevich K. objects, saying every problem would definitely be overcome by 1965! He made it clear that he was the Central Committee and the Central Committee was Khrushchev. The Soviet Union is united and indivisible! Surely these figures must have been run past the Politburo and nobody could have a shadow of a doubt that they're genuine. In 1958 he said we would overtake capitalism within seven years. In an impassioned speech, Comrade Khrushchev said we'd managed to meet more complex challenges than the miserable thirty or forty per cent that remained to make up the difference! The crucial starting-point for launching a decisive attack is Siberia! When Nikita Sergeyevich starts listing all the riches in the depths of Siberia as well as just below the surface, it sounds like the most wondrous fairy tale. There's oil, iron ore, bauxite for aluminium, uranium. There are billions of tons of all these strategic raw materials. What gives him even greater grounds for optimism is the fact that the Soviets have finally discovered enormous diamond deposits – the only element they had been missing so far. Comrade Khrushchev claims that

Kazakhstan will inundate the world with wheat and corn and in the near future the Soviet Union will be able to feed starving continents. What a glorious ideal! Long live communism! This is what the voices say, too. But they also say – don't worry, you won't live to see that! The voices I mean.

After being discharged from the sanatorium Peter's illness seemed to be generally under control. One part of Peter engaged in good-humoured, almost light-hearted banter, laughing and cracking jokes, while another part of him descended into depression and anxiety. The more jokes he told the deeper he sank. The more laughter, the more sadness.

Peter kept moving from one address to another. Father nursed a faint hope that he might come back to live in our house in Brežany but he moved in with a friend in Nitra instead. He cut off all contact with our family, which Mother found particularly hard to bear. As far as I could tell, Peter spent his time wandering around, drinking and accosting strangers in the street cadging cigarettes. Every time he was about to be arrested as a layabout he'd find a bogus job for a few days.

Later he referred to this time as his period of hibernation.

11.

The night before Bony was born Zuzana was tossing and turning in bed. As she turned to the other side, she touched my forehead, and I started to dream about her.

No woman has ever understood me as well as Zuzana. Once I told her that I felt an irresistible urge to take off all my clothes and run out into the night. She just said: Go ahead, then!

Bony was a sickly baby, spending his first days in this world balancing on the tightrope between life and death, and Zuzana had to stay in hospital with him. Thanks to Father, who was overjoyed at the birth of his first grandson and knew people at the Bratislava maternity clinic in Zochova Street (a stone's throw from my office), she was assured of the best possible treatment.

In those days we both had peculiar dreams. Zuzana once

dreamed she was standing in a swimming pool full of water, with Bony in her arms – he was made entirely of bread, a soft dough encased in a crunchy crust. He began to melt and fall apart in the water. She woke up screaming.

I dreamed that I cheated on Zuzana. With Zuzana. She was still a virgin.

After they came home from hospital, in the small hours when Bony wouldn't stop crying, I sometimes caught a desperate glance from Zuzana. For a mere second or a fraction of a second a shadow passed across the enchanting high arch of her brow. I suspected she was thinking of the moment when we conceived this tiny screaming creature, wondering if it had really been worth it. But she would always pull herself together and patiently attend to the chores.

It would be unfair to say she didn't enjoy motherhood; she just enjoyed it in her own inimitable mad, maddening Zuzana way. She told me that after Bony was born and the commotion was over, she fell asleep with him in her arms and tried to get used to the sensation of being a mother. She watched him turn his head every which way, scrunch up his eyes as he tried to get used to the light of the day, and sniffle, wrinkling his little nose until he found her nipple and latched on. She nicknamed him "little hedgehog" and "little mole", imitating the way he wrinkled his nose.

When Bony was about six months old he started smelling like peaches – this was my favourite period and I kept looking for excuses to smell him – and Zuzana called him her peach baby and later just "my peach". This nickname, too, failed to stick and was replaced by others of which only Kabiko survived into adulthood, used only by his two best friends who had no idea how it originated.

It was the first word he uttered.

Bony's arrival made our tiny flat in No. 43 Malinovský Street shrink like freshly laundered clothes. But we managed somehow.

Our flat was one of the seven comprising the so-called Unitas block, built about the time I was born. Architect Fridrich Weinwurm designed it in the 1930s, at the height of the housing crisis, as part of an affordable housing campaign. It was light and airy with the windows facing both east and west, so that one side had the sun in the morning and the other in the evening.

Just the other day I came across a photo of Fridrich Weinwurm in a magazine and was startled. The man in the black-and-white picture – the strong nose, thick eyebrows, light-coloured suit and striped tie – was the spitting image of Uncle Armin. Weinwurm, too, was Jewish. In spite of his renown and reputation the Weinwurm-Vécsei studio had to close down in 1939 because of the new anti-Jewish legislation. He was arrested the same year and after being held for a year in Ilava Prison he perished in unexplained circumstances, probably trying to cross the Hungarian border, in no-man's-land.

Sometimes I imagine that he was shot by someone – a Hlinka Guardsman or a border guard – who lived in one of the flats Weinwurm designed. Perhaps in this very block, the Unitas. Coming home in the evening this man would kiss his wife and she'd ask him how his day had been. And he'd say, nothing special, a day like any other. Then he'd join her on the sofa with a glass of beer and they'd chat about their child, perhaps in the very place where Fridrich Weinwurm had stood ten years earlier when he came to inspect the building site, admiring the fine craftsmanship and tapping the walls, nodding in approval. And after finishing his beer, the man might have stood by the window in just his vest, looking out into the night, at the young trees and the paths criss-crossing the blocks and leaning on the parapet, which had been designed and drawn in a single, perfect line, by Fridrich Weinwurm, no longer among the living.

I often thought of him when I was at home alone. Of him and Uncle Armin.

Besides, it was from the Filiálka station located right behind our block – these days it's used only rarely, to shunt freight trains – that several transports taking the Jews of Bratislava to the camps were dispatched.

Actually, Malinovský Street was ideally situated if you wanted to study the Doppler effect, with rushing ambulances, police cars and fire engines ploughing their way through the city's main artery. As they drew closer, the noise of wailing sirens would reach its peak and then gradually die away with the frequency of the sound waves.

The block was full of people who had recently re-located to Bratislava. They had only just cut loose from preceding generations of uneducated ants living in small villages, where marrying out was strongly discouraged and the population was united in its hatred of those living in other villages, and where people chewed on soil and grass, only occasionally managing to snatch a chunk of meat. Where everyone watched everyone else to make sure they toed the line, where people envied one another and drank together. And drank and drank and drank. Crushing everything that was the slightest bit different. They couldn't see further than their own nose, nor did they feel the slightest desire to do so. More than anything else they were scared of everything that was alien. They hated change and innovation and all that modern jazz the wind would sometimes blow in from the city... And they drank.

People like that have always fascinated me.

My neighbour Igor once surprised me (over a drink, naturally) with the following theory. He claimed that there is always an individual in whom all the deviations, aberrations and conflicts of the preceding generations that have been bubbling under the surface materialise in a concentrated form. The dark undercurrent, so to speak. The Bible says that the Jews, too, used to send a goat into the desert once a year to symbolically expiate their sins.

And one fine day this individual realises that he's different. He leaves for the big city, goes to university, builds a career as an engineer, artist, or psychologist, severing all family ties and disrupting the chain of cowering people. The first harbinger of the appearance of the family Saviour, Black Sheep or Goat in a family is the prevalence of suicide or serious alcoholism in a previous generation – these are the imperfect, unfinished specimens who have yet to get over their teething troubles. In Igor's family this role was performed by an uncle who, at the age of forty, hanged himself from a hook on the kitchen door, having first tried and failed to set fire to it. This kind of family cleansing facilitates progress. What you get are homosexual saviours. Abstract painters descended from illiterate grandfathers. Serfs freed in centuries past making a leap straight into the foul-smelling and gruesome twentieth century.

And that's the big city for you. Such are its snares and its corruption. And thank God for that!

The typewriter on the kitchen table clattered away late into the night as I revised scripts over countless cigarettes and cups of coffee.

340

The dawn chorus was a sure sign that I was in trouble and wouldn't meet my deadline.

Back then life seemed to move at a slower pace and the passage of time followed quite a different rhythm than it does today. It took time to get hold of somebody by telephone – provided, of course, that the person in question was at home or at some other specific location. It took time to write a letter and to have it delivered to its destination by post or by hand. You couldn't sort things out just like that, in a couple of hours. Compared with the present those were days of almost divine peace, yet I kept feeling I was only just keeping my head above the water. Being disorganised didn't help either.

But it's useful to cultivate one's bad traits if you don't want those around you to grow too comfortable. Father, too, subscribed to this view.

Family life (despite the drivel you read in Mills & Boon novels) tends to soften one's rough edges somewhat. The greatest mistake you could make is to marry your femme fatale. She should always remain loftily unattainable or you should stay separated from her by some tragic misunderstanding that can never be undone.

All those years I was convinced that Zuzana was indeed my femme fatale, as we negotiated various twists and turns or teetered at the edge of a few precipices, often tumbling into them and coming to blows. It's rather easy and convenient to blame all your mistakes on "the times" – you yourself usually have the key to everything.

As Pascal said: Man's greatest tragedy is that he can't sit quietly in his room. How right he was!

The TV set in our only room was turned on, although nobody was watching. President Novotný was addressing Czechoslovakia's two nations:

Comrades! Our beloved Fatherland has been a socialist country for a year now. We mustn't waver in pursuing our chief goal: ensuring that relations between people are always straightforward and honest and that man remains a comrade to his fellow man. Let us pursue our struggle against the curse of war! Let us ensure that all the weapons around the world are destroyed! We have devoted our lives to the struggle for peace. Let us put all our endeavours at the service of peace, so that peace may dictate the swift and powerful rhythm of our life, our work and our hearts. This is what profound happiness consists in. Best foot forward, comrades! Towards our nations' shared joy!

12.

Vojto and I would often declare, somewhat theatrically: Gone is the joy and simplicity of our younger days; it's vanished without a trace. These days we prefer coarser and more pedestrian joys and pleasures.

Such as wine, beer and television. And women…

Vojto would often quote Uncle Rudo: "If you have to calm down, think of food. It's a wonderfully uncomplicated topic."

After his time in Podbrezová where he did forced labour, as he used to call it, Vojto was at last allowed to return to Brežany. Luckily, he didn't have to sacrifice any of his fingers at the altar of the communist deities, the holy trinity of Marx, Engels and Lenin, which made him very happy. He came home at Easter, when the local men – fortunately represented primarily by young boys – go from house to house as part of the traditional custom of spanking women and girls with a willow whip, for which they are rewarded with food and drink.

When Vojto arrived, Mrs Roško was absorbed in re-living Jesus' last supper while continuously sampling her eggnog to make sure she got the taste right. So as the male population went on their rounds, they found this devout Brežany lady in a happy and chatty mood. Vojto's younger brother Teo ended up carrying the can as usual. His mother went on and on telling people that he was slow-witted because he had had meningitis as a child. That was why they sent him to horticultural college even though he could have studied law or maybe even medicine. Times had changed. She would have helped him get a place by pulling a few strings, since that was the only way to achieve anything nowadays.

Though accustomed to this kind of talk, Teo fortified himself with alcohol from early morning onwards. As for Roško senior, he preferred to disappear for the day.

"So when are you going to join the party at last?" Mrs Roško shouted at Vojto. "Or are you going to spend the rest of your life like this?"

Vojto just smiled and topped up her glass. It was all part of his plan to have her nod off in the armchair as soon after lunch as possible.

The only one who managed to escape unscathed was Vojto's little sister Ela. She pretended to practise declaiming the *Ode to the River Váh* by Mária Rázusová-Martáková (as a member of the Young Pioneers endowed with huge blue eyes she was often asked to perform this piece at school concerts and party meetings, invariably to rapturous applause). In reality she invented a new pastime, which kept her happily occupied for hours. She picked tomatoes that her father, former elite fighter pilot Roško, was growing in pots, and hurled them into the open windows of the passing long-distance coaches, nicknamed Cucumbers.

Uncle Rudo had to keep to a strict diet ever since he lost a third of his stomach to surgery. The doctor told him to eat frequently and keep the portions small. Against the doctor's advice but true to his habit, Rudo ate frequently but copiously.

The Sunday lunches at our house offered him plenty of opportunities to indulge. There was juicy pork, crunchy chicken (a drumstick or two), succulent beef, ham, soup… He relished it all. Only when he got to the dessert would he stop to think for a moment, take out his pocketknife and cut the dessert in half. He would eat one half, leaving the other half on his plate. A little later he would surreptitiously cut off half of the remaining piece and put it in his mouth. Then he'd cut off another piece… until the dessert was gone.

At that point he would take a breather and say: "This dessert doesn't seem to agree with me."

And he was basically right, because eventually – out of the many options available – he chose to die of diabetes.

He liked to say that we commit ritual suicide by means of food. He didn't mean just himself. He meant all of us. It all comes down to the same thing in the end. Sometimes he would gleefully recall that Uncle Oskar used to call him *fresser*, a guzzler.

He used to say: "There are two kinds of people in this world, Adam – happy people and thin people."

He celebrated his last New Year's Eve on this weird planet of

343

ours by drinking champagne through an enema. He kept complaining that his stomach couldn't cope anymore, and although he couldn't taste anything, he said the effects were spectacular. I guess the tickling bubbles hit the spot.

Someone worked out that we spend four to five years of our lives eating. That someone was Uncle Rudo. If we applied his theory to his own life and subtracted the years he spent eating he would have died as early as 1980.

While Uncle Rudo was happily munching his way to his death, the town of Brežany was blessed by a visit from a guardian angel. Gustáv Valach, a famous actor in real life, was blissfully unaware that the locals had cast him in the exalted role of an angel. What had brought him to Brežany was the leading role in a historical film about Slovak highwaymen that was being shot near Nevedovo, at the foot of the Volovec Mountain.

Valach was staying at the Stag Hotel and he spent his days strolling up and down Brežany's high street until he found his way to the Tower pub. He was immediately mobbed by the regulars, who couldn't believe their eyes. Everyone recognized his face from TV plays and his sonorous baritone from radio plays and readings. And suddenly the owner of the famous voice was sitting next to them, just like that! It was almost too good to be true! People were reduced to blushes and stutters.

Towering above them like Jesus Christ, he freely handed out advice to his enraptured listeners in his soft Central Slovak accent and precise slow diction.

"That's not the way to do it," he admonished Vencel the vintner. "The Irsay grape has to be harvested in early September, otherwise it falls off the vine."

Vencel gave an erudite nod but couldn't bring himself to utter a single word.

"What are you sobbing about? Forget about her, you'll find another woman!" he'd say to another man, moving him to tears.

A few days later I witnessed a case of truly miraculous healing of the stand-up-and-walk variety. Everyone had long given up on Klaudius Kolár, as it was pretty clear that he would drink himself into the grave. Suddenly there he was, at the Tower, drinking a glass of mineral water, almost a caricature of himself.

"I ought to stop drinking, I know!" he said in a contrite voice.

"But why all of a sudden?"

"Because he told me to. Alcohol is a poison! And he's right; he's dead right!"

That was when it dawned on me. Television is really a blessing. It can save human lives.

13.

"I make cheep-cheep 'coz I'm a birdie!"

"So how can you tell that you're a birdie?"

"I'm a birdie... 'coz I make cheep-cheep!"

This was my conversation with Bony, who was growing up in front of my eyes.

One of his favourite things was putting his tongue between the plus and minus metal plates of a battery. He loved the weird taste and the sensation of a weak electricity current surging through him.

"So that's why it says BATERIE SLANÝ, doesn't it?" he asked a few years later, when he was able to read the label, which linked the battery-maker to the Czech town of Slaný, which means salty.

It tasted salty to him. Or perhaps sour. No – salty.

Once he started walking, he loved to go on outings.

On that particular day the three of us – Zuzana, Bony and I – headed for Devín Castle. Zuzana's cousin asked us to take her seven-year-old daughter Marínka along. Although she was supposed to have Saturdays off, she had to work that day and had no childcare.

The May sun was warm and the horse chestnuts were in blossom. The eighth-century castle ruin towered above the broad, winding border zone surrounded by barbed wire. On the other side of the river Morava lay Austria, clearly visible from the castle hill, yet so incredibly far away. Marínka asked who was behind the fence, them or us. I didn't know what to say. She shrugged and declared that there must be great treasures on the other side of the river if they had to guard them so carefully.

I didn't respond to that either.

The sun was beginning to set as we walked down to the car park

345

below the castle. I went to open the car but the front door on Zuzana's side was stuck. While I tried to fix it the children were fooling around. Everything was quiet; only the odd hiker passed by. The thrushes and redstarts had launched into their evening song.

Bony ran off and stepped over the low wire fence along the side of the car park. We heard a crack and an explosion from the top of the Devínska Kobyla Hill. Someone had fired a signal rocket. Within a few minutes the river was swarming with motorboats and people armed with automatic rifles were combing the riverbank. Chaos and commotion.

Panicking, I finally managed to pull the door free. Zuzana cried out when she realised what Bony had done. She tried to grab him and bundle him into the car. But a group of armed men was already marching up to us.

One of them pointed to Bony: "That's the one, in the green jumper!"

Bony's jumper was blue, not green, but they obviously meant him. We were surrounded by border guards with their guns pointed at us.

"Explain yourself!" they shouted at me.

"What?"

"What are you doing here?"

"We've come for a walk."

"Your papers!"

We showed them our IDs. The border guard who had pointed to Bony raised his voice.

"Do you have any relatives abroad?"

I shook my head.

They hung around for a while, not sure what to do or what to ask. Finally they threw our IDs onto the car bonnet, turned on their heels and marched off.

"Keep an eye on the boy! This is a border zone!"

On the road back to Bratislava a lorry full of soldiers passed us at high speed.

I laughed: "I bet they were all called out because of us!"

"Adam, stop the car! Quick!" Zuzana screamed.

Marínka had gone as white as a sheet. I pulled over, and she dashed out and vomited into the murky waters of the shallow arm

346

of the Danube. Zuzana said it was shock. She got out of the car and tried to comfort her.

And that was the end of our lovely Saturday outing.

I was walking from the TV station down Slovak National Uprising Square, known until recently as Stalin Square. A storm must have been brewing because the sticky heavy air hung between the houses and my clothes clung to my skin. As I reached the corner by the Polish Cultural Institute I slowed down when I spotted a woman standing by the curb. At first I didn't recognize her, then my heart skipped a beat, my pulse quickened and I realised it was Ada.

I hesitated to approach her. I stopped some ten metres off, breathing in the cigarette smoke she exhaled, aware that only a few seconds ago the same smoke had been coursing inside her. It made the hairs on the back of my neck stand on end and made me feel as if we had established an intimate connection. But I couldn't bring myself to speak to her. The smoke teased my nose. I started to cough and turned away to avoid being recognized.

She was heartbreakingly gorgeous. I wondered how difficult this must have made her life. Looks are part of one's fate (in addition to being part of our character, which few people realise).

Gratuitously eloquent at times when I should stay silent and tongue-tied when it really matters, I just stood there until a taxi pulled up, she climbed in and disappeared from sight.

So close. Yet still so far away.

Part 4

The Half-Submerged Dog

Another of Goya's series of murals from the *House of the Deaf Man* is known as *The Half-Submerged Dog*. It depicts a dog's head, raised above a dark river, against a sepia background. The dog is swimming, although it is far from clear if it really is a dog and if what he is swimming in really is a river. It could just as easily be a stain on the wall. Goya left no clues.

In my imagination the image blends with another snapshot – a poor quality sepia-tinted photo showing a black dog struggling against the river current, with a lot of water splashing about. As the camera zooms out it reveals a young Alfonz Trnovský, my father, standing on the riverbank smiling. He is proud of the dog's performance. The dog's name is Polyester, possibly the first in the long line of Polyesters we have owned.

In my mind I'm back at the summer lido on the Sálava River.

Father is looking across to the far side where I'm swimming, strapped into a harness. A guard is slowly walking along the side of the pool holding a long pole attached to my harness. Father – wearing his off-white suit complete with waistcoat and jacket, and a hat pushed down his forehead to protect him from the sun – comments occasionally:

"Adam, why don't you do proper full strokes like Mr Kopasný says?"

But the water seems to resist.

The photograph melds into the next picture in the album.

Each clock in this house shows a different time. The clocks completely defy time, making it scatter every which way like a handful of marbles.

Yesterday, after I arrived, I set the time on the wall clock in the drawing room and on the alarm clock in Father's isolation cell. But in just one day time has set out in a direction of its own on both of them.

Soon all the clocks will stop ticking, depending on how much energy they have left to move ahead and propel moments yet to come, the inevitable future. Each clock will freeze in a different time. Eleven-thirty, three o'clock, a quarter to seven... I'm beginning to feel like a drowned man at the bottom of the sea. Submerged and dead.

I'm packing the few bits and pieces that are worth rescuing from here. I have come to say goodbye to this place that I am about to leave forever. I do it in my own way. Before Vojto moved out of his old flat in Szabó Street we covered all the walls with drawings; before handing over his patisserie Puškár stuffed all his cakes with beetles. I pass my hands along the walls and follow the colour lines left by furniture, trying to figure out what it was about this house that cast a spell on me, because it can't be anything but a spell.

Corners are wondrous things; they live a mysterious life of their own. You wouldn't expect to find anything much in corners except for the odd walnut that had rolled in there at Christmas. But you'd be wrong.

There's Father's lost sock, appropriated by Polyester number five or six... Here's a fossil that belonged to Peter, an ammonite he had picked up somewhere only to forget about it very soon... A battered dark red toy car I used to play with...

And dust, hairballs, dead insects, spiders.

The first time Peter showed his face again in Brežany after a year, like a bear emerging from hibernation, he crouched down and huddled in a corner of Mother's room. That was where he said he felt safe.

I've heard people say it's not nouns but adjectives that define the world. Lately I've been haunted by adjectives.

Railway stations, oh, all those railway stations! In this country, they all boast an identical plaque with the identical text: *They have died so that we might live. 1939 – 1945.* The identical black basalt, the identical grey marble, the same small branch as a symbol of mourning. Only the names vary... All these plaques must have been mass-produced in the same factory and solemnly mounted on the anniversary of the Slovak National Uprising – with music and bouquets of identical red carnations. Who knows why they always had to be mounted at railway stations, of all places?

The word "they", in gilded lettering, is in the plural, although here, in Brežany, it is followed by only one name. And even that one name was very hard to come by. The deceased are a rare commodity, particularly the desirable kind of deceased, preferably those who perished in the winter of 1944. Eventually, Brežany found its hero. And promptly misspelled his name. It didn't really matter. Nobody cared about him as a person. The band played the *March of the Fallen Revolutionaries*; the Chairman of the National Committee delivered a speech; a couple of war veterans, their chests decorated with medals, stood around for a while, as did a delegation of dignitaries who had been rushed in from Bratislava in a Tatra 603, and a bunch of young pioneers, dragged out of school at the last minute, so overjoyed at skipping class that they found it hard to appear suitably respectful. When it was over everyone went their own way.

Vojto's father shuffled past the ceremony without raising his head, quickening his step as he crossed to the far end of the station with his broom. He had recently started working here as cleaner. After being merged with another forestry enterprise, the entire staff at Brežany was fired. Mr Roško had finally been awarded a military pension, which paid peanuts. However, as he'd never been convicted of a crime or imprisoned, he wasn't entitled to be legally rehabilitated. It was as simple as that. So he was sweeping floors: crumpled paper flags, cigarette butts, crepe paper left over from parades, dog shit.

The former Reverend Čerešník was sitting in the railway bar, drunk, banging on the formica-topped table and shouting at the top of his voice: "Gregorian chants don't follow any old rhythm: it's the rhythm of… a Pioneer motorbike engine when it's idling!"

He and Vojto's father had lost one of their drinking pals now that the communist Németh had been pardoned, received an official apology and was allowed to return to Bratislava. He got an office job at one of the ministries and turned his back on his old pals.

Father Čerešník from the village of Vernár would chat up everyone who came up to the bar, and go on and on about doing time at Leopoldovo in 1951, and how he and his fellow priests were forced to stagger around the prison yard endlessly repeating: "There is no God! There is no God!"

Who knows what went through his head when he learned that Lieutenant Colonel Vojtech Roško stopped his car on the railway tracks in the path of a fast approaching train.

Father was summoned to the scene of the accident. The railway tracks, the smashed up car, Vojto's father… it was all one big blur. When the police doctor finally arrived, Father turned on his heels and left without a word. People shouted after him but he didn't hear anything.

Apart from the unbearable whistling in his ears.

Increasingly he would nod off in his consulting room (now I know that his old friend Luminal had something to do with that) leaving the patients standing in front of him stripped to the waist.

He'd wake up after a while and frown:

"He comes right up to me and talks into my ear! What's he muttering under his breath? What's his problem? He must speak up, louder!"

All the joy had gone out of our family gatherings and Sunday lunches. They were reduced to an ill-rehearsed theatre production whose actors regularly forgot their lines as their thoughts kept wandering off. Everyone just tried to finish their meal – "Ah, there's still coffee and dessert to come" – and leave as soon as possible. Surely we've done our duty? At moments like these Father pretended to be at ease, to act naturally and without affectation. He would chatter, crack jokes, cajole and dispense advice. He revelled in the role of paterfamilias.

Whenever I managed to escape from the hubbub, get hold of a magazine and withdraw into a corner with a crossword puzzle, Father would sidle up to me and peer over my shoulder.

"How is it going? – let's see where you've gone wrong… State of tumult, poetic… there are no other hints, hmm… Actually, you're not bad at all… Hang on, this isn't right, it should be… Let's see now… A female Christian name… You must check the calendar, 15 September is Jolana's name day. Oh, now I see why you've gone wrong! – your Ns look like Ws, you've got to write every letter clearly… An iron utensil for grilling. That's too easy! Now, that's more like it! Why isn't your pen working? Is the paper greasy or what…? You've invented a new word here… A practitioner of extreme rigour. Ascetic… We've got that one right. Hang on a minute… Hang on…!"

He was driving me to distraction.

As if he had guessed how I felt, he smiled and broke off, walked past Zuzana who was talking to Tina, ruffled little Bony's hair and started to discuss with Uncle Rudo the rumour that Khrushchev, on a recent official visit to West Germany, had received the latest Mercedes as a gift from the Chancellor. They heard he'd taken it for a test drive and promptly crashed it into the nearest tree. The cartoonists at *Der Spiegel* had a field day.

Mother flashed him an annoyed look as she cleared the coffee cups from the table. When we're not around, she whispered into my ear, Father spends most his time in silence, locked in his isolation cell or pottering about. Sometimes days went by without him exchanging a single word with her.

A few days before he took his last train journey Lieutenant Colonel Roško received a typed invitation:

Dear Comrade!
This year as usual, to mark the twentieth anniversary of the liberation of the Czechoslovak Soviet Socialist Republic, the May Day parade will be led by anti-fascist combatants. You are expected to do your fellow resistance fighters proud by taking part in the parade. Let us put on public display our solidarity with our working people on this day, which marks the twentieth anniversary of our country's liberation. Join us in the May Day parade! Medals should be worn. Your place in the parade will be allocated at the assembly point.
We trust that you will join your fellow resistance fighters in the parade. Your comrades-in-arms await you!
Confirmation slip. Name… Address…. This is to confirm that I will take part in the May Day parade and that I am the recipient of the following medals… I will wear my full dress uniform: yes/no (cross out what is not applicable). Signature.

This was the first time he had received this kind of invitation. And in keeping with his mercurial nature (Vojto told me that his father had once flung a brand new telephone out of the window because he couldn't get through to someone), he returned the confirmation slip without delay.

The 1965 May Day parade in Brežany was a grand affair. Those invited included the youngest Slovak partisan, Janko Giertli-Šokove from the village of Čierny Balog, a recipient of Slovakia's Heroism

Medal. In 1945, as a nine-year-old, he ran through snowdrifts to the next village and summoned partisans to help defend his own people against the Germans. By now he was thirty and looked fifty. He delivered one of the speeches from the rostrum.

Later that day I saw the poor guy, his chest laden with medals, blind drunk at the Tower pub, banging his fist on the table and insisting that he had personally saved the lives of twenty Soviet partisans. When he finished his drink and got up to leave, a Tatra 603 came to collect him.

A few minutes later another man, also sinking under the weight of his medals, stood up and started to whine: "But I am the real Janko Giertli…!"

He beat his chest and bewailed how someone else wanted to steal his thunder and credit.

Vojto's father, fortified by five shots of vodka, which worked miracles for his headaches, walked over unsteadily to join the parade. Though he had destroyed many of his decorations after the war, he did keep a few. He couldn't part with his Iron Cross, First Class, nor with the German Golden Buckle. His chest was adorned with the German Golden Cross and the Order of the Slovak National Uprising, First Class, and the Participant in the Slovak National Uprising Award.

He marched proudly, carrying a Soviet banner, looking neither left nor right. The crowd, horror-struck, parted to let him pass. Someone made a grab for him but he broke free and marched on, singing:

How quiet the night, so dark and fair / The partisan fights in his forest lair / The moon sleeps not a wink all night / The partisan it must guard with light / When he leaves the forest's shade / With fighting spirit his heart does blaze / Slovaks, onward! Into battle's might / Our homeland summons us to fight!

The march broke up. Monako and a few of his friends tried to take him out of circulation but Vojto's father insisted on returning to the parade. He had, after all, duly completed and returned his confirmation slip, listing all the medals he was now wearing.

Colonel Gajdoš, who had drafted and sent out the invitations, should have been alerted by the list of medals but he had obviously just glanced at the names at the top without bothering to read the slip all the way to the end. But the last straw was Lieutenant Colonel Roško's fighter pilot-officer uniform, also mentioned in the confirmation slip. It was the one he had proudly worn while serving in the army of the wartime Slovak Republic.

It took four policemen to overpower him and take him home. They tried to make him see sense and promised not to pursue the matter provided he never showed his face in a parade again. A horrified Vojto put his father to bed, trying to calm him down and comfort him with cold compresses.

As the sun rose the next day, retired Lieutenant Colonel Vojtech Roško climbed into his car and drove it onto the railway crossing where he stopped to await the express train to Bratislava.

The train was seven minutes late.

2.

The first time Tina showed it to me I had no idea what on earth it could be. A flexible, grey-blue round thingummy. Father held it up to the light and managed to make out a tiny cavity on someone's left lung. When we placed the object on Father's new record player, the room was filled with fabulous pounding rhythm the like of which I had never heard before. Tina explained it was "Jailhouse Rock". Elvis. I still had no idea what this was all about.

Tina sighed wearily and explained that this was "music on ribs", a peculiar method of recording music that was all the rage in the Soviet Union. Her pen friend Svetlana had sent one from Moscow, explaining in her cover letter that it was made by trimming an X-ray to the shape of a record. The thick plastic was particularly suitable for this purpose: you just had to punch a hole in the middle and make your recording. When Tina said that Svetlana had nicked this particular X-ray from her *babushka,* Father shouted from the other room that next time she wrote she should enquire about her friend's grandmother's health and ask if she was aware she had TB.

The recording crackled as if Elvis was singing in the middle of a roaring sea.

Svetlana had it made by a stranger who stood outside the GUM department store offering his services to young passers-by for a few roubles. The man kept a stock of records rolled up in his sleeve. They fitted in easily, being very flexible, and Svetlana referred to them as *plastinky*. That's what these things are called in the Soviet Union, she explained.

When Elvis finished singing we put him on again. And again. The first rock-and-roll recording of my life blew my mind.

As we listened, Tina suddenly remembered that about a month ago a long-haired chap who tried to chat her up at the skating rink had given her a black-and-white photo. The picture, which he clearly thought was something special, showed Elvis dancing. His name didn't ring a bell for her.

Unimpressed, she mumbled… "I see… Nice… Thanks…," and slipped the photo into her pocket. Taken aback, her suitor stood still for a while, turned around and offended, skated off into oblivion.

But now, with a slight delay, Elvis had found his rightful place in a gilded frame on her desk.

Soon this kind of music swept in from the other end of Europe. You couldn't hear any rock and roll on our radio or TV, the communists not being great fans of rock music, but Radio Luxembourg made up for that. Elvis, the Beatles, the Kinks, Little Richard, Chubby Checker… Tina and her girlfriends were forever giggling and repeating in a nasal voice:

Here is Radio Luxembourg! The station of the Stars!

Her ear was glued to "Luxie" day and night.

My sister Tina grew up to be a striking and stylish woman you couldn't fail to spot and especially, hear, from afar. She felt the need to "hear herself" walk so an assortment of objects was always rattling in her pockets or hanging from her clothes "to make sure she didn't get lost in the urban jungle".

It took great ingenuity to dress with style and avoid the conservative allure of grey socialist fashion designed by people whose taste was defined by opposition to the corrupt influence of capitalism. Like all her girlfriends Tina used to wear her hair à la Brigitte Bardot: a huge beehive with a bread roll in the middle (it tended to fall out whenever she let her hair out and sometimes also when she didn't), to make the hairdo look bigger and fluffier. For make-up she used thick eyeliner and enhanced her eyelashes with a toothbrush refashioned into a mascara stick, which she would spit on before applying it to her eyes. Although our shops didn't carry any Christian Dior merchandise, she took her inspiration from pictures in colour magazines. Tina coaxed Father into giving her a window net that he had used to stop flies and mosquitoes from flying into the house. She tied it tightly around her waist with an elastic band, and sewed it around the hem of her dress. Thus adjusted, the dress would maintain a tight fit around the top while staying wide and airy at the bottom. She complemented her outfit with stiletto heels and nylon stockings, a rare commodity that kept laddering. A bundle of energy, Tina didn't mind daily visits to the stocking repair shop run by Mrs Malánek. Payment was according to the number of ladders.

Our teachers launched a crusade against the pernicious influence of the West, to which Vojto's sister Ela fell victim. Their main goal was a "neat appearance", and in pursuit of this elusive criterion the teachers stopped students in front of the school to check with a ruler whether the bottoms of their trousers were too wide or too narrow, as the case may be. The same approach was applied to boys' hair, which couldn't be worn too long. On the other hand, crew cuts of the kind popularised by the Canadian hockey legend Al Dewsbury were also discouraged.

Tina couldn't wait to get her driving licence, which came as a shock to our family, since women at the driving wheel were still a rare sight in our town. I was soon to discover quite how rare when Father managed to get a good deal on a new robust Skoda 1202 estate and passed our old Chevy on to Tina, who asked me to be her instructor when she first took the wheel. Right on the corner of Voroshilov Street she blasted through the intersection without giving way to a lorry that came hurtling towards us. The driver jammed on his brakes, only narrowly avoiding disaster, and poked his head out of the window, yelling:

"Learn to drive, you prick!"

Winding down her window, Tina had the presence of mind to respond daintily:

"Excuse me – you mean to say: you cunt!"

She has always reacted very sensitively to gender issues.

She also dreamed of travelling. Frozen Czechoslovakia, like a snowman at the beginning of spring, slowly began to thaw. In 1966, in the middle of summer, a letter of invitation from Tina's friend Paulína came in the post. Following a brutal encounter with Russian soldiers at the very end of the war, which had left a permanent scar on her sex life, Paulína left Brežany in the autumn of 1945 and moved to England with her parents. She lived in the London suburb of Barking and offered to take Tina on a trip across the country, all the way up to Scotland and the islands in the north, the Orkneys or the Shetlands, I forget which.

Although those were happy times and the Iron Curtain was getting quite rusty by then, it took ages to sort out all the formalities. It seemed almost as if the authorities were determined that my sister should not travel abroad. So Father took matters in hand.

He wasn't convinced that England was a great idea but he did have a soft spot for his daughter and must have been torn between the desire to hold on to her for as long as possible and the longing to fulfil every wish that sprang from her lovely little head.

The minutes of a meeting that took place in the safe house include the following passage (covered in dark stains left by spilled fruit juice or perhaps red wine):

Comrade Trnovský: My daughter would like to make a trip abroad. To England. For a summer job.
Lt. Ďuratný: We might be able to help. Times are changing after all, aren't they? The atmosphere has relaxed… We are very interested in information on this issue, as you will appreciate. The mood in émigré circles. What they think of our rising star, Alexander Dubček.
C. Trnovský: I understand.
Lt. Ďuratný: I attended a meeting a few days ago. I have a few assignments for you. Take a look. What do you think?
C. Trnovský: I think that could be done.
Lt. Ďuratný: Pleased to hear that. It's in our common interest, isn't it?
C. Trnovský: And what about my daughter? She's a bright girl. I think…
Lt. Ďuratný: We'll see what we can do, trust me. Unless, of course, she fails to come back.
C. Trnovský: Why on earth shouldn't she? She has no reason not to.
Lt. Ďuratný: I'll take your word for it.

In 1967 Tina travelled around England with Paulína and some friends. She would send us postcards, telling us about various jobs she found and the places she visited. She wrote a lovely poem about the streets of London, I might still have it somewhere. She also wrote one about the streets of Edinburgh and another one about the streets of Kirkwall, in the Orkneys. She had a great time and revelled in her freedom.

On one of the postcards she said she might not be coming back, unleashing a firestorm in our house.

The next time she wrote she denied it all and mentioned a new acquaintance, a young man by the name of Trevor Tompkins, a recent graduate who played the piano in jazz clubs. They met at a camping site.

Her next postcard said that she was going to stay after all, in Trevor's tiny flat in London's East End. And that she was thinking of marrying him.

Father had a nervous breakdown when he read the news after coming home from his consulting room one evening.

Sometimes time inches along as slowly as a snail; then, when you least expect it, it lunges forward faster than a racehorse.

3.

Monako was a heavy smoker, as became obvious when he was admitted to hospital with a complicated leg fracture. Father came to see his old acquaintance and found a heap of quivering jelly. He sat down on the edge of his bed and watched Monako struggle, his legs held down, by turns screaming and whispering unintelligibly.

At first everything seemed to be going well. Monako underwent surgery and had his leg put into plaster. But on day four, when the effect of the painkillers had worn off, he suddenly felt as if the ceiling had caved in on him.

"Delirium," the consultant drily informed his wife. "Years and years of daily drinking have taken their toll! I just hope he makes a full recovery."

Father watched silently as Monako put his hand to his mouth, taking a drag on an imaginary cigarette and exhaling imaginary smoke. In a shaky, terrified voice he said he saw flour bugs and ground beetles crawling on the bedsheets, a veritable insect invasion, that he had tried to get rid of them but didn't have the strength to go on. He asked Father to help drive them away. He claimed he'd seen an old man being bludgeoned to death on the neighbouring ward and his bloodied body dragged down to the basement – the red smudge was still visible, over there! Look!

Monako later didn't remember any of this, just extreme exhaustion. Father prescribed tranquillizers.

Luminal was a perennial favourite, as I could tell by the number of empty boxes and blister packs in his bin. I was just discovering dexphenmetrazine whereas he had a predilection for Tacitin, a Swiss tranquillizer, sent by a colleague from abroad. He once told me it brought him great relief and profound peace. Profound peace. That was what he was looking for.

Everyone in our family tended to resort to medication, and each one of us had our own way of getting hold of drugs and concealing them. If someone had turned on a light and happened to choose the right moment, he might have caught us with our hands behind books on bookshelves, inside vases or in Father's medicine chest, which was full of empty packets and silver foil left over from sleeping pills, painkillers, stimulants, tranquillizers and antidepressants. No one had ever admitted to this openly, but now and then we had an inkling. Peter, Tina, Father and I.

Mother also spent the last days of her life clutching a packet of 400-gram Ibuprofen in one hand and some diazepam in the other.

Sometimes I think this might be just a modern version of the familiar phenomenon that drives the Slovaks to alcohol as a way of lifting their spirits.

Entries documenting the last period of the Ďuratný era are missing from Father's file. Some have been shredded, while others are lost, as handwritten notes on the margins of the surviving papers suggest. Tina's failure to return home from England must have got him into trouble. But perhaps the trouble was not too deep, as by then the Prague Spring was already in the air. I shall never know.

4.

Czechoslovakia was in ferment in April 1968 when Tina and Trevor met me at Heathrow airport. To my immense surprise it had been quite easy to get an exit visa and all the other permissions.

It was raining. I arrived with my camera. The tall, lanky, blue-eyed Trevor had ginger hair and freckles. He and Tina look happy in the photographs. They had recently got married, making Tina's stay in England legal. They lived in a small but cosy flat in the East End, in a terraced brick house in Brady Street in Whitechapel, close to a Jewish cemetery.

Tina had found a job in a small dressmakers' shop and was doing rather well. (Five years later she would open her own salon, *Double T* – for Tina Tompkins, although at this stage the idea wasn't even a twinkle in her eye. That's what's so wonderful about the future. And writing about the future.)

Although I could never fully understand why, whenever people see cascades of water, they feel compelled to toss coins into them. In London, with its many parks and fountains, sometimes even I succumbed. The awe-inspiring ancient trees made me feel at peace with myself and the world. I was surprised to discover that all you need to do is stray off the beaten track and the world seems a whole lot simpler.

Tina told me that on her first day in London she walked into the first butcher's shop she saw and innocently asked for bacon. The owner was livid and chased her out with a stream of abuse. Cursing and waving his fist, he screamed this was a provocation and an attempted assassination. Once outside she looked back and realized it was a kosher butcher.

It made me think of *zeyde* Blau and *bobe* Sara and, of course, Mr Stern the shochet with phylacteries wrapped around his arms, praying in the church because the synagogue had been closed and trying to make his voice heard over the Lord's prayer. And being carried out without a word.

We took a walk around Battersea Power Station on the south bank of the Thames, its four chimneys like fingers pointing menacingly at the sky. Tina mentioned in passing that this was the largest brick building in Europe. Nine years later, in 1977, it was to feature on the sleeve of Pink Floyd's album *Animals*. In a burst of enthusiasm and nostalgia I bought the record for what was then an astronomical sum.

A light but steady wind was blowing as we stood on the riverbank, and Tina gazed down at the water dreamily. Something about its flow reminded us of the Sálava. A ship under the US flag was sailing down the river, the sound of its horn bouncing off the walls of the power station.

"America must be a wonderful country. Trevor says their train horns are perfectly tuned. The Pacific Western railroad's passenger trains use the jazz six-chord in F major, freight trains are tuned to C major and the North West Pacific trains from Alaska use the extended septachord."

I looked at the Thames and nodded in surprise. Tina had never been into music theory. The miracles that love can perform!

Needless to say, I spoke almost no English and had to get by using phrases from song lyrics that I'd picked up listening to Radio Luxembourg. I could recite them by heart. Of course the cliché *All You Need Is Love* wasn't quite enough to get by on, even in these days of flower power. But *Wouldn't It Be Nice* and *It's Gonna Work Out Fine* often come in handy. All that mattered was that I managed to make myself understood. *I Heard It Through The Grapevine*.

During a ride on a double-decker bus Tina pointed out something in the street below and as I leaned forward the driver suddenly stepped on the brakes. I hit my head.

Tina dashed into a pharmacy to get some plasters, while I waited outside in the street.

A procession of schoolchildren was passing by. Their teacher made them give this weird man with a bloodied forehead, dressed in rather outlandish clothes, a wide berth. But one little boy turned around, walked back to me and asked me politely:

"Can I have a look at your bleeding, please?"

His pronounciation was so clear that even I understood – thanks to Bob Dylan, of course (*It's Alright, Ma, I'm Only Bleeding*) and The Kinks' (*You Really Got Me*).

We stopped at a tiny second-hand bookshop tucked away in an alley near Brady Street. Its bookshelves were overflowing and the books were in a jumble. The dust stung my eyes. Because of my poor knowledge of real English I couldn't enjoy it as much as I did similar places back at home. Nevertheless, after browsing for a while and feeling several book covers (which visibly irritated the stuffy, shrivelled bookseller, who didn't find the plaster on my forehead too confidence-inspiring), I finally picked up a worn book with a greenish cover and a title in white: *George Orwell, Nineteen Eighty-Four, a novel*. I'd heard about it before and a chill went down my spine as I paid, because I knew that Orwell's books were banned in Czechoslovakia. I was dying to find out what dangerous secrets the book held and decided to discover them at any cost.

On the very first page, it read, in bold: ***Big brother is watching you***, *the caption said, while the dark eyes looked deep into Winston's own.*

And on the next page, three lines declared: *WAR IS PEACE. FREEDOM IS SLAVERY. IGNORANCE IS STRENGTH.*

Next on my list was Abbey Road, where the Beatles had their recording studio, but I was a little disappointed to find an ordinary London street. I don't know quite what I was expecting.

On our way back we crossed the vast green expanse of Hyde Park, with its long, narrow pond. The city was full of long-haired people in colourful clothes, with bead necklaces and guitars. This was where they seemed to congregate.

I had always thought it was just a myth but at Speakers' Corner near Marble Arch small groups of people really did gather around speakers, some of them on raised platforms. They were allowed to speak about anything, apart from the royal family and overthrowing the government. I surprised Trevor by bursting into hysterical giggles when he said that Marx and Lenin had also spoken here once.

A man walked up and down with a banner that proclaimed: *Don't trust anyone, including me!* A balding chap at the edge of the crowd was holding forth about Vietnam. A small group of people listened to him, nodding earnestly as he worked himself up into a frenzy and his ears turned red. I watched him, spellbound.

Shortly afterwards a shabby old man with a Tesco carrier bag joined the group. He listened for a while, scratching his ear, and after a few more sentences he replied to the speaker's rhetorical question. The speaker became agitated but responded to the heckler and then carried on. The old man shouted something again. The speaker hesitated, said a few words in reply, evidently discomfited, for the old man had interrupted his flow. He continued, fumbling for words. The old man waited for a little before interrupting him again. He was obviously enjoying it.

The audience started to grow. The speech disintegrated into desperate ripostes to the old man's heckling. Trevor laughed. Tina just shook her head. She said the old man wasn't really disagreeing, he just enjoyed winding the speaker up.

Finally, after another comment from the old man the balding speaker gathered up his things, stepped off the platform and left in a huff, waving his arms and muttering to himself.

People sensed there was potential for more fun and followed the old man to the next speaker. This time the old man took aim at a gaunt man pontificating about vegetarianism. The speaker produced a chart and stabbed at it with his pencil until the old man's rasping voice interrupted, commenting sarcastically on his diagrams. The speaker blinked and offered a civilized explanation before returning to his chart.

When he had achieved the same effect as with the previous speaker, the old heckler smiled and shuffled off, followed by the whole cheerfully chattering crowd, including the three of us.

A third speaker was expounding his views on America, that evil and corrupt country. The old man threw in a caustic remark at the very beginning. But the speaker pretended not to hear. The heckler shouted but the speaker just raised his voice and went on. The old man elbowed his way closer and started talking right at him – I only caught the names Martin Luther King and Robert Kennedy. He tried to interrupt but the speaker just moved a few steps further away and continued undaunted.

The old man stopped in his tracks, then beat a retreat, dismayed. The speaker finished his talk, to considerable applause. He gave a bow and walked off. The audience began to drift away.

The old man shouted in desperation.

"What the hell you staring at?!"

In a nearby garden restaurant a black waiter presented the posh guests with their bill. The old man bellowed in their direction. Tina and Trevor wanted to leave but I wanted to know what he was saying.

Tina translated: "Don't pay, don't give him anything! I've lived for fifty years and look at me! Look how I ended up! And it's all because of people like him!"

He walked off grumbling and waving his Tesco carrier bag. He turned around once more and shouted something. Tina translated: "Stinking niggers!"

The man's odour stayed in my nostrils for a long time. Alcohol, sweat – and perhaps just a tinge of urine as well. An exquisite human bouquet.

Although Tina had become a fully-fledged British citizen she still felt homesick. It was no surprise that it wasn't the stereotypical national dishes such as *bryndzové halušky* the potato gnocchi with ewe's cheese, which she had always hated or *kapustnica*, the sauerkraut soup she had always tried to avoid, that symbolised Slovakia for her. Instead, we had to supply her for years with Horalky wafers. She claimed their chocolate and peanut filling epitomized the genuine taste of home. Tears welled up in her eyes whenever she took a bite, at least so she claimed. She had inherited Mother's histrionic streak. It was something Trevor never understood. And there was no way he could.

He thought the good old British Kit-Kat was a hundred times better. He had his own reasons for that.

When I returned from England, I gave Bony his first taste of 7-Up. He was fascinated by the very process of opening the can, the magic little piece of metal you have to flip before the click, followed by a hissing sound; the green colour of the drink, the lettering, the smell... He even loved the wonderful polystyrene cups I brought him from the plane. He just adored 7-Up and thought its unique citrusy taste was out of this world. He savoured it drop by drop, making it last a whole week, and he cherished the tin as if it were some precious relic for years to come. 7-Up tasted of freedom and of distant, inaccessible, exotic countries.

His friends tried to steal the precious object a few times. It brought him enormous respect in the eyes of his peers. The cans had a number of uses: for example, if you cut off the top you had a luxury pen and pencil holder. Coca-Cola cans acquired a similar fetish status: in the seventies some women carried them around in their handbags like pieces of jewellery.

Bony always managed to catch the thieves and get his tin back, although his friend Lego once nearly succeeded in smuggling it out of our flat hidden in the lining of his coat.

As for the Orwell novel, I hid it under my shirt before going through customs, just to be on the safe side. The book lay about in our wardrobe for some time and then I passed it on to Vojto, asking him to find someone to translate it.

5.

As soon as Bony learned to talk he grew very cheeky.

"Bony, would you like to earn ten crowns?" I would shout from the kitchen if I wanted him to do something.

"No. I want more!" came the answer.

Once a week I took him on a ramble around town, to visit the TV studios or for a cream slice at the Children's Patisserie in Hviezdoslav Square.

When I picked him up from nursery school the smell in the lobby brought back memories of Brežany. Cocoa, milkshake, sunlamps, it all came back like in a rewound film. Children are handed dark glasses and told to strip down to their shorts. They are asked to enter in small groups. The teacher issues an order – *Turn around! Out with you now, chop, chop!* – The lingering smell of ozone from the sunlamps. The alluring violet light you're not allowed to look into. The buzz of the enormous sunlamp. Just like the one Father had in his consulting room right after the war.

At nursery school Bony used to have visions of a big black spider coming to him during their compulsory afternoon nap, which had just become the trend in nursery schools. All the other children fell asleep but he never could. Keeping his eyes firmly shut he waited for the big soft furry body to creep up on him, slowly descending from the ceiling on its spider silk, ready to pounce the moment he made the slightest move…

"And then you woke up with your hand in the potty!" I would say trying to distract him from the nightmare.

But the fact was, in those days we all had our hand stuck in the potty, so to speak.

The regime suddenly loosened its iron grip. Dubček indulged in fantasies of "socialism with a human face". Vojto doubted that socialism could ever have a human face – he thought it bore more of a resemblance to a huge arse – but he threw himself into the thick of things nevertheless. He even managed to have his father fully rehabilitated and posthumously promoted to the rank of colonel. I thought he might just as easily have asked for him to be made general, which had an even better ring to it, but Vojto didn't think that was very amusing.

He was exhilarated and shocked at suddenly being able to take a deep breath. He could hardly believe it was true. He nearly choked. After years of aimless drifting he finally got a proper job with a magazine in Bratislava. He launched himself into writing essays and articles about atrocities committed during the 1950s show trials. He was in his element.

He was astonished to discover books that had been inaccessible before. *Doctor Zhivago* was published a year earlier – the translators had allegedly found it in a bookshop in English translation. The original was said to have been published by the Russian Ministry of Agriculture, and Vojto claimed that this information featured quite prominently in the book to legitimise translations into other languages. The Slovak translation sold out immediately, but Vojto kept a copy hidden out of sight somewhere on his bookshelf. Just to be on the safe side. He devoured *One Day in the Life of Ivan Denisovich,* with its portrait of the Russian gulag, and lapped up Henry Miller and Borges.

Our tipple of choice at the Czechoslovak TV studios in the main square was Myslivecká bitters. The picture of a cheerful woodsman on the bottle symbolised the "human face". We did a lot of filming in the streets, as galvanised citizens were happy to air their grievances on camera. Sometimes it almost looked as if things could really change.

Dubček shared a passionate kiss with Brezhnev. The legendary 1968 Summer of Love was about to begin. But we were soon to discover that it was really a slobbery kiss of death, like the one the female praying mantis delivers to her male.

I narrow my eyes and the two men in the photo seem to be moving almost imperceptibly. They launch into a tango to the quickening pace of the old song, in František Krištof Veselý's rendition:

> *Before you leave me, at least say goodbye*
> *Before you leave me, at least give me a kiss,*
> *Give me your dainty hand, rub your fanny on my…*

The tango turns increasingly lewd, spinning faster and faster. In its frenzy it begins to sound like the Russian song 'Kalinka'.

On 21 August 1968 I was visiting my parents in Brežany. I got up in the middle of the night to fetch a glass of water from the kitchen. Suddenly, as in a waking dream, everything started to shake, even the glass of water I had placed on the kitchen cabinet kept moving until it worked its way to the edge of the table and smashed on the floor. An earthquake – that was my first thought.

Quickly throwing a jacket over my pyjamas I went out into the balmy night. Stars were blinking in the sky above the house. And tanks, with their distinctive white stripes, rolled down the wide street (formerly named after Hitler, then Stalin and most recently, after Štúr).

I suddenly remembered that the workers at the Martin machine factory had given their tanks the sarcastic nickname Peace Doves.

I was also reminded of 1941, except that this time the tanks were moving in the opposite direction. *Whose eyes are these? Whose feet are these…?* I asked, just like during the parlour game of my childhood.

A column of tanks crossed the southern section of the park, deliberately sweeping everything before them. One tank uprooted an ancient plane tree, and as its branches fell they shattered the stained-glass windows of the manor house.

It was the height of summer. The Perseids meteor shower, which Catholics call the Tears of St. Lawrence, kept appearing at night. Not because of the invasion – after all this was its time of the year – but the symbolism-prone poet Klaudius Kolár would certainly have seen the connection.

The sun beat down mercilessly all through the next day, and the tarmac in the streets of Bratislava was melting. I had a contract to deliver to the accounts department at the TV studios in Slovak National Uprising Square. Someone had mounted a tiny portable TV in the window of a ground-floor office facing St Ursula Street. People clustered outside eagerly, watching the broadcast.

The entrance to the TV studios was guarded by Russian troops. A soldier with a machine gun barred my way and told me to go back home. On my way I passed the Technical University's Department of Engineering. The whole square was swarming with tanks. The soldiers didn't seem to have a clue where they were. This was confirmed by a soldier whom I chatted up on a whim. They were hungry, unwashed and stressed. They had been given their orders and off they marched. As someone who'd been exempted from military service, I didn't get the military logic. It seemed that for this wretched person it was enough to receive an order and he would dutifully occupy a strategic building and stand guard at its doors. No explanation needed.

The only person who was really happy was Bony. Until then he had seen Soviet tanks only in films and was desperate to go out and take a look. His eyes shining, he felt the armour plating and a soldier even let him touch his machine gun.

At night thousands of candles were lit in windows all over the city. They were candles of mourning.

Tanks were positioned outside the Slovak National Theatre as well. The doors of the Carlton Hotel's Cercle Bar were closed for several nights but once they re-opened the place was instantly crowded. Dozens of hopeful hookers turned up all dressed to the nines. Rumour had it the Russians had their headquarters in one of the hotel rooms.

The Russian officers finally worked up the courage to come downstairs. The other guests pretended the soldiers were invisible and tried to move away from them. The resident Gypsy band was ordered to play Russian songs and the musicians were shaking in their boots. "We'll be branded collaborators. We'll never play another gig!" I heard the band leader moan at the adjoining table.

The violinist, drenched in sweat, came up with a solution. They would play, but they would steer clear of their usual repertoire. They would only play songs that sound vaguely Russian. I nearly cracked up as they struck up *Smile, Captain* from *Captain Grant's*

Family, a Soviet film of 1938, followed by Charles Aznavour's *La Bohème*.

I had come to the bar to meet Ludvo, who wanted to borrow my camera. He whispered that all over the town of Gottwaldov and its vicinity people working at the local film studios had taken down road signs or switched them around to confuse the Russian soldiers. The tanks kept going around in circles.

I finished my brandy, paid up and was about to leave when the band started playing Grandma Mária's favourite partisan tune. Only the lyrics had been adjusted slightly, as I gathered from a few timid drunken voices from behind a pillar:

How quiet the night, so dark and fair / Šalgovič and Bil'ak, traitors in their lair. / When the night is over and the day breaks / Our nation won't forget these treasonous snakes.

A desolate Vojto joined the guard of honour at the entrance to Bratislava University, where a girl of fifteen, Danka Košanová, was shot dead by the invaders, for no particular reason. The ground was carpeted with flowers, a sea of candles had been lit and someone had brought a cross. Vojto stayed there on his own for a few hours after everyone else had gone home to bed.

A policeman came up to him: "Citizen, disperse!"

Vojto didn't move. Even if he had wanted to comply, he had no idea how. Was he to dispatch his right arm down Štúr Street, sending his left leg marching up Dostoyevsky Avenue, while his head set off for Šafárik Square?

"Move it! Disperse!"

Vojto wouldn't budge so it was up to the policeman to make a move. Vojto landed in detention for a few days.

Zuzana and I were eating dinner when Vojto turned up at our flat, just a few streets from the prison. He had stopped for a drink or two on the way. We also needed a drink and a bottle of wine was opened. Then another. It was a fine wine, a gift from Brežany, from Father – that is, from a patient of his.

Vojto started to pontificate:

"We start off united in resistance and full of resolve but our resistance gradually melts like butter left on the table for too long. It turns yellow, shapeless and turns rancid. Or like an ice cube: the hard blocks melt into ordinary water that drips under the furniture."

I jumped up: "One more simile and you'll get it from me!"

But he was right, of course.

Living up to our reputation as a nation of peace-loving doves – complete with fluffy down and gentle beaks, tiny claws and much cooing – our resistance took a very distinctive form. Rather than real, hardcore stuff, we put up a dove-like, symbolic fight. Everything, including a morning visit to the toilet, could be regarded as an act of resistance. Never mind that nobody saw you. Growing a beard was another sign of protest, with the added advantage of saving on razor blades. The National Theatre ballet made a profoundly symbolic gesture of protest with its new production of *Romeo and Juliet,* building on the message presciently encoded in Shakespeare's play – Juliet's (read Czechoslovakia's) flirtation with Romeo (read the dream of joining the West) was thwarted by evil members of the socialist bloc family.

Symbolic protests abounded. People protested by brushing their teeth and putting on their shoes, by smoking or by quitting smoking, they protested sexually (by experimenting with more daring positions) and by making pea soup.

I am bound to confess that I, too, found this form of protest more to my taste.

In those heady days I received a letter from Aaron Gronsky, the son of the dentist who had heeded Father's advice not to return from South America after the war. We had begun a nostalgic correspondence a few years back.

Montevideo, 26/2/1969

Dear Adam,

This is just a quick note in response to your letter, to make sure my reply catches the flight back to Europe that it came on.

We were sorry to hear that your travel plans have hit the rocks, we hoped to have a date for your arrival soon. But now things have got a bit tricky at my end. I received a Venezuelan visa a while ago but was putting off the trip, partly because of you. In any case, I have to travel by the end of March at the latest, which means I will be away virtually all April because, as well as Venezuela, I'm planning to visit neighbouring Guyana and throw in Trininad and Tobago for good measure. This will be my last trip on this continent as we have already booked our return trip to Europe. We're sailing on 3 August, arriving in Barcelona around 1 September.

So the best time for you to visit would be May, when I'm definitely back in Montevideo, in June. July is not so good any more, things will be chaotic before travelling, with packing and whatnot. As for filming, May or June certainly aren't ideal because it won't be so sunny any more. But I don't think it'll be too bad – you don't need permanent sunshine for shooting after all, and there's always some sun at that time of the year. Well, think about it, Adam. It would be a shame to miss what is basically the last opportunity.

That's it for now, I have nothing else to report. I'm looking forward to hearing from you. Please let me know how things are and what it's like at the TV studios now that the country has become a federation and Dr Husák is in charge. I wonder what the Communist Party congress will decide. Keep us posted, please!

With lots of love from all of us, your Aaron.

6.

On the last weekend in March 1969 I went to Prague to visit Arnošt and invited Vojto along. We spent Friday evening going around the Barrandov film studios and then went back to Arnošt's cubbyhole of an office to watch the ice hockey championship in Sweden on TV. Our team was to play the Russians and passions were running high after our two-nil victory the previous week.

The outcome of the game was keenly anticipated. Every one of the four goals was greeted with whoops of excited yelling. We beat the Russians 4:3 and Arnošt reached for the bottle of Becherovka he kept in his make-up case and poured the liquid into plastic cups, filling them to the brim. The drink went straight to my head even before the forward Golonka had time to kiss the ice (remember, this was the lovey-dovey sixties!) I listened to the national anthem with tears streaming down my cheeks. It was the first time in ten years that I had cried.

"Let's go…!" Arnošt commanded.

We took a cab to Vodičkova Street in the city centre and continued on foot. We fought our way through the ecstatic crowds along with – as I later learned from the news – half a million people across the country. We were yelling, and drinking Becherovka straight from the bottle.

Drivers hooted their horns and waved their arms from car windows giving the victory sign. We spotted some graffiti hastily daubed on trams: ČSSR 4, INVADERS 3. People wandered around carrying banners and flags, car horns blared, and the sounds of the national anthem fused with all the other sounds in an extraordinary cacophony. The closer we got to Wenceslas Square the more crowded the streets were, and in the heat of the moment I nearly forgot my usual fear of crowds. There was no turning back. A steady stream of bodies circled around the statue of St Wenceslas, carrying everyone on the waves of the stormy night. I took another swig of the syrupy Becherovka and passed the bottle to my companions, who kept disappearing and reappearing a few steps ahead of me. The surrounding streets, too, were filled with revellers. The crowd became a single animal with an unpredictable will of its own.

It must have been shortly after eleven that we somehow found ourselves outside the shopfront of Aeroflot, the Soviet airline, illuminated by a big, shining neon sign. Over the deafening racket of car horns and shouting I could hear the sound of shattering glass. I tripped over some loosened paving stones that lay scattered on the edge of the pavement although I saw no sign of roadworks anywhere or any of those triangles showing a labourer.

"*Shayba, shayba*. Goal, goal! One, two, three, four … Goal!" people howled. Someone bent down and hurled a rock into the shopfront. There was more shattering of glass and a few shards flew past my face.

Suddenly I wondered if I was hallucinating because I seemed to recognize the man who hurled the rock. He had grown much older and greyer, of course, but there was no mistaking those saucer-like blue eyes – it was Usačev, the Gestapo grass from Brežany. He used to be friends with everyone, chatting to all and sundry and constantly asking questions, but those who had fallen for his charm tended to disappear. He vanished after the liberation and the locals assumed he'd been executed. And now here he was in Prague! I tried to convince myself that I was wrong, that the man just happened to bear an uncanny resemblance to Usačev. He kept shouting and hurling stones.

375

I heard Vojto roar into my ear. "C'mon…!" as he dragged me off by my sleeve. "Let's get out of here, quick! I don't like the look of this – something's not quite right!"

I tried to break free. The Becherovka splashed about my head like in a torpedoed boat, tempting me to go with the flow.

"Hang on!"

I took a coin out of my pocket. If it's heads I'll go, if it's tails, the picture of the girl planting trees, I'll stay. But before I managed to toss the coin in the air someone bumped into me and I dropped it.

I raised my head and spotted the runt Gajdoš in the crowd. Astonished, I watched him bend down, pick up a paving stone and fling it at the big neon sign, which crackled and expired with a hiss.

The crowd lurched in through the broken shop window and began to smash up the interior. Desks, chairs, typewriters, cupboards, metal plane models. With great difficulty we managed to elbow our way out of the intoxicated mob, trying to ignore all the pushing and shoving. It was like being inside a whale whose guts had spilled across the entire square. I heard a collective gasp. When I turned around I saw flames rising from the buildings in the street.

We ran in the direction of the National Museum, pursued by the urgent wailing of a siren. The crowd lunged at the policemen in uniform and reinforcements leapt out of a police van that stopped nearby. No sooner did they touch the ground than they started hitting out at everyone with truncheons and batons without a word of warning, their faces lit up by the fire blazing into the night.

"What an inferno!" said Arnošt, panting.

"Gestapo! Gestapo!" someone very close to us shouted. But by then our view was obscured by St. Wenceslas and we pressed on until the crowd thinned out and we were able to walk away.

I was told that similar scenes had played out in the Slovak National Uprising Square in Bratislava. The enraged mob came face to face with the police outside the Soviet military headquarters in Miletič Street. Ludvo later showed me the footage he took with my camera and had secretly developed at the TV lab. Afterwards, when the wholesale purges started, a technician in charge of colour correction ratted on him and Ludvo was out on his ear.

The Russians eventually planted their people in the Politburo, headed by Gustáv Husák, the great shape-shifter, adept at navigating dark swamps without getting caught. As opposed to Dubček. The situation had to be "normalised", went the new official line.

Meanwhile a a large chunk of Bratislava's historic centre had been razed to the ground, including the neolog synagogue in Rybné Square that had served as a TV warehouse and studio. It had to make way for a new bridge across the Danube. Vojto and I watched the devastation and felt as if we'd been transported to a different, imaginary town.

"Synchronicity," was how my mad Zuzana laconically summed it up. She has always dabbled with faith in invisible transcendental forces.

When the the houses in the old Jewish quarter and the streets on the Castle Hill above it were demolished, comrades had their villas constructed there.

"Synchronicity," Zuzana commented wryly once more.

When the woods at the foot of the Volovec Mountain were felled, weeds immediately overran the clearing.

We all had to take part in the May Day parade.

It wasn't too bad: if you ignored the flags, banners and parade batons, the chanting crowds marching past the rostrum, the early morning start and music reminiscent of the Austro-Prussian war, you could think of it as going on a picnic with friends with lots of cheap booze and half-price sandwiches.

The orderly crowd moved up Slovak National Uprising Square at a stately pace. People waved their little flags, demonstrating their enthusiasm like well-trained extras. The main rostrum had been erected in front of the former city market hall where I had spent hours in the editing suite.

On the rostrum stood Gustáv Husák, Secretary General of the Communist Party Central Committee, in all his glory. He was flanked by the city communist party committee bigwigs, their greasy, cheery faces, suits and ties identical to thousands of others I had captured on film. They smiled, waving their hands mechanically like puppets.

All of a sudden I noticed five faces of unknown revolutionaries among the banners with the obligatory portraits of Lenin, Marx and Engels. My first thought was that they depicted Che Guevara with his comrades-in-arms since they all sported short beards and long hair. I assumed this was the latest addition to the communist pantheon, brought by the winds of a new era.

A ripple went through the crowd and as it lurched forward I got a good view of the people carrying the five banners. Proudly marching side by side, they were carrying their own enlarged and stiff likenesses. They must have been in their twenties.

They had just reached the rostrum. And amid the cheerful hubbub, chanting and brisk military music, time suddenly stood still.

As Gustáv Husák greeted the exultant crowds, his glance moved down to the five huge banners passing below his feet. A cold shudder ran down my back. The other comrades also turned their heads, following the boss's glance. Everyone waited to see what would happen. I had no doubt that the square was full of informers and plain-clothes police.

But then Husák's face broke into a smile. He whispered something to a companion who frowned and seemed ready to have the five long-haired troublemakers arrested. But he, too, started to laugh, and the other comrades joined in.

By then the five revolutionaries had passed the rostrum. A photographer positioned below it looked at them incredulously. I felt another cold shudder. They would be identified from the photographs.

I could still see the long-haired heads in the crowd when they tore their likenesses off the banners and tossed them to the ground near the Polish Cultural Institute. As I elbowed my way in their direction, I saw they had scattered to the winds, melting into the crowd.

By the time Bony was four he had already learned to live a double life. He was able to read but since we had warned him that he wasn't to flaunt his skill, all through first form he pretended he couldn't read. He put on a great show of pretending it was really hard to decipher basic phrases like *The hat is on the man. The man is on the van,* and so on.

That's what we all did in those days.

As homework Bony was told to have his parents help him read an article entitled 'The Soviet Union Through Children's Eyes', in the children's magazine, *Ohnik [The Bonfire]*:

There are many different countries on this planet of ours. In some countries it is hot even in wintertime and it never snows. Other countries have long, harsh winters and the sun hardly ever comes out. Some countries are nothing but bare, sandy deserts, others have vast fields of rolling wheat. Flax blooms in countries of the north, oranges ripen in the south. There are countries where tigers and camels live and also countries where polar bears roam on floes of ice. Animals or plants that you find in one country you don't always find in another.

Yet there is a country not far from ours that has everything: eternal spring and eternal winter, oranges and ice floes, as well as tigers and polar bears.

This amazing country is the Union of Soviet Socialist Republics. It is almost three times the size of the United States of America, ninety times bigger than Great Britain and a hundred and seventy-five times bigger than Czechoslovakia. The Soviet Union is the largest country on earth. It covers nearly half of Europe and a large part of Asia. It covers a sixth of the planet. For thousands and thousands of years Russia's mineral riches lay deep in the earth. But after the Great October Revolution New Communist Man learned how to extract all these riches – as if the Earth sensed that it was handing them over to good and wise stewards.

Wave after wave rippled along the bay of St Petersburg, not far from the shore, shaded by thick bushes, where a slightly-built man with a beard sat on a tree stump, writing. Five years later a crowd of armed workers gathered around the man with a twinkle in his eye at the Smolny Palace in the centre of St Petersburg, a city in tumult. He led the Russian people to a victorious revolution. His name was Vladimir Ilych Lenin. He was the brilliant leader of the working classes and founder of the Bolshevik party that liberated the peoples of Russia and founded the first workers' state in the world. Vladimir Ilych Lenin was a great man. His life is an example of modesty, hard work and courage and his teaching will forever be a source of inspiration for all progressive people.

The article was illustrated with black-and-white photos. *A shock worker in the Donbass Region. The construction of a hydroelectric plant. New housing for working people. Soldiers marching on Red Army Day. Comrade Leonid Brezhnev shares a friendly kiss with comrade Erich Honecker.*

Comrade Brezhnev looked almost as ardent as when he had

kissed Dubček, and the thought of his slobbery, hungry lips made me gag.

7.

Uncle Rudo rarely came to Bratislava so I was surprised to hear him outside my flat one Saturday morning in the summer. He rang the bell and when I answered he announced that he had arrived with Aunt Julka, her sister Marika and her husband Štefan who lived in the Kysuce region west of the capital. From their cheerful chatter we gathered that it was Marika and Štefan who had cooked up the brilliant plan to throw an impromptu birthday party for Rudo's son Filip, and to drag us along. Filip was about to take his family on a holiday at the seaside so they had to celebrate his birthday before he left. They hadn't told him until the day before and he didn't know when exactly they would arrive, so hush, not a word!

There was no point being angry. I grabbed a book off my bookshelf and a bottle of wine from the larder so that we didn't arrive empty-handed. Zuzana got Bony ready and we followed the crowd. It crossed my mind that I ought to give Filip a ring to warn him but in all the commotion I forgot.

My cousin Filip and his wife Veronika were five years younger than me. They lived in a large flat in Fučík Street with their two young sons, eight-year-old Juraj and Ivan, who was ten. Filip was a doctor at the internal medicine department of Bezručova Street hospital and Veronika was an accountant with a state enterprise. Even though we lived in the same city we saw each other quite rarely apart from the occasional chance meeting in the street. People tend to lose each other and then find each other again. Unless I feel a bond with someone I really don't care that we happen to share the same blood. Or a surname. But I have always loved Uncle Rudo. That was why I decided to go.

We slowly approached Filip's flat, anticipating that this would be just another boring family celebration. For Filip, however, it was something else, as I was to discover much later.

Filip and Veronika had decided to defect to the West some time before and were just waiting for the right opportunity. This had finally presented itself in the form of a holiday in Yugoslavia. They had managed to cross the minefield of gathering the reams of permissions involved in foreign travel. They planned well ahead, applying a year in advance for the official foreign currency allowance of a paltry sum in Yugoslav dinars. They received their Yugoslav visas and finally also an "exit visa". Years later, on the trip to Spain with Father's ashes, Bony would ask me what on earth an exit visa was.

I remembered that before my trip to England I had also needed this coveted and vital document, which listed the countries you were allowed to visit, as well as the purpose and duration of the visit, and contained encoded information on the prospective traveller, including the degree of scrutiny he or she was to be subjected by the border guards. These things really weren't easy to obtain. To begin with, you needed the approval of several institutions – your employer's communist party cell, the party cell at your place of residence, and the Revolutionary Trade Union organisation. If you had children their school headmaster had to add his imprimatur and, last but not least, you needed the opinion of the Special Tasks Department, which I knew from my TV work to be a a branch of the ŠtB. Its agents were known to visit you and rummage through your desk the day before departure. Empty drawers and a suspiciously well-organized desk were enough to raise doubts and prevent you from travelling well before you got anywhere near the border.

Filip had thought of everything. A couple of years ago he told me that he had left patient records scattered around his office and warned his nurse not to touch them under any circumstances. He went so far as to leave his precious watch, a present from his godfather, lying next to the gilded photo frame with a picture of his family.

Preparations were well under way.

Their friends and family were kept in the dark about their true intentions, with Veronika's mother the only person in the know. They felt it was advisable not to trust anyone. And since defectors' belongings were usually seized by the state, they began to get rid of all their possessions.

There was no lift in their block in Fučík Street and their third flat floor was crammed with huge items of furniture. Years ago, on a whim, Veronika had decided to learn to play the piano and her mother had given her the August Förster upright she had inherited from her parents. Now all that stuff had to be carried down the wide staircase without attracting attention. This was no easy matter. Their nosy second-floor neighbour Mr Martinka would peer out of the door at the slightest rustling, showing a lively interest in the goings-on. Everyone in the building knew he was an ŠtB informer.

When the removals men were about to lug the bulky and heavy cast iron Förster down the stairs, Veronika dropped by Mr Martinka bearing a bottle of liqueur and a Karel Gott record, which she played at full blast. Filip summoned the neighbour for a check-up at the hospital and while he was out of the way they got rid of wardrobes, a big sofa and their king-size bed. They told their other neighbours they were redecorating.

They also had to invent a plausible excuse to explain to their sons why their friends from the upstairs flat could no longer come and visit them and why various objects – such as the beloved train set they had spent several years building – started to disappear, and also to make sure they didn't let anything slip at school.

Veronika, once a popular hostess at ladies' gatherings, now pretended she had contracted a long-term contagious disease. She was so convincing that her girlfriends kept phoning to enquire about her state of health.

Then, suddenly, Filip started having doubts. He began to wax lyrical about his beloved Slovakia, would come home drunk late at night, in an "unspeakable state", in Veronika's words.

Despite all these minor setbacks everything seemed to be going to plan. Until we dropped in, a couple days before their departure.

"We're redecorating," Filip burst out as he let us in.

"Now, before going on holiday?" Uncle Rudo asked, puzzled.

"Well, we hope it'll be all done in time."

"But what's happened to your furniture?" Uncle Štefan chipped in.

"It's been moved to the children's room… and…"

"…and some is with our neighbours," added Veronika.

After these preliminaries we entered the living room. Newspapers and tins of paint lay scattered about the floor. Some of the walls had an undercoat already, and Filip was in the middle of painting the rest. The outlines of where the furniture had been were still visible.

"That's quite a big job you've taken on," the relatives from Kysuce commented at the sight of the lone dim light bulb dangling from the ceiling.

"What's happened to your TV set?" Uncle Štefan asked, looking around disoriented as he tried to locate the central point of every modern dwelling.

"So, cheers everybody!" said Veronika, who appeared in the doorway carrying a pre-war brass tray with shot glasses and a bottle. The powerful aroma of plum brandy filled the room.

We downed our drinks and Filip refilled our glasses immediately.

"Come and sit down!" said Veronika with a smile, leading us to a folding camp table covered with a plastic tablecloth and surrounded with canvas fishing chairs. The children were served orange Sunquick diluted with water.

"Right then, let's get going!" commanded Uncle Štefan, rolling up his sleeves and looking at me and Rudo. "We could get it all done in a couple of hours!"

"No, no, absolutely not," protested Filip, pushing his uncle back into his chair. "I won't have that! It's my party so let's celebrate! And now, some chasers! Veronika will be back in a minute with some garlic dip and canapés."

A few hours later uncle Štefan was singing bawdy songs at the top of his voice. Aunt Marika tried to intervene: "Keep your voice down! You're croaking like Radio Free Europe!"

She went on at great length about a noteworthy event she had recently organised in the library in Kysucký Lieskovec in her capacity as the manager of the local House of Culture: a discussion with the great pop star Dušan Grúň. However, when I asked what she thought of another Dušan, the writer Dušan Mitana and if she liked his short stories, that name didn't ring a bell. She sang the praises of the fabulous open-air museum that was being built in the nearby village of Vychylovka, with its charming wooden cottages, church and old mill, assembled from all over the Kysuce region. When it was ready, she said, she would personally see to it that all primary school children were taken there on compulsory visits – surely children must be familiar with their region's history?

Everyone nodded in unison. Inspired by the plum brandy, she continued, without stopping to take a breath, and informed us that her village of Lieskovec, too, was finally beginning to look presentable, with the old shacks disappearing and replaced by beautiful modern blocks. The process was accelerated in the spring, when the local stream broke its banks, inundating half the village. But this kind of progress was quite rare. For instance, the neighbouring village of Lodno was hopelessly behind the times and the locals still lived in disgusting hundred-year-old hovels and couldn't afford modern housing. Veronika suggested that it might be a nice place to take the boys for a romantic walk but Marika stopped her in her tracks and said there was no point.

"What would be the point of that?" she repeated.

I fancied the thought of subjecting her to a slow, sophisticated torture, which would involve rolling her face in the garlic dip and then banging her dumb, back-combed head on the table but Zuzana gave my hand a firm squeeze to stop me from blurting anything out or doing anything rash.

To change the subject, Uncle Rudo announced with a poker face: "I heard Husák has been elected pope!"

"No, really?"

"Really. He took the name Augustus The Twenty-first."

By midnight the police were at the door, saying a neighbour had complained about the noise. We saw Mr Martinka standing behind one of the officers, craning his neck to get a look at what was happening but Filip had the presence of mind to close the living room door. He explained we were having a party, that he was really sorry and would keep the noise down. The policemen gave him a ticking-off and left.

We took the opportunity to leave. We woke up Bony, who had fallen asleep on a folding bed in the kitchen and said our goodbyes.

The others had to go to a hotel for the night as Filip had no beds left and couldn't put them up.

Filip later told me how relieved they were to see everyone go.

They had contrived to smuggle some money out of the country in advance, and had only enough left to cover the bare necessities for the journey. Two days later they stoically parted with their flat and drove off.

A couple of hours later they were back.

It was Uncle Štefan who had messed everything up. He bumped into the nosy parker neighbour, Mr Martinka, who was walking his dog and relieving himself in the nearby bushes (he regarded the discharge of bodily functions outdoors as edifying). In his drunken state Štefan mentioned something about decorating and the empty flat. That was enough. Filip and his family were sent back from the border.

All that was left at home was a single bare light bulb and a wooden spoon. And a couple of bottles of wine left over from the party, though no glasses. They decided to open the wine.

Veronika remembered packing some instant soup. Filip fished out the immersion heating coil and boiled some water. This was their dinner, with some cooked meat they had also packed for the journey. They sat there eating in the bare flat and drinking wine from the bottle, while Juraj and Ivan ran around the empty rooms dressed up as a water goblin and a devil, in the masks they had worn for a fancy-dress party at the end of the school year.

8.

The records that survive of the partially destroyed intelligence file on Secret Informant Luminal indicate that Father was put under pressure to sound out the mood and attitudes of the population and to report on the dissemination of "offensive literature". In a handwritten note, his handler stated that the informant had filed a few reports but was using his increasingly deteriorating hearing as the reason that he was becoming increasingly isolated from the outside world.

This was regarded as an excuse. As if the informant had chosen to go deaf just to spite them.

All the Czechoslovak Television employees, like everyone working for a state-run institution, had to undergo screenings. Communist party members were vetted first, followed by non-members. The screening panel comprised mainly fat old comrades with typically sagging Slavic physiognomies (I've seen faces like these in Poland,

Russia as well as in Yugoslavia), dressed in drab grey suits. There were twelve of them, like the Twelve Months brothers in the Slovak fairy tale. It was truly a scene from a film.

Brother January starts off with the key question:

"What is your view of the Warsaw Pact armies' fraternal aid to Czechoslovakia?"

Ludvo is facing the committee fully aware that the wrong answer means he can say goodbye to his job.

"My view hasn't changed," he says, turning to a committee member, jolly Brother July: "Palko, surely you remember that we both thought the Russians should be denied food and drink?"

Brother July replies:

"It was wrong of us to think that."

Ludvo falls into the trap and flails about desperately. Brother October and Brother March mutter their disapproval as he says:

"OK, they may have come to help us but why on earth did they have to arrive in tanks? They've destroyed our roads!" And he repeats: "They've destroyed our roads!"

Ludvo has to go. Esteemed Brother July stays on, commanding the TV branch of the People's Militia until 1990.

The harshest condemnation came from comrade Peter Trnovský, my brother, who served on the panel on behalf of the City Communist Party Committee. Therapy sessions and a prolonged stay in a psychiatric institution had clearly worked miracles, replacing his fear of death with a fear of life. His coping strategy was to escape into the world of theories as unshakeable as the four solid walls of a house, never mind that they were just mental constructs. They were enough to lean on for support.

I heard Peter give a speech at a TV employees' Communist Party meeting:

"With sensitive programming, a TV adaptation of a Goldoni farce, provided it is suitably blended in with the rest of the evening programmes, will help enhance our optimistic message, which forms an integral part of the socialist way of life. In case of insensitive programming, on the other hand, the same farce – whose intrinsic ideological values do not contribute to raising socialist consciousness – may have the effect of glorifying a way of thinking typical of the past and distracting the viewers' attention from the remainder of the evening programme. While the first scenario provides an example of the positive propaganda value of an entire evening's shows,

including the Goldoni farce, the other scenario is an example of how an entire evening's programming, or part of it, can be deprived of propaganda value. Demanding, ideologically principled and professional performance on the part of the management ensures that positive propaganda value is extracted from every available form of artistic expression."

I was bored rigid but couldn't leave. I kept repeating with Cain: *I am not my brother's keeper!*

Communist Party of Czechoslovakia Central Committee member Vasil Bil'ak objected to magazine covers carrying photos of pop music and film stars.

"It is a sign of dangerous capitalist influence on our wholesome youth and our socialist ideals…!"

In 1972 a decree was issued requiring magazine covers and the front pages of newspapers to show only working women and individuals who could serve as role models for the youth.

I thought I caught a glimpse of my brother Peter's shadow behind this. Like when a mouse runs along a wall and you spot it out of the corner of your eye.

I had many more opportunities to hear speeches of this kind. My new editor-in-chief, Comrade Cesnak, made me enrol at EMLU, the Evening University of Marxism-Leninism. Luckily, it was located just around the corner from our flat, next to the Steiner brewery.

In addition to an introduction to political economy, I learned a great deal about significant meetings of old comrades and conspiratorial meetings in the interwar period. The professor made us pay particular attention to such crucial information as whether a particular meeting had taken place in the morning or in the afternoon.

For some reason, he omitted further vital details, such as which of the comrades had got plastered the night before, how much alcohol had been consumed or how many four-letter words had been used. And of course, he never mentioned that the main purpose of these meetings was for these great fighters against the exploitation of the working classes to make others work for them.

Comrade Cesnak helped to get me an extremely interesting job. Every now and then some high-up comrades would invite me to

387

film a key meeting, in a purely private capacity. It was just me and my camera, and I had to hand in the film, still undeveloped, to someone at the secretariat. It was well paid and I was expected to keep everything about it to myself.

The meetings were often held at the Slovak Communist Party retreat in the mountains, in a villa at Biela Skala. The comrades were jolly, affable and drunk. On one occasion Hungary's leader János Kádár made a brief, inebriated appearance. He lavished bottles of the finest Tokay wine on waiters who had been brought in all the way from the Carlton Hotel in Bratislava.

And since vodka raises your blood pressure, the comrades would stuff themselves with cloves of garlic all day long, allegedly on doctors' advice. The minute I walked through the door I was greeted by a distinctive aura: the smell of spirits and garlic.

I was strictly forbidden, however, to film them while eating or performing any bodily function. No sneezing, hiccupping, coughing, vomiting, not even innocuous chewing was to be captured on film. Under no circumstances was I to shoot from above (revealing bald spots, thinning hair, etc.) or from below (exposing double, treble or quadruple chins, oversize nostrils…), and in some cases even from the side (drawing attention to a large or irregularly shaped nose, a scar…), and in one extreme case not even *en face* (because of a glass eye of a hue different from the real one).

Then there was Comrade Poláková who, for some mysterious reason, objected to being filmed from behind. Not because her behind was too big, in fact its size was just right, nor because of a curvature of the spine or bad hair. I supposed she just wanted to appear perfect, mysterious, elusive. A woman of her proclivities and proportions would have thrived under any regime. I can easily imagine her by Hitler's, Stalin's or Mečiar's side, or as a steadfast human rights advocate at the White House. She was born a predator and had had to fight to get to where she was. By fair means or foul.

After one of these events I had dismantled the equipment, folded the tripod and replaced the camera in its case and was about to leave when I felt comrade Poláková's hand on my shoulder.

"Comrade Trnovský, don't go yet. I'd like to get to know you better! Take a seat. You don't have to work so hard all the time."

Taking me by the sleeve, she led me to some leather armchairs by the window, lit a cigarette in a long cigarette holder and gracefully exhaled the smoke.

"So, tell me a little about yourself. What are your plans and your dreams? I suppose you'd like to make a feature film one day – am I right?"

"Yes, of course – that's my great dream! I... I've always regarded myself as a film-maker and..."

"You're just like my son! He's been like that ever since he was a little boy. I keep telling him – you must finish secondary school first, then we'll think of something. All my life I've championed the idea that everything is possible. When I was cultural attaché in Paris I received a state prize for promoting our culture abroad. It's not been easy, let me tell you. I have to keep knocking on doors, arguing my case over and over again. The arts are a nation's greatest wealth, we must never forget that, Mr Trnovský! What do you think?"

"Certainly, I mean..."

"But of course, it's not all that straightforward. It's largely thanks to me that anything is happening this area, that our socialist cinema has a presence abroad, that our great artists are exhibited, readings take place... But I don't mind staying in the shadows, you know. I'd rather sit at the back keeping quiet and enjoying the fruits of my work. I don't need any tributes and everyone who knows me will confirm that. Anyway, these are indisputable facts. What do you think?"

"Absolutely, I also..."

"For example, take the series of concerts in Turin! I was the one who arranged everything. The *éminence grise*, my mummy used to joke – being the *éminence grise*, that's your role, Vieruška. You help pave our way to happy tomorrows! Well, enough of this chatter; I must rush. Please don't take this personally!"

She took my hand with a friendly smile:

"You're a very nice and talented young man, Mr. Trnovský! I'll see what I can do for you!"

With that she stood up and left. I've never seen her since – except, that is, on TV. Within two years she was pushed out by another communist predator. These things happen. Life is a game. A very human game at that. Angels exist only in heaven. We're just animals. Slightly more developed animals. Although we might be endowed with the capacity to put on a serious and dignified air. An air of importance. Nature takes care of everything else.

It was not so much characters like Comrade Poláková who surprised me at Biela Skala – she was far from the only one of her ilk there – but rather a certain distinguished gentleman with slightly greying hair and a carefully trimmed moustache. The first time I saw him sitting in an armchair wreathed in thick pipe smoke I was so startled I started coughing and the Blue Portuguese I was drinking almost spurted out of my nose. It was Rehor Kohút in person, as ready to perform miracles under socialism as he had been under previous regimes.

Sure, we live in a material world, that's an indisputable fact – but you never know and it can't do any harm to leave the door slightly ajar, onto worlds that are slightly different. There's nothing wrong with that. When I saw Kohút in the middle of a tête-à-tête with my brother Peter at one of the party functions, I gently tried to jog my brother's memory and remind him of the miracles Kohút had performed in Brežany before the war. Among other things, I mentioned his love affair with Klaudia Horváthová and its aborted consequence, and Vojto's mother Natália's adulation bolstered by astronomical bills for miracle potions. But Peter's response was a frown or a puzzled smile. He remembered none of this.

Along with other Central Committee comrades he made use of Kohút's latest contraption, which relied on the healing effects of a mysterious radioactive isotope developed by Soviet experts. Rehor installed it in a small room next to the big hall, admitting clients strictly one at a time. Each comrade could have his or her "internal radiation synchronized" on demand.

"The human body acts basically as a big radiator. We are living batteries, primary cells," he proclaimed, letting a weak electric current pass through a piece of rock in a glass tube, making it glow red.

Our TV editing studios were located in the old market hall in Slovak National Uprising Square, high up on the gallery. The studios were tiny, with only enough room for me and my cutter Džony, a man with thick shiny spectacles, whose amazing memory I came to appreciate. Any visitors had to sit on the floor or stay in the corridor. Džony had pride of place at the big editing suite and film clips hung above his head like laundry on a line. He knew exactly what was in each clip, a skill I greatly admired when we had to splice them together for a documentary or a report.

We would often spend all night in the editing studio. From time to time I would pop down to Tempo, a deli on the corner of the square, furnished with tall counters where people ate and drank standing up. It was always full of human wrecks dozing over a glass of beer and making the most of the late opening hours. I would buy a couple of rolls and some chicken salad or – on those rare occasions when we finished a job – a celebratory bottle of bubbly.

On my way out I had to pass a studio that took up the whole of the ground floor. It was packed full of props and lights, with tired actors hanging around in historical costumes smoking on their break.

Hands off Vietnam! and slogans of that nature would echo in my head after I passed the neighbouring suite where another team was editing a report, in which incensed citizens collected signatures for a petition in the streets. They were handing out a postcard with a picture of a desperate Asian woman on the run, a starving baby in her arms, pre-printed with the address of the US Embassy in Bratislava, text in Slovak and English, and a space for a signature and return address.

There were also other petitions targeting nasty Israel and friendly Lebanon, or nasty Iran and friendly Iraq.

9.

Vojto found a job as projectionist at The Future, a fleapit of a cinema on the outskirts of Bratislava. He thought it was ironic: "Who's to say I've got no future…?"

I went to see him, together with Mário Tóth, son of the man who used to own the Stag Hotel in Brežany. Mário had also moved to Bratislava and had a job operating overhead projectors at the university's science department.

"Let me show you some amazing footage from last winter!" said Vojto, threading film into a Super-8 projector pointed at the big screen.

He said it took him this long to understand how film language had changed over the years – scenes set in the present used to be shot in black and white, while flashbacks were in colour. These days most films were in colour and the flashbacks had become black and white. As if actual memories were also black and white.

He turned off the lights and the projector started to rattle and purr.

At first we saw nothing, only whiteness.

"This is snow falling. It was last winter, when we had those blizzards."

Nothing happened for another five minutes.

"It's snowing, can you see? It just keeps on snowing."

"Yes, and so what?" Mário asked impatiently.

"Now watch, watch, there will be a snowplough going past!"

We stared at the bright white screen holding our breath.

"Hmm, maybe that's on another reel. It must be. No, here it is! Now! Did you see it?"

"No," Mário said.

"Let me just show you again!"

Baudelaire, whom I read in those days, in a 1960s translation called it *ennui*. The Slovak language doesn't have a single word for this but what he had in mind was the deadly boredom that can be banished only by alcohol or other artificial means.

Many people felt that the only thing one could do in those stagnant days was drink, chase after women or throw themselves into DIY at their cottages at weekends.

Vojto withdrew into his shell like a snail. When he came home from work he spent hours at his typewriter committing a crime. He tried to squeeze in as many sheets of paper and carbons as possible. He began by typing the words George Orwell 1984 on the front page. The book had long since lost its green cover and wasn't even in English. Someone had translated it.

Vojto was copying a banned book.

On Friday mornings he used to go to a second-hand bookshop and spend several hours browsing. He would buy five or six volumes at a time, enough to last him a whole weekend. He didn't go out much because he noticed he was being tailed, and there was nothing to watch on TV. Vojto had chosen internal exile, emigrating into his own head, amid the four walls of his flat. But that wasn't his only place of exile.

Women had always found him attractive (they used to say they'd been "seduced", as if their own minds and bodies were not to blame: "He insisted until I gave in!" although, as we know, it takes two to tango). It certainly wasn't because of his looks. It must have been his charisma.

He became what one could call a collector. Some writers, such as Henry Miller, use the term whoremonger, others (Janko Jesenský, for instance) call men like these skirt-chasers, while others (including the fairy tale writer Dobšinský) prefer the word womaniser, and yet others (such as Maupassant) opt for old rake. I have looked into this phenomenon and discovered that it's hereditary – Vojto's father was notorious, for understandable reasons: what else would you do if you were a dashing soldier in uniform, and a fighter pilot to boot! It was fun to watch Vojto's eyes light up at the first sight of an even halfway attractive woman going past or entering a room. Sometimes the attraction had lasting consequences – by the end of his life Vojto had been through four wives and had fathered a child with each.

His modus operandi seemed quite simple: he cheated on every one of them, or let them down in some other way. Nevertheless, every time he came back contrite, not only would they take him back but they would end up comforting him. Reformed sinners are always sexy – just check the Bible and read the story of St Paul or St Matthew. This is what makes the world go round. What struck me in particular was that all the women wanted – in their own words – "to save" him. – "Oh but he's so miserable, that's why he has to drink so much! The poor thing!"

At the end of a bender, this martyr to family life would sometimes drop in on us at Malinovský Street. He would turn up on our doorstep looking like an old tomcat, just as we would be sitting down to our Sunday lunch.

I went to open the door. He reeked of drink.

"What's for lunch?"

"Goulash."

"Oh, my favourite!"

"Come on in then."

He would ruffle Bony's hair, give Zuzana a peck on the cheek and join us at the table, wolfing down everything on his plate.

Zuzana opened another of the bottles of wine from one of Father's patients and filled our glasses. We clinked and Vojto downed a whole glass in one gulp.

"Not bad," was his verdict.

Reaching for the ladle he helped himself to more goulash.

"There's not enough meat in it," he remarked.

Zuzana bristled. "What do you mean? I followed a recipe – let me show you." She rushed to the kitchen. "Look, it gives the exact quantities! Half a kilo of pork!"

Bony hid a smile behind his spoon, happy that the grown-ups had lost interest in his unfinished food. He loved Vojto's unexpected visits.

"All right, all right, Zuzana. Any wine left?"

"I'll go and get some."

Vojto downed three more glasses and got up. He planted a juicy smacker on my sweaty brow, pinched Zuzana's cheek, pretended to pull Bony's ear and off he went.

Later that day Peter dropped by. He had promised Father some papers and wanted me to deliver them. Bony let him in.

I went to meet Peter in the hall. While he was taking off his shoes he spotted a thick plastic folder that had fallen behind the shoe rack and was now studying it with great interest.

"What's this?" I asked.

He showed it to me without a word.

"Is it yours?"

I shook my head.

The top sheet of tracing paper said, in letters copied through carbon paper: *GEORGE ORWELL, 1984.* It was a manuscript. It must have fallen out of Vojto's raincoat when he bent down for the shoehorn. A chill ran down my spine.

"Let me see," I said, reaching for the yellow folder.

But by now something had caught Peter's attention: the words *ALL FURTHER COPYING EXPRESSLY FORBIDDEN.* Their acronym in Slovak was *VZDOR*, meaning defiance. It was a secret code for samizdat. Actually, it seemed it was no longer secret, as Peter had recognized it. Without a word, he stuffed the manuscript into his pocket. Then he said:

"All right. I won't say a word to anyone. But I'm confiscating this."

Zuzana called out from the kitchen, "Can I offer you some coffee?"

"Yes please, Zuzka. Do you have any rum?"

Judging by Peter's diary, which I read during his next psychiatric episode, my brother was enthralled and stunned by George Orwell. Quite an achievement for a chap who had been dead for over twenty years.

So communism is going to prevail after all – once people have understood everything. If you know how to read this book you'll find it's incredibly valuable to people like us. Orwell was a genius, a visionary!

I suggested to VB, for a start, that opponents of the regime shouldn't be just punished or exiled. Instead, by psychological manipulation and maybe some coercive means, we should turn them into orthodox communists unconditionally devoted to the party. Because, surely, we don't want their devotion to be fake! VB liked my idea, although he was concerned that it might not be easy to implement, especially the technical side. But he said he'd discuss it with EP. For the time being, I pretended the idea was entirely mine.

Peter stayed up all night, making feverish notes:

In spite of its overall negative message this is undeniably an extremely inspiring book, even though, overall, it is quite harmful.

What this book shows first and foremost is the great importance the ruling party attaches to promoting its ideas and strengthening its position. On each landing, in each block of flats, and at all house fronts "one of those pictures which are so contrived that the eyes follow you about when you move" *gazes down from the walls. The slogan* "Big Brother is Watching You" *might be slightly over the top but the basic idea is very apt. (NB It would be preferable to avoid using the picture of the same person as that might smack of the cult of personality.)*

The other great innovation is the telescreens installed in people's homes. First of all, they serve as a propaganda outlet, disseminating information on economic achievements, of which, of course, there can never be enough. Second, they can never be shut off completely, only dimmed. Obviously, this may pose a challenge in terms of electricity usage but it should nevertheless be considered, particularly because of a further important advantage that compensates for many other disadvantages: this new type of TV set captures any sound "above the level of a very low whisper"*!*

Moreover – the screen also serves as a kind of camera or a recording device, which can be turned on by the secret services at any time and those who find themselves in its field of vision can never be sure when exactly they are being watched. I doubt Comrade VB has ever read Orwell but I'm sure he'll like it, not least because this can radically lower the crime rate, reduce economic damage and improve quality of life! I'm convinced the Comrade will be impressed… Because the book states, and I quote: "You had to live – did live – from habit that became instinct, on the assumption that every sound you made was overheard, and, except in darkness, every movement scrutinized." Of course, you could turn your back to the screen, as the main character often does, but it's still a brilliant idea.

We should also consider establishing four ministries (abolishing all others), which will be quite sufficient to manage the state – a "Ministry of Truth" which is in charge of propaganda, a "Ministry of Peace" that wages war on imperialism and hostile individuals. The "Ministry of Love" will deal with law and order. And a "Ministry of Plenty" would deal with the economy. The names are important, as they embody the very essence of the ideas involved.

Names such as "Victory Gin" or "Victory Cigarettes" sound rather like a parody of our products but it's definitely a good idea to eliminate an unnecessary diversity of brand names and replace them with a small number of labels that carry a clear and correct message. Browsing through an encyclopaedia I came across the name "Sparta". To an ordinary person, someone who ought not to indulge in amoral pleasures, this simple name will evoke Spartan attitude, austerity and discipline. Similarly, the name "Domestic rum" will drive home the message that socialist Slovakia, too, can feel like a Caribbean paradise. Both brand names are definitely worthy of consideration.

The ruling party depicted in the book has a very strict – and, we might say, highly appropriate – position on sexuality, because the sex act distracts people from their mission of building socialism, instead of indulging in it exclusively for the purposes of procreation. However, our system is still too soft and it will take some time before our society reaches the stage when men and women learn to interact in a dispassionate way, with the requisite prudence. But I'm convinced that this time will come. There's still some time to go before 1984 and a lot remains to be done to make it happen. The "Anti-Sexual Youth League" would work well as a name.

This book is prophetic, visionary even!

As part of the compulsory "Two Minutes of Hate" (this is also slightly over the top but we have to bear in mind when the book was written), people participate in a collective session – a kind of seance or a training workshop

396

perhaps – during which class enemies are named and shamed. In the book they are represented by Emanuel Goldstein. In our context his name could be substituted with names of individuals associated with the so-called Prague Spring such as Dubček, Kriegel or Smrkovský. It might, therefore, be worth launching a concentrated propaganda and promotional campaign to this effect. This is great, brilliant!

But by far the most ingenious idea is "Newspeak"! VB asked me how I was getting along so I told him that by reducing language to a minimum we could put a complete stop to the dissemination of anti-party propaganda by counter-revolutionary and anti-party elements. He frowned a bit, so maybe he hasn't yet grasped the full significance of this idea and I'll have to find an opportunity to explain it to him in more detail. But surely to communicate we need only the most basic, limited vocabulary! History has repeatedly proved that once vocabulary expands, becomes refined and over-sophisticated, instead of conveying matters accurately and straightforwardly it leads directly to hell – i.e. it facilitates corridor talk, gossip and slander. If, however, people lack suitable terms for expressing anti-state ideas, because they simply don't exist, have been eliminated, thoroughly uprooted, mocked and drained of any content, we'll have won a resounding victory. It is common knowledge that "language" is tantamount to "thinking". The minute the enemy loses his ability to express harmful ideas they will disappear altogether. Harmful ideas will become literally "unthinkable", as Orwell has said. I believe that one day this genius of a writer – in spite of what he stood for – will be regarded as one of the key ideologues of Communism. We need a straightforward, accurate language, purged of any hidden meanings and double entendres, without allegories and symbols, where each word denotes a single, specific and simple thing or concept. We must reduce our vocabulary! VB tried to change the subject, but I kept coming back to Orwell. Oh, I so wish he understood what I mean so that we could start implementing these ideas.

English has a slight advantage in this respect, being more flexible and predisposed to simplification, but I am certain that, if we could get a team of linguists to put their minds to it, the Slavonic languages could also be simplified in this way. What matters is accuracy, melodiousness and simplicity of explanation. VB liked that. I could see his eyes light up.

I recommended that we should have 1984's appendix on "Newspeak" professionally translated and studied by scholars.

VB, my brother's interlocutor, was none other than Vasil Bil'ak, the notoriously uneducated member of Czechoslovakia's Communist Party Central Committee. I learned from an entry in his diary that Peter had gone all the way to Orava in northern Slovakia to consult the research and development staff at the Tesla factory in Nižná on secretly developing a TV set that could double up as a camera. He was also a frequent visitor to the Institute of Linguistics at the Slovak Academy of Sciences, where he consulted experts on a kind of communist Esperanto that would gradually drive out and eventually completely replace the standard Slovak language as we knew it.

Peter himself made a few experimental forays into linguistics. In his diary I found a folded sheet of paper containing a political speech in *Newspeak* or, as he called it in Slovak, *no-rek*. It read as follows:

Look! See! Praise! Forward socconstruct plan overfulfill good Czechslov plus Sovuni eternal. Work reap think all ComPart Czechslov, everything, everyone econcult welfare.

Eventually an unmarked van stopped outside Peter's house and two gentlemen in white coats alighted discreetly. They brought a straitjacket along, just in case.

10.

I have always loved the view from a train window.

En route from Bratislava to Brežany the train passed some low buildings around the Central Station, the sweep of Malinovský Street, followed by rows of long three-storey 1950s blocks, then the huge white State Security compound with its barred windows facing an internal courtyard, followed by the Figaro chocolate factory, then the uneven buildings of the Dimitrov Chemical plant, new high-rise blocks as far as the eye could see, the tramline, vineyards and finally the slopes of the Lesser Carpathians.

Bony was asleep and Zuzana was looking the other way, lost in thought, drowsy from the journey. *Millions, millions, millions of scarlet roses!* – Russian pop star Alla Pugacheva droned on and on. Surely this habit of carrying around a small transistor radio and listening to the awful crackling interspersed with music and the spoken word must cause lasting damage to your ears, I thought as I dozed off.

Even when I was half-asleep, I still knew instinctively when the journey was about to come to an end and woke up just before we reached Brežany. The train was passing a new housing estate. Both the Karl Liebknecht factory and Slovlina desperately needed housing for their employees. Old people sat outside their blocks of flats on benches, just like they used to sit in front of the cottages before their villages were devoured by the city; from time to time I caught a glimpse of someone in folk dress. A few mobile beehives were parked behind the blocks, ordinary trailers as well as blue, yellow and red caravans. People moved them around to be closer to the acacias and the linden trees in bloom.

This Sunday Father had decided to combine lunch with a celebration of his sixtieth birthday. I found him in his isolation cell, the perennial thick cloud of smoke illuminated by rays of the afternoon sun. He was studying the medical records of a local woman.

"These three words sum up her medical history: discharge, chlamydia and depression. A whole life in three words, Adam.

"Her husband is away most of the time, leaving her alone with their three children. Sometimes despair drives her to seek a brief, entirely physical and sweaty encounter with a random man. Names and faces are immaterial, anyone will do, just to keep loneliness and anxiety at bay. She keeps a cross in her handbag, and takes it out to kiss the face of Jesus Christ, that's how desperate she is. She despairs at the enormity of the conflict between body and soul that people have grappled with for millennia."

"Why are you showing me this? Is she someone I know?"

Father shook his head.

"What about you, do you know her well?"

"Let's go," he said as if he hadn't heard me. And maybe he hadn't – the thick cloud of smoke must have swallowed my words, preventing them from reaching him.

"It's party time!"

I glanced at the medical report he left on the desk. The name Klaudia Horváthová didn't mean anything to me at that point.

Soon Father blew out the sixty candles which had been painstakingly inserted into the birthday cake. Aunt Tonička was the first to sing Happy Birthday: *Mnoga ljeta, mnoga ljeta, mnoga ljeta, živio…!* Mother and Zuzana followed, then Uncle Julka and Uncle Rudo and eventually, gritting our teeth, Bony and I joined in. The two of us shared a hatred of this Happy Birthday song and our singing was deliberately flat. We exchanged meaningful looks but our fun was soon cut short by the insistent ringing of the doorbell.

I opened the door to find Mrs Vašíčková on the doorstep. Red-faced and out of breath, she gasped: "Please get the doctor! My husband is very ill!"

Her husband Július Vašíček, also known as Monako, had recently risen to great prominence. To everyone's surprise he had survived the screening and subsequent purges, becoming Chairman of the Brežany City National Committee. He had the reputation of a competent and dutiful bureaucrat who had managed to move up in the world without asking too many questions. He enjoyed saying: "I'm just a rank-and-file official, a small cog in a big wheel. I don't really have anything to do with the system, but I have a piece of advice for you." Like he did during the war, when Mother's Jewish relatives needed help.

After a substantial Sunday lunch and a cigarette, he suddenly sidled up to his wife saying, how about… if they tried… a little… just a little you-know-what… He purred into her ear like an old tomcat until she let him take off her clothes although she pointed out that at their age – she was sixty and he was five years her senior – it was not perhaps not quite the done thing to indulge in certain activities. But he wouldn't listen.

She was sitting on top of him when suddenly his lips turned blue. Taking this as a sign of appreciation of her performance, she smiled and went on until they both reached climax, or so she thought. She collapsed onto the bed, her body shaken by a spasm of delight. Only then did she hear her husband rasp and realised he was clutching his chest.

She panicked. Convinced that it wouldn't do for a doctor to see a naked National Committee Chairman *in flagrante*, with an enormous, unflagging erection, she hurriedly squeezed her husband into his trousers and shirt and even – against his feeble protest – put a tie on him and combed his hair. Then she smoothed down the sweaty bedsheets and opened the window, dressed in her Sunday best, adding a necklace and some rings for good measure and then – what would people say if they saw a National Committee

Chairman's wife in the street without make-up – she proceeded to refresh the lipstick smeared by passionate kisses, re-applied make-up to her eyes, did her hair and finally ran out into the sunlit street.

We lived quite close so she was back home within five minutes, accompanied by Father. He diagnosed myocardial infarction, adding the word *Exitus.*

Father gradually managed to prise out of the widow of Comrade Vašíček, the National Committee chairman, an account of what had happened.

"Well, in addition to the expressions of my deepest sympathy I have to say, congratulations. What a wonderful way to go," Father said, putting away his stethoscope.

Back at home he remarked that Monako could have survived if…

A week after the funeral Father received a letter.

Brežany, 4 September 1975.

Dear Comrade Trnovský,

The Brežany City Communist Party Committee feels compelled to give you the following urgent notice:

It has come to the attention of the local party cell committee and indeed, all of our cell's membership, that for some time now you have been neglecting to meet your basic party obligations arising from the party statutes and failed to attend party meetings (the last time you honoured us with your presence was during the AGM) and that you have maintained no links with the organisation apart from paying your membership dues, and have not participated in its activities. While we understand that you are not in the best of health, we believe that the profoundly passive behaviour you have exhibited cannot be justified, particularly nowadays, when each and every party member is expected to step up his activities and take on specific party commitments. You are strongly advised to reactivate your links with your local party cell and with the Committee at your earliest convenience and to the greatest extent possible, offering a plausible explanation for your recent passivity and proposing a suitable way of participating in the life of our party organisation and of contributing to its activities.

With comradely greetings,

On behalf of the Brežany City Committee of the Communist Party of Slovakia

Emil Jedenástik

Father was livid. He paced up and down his isolation cell like a caged beast with a cigarette in his mouth. When he had calmed down somewhat, he sat down to compose a reply.

To: The Brežany Committee of the Communist Party of Slovakia

I am writing in response to your "urgent notice" dated 4 September 1975, in which you demand a "plausible explanation" for my "profoundly passive behaviour". I regret that I had wrongly assumed that my contribution over the past twenty-five years spoke for itself.

In the past two or three years I have provided two medical reports, which I suspect have not been read (!). That is the only possible explanation for making allegations of the kind I do not wish ever to read again, since your letter has given me a bout of angina pectoris. *Nevertheless, I am willing, for the last time, to provide you with a detailed explanation.*

The medical reports mentioned above certify that I am wholly unable to participate in meetings of any kind for the following reasons:

damage to my spinal marrow cells which has a detrimental impact on my ability to concentrate inability to spend any length of time in a room that is not sufficiently aired inability to spend any length of time in an environment contaminated with the slightest trace of nicotine

considerably impaired capacity to stand upright with my lower extremities in a vertical position

inability to spend more than 2-3 minutes in a sitting position, with my lower extremities in a vertical position

continuously deteriorating and inexorably progressing issues with my cochlear implant, resulting in a gradual loss of hearing

Were you familiar with the comments made by Comrade M. Jakeš in a recent speech broadcast on radio and television and reprinted in the press – to the effect that "elderly and sick pensioners must not be coerced into attending party meetings" – I wouldn't have to go to the trouble of explaining all this to you.

Thank you for your understanding. I am particularly grateful to Comrade Jedenástik for being so accommodating and managing to last for a full hour without smoking on those rare occasions when I was able to attend a meeting.

Sincerely yours,

signed: Dr Alfonz Trnovský

11.

Mr Navrátil had no idea that the real object of my enquiry was a pile of bones.

Mr Navrátil kept smiling. He smiled as he opened the door for me, he smiled when I introduced myself as a relative of Klaudia Horváthová's, who wished to to locate her after many years. He smiled as he served me cheap coffee and informed me that he had lived in this flat as a widower for the past fifteen years. His wife had died of pancreatic cancer and their children lived in Bratislava.

"Can I ask how long you've been living here?"

"It must be... let me see now, let me see... forty-six years."

I had come across a man with his name and codename "Informant Samaritan" in the ŠtB files. And sure enough, the man was still living at the same address, in a block of flats in what used to be known as Voroshilov Street and has reverted to its maiden name, Nitrianska Street, after 1989. He lived in the same flat on the third floor, like an old palm tree that had put down very deep roots. A short, bald and very ordinary pensioner.

"Do you remember when she moved away?"

"Who is it you're asking about?"

"Mrs Horváthová."

"Oh, I see. That would be at least twenty years ago!"

"She lived here with her husband, right?"

"Yes she did, but he'd left her."

"And I understand from my cousin that there was someone else... a man."

"Well... That's quite possible. That's entirely possible. Wait a minute, I have to let the cat in, it comes back from its stroll around the block at this time of the day."

"Do you have any more information?"

"About what?"

"I mean... about the other man..."

"Is that a tick you've picked up, my pet? Mici!"

"Do you remember what Klaudia Horváthová was like in her young days?"

"Beautiful. A gorgeous woman she was. What more can I say...?"

"So I guess men were attracted to her?"

403

"That's right."

"And what about her?"

"Well, yes… she did have a lover."

"Do you know anything about him?" I leaned closer, lowering my voice as if to bond with him, two men sharing a secret.

"He used to wear an off-white suit. And a hat."

"Anything more you can tell me…?"

"Excuse me, I have to take my medication. Anything else I can do for you?"

"Do you know where she moved to?"

"I can't remember any more. Please make sure you don't let Mici out as you leave," said Mr Navrátil, still smiling broadly.

12.

The secret police file on Puškár classfied him as a hostile element. For some strange sentimental reasons Father had spared him in his reports, not mentioning certain things or providing only vague information nobody could make head or tail of.

At the time, nothing that came to pass on that fateful day in June 1976 made sense to me. Or rather, I never gave it a second thought, as I was aware only of a few snippets of information as well as of the final act of the mysterious drama. It wasn't until much later that I discovered how the various pieces of the story fitted together.

At around six p.m. Puškár's phone rang.

Ten minutes later the phone rang in our house, too. Father grunted something into the receiver and hastily pulled on his jacket.

He rang the doorbell of Puškár's flat two streets down.

Before he even sat down Father began:

"Tell me who phoned you just now and what you talked about. I've just had a call from… you know where. We've known each other for a long time so I'm telling you like it is."

The situation had apparently made Father very uncomfortable and I'm sure he would have been shuffling his feet, maybe also biting his nails. For some reason he decided that honesty was the best policy. It seems that Father felt cornered by the ŠtB and was beyond caring what Puškár might think.

Puškár was beaming with joy and had no idea what Father was on about. "The God of love has granted me a woman!" He was over the moon and failed to grasp what was at stake or how on earth his friend the doctor knew about the phone call or why anyone else should be interested in it.

Unable to contain his happiness, he blurted out:

"It was Lila!"

"How do you mean?" Father asked.

"Lila has just rung me!" he said with a flushed face, beside himself with joy.

"I don't understand. You've got to speak up!"

"It was Lila. She is living in West Germany now. She said she just had to hear my voice!"

"Wait a minute, wait a minute... Did she say it was her?"

"I know it was her!"

Father collapsed into a chair, cracking up. He hid his face in his hands and roared with laughter. He couldn't stop. Puškár joined in – partly out of embarrassment but mainly for joy. He felt relieved and exhilarated after all those years of futile waiting and daydreaming.

Father stopped laughing.

"There is no Lila. She's just a figment of my imagination."

"What do you mean...?"

"I made her up."

Puškár went on smiling. He couldn't take in what Father was saying and thought his friend, the poor chap, had gone crazy.

"But that's impossible, I've just spoken to her on the phone."

"Pour me a drink and I'll explain everything."

They drank some plum brandy.

I have no idea why Father was so hard on him but he told him the whole story. The ad, the letters, the photo. Of course, at first Puškár didn't believe a word. He thought that for some strange reason Father just wanted to spoil his fun, just when the woman he'd been waiting for all those dull, empty years had finally got in touch.

Infuriated by his response, Father went on to give him a detailed account of things he couldn't have known otherwise – quoting words and situations, a flattering nickname, intimate details from

405

the correspondence… Puškár's face turned paler by the minute until it was almost transparent. He sank deeper and deeper into his chair and kept refilling his glass. Just before he left, Father must have realised he'd been foolish and that he'd done something needlessly and pointlessly cruel but it was too late to take his words back.

In the early hours of the morning Puškár hanged himself. I saw his swollen blue tongue. He was discovered three days later, when the postman who tried to deliver a registered letter roused the neighbours.

Father was the first person to be called in. The sight of Puškár's face made him freeze, as if he head seen the head of Medusa. He refused to touch him. Babbling incoherently he stated the obvious cause of death before the arrival of the coroner who confirmed that nobody else had been involved.

Father didn't come home until late at night. He was drunk, which happened only rarely.

All he said was: "He had such a beautiful sub-sternal struma that the pathologist decided to keep it for his collection," then he locked himself in his isolation cell.

13.

The town of Brežany grew and so did its significance.

Boris Tóth, the other son of the former owner of the Stag Hotel, now worked at the hotel's reception desk. He was more Tina's friend than mine, but if I was passing I usually stopped for a chat. On one occasion he pointed out a man in a grey suit hanging round the reception area. He was the hotel informer. It wasn't an official position, but everyone knew he worked for the ŠtB. He would loiter in the lobby or have coffee at the restaurant, sometimes exchanging a few words with the staff. He spent all his days here. His job was to keep an eye on all the prominent guests who happened to honour our town with their presence. Apparently he took pictures of them but Boris never saw him in action. Every now and then the hotel manager asked Boris to compile a list of guest names, addresses and ID numbers. This was meant for the man in the grey suit.

Otherwise our town could boast no more than a couple of

murders, one case of child abuse and the usual number of rapes per year. A decent statistic, comparable with other cities, Trenčín, for example.

Scores of houses were demolished. The street outside the hotel resembled a mouth that had its teeth knocked out in a big street brawl. It was around this time that Brežany acquired the same unalluring, makeshift appearance as many other cities of Slovakia. Its suburbs had grown strangely flabby, like dough that's been left too long to rise. Everything was covered in dust.

My allergy also got worse. Every time I visited our house I would start sneezing and sometimes couldn't catch my breath, as if something had lodged in my throat and I couldn't get rid of it.

On the outskirts of town, near the place known as Mislovič's Island, a new hill grew out of material left over from building the high-rises and regulating the Sálava. Soil and debris, brickwork and stones had been tipped out here, making a big heap that was eventually covered over by grass. The locals called it the Blue Hill – Vojto told me that the grass that grew there had a strange bluish hue – and in winter children would come here with their sledges.

In the summer Bony pretended this was the Wild West. Children shouted at each other in Czech, the language into which TV films about Winnetou the Indian chief had been dubbed, making them believe that Czech was what real Indians spoke. A few goose and chicken feathers sewn onto knicker elastic and a few bits of buckskin were enough to complete the illusion.

Before the Sálava was regulated, there was an explosion at the Slovlina factory, located a little upstream. Built in the 1950s, Slovlina sported a huge sign above its entrance: *Brežany – the Pearl of the Socialist Chemical Industry.*

Few rivers in Slovakia could boast a greater abundance of fish than the Sálava. After the explosion we could see for ourselves – the banks all along the stream were littered with dead fish of every kind and size. A true ichthyological paradise. They hadn't been poisoned. Some kind of gunge had glued their gills together making them suffocate.

Rumour had it that Comrade Jančo, the director of the chemical factory, hanged himself when he saw the devastation.

"Now that's what I call integrity…!" Father commented drily.

There has always been something treacherous and inscrutable about the Sálava. One year it was shallow, barely reaching your waist, the next it would swell and its perilous waters would run four metres deep. The water snaked around, forming meanders and blind channels. Willows and papyrus plants grew along its banks. For many years a ferry ran across the river, made of three interlinked pontoons left behind by the Russians, big enough for a few cars. The ferryman, Mr Lucký, lived on the riverbank in a small house sheltered by enormous oaks, where he used to tie up his ferry. The 1975 floods swept the trees away. To make things worse, the Sálava inundated the town and people lost patience with it.

In 1976 the river was tamed, its bends realigned in a straight line. The meanders were dug up and the area was cleared out. The river now flowed at a faster pace, as if it wanted to get away from us as quickly as possible. In its newly regulated state its level sank by three metres, as did the groundwater in all the surrounding wells. Not many fish were left in this fast-flowing, nondescript shiny ribbon. Water almost completely disappeared from Behy, the small pond by the old brickhouse. It became a haven for frogs and thick green algae. People threw rubbish into it and it began to give off a disgusting stench.

People no longer enjoyed the manicured grey wasteland along the Sálava. The beautiful grove had been cut down, including our favourite tree in whose branches Vojto and I once had our hideaway. Five years ago we went down there with a bottle of wine and argued about where exactly our tree had been.

Neither of us got the spot right, as I discovered when I checked the map afterwards.

14.

The new building of the state TV in the Bratislava suburb of Mlynská Dolina was almost complete, but the current affairs and documentary departments were still housed in the old building, the former Tatrabanka, in Slovak National Uprising Square. The editor-in-chief, Comrade Cesnak, was waiting for me impatiently at his desk. When I presented him with my diploma, he grinned happily and said he was glad I'd finally made it and he, too, would now be off the hook. He admired my diploma:

The Political University of the Communist Party of Czechoslovakia Central Committee.

Comrade Adam Trnovský, d.o.b. 25.6.1934, Brežany

Attended from 27 November 1976 to 21 December 1976, a training course on cultural policy issues for editors of culture desks of central press, radio and television.

Prague, 21 December 1976
Enrolment number K 17/23-76

Diplomas or not, our internal life had been driven deep underground. The surface was a desert covered in grey ash, a sight that was pleasing to the eyes of those who longed for clarity and order in all matters, and preferred silent, ash-grey, identically faced individuals.

"What is left for us to do? There's just alcohol or sex. Take your pick," Vojto used to say.

We had just rung the bell at someone's flat. A party was in full swing. A woman in a tie-dyed T-shirt who neither of us knew let us in. She wore a wilted flower in her hair.

"Come on in! Help yourselves."

There was no trace of the traditional welcome of bread and salt. Instead, she held out a plate full of pills. Dexphenmetrazine. We each took a pill and mingled with the other guests. The last shall be the first and the first shall be the last: that was the slogan of those wild parties.

We arrived on Friday and didn't leave until Sunday night. At lunchtime on Saturday we were still in the middle of a heated discussion but then the volume went down as people collapsed in a heap wherever they happened to be standing, between the low chairs and the carpet.

Someone put on *Wild Horses* for the hundredth time. Vojto got up and said with a big smile:

"I want to make a living by listening to The Rolling Stones!"

We scoured the newspapers until midnight but none listed any vacancies with that job description.

By now Vojto was a heavy drinker but he hated boozing on his own. He had taken to stopping strangers in the street and urging them to take a swig from his hip flask. If you ran into him when he was on a bender your chances of staying sober were nil. He used to sit on the low wall outside his block of flats in Szabó Street and, like a spider, look out for passers-by to trap.

He had the odd spell on the wagon but to be honest these were very brief.

Soon enough he'd be yelling out of his window, drunk out of his head:

"I love you, vagina! You're like a blooming rose!"

We tried to drag him back inside before someone called the police. Instead he would wind up any female present with his tirades:

"There are three things that need to be well developed in a woman: the milk bar, the gas plant and the amusement park!"

Then he'd pull his old contrition trick, invariably ending up in bed with one of them.

One party in particular I still remember quite vividly. The sun was beaming through the windows like a spotlight in a film set; wine and vodka flowed by the barrelful.

Vojto told us that he'd been to see a friend, an acclaimed painter, in his studio. When he went to the bathroom he spotted some paintings drying in the bathtub. They all looked the same: multicoloured stripes with the paint blurred at the edges. He asked what on earth they were.

"Oh, this is just something I paint for the doctors. They have no idea about art. The pricks are willing to pay me ten thousand a piece!" the painter laughed.

"So I pissed on them!" Vojto concluded. No doubt that increased their value considerably.

The doorbell rang.

Vojto opened the door to find two canvassers outside.

We were in the middle of a general election and this was the third time the two suits had called on him. Their first visit had been a month earlier, and they had knocked again three days ago. They waved ballot papers in his face.

"But what if I want to vote for someone else?"

"You can't!"

"What do you mean, I can't?"

"Well... You can't vote for anyone else. We have a single National Front candidate list."

"So what's the point of voting then?"

"The Comrade Chairman of the Electoral Committee has sent us. We must make sure the turnout is a hundred percent. Otherwise he won't get his bonus."

"But I want to vote for someone else!"

"You can't. Those are the rules. And whoever heard of having a choice anyway? Where do you think we are? Here's your ballot paper!"

Knowing what kind of customer he was, they brought the ballot box along. Vojto shook his head.

"It's up to you. You don't have to fill out the ballot paper, just put it in as it is!"

"Take it away! Oh, listen, let me tell you this great joke...! An outraged citizen comes to see Husák and shows him a postage stamp with his likeness: 'Comrade President, this stamp won't stick!' Husák frowns. 'Let me see!' He licks the stamp, puts it on the envelope and presses it down with his fist. 'See, it does stick, no problem.' The citizen's eyes light up: 'Oh I see! I was spitting on the wrong side!'"

The comrades in suits put on forced smiles.

"OK, that's enough now, let's get out of here!"

He slammed the door in their faces: "And remember me to the Comrade Chairman of the Electoral Committee!"

Late that night, after everyone else was gone, Vojto and I were lounging on his bed with a bottle of Romanian Traminer, staring out of the window. The majestic, thick-branched linden tree, mysterious in the dark courtyard, could have been planted by Magritte himself.

"There's just one thing I'd like you to tell me, Adam..." Vojto turned to me. "Do you really believe that crap in your films?"

"No, I don't."

"Oh good. Just checking."

He could see I wasn't keen to expand on this topic.

Vojto sometimes had visitors when he was out. The uninvited

411

guests made a point of moving his TV set onto the bed or leaving bedlinen scattered on the floor. Or they would rip a few pages out of his beloved Kant and wrap cigarette ends in them. One night he came home from a screening at The Future cinema to find the bedroom wardrobe door flung open. The Caucasian mountain-dog fur coat he inherited from his father had been meticulously cut into thin strips.

This was how mysterious beings from another world made their presence known.

The State Security spread like a contagious disease in its early stages, before it is diagnosed. You may cough up a little blood or feel a pang of pain, and dismiss it as a light case of flu. But you're wrong.

A guy in a leather coat, just like in movies, would come to see me from time to time and ask about Vojto. He recommended that I stop seeing him. The all-powerful head of the TV personnel department took me aside in the canteen and gave me a friendly talking-to. As he spoke, the glasses on the golden chain hanging from his neck kept dipping into his boiled cabbage.

Vojto was summoned for interrogation to Februárka, the Bratislava secret police headquarters. They knew all about the two canvassers, the dexphenmetrazine and marijuana – someone must have squealed. Trying to guess who the snitch was was a popular game at parties – was it the man in the ill-fitting jacket? No, not likely. Or the one by the window? Could be him.

When Vojto's passport was confiscated and he was banned from travelling abroad, he just grinned: "At least I have something in common with Kant. He never left Königsberg all his life. I, on the other hand, will never set foot in Kaliningrad, as his birthplace is now known."

The only thing that disturbed his quiet days in Szabó Street was the old woman who lived one floor above and must have had a hundred cats. OK, maybe not a hundred, but she had never let anyone into her flat to count them.

In the middle of the night Vojto would be woken up by the sound of the cats walking on the parquet floor above. He would hear the patter of their paws or a gentle thud as the cats knocked something over or landed on the floor.

At least ten pairs of eyes would gaze at him from the window when he went down to the courtyard for a smoke. He was mesmerised by the yellow discs with black slits that followed his every move attentively. Stony faces. Guardians of the territory. They had an overview of everything that went on. On his way back, after he finished his cigarette and stamped the butt into the ground, he could feel the cats' gaze turn away as they retreated from the window one by one and disappeared into the flat.

Vojto's resolve to resist the regime weakened only once. By now he had two children, a girl and a boy by two different women, but neither mother showed great enthusiasm when he turned up on their doorstep drunk and penniless.

I recently came across some evidence of wavering.

A reference for Comrade Vojtech Roško
I have known Comrade Vojtech Roško and his family since our schooldays. I believe that his personal development as well as his professional and creative achievements demonstrate that he is worthy of the party's confidence and has the potential to become a valuable member. I fully support his nomination as candidate for Communist Party membership.

A comradely reprimand:
The Board of the District Committee of the Communist Party of Czechoslovakia hereby issues a comradely reprimand to Comrade Trnovský for providing an inadequate assessment of Comrade Roško's political views with regard to the crisis years of 1968–1969 as well as the present in his recommendation to be accepted as candidate for membership of the Communist Party of Czechoslovakia.

15.

"Each time you buy something new you have to get rid of something old," Grandma Mária used to say about clothes.

This has stayed with me as a kind of superstition. I believed in the ultimate balance of things, and this had caused me a lot of anxiety as a child. When I was in primary school I began to lose things deliberately. Whenever I got an A in a test I would destroy a favourite toy, fearing that otherwise I'd run out of good luck.

At one point, in the mid 1970s, I suddenly felt all the gods were giving up on me. But there was nothing I could do about it.

I have always enjoyed hanging around TV studios, backstage with the propmen. I was particularly fond of Gusto, who was two fingers short on one hand but no less dextrous for it. He was just in the middle of making a marble obelisk for a TV drama.

He started by dipping pieces of brown card into a bathtub filled with cream, ochre and beige paint, which he had mixed gently by blowing with a hairdryer without letting them merge into a single colour. He was after texture. He submerged a piece of card and pulled it out skilfully. A thin layer of paint trapped on the surface really looked like marble. He set it aside to dry before glueing it on a concrete pillar.

Just as he dipped the second sheet in the bath I happened to raise my head. That's when I spotted her behind the set, not far from where I was standing. An apparition from a long-forgotten world, almost. Tina's friend Ada, the one whose pheromones were capable of driving our entire family crazy. An assistant producer, as I later learned, she was having a heated argument with the production designer.

There she was, with her husky voice, her blonde hair tied back and eyes of an uncertain colour, exuding that feminine fragrance mixed with a perfume I didn't recognize. I reached for a coin in my pocket even though I knew the outcome in advance. Three times the coin said: "Don't go", but I couldn't stop myself from moving away from the bathtub and approaching her.

Something in me revolted against a purely physical relationship, whereas Ada didn't mind that at all. She had no expectations and knew I wasn't going to divorce Zuzana, since I told her so right at the start. Besides, there was another man around, maybe even more than one. We were all pawns on a chessboard.

I should have known better and realised it wouldn't work. What do you make of a person who shows you their favourite place that means a lot to them but all you can see is a boring pine forest with trees planted in straight lines, with sand so hard and compacted it doesn't make any sound under your feet, the paths disappear into the distance and there's nowhere to hide? You're bored while she's happy to be there and you can't understand why, while she doesn't understand why being here isn't making you happy too. A perfect wordless lack of understanding.

This is what it was like between me and Ada. But by then it was too late: Zuzana had left me, having packed her stuff and moved with Bony to a tiny pied-à-terre in Dulovo Square that she inherited from an aunt. Time refused to stand still and wait for me to point it in another direction.

Ada laughed at me and thought I was showing weakness. It had never occurred to her to move in with me. And I was getting sick and tired of her repeating different variations on the word "freedom".

Stage and film dramas commonly involve sombre-looking characters shedding tears and sometimes sharing hugs and resolving their life crises in the course of "a long day's journey into night". Everything suddenly becomes clear.

But their authors seldom go on to show what happens afterwards – the boredom, routine and silence, the cooling off, alienation, the process of leaving, abandoning as well as aging, as bodies turn increasingly decrepit, ending up on a drip or suffering other indignities. They leave out the "they lived happily ever after till life did them part". The real mystery.

In those days our Brežany house started exerting its pernicious and hypnotic influence on me again. I took two weeks' leave and went home to have at least a short break from everything, both the world and myself. Our childhood rhyme, *čik-čik, domček!*, rang in my ears as it did every time I returned. My allergy, too, came back with a vengeance, but it calmed down slightly after a few days. My body accepted that I was going to stay here for a while.

By that time Father was alone. Or rather, the moment was approaching fast.

That time, I climbed to the top of the church tower just as I did yesterday, and looked down at the town of Brežany spilling into the distance. A sea of dilapidated and hole-riddled roofs gave way to stark new housing estates. The minuscule town square crouched below me and the wide Štúr Street – the street of changing names – snaked around the square before heading south. I wetted my finger with saliva and waved it the air: following the direction of the wind I found a gap in the buildings in Štúr Street where our house stood. My house, my father's house, my father's father's house. The house. At this time of year the wind usually blew from the east.

Father and I were sitting in the drawing room, bathed in a soft autumn glow. In the empty house, battered by the wind, with Gershwin softly playing on the record player. *It Ain't Necessarily So*, followed by more Gershwin.

"What do you think is the limit for what one may do and what's no longer permissible?"

"I don't know what you're talking about."

"I think you do."

"You see, Adam… Things could have turned out differently but… But the times caught me unawares."

"The times always catch you unawares. That's life. You just have to learn to deal with it."

"You never learn to deal with it; you've seen that for yourself. You're always surprised by what happens, whether you like it or not. And sometimes all you can do is survive. Will you have some soup?"

"I'm not hungry. Tell me about Armin, what actually happened."

"You have to speak up. I can't hear you."

"Armin."

"Well… they came to take him away… That's how things were in those days."

"I see."

"It wasn't my fault."

"And can you tell me why Mother has left you?"

"You know what she's like… She's overemotional, lives in a world of her own and isn't interested in anything else."

We stayed silent for a long time. I wanted to take him up on everything, I really did. But nothing specific occurred to me. Nothing that I wasn't guilty of myself.

It was 17 November. Klaudia's name day.

16.

Eventually I had to return to Bratislava.

I stayed in the flat in Malinovský Street alone. Bony was looking after Polyester number six, who for some reason was known as Bret. The dog and I suffered in equal measure. The dog refused to eat, and its fur fell out in clumps as it scratched itself furiously. Bret missed me badly, but when I came to visit he avoided me as punishment for my betrayal and for leaving him at the mercy of a cruel world.

What kept me going in those days was vegetable soup. It was my safe haven, its colours alone offering a refuge from the drabness of life. I loved watching the bubbling pot with the red carrots and white parsley roots, pieces of chopped celeriac, the light green kohlrabi, a whole onion tossed in with its brown skin and lots of green vegetable tops… Inhaling its invigorating fragrance made me feel that the world couldn't be all that bad if things like this soup were possible.

Preparing the soup became a ritual. I stopped for the vegetables at the recently completed New Market Hall at František Župka Square, which still smelled of fresh brickwork and chemicals. The stallholders and shoppers, all the regulars – simple, uncomplicated folk – were a never-ending source of fascination to me. Free of major problems of the kind I was plagued by (at least I was trying to convince myself that my problems were really major), these people – always looking the same and always contented and in good humour – had been coming here or to some similar place, in every era since the beginning of the twentieth century, during the two wars, after February 1948, in 1968. They were here three hundred years ago and would still be here a hundred years from now. As long as they didn't go hungry, were able to get a drink, had a few friends and some kind of a job, they weren't affected by history at all. The market hall was an anthill and those inside didn't care whether outside there was a raging storm or the most brilliant sunshine.

Sometimes I'd stop at a makeshift wine bar for a glass of dreadful plonk – divided, crudely, into two simple categories: *white* and *red*. I didn't really drink it; it was just an excuse to hang around at the bar watching and listening to the regulars. This was the real world, so distant from mine. I had spent too many years gazing at my own navel. I envied those people.

At home I would unload the shopping, neatly cut up the vegetables, fry them in oil and make the soup. It offered security, the only firm reference point in my precarious world. It gave me peace of mind and helped me regain my composure. In those moments savouring the fragrance and the taste of the vegetable soup was the only thing that seemed real.

I listened to the radio a lot, especially at night, when I put classical music on to play softly. It reminded me of our midnight raids on the fridge back in the old days in Brežany and I often wondered what Peter and Tina were up to at that moment. The empty flat, the radio and sometimes, after the rain, the overwhelming moist fragrance of elderberry blossom. People say that in the old days elderberry branches were used to measure people for their coffins. I, too, was dead, in a way. Agreeably dead. Or so it seemed at such peaceful moments.

Sometimes I just stared at the fruit flies. They proliferated in the summer, leaving hundreds of brown dots on the wall before some mysterious illness suddenly mowed them down. Another lost generation. All that remained was dried up little carcasses on the walls. *Lost generation.*

There was a dreamy, somnolent quality to the early summer evenings on the courtyard balcony. Somebody was playing *Besame mucho* on a flute by an open window – the sound bounced off the walls, ingeniously finding its way in through cracks, air vents and around corners so that you couldn't tell where it came from. Nor did it really matter. The Spanish tune was followed by Charles Aznavour's languorous *La Bohème*. Sad sounds drifted from house to house.

Every now and then joyriders would send ripples down the smooth surface of the daily routine. These were young hooligans who, in the absence of anything better to do, nicked cars and took them for a ride before returning them. Sometimes they crashed them and left them where they were. There were constant complaints and a couple of people in our block were questioned by the police. I overheard the conversations as I sat on the balcony with my feet up on the railing.

In the background I could hear the clattering of Scrappy Paul, as local children used to call him (his nickname was taken from a character in *Golden Gate*, a children's TV programme, who urged them to collect waste paper and scrap metal). He was struggling to smash up an old fridge so he could lug it to the recycling centre. His heavy hammer seemed to be pounding my skull. He lived in the caretaker's flat, never said hello to anyone and the only thing I'd ever heard him utter were curses when he had to shovel snow or sweep up the fallen leaves around the rubbish bins.

He was quite useful. Like a clever forest creature that sniffs out any carrion or rotten tree stump and then gets rid of it, Scrappy Paul stripped our neighbourhood of all kinds of metal, paper, bottles and glass. Once he dragged a reel of copper wire under our courtyard balcony. I'm sure it wasn't scrap but nothing left within two hundred metres of our block was safe from his hands. Not even a car. If it was left for too long, he'd start by tentatively knocking off a side mirror, and if that elicited no response he'd let the air out of the tyres and wait a little longer before smashing a side window. If even that failed to provoke a reaction he'd proceed to take it apart and carry it off to the recycling centre, bit by bit.

I had plenty of time to reflect. Memories of dramatic events from the past came flooding back to me like recurrent bouts of malaria, something Uncle Rudo had suffered from (and which had eventually contributed to his demise, although he always claimed that life itself was the deadliest of all illnesses, and one with a very bad long-term prognosis at that). These attacks tended to come especially when I least expected them.

Sometimes I would just lie in bed tossing and turning. I'd remain lying on one side until all the snot flowed from the upper nostril to the lower one. I imagined a timepiece, my very own sand-glass or, rather, water-glass. I managed to spend a whole day like this, incapable of getting up and doing anything. I even timed it: it took six minutes and fifteen seconds for the snot to flow from the right nostril to the left. It took a little longer in the other direction because my left nostril was slightly smaller as a result of a childhood accident, when I had to have stitches in my nose. That took seven minutes and three seconds.

419

People choose different ways of slowly killing themselves, each appropriate to a particular phase of life. In the 1970s Analgon tablets did a great job. You washed them down with a small beer if necessary. That was quite enough to knock you out. It would add colour to your day, especially if you were spending it in front of the TV set. Back home, after a decent day's work. When everything was done and dusted, as people say.

A female voice droned from the TV set. The programme I'd finished editing three weeks earlier happened to be on.

What should I prepare for dinner today? This question comes up constantly, day in, day out. Some people love cooking, it's their hobby, while for many women it's just a daily chore and part of their routine.

Statisticians have calculated that the workload connected with food preparation in Czechoslovakia's households adds up to some sixty million hours a week. If we convert this total into statutory weekly working hours we arrive at an interesting conclusion: activities related to food preparation in an average household are equivalent to a full-time job performed by 1.5 employees.

The preparation of a simple main course meal involves 150 distinct tasks. This figure can rise to 500 in the case of more complicated dishes. A cook has to cover the distance from the stove to the worktop alone fifty times; she needs water at least fifteen times, and puts the used utensils away twenty times. Then there are various additional tasks on top of that. The greatest number of activities takes place between the stove and the worktop, and the next busiest route is the one between the worktop and the kitchen sink.

I walked over to the kitchen to ladle some soup into a bowl.

When sitting at the table each individual needs to enjoy sufficient freedom of movement. Experiments have shown that the amount of space an average person requires during a meal ranges from fifty-three to sixty-five centimetres in width. That means that an average elbow-room of fifty-eight centimetres should be sufficient for any diner. The average table space allocated to each diner should be no less than fifty-four centimetres, to enable a person to reach for the bowl, butter a roll and pass the ketchup or mustard.

My only pet – apart from fruit flies, silverfish, moths and black flour beetles – was a red fish in a round fishbowl. It kept me silent company. It was most active at night, when it tried to commit suicide, or at least that was what it seemed to be doing. At around one or two in the morning I would hear a splash as it flung itself out of the fishbowl. This was followed by a smack as the fish hit the floorboards. I wondered how it would survive once I started sleeping well again. It might at last be successful in its attempt.

I had trouble falling asleep. The moon, which was yellow as rancid butter, shone through the window, projecting the pattern of the curtain onto the floor. Busy Malinovský Street had long gone quiet and a voice in my head whispered at first, then roared in a never-ending chorus:

Nessun dorma!

Nessun dorma!

No one is asleep. *Turandot* in the depths of night.

17.

The beige marble lobby of the brand new high-rise TV studios in Mlynská Dolina signalled to visitors that some mysterious and significant activity was taking place inside the building.

The same image was conveyed by the large conference room. Comrade Cesnak sat at the end of a long table, nodding contentedly.

He was admiring the white plaster model of the state of the art Czechoslovak Television compound. Then he asked his secretary to come in.

"Janka, take a look, please. What's that thing in there?"

Together they examined something inside the airshaft of Studio 4. Janka extracted it with her eyebrow tweezers. The thing had wires sticking out of it.

"What on earth is that?"

"It's a bug," Comrade Cesnak sighed.

Producers and camera operators were assigned corner meeting rooms but hardly spent any time in them. They tended to congregate in the snack bar on the top floor, the 28th, which had panoramic views. But the best place to hole up was the Green Bar, a room in the sound technicians' wing, decorated in orange and green, where ordinary mortals never set foot. If they did, they never came out again.

Getting footage of the Tatra Mountains required a day-long drive along potholed roads in a dour GDR-built Robur minibus that spluttered clouds of smoke, followed by a day's shooting and then another day for the return journey.

I preferred to go to the TV archive instead, where I would dig up some suitable old footage. I would choose some sections, mark them laboriously with slips of paper and then insert them into the new film. Everyone resorted to this technique, which is why every documentary made in those years features identical footage of mountain peaks covered in snow.

There were some occasions, however, when a trip in the TV Robur couldn't be avoided. For example, there was the time when we were sent to shoot a documentary about a town centre somewhere in the heart of Slovakia that had been redesigned in the spirit of socialist aesthetics. With the equipment loaded up in the back of the minibus, we sat on the kind of double-seats you find on coaches, only far worse for wear, and were tossed about from one side to another. The air vent in the minibus ceiling was broken, generously letting in dust or rain. Exhaust fumes swirled around the vehicle. It was just about bearable with a good supply of wine and pastries.

When we arrived the locals gathered around us, attracted by TV's magic pull.

"Who's the producer here?" somebody asked.

Without thinking twice I pointed to our fat driver, whose pockmarked face was covered in festering pimples and whose builder's bum stuck out of saggy corduroys as he unloaded the tripod and camera. He wiped his forehead on his sweaty T-shirt, sat down behind the wheel and couldn't believe his luck when the most enterprising of the local girls tapped on his windshield.

For the next two days he was mostly out of circulation. He would turn up at random in the most unexpected places, with several lovelies in tow.

His hotel room was next to mine and at night female moans kept waking me up from my light sleep. In the morning a crew member enquired if the lady was a virgin but the driver brushed him off, saying she'd recently broken her arm and was in pain whenever he put his weight on her.

I've always found it hard to do things the straightforward way. Like a lead guitar player who got so used to fancy ballad-and-blues riffs he can no longer pull off an ordinary solo in a major key.

That is why I envied straightforward people. And hated them, too.

I hooked up with a woman who lived in the same block, one floor above me. We met after the duvet she was airing fell onto my courtyard balcony. She stuck a note in everyone's letter box, asking whoever found it to bring it back. Since it landed outside my window the task fell to me. Admittedly, curiosity also played a role as the note bore a female name, and there hadn't been any interesting women in my life lately. I returned her duvet and we got talking.

Her name was Dorota. She was a handsome, mature woman, twelve years older than me. By saying mature I mean kind of like a juicy plum you've been saving until its sun-soaked flesh turns orange and sweet. Her husband's name was Igor and he was a doctor, a coroner who seemed to work lots of night shifts. I would visit her during the day, when the building was empty apart from a couple of deaf pensioners and dogs howling because their owners had locked them indoors.

A few years went by in this fashion. I could hardly tell if I was alive or dead. My world resembled the asphodel fields of the ancient Greek underworld populated with dead souls of those who had been neither good nor bad in their lifetime and now wandered around a grey landscape, drained of feeling and expression, while everyone else was burning in Hell or having a great time in Heaven. I would have opted for Hell if I'd had the choice and the courage, but I possessed neither.

People in our block developed various strategies for getting by. For instance, the shrivelled-up woman who lived on the fourth floor kept popping to the corner shop to buy ingredients for her rum-laced cakes. Her cupboard was filling up with supplies of flour and baking powder. And lots of vanilla sugar and eggs. If only the damned rum didn't run out so fast.

That called for another visit to the shop.

18

It was one of those hot, lazy, yawning Saturdays that make your eyelids droop. Vojto and I were sitting in the Luxorka cafeteria, like two lone wolves with slightly moulting fur, looking out of its huge windows as the occasional tram cut across a half-empty Štúr Street. A young woman out on a stroll with her family fell behind them and stopped by the café window to touch up her lipstick. When she realized the place wasn't empty and saw two curious men staring back at her, she gave a start and ran to catch up with her husband. Apart from us, only a couple of other similar human wrecks were having lunch here. All the other regulars preferred to eat at home at weekends.

Once in a while I'd get a visit from the secret police to persuade me to stop seeing Vojto on account of his hostile attitude. Then they changed tack and said it was fine, I could go on seeing him if I insisted, but I'd have to return the favour. They brought up Father, too, but I didn't understand the significance of that until later. I refused and decided to be more careful. But that wasn't the end of the story. For years I'd been dreaming of making a *real* documentary and had just come up with the idea for an hour-long film that would include in-depth interviews (albeit with the requisite ideological veneer) with the poor wretches who had been uprooted from their cottages in Nevedovo and other villages in the area and resettled in Brežany, on the Brehy housing estate. When I pitched the idea to my editor-in-chief he said it was "out of the question, and surely I don't need to tell you why". I did know, of course. It was because of my friendship with Vojto. It was a painful choice but I didn't want to lose my best friend.

Still, Vojto and I found ourselves on opposite sides of the barricade. He signed Charter 77 protesting against human rights violations in our country. I, on the other hand, signed the so-called Anti-Charter, like everyone else who didn't want to be out of a job. Vojto socialised with intellectuals in baggy sweaters, distributed samizdat and his flat in Szabó Street became a depository of journals and books published in exile. The State Security regularly hauled him in to Februárka for interrogation. They would keep him for hours, asking endless questions and trying to prove that he must have said something or known something. They demanded to know what so-and-so had said to him and what Vojto's response had been, claiming they had witnesses for everything and even if it might take a while, one day he was bound to make a mistake and give them something they could use.

After that they usually let him go.

The potato salad at Luxorka wasn't anything to write home about either. The cook scowled at us from behind the counter and kept banging the dishes she was cleaning as a gentle hint that it was high time we left.

Vojto told me that when he was young, his harsh martinet of a father, Lieutenant Colonel Roško, used to tie him and his brother Teo to the backs of the kitchen chairs so that they would sit straight while eating. And to make them keep their elbows by their sides, he would make them hold china plates under their arms. Things improved slightly when he swapped china for unbreakable plastic.

Vojto put his fork down and reached for a toothpick. A bit of beef was stuck between his teeth.

We decided to take a ride on the rickety old bus to Devín, along with cheerful day-trippers and squealing children.

Vojto told me he'd recently been there with his mother Natália. She now spent most of her time at home in Brežany wandering around the empty house, usually drunk. She wouldn't drink just anything; she insisted on Georgian brandy. Her beauty had long since faded although flashes of it were still visible now and then. Vojto hadn't seen her without make-up for years. On her bedside table she kept her own photograph from her prime, capturing her radiant smile and peroxide blonde hair. Every time she looked at it she would sigh and say:

"I was a beauty, wasn't I? In the old days in Prague – the only people who had blond hair were me and the tarts!"

Her favourite reading was her Guest Book, which she had been keeping since the 1930s. Most of the eminent guests who frequented her fancy salon in Brežany and in Prague had written a few nice words or contributed a drawing. After Mr Roško was dismissed from the army the entries became rarer, and prominent guests disappeared altogether; the last pages contained only scribbles from Father Savický, who lived out his days writing about things he no longer remembered. She didn't have the heart to tell him to stop coming.

Vojto and I spent a few hours in a wine bar under artfully twisted vines. We were rather mellow from sweet redcurrant wine, the Devín speciality that looked and tasted as sweet and heavy as a diabetic's urine.

It was after sunset. We went for a drunken stroll around Devín, under street lamps that crackled as they were switched on, shedding a purple neon glow over the streets. We passed a phone box. Vojto went in, pulled out a crumpled piece of paper from his pocket and started to laugh.

"Who are you calling?"

"Bil'ak."

"How come you've got his phone number?"

"I'll tell you later."

He moved the receiver closer to me so that I could listen in – it was ringing.

"Who is it?" came a feeble, sleepy voice.

"This is Stalin speaking!" Vojto thundered, putting on a Russian accent.

"Who...?"

"Zdes Stalin, yob tvoju mat'! This is Stalin, you bastard!"

There was a startled silence.

"Izvinite pozhaluysta, please excuse me, Joseph Vissarionovich," the voice on the other end of the line said after a while. Apparently Bil'ak couldn't decide if this was a dream. I imagine he was standing to attention next to the phone. Perhaps he wet himself a tiny bit too.

The feeble little voice came again: "And what is it you're calling me about, tovarish..." We could hear he was concerned.

"I'm calling to praise you! You're doing a great job, comrade! A great job indeed!" Vojto thundered.

The voice at the other end trembled with emotion. "Thank you, Joseph Vissarionovich! Thank you so much! Thank you...!" Bil'ak was lost for words.

"No need to thank me, Vasil! You are a good comrade! Keep it up!"

"I can't tell you how much this means to me! Your praise..."

"I may be dead but I know how a true communist's heart beats! Do svidania, tovarish!"

Vojto put the phone down and roared with laughter. He just couldn't stop. His face went all red and I thought he would burst a blood vessel.

I shook him. "Where did you get the number?"

"I have this mate… He works for the phone company and has access to these secret lines. He had done some repairs in his house. I knew it would come in handy one day. But not a word to anyone. They could arrest him. And us too," said Vojto, still choking with laughter.

Inadvertently my hand reached for the stone in the pocket of my windcheater. It was there, as always. I played with it whenever something was on my mind; it had a soothing effect on me. The black onyx from the countess's earrings that Vojto and I had found behind furniture in the mansion house after the war. He had the other one.

The stones represented our friendship, and back in the old days we'd made a deal. If either of us ever decided our friendship was over he'd hand his stone to the other one without having to say a word.

Not long afterwards I learned that Vojto was seeing my former wife, the mad, maddening Zuzana.

Actually, I found out very early on, when I spotted Bony's favourite model airplane in Vojto's flat in Szabó Street. Vojto had tried to push it under the wardrobe but I noticed it anyway. In a subsequent conversation I mentioned the eczema on Zuzana's hand – this was something she'd been fighting for years – and he knew what I was talking about even though I'd never said anything about it to him before. Trying to cover it up he came up with all sorts of stories.

I said nothing and waited to see how things would develop and how long he could keep it secret. It didn't take long. One day we got drunk and he finally came clean.

"I'm aware of it," I said.

"Why didn't you say anything?"

He was cross with me for a while.

It was he who told me that Bony had started cutting himself.

Whevever he wanted to punish himself or was upset about something he'd take a razor and make a few shallow incisions on his wrist.

During our trip to Spain he told me it had made him feel calmer. It felt good. It's a family affliction, I thought to myself. With parents like us he didn't have an easy life.

I felt guilty and I started bringing him treats from my business trips. Tinned Prague ham was a rare commodity. It was produced only for export and you couldn't get it in ordinary shops.

What will you have for breakfast? A ham sandwich. And for elevenses? A ham sandwich. Coming home from school he'd head straight for the fridge to make himself... a ham sandwich, Zuzana later told me.

From a trip to Budapest I brought him vegeta, the Yugoslav condiment, Hungarian salami and Rama margarine. A sandwich made with these three things was his favourite. Nothing pleased him more.

When I reminded him of this recently he just laughed.

19.

I was shooting a documentary about an extraordinary communist party meeting for the Short Film Studios. Editing it required great skill because we weren't allowed to use most of the footage. The comrades kept sending someone to make sure they weren't shown chewing, laughing their heads off, picking their noses or scratching their ears. We were given a list of images that were forbidden. My cutter Džony and I called the footage that had to be edited out *CCUV,* short for Central Committee radiation.

The meeting was held at the count's former manor house in Brežany, now refurbished and used for special functions.

A ministry official attended the opening. She arrived at the last moment in a shiny black Tatra 612 limousine with two drivers in oilskin jackets who hung around the car waiting for her, smoking.

Her opening speech included heart-rending allusions to the plight of exploited workers in the USA and the West, unhealthy bourgeois imperialist habits and the successful building of our socialist society.

The manager, Mr. Brezanský, shook his head as he whispered to me that a day before the official's arrival a note from the ministry informed him that the comrade from the ministry felt like some roast suckling pig. Mr. Brezanský had to spend a whole day procuring it, then have it roasted on the sly at the Brežany bakery. He only just managed to get everything done in time and was now totally exhausted. The comrade savoured the suckling pig served on a silver platter in a private booth with antique furniture.

After lunch the comrade from the ministry was in a great hurry to return to Bratislava. She and her secretaries carried the remains of the suckling pig to the limo in two bags. Fat, greasy and well lubricated, she slid into her leather seat as the entire manor house staff stood to attention.

For a brief moment the brooding chief of staff of the Slovak Communist Party's Central Committee graced the extraordinary meeting with his presence, his regular Gitane between his lips. It was an open secret that he loved Paris above everything else (including human beings). He would summon his driver on the spur of the moment and take off. A few hours later he'd be breathing the air of Paris. He stayed at a hotel in Boulevard Magenta and savoured rotting capitalism in great big gulps. For all I know, he may have tried to imagine his beloved city under communist rule, no doubt realising that it would be a real shame. It would mean the end of hookers, the Moulin Rouge would run to seed with its former staff scattered around labour camps, the venue would be converted to a campaign centre or an evening university of Marxism-Leninism; only two kinds of unexciting cheese would be available, and in true egalitarian fashion, the only wine you could get would be a cheap plonk, which would try to pass itself off as vintage wine, its label bearing the name of some King Louis or other although it would be the product of a cooperative farm somewhere in Brittany. The whole country would be collectivised. Snails and truffles would be for export only. Endless Labour Day military parades would pass under the Eiffel Tower...

"No," he said, abruptly turning away from the window, noticing my glance, exhaling smoke and saying almost audibly: "The division into two worlds must be preserved!"

There had to be one place left to get away from our glorious progress. An escape from our glorious tomorrows, a place that was truly glorious.

There was another familiar figure moving around in the shadows at the back, though this time his presence didn't surprise me. Rehor Kohút, veiled in a cloud of mystery. With his perfect smile, pointed shoes, well-groomed greying curly hair, sharply lined face and manicured hands, he resembled an ageing star of the silver screen. A pinch of idealism was needed, after all, to complement the prevailing materialism. Like that little outing to Paris.

None of this ended up in my documentary, of course.

In the autumn of 1989 I found myself once again at the manor house with my camera. It so happened that the building had just been taken over by the National Property Fund, and I was there to film their annual conference. A lady from the ministry arrived to deliver a speech.

The déjà vu that followed trumped everything I'd ever experienced. The manager, the now elderly Mr. Brezanský, came up to me. Shaking his head, he whispered that a note had been delivered from the ministry a day earlier, informing him that the lady from the ministry felt like some roast suckling pig. It took him a whole day to procure one, and he had it roasted on the sly at the Brežany bakery. He only just managed to get everything done in time and was now totally exhausted. The lady asked for the suckling pig to be served on a silver platter in a private booth with antique furniture. After lunch she was in a great hurry to return to Bratislava. She and her secretaries carried the remains of the suckling pig to a BMW limo in two bags. Fat, and greasy and well lubricated, she slid into her leather seat as the entire manor house staff house stood to attention.

His account became more and more hesitant, as if he realised that the two of us had had this conversation before.

20.

All through the seventies and eighties my sister Tina made occasional visits from London to Brežany.

Everything in her home town seemed to her drab, dark and sad, including the people. The restaurants and bars closed by seven in the evening and there was nothing to buy in the shops. She'd get used to it within a week and go with the flow. On her return to London (her suitcase, naturally, stuffed with Horalky wafers, her remedy for homesickness), she was overjoyed to see the lights of the big city, the bright shop windows, people with smiles on their faces and music everywhere… Two weeks later she'd write saying she was fed up with all the noise and commotion.

In the summer she used to go to Sweden with Trevor and their daughter Jenny. She loved the northern summers. Once she sent me a souvenir, a tin shaped like a fishbone. The label said: *Genuine Swedish air*.

The package was delivered opened and pierced in several places. I was summoned to Februárka and got shouted at:

"What's this supposed to mean? Are you trying to smuggle in drugs or what?"

Tina was the first to notice that things were not right between Father and Mother. I guess because she saw them less often.

"I wonder if Dad has a girlfriend," she kept saying. "Or do you think he's not well?"

She wouldn't be fobbed off by my litany of clichés along the lines of – *you know what he's like* – or – *he's always been a bit…* – I couldn't find the right word – *one doesn't get to choose one's parents, we have to accept them as they are* – or – *I wash my hands of any responsibility for him* – or – *I've given up on him* – and similar meaningless drivel. I usually finished by saying – *I really don't want to talk about him!*

And then it all came pouring out.

I mentioned Klaudia Horváthová, who was an important woman in Father's life, if not the most important one. Yet everyone pretended she didn't really exist. Surely Tina would remember that this woman had turned up when we went for a walk, the cakes she used to bake for us, or the sweets she used to ply us with.

"So this had been going on for years…?"

"Apparently."

I hadn't seen her for ages but was sure she was still beautiful.

"All those years…"

"All those years!"

431

I also remembered what Mother used to say sometimes when the three of us went swimming in the old gravel lake and Father stayed on the shore.

"See what he's like? He'll never come here with me. He says swimming is boring. But who knows, he might actually enjoy it with someone else…"

I tried to change the subject as it made me feel uncomfortable. I didn't want to know. I had no idea whether Mother knew about Klaudia Horváthová or whether she was just bluffing.

Only later did I discover that the beautiful and ravishing Klaudia was another constant and shadowy presence in Father's life. While he regarded it as purely a physical relationship it had meant much more to her. They went on seeing each other even after she realised this and found herself a husband. (Did she think Father would be hurt? Perhaps. Except that he hadn't seen it that way. He once told me scornfully that she'd made the announcement dressed in red and blue like a village Madonna.)

As the years went by Father began to use her to spite his own wife. Whenever they had a row, or Mother reproached him for anything, he'd visit Klaudia and go to bed with her. He thought he was the only one in the know and it gave him a sense of sweet satisfaction.

Years later, in one of the rare moments of intimacy we shared, Father told me that in a weak moment he had confessed everything to Mother. He had to come down from his high, sun-drenched pedestal. It was like God admitting he'd been lying and had been just an ordinary mortal all along.

The next morning Father got up and pretended nothing had happened.

Soon after that he broke up with Klaudia Horváthová and she moved to another city, where her daughter lived.

"I might not even recognise her today. Human cells keep changing, Adam. Every seven or ten years we shed our entire body and replace it with a new one. It's been ten years since I last saw her," he told me then.

He felt that Klaudia was watching over him, right up to the days before he died. He felt she kept an eye on him even though they hadn't spoken to each other and lived far apart; that Klaudia knew exactly where he was and what he was up to at any given moment. She knew his habits, good and bad. She'd been tracking him for years.

And she also appeared in our old photographs, as I've just discovered.

But I'm getting ahead of myself again.

Part 5

Saturn Devouring One of His Children

1.

A large naked male body. A deranged-looking man on his knees is taking a bite of a small child's bleeding torso. I remember Father holding the book in his lap and studying the reproduction. He wasn't familiar with the myth.

"Kronos, the ruler of the skies in ancient Greek mythology, better known by his Roman name Saturn, was destined to be overthrown by his own son," I explained. "To prevent the prophecy from coming true, he decided to devour all of his sons. But because of their divine origin they continued to live inside him. And the prophecy was eventually fulfilled by his son Zeus, whom his mother had managed to hide."

Father listened pensively, staring into space.

"It can't have been easy to eat one's own child," he observed laconically.

He raised his head.

"Every clock in this house shows a different time," he said with a sigh, tapping the pendulum of the large grandfather clock in the drawing room. "You wind it up but it will stop before long!"

I go to the window and look out, trying to stop my attention from wandering. There are too many distractions out there and I can't focus properly. Normally it doesn't take this long. I guess my eyesight isn't helping either, not being what it used to be, although I can't say that has always been a bad thing.

Found it at last!

A tiny bubble, a minuscule blemish in the pane of glass. A translucent oblong shape, like the pupil in a cat's eye. A small fish imprisoned within the window.

When I was young I would spend ages gazing at it, observing the world locked inside a tiny atom. The universe hidden in glass.

Ever since I left home, whenever I came back the first thing I'd do was go to the window and look for the bubble. And stare.

"Come over here, Adam! What are you doing there again?"

I could see the outside world as well as a reflection of the world within.

I've only had one truly frank conversation with Father about all the

437

serious and important things in life. It may have been late autumn. I remember shivering from cold after touching the windowpane.

Gershwin's music was playing on the record player in an endless loop. Aretha Franklin was singing *It Ain't Necessarily So* on a record Tina brought Father from England. The basic tune always reminded Uncle Oskar of another musical motif – sung to the lyrics of *Baruchu et adonai hamevorach,* a blessing for the person called upon to read from the Torah.

Aretha kept insisting "it ain't necessarily so".

How true.

"Turn it up, Adam!"

All you had to do was walk along the wall to find the gate. The wall surrounded the park, in all its English garden architectural glory: venerable trees and bushes, and lawns with endless intersecting white gravel paths.

When a descendant of the former count came for a visit from Switzerland in 1967, he walked around outside the manor house like a ghost but wasn't able to get in. In the end he was allowed to take a look at the cellars, now used for storage by the Brežany Wine Company. He spent the day in the park without anyone showing any interest in him.

On that day my parents spent hours walking in the park, talking. In the evening Mother packed her bags and left. Apparently she claimed she'd had enough of everyone and everything and couldn't bear to stay in this house for a minute longer. She has never told anyone what it was they had discussed that day.

And they lived happily ever after, until life did them part.

There were three weddings at the manor house that day. The ceremonies were usually held in the great drawing room, attended by a national committee representative, accompanied by the caterwauling of the Brežany choir and followed by a female official's heartfelt rendition of an ode to the glories of family life, penned by a comrade writer.

That was why my parents kept coming across jolly wedding guests on their walk. There were best men leaping out from behind hundred-year-old elm trees at the most unexpected moments, and radiant brides and bridegrooms happily posing for pictures in the clearings. Everyone was happy, but a cloud of sorrow seemed to hang over my parents. They tried to seek out the more secluded sections of the park, off the beaten track, in order to avoid meeting people, but to no avail.

At the end of the walk Father said: "I know you've always been faithful to me." Mother declared defiantly: "I have most certainly not!"

Father didn't hear her. He had no recollection of her saying anything like that.

When Mother moved out one of the things she packed was the blue album containing the banknotes. Just in case.

Father showed me a letter she had sent him shortly before I was born. It was his revenge. The letter said the child meant nothing to her, that she was unable to relate to it and would rather it had never come into this world. It came as a surprise to learn that Peter had spent the first years of his life living with Grandma Mária and that it wasn't until I was born that my parents finally decided to get married.

This was the first time I'd heard this version of the story.

2.

The banknotes in the blue album were a bit like the fairytale golden ring with the power to make your wishes come true. A passport to an uncertain future, something you keep saving for the one truly rainy day. That moment hadn't quite arrived after the war, nor in 1953, in the 1960s, nor later. My gullible parents were convinced that the strange little bits of printed paper would continue to increase in value. When Mother announced she was taking the album, Father agreed, through gritted teeth.

A few years later Mother wanted to give Bony something really valuable for his eighteenth birthday. She showed the album to Mr Míka, who ran a stamp collectors' shop in Brežany. I was shocked to hear he valued it at only five hundred crowns.

I phoned him straight away, said the album belonged to me and I was going to buy it back. I was happy to pay a thousand crowns more but old Míka refused to sell.

"It has no value. I'm going to give the banknotes away for free, with stamps."

I didn't believe him but there was nothing I could do.

I didn't visit Mother all that often. She lived in Armin's old flat, which Father somehow managed to get back after the war.

I was too busy to feel like playing her favourite game, which went roughly like this: you tell me you've been to the dentist and in return you'll get a litany of all my ailments: *Head, shoulders, knees and toes, knees and toes, knees and toes…* Illnesses were the only topics of interest to her. In those days she was already turning into an old lady with unruly blue-rinsed hair.

She was enjoying the happy autumn of her life… caressing her silvery hair with her work-worn wrinkly hand … Fill in your favourite cliché. She shared the nuggets of wisdom she gathered over the long years of her hard life… with anyone and everyone. I'd rather she had kept some of them to herself.

Peter was still her favourite. When I came to see her, she spent most of the time talking about him. He would make only the occasional visit himself, the noble gentleman in white gloves, the spoilt firstborn.

She pumped me for the latest news. I was beginning to suspect she didn't really believe what I told her. In her recollection people didn't get older. And since she hardly ever left the house, she let the incomprehensible outside world rush by with the condescending smile of someone who knows better.

Nevertheless, when she did go out, she made careful preparations. The small utility room had been turned into a walk-in wardrobe, and a cupboard in her room always contained clothes appropriate for the season.

She regularly switched the clothes between the walk-in wardrobe and her room. "It's almost summer and my spring clothes are still out here. Could you bring me that pair of shoes… and that skirt please?"

Mother would have me run back and forth, fetching clothes and then putting them back again. She claimed she couldn't manage on her own and I was saving her time. "Don't forget the fur coat, there's a blizzard out there!"

She smoked like a chimney. Each visit was a torment for my

asthmatic lungs because even if I opened the windows wide the room was filled with smoke.

"I'd ban smoking worldwide if I could!" I would rage.

Bony's riposte usually went:

"But then you'd still slip grandma some cigarettes on the sly."

Sometimes, when she was in a sentimental mood, she'd recall stories from my childhood.

For example, whenever I lost a milk tooth, Mother insisted that we plant it under the big yew tree by the kitchen window to make sure a new tooth would grow in its place, claiming a gap would stay in my gums forever if we didn't. I had no idea why she picked the yew tree. It was quite a coincidence, as this was where I found the bones years later. She was right. Every time we buried a milk tooth a new one would sprout from my gums. That was all the proof I needed. I trusted Mother implicitly.

After she moved out she never had a good word to say about Father. Just the mention of his name was enough to unleash a string of invectives.

"I always knew it. He worked for the ŠtB! He spied on me, too, and informed on me!"

Who on earth would have been interested in you? I thought, though I never said so out loud. Besides, it sounded like sheer nonsense at the time.

"He had hundreds of women, one on every corner! Even fat, old ones. His own patients! Dirty peasants! I looked the other way."

I felt embarrassed.

"And as for the bed department, well, you know what I mean, that was an ordeal. All those times I had to bite the duvet!"

At that point I'd usually interrupt her, sometimes quite brusquely, saying I'd leave if she didn't stop immediately. Or I would quickly change the subject. She had such a knack of exaggerating that I sometimes believed her.

"He killed his own mother, he admitted it to me once!"

I stood up, beetroot-red.

She went on, undeterred. Surely I remembered that Grandma Mária had suffered from an incurable disease. It was Uncle Rudo who'd asked Father to do it. So did his mother, apparently. She couldn't take the pain any longer and he gave her some medication.

441

"You can ask Rudo! Go ahead and ask him if you don't believe me!"

I've never found the courage.

The cause of death on Mária Trnovská's death certificate was given as intestinal haemorrhage.

3.

All my life I've sat on the fence. Trying to balance between two worlds. Which is why, whatever I tried to do, I only ever got it half-done. When a numerologist said two was my number, it came as no surprise. Most things happened to me in pairs.

No wonder that I managed to visit two very disparate places in the space of a single week.

To my surprise, I ran into my Prague friend Arnošt in Bratislava. He passed me in Hviezdoslav Square without noticing. Then he introduced me to Jirka, a painter friend of his who fancied wood carvings and tapestries, and men as well as women. While he flirted with me, which I found deeply embarrassing, Arnošt let slip that they had come to pick up a "shipment" and were taking the next train to Prague. If I was interested I was welcome to join them – they were going to a party I'd never forget.

The house in Hradčany Square was like a black hole. In every sense of the word. None of what took place inside would ever get out into the outside world, and even if it did, nobody would have believed it anyway. The house belonged to the son of a famous painter, who had inherited it from his father. Not far from the entrance I tripped over a couple having sex, though it was too dark to tell the gender of the individuals involved. We were greeted by the host, who was wearing an oriental garment. He surveyed the bedlam, puffing on a hubble-bubble. Jethro Tull, The Doors and Led Zeppelin records played all at the same time and I felt as if I was on a set of a bizarre experimental film. A well-known though not particularly acclaimed film director grabbed me by one knee, while a well-known and highly acclaimed actress grabbed me by the other. I admired the stunning art nouveau posters on the walls, which looked suspiciously like originals.

In the middle of the table lay a cut crystal bowl piled high with a variety of pills, capsules and tablets: red, blue, yellow and white, oblong and round... A neatly bound booklet next to the bowl contained all the dosage leaflets, complete with realistic, hand-drawn depictions of individual pills. Very impressive. The host had thought of everything. In view of our family affliction I didn't hesitate. For that reason I don't remember much about what happened later. An oasis in the grey desert welcomed me with open arms.

Back at home I got a phone call from Peter. He was in great shape. He had his better moments, when he seemed completely sane, particularly if his medication was working. He didn't wait for my reply or consent: he just dragged me off to the diplomats' shop to pick up supplies for the night, as he put it. The shop, tucked away in a courtyard in Tobrucká Street, looked unassuming from the outside. Peter waved his ID and an obliging staff member let us in.

Flabbergasted, I ran my fingers along jars of Vegeta, bottles of Cuban rum and Veterano brandy, the likes of which were never seen in the ordinary shops. Peter grinned when I picked up something brown and furry and asked what on earth it was.

"A kiwi," he said calmly. "Get a kilo for Father. He'll love them."

Peter's chauffeur drove us to the hill above Bratislava, stopping in front of a small cosy-looking mansion. A prominent graphic artist had received it from the authorities ten years earlier on condition he had it fixed up. He could easily afford this on his income, which was so lavish that he never worked or sold his output between October and the end of the year to reduce his tax bill.

To return the favour he showered the comrades from the Central Committee and artist organisation officials with gifts, and threw expensive parties with copious quantities of food and drink. His personal poison was strong vodka, which made his hands shake uncontrollably. It was rumoured he stayed on the wagon while working, otherwise he wouldn't have been able to produce his delicate engravings and prints.

Classical music was on the record player: Händel, Haydn and a touch of Mozart, though not all at the same time. Virtually the entire Central Committee of the Communist Party of Slovakia was present. The ruddy-faced officials discussed art, pretending to be great connoisseurs.

I spotted the artist's haggard face. He was quite sociable for about an hour, before withdrawing into himself. The more he drank the quieter and more depressed he became. His guests seemed to be used to it and didn't pay much attention. Drawn by the smell of paint and turpentine, I found him in a little cubbyhole by his studio, motionless among his pictures, spotty palettes and grubby painting brushes.

Sitting there with his heavy head in his hands, he smelled of alcohol and depression.

"Are they still there?" he asked.

I nodded. He waved his hand and fell asleep with his head on the table.

Bony's friend Lego lent him a copy of *Hustler* magazine, which he had managed to smuggle in from Yugoslavia. Bony found the lubricious blurred pictures tantalising. Many years later he confessed that his fascination was so great that on one occasion he had to resort to his Socialist Youth League tie to relieve the excitement, as it was the only thing he had to hand. On that day they had been told to come to school in their Sunday best to watch the TV broadcast of the Soviet Secretary General's funeral.

In 1982 Brezhnev died – people had been whispering for years that he ran on batteries and was only kept alive by machines. Rumour had it that during speeches only one of the microphones placed before him actually worked; the remaining nine were actually fans to keep him refreshed.

According to a joke that made the rounds at the time, Radio Moscow regularly broadcast news on Comrade Brezhnev's daily routine: 6:30 a.m. – Comrade Brezhnev has had a pee, the urine is clear and clean, lab tests detected no pathogenic materials. 6:50 a.m. – Comrade Brezhnev has just done a number two, the stools are of the right consistency and composition. 7:30 a.m. – comrade Brezhnev has just woken up.

Moscow was in mourning. For hours on end, his coffin traversed Red Square and the nearby avenues. Students at school had to watch the funeral live and they had to keep quiet even when a strap tore as the coffin was lowered into the grave. The funerals continued as if on a conveyor belt: Yury Andropov came next, followed by Konstantin Chernenko, each with his own big crowds and mourning on the TV. The waxen faces of the deceased General Secretaries were bathed in sunshine, perhaps facing the good Lord, in whom they didn't believe in their lifetime. They tended to die in early spring.

When I came to see Bony, I heard him singing under the shower, improvising to the tune of the *March of the Fallen Revolutionaries*:

> *You fell asleep in fatal battle,*
> *knocked out by my vampire fangs,*
> *You gave away your life and freedom*
> *Welcome to the undead lands.*

It was a time of some truly great songs.

More joy, in addition to the spring delights ushered in by the Three Kings from the East, arrived in May 1986 courtesy of the exploding nuclear power station at Chernobyl. After first heading for Scandinavia, the radioactive cloud veered in our direction. Kindergartens were told not to let children play outdoors. TV programmes that normally pretended everything was hunky-dory and we were living in the best of all possible worlds, suddenly carried a casual recommendation that people should buy UHT milk with an older sell-by date instead of the usual fresh milk in bags. Any real concern was only voiced on Austrian TV, which we were able to watch, even though the reception was patchy depending on which part of Bratislava you lived in, and later on Hungarian State TV, which offered down-to-earth advice on what one should and shouldn't do.

"Lego says no more mushroom-picking for the next twenty years," Bony said, frowning. Lego got his nickname after he fell from a fifth-floor window, smashing every single bone in his body. His bones grew together in a funny way, making him look as if he'd been put together from pieces of Lego.

He would never have got this nickname if Tina hadn't sent Bony a Lego set from England. It was a great rarity and all his friends loved it. Especially Lego.

I wallowed in my solitude until my second wife burst into my life, disrupting my quiet exile at Malinovský Street. I got hooked on TV

445

programmes such as "Chef Svatopluk Hesitates", a soap opera whose viewers decided the storyline by switching their lights on and off. And unless I wanted my colleagues to take me both for a snob and an ignoramus I couldn't afford to miss "Ein Kessel Buntes", the East German show featuring the latest in Eastern bloc pop. The next day there was just one topic on everyone's lips: had the ageless diva Helena Vondráčková had a facelift?

My favourite occupation was reading on the toilet. In the Middle Ages good Christians were discouraged from tackling secular literature before they reached the ripe old age of seventy, well perhaps fifty, but definitely not earlier than that, lest they be led astray. Those who couldn't wait that long had to resort to reading in secret, while attending to the call of nature. This must have been how this habit, or rather passion, got into my genes.

The only one to disturb my peace and quiet was Scrappy Paul. He had got hold of another washing machine and was dismantling it down in the courtyard.

4.

Losing your eyesight is supposed to isolate you from things while the loss of your hearing isolates you from other people.

Father's hearing was deteriorating rapidly and even at the best of times he was plagued by tinnitus. He refused to use a hearing aid, which he claimed was uncomfortable and undignified. He complained that it made a whistling noise and amplified the sound of his chewing and swallowing. First Uncle Rudo, then Tina, Peter and Mother also remembered that their paternal grandfather or great-grandfather kept asking people to repeat what they'd said, and constantly upbraided them for muttering under their breath.

A maternal aunt whose name I forget couldn't hear high-pitched sounds and kept shouting: "Turn the radio up – louder!" She understood men but had trouble understanding women. I wonder if hearing really had anything to do with it.

Father still sat at the head of the table at family celebrations but if you tried to talk to him, he wouldn't understand you in the midst of the general hubbub. Trying to listen to other people's conversations drove him crazy. The voices got all jumbled. To avoid interference from behind he preferred to sit with his back against the wall. It didn't help. Eventually most of his friends, apart from the most diehard ones, stopped visiting him. One fine day, Uncle Rudo also stopped straining his diabetic legs and stayed at home saying: "I'm not as young any more as I think I am".

One Sunday when I came home, I took my coat off in the hallway, held my breath to listen but found the house empty and bereft of any voices.

By now Father had long stopped going to his practice, which had given his life some semblance of a routine. He had reached the stage when he no longer cared about anything. The house succumbed to the anarchy of objects. Light bulbs that normally lived in the larder would suddenly turn up in the bathroom or on the terrace. The carving knife found its way into the bedroom; gardening shears appeared in the isolation cell, the chopping board in the living room. Objects acquired a life of their own and refused to respect their established places.

Father started his days with a drink of milk infused with a drop of brandy from the cellar, stocked with a bottomless supply of the bottles he'd received from his patients. The cocktail tasted quite good, once you got used to it. Sometimes he would keep sipping it until the evening.

One night Father was woken up by some strange and scary rustling in the empty house. Perhaps it was just his imagination, for Father had heard imaginary sounds before. He got out of bed and padded through the dark rooms.

He went to the cupboard and took out the revolver Dr Atlas had given him in the final days of the war. He loaded it and fired a few shots in the direction of the noise, the creaking of the old parquet floor that he must have taken for footsteps.

The otolaryngologist later concluded that the sound of gunfire in an enclosed space had caused irreversible damage to Father's eardrums.

And the house kept making all sorts of gentle noises – water dripping from the bathroom tap, the wind rattling the shutters, the scratching of pigeons nesting in the attic. But Father could no longer hear any of it.

447

Today, too, the windows shake as the wind blows through the cracked window seals. A spooky wailing sound fills the emptiness of the old living room, like Miles Davis playing the trumpet through a muffler. As usual, it seems to come from the far right corner.

I go up to the old piano that hasn't been tuned for ages. I have yet to decide what to do about it. I lift the cover and listen.

A sharp. B, C, A sharp. G sharp...

I try to pick out the tune of the wind. I can't do it. The tune consists only of half-tones, vibrating around the one-line B-flat. And it's all out of tune. The wind responds with another tune of its own.

B flat. C sharp, D flat, B flat... I repeat the motif.

I listen again. Somewhere the shutters are banging, the furniture is groaning. A storm is raging in the old fridge, gusting even louder as I open the door and let its icy breath stream out. This is how an old engine works. It's a familiar noise; it's always been a part of this house, like fierce winds whipping round the alcoves and gargoyles of a cathedral.

I get myself something to eat. And a beer.

For many years now I've watched the house slowly moulder, fall apart, go to rack and ruin. The plaster is damp, the roof leaks. But I've never been up to having it fixed. It was as if I was held back by some invisible force.

When I confided in Vojto, he said, why waste money? One shouldn't recklessly interfere with the natural course of events. This house was destined to fall apart. There was nothing I could do to save it. There was no point trying to resist. All you could do was silently watch it disintegrate.

One day in the summer, after torrential rains, the house looked as if it was drowning. I had to get the builders in. Treading on Father's carpets in their dirty shoes, they moved his stuff from one place to another covering it with polythene while he sat in an armchair without saying a word. Who knows what was going through his head? By then he was almost completely deaf.

The presence of the builders changed the atmosphere in the house. It now smelled of a characteristic mixture of sweat, alcohol and scraped plaster, with a hint of solvent. The workmen invaded the house like a horde of barbarians storming a no-man's-land, a place where ordinary mortals had never before set foot. They repaired what they could, but it didn't last long. The house had long been doomed to fall into decline, disintegration, *Verfall*, as the Germans so aptly put it.

Father wouldn't let us have the house fixed properly and agreed only to some small and absolutely essential repairs: "Don't you dare touch that!" Everything seemed important to him, nothing could be thrown out. Including his useless old medical bits and bobs or his black bag, which still contained his stethoscope and enemas. Now it's all mine.

"A clean house invites death," was Father's refrain. He was right. Mother would have concurred. If she had still been alive.

As would her brand-new fridge that stayed in the middle of the kitchen, still in its wrapping. She had burned the books. She had sold Father's records. Gershwin et al. *It Ain't Necessarily So.*

I've always hated this house, kept fleeing from it, but something inexplicable kept drawing me back. The umbilical cord had never let me get too far away.

But if I wanted to stay here I would have to clear out all the invisible stuff that's still here, and the only way to get rid of it completely is by tearing down this ghastly edifice. It's been the nightmare of my life and the cause of all my anxieties, forcing me to keep revisiting this dangerous terrain. What a relief it would be if the house just disappeared.

And now, finally, I know that this moment will soon come. And it's making me very apprehensive.

5.

The early spring nights are still quite chilly. The outside temperature is around zero.

The oil radiator I brought to heat the place on the first night has blown its fuse for the third time. The old power lines in the house are in mutiny and I've had enough. I've fetched some damp mouldering logs from the shed, all I could find there. I've lit a fire in the fireplace in the drawing room. It took a while for it to get going.

The heat radiating from the fireplace has awakened the insects that have sought shelter in the dead house over the winter months. There's a green lacewing, some ladybirds and a peacock butterfly that seems somehow to have survived the frost and is now desperately flitting from one end of the room to the other in the middle of the night.

Some of the creatures are headed for the source of the heat, perhaps driven by the same instinct that makes them seek the sun. Either way it means the end for them.

I feel it's not my place to interfere with the inexorable course of nature, although I have already done so just by starting the fire. All these reasons and causes, instincts and drives. Consequences.

I get through another night with the help of my good friend Noax. It's cosily comforting, I just have to be careful not to climb too far up the tree. The higher I get the more painful the fall will be.

The house used to stand in a quiet street. Over the years the town around it has changed, engulfing it like mould. Tall buildings have blocked much of the view except for one house that has disappeared, offering a vista stretching as far as the hotel.

I light a cigarette, remembering in passing the doctor's warning, and go out onto the balcony, into the night air. Oh yes, it used to be fragrant. Now all the fragrance is gone, sucked out by the busy alien town that feels as if it has been brought here from somewhere else, replacing the original Brežany of old.

It started under communism, this wrecking of the town by people with no regard for memory, who did indeed try to eliminate every trace of it. Then, after 1989, their successors, a new lot with no regard for memory, continued the work of destruction. The town I am looking at now might just as well bear any other name. All right, let's keep calling it Brežany. For the sake of maps which would have to be redrawn otherwise.

The Golden Stag hotel has been renovated and refurbished. A car with an Austrian number plate has just pulled into the almost empty car park. The obliging receptionist has come out and tries to point the driver to a parking space but is really just getting in the way. When the car stops he stands there, hands folded behind his back, waiting for a tip. But the man in glasses and a smart suit just hands him his luggage. The receptionist shakes his head, the job is

450

beneath his dignity. He leaves the suitcases on the pavement and motions to a young bellboy.

The chimneys of the nearby paper mill that until recently bore the proud name Karl Liebknecht Mill belch out their fumes. For a while I watch the endlessly changing patterns made by the smoke, white against the backdrop of the dark cloudy sky. I see skulls, skeletons, monsters and fantastical grimaces. An endless streams of cars hums past the house in the street below. I think of Father and bite my lips until I draw blood.

I flick away the unfinished cigarette and walk slowly back into the empty room, like I did that time when I was here trying to get over Ada and Zuzana, and heard Father looking for me in the bowels of this enormous decaying whale.

I found him at the kitchen table, lit by the last remaining functioning lamp. Father was sitting there wearing a brushed cotton shirt and a hearing aid he had reluctantly consented to use from time to time.

The hearing aid never worked properly because he kept fiddling with it, turning the volume up and down until he could no longer tell what was a real sound and what wasn't.

He could lip-read as my face was illuminated by the lamp.

"You're the one who introduced me to eau de colognes," he said. "Remember the French one you brought back from a business trip…? I'd never used eau de cologne before."

I was taken aback. I became fond of colognes precisely because Father had always exuded their fragrance. He was the one who bought me my first one. I thought it was a sissy thing to use at first and kept it locked in a cupboard for about a year. Then I happened to come across it and came to like it. He was the one who introduced me to wine, too. I owe most of my proclivities to Father.

"And it was from you that I got the taste for wine," he went on.

"But wine has always been your thing…!"

"Oh no, definitely not! I got it from you."

All of a sudden he started telling me that he used to escape to the garden or the vineyard to get away from his patients and family, to have some peace and quiet. He said he hadn't actually been all that keen on mucking about in the soil as everyone else. All his life he'd pretended to care about family life but in reality he just wanted to be left alone. That was all he ever wanted, to be left alone. He began to sound pathetic. I didn't really feel like listening to him but I kept quiet, watching a big, black fly crawling on the lampshade.

"And wine… You're the one who taught me to drink!"

I shook my head, thinking of the games we had played together in the bathtub. Of tasting the imaginary Veltliner, St Lawrence, Blaufränkisch, Tokay Szamorodni, Irsai Olivér…

"Don't talk back, I'm your father!" he said, getting up abruptly, only to collapse back into the chair, so weak were his legs.

In a house nearby I heard someone trying to coax a simple tune out of a piano but failing miserably. It was unbearable. Whoever it was kept going back to the beginning again and again, going wrong and starting again, equipped with just the first few notes and endless patience.

I sipped my tea and watched Father's face.

"You know… I've always felt like you weren't really here. Like you were constantly absent."

"Absent…" he exhaled the word thoughtfully.

"Yes, you did make an effort to spend time with us. But you were always somewhere else! Absent. You were here in body but your mind was elsewhere!"

"Where do you think I was?"

"I don't know… With your patients… Lost in thought… Certainly not with us."

"If you say so…"

"Will you tell me about Klaudia?"

"What Klaudia?"

"Klaudia."

Instead of responding he slowly got up and went out of the room. He rummaged around his isolation cell for a while. When he came back, he thrust a pile of letters into my hands and left the kitchen.

My dear Alfie,

As promised, I'm sending you the paperweight that you admired the other day. At first I thought I would deliver it today (Tuesday is a long day) in person and hand it over to you at Behy, by the pond. I'd love to ask you how you've been these past two weeks – you know what I mean, you know everything… I've been thinking about you a lot during the holidays, especially the first few days when I went for walks on my own (Z. stayed with his parents and didn't join me until Wednesday).

Kla.

452

Alfie dear,
It's been a long time. Are you alive? Please forgive me for not writing earlier, I was rather tired for the first few days (by the way, I "risked my life" to place a direct call to you from the hospital in Nitra but you were out). I didn't know who to ask to post the letter, I didn't want to ask Mum or Edit. It just didn't feel right. I haven't been out yet. I couldn't while Mum was here. In any case, I hope I can see you soon. I'm sure you'd like to see us – my little Minka Petrovská and myself, although I've put on some weight – please do come whenever you can. Any time, morning, afternoon, but not after nine in the evening. That's when I'm trying to get some sleep because the baby sleeps best after its bath, from nine o'clock to about half past midnight or one o'clock. That's the only time I can get any sleep.

Kla.

Alfie,
The last time you went away I felt so strange, so low – not because of what had just happened but because of what might happen – and I thought you didn't understand. And that hurt. But I don't blame you for anything, not at all. I don't hold any grudges either. Although I can see today that I was right not to send you the letter in which I had bared my soul to you as I tried to make sense of my own actions, thinking there might still be a flicker of hope. Nothing that has happened stems from a lack of restraint or selfishness – certainly not on my part, and I would like to believe that it wasn't so on your part, either. Surely nothing has really changed, otherwise I'd have to regret everything that has happened. It hasn't been easy for me and my soul has been troubled for a long time, nevertheless I treasure what we had and think it was pure and beautiful. At the same time, I realise that I must be more cautious and stricter with myself in future, and make sure I avoid similar "miracles" in my life. Because then this "first miracle" would lose its spell and its true value – but, more importantly, it wouldn't be fair to Z. Although, luckily, it hasn't really affected him.

Kla.

Alfie,
I feel very humiliated as I scribble these few lines in haste (I don't even have a pen on me). But I feel that I may have inadvertently offended you, and the thought that I have hurt you is more unbearable and painful for me than any sense of my own pride, which has suffered so much

humiliation before – I keep apologising without knowing what it is that I'm apologising for. I just feel all the time that my behaviour is foolish but that's only because I'm scared to be honest, and because I'm trying to conceal the fact that the wound inflicted by a painful, albeit necessary, surgical intervention, takes a very long time to heal (I'm thinking of the abrupt end in January) so that you don't reproach me and say "women can't manage without it". Yes, these things are more difficult for us women because we offer more than just "some emotion", we offer up everything we have, our peace of mind and our so-called moral purity, and that is why we are in the difficult position of not only keeping quiet – in order to avoid hurting others (I'm thinking of Z. now) – but also of always having to look happy and pretend to be "exceptionally well-balanced", and then we get over things by crying our eyes out at night, when nobody can see us. And the only person who knows the cause of the turmoil in my soul shows indifference or rather, not just shows indifference but acts indifferently.

Kla.

Alfie,
I can't help thinking back… It's surprising how vivid the memories are, as if it was not a whole shocking year that has passed but only a few calm days. There's so much I'd love to tell you. In fact I have written you a long letter – but I don't want to upset you unnecessarily. The only reason I'm sending you these few lines is because it's your birthday and I want to wish you good health (no more headaches!), contentment and, above all, constancy (may your "happiness batteries" stay charged for a long time) and an abundance of joy – all those things you had never wanted me to give you but I would have loved to give you if only you had let me.

Kla.

An owl hooted in the garden outside the window, a portent of doom.

"I've died so many times in my sleep that it won't feel like a new experience," Father used to say.

In the early 1990s a young journalist from a newly-founded Brežany paper contacted me. She wanted to write a report about Father, a venerable and upstanding citizen of this town who had lived through so much history. I told her I'd have to accompany her, just in case, and that's why I was present when Father met her in the small café in the Golden Stag's lobby.

They spent an hour talking about the old streets, how many original houses still stood in the square, who had owned the military vehicle that had been mouldering in the woods under the Volovec Mountain for years, what had happened to the gilded golden stag that used to adorn the hotel portal, as well as the fact that Brežany was where the great Klaudius Kolár spent the last years of his life – a man who had suffered under the previous regime and was now included in the school curriculum, his long-forgotten poetry widely translated.

I was starting to yawn when she turned to me and asked what I admired most about my father.

"Hmm, I guess… that he's always acted like a real man. A great and proud man."

"And what do you admire about your son?" she asked, pointing her dictaphone at Father.

"He has a kind heart," Father said after thinking for a while. "And he is capable of forgiving."

"Thank you. That will be great. I'll send it to you for your approval within a week. By the way, are you aware that the two of you have similar gestures? Even your facial gestures and voices are similar."

We both nodded.

When she left, we sat in the café without saying a word. We were moved. Neither of us understood why we felt so awkward.

I spent the rest of that day thinking about it and realised this may have been the only time that Father and I expressed our love for one another. We had never done so before. Or since.

6.

Another huge piece of plaster that once fell off the ceiling after the torrential rain made me realise that the house was like a sinking ship that nobody had any strength to salvage. All one can do is grab a lifebelt and jump overboard.

Today I feel as if I'm walking aboard a wreck buried at the

bottom of the sea. Nothing moves here, everything is dead, every soul has vanished.

I go around humming Father's beloved Pastoral symphony. The music rings out with carefree joy, serenity and hope. I believe that for Father it epitomised the kind of life he had always longed for but failed to have.

"I'll get my hearing back in heaven!" he yelled, inspired by the symphony's composer. But he couldn't hear himself yelling.

Certainly not with his own ears, because of those little bones in his skull.

He kept putting on Beethoven records out of habit, even when his hearing was almost completely gone. He would sit in his armchair, sometimes conducting an invisible orchestra with sweeping gestures, surprising chance visitors. The whole house roared.

"This is sheer horror," Father said, "having to listen to this music through a stupid gadget in my ear!

The garden fell prey to hoodlums from the vicinity who came to steal plums and apricots. Slowly it ceased to belong to us.

The only creature still alive seemed to be a big spotted cow grazing behind the neighbour's house. Father used to watch it through the kitchen window. It would spend endless hours lying in the grass. Then it would rise to its feet, lie down again and get up, never moving away. It just stayed there all day, ruminating.

The only time the owners took the cow away was when it rained. They would bring it out again when it stopped raining. It would lie there ruminating, get up and lie down again…

And then it was killed. It was the last animal to go. The neighbour no longer wanted to keep any living creatures.

It happened on that day in the autumn, way back in the eighties, when I came to check on the empty house because Father was in hospital. A seemingly endless flock of wild geese sailed across the sky, squadron-like. Through the icy clouds ready to disgorge snow I could hear the birds reassuring each other that they hadn't lost their bearings and were still all together.

This was when I dug up my childhood treasure and human bones from under the yew tree.

I was beginning to discover my father.

Part 6
Two Old People Eating

1.

"This wall painting from Goya's black series in the House of the Deaf Man, known as *Two People Eating*, shows two old men. Bent over a meal, they seem to be deep in conversation. The room is dark," the curator at the Prado intoned, and I wondered why – like everyone else in his profession – he would waste his time describing things that were plain for all to see.

"Every clock in this house shows a different time."

I keep having this weird dream. Horror-struck, I realise that I've forgotten Father. I've forgotten him, I haven't been feeding him and have totally failed to look after him. He's been left all alone in the big house, with no one to help him. How could I let that happen? Hang on, when was the last time I went to see him? I don't even know if he's still alive...!

In my dream I dress hurriedly, intending to go to Brežany straight away. But then I decide to wait a few more days, so that it doesn't look so bad. What would people say otherwise? If he has indeed died, I'll just find him there on the quiet and act surprised, I'll figure out a way to carry it off. I'll think of something. And perhaps people will believe I wasn't able to come earlier. They just might...

At that point I usually wake up in a sweat, still wondering what to wear and what the consequences will be. It wasn't my fault, I swear! I didn't mean to forget about him!

And then, almost by chance, I remember it's been nearly a year since he died.

Three old men sat on a hill. Uncle Rudo's former vineyard, known for its Zákrivné lúky appellation wines, had run to seed and was now such a jungle that it took them a while to find somewhere to put down the three chairs they had lugged all the way up the hill. The straight silver ribbon of the Sálava flowed lethargically below them. They had a view of Brežany and the enormous full moon, orange as it rose. They took swigs from bottles of beer they clutched.

One of the men had a transistor radio in his lap. He didn't seem to mind that the sound it made was more of a tinny rattle than spoken words or music, and kept pressing the receiver to his ear from time to time, out of habit. The men were talking.

"How beautiful!"

"Yes, it's beautiful!"

"I'm glad we've come."

"Look, that derelict house over there – isn't that where old Mislovič used to live? He survived all the floods and just laughed at everyone. He was up to his shoulders in water and when they sent a boat to rescue him, he just waved them away and said he wasn't going anywhere. And how right he was! He never came to any harm."

"When I was small, we used to play football in that street down there."

"That one over there?"

"Yeah, that's the one."

"Surely not, there's too much traffic!"

"There is now, but when I was little there'd be no more than a car an hour passing through."

"By the way, did you know that Milan died last week?"

"Milan? Milan who?"

"Oh, you know – the one with the gammy leg."

"Oh, him! But he was so young!"

"I agree. Not quite seventy-six…"

"And Puškár's gone, too…"

"You mean the patissier?"

"Yeah, him. He hanged himself. But that was a long time ago. Remember his scrumptious cream slices?"

"Jožko died two years ago. I heard he choked on a fish bone."

"And Jano had a heart attack."

"Mr Levendovský has died, too… The one who lived on the second floor."

"You mean Mrs Levendovská, don't you?"

"Oh yes, you're right, Mrs Levendovská… The one on the second floor."

"We're all headed there, one day."

"Yes, we all are, can't be helped."

"And what about our friend, the doctor?"

"Which one?"

"How many doctors have we had?"

"Oh, him!"

"Haven't seen him for ages. Is he still alive?"

"I think so. He delivered all my children."

"I heard he was an ŠtB agent. Can't remember who said that."

"Nonsense. Why would he have been? I'm sure the communists left him alone."

"I don't believe it either."

"Nobody believes it! Nobody in Brežany does!"

"The doctor is a good man. He's helped so many people."

"The only decent man in Brežany! Let's drink to his health!"

They clinked their bottles and silently watched darkness envelop Brežany in the valley below.

2.

The heading on top of page 24 read: *Using the baton*, and a subheading underneath it ran: *Vulnerable points of the human body*, followed by the explanation: *By vulnerable points are meant those parts of the body where a blow causes considerable pain without leaving any major, lasting signs of damage. Vulnerable points should be struck with the tip of the baton.*

A drawing illustrates sixty such points on the human body:

Eight cranial bones, frontal bone, temples, eyebrows, bridge of the nose, eyes, external auditory canal, zygomatic arch, tip of the nose, upper lip groove, cochlear nerve, small hollow behind the jawbone, jawbone, point of the chin, jugular artery, Adam's apple, jugular notch, supraclavicular fossa, collarbone, subclavian fossa, subscapular fossa, sternum, heart apex, brachial nerve, metasternum, solar plexus, floating ribs, spleen, stomach, navel, bladder, groin, scrotum, quadriceps femoris muscle, patella, side of the shin, front of the shin, inside of the ankle, instep bones, shoulder blade ridge, fifth breast vertebra, seventh breast vertebra, kidneys, sacrum, gluteus maximus, tailbone, great sciatic nerve, popliteal fossa, calf, outside of the ankle, Achilles tendon, toes, radial nerve, palmar finger nerves, metacarpals.

I was trying to remember where I read this, as Vojto and I ran down Hviezdoslav Square. It was 25 March 1988 and our hair and trousers were drenched after an encounter with the water cannon. Vojto was clutching his elbow where he had been hit by a baton. He'd convinced me it was time to stop messing about and join him at the candlelight vigil, which turned out to be huge, the first major rally for religious freedom under communism. It was a last-minute decision, similar to the one Lego's parents made when they decided go through the ordeal of defecting to Germany the following September, only to return home two months later, after the Velvet Revolution.

People sang a few songs, albeit rather quietly. Grandma Mária's favourite – the 1968 version – got another airing: *How quiet the night, so dark and fair / Šalgovič and Bil'ak, traitors in their lair / When the night is gone and day breaks/ Our nation won't forget these treasonous snakes.*

Every country in the world is only five or six meals away from a revolution. Just let your loyal citizens starve for a few days and they can be persuaded to do anything. Who was it that said that...? It was Peter. My brother Peter. I'm sure it was him.

He was the last person I expected to lecture me on free will.

The events of those days had the texture of a thickly woven rug. They sounded like an orchestra playing several symphonies at once. I recall only some isolated fragments.

For example, I remember the day in late November 1989, in the middle of the turmoil of the Velvet Revolution, when everything had an aura of freshness and innocence, when I went to the Mozart House in the heart of the Bratislava Old Town, in Jirásek Street (soon to revert to its pre-war name, Ventúrska Street), formerly the House for Political Education (where I'd collected my University of Marxism-Leninism diploma), which now housed the headquarters of Public Against Violence, the movement that spearheaded the revolution in Slovakia. I had brought something for Vojto, whose day had finally come. He'd been plucked from obscurity because the movement was in desperate need of experienced people. My admiration for him grew – he hadn't been broken, he'd kept his integrity, never kowtowed or compromised: in short, I envied him for behaving the way I was never able to. I used to have grand plans, that's for sure, but I never managed to step over my own shadow, remaining a grey specimen of humanity drifting with the flow. A coward, careful not to stick my neck out.

Inside the building I found a throng of stunning young women busy typing up manifestos and declarations, ten carbon copies at a time. The room was filled with the sound of typing and an exquisite, almost unearthly fragrance. A few weeks later mimeograph machines arrived and the documents could be reproduced mechanically. The room was now deserted and ordinary, almost ugly.

My thoughts were interrupted by Vojto's arrival. Tired from all the excitement of the talks and negotiations, he gave a deep sigh:

"Democracy may be the dictatorship of the mediocre but it's still the best solution there is."

Let me now fast forward a bit – it's 10 December, the ice is breaking up on the Danube and we're in Devín, the venue of our redcurrant wine expeditions and Stalin phone calls. Vojto and I are vying for a piece of barbed wire from the tall fence that's being dismantled. I've managed to get hold of the most coveted prize and walk off with a notice saying "Border zone: entry strictly prohibited". The fence was gone within days of travel restrictions being lifted by the government.

People sing while wielding their wire cutters; nobody can believe that this is really happening. Less than a month ago this place was surrounded by watchtowers; electric current ran through the barbed wire, and a road roller patrolled the area between two fences so that the guards could immediately detect any "border violators" and eliminate them.

Urban legends started circulating again, this time loudly and with relief, about the daredevil who managed to fly from the Devínska Kobyla Hill all the way across to Austria on a hang-glider, and of a contraption that could drive along the high voltage wires suspended high above, and carry people across the border.

Vojto and I decided to walk to the Austrian town of Hainburg, after years of just staring at it enviously from the Devínska Kobyla Hill.

Shivering with excitement, we passed the Petržalka-Berg border post, which until recently had been one of the most closely guarded and impenetrable in Europe. We hesitated for a while, not sure if we'd be allowed to cross without anything more than the passports we'd hastily applied for and just received.

As soon as we entered Wolfsthal, the first village on the Austrian side, everything seemed affluent, beautiful and bright. This was our first whiff of rotten capitalism in years. The Austrians weren't all that keen on the fall of the Iron Curtain, as we gathered from the ad hoc signs pleading: *Please: no pilfering!* posted in the shop windows.

Elated, we went into the first café we found in Hainburg and studied the drinks menu. The prices made us a bit nervous, as we had only a few schillings that Vojto had dug up somewhere. Luckily an enterprising soul had put together a little picture dictionary so visitors whose German was as rusty as mine could communicate by pointing. Vojto kept one as a souvenir.

With the help of the drawings we managed to place our order – a small coffee with milk.

The waiter brought us a *piccolo* – a few drops of coffee at the bottom of curiously shaped, oblong cups. I was offended. The waiter must have figured out we'd come from the East and was trying to rip us off!

We downed our coffee in one gulp. It was strong and heady. Vojto was moved to declare that this was the first real coffee he'd ever tasted.

Panting middle-aged fellows that we were, we climbed to the top of nearby Braunsberg Hill to look at the Devín Castle from an unusual vantage point. I was rather taken aback to notice that a 1980s map carved there in marble referred to Slovakia as *Nordkarpatenland,* which more than smacked of Nazi terminology. As far as I know, the map was still there as recently as six months ago. Only right at the bottom, where dogs go to piss, the word *Slovakia*, has been discreetly added. For the rest of the day Vojto and I referred to Austria as *Südalpenland*.

In a sex shop in Vienna's Mariahilferstrasse we discovered another world. This was the first time I saw an inflatable doll that boasted of having "three love openings" although, as Vojto pointed out, a penknife would have been enough to produce a few more. I shivered with excitement and sweated as if in a trance. Things I'd only dreamed of were right there before my very eyes.

The former Gottwald Square in Bratislava was deserted. One day the oversized statue depicting the permanently drunk and syphilitic president and his pals was blown up by persons unknown.

Unfortunately, I've only seen amateur footage on Austrian ORF TV, shot by a bystander from the entrance to the Technical University. The statue was no great loss, although perhaps the raw materials could have been put to some more sensible use. But it's the same conundrum as with Ceauşescu – when he was shot, should his body parts have been used for organ transplants? Or would they have retained his thoughts and emotions? Wouldn't Gottwald's past have remained carved in the stone? The swelling of the aorta, the alcohol-soaked nights after signing a few more death sentences, the vagina of an infected prostitute, the dread of the bewhiskered man from the Caucasus, whom he eventually followed on this last journey, having caught up with him in the antechamber of communist Heaven (instead of St Peter, I imagine Lenin himself met him at the gate in all his five-foot two glory, with his shiny bald pate and a red star on his brow, holding an allegorical sickle in one hand and a metaphorical hammer in the other, mobbed by eager cherubim with young pioneer scarves), the smell of vodka and red carnations, flowery speeches on equality and justice and an artificial arm with the artificial fist of the working class which Arnošt had once showed me at the Barrandov studios. These were the thoughts going through my head.

In January the postman delivered new Ministry of the Interior guidelines:

Dear Mr Roško,
Following the suspension of Article 4 of the Constitution of the Czechoslovak Socialist Republic and until relevant department guidelines are updated, the forms of address are being changed as follows, effective 15 January 1990:
   The form of address "comrade" is to be replaced by "Mr"/"Mrs"
   The form of address "comrades" in meetings is to be replaced by "ladies and gentlemen".
   The greeting "Hail Labour" is to be replaced by the civilian "hello" ("good morning" or "good evening").
   You are hereby instructed to ensure that all the subordinate staff within your remit are acquainted with this change and comply with it.

Richard Sacher
ČSSR Minister of the Interior

The following spring was full of joy. Nature enjoyed its yellow period, gradually blending into the green, followed by the purple and the blue period, only to be superseded by the red, yellow and brown period, followed by the orange, and ending up with the grey and the white. Then the cycle will begin all over again.

On Thursday 12 April I phoned my brother Peter to ask if he was planning to spend Easter in Brežany.

He came to the phone after several rings, just as I was about to give up.

"Hello," he said in an otherworldly voice that gave me the creeps.

"Hello... What's happened, is anything wrong?"

"I'm sorry, Adam, I can't talk right now. I'm having the Last Supper."

I put the phone down without even saying goodbye.

3.

And that's when, all of a sudden, it happened.

Mrs Roško was reading her cards. She drew a red nine followed by a red ten, meaning anger and sorrow. The next card, an acorn eight, meant it would happen suddenly.

In the midst of wrangling over whether the ŠtB archives, including the lists of agents and informants, should be opened to the public, someone dug up Vojto's file. A former high-ranking ŠtB officer decided to crawl out of his cocoon like chrysalis turned butterfly, and go into politics. Vojto opposed his candidacy on principle as this was the same man who had interrogated him several times at Februárka and had held him in unlawful detention. Vojto could still feel the slaps across his face.

The reaction was swift.

Vojto took the matter to court but soon discovered that this wasn't a game he could win. The ŠtB man who had opened the file on Vojto and signed all the reports was called as a witness. Vojto had to accept that once a single drop of coffee has been spilled into a cup of milk, it would never be white again.

He was stripped of every office and his political career was over. He was a dead man.

During one of Father's many hospital stays Vojto and I sat in the living room of our Brežany house. The street outside was humming away and the house sank deeper and deeper into the night. Everything around was going quiet, only a tireless nightingale sang somewhere in the distant darkness, oblivious of the cold night wind. Our wine, too, steadily ebbed away, until I brought another bottle. And then another.

Vojto did most of the talking, while I mostly kept silent. He admitted that at one point, in the 1980s, the ŠtB had tightened the screws on him, after he applied for a passport. They made him sign a piece of paper agreeing to cooperate. But he'd never harmed anyone and the information he'd provided was so misleading that they had eventually dropped him as unreliable. All this would have been confirmed by the file, which allegedly no longer existed, as it was one of the many said to have been destroyed in the heady days after November 17, when the ŠtB frenziedly removed evidence, shredding piles of documents, leaving only his name on the list of informants, with the word "agent" added by hand.

"But you do believe me, don't you?" Vojto said imploringly, as if I were the only person who could absolve him. "I've never hurt anyone!"

"Yes, I believe you... I believe you..." I said softly.

He cried on my shoulder. We'd never touched before, not being the touchy-feely types. I threw my arm around Vojto and listened to him sigh. His tears soaked my jumper.

I look back at myself sitting here that night. This past version of Adam is still unaware of many things about his father, but he can't help thinking of him because in this house his old man is on his mind all the time – this house is the embodiment of his father and he is present in its every atom. The place is forever haunted by the soul that had gradually drained from his decrepit body.

We agreed to meet for lunch the next day.

After reverting to its respectable old name, the dilapidated old Golden Stag hotel in the centre of Brežany was in free fall as a guest who was about to have a bath suddenly heard an almighty roar. The bathtub, along with half the bathroom, landed one floor below.

The hotel became a no-man's-land for a while. People regarded it as some kind of communist cadaver, whereas under communism it had been branded a bourgeois relic. Eventually it was bought and rebuilt by a Belgian company. Ignoring a report by the Brežany conservation society that listed all the features that had to be preserved, the Belgians tore the building down, gutted it like a dead frog and rebuilt it so thoroughly it ended up looking like any number of buildings anywhere in the world, with gilt door handles and pastel-coloured upholstery, where discerning guests could be under the illusion they had ended up in Acapulco, Johannesburg, Khartoum or Helsinki. When the builders uncovered a bricked-up eighteenth-century room at the back, complete with stuccos and frescos (just the kind of stuff that was trendy at that point) they quietly demolished it because it would have disrupted the building work. Old Mário Tóth told me about it. He was the one who had shown the Belgians the secret cubbyhole next to the reception, which had been kept under lock and key and contained the equipment used to eavesdrop on hotel guests.

Finally, a week before our meeting, the hotel had been ceremonially reopened. Vojto and I could not recognize anything as we wandered around like two zombies who had lost their memory due to head injuries. And not just memory: the food tasted of nothing and at the bottom of the menu we found the reassuring notice: "The waiting staff will present you with the allergens on request."

Great, so now I can have allergens on request. That might be a step too far.

I graduated to producing a regular programme on health issues for state TV, which was pretty innocent and harmless stuff compared with my previous work. We filmed heart, intestinal or prostate examinations and surgeries, and the footage was then used to illustrate studio discussions by experts.

I had lots of time on my hands. Taking advantage of this, Bony would lumber me with nine-year-old Matúš, my grandson. He would pick him up from the boy's mother – from whom he was separated at the time – and pass him on to me straight away because something urgent had usually cropped up all of a sudden.

That's how I ended up helping little Matúš plough through a magazine article he was asked to read for his homework.

Since the fall of the communist regime our hopes have been pinned on

468

our great model – the founder and guarantor of global present-day democracy – the United States of America. The first North American colonies were established by Christians who had been driven from Europe by their rulers' tyranny and religious intolerance, and it was these people who founded the USA, the cradle of democracy, freedom, the free market and an open society. The ideas of the Pilgrim Fathers, who arrived in a free country in order to found a "city upon a hill" and a "beacon of freedom and faith" found their expression in the Declaration of US Independence, which was drawn up by Thomas Jefferson and signed on 4 July 1776.

The United States of America is the third most populous and third largest country in the world, stretching across four time zones, between the Atlantic and the Pacific Ocean and including some Pacific and Caribbean islands.

After the end of Word War II the USA became the world's most powerful economy and since the end of the Cold War it has become the dominant global economic, cultural, political and military power. The country generates one quarter of the world's total economy.

The article was illustrated with colour photographs of the White House, Yellowstone National Park, Mount Rushmore, and San Francisco's Golden Gate Bridge. Most striking was the moving picture of American schoolchildren holding hands on Thanksgiving Day – one black, one white, one Asian as well as a little girl whose features were clearly native Indian. The captions under a few additional snapshots read: A New York City policeman, strict but fair. A happy celebration on a Native Indian reservation. US troops lined up in front of President George Bush honouring the dead at Arlington Cemetery. Workers on a Ford factory assembly line. A black fisherman pulling a net full of prawns out of the sea.

As I read this I remembered what Juraj – cousin Filip's younger son and now a law graduate – had told me after returning from a six-month language course in the UK. He had stayed in Tina's large Hampstead house eagerly lapping up everything he was told.

"We've got to take from the rich, otherwise there won't be justice in the world. I support the introduction of progressive taxation."

"How about taking from the rich lefties," I said, teasing him, but he wouldn't listen.

"Just look how it ended all over the world! It hasn't worked out anywhere. Rather than in a backward Asiatic country like Russia,

469

socialism should have prevailed in the US: that would have been something!"

Fascinating. I'm sure the only reason his father wanted to defect to the US in the 1970s was to test this hypothesis. I had to quote his grandfather, the late Uncle Rudo:

"Christianity and communism are great ideologies but they're not for human beings. If angels walked the Earth – why not, be my guest!"

But Juraj wouldn't listen.

One day, as Vojto got off a tram in Krížna Street, a man ran up to him, smiling broadly.

"Hello! My father sends his regards. He's in hospital right now, poor man. I'm so glad I ran into you!"

The man gave him a hug. Not wishing to hurt his feelings Vojto asked how his father was doing, although he had no idea who it was.

"He's feeling a bit better," said the friendly man. He patted him on the back a few more times and quickly said goodbye as his tram was approaching.

When Vojto got home he discovered his wallet and documents were missing. All that was left in his pocket was a note he'd found in his postbox earlier that day:

GOOD FORTUNE. You've been sent this letter to bring you good fortune. The original was posted in Holland and replies have come from all over the world. GOOD FORTUNE beckons. It will reach you within eight days of receiving this letter. Send a copy of this letter to those you know are in need of good luck. Do not send any money, do not throw this letter out. You must send it on within 96 hours of receiving it at the latest. – A certain Mr Kuscha received this letter in 1965. He asked his secretary to send out 10 copies. A few days later he won the lottery. A friend of his threw the letter away and died a few days later. An SPT officer received 7,000 US dollars after posting the letter. Another gentleman forgot to post the letter and died 6 days later. Send out 10 copies and see what happens in four days. A surprise awaits you in a few days' time. This is really true even if you are not superstitious. – Do not throw this letter away and don't break the chain whatever you do!!!

Don't forget – you have 96 hours.

4.

A big yellow Avia has reversed through the garden gate. Four removals men have started loading up. They've been kicking up the dust and stomping on the wooden floor, panting and cracking jokes. For the first time in years the worm-eaten wardrobes are carried into the sunlight. As is the large mirror, which now carves out a strangely shaped piece of the garden. The piano is next, then chairs, shelves, boxes...

It's all going to a warehouse in Bratislava, on the other side of the Danube in Petržalka. I've rented some storage place there until I figure out what to do with it all. Peter didn't want anything, and neither did Tina.

Very soon only the empty house will be left. The empty shell of a dead snail.

The mad, maddening Zuzana had stuck it out with Vojto although he kept drifting away. His image seemed to be shrinking in the picture, as if in perspective he appeared smaller and smaller until he almost fitted into the palm of her hand, tiny and distant at the same time. She bore him a child, her second.

After 1990, she managed to make her mark at a magazine where over the years, step by step, she rose up the ladder and it seemed that by the time she reached retirement age she would climb high enough to feel a sense of satisfaction with her career.

But the beautiful dream vanished, as if by the stroke of a magic wand. She was over fifty and the old tradition linking a worker's value to increasing age was suddenly replaced by a cult of youth. Suddenly she was too experienced – after being told for years, with a smile, that she had to wait a little because she lacked experience. Like many women of her age at the time of the revolution, she found herself with a chunk of her life torn out, wandering in a no-man's land, often with a bottle of wine or vodka and frequently contemplating taking an overdose or putting a razor blade to her wrists in a hot bath. Women like her were no longer needed.

Vojto no longer needed Zuzana either. And just as he'd once been afraid to admit to me that he was living with her, he didn't dare to tell me for a long time that he'd left her. He had a lot of stamina but he could no longer take her drunken babbling, aggressive shouting and the bottles stashed away in cupboards. So he upped and left her. For another woman – as was his way. The world is full of women, after all.

His latest conquest, too, just came walking into a room or he passed her in the street, his eyes lighting up when he got a whiff of her perfume. Well, actually, he found her, abandoned and attractive, in one of the flats where he woke up one morning. So he just stayed.

According to Tina, after Mother left Father, they continued to talk on the phone for a while. The phone would ring and Father would pick up.

"Hello…?"

Silence greeted him at the other end. He put the phone down and dialled Mother's number.

"Why didn't you say anything?"

"I had nothing to say."

"So why did you call?"

"Mind your own business!"

After his hearing deteriorated there was no point phoning him, he wouldn't have heard it anyway. And soon he wasn't able to hear the phone ringing either. He stayed locked in his own silence.

Utter silence.

Our mother, on the other hand, as she grew old was like an overripe pear – whichever way you turn it, it will go brown. Soft and squishy all over.

She gave her tomcat the name Alfonz, instead of the customary name Ikebana, which she used to give to all cats, regardless of gender. Alfonz's predecessor, for example, was Ikebana VIII. This time, however, she decided that enough was enough and instead of taking number nine she picked Father's name. As she told me several times – she'd done it on impulse, without realising its significance. She just liked the name.

She spent entire days in bed, moaning about everything, going on and on about how unwell she was, and chain-smoking. She said the damned tomcat had exactly the same character as Father. Including his favourite food and foibles. She would watch the cat, and depending on its behaviour would predict what its namesake was up to at that moment.

472

Whenever I went to see her – which, admittedly, wasn't very often – I envied the animal that could just live its life, without any emotional ties to relatives (who knows if it would even recognize its parents) or responsibilities. All it had to do was exist and that was enough to earn it food and shelter. I realised we give the animals of the *Felis domesticus* and *Canis lupus familiaris* species much more love than we give the members of our own *Homo sapiens*.

When Father died, the cat fell gravely ill. It could barely walk and vomited tapeworms. And soon it died.

All her life, my sister couldn't stand Mother, so it surprised me that she ended up being uncannily like her. I came to see Tina in the flat she and Trevor had just bought in Bratislava and found her lying in bed fully dressed. She smoked throughout our conversation. Just like Mother. And just like Mother and equally ineffectually, she tried to blow the smoke the other way, away from my face. If she absolutely couldn't avoid getting out of bed and going out, she would prepare meticulously, always changing her mind at the last minute. She started to collect porcelain figures obsessively, the kind she had hated years ago. (I remember she once swore to take a hammer to Mother's collection at night when nobody was looking.) Tina's flat began to resemble Mother's and I thought it was just as well that she wasn't aware of it. Like it or not, we all turn into our parents.

Mother used to tell Tina: "Stop laughing like that! You look so ugly; why don't you do something to your hair?" And most often: "You're stupid, you're so stupid!"

And now I heard Tina say to her daughter Jenny: "Why do you laugh like that? Stop it! You look so ugly; why don't you do something about your hair!"

Her daughter Jenny was secretly planning to leave her mother as soon as she could although she wasn't yet sure how. Just like Tina years ago. And just like Tina, she would later wish she could make peace with her mother. But it was not to be.

At least Tina had finally had a proper talk with Peter. Mother always used to hold him up as an example, which drove her mad. Now they fell into each other's arms. Each was wary of upsetting the other and was on their best behaviour whenever they met. I found it sickening.

473

One of their meetings took place when Tina's Trevor and his band, the Joker's Smokers, played the Bratislava Jazz Days.

My second wife Ingrid mastered the sophisticated art of emotional withdrawal and the cold shoulder, and trained me to patter up to her like a puppy begging to be stroked. A puppy that will do anything for her.

I was so smitten that before going to sleep I imagined serenading her with *Bona nocte, mea amata. Bene dormire. Good night, my dear…* In Latin. Or in any other language for that matter.

Sometimes it all got too much and I would have my sweet revenge in the form of the occasional passionate secret encounter with a certain Nataša.

Ingrid and I often went for walks in the Brežany park.

"I must have been a warm breeze in a previous life – I can sense its profound sadness," she said.

"Why not a cold breeze?"

"Because that is rough and disagreeable. But there's something profoundly sad about a warm breeze. Whenever I feel it, it makes me want to die." Ingrid had plenty of reasons to be unhappy. Before she met me she had lived for ten years with the director of a publishing house where her poetry appeared. They split up after the revolution and he moved on. His secretary – who had always been friendly, generous with smiles and praise – sent Ingrid a fat envelope marked: Found this while clearing up the office. Inside was a bunch of scathing opinions and reviews of Ingrid's poetry. The secretary must have been collecting them for years.

5.

Father was a collector of deaf men. It started with Beethoven. Goya came next.

A doctor to the end, he informed me that Francisco must have been poisoned by the lead in the paint, which he used to apply to the canvas with his fingers and thumbs, dipping them into the little cups and containers until he developed some kind of brain disease, which led to loss of hearing, depression and even madness.

"Burnt Sienna, Prussian blue, Cyprus green, chrome green, Windsor green, Havana black, ivory black, bone black..." Father silently mouthed the names of colours.

It struck me that Bony and I were actually visiting the Prado in Madrid vicariously on Father's behalf, as he was no longer able to come himself. That is why we made such a big detour on our expedition with his ashes. In a way, he was with us on this journey.

Our tourist group followed an elderly museum guide. With his eccentric moustache and suit he looked as if he had stepped straight out of a Velázquez painting, rather than one by Goya. The restored Black Paintings were displayed over two floors, with scattered rays of sun shining on them through the gallery's high windows.

The guide's commentary proved too much for my English, which I had picked up from songs, and his thick Spanish accent confused me even more, so Bony had to whisper a translation:

"At the age of forty-five Francisco Goya fell gravely ill and although he later recovered, he was left profoundly deaf. It was this handicap and his deteriorating mental health that drove him into increasing isolation, causing existential anxiety as well as recurrent episodes of mental illness during which he heard voices and suffered nightmares. When his wife died he moved to a country house near Madrid, now known as the House of the Deaf Man – ironically, it had got its name from its previous owner. It was here, between 1820 and 1824, that Goya painted the fourteen mysterious and spine-chilling painting while having a relationship with the young and lovely Leocadia Weiss, whom he was teaching to paint. He was seventy-five by the time he finished the paintings. It was not Goya who called them the Black Series; they received their name from art historians."

I went right up to the paintings and then stepped away again, examining them closely. *Saturn Devouring his Son*, *The Witches' Sabbath* and *Doña Leocadia Zorilla* were exhibited on the first floor. On the wall facing *The Witches' Sabbath* was *The Fear of Flying* and to its left, *Two Old People Eating*. On the first floor, diagonally opposite each other, were the *Half-Submerged Dog* and *The Reading*, with *The Fates* between them.

The guide continued:

"Scholars consider the black paintings an extreme manifestation of the growing lack of understanding and alienation between the artist and society of his day. Goya painted them directly onto the plaster walls of the house he lived in. He did not expect anyone would see the pictures and probably did not want anyone to. He regarded them as private images that had sprung from the depths of his soul. This seems to be borne out by the fact that he suddenly took to wall painting instead of painting with oils on canvas. He created the scenes in great haste, using broad strokes with a thick brush and a variety of spatulas and sponges. However, he made a technical mistake that more or less doomed the wall frescoes. He applied oil paints onto plaster, making things worse by drawing in chalk – oil and chalk are not supposed to be combined. Seventy years after their creation and long after the artist's death, a special technique was needed to transfer the paintings to canvas, after which they were donated to the Spanish government."

Father had often thought about this and disapproved. He believed Goya would have been outraged to see the paintings exhibited at the Prado. Things that are meant to stay hidden should not be "rescued" and put on public display. Particularly since the House of the Deaf Man itself, with the original paintings, had since been torn down.

"They should have been left there!" he fulminated, drawing me into an argument. "It was an intrusion into his privacy!" he concluded implacably, and stood up abruptly to indicate the conversation about Goya was over.

Part 7

The Reading

1.

This particular painting, *The Reading,* also known by various other names, shows a group of men against a dark backdrop. They are all bending over looking at a book except for one, whose gaze is directed upwards.

This was the position in which Father used to examine the X-ray of a rib cage or lungs.

Holding a cigarette in his other hand and exhaling clouds of smoke.

Every clock in this house shows a different time.

The furniture is slowly disappearing and before time itself has also evaporated, my eyes wander over to the wooden staircase leading to the attic. I see Vojto sitting there again, all by himself. He likes this place. He has sneaked in quietly, as usual.

Father, who has always reprimanded his patients for smoking, is standing by the window with his after-lunch cigarette. He gives a start at the sound of Vojto's voice.

"You're a smoker, doctor?"

Father turns around.

"One cigarette won't do you any harm, my friend. But you have to be careful not to inhale too much – you just exhale from the corner of your mouth, like this, see…!"

"Are you serious?"

"Yes. But it does have some health benefits, too. For instance, because I smoke I'm never ill. Whenever I start sniffling or coughing, I just light up and that's it. I feel better right away."

I've heard this story many times from my best friend Vojto, who later died of lung cancer.

I doubt that Father would have put it quite like that.

2.

Peter was among the first to help organise rallies in support of the petition *For Slovakia's Sovereignty,* initiated by Matica slovenská,

Slovakia's most venerable cultural institution, now in the vanguard of the new nationalism. The news rather surprised me because I remembered that back in the 1980s he often told me how much he liked his trips to Prague, that it was like a breath of fresh air that helped him escape from the mustiness of Slovakia. But that's what my brother was like. Like Ikebana's fur, he would pick up everything that floated past.

Vojto gleefully drew my attention to Peter's articles in the nationalist press, the weekly *New Slovak* and later in the daily *Republika*. Overflowing with new-found patriotic fervour he presented learned theories about who was a genuine Slovak and who wasn't – he had a good eye for renegades and cosmopolitans, just as in the past he had never failed to spot a Trotskyite, right-wing opportunist or reactionary. He just had a sixth sense for it.

As 1992 drew to a close and Czechoslovakia was about to be divided, some people expressed their disapproval by singing the Czech national anthem on New Year's Eve. Slovakia started again from scratch. But then it's something we're used to. This country has had several new starts so we've had plenty of practice. We're a nation of perpetual beginners, you see. Nothing here lasts forever. We must crush our predecessors and then it's back to square one.

We made a fresh start back in 1918, in 1938, then again in 1945, then in 1948, in 1968 and again in 1969; we had a brand new start in 1989 and another in 1993, then in 1994 and yet another in the same year, and again in 1998, after Vladimír Mečiar lost the election… Acute memory loss is our national malaise. And this is what makes it possible for the same people to keep popping up again and again, pretending they had stuck on new heads. Or behaving just like before and sticking new heads on everyone else. Whichever is easier.

We are a fascinating nation of eternal infants, eternal toddlers who keep going through the same children's diseases: mumps, scarlet fever, measles, rubella and then all over again. Here you are, here's your rattle and your bib. Fingers are not for eating! We keep learning to speak all over again. We keep having to learn to walk all over again.

And we always make sure our tracks are properly covered up.

The statues gracing Brežany's main square kept changing, although the material of which they were made remained the same. National hero Milan Rastislav Štefánik's bronze statue was fashioned by a gentleman with an insufficiently Aryan-sounding name so in due course he had to be replaced by Hlinka, who, in turn, was replaced by Gottwald, to be briefly replaced by Hlinka again who, in turn, was again replaced by Štefánik.

The game of musical chairs came to an end when the statue was sent for restoration, and a huge wide billboard was erected in the middle of the square, its red and white letters proclaiming: *TESCO, 1.2 km*. The sign pointed in the direction of the mushrooming satellite suburbs, the new ghost towns. Silent, uninhabited houses reminiscent of Potemkin villages. Pastel colours, identical roofs, lawns without a single insect… and silence. With very few lights on at night. The houses looked as if they had been built by some sinister creatures hostile to humans, intent on driving mankind off the face of the earth.

On the mayor's orders ornamental paving was laid around the billboard, giving the square the same appearance as every other square. Smiling Chinese and Vietnamese tradesmen pitched their tents here during the traditional Brežany annual fair.

Mário Tóth leased the Tower after the Velvet Revolution revolution and turned it into an English-style pub, making a point of featuring the English word "pub" in its name. It has the same meaning as its Slovak equivalent, *krčma*, except that it is a syllable shorter and much easier to pronounce, particularly when, after six beers, you're trying to explain to you pals over the phone where to find you. Vojto and I went for a drink there for the first time, and soon for the last time. In the meantime the Tower Pub "went down like a Led Zeppelin" to quote Mário's favourite drummer with The Who – their music played in the pub from morning till night.

It took Mário a while to figure out that his waiters had set up a parallel book-keeping system and that they were selling their own drink to his customers. Trusting and naïve, Mário never checked on them. There were days when the pub was bursting at the seams, yet the takings were dismal. He didn't last long.

On his last night he invited all his friends, including Vojto and me, to finish off his bar stocks. Mário walked from one table to another, smiling and cracking jokes – and then popped upstairs to his office. A little while later he was back, cracked a few more jokes, laughed and disappeared again.

"I bet he keeps going up to play Russian roulette," I whispered to Vojto. "He loads the gun with a single bullet and puts it to his head. He pulls the trigger. Click. Nothing. He puts it away, sighs and goes back to the pub. Half an hour later he's back in the office and tries again. Click. Nothing happens so he goes back, tells a few jokes, gives someone a slap on the back. Then he goes off again."

Vojto roared with laughter and said he absolutely had to ask Mário about this next time he came back.

Thirty minutes passed and there was no sign of him. An hour later he still wasn't back. Two hours went by.

Then his horrified wife came in and said he had done it. "There's blood all over the wall," she said.

One day, I went for a walk on the Slavín Hill in the villa district of Bratislava, and on my way back I ran into Peter. He was just coming out of the mansion to which he'd once taken me for a party. We stopped for a chat on the street.

He had sad news. The artist who had owned the mansion had died. The poor chap had cirrhosis of the liver. Chained to a rock, Prometheus-like, he had his liver eaten away by daily shots of vodka, only for it to grow back by the morning (Father used to say the liver regenerates very fast, provided, of course, you're not even faster.) Day after day he would await his 60-degrees-proof bird of prey.

"A really sad story," Peter said. "But never mind, life goes on."

He explained that the artist's wife had moved out of the mansion after the son of the original pre-war owner got it back when property was returned after the fall of communism, but he wasn't able to keep up the payments on it so he sold it to a friend of Peter's, a former top communist party official. This man was now an entrepreneur, like most of Peter's friends, the erstwhile communist aristocracy. Their children have the money and the contacts, they own restaurants and are having the time of their lives.

Peter waxed lyrical about the mansion, which still contained all the original prints and fine pictures on the walls. Nothing had changed. The turrets, the rugs, the drawing rooms were the same. Only the former studio had been cleared out, the palettes and easels thrown out and the room turned into a reception hall. A kind of bar.

482

He would show me one day, he said. And could I give Father his regards – he was too busy now but was sure to stop by Brežany and drop in.

Sure.

I'm not my brother's keeper, to quote Cain once again.

3.

"Leocadia, please…!" The blanket had slipped off Father's lap and he was cold.

"My name is Mária."

Father could no longer be left alone in the house so I found him a carer, splitting the cost with Peter. Her job was to keep the crumbling household running as far as possible.

She was able to communicate with Father as he mastered sign language and learned to read her beautiful lips (they really were), provided she spoke slowly. Very slowly.

Father's words immediately conjured up the image in Goya's painting, a dark-haired young woman in a black dress leaning on an unmade bed and looking at something outside the picture.

Mária was propped against the unmade bed, just like Leocadia (to whom, apart from her clothes and hair she bore an uncanny resemblance), watching the aged owner of the house, seated in an armchair. She was trying to figure out what he wanted. She came closer, picked up the blanket from the floor and after tenderly covering him up, she continued making the bed.

"Leocadia…!"

"My name is Mária!"

She couldn't understand why he couldn't remember her name. She even wrote it down on a piece of paper and waved it at him when necessary. But it was no use.

She kept telling him that in spite of her youthful looks she had a twelve-year-old son, and Father received this information with the same surprise and interest every time. Her son was a talented violinist and had already begun to make a little money. He played at funerals and weddings in Brežany.

483

Funerals pay better, perhaps because death is forever. It's a better investment. So the mourners are more generous.

Father fantasised about starting a new life. He was going to learn French and to play the piano.

"I've always wanted to play the piano. Do you remember?"

"No, I don't," I said.

"This is the best time for it; I have plenty of time on my hands."

I just shrugged and looked out of the window through my little bubble, my cat's eye.

Within a few days the trees had shed all their leaves, dozens of them ripped off by a single powerful gust of wind, and before long the ravens arrived from the north. They would perch on the vineyards' wiring like some ominous dark beings, or navigate clumsily among the houses in the grey fog. In the cemetery, they strutted around like dignified funeral guests, every now and then dipping their beaks into the soil, newly hardened by frost.

Our garden still contained a few tangled clumps of greenery that had long smothered any traces of man-made order. The last remaining roses mingled with thistles and elderflowers that exploded into fragrant blossom in the spring and then covered the ground with tiny intruders, their purple-black berries. Some of them have taken root and their ubiquitous branches will sprout next year. I heard that the guilt-ridden Judas had hanged himself on an elder tree. His ears sprout from time to time on trunks of old elder trees: the fungus, known as Judas's ear, really does resemble supple black cartilage, an earlobe of soft skin. A mysterious black creature hidden inside the tree. Judas.

I watched martens cowering in the tall grass sending signals to one another as they prowled about, edging towards the neighbour's chicken hatch.

Father didn't see or hear any of this.

He was sitting in his armchair with the TV bawling. Assorted scenes of demonstrations and military conflicts flickered on the screen, interspersed, without any transition, with throngs of naked people who had gathered somewhere trying to break some kind of Guinness record.

Father shook his head. None of this made any sense to him.

The nudists were followed by the news of a lunatic who claimed to have seen extraterrestrials. As evidence he'd sent in a photo showing his house with a circle around the window from which he'd observed them.

"God must be laughing his head off at the sight of his creation," mumbled Father, turning his back to the TV set, preferring to watch the wall instead.

He fell asleep almost instantly.

I salute you, wonderful blue glow of living rooms at night! I salute you, the opium electric that befuddles mankind. I salute you, television, for preventing your viewers from getting up to mischief because they're bored and have nothing better to do. I salute you, the sweet trance to which criminals, layabouts and violent people succumb, that switches off the brain, dampens dangerous passions and offers distraction. I salute you, oh television, I salute you!

Had you arrived earlier, I am sure history would have taken a different turn.

When he wasn't sitting in his armchair, Father roamed the house like an overgrown toddler in a nappy. Where's everyone gone? He kept looking for people. Everything seemed to have suddenly become desolate.

Objects that had served him all his life suddenly lost their purpose. Sometimes he had no idea what they were for and couldn't find the right words. There were moments when he hated this house that had become his prison, even though he'd built it in his own image many years ago. The house used to be him.

He claimed that there were intruders in the house. He was scared it would be invaded through doors reflected in mirrors. Mária and I had to cover the mirrors up. That didn't stop him believing that someone kept pushing under the door small notes with ominous, unspeakable messages.

I was the only person allowed to cut his toenails. Toenails and hair have always reminded me of time stashed away, insects sealed in amber.

Touching Father's feet felt banal and very intimate at the same time.

Bits of hard toenail would shoot off in all directions and stay hidden in corners for many years. I have found some over the past

485

couple of days. Lodged under the carpet and behind wardrobes. I used to get on all fours to try and pick them up but never managed to find them all.

Father would try to help, whispering feebly:

"Here's a bit… And there's another…!"

He sat on his bed motionless, staring into the void and murmuring:

"The person of interest maintained suspicious contacts with former insurgents, who harbour hostile sentiments towards our system, as I learned mainly from his son Vojtech, who is a friend of my son's. They visit him under the pretence of playing card games. The person of interest has further told me that his wife is prone to fits of hysteria and excruciating headaches. I promised to visit him again with my son, who also accompanied me on this occasion. My handler instructed me to bring him a small gift on his name day and, if possible, secure an invitation to his party." By now I was beginning to understand what he was talking about.

But I didn't know how to tell him that I knew.

The removals men are loading up the last item, the huge astronomical telescope from the count's manor house. It had been gathering dust in the attic for years. I only brought it down last night.

Incredibly enough, it never occurred to us to use it to look at the stars.

Until last night. I lugged the telescope down to the terrace and waited for the moon to slip out from behind the clouds. The divine peep show, an opening in the heavenly dome through which someone is observing us. That's what Peter used to tell me when I was little. And I believed him. I believed every word he said.

I couldn't help myself; the dark lunar seas reminded me of a face. Father's face.

This is beginning to drive me insane. It's high time for me to leave this place.

4.

General managers of Slovakia's state TV rotated like statues of the apostles in an astronomical clock. A director would appear in the little window, pull a few grimaces, bow and disappear. The next one would pop out, scratch his head, smile and disappear too, immediately followed by a third ... His predecessors would be immediately forgotten by ordinary mortals.

As far as I could tell, the impact of this rotation on the goings-on inside the TV's high-rise building could be summed up as follows: an enthusiastic start, usually involving statements along the lines of "You are all incompetent idiots – I'll show you how to make television!" was followed by gasps of amazement a month later as the hopeful saviour discovered that trying to fight the mysterious machinery is futile, and a sense of resignation and depression eventually culminated in the realisation that all he could do was get as much as possible out of it for himself and that Madame de Pompadour had been quite right when she said: *Après moi le déluge!*

An illustrious director who had made dozens of films lamented in a TV interview about the persecution he'd had to suffer under the previous regime.

Over at the Tower pub in Brežany, Vojto commented:

"People like these brag in their memoirs of having bravely stood up to the communists. I have no doubt that at the end of a successful and exhausting day of filming, back in their villa or an enormous posh flat, they had their dinner, skimmed a few newspaper headlines, sighed and said to their wives: 'Fuck Husák... !' Then they went to bed because they had to be back at the studio early the next day. I don't blame them for wanting to live a comfortable life. There's nothing wrong with that. I just wish they didn't go on about it."

After toying with the idea for years I decided now was the time to finally create something that would really count instead of the claptrap I'd been producing for years. Looking back, all I could see were a few attempts that had failed hopelessly.

I was going to make a full-length documentary on the ŠtB,

487

featuring interviews not only with officers and operatives but also agents, informants, custodians of safe houses as well as ordinary people whose lives have been destroyed. I would supplement it with hidden camera footage, surveillance recordings, photographs – the very thought chilled me to the marrow – and I would be the first to bring all this to light.

Juraj, my cousin Filip's son, started dabbling in these issues when he began to practise law. The first time I went to see him was in the spring of 2002 – one year before Father died. At that point I wasn't sure how to go about it or where to begin and just wanted to establish what material was available.

I started looking at the ŠtB archives, made available by the Institute of National Remembrance. After my third or fourth visit I decided to enter my own name into the system and was amazed to find myself listed under the category CI, a candidate for informant. Juraj explained that this just meant that they had shown preliminary interest in my person, and it was nothing to worry about. There was no mention of Peter Trnovský in the files – Juraj said that as far as he knew, high-ranking party officials were never formally recruited or registered. My sister's name – negative. Then I tried Father's name. Mainly because of the human bones puzzle. I wasn't getting anywhere near solving it, and was clutching at razors (in this case, it seems a more appropriate expression than the proverbial straws). Soon I stumbled across the first clue.

I was staring at the words: Alfonz Trnovský, labelled AGENT.

That night I couldn't get to sleep – my first impulse was to get hold of his file, one of those that fortunately (or unfortunately) wasn't destroyed in 1989. Fortunately – unfortunately.

I realised I had no right to produce a documentary of this kind.

5.

Vojto had spent his whole life drifting about and eking out a living. When his old Fiat gave up the ghost and he found a replacement in the classifieds, the only thing that mattered to him was that it should be cheap and that the engine should start. The owner lived in a block of flats in the Bratislava suburb of Dúbravka.

Vojto was sitting on a worn-out sofa in the most ordinary living room in the world looking at a ceramic stag on the mantelpiece. He felt awkward under the distrustful stare of a fifty-year-old woman in a white blouse and brown plaited skirt, her hair discreetly streaked with the first signs of grey. She took great care not to look Vojto in the eye. She didn't know what to do with her hands while they waited in silence. They heard rustling from the other room. Vojto fidgeted with his cup of undrinkable coffee.

"It's a 1984 model," said the balding man in a baggy old jumper as he brought in a pile of papers.

"Here's the paperwork…." he added, smoothing out a bent corner that kept stubbornly curling, trying to return to its original shape.

"And here's the… the MOT certificate."

Vojto started examining the papers. The man and the woman watched him intently. The woman sighed. He looked up. Hesitantly, the man placed a crumpled orange notebook on the table and pushed it towards Vojto.

"This is where I noted all the… all the… Actually, everything about it… Right from the start."

Vojto reached for the notebook and started leafing through it under the man's inquisitive gaze.

Our little Janka was born today… 325 kilometres. 20 April… Janka has lost a tooth… Carburettor repair, oil change… Košice and back. Janka's wedding… Followed by illegible numbers. At the end the word DEADLINE and today's date had been scribbled in a shaky untrained hand below a thick red line.

"It's been with us through the best years of our lives…" the man said in a low voice. The woman pressed her lips together and stared at the floor.

"If you wish… you can take this as well."

"You really want to give him the notebook as well?" the woman piped up suddenly. This was the first time she had spoken since Vojto arrived. Her voice was low and a little hoarse.

She stared hard at her husband. He wouldn't take his eyes off the stranger who'd come about the ad.

"It's all or nothing…!" he said over his shoulder, trying to sound casual.

Five minutes later they stood by the window silently watching the red Skoda slowly splutter out of the car park and disappear forever around the corner. The man turned around and slowly walked back to the table where there lay a 5,000 Slovak crown note.

General Štefánik gazed out from the banknote, looking serious and dreaming of distant stars, islands in the desert and an endless expanse of azure ocean.

Under the influence of his new wife Vojto took up painting. He had no interest in keeping his canvases so he organised an exhibition in the corridors of his block. It lasted one day, a Saturday (in keeping with our old adage that a collection of poetry should be published in a single copy and a play ought to be performed without an audience, if at all possible). I got there at the last minute. Vojto and his wife showed me around the exhibits, up and down the stairways and around corners. We met some neighbours who admired Vojto's landscapes and still lifes. I said it was wonderful to have such supportive neighbours. Like this nice old lady.

Zdena, Vojto's fourth (and last) wife frowned:

"You think she's nice? She squealed on a young family back in 1982, claiming that a three-bedroom flat was too big for them. They were evicted and she lives there alone now. – Oh, hello, how are you?"

One floor below a man with a camera was lingering by a painting of a blue banana.

"He looks like a professional photographer."

"He tormented his wife to death, she jumped from a third-floor window. Their children have run away. He's a violent thug. I'm surprised he's even showed up."

"Our lovely neighbours," Vojto said with a smile. "Let's go in."

Zdena was a cultural sociologist and cat lover. There were cats sprawled and wandering all around their flat. Cats of both genders. The females were named Fulla, Benka and Mucha, after famous Slovak and Czech painters, while the toms were named after composers Cikker, Suchoň and Schneider. Cikker was the largest, Suchoň was rather emaciated, Mucha was smarmy and annoying, constantly begging for food and asking to be stroked. Another painter, Galanda, didn't live long and had a fine burial under the plane tree in the back yard.

In his dotage Vojto fathered another child. Zdena was twenty-five years younger and was raising the child like one of her cats.

Vojto and Zdena smoked a cigarette by the window in the sweltering summer kitchen. Our T-shirts clung to our bodies, the courtyard echoed to the sound of children and Schneider and Fulla were lazing about on the windowsill. It was getting dark and their baby was asleep. He slept almost all the time and at the most unlikely hours, like the cats.

Zdena was in her element, elaborating in great detail how everything in this world could be seen as part of the creative process – from rudeness, withdrawal, inability to communicate, bizarre behaviour to misanthropy… The only thing that matters is the outcome. People who are not creative have no right to be eccentric, patronizing and difficult. She gave as an example the son of a famous musician who lacked talent. Both father and son were notorious for their terrible manners – but in the father's case this was justifiable because he was a genius who had created something powerful and uplifting.

Vojto knew this monologue by heart; he could have recited it himself. Instead he just smiled and topped up my glass. As a recovered alcoholic he still saw everything from the vantage point of alcohol – everything good was like wine: you had to distil the essence of everything, and some people could never agree whether a glass was half-full or half-empty. Unlike his fellow sufferers, who mostly turn into holy warriors against this "scourge of humanity", he enjoyed drinking vicariously: he wouldn't touch a drop himself but was generous in topping up other people's glasses and encouraged everyone to drink their fill.

During his worst period, when for days on end he stayed marinated in vodka like a lizard prepared for dissection, he left his wife, moved back to Brežany and virtually lived at the Tower. The new owner had converted the cellar into a games room with fruit machines, with constantly blinking lights in all colours of the rainbow and little lemons and oranges to encourage players who had lost all hope: "This time you'll be lucky, you'll hit the jackpot, you'll get rich, come on, play just one more time, one last time. If you don't, you'll be missing the chance of a lifetime! Untold wealth awaits! Don't be scared!" The rest of the time he spent trying to scrounge money off anyone within a ten-kilometre radius.

"Adam," he sighed. "Life feels sort of bland these days."

He showed me a letter he'd just received:

Shop security has been keeping an eye on you for some time, and we have repeatedly drawn your attention to the disorderly conduct you have demonstrated in our hypermarket.

We have recorded the following specific incidents: on 12 May at 5:30 p.m. you wound up all the alarm clocks in the clock department, setting them all to the same time, 5:40 p.m., which resulted in all the alarms going off simultaneously. On 16 June you removed a bottle of ketchup from the grocery section and squeezed out considerable quantities of it on the toilet floor between washbasins and cubicles. On 25 June you hid among hangers and shouted at female customers shopping for coats: "Please take me as well…!" You smeared yogurt all over your face and when confronted by the cashier at register no. 12, you claimed it was an ointment for treating psoriasis. Having entered the white goods storage area without authorisation, you intentionally set off the fire alarm with a lighted cigarette.

Since you have failed to desist from these activities, in spite of repeated warnings on the part our hypermarket's security service, claiming by way of justification that your wife forced you to accompany her on shopping trips and that you were bored, we have reached the following decision: both you and your wife are banned from entering our premises for the duration of one year. There is no appeal against this decision.

Vojto fell gravely ill but didn't take his condition seriously. He shrugged off the persistent coughing, didn't seem to feel any pain and ignored the fact that he was short of breath and was coughing up blood. His mother, Mrs Roško, thought the doctors were too non-committal and woolly, and she came up with a solution.

Enter an old acquaintance of hers: the aged but still dapper and well-preserved Rehor Kohút in his old-fashioned suit, off-white shirt and waistcoat. He walked into Vojto's flat wearing his indispensable pointed shoes and walking stick.

He advertised his services in the tabloids, and photographs accompanying his ads for long-distance treatment showed him directing the fierce gaze of his half-closed eyes and the palms of his hands at the reader. During personal consultations he would concentrate deeply and move his hand up and down above his prostrate customer. Next he would hold his hand over a candle and show the client that his palm had gone black, from drawing out the bad energy. He synchronised chakras by attaching a tiny computer to his clients' bodies by means of electrodes. He claimed that by using a certain frequency he was able to cure a certain gentleman's haemorrhoids – they disappeared completely after a few days of treatment. Another device, allegedly developed by NASA, consisted of two electrodes, which produced a whistling sound when placed on the body, indicating the location of an unhealthy nidus.

"He has diagnosed heart attacks, ulcers, diabetes and multiple sclerosis – that's how good his equipment is!" Vojto's mother said over the phone.

"Isn't it just a load of baloney?"

"I believe in him – he has an engineering degree after all! He told me so himself."

"Really?"

"He's been mainly working abroad. His phone number isn't listed, he only gives it to select customers. And even then you have to let it ring five or six times before he answers. He's very hard to get hold of. But I've managed it! He said he remembers me from before the war."

Rehor Kohút listened to Vojto and felt him all over. Then he opened a smart alligator skin bag and took out a fancy little box containing a fine white powder. He explained this "medium" was a highly effective extract of rare Egyptian herbs and he had to charge eight thousand crowns for it.

He had proof – a previous client whom he'd cured of terminal cancer. The cancer had spread through the man's entire body, he had been put on a battery of the most powerful drugs and eventually the doctors had given up on him. Then the fellow came to see Kohút who cured him completely.

So Vojto bought the powder. It cost him every penny he had.

Later he heard that Mr Kohút was often seen at the crematorium in Bratislava enquiring about the content of uncollected urns.

Meanwhile I was feverishly studying photocopied papers in Father's file. I was determined to tell Vojto about it on that summer evening as I was sitting in his kitchen with the cat Benka in my lap and a litre of wine in my head. I decided to tell him what I'd grandly dubbed "the truth about my father" although later I had to admit that things are rarely black and white.

But his wife Zdena jabbered on about art and geniuses, human character and works of art and I couldn't pluck up the courage. Every time I went to the toilet I tossed a coin. I kept getting heads. No. No. No. I so much wanted to tell him and kept waiting for a damned tails, a YES, but it wasn't coming. It was unbelievable.

Eventually Zdena put out her umpteenth cigarette and went to check on the baby, who had woken up in the middle of the night and started crying.

That's when I told him everything.

Vojto was shocked but he made light of it all. He said he understood and that he'd been through the same thing himself. I was still his best friend and couldn't be held responsible for my father's sins.

When I left in the early hours, he gave me a hug.

A week later Vojto suddenly showed up at my door, handed me his onyx from the Countess's earrings and left without a word. That was the last time I saw him.

Two months later he died of lung cancer.

Just the other day, as I was sitting in a café in the centre of Bratislava, I thought I caught sight of a familiar face among the cheerful crowd of shoppers and gossiping folk. A contented, prosperous pensioner with glasses, in a suit... He was smiling and chatting to the waitress. He asked her what pastry she would recommend and said the coffee was excellent... After complimenting her on her perfume, he left a generous tip.

I looked at him again and recognized a retired general, the most powerful ŠtB man before the Velvet Revolution, the organisation's all-powerful boss. These days nobody blames him for anything, he basks in the sun and greets friends he passes in the street. He has become a successful entrepreneur, wealthy and influential.

He walks down the street without a care in the world and the sun shines brightly on him.

Part 8

A manola, doña Leocadia Zorilla

1.

La Leocadia in Goya's painting has always reminded me of the Grim Reaper in a dark robe, propped against a bed, as if waiting until your life's work is done and he can cosy up to you saying tenderly: "It's time we had a talk, my dear!"

Every clock in this house shows a different time.

Actually, there was only one time left for Father. Everything merged into a single shapeless mass, in which the past, present and future blurred into one another and everything was happening simultaneously.

"Where is SS-Hauptsturmführer Atlas? We have to operate on Captain Roško without delay!"

Here's Monako, smiling from a dark corner:

"I'm just a lowly pawn, a tiny cog in the machine, I don't really have anything to do with this but I can offer you a word of advice."

And here's Puškár, standing behind him, whispering into his ear, unseen:

"The God of love has granted me a woman…!"

For me the house had turned into something between bedlam and hell. I hated going back there. I felt anxious amid the decline and destruction since the process of disintegration could apparently go on forever.

"I heard you fell over yesterday," said Mária.

"I did, but not here, it was in Nitra."

"But you haven't been to Nitra."

"That was a long time ago."

"Oh, I see."

And then, all of a sudden, Father started running away.

Every time it happened I had to think hard where to look for him. It usually depended on what he had been talking about the day before and what memory had caught up with him. I was concerned about him as if he were a small child who might get up to some mischief or into harm's way.

Once I found him where Vojto's house used to stand. Wearing only his robe, Father was about to step into a busy road, and passing cars hooted at him.

On another occasion I didn't find him until late at night. I drove up and down the streets of Brežany but there was no sign of him anywhere. I was beginning to despair when I saw him walking down the pavement outside the Golden Stag hotel, which had by now changed beyond recognition.

I jammed on the brakes and ran up to him.

"Dad, where have you been?"

"What do you mean, where I've been? I went for a walk."

I hit the roof, grabbed him by the hand and dragged him to the car. I had to give him a shove because he refused to get in. I felt terribly sorry and guilty afterwards. But we no longer had a language in common.

Things couldn't go on like that anymore. Once he fell down the stairs when Mária was out of sight. He suffered multiple fractures and needed full-time medical care.

It was time to take him to a hospice.

2.

My only distraction in those endless days drowning in time came from What's-her-face – everyone called her that because she could no longer remember anyone's name, they had all dissolved, disappeared into the ether, – and when she talked about someone she would refer to them as What's-his-face or What's-her-face. She used to run up and down the corridors of the hospice like a Fury, opening every door and incessantly asking questions.

I came to see Father and found him slumped in a chair in the hospice's tiled bathroom, wearing hospital pyjamas. As he sat there waiting, with stooped shoulders, his face waxen and his eyes faded, he looked like a corpse. There was only the tiniest spark of life left in him.

His tousled grey hair was being cut. Samson losing his strength along with his hair.

"My eyes have been watering lately."

"But you're crying, Father…"

I was the only person who ever came to see him. Everyone else always had a ready excuse as to why they couldn't come or what had held them up.

A huge procession was passing by the hospice building. May 9 had been declared the Day of Europe and a medieval fair was being held in Brežany's main square and the surrounding streets. Slovakia had just signed the accession treaty to the European Union and the local authorities wanted to make a show of marking the occasion.

There were actors in masks walking on stilts, and brash music from drums, flutes and pipes. The reflections of the masks, some funny, some scary, flickered in the windows. The actors were sweating profusely under their costumes.

The day had started with a drizzle, which gradually gave way to glorious sunshine. People were sitting in cafés, strolling in the streets, pausing to admire the floats. They were alive.

The last person in the procession was a scythe-wielding Grim Reaper in a hood.

The windows in Father's first-floor room looked out onto the street. Monster heads peered in, as in his nightmare of old.

There was a tomcat called Hermi at the hospice. He spent most of his time around the kitchen, snooping around the pots and behind the back door. He had a strange habit of snuggling up to patients whose end was nigh.

Once I overheard a snippet of a conversation in the corridor. A woman in a dark dress asked:

"How much longer has he got?"

"Well, according to Hermi, a few hours max," a nurse mumbled over his shoulder.

"According to Hermi? Who's Hermi?"

"Well… basically, it won't be long now. I'm sorry."

At dawn Hermi crawled into Father's bed and positioned himself by his feet. A few hours later the cat moved up to his head and pushed his way under the blanket. The only part of him sticking out was his grey nose. He was purring loudly.

What's-her-face was telling her beads in the corridor, by popping those little cushions from the bubble wrap she had picked up somewhere. It was the closest thing to beads that she could find.

Our Father, Who art in heaven, hallowed be Thy Name. Thy Kingdom come. Thy Will be done, on earth as it is in Heaven. Give us this day our daily bread. And forgive us our trespasses, as we forgive those who trespass against us. And lead us not into temptation, but deliver us from evil. Amen.

Father's hearing suddenly became acute. The popping of plastic bubbles sounded like a heart that stopped abruptly. His vision became blurred.

He breathed his last with the final pop.

All right – this is how I imagine it. Don't give me struggle, agony and body fluids and all the other indispensable accoutrements of dying. I don't want to see that. I don't see it.

Instead I follow the float marching to the drums as it crosses the town. The hooded Grim Reaper walks on stilts swinging his scythe wildly.

People are sitting in cafés, strolling down the streets, pausing to window shop.

3.

That night I got totally smashed at the Tower. I couldn't help it. I remember singing and shouting around midnight:

"All together now! In the Brežany Tower / Two badgers fucked for an hour / Then they did it all over again / And never needed a shower!"

The pub had changed – instead of formica tables, there were now rustic wooden benches, bright plastic fittings and Czech hard rock.

Monako's younger son, Oleg, staggered up to me: "Do you know Magda Levendovská? Her daughter married an African. They're walking down the street, and what do I see – a nigger! As black as my shoe!"

I shrugged and downed another vodka. I lost count of how many I'd already had. My head was throbbing.

Oleg went on: "What I'd like to know is which filthy Jew is going to take over the Slovlina factory when it closes down!"

I patted him on the back: "I've got to go, Oleg."

A silent, empty house awaited me.

I went into the kitchen, turned on a gas burner on the stove and held my hand in the flame until the skin came off.

In the morning, I managed to go through Father's clothes in the wardrobe, with my old friend Noax helping me to cope with the burns and a splitting headache. I chose Father's favourite off-white suit, a white shirt and a dark tie. And a pair of black socks.

I walked across the park carrying my deceased father's clothes in a Tesco carrier bag, the only one I could find. The staff at the funeral parlour signed for the clothes and asked me what music I wanted played during the ceremony. *Gershwin*, I said, *It Ain't Necessarily So*. Nothing else would do. I had to repeat the song title because the clerk didn't understand me. Shaking my hand and muttering the same words of condolence he'd already said several times that morning he turned Father into another statistic.

"What happened to your hand?"

"Oh… I just caught it in the door."

It ain't necessarily so.

I spent the evening mindlessly staring out of the window. In May the three Ice Saints rapidly brought the night temperatures down. A discarded crisp bag lay on the pavement on the opposite side of the street, looking like a glowing flame in the light of the blazing street lamps. There was something mournful about the scene, more like November than May. The cold air held the promise of spring. Maybe that's what made me feel sad.

I remembered the note found in the drawer of Father's bedside table at the hospice. It was handed over to me with all his other things.

I sat down in the armchair, assuming Father had left it for me and that it was written a long time ago.

It concerned the day when the Hlinka Guardsmen came for Mother's brother Armin. Father had officially notified the

501

authorities that he didn't need him at the hairdressing salon, which meant he would be included in a transport. When they came to arrest him Armin had a heart attack. But nobody could figure out why his dog Gaštan was found dead in the courtyard below. Father told everyone that Sára Silberstein had thrown the dog's ball out of the window and the animal had made the fatal mistake of jumping after it. It sounded strange and mysterious.

Most of what the note said I had already learned from other sources. The only new piece of information was the admission that the night Gajdoš came to arrest Armin, Father was also there, visiting. I couldn't understand why. What on earth had made him go to Armin's place in the first place? Did he want to make a show of his hatred? The note didn't explain that. But it said that the dog, Gaštan, who could never stand Gajdoš, kept attacking him and eventually bit his hand. Gajdoš got angry and flung the dog out of the window.

Thanks, great! Here's another bit of information I didn't really need to know.

The night before the funeral I dreamed that Father didn't die, we'd just forgotten about him and he was still in his room, under sedation. I hadn't been to see him for a few days and I felt I really ought to make a visit. After waking up with a start and a sinking feeling in the pit of my stomach, I stared into the darkness.

Death as a form of forgetting. What an interesting idea.

Ingrid and I arrived at the crematorium a little ahead of the ceremony.

A speckled cat peed on the soil of a nearby grave, followed by another. Shiny brass instruments and sheets of music had been left on a large granite gravestone by members of the funeral band. Sweating musicians sat by the gravestones, smoking.

A ceremony was taking place inside.

Ingrid listened. "I like that song!"

Inside the funeral parlour, Elvis was singing *Always on my mind*.

A dead man singing for another dead man.

I made sure to notify everyone in the family, and nearly all our living relatives gathered for the funeral. This conference of the birds was the result of the letters I'd sent out and phone calls I'd made.

Bony was there, supporting his grandmother, our Mother, who now found the stairs too much. Tina and Trevor arrived from London, and their daughter Jenny came from Bratislava. A now aged uncle Oscar with the new Auntie Rózka had come all the way from Israel – afterwards he dragged me around all over Brežany in search of the mythical synagogue, whose destruction his misguided faith help to bring about. His kippah-wearing grandsons didn't speak any Slovak and spent the whole time sulking, angry about being forced to travel to such a cold place. Peter was also here, wearing a serious expression and with his family in tow. Rudo's son Filip came with his wife and sons, and looking at Juraj I couldn't help feeling that he'd been complicit in my bringing the family skeleton out of the closet. I sincerely hoped he hadn't mentioned it to anyone. A swarm of children was running around among the assembled guests.

The opening music was played, the official in charge entered sedately and turned to face the guests. I had taken great care in writing his speech but he embellished it with so many kitschy phrases and cheap bathos of his own, that I mentally had to beg Father's forgiveness.

My nephew Fero, whom Peter had fathered in the autumn of his days, elbowed his way over to Bony, happy to see someone he knew at least by sight.

Bony leaned over to him and whispered: "Hiya, how have you been?"

"We're developing a predictive dictionary for a mobile phone company."

"What…?"

"Well, to write a text message, you have to type in every individual character or, alternatively, you can use a T9 dictionary – when you start typing it offers you a number of options. It contains around ten thousand words but you can add some more. Basically, it consists of the most frequently used expressions that contain the given characters. Right now I'm working on a predictive programme for mobile phones. The vocabulary is based on words older people use most frequently, according to surveys. I'm including words like: slog, ungrateful, spoilt, youth, mum, brat, Gypsy, Hungarian, Mečiar…"

He grinned. "The dictionary we have for young people is completely different: love, music, sex, school, condom, gay, weed…"

"You must be joking!"

"No, I'm not."

"Keep it down, boys," Uncle Oskar hissed.

Bony looked at Fero's outfit. It seemed far too big for him. Fero noticed his glance:

"Oh, I get all my gear in hip-hop shops. The jacket is four sizes too big!"

Father's coffin disappeared into the depths of the crematorium and Aretha Franklin sang Gershwin. Fero jerked his head in the direction of the coffin.

"D'ya know what… I never really knew the man."

Tina was sobbing, while Mother looked uninterested, scrunching up a handkerchief in her hand and dabbing at non-existent tears. The children were having the time of their lives and their parents kept shushing at them trying to keep them under control.

The only ones who actually wept were people I didn't know at all. Locals, old-timers. And Vojto's second son Sebastián, Basty for short.

The funeral reception was held at the old house. We had moved the sofa and armchairs from the drawing room and laid out a long table with chairs. Peter had some food and drinks brought over from the Golden Stag, whose new manager was an old schoolmate of his.

My cousin Samuel joined me at the table. We reminisced about our time building the Youth Dam. Our memories were so different we might as well have lived on two different planets. And we did, really. His memories were bright red and he had mercifully forgotten all the other major details. I chose not to remind him. Oh, the good old golden days of our strange youth!

He showed me a photograph of his eldest granddaughter, a stunning redhead who had just started studying choreography in Jaffa. She'd confessed that she was earning her upkeep by working as stripper in a nightclub.

"At least that's what she says. She claims it's nothing more than that. Can you imagine?!"

His grandson, he went on, was studying graphic design. He was a quiet, smart boy, always a good student, introverted, had never had a girlfriend and all he did was mess about with pictures – they were all he cared about. One day he'd left a printout on the table.

It was a picture of Santa Claus standing with his back against a wall, with a lustful look in his face, his coat upturned and a prostitute kneeling in front of him, giving him a blow job.

"That sort of thing didn't happen on in our days!"

"If you mean computers, I agree."

"Come on, you know very well what I mean."

"As far as I remember, Shmuli, sex already existed in our time."

"Come off it, Adam, not the kind of crazy stuff you see today; we weren't into that sort of thing! You must admit that!"

"Striptease is an invention much older than us and what the lady in the picture you described was doing was a popular pastime in Ancient Rome. But I do understand – when Ben and Esther grow old they will be saying the same things about their grandchildren."

Our conversation was fittingly complemented by Fero's monologue, which I partly overheard – he was telling Bony that he had just bought a transparent designer chair. Just the other day his girlfriend sat on it while having her breakfast cereal. He lay down on the floor and watched her pubes, appropriately trimmed, the two cheeks of her perky little bum and her skin sticking to the seat because she had just had a shower. For a while I let myself be carried away by this tantalising image.

Cousin Filip broke my pleasant reverie as he battled his way back to his seat, to his unfinished dessert, holding his wife Veronika's hand.

"How sweet, you still go around holding hands!"

"I'm just supporting her so she doesn't fall over," he replied.

Uncle Oskar praised me for having organised everything so well. The funeral reception happened to coincide with Lag BaOmer, which he explained was the thirty-third day of Omer, the period between the holidays of Passover and Shavuot, when mourning is suspended and the cutting of hair, marrying and celebrating is allowed for one day. I told him it wasn't intentional but if it made him happy he should savour the funeral party to the full.

As I went round making small talk with everyone, I asked him what things were like in the turbulent state of Israel. He sighed:

"What can I tell you? Golda Meir once said that Moses had spent forty years looking for a land that has no oil."

I was surprised to learn that a distant relative, a Mr Blau, had

505

tracked down Tina's daughter Jenny, who had married a Slovak and settled in Slovakia. Mr Blau was putting together a family tree and wanted to post it on the Internet. Jenny was horrified, because she often heard people at work, otherwise friendly and quite ordinary, make casual remarks such as: "Oh well, what can you expect from a Jew?!" or: "Typical Jewish behaviour!" Comments that sounded like scenes in a porn movie someone had inserted into a romantic soap opera by mistake.

So Jenny picked up the phone and asked Mr Blau to kindly remove her from the online family tree since her grandmother had only been adopted anyway – basically, she made it clear that she didn't want to have anything to do with this idea.

The issue must have been hanging in the air because a little later my brother Peter got into a heated argument with Uncle Oskar. He claimed the Jews had their fingers in every pie, that they controlled the world and everything was one big Jewish plot. Oskar countered by saying he'd never met any conspirators.

"That's is what you Jews would have the rest of us believe."

"You should be proud you don't have a single drop of Jewish blood in your veins."

"Of course I don't."

"How can you be so sure? You don't know your mother's full story. Just ask her."

I pricked up my ears, for this was something I was also interested in. But by then time had speeded up, its flow reduced to a thin trickle that threatened to dry up very soon.

The doctors had prescribed Mother a mountain of medications. Her favourite game of *Head-shoulders-knees-and-toes*, moaning about assorted pains and illnesses from head to toe, was becoming all too real. I had to keep checking:

"Did you take your medication?"

"Yes I did."

"So what's this here then?"

She behaved like a naughty little girl. She would wrap her pills in a napkin and hide them in her bedside drawer. She refused to take them, claiming they didn't agree with her. She invented lots of other reasons. Mind you, she had no problem with Xanax or Alprazolam, quite the contrary. She kept begging her doctor for more.

I see her again walking down the gravel path to the Dominican church on her way to the requiem mass, looking imposing even as she leans on a stick. She can't wait to savour her glorious revenge for all the wrongs, imagined and real. She projects Father's face onto the faces of the fallen angels.

I see her standing in our garden at dusk, with her unruly grey hair with its artificial bluish rinse. She is raking the edges of the fire while Dostoyevsky, Rimbaud and the collected works of Tacitus burn at her feet.

Was that a slight cough?

Yes, she is coughing. The night is unusually chilly for May.

Earlier that day a vendor came to pick up Father's unique record collection.

The new fridge, still in its wrapping, has stayed in the kitchen. White and beautiful. A symbol of new life.

4.

Each time I escaped from this house, I'd shake off some anxiety of which I wasn't even aware until it was gone. It would return as soon as I approached the house again, as if something dark and sinister had penetrated its walls.

After both my parents died, the house was ransacked by Gypsies. The massive iron stove, which Grandpa Albert used to heat the house, was too heavy for them to carry away. When it started to rain they left it behind. We had to lug it back across half the garden. They discarded the telescope, too. They wanted to take it but then realized they didn't know what to do with it, whether to have it recycled it as glass or as scrap metal.

The removals men have carefully fastened it to the deck of the Avia. Is that it, they ask and I nod.

I could go back to Bratislava with them but I prefer to stay to the bitter end.

Development plans that I saw soon after Mother's death show that the site of the house would be affected by the construction of a new bypass and a motorway link road. During Mother's funeral reception Peter took Tina and me aside and said we had to sell the house.

A month later I went to see Peter in his weekend cottage in Čierny Balog. I wanted to negotiate, persuade him to change his mind but he was adamant. He said we would get another plot in exchange, somewhere in Saliny, in the foothills. And I realised I didn't have any arguments to in my favour. Except for some strange nostalgia that had suddenly gripped me.

"What's gone is gone, Adam – photos are enough to remember things by," he said with a smile.

Proudly displayed on his wall was the Slovak national emblem carved out of linden wood. He made me admire it as soon as we entered the cottage.

Peter had the cottage built as an exact, authentic replica of a traditional wooden dwelling common in the Orava Region, only relocated some 100 kilometres south, in the foothills of the Pol'ana Mountain. A minor difference, from the point of view of a satellite in outer space. Peter's half-naked grandchildren with huge brown eyes were cavorting in the garden. I envied their blessed innocence about themselves and the world. They were yelling and splashing about in a plastic paddling pool, occasionally calling their grandfather in a mixture of Czech and Slovak:

"Stop it! Leave me alone! Cut it out! Grandpa, grandpa, tell her not to take my things!"

"That's because they watch the TV series on satellite," he explained and then turned to the children: "Let's pretend I'm not here right now, OK? Remember what I told you? Give it back to him, did you hear me? There's a good girl! I'll get you something to drink. In a minute, OK?"

"I'm going to kill you!"

"Come over here; sing our national anthem to uncle. Be a good boy!"

One of his grandchildren, a little boy with the trendy name Sean, was a bit shy at first but then started belting out the Czech national anthem:

"Where is my home, where is my home...!"

"It's because of the hockey championship," said Peter and slapped the boy's naked bum by way of warning. The boy started to cry and ran off, offended.

We fell silent. I was wondering what was left to say. Coming here had been a waste of time. I noticed the room we were in was full of murdered animals. The walls were covered in trophies: mouflons, fallow deer, roe deer, harts. Skulls, antlers and stuffed heads with labels. Peter had shot many of them himself, in the old days when he used to go hunting with the comrades.

A photograph on the wall showed Peter hugging Brezhnev. He noticed I was looking at the photo and laughed:

"Wasn't it crazy, the times we lived in?"

There was a knock on the door. It was a forester, bringing a young wild boar. Peter invited him to join us and poured him some plum brandy. I knew he wanted to get rid of me, our conversation was making him uneasy. But I stayed on, still hoping I could make him change his mind.

"You've got to believe me! Honest Injun!" This was the argument I used as my trump card when we fought as children. I doubted it would work now.

I gave up once they moved on to discussing the details of the Great Bonfire of Slovak Sovereignty planned for 17 July. Peter had invited many friends from Bratislava and was concerned that there should be somewhere safe for one of his pals to stick his Hummer.

As he said goodbye to me, visibly relieved, he whispered that he was writing his memoirs and would be in touch soon because there were a few details he couldn't recall.

"Speak to you soon," he said with a wave.

I was tempted to suggest that his first sentence should read: In the beginning I created Heaven and Earth!

5.

Since the most recent floods the Sálava has returned to its origins. It is back in its old bed. When it was regulated the banks had been cleared but now they are lovely and green again, overgrown with bushes, willows and poplars. The indestructible elder and ash trees have begun to sprawl everywhere.

I'm walking slowly along the bank up to the Volovec logistics centre, built over the count's vineyards with their winding paths,

509

where the acclaimed Château Sálava was produced until 1920. Then I turn around and walk back.

It occurs to me that, strangely enough, Bony had no idea what had actually happened in 1968 until he was called up to do his military service. At home we didn't talk about politics but once in the army he was enlightened within a few days.

It took him less than a week to decide that he didn't want to serve this regime – he feigned mental illness and a psychiatrist friend had him exempted on grounds of insanity. He spent a few weeks in a hospital and was free to go.

His first son Matúš, the child of a great love that vanished in a matter of months, once told Bony he didn't believe that anything really interesting could have happened before he was born. Of course, he knew the stories from history lessons at school and newspapers but he thought it was all just old hat, stuff meant to amuse or scare people.

"A load of codswallop!" he declared.

"Are you seriously telling me that there was this *Bravo* magazine that people used to smuggle in from Germany, that it came with bubble gum for blowing coloured bubbles and that because you couldn't get it in Czechoslovakia, you and your friends would crush coloured pencil lead into ordinary chewing gum to show off? Pull the other one!"

"But it's true – some of us had to have our stomachs pumped out," his dad told him.

For Matúš's generation the Slovak National Uprising was something out of *Warcraft,* with the Nazis playing the role of Orc Warlocks and the partisans that of Water Elementals.

The northern cemetery has long been my favourite. All my family is here. Father, Mother, Grandma Mária, Grandpa Albert, Uncle Rudo… Black thrushes sing their fancy operettas in the trees and ant motorways criss-cross the paths of humans.

One day I came here with Bony. I showed him Grandpa Albert's grave and the old apple tree that grows above it. I picked two apples and handed him one.

"This is what your great-grandfather tastes like."

Bony was taken aback and examined the red skin of the fruit while I bit into it with gusto. On my tongue I could definitely taste the cigarettes, soap and eau de cologne, which is how Grandma Mária used to describe his smell. I shuddered. The apple tree grew from his flesh and bones.

Hesitantly, Bony took a bite. He chewed slowly.

"He tastes good," he said. "I can taste something smoky."

Clouds scudded over the cemetery.

"Do you remember that time we went for a pee together when you were little?"

Bony shrugged.

"You saw I was going to the toilet and shouted – wait, wait, me too! I spread my legs above the bowl and so did you, you were just this tall – and off we went. Two streams. We laughed. You shook out your little pecker, weeny compared to mine. I have no idea why I still remember it."

"Let's do it again."

We went up to the cemetery wall, stood next to each other and unzipped.

"Wonderful!"

"Great!"

It reminded me of the time Father and I stood in our garden. The sun, hanging low over the horizon, had just begun to set behind the Volovec Mountain. Its shadow moved across the hillside opposite like a coastline, a moving boundary between light and darkness, bathing everything in a honeyed glow. I imagined that if I kept following the shadow and walked very fast, I would eventually reach the edge of the world.

Bony zipped up his flies and said: "D'you know, when I was a little boy and came to Brežany with you, I used to play this game where I imagined that if I kept following the shadow of that hill over there – look, it's moving up slowly right now – well, that if I kept pace with it and followed it over the hill and the next hill, and kept going really fast, I would reach the end of the world."

I was silent for a while, before saying:

"When I was a little boy, Kabiko, I imagined exactly the same thing."

He shot me a surprised look. It had been years since anyone addressed him by his childhood nickname.

Evening came and dusk slowly fell over the cemetery. The wind had stripped the trees of their leaves and only a few apples that nobody could reach hung from the topmost branches. Wrinkled, yellow and glowing, they gleamed in the thickening twilight like streetlamps, pointing the way. Even after the lights in the windows all around had gone out and most people were asleep in their beds, they shone into the depth of night, giving encouragement to all those kept awake by overexcitement or insomnia.

The next day snow fell and the apples kept sparkling under its white covering, lighting up the day, emitting tiny yellow patches of light, short flickers in the endless whiteness until they were completely covered the following night, which was no longer dark.

6.

Kabiko, aka Bony, is tall with chiselled features. The kind of looks I've always longed for. Handsome and tanned, he takes after his mother. He likes to wear a bandanna around his neck or on his head, like a biker, and sports permanent stubble and a greying crown of hair. In that respect he doesn't take after me, as I've always fallen rather short in the hair department.

A month or two after Father's funeral Bony and I set out for Santiago de Compostella. With Father's ashes. It was a crazy idea, but the real point was the journey.

"If you want to get to know someone properly you have to go on a journey with them," Kabiko used to say. *Experto crede*.

We could have picked any place but Kabiko liked the idea of following the Milky Way like medieval pilgrims on the way of St James. They used to make the pilgrimage in penance, to purge themselves of their sins. Bony liked St James's shell, both the scallop and the legend according to which the apostle had miraculously saved a wrongly accused boy from dying on the scaffold and brought back to life the chicken on a judge's dinner plate. Bony found this particularly amusing. He thought it was a really charming story.

We took Bony's car, a present from Zuzana.

The sun visor on the front passenger side displayed the existential sign: *Mort ou blessure grave. Death or serious injury. Morte e lesioni gravi. Muerte o heridas graves. Or Dood of zware verwondingen.*

It served as a constant reminder of implacable faith for every passenger, including those in child seats. When I turn the visor around I found that the same text had been considerately printed on the other side, too. As someone who hadn't travelled much in his lifetime I kept compulsively glancing up and thinking of this little *memento mori*.

Kabiko saw me and remarked casually: "Our idea of what is a threat to life has been primarily shaped by films. I can't imagine what things were like during the war! It all looks so simple in the films. Dying is like being stung by a tiny bee."

"I see… yes."

He was working himself into a rage: "How dare old people claim the times are getting more and more savage? That young people are more prone to violence now, even infatuated with violence, when in fact they and their ancestors went on a revolting murderous rampage in two world wars! Who are they to preach to us about violence?!"

"I see. Yes, yes, I see what you mean," I said with a smile.

We were overtaken by two speeding, shiny BMWs that looked like luxury coffins.

"You don't have to agree with everything I say, Dad."

"Yes, Kabiko, you're right."

I have always felt there was something very strange about travelling. It alters your perception of the world. It's a state of altered perception of the world. I've heard someone say that junkies often die of an overdose while travelling, far away from their well-trodden paths. Their bodies are accustomed to certain rituals that precede the taking of their actual dose and if they fail to follow them even the usual amount of the drug can easily kill them. The body just isn't prepared for it. It's not tuned in.

At the end of a day's journey the front windscreen was covered with tiny shattered coloured balls, white and red, yellow and green. The bodily fluids of insects whose aerial paths we had crossed. Constellations of dead time.

As he drove Bony talked about his many years of travelling that hadn't quite come to an end. Bony told me about his many years….

One year after the Velvet Revolution he started to itch to see the world, although not the way others see it. He gave up his job at the company where he'd risen to a decent managerial position. Everything suddenly seemed ridiculous and futile: he had gone off civilisation, as he put it. So he set out to walk to India. Yes, walk all the way to India. Without saying a word to anyone. If I had known it at the time I wouldn't have let him go. And Zuzana would have been even less inclined to do so. He left two children at home. Along with their mothers.

We would hear from him from time to time. Until he worked up courage for the big journey, he lived on the beach on a Spanish island, in a tent patched together from bits of rags. He eked out a living by scavenging for wire, mostly copper. He would strip off the plastic with a knife and sell the wire for recycling. One day a huge black dog stole up to him. Someone must have thrown it out of a car; maybe it had grown too big for its owner. ("Don't cry, my child. I'm sure it'll come back!" Oh yeah, like dead goldfish, tattered old teddy bears and chocolate.) Kabiko said the dog had been disgorged by civilisation, just like himself. So he took him along on his travels, with just a few coins in his pocket.

I listened to my son wide-eyed and with growing admiration. He did something I'd never dared to do: just get up and go, not knowing where you'd stay the night or where your next meal will come from. Without planning, just following your nose. I've never found the courage. It suddenly dawned on me that this might have been the greatest mistake of my life.

Kabiko sat next to me at the driving wheel, talking. He talked about travelling along the coast, the day his dog disappeared in Pakistan and how he spent three days looking for it. About communities of aged hippies in India whom he couldn't stand. About the time he was fishing in a river wearing tattered clothes, when a man in a suit came up to him and asked why he was wasting his time sitting there doing nothing, even though he seemed to be a smart chap who could easily find a good job, start his own business, any business, hire people. And then, eventually, he would no longer have to work and could just sit there looking at the sea, enjoying his peace and quiet. And Bony told him: But that's exactly what I'm doing now! The man in the suit turned on his heel and left without a word.

514

"This isn't actually my story – it's just an anecdote I've heard, but I like it," said Bony, laughing.

The engine purred steadily.

"When you travel alone you have to learn the basics of self-defence," he explained. "If you're assaulted you have to disarm the attacker within the first five seconds – get him in the eye, hit him hard in the Adam's apple or ear, break his leg, stab him if you have a knife. If he feels pain, sees lots of blood or can't move, he'll get weaker. He'll back off. It's the only way."

"Ever had to use self-defence?"

"Of course. Lots of times."

I popped a white pill from a blister surreptitiously and swallowed it. He looked at me.

"Noax? Oh yeah, I know it very well!"

He had caught me out.

"The good thing about growing old is all the medication you can take legally. Medication for pain, for your mood…"

To my immense surprise he confirmed the well-guarded and secret family weakness:

"Compared with this stuff alcohol is just a sackcloth patch on a silk shirt!"

7.

For many years Bony had lived far away, paying only occasional visits to Slovakia. He communicated via his website. It was the only way he kept in touch with his parents, ex-wives and friends. He usually wrote about trivial things: how much he got for recycling copper wire, what the weather had been like yesterday, that his dog had fallen ill and died and he'd held a splendid funeral for it in the dunes, things like that. He would stop at an Internet café near the beach when he went shopping.

He never replied to the emails I'd cobbled up with great difficulty. That's why I was surprised to see him suddenly standing in the cellar door and saying: "Well, are you ready to go…?"

He had come back.

As he opened the door I was blinded by the sun and I could only see the dark outline of his body.

515

"What's this, a jam session?"

I was in the middle of making plum jam in a huge pot and my face was covered in sticky purple blotches from waving the flies away. I didn't want to let the plums from our garden rot away. Nobody else would use them and I wasn't really into making plum brandy.

An old radio, discarded years ago, was hissing in the cellar. Whenever I turned it on, the characteristic sound of dying speakers would immediately conjure up the ritual of pickling cucumbers. The acrid odour of vinegar on a warm night. Sweat drying on the body, hot air streaming in through the window as the huge tin pot slowly cooled off.

I was listening to Slovak Radio. The same old voices, the same old news, water level reports. 384 metres at Medved'ovo. When Bony was little he always asked: how can they know it so precisely? And why do they report it on the radio? And why are they talking about bears? Why not about foxes or deer? Why does it have to be bears all the time? I had to explain that Medved'ovo is a village on the Danube and its name just happens to have the word for 'bear' in it.

He roared with laughter:

"Gosh, the water level report! It's still being broadcast?"

The announcer's voice was followed by a 30-second pause and the water level report, next came the time signal and after another 30 seconds of silence a soporific voice introduced the next programme. A fastidious female announcer, sounding rather elderly, made an enormous effort to enunciate clearly and comprehensibly as she read a convoluted text bristling with words like "flexibility", "mobility" and "hyperlink". She sounded like one of those schoolteachers in the 1970s giving a detailed explanation that included words she had never heard before. She was talking about a modern painting called, if I remember it rightly, *A large penis suspended from the moon*, painstakingly avoiding the word "penis", and using a circumlocution instead. It sounded so absurd that I had to turn the radio off.

Kabiko and I talked a lot during my parents' funerals. He left me his e-mail address and website details. I told him we had to figure out what to do with Father's ashes – we couldn't just bury him in a grave. It had to be something special.

"It's obvious. We'll toss Grandpa into the sea. We'll take a trip."
And now he had come to collect me.

At the end of a sweltering, scorching day absolution arrived in the form of a ferocious summer storm. It cleared the air.

I got changed and suggested we go for a walk. The damp streets smelled of rain. We walked around avoiding the puddles.

"Just around the corner is a place where they used to sell delicious mignons and cream slices."

I came to a halt at the spot where Puškár's patisserie used to be.

A passer-by, a man in Bermuda shorts, confirmed that yes, this is where there used to be a patisserie, then it became a newsagent's and tobacconist's, then a small supermarket, a shoe shop and now it's a pet shop.

"Don't worry, dad. The next time you come it will be a patisserie again."

8.

Time ceases to exist when you're travelling. The only thing that exist are the two points between which you are moving.

We drove along the Gulf of Lion coast, and while we were passing Narbonne I reflected that as you progress through life, all that you leave behind is wreckage, desiccated objects. I was thinking of Zuzana, Vojto, of my sister and brother... And then of the dreaded house again, to which I've been bound my entire life, whether I liked it or not.

Bony and I agreed that the urn was too conspicuous and poured Father into a cigar box we'd found in the house. He'd spent his whole life pretending he wasn't smoking, after all. The cigars had been a birthday present from Vojto's father.

Somewhere near Figueras (I was holding a map in my lap) Bony put on the radio to listen to the weather forecast, just as a new cover of *It Ain't Necessarily So* was on. I turned the sound up.

"Bronski Beat. You know it, dad?" Kabiko asked in surprise.

"It's Grandpa's favourite song."

"This?"

"As sung by Aretha Franklin," I said with a smile.

An enormous Hummer roared past us on the dark motorway.

"Just look at that!" Kabiko pointed to the car.

The car twinkled with so many little lights it looked like a Christmas tree.

We decided to stop in Madrid. It was a bit of a detour but I was sure Father would have liked to see his favourite paintings live, as it were, at the Prado. This was his trip, we wouldn't have taken it without him. Everything fitted.

We stayed the night at a motel where Kabiko read up on Goya's biography on the Internet, taking quick notes on his laptop. I looked at his notes when he went to the toilet. I clicked on a name and Word created a "smart tag": *La Leocadia*.

The programme continued with prompts:

Contact Name: La Leocadia
Send Mail
Schedule a Meeting
Open Contact
Add to Contacts
Insert Address
Stop Recognizing "La Leocadia"

I wondered if I could meet her. Perhaps in the nether world?

Although we didn't have the slightest shred of evidence to prove it, after two bottles of wine Bony and I fantasized they might have been lovers by the end – Father had the kind of strange and indefinable charisma that appeals to women and doesn't diminish with age. We decided that Leocadia must have succumbed in the end. I never had this kind of appeal, all my relationships with women were based on honest slog – but the gene has obviously skipped a generation, from grandfather to Bony. He didn't have to lift a finger to have women flocking to him.

I'm afraid my imagination is too limited to be able to picture a declaration of love in sign language.

The coincidences continued to pile up.

One day we were sitting in an Internet café and for lack of something better to do Bony showed me the Google Earth website, which has allegedly mapped the entire surface of the Earth down to the last detail. He said it's supposed to be so accurate that you

518

can find pictures on YouTube of people having sex on top of skyscrapers. I didn't believe him.

The picture of Earth we were looking at had been recorded in March 2003. Father was still alive then. I asked Bony to home in on our house. Bony magnified Europe, Slovakia, found Brežany and our street… Then our house. It took me a while to get used to its shape from above but everything was where it was meant to be. There was our street and the surrounding houses. I noticed a tiny speck in the garden, almost covered by trees and bushes.

"When you look at New York City you can tell white people from black ones," said Bony. He enlarged the spot but it was getting less distinct and more blurred with each enlargement. It could only have been him, Father. Was it him? It had to be him.

A picture from outer space shows my dead father standing in our garden. Leaning on Mária. I salute you, Leocadia, wherever you may be!

The following morning I woke up very early. I stared out of the window for a while, then I got bored and started rummaging in the bedside drawer.

I opened the Gideon bible at random. Like an oracle my eyes alighted on a passage in English: THE NEW TESTAMENT – LUKE 19:1 *Then Jesus entered Jericho and was passing through.*

Our journey was coming to an end, the journey of fathers and sons, in which I was both a father and a son.

Then I heard the sound of Brahms's Lullaby – it was the ring tone on Bony's mobile phone alarm. We went down for a quick breakfast, or incontinental breakfast, as Puškár would have said. God, how I miss him!

The receptionist praised Kabiko's leather wallet, which had an unusual black and white pattern. It was a present from Bony's friend in Prague with whom he'd stayed for a few days. His father, who worked as a cleaner on the underground, often found discarded wallets because pickpockets usually kept just the money and documents and threw the empty wallets away. He had dozens of them and handed them out to all his friends. This one had served Kabiko for ten years and was still as good as new.

"*Si usted tiene gusto – disfrute!*" said Bony and started emptying the wallet. The receptionist raised his arms with a smile.

"*No, señor, muchas gracias!*"

In the car Bony explained that in Spain if you like something, it's considered good manners to praise it. And it's also regarded as good manners for the owner to offer the object in question. However, it's very rude to accept. A nice game.

I was nibbling some Horalky wafers, a habit I had picked up from Tina. They represented the taste of home, something intimate and familiar. We'd brought more than thirty packets with us, and stowed them all over the car.

We still had a long way to go to Madrid.

As he drove, Bony was telling me about the late-night show he used to run on Radio Gondwana before he left Slovakia in 1990. The station had started as an underground channel for more discriminating listeners, with programming that would be out of the question nowadays – unconventional music, literature, classical music, jazz, long interviews – but in those days everything was possible, the air was pulsating with new opportunities. It felt like living in the Tertiary when the atmosphere contained much more oxygen than it does today, and meter-long dragonflies and giant butterflies flitted above the vast meadows. The university's arts department donated the space, and the equipment was a gift from a US foundation. Bony had run into an old friend who dragged him into a studio, and before he knew it, he had his own show. It was on the air for three hours every Wednesday from eleven at night. He used to go in empty-handed, having only prepared a general theme to discuss with people who phoned in, and would find music to match. Today it seems unthinkable!

There were all sorts of weirdos floating around. Some weird girls, too.

"And now I have a son with one of them," Kabiko laughed.

But then the level of oxygen started to fall, partly because the radio station had to earn its living. Gradually the programming began to change and the music became increasingly commercial. Eventually Gondwana ceased to exist in its original form.

"Some of my former colleagues now work for commercial radio stations and advertising agencies. They're happy because they've never noticed that something happened to them."

9.

To be honest, we didn't spend that much time in Santiago. After visiting St James's Cathedral, which was awash with pilgrims, we got back into the car and headed for Balo and Corcubión, just a stone's throw (if indeed we'd had a stone) from Cape Finisterre.

I had read about the place in a poem. A pilgrim rides his horse until he comes to a halt at Europe's westernmost promontory. In the Middle Ages this was considered the end of the world as people knew it. So this is where we would end up if we followed the shadow of the Volovec Mountain...

A strong wind blew salty and humid air from the ocean, constantly changing direction.

I ran my fingers through Father's off-white ashes, wondering what happens to the energy of human organs and tissues.

Like a coil, the DNA spiral shoots from two cells, a male and a female, two tiny, flimsy, almost invisible cells, growing to enormous dimensions. This is our genetic print, our replica, imitation, a fake that will keep propagating... Changing, repeating, varying. Making the same mistakes and feeling the same desires.

All of a sudden I saw all this human swarming in reverse. Back to front. Men suck their seed back from women in a sweet convulsion. They sway to and fro in rhythmical motion, they are less and less aroused until the couple hardly recognizes each other and eventually become complete strangers. They disappear into other male and female bodies, going back all the way back to the beginning of the universe until they vanish in the twists and turns of time.

Bony later confessed that he had scattered a handful of Father at the Prado. He pretended to go to the toilet but he'd actually sneaked into the engine room and threw the ashes into the air conditioning system. So Father now circulates around the museum exhibits, inhaled by visitors and being deposited on Goya's paintings.

I had seen the sea only a couple of times in my life so I really relished this experience. I wanted to savour it for a while before we climbed up the cliff again. I waded along the coast picking up translucent little stones out of the water. I showed them to Bony, happy as a sandboy.

Sailing ships used to bring piles of stones from faraway countries to the ports of Europe. They began their voyage loaded to the gunwales with merchandise, with a deep draught. To make steering easier they had to be loaded up for the return journey as well, so sailors filled the hold with rocks from exotic countries. To this day ports like Bordeaux, Bristol, Lisbon, Marseille, and Le Havre are full of bits of other continents.

Maybe these pebbles, too, have come from the far ends of the planet.

"These are just pieces of glass, dad. The sea has just smoothed their edges," Bony said.

Kabiko and I grabbed the cigar box and tossed it into the sea in a wide arc. It opened up in the air and spun around, spilling Father's ashes. The wind slowly carried him away into the distance.

A few inquisitive eider ducks gathered around the box in the water below. Large numbers of the birds had built their nests on the cliff below. Apparently the female plucks feathers from her own body to build a soft, warm nest for her young. If someone removes the feathers from the nest she starts all over again. Once she has shorn herself, exposing raw flesh and drawing blood, it is the male's turn to start plucking out his own feathers. The young eiders grow up clothed in their parents.

Kabiko and I hugged each other and stood on the coast for a long time.

10.

It was only at the fifth attempt that I got through to Igor.

"Ah, your bones," he said by way of a greeting.

"Have you got anything?"

"I've been through the lists of missing persons several times but haven't found your mysterious beauty. I'm sorry."

I was convinced that something must have happened between

Klaudia and Father. Something in the letters made me think that their relationship didn't end in a straightforward way. The best Igor could do was track down, through a policeman friend of his, her last registered address in Brežany. I went there several times. The house was overgrown with roses, breathing an air of mustiness and emptiness.

The first time I rang the bell nobody came to the door, but on my third visit I heard a lawnmower buzzing behind the neighbour's fence.

"Hello there," I shouted.

The lawnmower fell silent and a muscular man, stripped down to the waist, came to the fence.

"I'm looking for your neighbour."

"It's been a long time since anyone has been here."

"How long?"

"A year. Or two…"

"And before that? Didn't an old lady live here? Mrs Horváthová?"

"I wouldn't know. But a younger woman comes sometimes. From Bratislava."

He gave me the mobile number the woman had left in case anything happened to the house.

I arranged to meet her in a bistro in Obchodná Street. I was first to arrive and as soon as I sat down, the door opened and an almost perfect replica of the woman I remembered from my childhood walked in. She had blue eyes and long black hair.

"Hello, I'm Ema Petrovská."

"Hello. I'm Vojtech Roško."

For some reason I was reluctant to identify myself.

"I'm a film director. I'm shooting a TV documentary about Brežany. What the town used to look like, how it looks now – and I'm looking for people who remember it before the war, during the war and so on."

"I see. But I rarely go to Brežany and…"

"Actually, it's your grandmother, Mrs Klaudia Horváthová, I was hoping to meet."

"I see. But that won't be possible."

Shivers went down my spine. I felt I was getting to the bottom of the mystery.

523

"She's no longer alive."

"Oh, she's not alive… So when did she die?"

"This year. On the ninth of May."

The day my Father died. I was speechless, and for a moment I lost all sense of time.

French music filled the air and laughter drifted over from the neighbouring table.

"But if you're interested in Brežany I have a friend whose grandparents come from there. His name is Matúš Trnovský, do you know him?"

My grandson. Bony's son. I shook my head.

"I went out with him for about a year, he told me lots of interesting things. Would you like his phone number?"

"Yes please."

Mechanically I wrote down the number and was beginning to admit to myself that the trail had gone cold for good.

I watched Ema walk past the window, flash me a smile and disappear around the corner. It was dawning on me that I'd have to rely on my imagination.

Dead people can be used like puppets. They don't resist. They agree.

11.

In the afternoon I take a nap on the old couch, the only piece of furniture left in the house – and Father comes to me in my dream.

There's someone at the door. I go down to open up and there he is, in his off-white suit, waistcoat with four pockets, with his black doctor's bag in his hand. – "Won't you come in?" – I ask. – "All right, but I can only stay for a couple of hours, until seven o'clock" – says Father, lighting a cigarette. – "Let's go for a drive, I'll show you the town." We climb into our old Chevy – in the dream I remember that Tina had smashed it up somewhere in Nevedovo but now it's parked outside the house again… Oh, never mind.

Zigzagging across the town, I show him the new Brežany: "Look, this is what they've built here, and that…" and Father says – "Hang on, isn't this where the pub used to be? Has it closed

524

down?" – I nod. – "By the way, what's it like on the other side?" – Father pauses to think: "Oh, I don't know, nothing to write home about. But I've got two friends there, Puškár and Krebs; we see each quite a lot of each other."

We keep driving around until it is time for him to leave. He gets off in the main square, smiles and walks away.

When I wake up I find Bony standing over me.

"When the pilgrims on the Way of St James reach the Cape of Finisterre they burn their shoes to mark the end of the journey," he says and I know immediately what he has in mind.

I rummage through the bag and take out Father's last pair of shoes: old-fashioned, scuffed and worn out.

Meanwhile Kabiko starts a bonfire in the garden.

We toss the shoes into the flames one after the other. They quickly catch fire.

I pick up his doctor's bag. I look at Bony and he nods. The leather crackles and the flames expose the insides. We watch in silence. The old stethoscope is on fire inside the bag, buckling and falling apart in the flames. At the end a few shiny parts remain in the embers.

Kabiko takes his own shoes off pensively and slowly tosses them into the fire. I undo my shoelaces and do the same.

We stand on the cold ground quietly until the last embers go out.

That's where the builders find us, the hollering and shouting barbarians. They don't understand what's going on and what the hell we're still doing there.

The world is in decline, everything is falling apart, I say to myself, sounding like an old man. I stop and realise that in fact, I'm old. Old.

Our house is falling to rack and ruin. The thick walls, all the rooms, the ceilings and the roof.

The dust takes a long time to settle.

One day we shall all live in this house. Like one big family, Father used to say. That was his dream.

Uncle Rudo, in turn, used to say: In the long run we're all dead.

EPILOGUE

Dear Mr Trnovský,

Yes, it's quite possible that we have met before but I definitely remember your father "Bony", as he was called, although I have only met him a couple of times.

I am sorry it has taken me so long to reply to your e-mail of May 2012 but I've been busy at work and my computer has been playing up. Right now I'm totally fed up with Facebook because I've just discovered it's sent out birthday wishes in my name to complete strangers and I had no idea this was happening! You see, I have a rather special attitude to birthdays and to fakes posing as originals. Although, admittedly, as my son has just pointed out, it serves me right for accepting as friends people who are not real friends. But there you go… You don't want to hurt anyone's feelings and this is what you get.

But I must stop bothering you with my old man's moans about modern technology.

I was truly sorry to hear that your grandfather Adam Trnovský (whom I knew very well) did not recover from his second heart attack. Please accept my heartfelt condolences. He was an interesting man, a bit strange, always smartly turned-out, interested in everything, and with a keen sense of irony. I completely understand your feelings – I never managed to have a proper talk with my grandfather either, he died too soon. I should add that even with my father I never managed to talk. Basically, we had never bonded and now that he's gone for good there's so much I'd like to say to him and so many questions remain. Please forgive me if I sound a bit sentimental.

For all these reasons I was very happy to hear about the manuscript, found among your father's papers, which records your family history and contains long passages devoted to your great-grandfather Alfonz, after whom you were named. I hope to learn more about the manuscript or borrow it, if possible. I expect my father also features in it. I will come to Bratislava as soon as I can spare the time.

As for the Trnovský family house in Brežany, I have to say I've only been there once and have only the vaguest recollection of where it might have been. All I know is that it was torn down in 2003 or 2004. You were only ten years old at the time so you wouldn't remember it. The reason for its demolition was the planned link road to the motorway but in the end it was built a few kilometres further down, near Nevedovo. The new shopping centre, Vesna, was built on the site and your family's house would have been somewhere in the southern part of what is now a car park, near the Štefánik Street exit.

I was quite surprised to learn that nobody in your family has kept any photographs of the house although I do remember that in 2006 a fire in your grandfather's flat destroyed a great many family mementoes. If I were you I'd try his brother Peter, if he is still alive: his son František is the co-owner of Sálava Group Developments. If I'm not mistaken it was they who built the famous Behy aquapark, as well as (without the proper permits) the loft apartments in what was the bankrupt Slovlina factory. Although you say you're not on good terms with this side of the family, there is a chance that Peter managed to scan some of the photos.

I found the attached photograph quite by chance while sorting through some papers (my father didn't really care about hanging on to souvenirs – he took very few pictures and many of them have been lost). This picture must have been taken in the early 1940s and the smaller of the two boys at the front (the one holding a boomerang) is presumably my father Vojtech while the one crouching behind him is your grandfather, Adam. I think they're standing in front of the Trnovský house in Brežany, although I might be mistaken.

I apologise for the bad quality of the scan but the original is damaged and rather worn.

With best wishes,
Sebastián Roško

ACKNOWLEDGEMENTS

The following people were of great assistance in collecting anecdotes and facts from the period: Kornel Földvári, Peter Smékal, Ivan Králik, František Hlinčík, Dušan Hlinčík, Norbert Uhnák, Štefan Ďurajka, Karol Feješ, Peter Getting and Ján Šimko. They deserve my heartfelt thanks. The medical records from Dr. Robert Viso's medical practice as well as my grandfather Vladimír Kriško's papers, including his notes, c.v.s and diary entries from 1944 and 1945, have also proved valuable sources of information.

I am grateful for the feedback and encouragement I received from Marta Šáteková, Tomáš Janovic, Dado Nagy and my mother Zora Krištúfková-Králiková.

Viktor Suchý, my copy editor, has my gratitude for his patience and attention to detail and I am indebted to Palo and Janka Bálik, who designed the book.

Last but not least, I am grateful to Roseline Deleu for her kind permission to quote from her Feng Shui blog (http://fengshuisteps.wordpress.com/)

Quotes from the following books have also been used:

Albert E. Kahn, The game of death : effects of the Cold War on our children, New York: Cameron & Kahn, 1953

George Orwell: 1984

ADAM TRNOVSKÝ'S FAMILY TREE

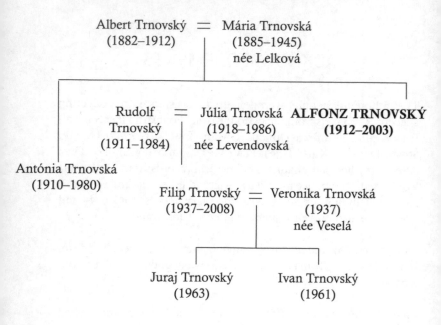

Albert Trnovský = Mária Trnovská
(1882–1912) (1885–1945)
née Lelková

Rudolf = Júlia Trnovská **ALFONZ TRNOVSKÝ**
Trnovský (1918–1986) **(1912–2003)**
(1911–1984) née Levendovská

Antónia Trnovská
(1910–1980)

Filip Trnovský = Veronika Trnovská
(1937–2008) (1937)
née Veselá

Juraj Trnovský Ivan Trnovský
(1963) (1961)

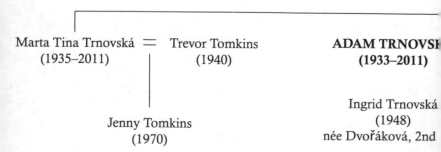

Marta Tina Trnovská = Trevor Tomkins **ADAM TRNOVSK**
(1935–2011) (1940) **(1933–2011)**

Jenny Tomkins Ingrid Trnovská
(1970) (1948)
née Dvořáková, 2nd

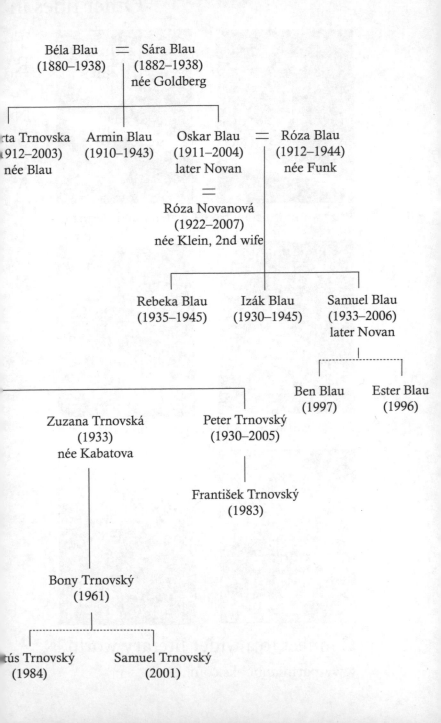

Béla Blau (1880–1938) = Sára Blau (1882–1938) née Goldberg

...rta Trnovska (...912–2003) née Blau

Armin Blau (1910–1943)

Oskar Blau (1911–2004) later Novan = Róza Blau (1912–1944) née Funk

= Róza Novanová (1922–2007) née Klein, 2nd wife

Rebeka Blau (1935–1945)

Izák Blau (1930–1945)

Samuel Blau (1933–2006) later Novan

Ben Blau (1997)

Ester Blau (1996)

Zuzana Trnovská (1933) née Kabatova

Peter Trnovský (1930–2005)

František Trnovský (1983)

Bony Trnovský (1961)

...tús Trnovský (1984)

Samuel Trnovský (2001)

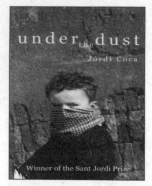

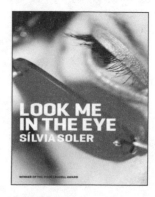
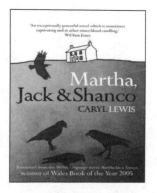
534

PARTHIAN EUROPA CARNIVALE

Featuring writers from the Basque coast at Donostia, to Slovakia, to Romania, to Germany, to Turkey and from Wales, the Parthian Europa Carnivale project represents a collection of new European fiction and poetry.

PEC Title List

Women Who Blow on Knots by Ece Temelkuran
Translated from the Turkish by Alex Dawe

Pigeon by Alys Conran

Pijin by Alys Conran
Translated into Welsh by Sian Northey

The Equestrienne by Uršuľa Kovalyk
Translated from the Slovak by Julia and Peter Sherwood

Goldfish Memory by Monique Schwitter
Translated from the German by Eluned Gramich

Washing My Hair with Nettles by Emilia Ivancu
Translated from the Romanian by Diarmuid Johnson

Clown's Shoes by Rebecca F. John

My Mother's Hands by Karmele Jaio
Translated from the Basque by Kristin Addis

A Glass Eye by Miren Agur Meabe
Translated from the Basque by Amaia Gabantxo

A Butterfly's Tremblings by Eleni Cay
Translated from the Slovak by John Minahane

Paper Spurs by Olga Merino
Translated from the Spanish by A. G. Thomas

Strange Language: an anthology of Basque short stories
Translated from the Basque by Mari Jose Olaziregi

Make sure you enter the code 'PECFREE' at checkout on the Parthian webstore to receive free P&P on your order.

parthianbooks.com

PARTHIAN